NEW VISIONS OF THE COUNTRYSIDE OF ROMAN BRITAIN

VOLUME 3:

LIFE AND DEATH IN THE COUNTRYSIDE
OF ROMAN BRITAIN

NEW VISIONS OF THE COUNTRYSIDE OF ROMAN BRITAIN

VOLUME 3

LIFE AND DEATH IN THE COUNTRYSIDE OF ROMAN BRITAIN

BY

Alexander Smith, Martyn Allen, Tom Brindle, Michael Fulford, Lisa Lodwick and Anna Rohnbogner

Series Editors
Michael Fulford and Neil Holbrook

Britannia Monograph Series
No. 31

Published by the Society for the Promotion of Roman Studies
Senate House Malet Street London WC1E 7HU
2018

BRITANNIA MONOGRAPH SERIES NO. 31

Published by the Society for the Promotion of Roman Studies
Senate House, Malet Street, London WC1E 7HU

This monograph was published with the aid of a grant
from Historic England

British Library Catalogue in Publication Data
A catalogue record of this book is available from the British Library

ISBN 978 0 907764 46 5

Front Cover illustration: Artist's reconstruction of an early Roman cemetery at Strood Hall,
Essex (by Peter Lorimer, after Timby *et al.* 2007a, 143, plate 3.24;
© Oxford Wessex Archaeology)
Back Cover illustration: Excavation of a late Roman cemetery at Bourton-on-the-Water,
Gloucestershire (Hart *et al.* 2017; © Cotswold Archaeology)

Printed by 4Word Ltd, Bristol BS13 7TT

Printed in Great Britain

CONTENTS

LIST OF FIGURES

LIST OF TABLES

PREFACE

Life and Death in the Countryside of Roman Britain is the third and final volume of *New Visions of the Countryside of Roman Britain*. It draws on data from the same excavated settlements that provided the resources for Volumes 1 and 2. These include farmsteads, villas, villages, roadside settlements, industrial and religious sites and a selected sample of defended small towns. These data – over a million fields – are available through *The Rural Settlement of Roman Britain: an online resource* (revised 2016): http://archaeologydataservice. ac.uk/archives/view/romangl/

Collection doi:10.5284/1030449

ACKNOWLEDGEMENTS

Our principal and warmest thanks for the production of the third volume of *New Visions of the Countryside of Roman Britain* are owed to the Leverhulme Trust, which, since 2012, has provided continuous support of the research project on the rural settlement of Roman Britain. Their research grant RPG 2014-227 has funded the research team of Drs Martyn Allen, Tom Brindle and Alex Smith at the University of Reading, and Dr Tim Evans at the Archaeology Data Service, University of York. At Cotswold Archaeology it provided for the completion of data collection with the inclusion of the evidence from Wales. We are particularly grateful to Dr Alex Smith for his day-to-day management of the whole team and the development of their respective contributions.

Thanks to a generous donation to the University of Reading by Paul Chadwick it has been possible to extend the original scope of the volume by including a major chapter on the osteology of the rural population by Dr Anna Rohnbogner (Chapter 7) as well as contributions by Dr Lisa Lodwick on gardens and plants, the ritual use of plants and plants in burials (see Chapters 3, 5 and 6). We are grateful to both, not least for their ready accommodation to the timetable of the project.

We also warmly thank Historic England for their continued support of the overall *Rural Settlement of Roman Britain Project*, in this instance for their grant towards the publication costs of this volume.

We thank the members of our Steering Committee, chaired by Professor Steve Rippon (University of Exeter), for their very helpful advice and guidance. The majority have been with us since the inception of the first project in 2012 and we are grateful to them for their unstinting support: Stewart Bryant (ALGAO), Dr Hella Eckardt (University of Reading), Professor Chris Gosden (University of Oxford), Dr Peter Guest (Cardiff University), Professor Mark Maltby (Bournemouth University), Chris Martin (Clwyd-Powys Archaeological Trust), Professor Julian Richards (ADS, University of York), Kathryn Roberts (Cadw), Professor Mark Robinson (University of Oxford), Barney Sloane (Historic England), Dr Jeremy Taylor (University of Leicester), Dr Roger Thomas (Historic England) and Pete Wilson (Historic England).

Individual authors also gratefully acknowledge help received in the preparation of their respective contributions:

Dr Martyn Allen thanks Umberto Albarella, Sue Stallibrass, Mark Maltby and Richard Chuang.

Dr Tom Brindle thanks Dr Hella Eckardt for her helpful advice on brooches and literacy and Dr Frances McIntosh for her assistance with brooches in Chapter 2.

Professor Mike Fulford thanks Dr Lisa Lodwick for her help with his contribution on food and drink in Chapter 3.

Dr Anna Rohnbogner thanks Professor Mike Fulford, Drs Alex Smith, Martyn Allen, Tom Brindle, Lisa Lodwick and Rebecca Gowland for their comments and feedback, also Drs Mary Lewis and Hella Eckardt who commented upon earlier versions of Chapter 7. Anna is indebted to Mike Luke at Albion Archaeology, Christopher Evans and Sam Lucy at Cambridge Archaeological Unit, Mary Alexander at Cotswold Archaeology, Imogen Gunn at the Museum of Archaeology and Anthropology, University of Cambridge, Ken Welsh, Stuart Foreman, Louise Loe, James Drummond-Murray and Lauren McIntyre at Oxford Archaeology, Peter Cox at AC Archaeology, Chris Webster at Somerset Heritage Centre, Mary Ruddy at Museum of London Archaeology, Ayesha Hussain at the Shakespeare Birthplace Trust, Vicki Score at the University of Leicester Archaeological Services, Pippa Bradley and Jacqueline McKinley at Wessex Archaeology, for providing osteological data, reports and tables, and helping in the location of skeletal archives.

Dr Alex Smith thanks Paul Booth, Professor Miranda Aldhouse-Green and Dr John Pearce for reading through early drafts of Chapters 5 and 6 and providing valuable comments.

We thank our principal illustrators, Sarah Lambert-Gates and Daniel Wheeler, and also Tom Brindle who produced the maps. We are grateful to Paul Bidwell, editor of the Britannia Monograph series, and Professor Richard Hingley, Durham University, for their very helpful comments and corrections of the draft text. Finally, we thank Val Kinsler, 100% Proof, who copy-edited and typeset the text, and Dr Lynn Pitts, who guided the volume through the press for the Roman Society.

Michael Fulford, University of Reading
Neil Holbrook, Cotswold Archaeology
September 2017

SUMMARY

The research presented here builds on the previous two volumes of *New Visions of the Countryside of Roman Britain*. Volume 1 set out a framework for analysis with its eight regions and range of different rural settlement types, while Volume 2 focused on the economic life of the countryside, making full use of the mass of recent archaeobotanical and zooarchaeological data to discuss the principal activity, agriculture. In this, the final volume, we have placed the people firmly at the heart of the analysis – how they looked, lived, interacted with the material and spiritual worlds surrounding them, and also how they died, and what their physical remains can tell us.

Many previous syntheses of life and death in Roman Britain have drawn mostly upon data from urban or military settings, with rural life being limited to the elite residing in villas. Thanks largely to the increase in new information resulting from developer-funded excavations over the past thirty years, this situation has now changed, so that we can place the spotlight firmly on the mass of the rural population living in farmsteads and nucleated settlements across the Roman province. This is a world that has rarely been explored before, and never in as much depth as has been possible here, resulting in a picture of the countryside of Roman Britain that is – for the most part – far removed from the bucolic scenes of villa-life.

The six main chapters in this volume each tackle a different theme relating to life and death in the countryside of Roman Britain, all combining to facilitate construction of a broad social archaeology of the province. Personal appearance is discussed in Chapter 2, using various categories of object associated with dress and personal display – particularly brooches – to highlight the diversity and social inequalities of peoples across the Roman province. A wider range of themes concerned with lifestyle and the domestic environment is addressed in Chapter 3, focusing upon variations in domestic homes, alongside evidence for eating and drinking, recreation and literacy. Chapter 4 explores the social connections between people and animals, domesticated and wild, suggesting distinct behaviours differentiating those living in villas, towns and farmsteads, as well as wider changes in attitudes between the Iron Age and Roman period. Religion permeated most aspects of Iron Age and Roman society and is explored in Chapter 5, focusing upon analyses of sacred space, along with the material culture, plant and animal remains that displayed religious associations. The diversity and dynamism of religious expression is readily apparent, and is matched by the rituals relating to burial practice, which are analysed and discussed in Chapter 6. Over 15,000 rural burials form the basis for this analysis, providing an unparalleled resource to assess regional and chronological variations in burial rites, and how these may relate to broader social changes in the province. Osteological data from a selected sample of these burials are used in Chapter 7 to examine the people of the countryside in later Roman Britain, providing important observations on the rural living environment, including aspects of diet and the range of daily stressors that impacted on their wellbeing. It is clear from this analysis that the inhabitants of the countryside, at least in certain parts of Roman Britain, were, for the most part, living very tough lives.

Overall, the analyses presented in this volume indicate a geographically and socially diverse society, influenced by pre-existing cultural traditions and degrees of social connectivity between settlements. There is no doubt that incorporation into the Roman Empire brought with it a great deal of social change, though it would appear that this change was largely to the detriment of many of those living in the countryside.

RÉSUMÉ

La recherche présentée ici s'appuie sur les deux tomes précédents des *Nouvelles Visions de la population rurale de la Bretagne romaine*. Le tome 1 expose un cadre pour l'analyse des huit régions qui la compose et une série de types d'habitats ruraux différents, tandis que le tome 2 se concentre sur la vie économique de la population rurale faisant plein usage de la masse de données archéobotaniques et archéozoologiques récentes pour discuter de l'activité principale, l'agriculture. Dans ce volume final, nous avons placé le peuplement résolument au cœur de l'analyse – à quoi ressemblaient-ils, comment vivaient-ils et comment communiquaient-ils avec les mondes matériel et spirituel qui les entouraient, mais aussi de quelle manière mouraient-ils, et que peuvent nous apprendre les restes matériels recueillis ?

De nombreuses synthèses antérieures sur la vie et la mort en Bretagne romaine ont puisé principalement dans les données issues de contextes urbains et militaires, la vie rurale étant limitée à l'élite qui seule réside dans les *villas*. Essentiellement grâce à l'augmentation de nouvelles informations générées par les fouilles préventives de ces 30 dernières années, cette situation a maintenant changé, nous permettant ainsi de mettre en pleine lumière la masse de la population rurale qui vit dans les fermes et les habitats nucléés à travers l'ensemble de la province romaine. Il s'agit d'un 'monde' rarement exploré auparavant, et jamais de façon aussi exhaustive qu'il a été possible de le faire ici. Cela nous a permis de produire une « image » de la population rurale de la Bretagne romaine qui est – en majeure partie – fort éloignée des scènes bucoliques de la vie en villa.

Chacun des six principaux chapitres de ce volume aborde un thème différent et relate la vie et la mort dans la campagne de la Bretagne romaine. Ensemble, ils facilitent l'élaboration d'une archéologie sociale générale de la province. La discussion sur l'apparence personnelle est l'objet du chapitre 2 grâce à des objets de catégories diverses relatifs à l'habit et à l'apparence personnelle – particulièrement les broches – pour souligner la diversité et les inégalités sociales des peuples à travers la province romaine. Une gamme plus étendue de sujets s'intéressant au mode de vie et à l'environnent domestique est abordée au chapitre 3 et se penche sur les variations des habitations domestiques et les restes alimentaires et de boissons, ainsi que les témoignages sur le jeu et l'alphabétisation. Quant au chapitre 4, il explore les liens sociaux existant entre les peuplements et les animaux, domestiqués et sauvages, qui suggèrent des comportements distincts différenciant les habitants des villas, des villes et des fermes, ainsi que des changements de comportements plus notables entre l'âge du Fer et la période romaine. La religion qui imprégnait la plupart des aspects de l'Age du Fer et de la société romaine est appréhendé dans le chapitre 5, axé sur les analyses de l'espace sacré, la culture matérielle, les restes archéobotaniques et les ossements animaux qui affichent des associations religieuses. La diversité et le dynamisme de l'expression religieuse sont vite apparents, comme c'est le cas pour les rituels relatifs aux pratiques funéraires, qui font l'objet d'une analyse et d'une discussion au chapitre 6. Plus de 15000 sépultures rurales forment la base de cette analyse et fournissent des ressources sans parallèle pour évaluer les écarts régionaux et chronologiques des rites funéraires, et la manière dont ces derniers pourraient être liés aux changements sociaux plus vastes au sein de la province. Les données ostéologiques d'un échantillon choisi à partir de ces sépultures sont utilisées dans le chapitre 7 pour étudier le peuplement des campagnes à la période romaine tardive. Ces données apportent d'importantes observations sur l'environnement de la vie en milieu rural, dont des aspects sur le régime alimentaire et la série de facteurs de stress quotidiens qui impactaient leur bien-être. A partir de cette analyse, il est clair que les habitants de la campagne, au moins dans certaines parties de la Bretagne romaine, avaient, pour la majeure partie, une vie très rude.

Globalement, les analyses présentées dans ce volume indiquent une société géographiquement et socialement diverse, influencée par des traditions culturelles préexistantes et des degrés de lien sociale entre les habitats. Il ne fait aucun doute que l'incorporation à l'empire romain ait engendré de nombreux changements sociaux, bien qu'apparemment ces derniers aient eu lieu largement au détriment de beaucoup d'habitants vivant à la campagne.

ZUSAMMENFASSUNG

Die hier vorgestellten Forschungsergebnisse basieren auf den zwei vorangegangenen Bänden von *New Visions of the Countryside of Roman Britain*. Im ersten Band wurde der Rahmen der Untersuchungen gesetzt, acht Regionen mit ihren unterschiedlichen ländlichen Siedlungstypen. Während Band 2 das ökonomische Leben der Landschaft in den Fokus nahm und sich dabei der breiten Masse der neueren archäobotanischen und archäozoologischen Daten zunutze machte, um die Haupttätigkeit, die Landwirtschaft, zu diskutieren. In diesem, dem letzten Band, wurden die Menschen in den Mittelpunkt der Forschung gestellt – wie sie aussahen, lebten, interagierten mit der materiellen und spirituellen Welt die sie umgab, wie sie starben und was ihre sterblichen Überreste uns mitteilen können.

Viele vorangegangene Synthesen des Lebens und Sterbens im römischen Britannien wurden primär aus urbanen oder militärischen Siedlungen gezogen, während die Analyse des ländlichen Lebens auf die in den Villen lebenden Eliten beschränkt war. In den letzten dreißig Jahren hat sich die Situation jedoch, dank der durch Bauträgerfinanzierten Ausgrabungen und der dadurch rapide angestiegenen Datenmengen, stark verändert. Mit Hilfe der neuen Daten ergibt sich nun ein detaillierteres Bild der Masse der auf Bauernhöfen lebenden Landbevölkerung und der Bevölkerung kleiner Siedlungen in der gesamten römischen Provinz. Dies ist eine Welt, die selten zuvor untersucht wurde, und niemals so detailliert, wie es hier möglich war, was zu einem Bild des ländlichen römischen Britanniens führt, das – größten Teils – weit entfernt von den idyllischen Szenen des Villa-Lebens war.

Die sechs Kapitel des vorliegenden Bandes beschäftigen sich jeweils mit einem Thema des Bereiches Leben und Sterben im ländlichen römischen Britannien. Zusammengenommen helfen sie uns ein breit gefächertes Konstrukt der sozialen Archäologie der Provinz herzustellen. Das persönliche Erscheinungsbild wird in Kapitel 2 behandelt. Verschiedene Objektkategorien von Kleidung und der persönlichen Darstellung – insbesondere Fibeln - wurden benutzt, um die Vielfalt und die soziale Ungleichheit der Völker der römischen Provinz hervorzuheben. Eine breitere Themenpalette, welche sich mit dem Lebensstil und dem häuslichen Umfeld beschäftigt, wird in

Kapitel 3 behandelt. Hier wird der Fokus auf die Variationen im Hausbau, sowie dem Essen, dem Trinken, der Erholung und der Bildung gelegt. Kapitel 4 untersucht die sozialen Zusammenhänge zwischen Mensch und Tier, domestiziert und wild, mit der Andeutung, dass ein deutlicher Unterschied zwischen Bewohnern von Villen, Städten und der Landbevölkerung bestand. Es wird weiterhin ausgeführt, dass tiefer reichenden Veränderungen, in der Haltung von Menschen gegenüber Tieren, zwischen der Eisenzeit und der römischen Periode zu erkennen sind. Religion durchdringt fast alle Aspekte der eisenzeitlichen und römischen Gesellschaft und wird in Kapitel 5 sondiert, mit der Analyse heiliger Plätze zusammen mit der materiellen Kultur und pflanzlicher- und tierischer Überreste, die religiöse Zugehörigkeit darstellten. Die Vielfalt und Dynamik mit der Religion ausgedrückt wird ist allgegenwärtig und findet ihren Ausdruck in den Riten der Bestattungspraxis, die in Kapitel 6 diskutiert werden. Über 15.000 ländliche Bestattungen bilden die Grundlage für diese Analyse und bieten eine beispiellose Quelle, um regionale und chronologische Variationen der Bestattungsriten bewerten zu können, auch in Hinblick auf umfassendere gesellschaftliche Veränderungen in der Provinz.

Osteologische Daten, einer ausgewählten Stichprobe dieser Bestattungen, werden in Kapitel 7 untersucht, um die Menschen auf dem Lande im späteren römischen Britannien zu untersuchen und wichtige Beobachtungen über das ländliche Leben, inklusive Aspekte der Ernährung und des Umfangs der täglichen Stressfaktoren, die sich auf das Wohlbefinden auswirken, zu liefern. Aus dieser Analyse geht hervor, dass ein Großteil der Landbevölkerung, zumindest in einigen Teilen des römischen Britanniens, ein sehr hartes Leben führte.

Insgesamt zeigen die in diesem Band vorgestellten Untersuchungen eine geographisch und soziokulturell vielfältige Gesellschaft, die durch bereits bestehende kulturelle Traditionen und Grade der sozialen Verknüpfung zwischen Siedlungen geprägt wird. Es scheint kein Zweifel daran zu bestehen, dass die Eingliederung in das römische Reich große soziale Veränderungen mit sich brachte und es entsteht der Eindruck, dass diese Veränderungen in hohem Maße zum Nachteil der ländlichen Bevölkerung waren.

CHAPTER 1

INTRODUCTION

By Michael Fulford

The combination of the increase in new information from the corresponding recent expansion in the number of archaeological investigations in England and Wales, especially since the implementation of PPG16 in England in 1990, and the enrichment of the knowledge derived from each one through the application of new approaches to environmental and material culture, now allows us to say much more about life and death in the countryside of Roman Britain. This research builds on the previous two volumes of *New Visions of the Countryside of Roman Britain*, the first of which, *The Rural Settlement of Roman Britain* (Smith *et al.* 2016), established a typology of rural settlement and a regional framework where material culture and environmental evidence played key, complementary, roles in its formulation (FIG. 1.1).

The regional framework continued to help articulate the evidence for the rural economy of Roman Britain that was set out in Volume 2 of *New Visions* (Allen *et al.* 2017). Here, the mass of recent archaeobotanical and zooarchaeological data informed a new understanding of agriculture in the province alongside a re-appraisal of other rural industries, while coins, ceramics and other categories of material culture allowed a more nuanced insight into the movement of resources and the development of markets.

In contextualising our third study, essentially trying to offer a richer characterisation of life (and death) in the countryside, we can look back at late twentieth-century syntheses of Roman Britain where the countryside was conceived very much in terms of the built environment of the elite, the villa

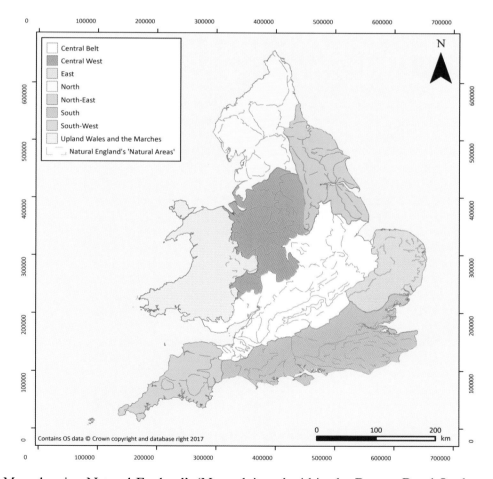

FIG. 1.1. Map showing Natural England's 'Natural Areas' within the Roman Rural Settlement Project regions

and its attributes, such as the bathhouse, hypocausts and the interior décor of mosaic pavements and painted plaster (e.g. Frere 1967; Salway 1981; Todd 1981). When Anthony Birley wrote his *The People of Roman Britain*, the chapter dedicated to the subject of 'country dwellers' drew exclusively on the epigraphic record from the countryside of Roman Britain to assess the (limited) evidence that names provided for identifying immigrants, estate owners, citizens and peregrines (1979, 137–44), with a further chapter considering the evidence, though much of it drawn from military and urban contexts, for slaves and freedmen (*ibid.*, 145–50).

Now it is possible to reach far beyond just names: the first decades of the twenty-first century have seen a sea change in approaches to the people of Roman Britain, with David Mattingly exploiting the first fruits of the new, contextualised and scientific approaches to material culture and environmental evidence to characterise a society separated into communities – military, civil and rural – and to introduce the concept of the rural non-elite in his *An Imperial Possession: Britain in the Roman Empire* (2006). This represents an altogether very different approach to the syntheses of the second half of the twentieth century cited above, which had privileged the military and political history of the province and only latterly the archaeology (Millett 1990). Also, in 2006 Hilary Cool published her *Eating and Drinking in Roman Britain*, bringing together the strands of new knowledge derived from archaeobotany, zooarchaeology, osteology and material culture studies to construct a rich, socially nuanced picture of eating and drinking (2006). Previously Charlotte Roberts and Margaret Cox had synthesised the evidence for health and disease in Britain, including for the Roman period, though their data drew almost exclusively from urban cemeteries (2003). Fresh approaches to material culture using quantitative techniques and taking account of context have enriched our ideas of identity and diversity far beyond what the evidence of names alone could offer in the late twentieth century (e.g. Cool 2016; Eckardt and Crummy 2008; Eckardt 2014). This has been taken significantly further through the application of isotope analysis to allow us to distinguish between locals and foreigners in the province and so deepen our understanding of mobility (e.g. Eckardt 2010b; Eckardt and Müldner 2016). The distance that the study of Roman Britain has travelled in the almost fifty years since the publication of the second edition of what may be thought of as the first handbook of Roman Britain, *The Archaeology of Roman Britain* (Collingwood and Richmond 1969), or of Liversidge's *Britain in the Roman Empire* (1968),

can be measured by the contents of *The Oxford Handbook of Roman Britain* (Millett *et al.* 2016), itself building on Malcolm Todd's *A Companion to Roman Britain* (2004). The contents of *The Archaeology...* and *The Oxford Handbook...* are almost mutually exclusive: the first, amply illustrated, is very much concerned with the built environment – military, urban and rural, inscriptions and key artefact types of the province; the latter, with proportionally many fewer visual references, is strongly orientated towards constructing the components for a social archaeology of Roman Britain.

Indeed, social archaeology is the linking theme of the contents of this, the third volume of *New Visions*. With the data collected from some 3600 records derived from 2500 rural settlements across Roman Britain, we can now apply some of the approaches, mostly developed in the late twentieth century, specifically to the people who lived in the countryside of Roman Britain, and who constituted the vast majority of the population of the province. Moreover we are able to develop further our appreciation of the diversity of that people through the perspectives of the regional framework and its categories of settlement type: from the small towns, military *vici* and roadside settlements, through to the villas and other types of farmstead, expounded in the first volume of *New Visions* (Smith *et al.* 2016).

The data (Allen *et al.* 2016) that underpin this volume are available online at:

http://archaeologydataservice.ac.uk/archives/view/romangl/

We begin our social archaeology with a study of what people across Roman Britain wore through the media of objects associated with dress and personal display, with particular emphasis on the evidence provided by brooches (Chapter 2). Other than copper-alloy coins or structural items like iron nails, the brooch is one of the most commonly found metal objects and there is a well-developed typology that has allowed Brindle to assess the frequency of the different types across the eight regions, contextualising the finds according to settlement type. He reaches important conclusions both about identity and the diversity of appearance across the province, but also stressing the inequalities in the social distribution of dress accessories. This study takes us to the early to mid-third century when the tradition of brooch-making and wearing almost dies out, such that, for the fourth century, it is principally through the differing burial traditions explored in Chapter 6 that we gain a further perspective on diversity and identity.

A wider range of themes concerned with lifestyle and the domestic environment is addressed in

Chapter 3. While subsistence was of over-riding importance, there is comparatively little that can be said about what people actually ate and drank, but the skeletal evidence explored in Chapter 7 reveals widespread malnutrition among the rural population. As the principal source of the majority of the food and drink consumed in Roman Britain, the countryside had the potential to support a well-nourished rural population. However, differential access is very much in evidence, with the elite benefiting at the expense of poorer households, whose diet was largely limited to the staple crops with some access to meat. Landowners appear to have exercised strict control over what was grown or reared, as well as over wild resources, on their estates in order to maximise the return from supplying the market and the needs of the state, particularly the army.

Inequality of access was not only limited to food and drink, but can be seen in household security and lighting, where the scarcity of locks and keys and lighting equipment is very clear outside the Central Belt and South regions, as well as among farmsteads more generally across the province. For the heating of houses, too, reliance on a simple, central hearth is most commonly evidenced with examples of rooms with hypocausts confined to the higher status villas. It was the rural elite, too, who mainly benefited from the provision of bathhouses, with a very small proportion, on the basis of the evidence available to date, enjoying the further pleasure of a formal garden. Recreational objects, mostly in the form of gaming counters, have been recorded from only about 12 per cent of all sites, the majority of these being nucleated settlements, but with villas also having significantly greater representation compared with other farmsteads. Finally, literacy: although there has been much recent research on the extent and character of literacy in Roman Britain, the evidence from the database of the incidence of graffiti on ceramics, of inscriptions on stone, of writing equipment, such as styli, wax spatulae, seal boxes and inkwells, provides a more nuanced picture of social distribution where, except for the incidence of inscriptions at military *vici*, the defended small towns clearly stand out above all other categories of settlement, with almost two-thirds producing some form of evidence of literacy. Except for inscriptions, roadside settlements otherwise follow defended small towns rather than military *vici* in the percentage of them with evidence of literacy. At the other end of the scale there is little to distinguish between the various types of non-villa farmstead; only in the single category of styli do complex farmsteads stand out a little, showing representation at between five and ten per cent of sites in this category. Together, this emphasises the importance of the road network and underlines a difference in the role played by the defended small towns (other than that of defence) in the infrastructure and bureaucratic management of the province.

Fresh insights into the ways that the Roman occupation of Britain changed the lives of people and of their relationship to animals, both domesticated and wild, are the subject of Chapter 4. There are indications of changing attitudes towards cattle, sheep and pig (the commodification of meat) as animals increased in number and generally lived longer before slaughter during the Roman period. Here a direct link can be drawn with patterns of occupation, where animals suitable for traction, particularly cattle but also horses, were required to meet the growing demands of arable cultivation and to move resources along roads and trackways to the towns and military consumers, with consequent impacts on their health as reflected in their pathology. Attitudes towards dogs, probably deliberately bred for a variety of roles, including as pets, and cats also changed over the Roman period. In the case of the wild, the importance of hunting as an elite activity among landowners and the military accounts for some of the change in the exploitation of wild animals, particularly of deer, but also of hare and some wild birds compared with the Iron Age. Mediterranean influences may also explain the increased role of fish, both freshwater and marine species, in the diet, also with a strong association with the elite. Virtually absent in the Iron Age, fish is particularly noticeable by the late Roman period. So, too, are shellfish, particularly the oyster, a notable feature of elite dining in the Roman world.

Animals also played an important role in the religious life of the rural population, which is the subject of Chapter 5. This brings together a mass of new evidence to enrich our concept of what constituted 'sacred' in late Iron Age and Roman Britain. Between the formal, Classical architecture of the temple to Sulis Minerva at Bath and the sanctity of space indicated by the repeated deposition of certain types of artefact or selected parts of animal skeletons within, for example, enclosures, or around prehistoric monuments, or in caves, shafts, wells or watery places more generally, there is great variety, much of it found within the Central Belt and South regions. In this context the Romano-Celtic temple, so familiar from earlier treatments of religion in Roman Britain, with its tendency for concentric arrangements of cella and ambulatory, becomes the exception not the norm. However, what may be considered to be sacred space often hinges on the interpretation of associated artefacts and/or animal bone and perceptions of difference from a domestic 'rubbish' assemblage. No certainties can be offered in this regard and one does not preclude the other; the sacred and the domestic were not necessarily mutually exclusive (cf. Eckardt 2006). This is nowhere more evident than in the treatment of certain, otherwise 'everyday' items like coins or brooches, where their recovery from some sites in their hundreds or thousands suggests a religious motivation. The chapter concludes with a major review of structured deposition – of deposits of artefacts, human and animal remains, the latter often articulated – which links back to the discussions of the identification of sacred space earlier in the chapter, but also relates to types of deposition associated with a wider range of domestic and agricultural buildings, such as corndryers, with no obvious sacred significance, but perhaps marking major events like their initial construction or their final abandonment. The wide-ranging scope of this chapter highlights the all-pervasive concern in all regions of Roman Britain with the appeasement of deities and the management of superstition.

The last two chapters are complementary; the one about the different ways people were treated after death over time as well as across regions and the settlement hierarchy (Chapter 6), the other about the characteristics of the population as revealed by study of their skeletal remains (Chapter 7). Over 15,000 burials recorded from excavated sites in England and Wales form the basis for these analyses, a resource that offers the prospect of further comparative research, such as of burial practice, or health and disease in towns in Britain, or across the north-western provinces of the Empire more generally. However, with the comparative lack of excavations conducted with modern methodologies of the higher status villa sites, as noted in Volume 1 (Allen and Smith 2016, 33–7), we should also be aware of the limitations of the data.

Although both inhumation and cremation burials are in evidence from the late Iron Age, the latter is the dominant mode until the late Roman period. From a fairly tight focus in the south-east of England in the late Iron Age, showing close parallels with practice across the Channel in northern Gaul, there is evidence of cremation right across the province by the second century A.D. Whereas there is a strong argument for linking the former with pre-conquest migration, in the case of the latter there is a clear correlation with the Roman conquest and the traditions introduced by the military and their associated camp followers. Explaining the shift towards a greater, but by no means exclusive, preference for inhumation by the late Roman period is necessarily more complex.

There is manifestly an indigenous context evident from the late Iron Age but, like cremation earlier, the trend in Britain is paralleled across the empire more widely. Within Britain itself, there is a much more apparent regional concentration of burial evidence in the late Roman period, with the great majority of examples found in the Central Belt and the west of the South regions. While we should always be aware of the influence of the varying intensities of developer-funded work, some of the patterning in the late Roman period correlates with changes in overall settlement density, such as the comparative lack of evidence for inhumation burial in the North Kent Plain.

One of the benefits of an assessment of the entirety of the rural burial record is that minority practices can be seen in context. For obvious reasons, the rite of decapitation and the debate over possible explanations for the detachment of the head from the rest of the body has attracted attention, but with this study we can see it as one of several minority practices in the late Roman period, which include prone and flexed inhumations as well as cremation, and which is represented across the associated settlement hierarchy. Study of the skeletal remains in Chapter 7 shows that these rites were not confined to particular sexes or age groups; for example, there are cases of decapitation among both young and old adults. These differing traditions are to be found alongside each other and in urban as well as rural contexts, particularly across the Central Belt and parts of the South region, but also in the East. If we can now see these practices as normative in late Roman Britain, they still imply differences among the living who chose these particular rites for their dead. What we do not know is whether the groups that chose to express their identities in this particular way were present in the early Roman period when cremation was the dominant rite and where their various identities might have been expressed in other ways, not necessarily evident in burial practice. The presence of these distinct traditions reminds us that we know very little about the movement of peoples, as opposed to individuals, between Britain and the Continent, or within Britain in the late Roman period. We can only speculate whether movements, like that of the Durotriges and Dumnonii to Hadrian's Wall, presumably enforced, in the second century, also took place in the late Roman period. Also, were the people who migrated into towns, as the isotopic evidence suggests (Eckardt 2010a, 112–20; Eckardt and Müldner 2016, 207–13), from the local or regional countryside replaced to ensure continued productivity on the land and, if so, how? Collectively the evidence of the various rites associated with late Roman inhumations shows a strong cross-regional clustering in the south of Britain, one which also transcends any boundaries that might be conceived of in terms of tribes or *civitates*. An important question for future research is the extent to which comparable expressions of burial identity, individually and/or collectively can be found across the Channel in Gallia Belgica or Germania, or yet further afield.

The complementary evidence from the analysis of the skeletal remains gives vivid insight into daily life in the countryside (Chapter 7). Compared with the Iron Age population we see elevated levels of pathology in the rural population of late Roman Britain, with spinal degeneration the most prominent. The incidence is also higher than in the contemporary urban sample (Lankhills, Winchester), with lesions reflecting the kind of labour associated with farming and present in both men and, to a lesser extent, in women. Degenerative joint disease is also widely observed in young adults, accounting for between 10 and 20 per cent of this population in the southern regions. When it comes to food, the rural population appears to have had a less adequate diet than its

urban counterparts, or in the Iron Age, with a relatively high incidence of metabolic disease, including among children, who were also affected by rickets and scurvy, particularly in the Central Belt region. However, even though the incidence of tooth decay was higher in the countryside in the Roman period compared with the Iron Age, it was significantly less than in the urban sample. Overall, the Roman period in the countryside saw a considerable decline in health from the Iron Age, a situation that was worse than in the urban sample. Given the nature of the evidence, with cremation the dominant rite in the early Roman period, we cannot yet determine whether the situation in late Roman Britain was better or worse than in the second century when, in other respects, *Britannia* appears to have been at its height (Smith *et al.* 2016).

To conclude this introduction, the contributions to *Life and Death in the Countryside of Roman Britain* show clearly that whatever might be perceived as the benefits of the Roman occupation of Britain, they touched only the rural elite, to the detriment of the rural population at large.

CHAPTER 2

PERSONAL APPEARANCE IN THE COUNTRYSIDE OF ROMAN BRITAIN

By Tom Brindle

INTRODUCTION

Evidence for the clothes that the people of Roman Britain wore is sometimes available to us through sculptural depictions on tombstones, and occasionally through wall paintings and figures represented on mosaics. Such representations are rare, however, even in urban, military and high-status sites, and while these may give an indication about the appearance of some occupants of military sites and towns, they contribute little to our understanding of the way people looked in the wider countryside.

There is also little evidence from the textiles themselves; fabrics survive only in exceptional circumstances, as in the waterlogged conditions at Vindolanda (Cool 2016, 406) and there is insufficient evidence from clothing to inform us about regional traditions of dress. Most evidence from the Roman world comes from the Mediterranean (cf. Rothe 2012), and from this we know that woollen and linen tunics were the principal types of clothing, worn by both sexes along with tube dresses, worn by women (Cool 2016, 409). Outer garments took the form of cloaks and capes for men and mantles for women (*ibid.*). Even in Rome the toga was essentially a formal item of clothing, worn only for ceremonial occasions (Allason-Jones 2014, 70; Cool 2016, 418). Tunics varied in shape between provinces; a type that is believed to have been common in the north-western provinces of the empire is often referred to by archaeologists as the Gallic coat, characterised by its long sleeves (Wild 1968, 168). The *birrus Britannicus*, a hooded woollen cape, is listed in the Edict of Diocletian (Wild 2002, 1), while a range of other garments are named on the writing tablets from Vindolanda and curse tablets from Bath (*ibid.* 25). Although these provide some evidence for a variety of types of clothing worn in Britain, the examples are not from rural sites, and we can expect there to have been considerable regional and social differences in the form of garments, as well as in the patterns and colours used (where they were decorated at all), which reflected varying cultural and social norms, including tribal tradition, religious affiliation, social status, gender and age (cf. Rothe 2009 for analysis of dress and cultural identity in the Rhine-Moselle region of the Roman Empire).

Although we usually lack visual depictions of dress, there is a wide array of objects that provide evidence for the ways people dressed and displayed themselves in Roman Britain. Although clothes themselves rarely survive, the brooches used to secure garments, hairpins for holding together hairstyles and dress accessories, such as finger rings and bracelets, often allow us to gain an impression of what some people may have looked like (FIG. 2.1). Common finds of personal grooming equipment, including tweezers, nail cleaners and cosmetic spoons, attest to the desire not only for personal hygiene (FIG. 2.2), but also for the wish to present oneself as clean and respectable to others, especially as such accoutrements were often worn together, sometimes grouped on a decorative chatelaine brooch (e.g. Eckardt 2008; Eckardt and Crummy 2008). Such objects are a widely recognised component of Roman finds assemblages in Britain. However, as will become clear in this chapter, they were by no means familiar to everyone. Indeed, the types of object that tell us most about the way people looked are very unevenly distributed, occurring most frequently at military, urban and villa sites and there is considerable variation in their geographical distribution outside of these settlement types. There is no doubt that the rural population of Roman Britain encompassed groups of people who looked very different from one another, and shared ways of dressing must have been an important aspect of formulating and maintaining common group identities (Allason-Jones 2014, 70). The purpose of this chapter is to examine the evidence we have for the variation in the way people presented themselves in the countryside of Roman Britain, by providing an overview of some important social and geographical differences that are evident across a range of objects associated with people's personal appearance.

For the purposes of this chapter, five broad groups of material culture have been selected to explore the appearance of people living in the countryside of Roman Britain – brooches, bracelets, finger rings, hairpins and personal grooming equipment. The last group covers a range of objects including tweezers, nail cleaners, cosmetic grinders, cosmetic palettes, cosmetic

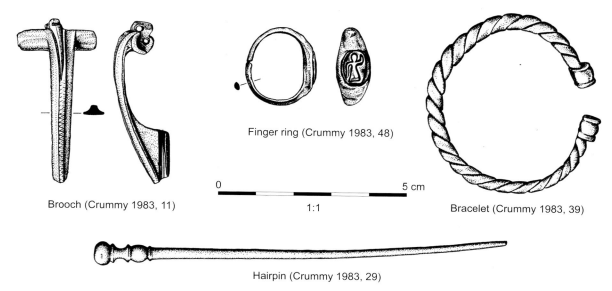

Brooch (Crummy 1983, 11)

Finger ring (Crummy 1983, 48)

0   5 cm

1:1

Bracelet (Crummy 1983, 39)

Hairpin (Crummy 1983, 29)

FIG. 2.1. A selection of objects associated with personal adornment, all from Colchester (Crummy 1983)

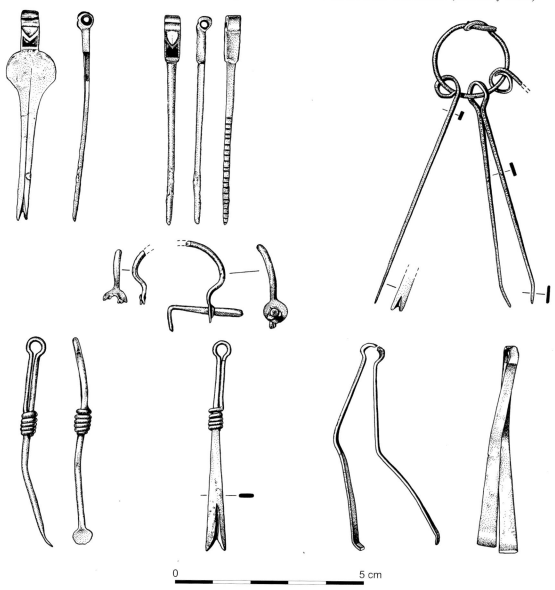

0   5 cm

FIG. 2.2. A selection of personal grooming equipment, all from Colchester (Crummy 1983). Scale 1:1

spoons, combs and mirrors, most of which are likely to have been associated with personal adornment (see Eckardt and Crummy 2008 for a useful overview, though also Morrison (2013) for an alternative perspective regarding the function of some object types).

These five groups have been selected because they are the most common types of object associated with personal adornment recovered from Romano-British sites, and their social and geographical distribution may allow us to recognise broad similarities and differences between people living at different types of rural sites, and in different geographical areas. The approach adopted in the subsequent discussion has been to present a brief overview of the social distribution (see Crummy and Eckardt 2003 and Eckardt 2014, 17–20, for discussions of the value of such an approach) of each of these object types in each of the eight project regions (see Ch. 1, FIG. 1.1). As brooches are by far the most common type of dress accessory recovered from Romano-British rural sites, these have then been selected for more detailed analysis, allowing regional and social distinctions in the types of brooches used to be recognised.

BROOCHES

Brooches are found in a bewildering range of different forms. Mackreth, in his recently published volume (2011), the culmination of nearly 50 years of study, identifies in his 'monster of a classification system' (*ibid.*, vi) 59 families of brooches, and over 1000 types and varieties in all (cf. Statton 2012, 107). Despite the multitude of types recognised by Mackreth, Roman brooches can, at the simplest level, be divided into three very broad types – bow brooches (often termed *fibulae*), plate brooches and penannular brooches. While each of these basic forms of brooch includes a staggering array of variation, there are enough similarities in form between many brooches to allow broad families and sub-types to be recognised, although there remain many hybrids and 'one-offs' that defy classification. No attempt is made to describe in detail the different varieties here, and the reader is directed towards the work of Mackreth (2011), Bayley and Butcher (2004) and Hattatt (1982; 1985; 1987; 1989) for descriptions and illustrations of the principal types.

The main function of most brooches was to secure clothing, although, like any aspect of personal dress, as highly visible objects they potentially also served as a means of displaying information about the wearer's social status and identity (Jundi and Hill 1998). The brooch pin could be sprung or hinged, and was essentially used to secure clothes in a similar way to a safety pin. Many plate brooches would have been ineffective for securing heavily woven cloth, lacking the space between the pin and the catchplate to secure bulky garments, leading Allason-Jones to suggest that they may have been decorative rather than functional, with some types carrying ideological messages (Allason-Jones 2014), although it seems plausible that some may have been used to secure very fine fabrics such as silk, which would certainly have been worn by the very affluent (Cool 2016, 419). Although usually found individually, brooches were often worn in pairs, as head-loops and chains found on some brooch types suggest, and as indicated by occasional discoveries from graves, such as a pair of disc brooches included as grave goods in the grave of a woman at North Lancing, West Sussex (Kelly and Dudley 1981).

Brooches were used in Britain from at least the early Iron Age (S. Adams 2013), although they are rare discoveries at archaeological sites for periods up until the first century B.C., at which point there was a well-recognised boom in the numbers of brooches being used and lost in southern Britain – Hill's 'Fibula Event Horizon' (Hill 1995a; 1995b; 1997; Jundi and Hill 1998). This increase in the use of brooches occurs rather later in central and northern Britain, not happening until after the Roman conquest, from the late first century A.D. onwards (Jundi and Hill 1998; Cool and Baxter 2016). It was suggested by Jundi and Hill that the increased number of brooches in the archaeological record during the late Iron Age and early Roman periods reflects not just that more brooches were in circulation at these times, but that they, as well as other objects of personal adornment, were being deposited in particular ways, frequently chosen as objects to accompany burials and often placed as ritual deposits (Jundi and Hill 1998, 128–9). The frequent use of brooches for religious deposition during the Roman period is attested by the recovery of many brooches from Romano-British temples and shrines, and several examples are discussed below (see also Ch. 5).

Recently, by ordering the brooches recorded in Mackreth's corpus (2011) chronologically, Cool and Baxter (2016) have used statistical methods to bring greater resolution to the chronology of brooch use in Britain. They demonstrated distinctive regional patterns for Hill's 'Fibula Event Horizon', with the increased use of brooches happening significantly later in the midlands and the north than in the south and the east of the province. Importantly, they were also able to recognise what they have termed a 'Fibula Abandonment Horizon', when brooches ceased to be such an important part of dress. This begins to occur from around the beginning of the third century A.D., although the authors demonstrated that the decline in brooch use was again regionally variable, with brooch use continuing later into the Roman period in the regions slowest to adopt them (i.e. midlands and north). Of additional importance was their identification of the potentially extremely long use-life brooches could have, with some types being recovered from dated contexts separated by many decades, occasionally even by centuries. Although the use-life of different types is certain to have been very variable, Cool and Baxter were able to suggest that few types were likely to have been short-lived fashions, and therefore cannot confidently be slotted into groups with tightly defined temporal parameters (*ibid.*, 87).

The following regional analysis of brooch use at rural sites utilises the method adopted by Cool for Mackreth's brooches, grouping bow brooches into five broad chronological bands, with separate groups for plate brooches and those of penannular form (Cool 2016). Plate brooches have been considered as one group for two reasons: first, as we shall see, they are fairly infrequent finds at Roman rural sites, and, second, many plate brooches are imprecisely identified in archaeological site reports and are thus difficult to date. Similarly, penannular brooches of broadly similar form were used throughout the late Iron Age and Roman periods (and beyond) and are notoriously difficult to date (e.g. Booth 2014, 53). The advantage of this approach is that it provides a pragmatic means of comparing brooch use between rural site types and between regions, which allows for some broad chronological resolution, but without the complexities of attempting to compare sites and regions by the large number of individual brooch-families.

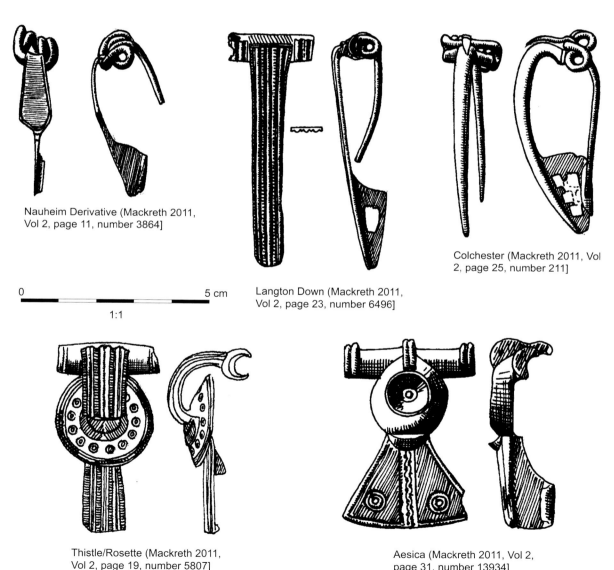

Nauheim Derivative (Mackreth 2011, Vol 2, page 11, number 3864]

Colchester (Mackreth 2011, Vol 2, page 25, number 211]

0   5 cm

1:1

Langton Down (Mackreth 2011, Vol 2, page 23, number 6496]

Thistle/Rosette (Mackreth 2011, Vol 2, page 19, number 5807]

Aesica (Mackreth 2011, Vol 2, page 31, number 13934]

FIG. 2.3. A selection of brooches within the Group A category (all illustrated by Mackreth 2011)

Although Cool's basic method for analysing brooches has been employed, the names of each group have been altered for the purposes of the following analysis, and the groups discussed are:

Group A – All brooches of Iron Age type, especially those common during the first half of the first century A.D., many of which continued to be used in the decades immediately following the Roman Conquest. The most common types are Iron Age La Tène I, II and III brooches, including Nauheim Derivatives and Colchester one-piece brooches, along with other broad families such as the Langton Down, the Thistle/Rosette and the Aesica types (FIG. 2.3).

Group B – The wide range of Colchester Derivative brooches and their variants, which began to develop in the early years following the conquest, and which continued to be used well into the second century A.D., including brooches

of Initial T-Shaped and Polden Hill types. Also included in this group are the new brooch types that came in with the Roman army during the mid-first century A.D. – the Hod Hill and the Aucissa and their derivatives (FIG. 2.4).

Group C – Brooches that began to develop in the later part of the first century A.D. and which continued until the late second century, predominantly brooches of Developed T-shaped, Trumpet and Headstud type, along with their derivatives (FIG. 2.5).

Group D – Brooches that are predominantly of late second to third century date – principally the Knee brooch and Sheath Footed types (FIG. 2.6).

Group E – Crossbow Brooches (FIG. 2.7).

Plate Brooches – plate brooches of all dates, including a range of types and forms (FIG. 2.8).

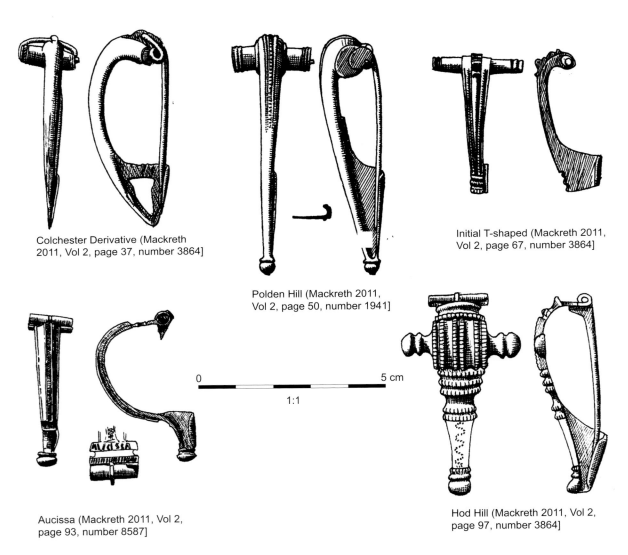

Colchester Derivative (Mackreth 2011, Vol 2, page 37, number 3864]

Polden Hill (Mackreth 2011, Vol 2, page 50, number 1941]

Initial T-shaped (Mackreth 2011, Vol 2, page 67, number 3864]

Aucissa (Mackreth 2011, Vol 2, page 93, number 8587]

Hod Hill (Mackreth 2011, Vol 2, page 97, number 3864]

0 ————— 5 cm

1:1

FIG. 2.4. A selection of brooches within the Group B category (all illustrated by Mackreth 2011)

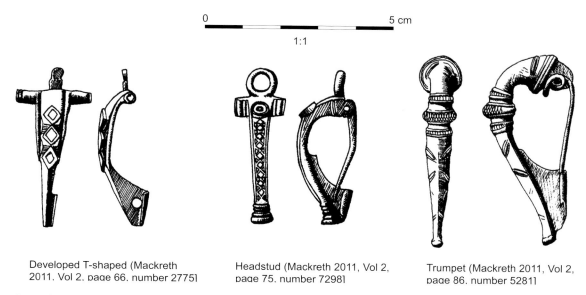

Developed T-shaped (Mackreth 2011, Vol 2, page 66, number 2775]

Headstud (Mackreth 2011, Vol 2, page 75, number 7298]

Trumpet (Mackreth 2011, Vol 2, page 86, number 5281]

FIG. 2.5. A selection of brooches within the Group C category (all illustrated by Mackreth 2011)

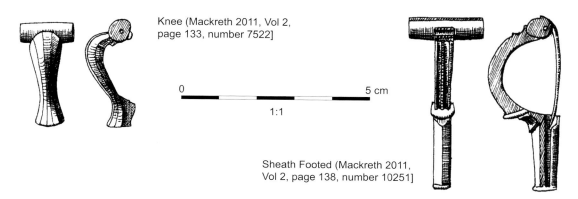

Knee (Mackreth 2011, Vol 2, page 133, number 7522]

Sheath Footed (Mackreth 2011, Vol 2, page 138, number 1025l]

FIG. 2.6. A selection of brooches within the Group D category (all illustrated by Mackreth 2011)

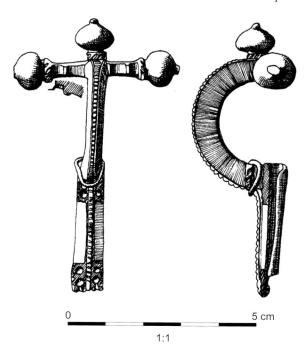

FIG. 2.7. Example of a Crossbow brooch in Group E category (illustrated by Mackreth 2011, page 141, 10438)

Penannular Brooches – notoriously difficult to date penannular brooches of all types (FIG. 2.9).

The above groupings provide a pragmatic way for drawing together and interpreting a very large body of data. However, a strong note of caution is required. Cool, using Mackreth's data, could be confident of the identifications of the brooches she was using, as all were identified by Mackreth himself. The brooches recorded by the Roman Rural Settlement Project were from a wide range of different published and unpublished sources, and were identified and recorded by a large number of finds specialists (and often non-specialists), with varying expertise in brooches. It is therefore inevitable that some brooches are misidentified, and, indeed, incorrectly identified brooches have frequently been recognised in finds reports during data collection. Although this brings an element of 'fuzziness' to the data, it is unlikely to have too drastic an impact on the broad patterns identified in the context of this review of brooch use. Nevertheless, there is one particular problem

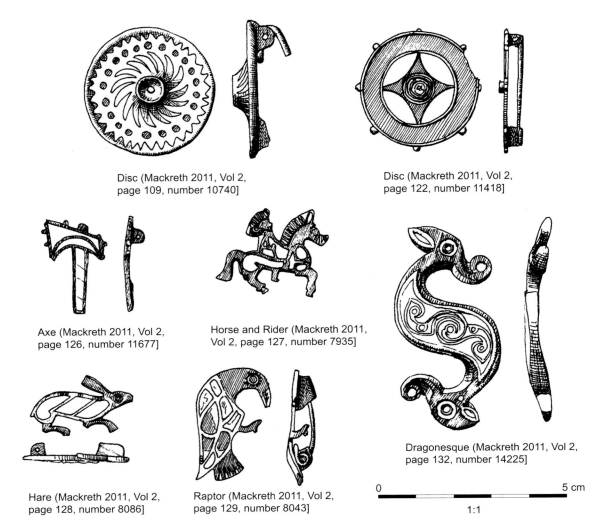

Disc (Mackreth 2011, Vol 2,
page 109, number 10740]

Disc (Mackreth 2011, Vol 2,
page 122, number 11418]

Axe (Mackreth 2011, Vol 2,
page 126, number 11677]

Horse and Rider (Mackreth 2011,
Vol 2, page 127, number 7935]

Dragonesque (Mackreth 2011, Vol 2,
page 132, number 14225]

Hare (Mackreth 2011, Vol 2,
page 128, number 8086]

Raptor (Mackreth 2011, Vol 2,
page 129, number 8043]

0   5 cm

1:1

FIG. 2.8. A selection of plate brooches (all illustrated by Mackreth 2011)

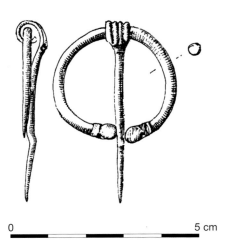

0   5 cm

FIG. 2.9. Example of a penannular brooch (illustrated
by Mackreth 2011, page 151, 12804). Scale 1:1

which needs recognition, and this concerns the
distinction between Colchester brooches and
Colchester Derivatives. This is particularly acute
because both types are among the most common
brooches recovered from the south and east of the
province, and because the two types are within
separate groups – the one-piece Colchesters falling
in Group A, and the two-piece derivatives in
Group B. Where brooches were described in a
report as being of Colchester Derivative type they
would have been entered into the relevant box.
However, often, two-piece Colchester brooches are
described in various ways – sometimes using
simple terms such as being of 'Colchester type',
sometimes as a 'Two-Piece Colchester', sometimes
as a 'Colchester Type B'. Given that only one
member of the Rural Settlement Project team had
a background in the study of artefacts, this lack of
standardisation in reports has undoubtedly
resulted in inconsistencies in the data, and it is
evident that the 'Colchester' brooch group contains
many brooches that should in fact have been
placed in the 'Colchester Derivative' category. This
means, of course, that the Group A brooches are
likely to be somewhat inflated, while the Group B
brooches may be somewhat under-represented. A
random check of several reports has confirmed
this. For instance, what appears to be a two-piece

Colchester Derivative brooch with a Polden Hill spring mechanism, illustrated in the site report for Tolpuddle Ball, Dorset, was identified in the finds report as being of 'Colchester Type', dated to the first half of the first century A.D. (Loader 1999, 102), and used as dating evidence to suggest that a burial was late Iron Age in date. This was included under the 'Colchester' category on the project database, and thus is included in brooches of Group A.

The issue is difficult to compensate for, but as Colchester Derivative brooches are significantly more common than one-piece Colchesters, with a ratio approaching 2:1 (even without correction of the misidentified examples), both Colchesters and Colchester Derivatives have been included in the 'Colchester Derivative' group. Inevitably, this has the potential to have a strong impact on the proportion of Iron Age types in each assemblage, and in the southern project region, for example, if all of those recorded as Colchesters were genuine one-piece Colchester brooches, removing them and placing them in Group B would reduce the number of Group A brooches from 742 examples to 578 – a reduction of 22 per cent. The likelihood is that several of these brooches were one-piece Colchesters, yet as the extent of the issue is unknown, it has been deemed best to accept that there is likely to be some bias against the Iron Age types in Group A, rather than to attempt to 'correct' for the issue statistically. The potential impact of this methodological issue is assessed in each of the case studies below, where testing has determined the difference that moving the Colchesters from one group to another makes on the overall patterns.

The issue is factored in to the interpretative discussions in each of the regional discussions where relevant below, particularly where Colchester brooches are most widespread (in the South, the East and the Central Belt regions).

Although the main method of brooch analysis has been to compare brooches by basic groups, the principal types of brooch in use are discussed in the text in each of the regional case studies, as the different types favoured in each region have the potential to provide some insights into regional variations in dress, and, perhaps, cultural and social attitudes. In broad regional terms the following analysis, as would be expected, for the most part supports the patterns recently presented by Cool and Baxter (2016). However, the principal significance of the following analysis lies in its presentation of the social distribution of the seven groups of brooches across different site types. Most brooch studies have a firm emphasis on typology and chronology, whereas this approach allows us to develop a considerably more nuanced understanding of the ways that brooches were used by different sets of people in the countryside of Roman Britain.

PERSONAL ADORNMENT IN THE SOUTH REGION

Objects associated with personal display are very unevenly distributed across site types in the South region (FIG. 2.10). There are too few open farmsteads from the region to consider by percentages so these are omitted from FIG. 2.10, but it is fair to say that objects associated with personal adornment are in general infrequent finds

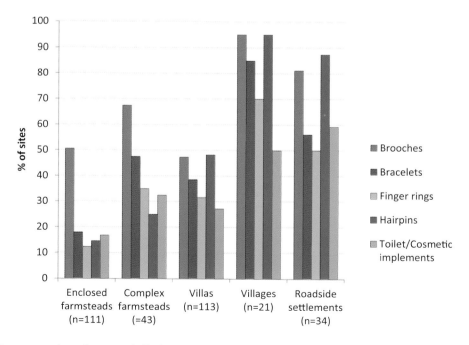

FIG. 2.10. Representation of personal display equipment in the South region by site type (n=no. of sites)

from these site types. Enclosed farmsteads are, on the whole, considerably less well represented by most types of dress accessory than the other site types, though they are reasonably well represented by brooches, which were recovered from 50 per cent of sites – more than at villas (likely reasons for this are discussed below, p. 16). Brooches are also well represented at all other site-types in the South, yet at these other types of site bracelets, finger rings, hairpins and toilet equipment are substantially more common than at enclosed farmsteads. The nucleated sites, roadside settlements and villages stand out over all other site-types, including villas, in terms of the frequency of most objects of personal adornment. This may partially reflect the size of some of these settlements – greater populations meant more people using objects, and therefore more opportunities for them to be lost and recovered during archaeological intervention – yet it is also likely to reflect a situation where the increased population sizes at some of these settlements meant that regular interaction with others in larger communities made presenting the self in particular ways more desirable. The recovery, for instance, of toilet equipment at 50 per cent of villages and nearly 60 per cent of roadside settlements, suggests that personal grooming was of particular importance for the occupants of and/ or visitors to these settlement types. The emphasis that many of these sites had on industry and production, with many likely serving as local market centres, suggests that they were places to go to and, importantly, to be seen at.

While villas in the South do not stand out as being especially well represented by most objects of personal adornment compared with complex farmsteads, they are substantially better represented by hairpins (48 per cent compared with 25 per cent of complex farmsteads), and some villas have yielded exceptionally large groups of hairpins (e.g. Barton Field, Tarrant Hinton, Dorset; Graham 2006). Some of this patterning may be due to chronological considerations, with many hairpin types being late Roman in date, and therefore falling within the main *floruit* of villa use. However, the role of hairpins as an important indicator of status is now recognised (Eckardt 2014, 174), and the phenomenon is also likely to reflect the wealth and status of villa occupants, perhaps indicating a situation where elite females had more leisure time to allow the creation of the types of elaborate hairstyles that can be recognised in surviving busts from across the Roman Empire (and as have convincingly been re-created, using hairpins and needles, by Stephens 2008). The increased frequency of hairpins may also reflect large numbers of women and girls at villa sites generally, where they would have been required to

perform the various roles, as slaves or servants, associated with the daily upkeep of the villa and perhaps as attendants to elite women. The large numbers of spindlewhorls recovered from some villas (see Brindle and Lodwick 2017, 226–8) may also suggest groups of females at some of these sites, as spinning was a predominantly female activity (e.g. Wild 2002, 8; Hersch 2010; Cool 2010, 274–6; 2016, 408).

BROOCH USE IN THE SOUTH

Brooches were recovered from 35 per cent of all sites in the database from the South region, making it among the best represented regions in the province for brooches at rural sites. Considering all brooches from all sites recorded in the project database together first, it is immediately apparent that brooches of the late Iron Age and the early Roman period (Groups A and B) form a large proportion of all brooch types from the region (FIG. 2.11). We must remember that the Group B brooches inevitably contain some one-piece Colchesters, and so the Group A brooches are probably more important than they seem. Certainly, however, Group A and B brooches are the most important types, with a distinct reduction for Group C onwards. We must also remember the potentially very long use-life of brooches demonstrated by Cool and Baxter (2016). While Group C brooches – the Trumpets, Headstuds, Developed T-shaped type and their derivatives – emerged slightly later than those in Group B, in the latter part of the first century A.D., many types in both groups appear to have continued in use long into the second century A.D., and thus had the potential to be in use at the same time. The dominance of Group B brooches over those in Group C may therefore say a good deal about regional preference regarding particular brooch forms.

Plate brooches and penannular brooches account for very small proportions of the brooches from the region, at just 10 per cent and 7 per cent respectively. It seems clear then that brooch use was at its height in the South during the late Iron Age and early decades following the Roman conquest, and this accords well with the first-century A.D. peak in brooch use, at around A.D. 60, recognised by Cool and Baxter for their southern region (Cool and Baxter 2016, 85). Brooches were an important aspect of dress for much of the population in the South during the late Iron Age and early Roman periods.

Given that there is wide variation in the chronologies of different types of Roman rural settlements, it is scarcely surprising that the broad pattern for brooch-use in the South is reflected in the types of brooches recovered from different site types. FIGURE 2.12 shows the variation in the types

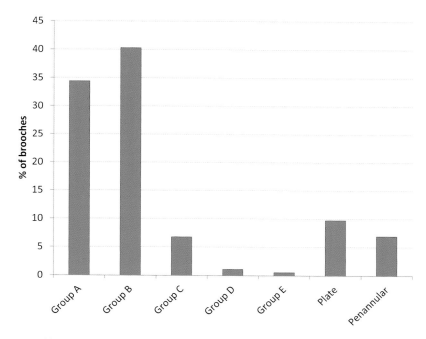

FIG. 2.11. Percentages of brooches from each group in the South region (total no. brooches=1679)

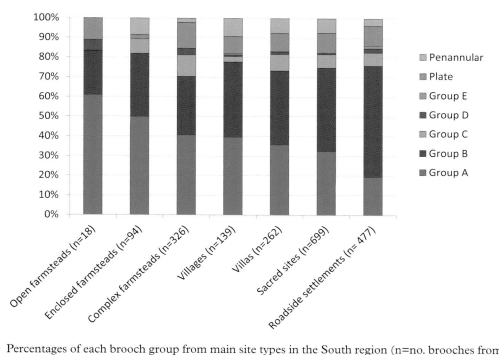

FIG. 2.12. Percentages of each brooch group from main site types in the South region (n=no. brooches from site type)

of brooch from the main site types. Brooches are less common finds in general at open and enclosed farmsteads than at many other types of site, and where they are recovered, those of Group A dominate. Although a range of brooch types are included in this broad group, they are dominated by the various types of Iron Age British La Tène III brooches, especially Nauheim Derivatives. Viewed as a proportion of all brooches from complex farmsteads, Group A brooches appear to be the most common, although this is partly accounted for by a small number of these sites producing quite large assemblages of these brooches (e.g. Balksbury Camp, Andover, Hampshire: Wainwright and Davies 1995; Ellis and Rawlings 2001). In terms of their representation across settlements, Group B brooches are the most widely encountered (FIG. 2.13). Complex farmsteads are also considerably better represented by brooches of Group C (particularly Developed T-shaped brooches and Trumpet brooches) and plate brooches than enclosed farmsteads, whereas

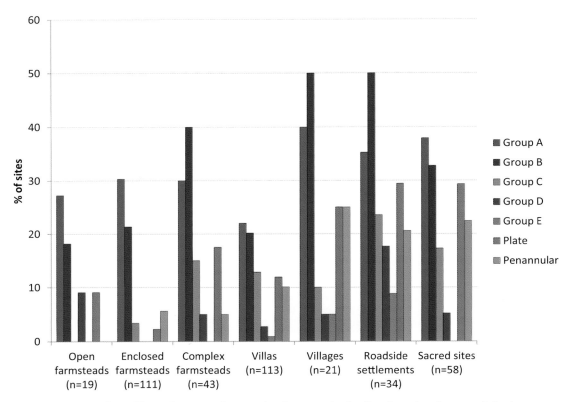

FIG. 2.13.   Representation of brooch groups from main site types in the South region (n=no. of sites)

enclosed farmsteads are somewhat better represented by brooches of penannular form.

Group B brooches make up much more sizeable components of the assemblages at villages, villas, sacred sites and roadside settlements, notably so at the last (FIGS 2.12 and 2.13). This, in large part, is likely to reflect the chronology of these types of site. While some have yielded evidence for Iron Age occupation, the majority of roadside settlements in the South appear to have been post-conquest in date (Allen 2016a, 97–8), and most, if not all, were therefore occupied at the point when brooch-use in the south was at its *floruit*. The fact that these sites are also well represented by Group A brooches is not necessarily because they were in existence prior to the conquest (although some were), but rather that many of the brooches in Group A had long periods of use, which continued well into the second half of the first century A.D. (Bayley and Butcher 2004; Mackreth 2011; Cool and Baxter 2016). Compared with the other site types, villas are the least well represented by all brooch types, primarily reflecting the fact that, although many villas in the east of the region were early foundations, and several developed out of Iron Age and/or early Roman farmsteads, many others, particularly in the west of the region, were established during the late Roman period (Allen 2016a, 90–7), and were therefore not occupied during the peak period of brooch use.

It is notable that Group B brooches are far more regularly recovered from complex farmsteads than either enclosed farmsteads or villas (FIG. 2.13). Although comparison of Groups A and B require caution owing to the issues of distinguishing between one-piece Colchester brooches and the two-piece Colchester Derivatives, it seems unlikely that the difference between the site types has been caused by this, as all should suffer from a similar bias towards brooches of Group B. The general scarcity of these types of brooch at villas is probably a result of the same chronological factors referred to above. However, there is a distinct difference between enclosed farmsteads and complex farmsteads that seems less likely to be accounted for by site chronology, and it is worth considering this in some detail.

Although there is a gradual reduction in the number of enclosed farmsteads in use over time in the South, these farmsteads remained the dominant type of rural settlement in this region until the late Roman period (Allen 2016a, 84). While some enclosed farmsteads did go out of use at around the time of the Roman conquest, around 80 per cent continued into the second half of the first century, and nearly 70 per cent remained occupied during the first half of the second century. Even if we exclude the enclosed farmsteads that were abandoned during the first century A.D., and which might therefore be

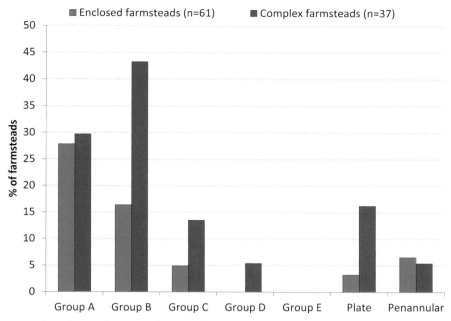

FIG. 2.14. Representation of brooch groups from enclosed and complex farmsteads from the South region occupied to at least A.D. 150 (n=no. of sites)

precluded on grounds of dating from receiving the newer brooches that emerged in the decades following the conquest, there is still a stark contrast between enclosed farmsteads and those of complex form (FIG. 2.14). While complex farmsteads see a large increase in the number of brooches lost, enclosed farmsteads see a reduction, and although complex farmsteads are better represented by all types of brooch than enclosed farmsteads (except penannulars), the distinctions are most stark for the Group B types and plate brooches. Given that all sites in the sample were occupied well into the second century A.D. there seems little chronological reason for them all not to have acquired these brooches.

If chronology is not the principal factor, then this pattern alludes to some important distinctions between the inhabitants of these different types of rural settlement in the south. One factor may have been related to changes in the ways that brooches were marketed, with differential access to the new brooch types. Indeed, in their metallurgical analysis of the composition of brooches, Bayley and Butcher recognised major technological changes, with a shift from the brass of the first half of the first century A.D. to leaded bronze during the middle part of that century (Bayley and Butcher 2004, 207). This change in composition was associated with an important technological development, from one-piece brooches of wrought metal to two-piece brooches that could now be cast, using what was probably a cheaper and more readily available alloy (*ibid.*). Although direct evidence for manufacture is usually lacking, it

seems likely that such technological changes were most widespread at towns and other newly emerging sites on the road network. Within the South region, for instance, the roadside settlement and religious complex at Springhead, Kent, has produced possible evidence for the production of Colchester Derivative brooches (*ibid.*, 37, table 11; Penn 1957, 70). Such sites had large populations who appear to have embraced fashions that required the use of brooches more than ever before. This produced a greater demand for brooches, and the change in alloy and increased use of casting seems likely to be a response to the increasing popularity of brooches for people at nucleated settlements, and for those who frequented these sites most often.

If markets at towns and roadside settlements became the places where new brooch types were typically acquired, this may have meant that there were more limited opportunities to acquire them for those who visited these sites less frequently. That the occupants of complex farmsteads were in general far more closely integrated with the new markets than those at enclosed farmsteads is suggested by a number of sets of proxy evidence. For instance, imported ceramics are considerably more common at complex farmsteads, with amphora sherds present at 70 per cent of these sites, compared with 22 per cent of enclosed farmsteads, while samian occurs at 65 per cent and 34 per cent of the different farmstead types respectively. Coins are also much less frequently recovered from enclosed farmsteads than those of complex form (see Brindle 2017a). The greater association of features interpreted as stock enclosures with complex farmsteads (65 per cent compared with 21 per cent at enclosed farmsteads) might imply higher numbers of livestock, while corndryers (28 per cent compared with 12 per cent) and pottery kilns (15 per cent compared with 6 per cent) also imply a greater level of surplus productivity for complex farmsteads. Any such surplus may have contributed to the increased wealth that facilitated the acquisition of new types of clothing and their fasteners. The need to market surplus produce is also likely to have led to increased opportunities for social interaction with a wider range of people, making the expression of self to others through appearance all the more important for the occupants of complex farmsteads. This may also be the reason for the low frequency of other objects of personal adornment at enclosed farmsteads, as shown in FIG. 2.10. If the occupants of most enclosed farmsteads were self-sufficient peasants, they may have had less reason to visit markets held at roadside settlements and towns, and therefore less desire or need to present themselves in the sorts of ways that were becoming socially prescribed at nucleated settlements.

As brooches (and indeed bracelets, finger rings and hairpins) could be a highly visible element of one's dress, and their display projected messages about their wearer's identity and status (e.g. Jundi and Hill 1998), it seems likely that their increased frequency at complex farmsteads reflects a greater degree of interaction with others. The greater representation of plate brooches may also be important in this regard. As discussed above, the utilitarian value of plate brooches has been questioned (Allason-Jones 2014) and their increased frequency at complex farmsteads suggests that people here had the desire and means to wear brooches that may not have functioned primarily as pins to secure clothing, but which carried decorative patterns (and possibly some ideological messages), and which, therefore, said something about wealth and status, where the occupants of most enclosed farmsteads did not. We cannot easily know whether the occupants of enclosed farmsteads coveted these new aspects of fashion but could not generally afford them, whether they seldom had the opportunities to acquire them, or whether they took active decisions to eschew the newer types of brooch and other objects due to an inherently greater level of cultural conservatism and adherence to pre-conquest traditions of personal display. The three scenarios may all have been related. Although the new types of cast bow brooch were in general of a similar shape to those of wrought metal, and might at first glance appear not to be substantially different, the change in alloy composition may

also have meant that they had quite distinctive appearances – brass being yellow, and bronze varying shades of brown (Bayley and Butcher 2004, 16). The increased use of enamelling as a method of decoration for brooches during the late first and second centuries certainly indicates that colour was an important attribute of brooches, and there has been increasing recognition that the colour of an object could be of considerable importance in the ancient world (e.g. Eckardt 2014, 94–6; Cool 2016, 415–16). Perhaps varying colours of these different types of brooches played a part in marking people out as different.

Whether or not this is the case, given the lower frequency of brooches in general at enclosed farmsteads it is likely that the very act of wearing a brooch of any type, and, perhaps more importantly, the changes in clothing styles that this might reflect, were in themselves an indication of the need to mark one's social identity in particular ways. Perhaps brooches were increasingly being used in new ways by people living at complex farmsteads following the conquest. They may have been worn differently, with new types of clothing, as those who engaged more extensively with markets at towns and other nucleated sites were exposed to new ways of dressing, this also being reflected by the increased representation of bracelets, finger rings, hairpins and personal grooming equipment.

Cool (1990, 176) has suggested how the proliferation of hairpins during the second half of the first century A.D. may provide archaeological verification of Tacitus' comment concerning the increasing adoption of Roman fashions in Britain under Agricola (Tac. Ag. 21). The increased evidence for a wide range of dress accessories at complex farmsteads, including those that were uncommon in Britain during the late Iron Age – especially finger rings (cf. Johns 1996a, 41) and hairpins (Cool 1990; Eckardt 2014, 154) – provide us with insights into the types of site where populations were the most influenced by the new and emerging ways of dressing. Given the evidence from the broad groups of dress accessories and personal grooming equipment discussed here, there seems little doubt that many of the occupants of enclosed and complex farmsteads in the South would have been quite clearly distinguishable from one another by their appearance (or indeed, by their consumption of other types of material culture including pottery), and it is possible that they may have viewed one another as distinct social classes (discussed further below, p. 44).

A final point to make concerns the use of brooches at sacred sites in the South, with some such sites having exceptionally large brooch assemblages. There has long been recognition that some types of brooch, particularly plate brooches, are associated with sacred sites and that some may have had associations with specific deities (e.g. Ferris 1986; 2012, 35–9; Johns 1995; Simpson and Blance 1998; Eckardt 2005; Crummy 2007; Allason-Jones 2014; see also Ch. 5). Bow brooches, too, appear often to have been selected as votive objects, with over 200 brooches, of a wide range of types, being recovered from the religious complex at Springhead, Kent, many seemingly deposited as votives at the sacred springs and temple (Biddulph *et al.* 2011). The religious sites at Cold Kitchen Hill, Wiltshire (Nan Kivell 1927; 1929), and Lamyatt Beacon, Somerset (Leech 1986), are noteworthy for having yielded a number of Horse-and-Rider brooches, a type with a well-recognised religious association (Ferris 1986; 2012, 35–9; Johns 1995; Eckardt 2005; 2014, 132; Fillery-Travis 2012, 158), and these are a feature of other probable religious sites in this part of the region (Brindle 2014, 42).

PERSONAL ADORNMENT IN THE EAST REGION

There is, to a certain extent, a similar social hierarchy in terms of the distribution of dress accessories and grooming equipment in the East region as in the South (FIG. 2.15), although the distinctions between different classes of rural site are considerably less marked. Open farmsteads are too poorly represented for percentages to be of

value, but again, those in the East seem often to be poorly represented by dress accessories, though brooches are reasonably common, present at three of the four examples. Enclosed farmsteads are less well represented by all object types than the other site types, yet there appears to be far less of a distinction between these and complex farmsteads than in the South. Complex farmsteads are also better represented by some types of object than the equivalent sites in the South, especially hairpins (59 per cent of sites compared with 25 per cent) and personal grooming equipment (53 per cent compared with 33 per cent). The sample sizes are small in the East, however, and whether this reflects a genuinely greater level of investment in personal display (at least that which is archaeologically visible) for occupants of both enclosed and complex farmsteads in the East than in the South, or whether it is a factor created by the small sample sizes (as well, perhaps, as increased metal-detector use during excavations) is slightly unclear. It is, however, of note that settlements in the East do appear to be represented by substantially greater quantities of material culture in general than other regions (see Smith 2016c, 235–7; and discussed further below), and there may have been differing, perhaps very long-lived, attitudes towards personal display, which meant that more of the rural population in this region were receptive to, and had access to and the means to acquire, objects that allowed presentation of the self in particular ways.

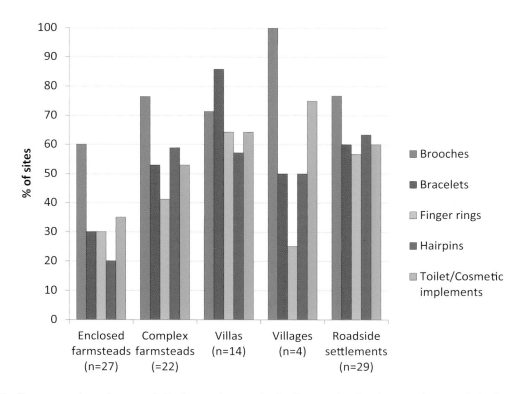

FIG. 2.15. Representation of personal display equipment in the East region by site type (n=no. of sites).

BROOCH USE IN THE EAST

Brooches were found at *c.* 50 per cent of sites recorded on the project database for the East region, making it the most well-populated region in terms of brooches. In common with the South, rural sites are totally dominated by brooches of Groups A and B, of late Iron Age and early Roman date, and those from the other groups are comparatively scarce (FIG. 2.16). Like the South, Group A brooches are dominated by simple one-piece La Tène III variants, especially Nauheim Derivatives. Langton Down and Thistle/Rosette brooches are reasonably well represented, although they are concentrated in roadside settlements and are seldom recovered from non-nucleated settlements. It is important to note that one-piece Colchester brooches are common in this region – indeed there is evidence for their manufacture at the roadside settlement at Baldock (Stead and Rigby 1986, 122) – and their inclusion with the Colchester Derivatives in Group B has undoubtedly created a bias against those of Group A. If all brooches recorded as Colchesters on the project database were indeed the earlier one-piece types, then the Iron Age types would overtake those in Group B. It may therefore be safest to regard Groups A and B as being of broadly comparable frequency in general in this region. Brooches of Group B are overwhelmingly dominated by Colchester Derivatives, even if the uncertain Colchesters are excluded. Less common, though present in some numbers, are the strip-bow brooches brought in by the Roman military – the Aucissa and Hod Hill types. As with the Langton Downs and Thistle/Rosettes, these are concentrated

at nucleated settlements on the road network. Other types are generally rare at rural settlements in the region. Together, Groups A and B totally dominate the assemblages from the East, suggesting a peak in brooch use in the first century A.D., which corresponds with the pattern recognised by Cool and Baxter (2016, 85), who identified a peak during the latter half of the first century A.D. for their East Anglia region.

As in the South region, there are some differences between the main rural site types (FIGS 2.17 and 2.18). All are dominated by brooches of Groups A and B, and, as noted, Group A are likely to be more common than they seem in the charts. Villas, however, are notably less-well represented by brooches of Group A. As in the South, this must relate to the chronology of the villas, and although not all are well understood, only around a quarter have produced evidence for occupation during the Iron Age, compared with, for instance, over half of complex farmsteads and nearly all enclosed farmsteads. Villas are, however, considerably better represented by both plate and penannular brooches than either type of farmstead, and the increased frequency of plate brooches in particular may be a mark of the wealth and status of villa occupants.

There is rather less evidence in the East for the strong distinction between enclosed and complex farmsteads when compared with the South, and this is also witnessed by some other types of material culture. For example, samian was recovered from every complex farmstead and 70 per cent of enclosed farmsteads, while amphora sherds were recovered from 59 per cent of complex

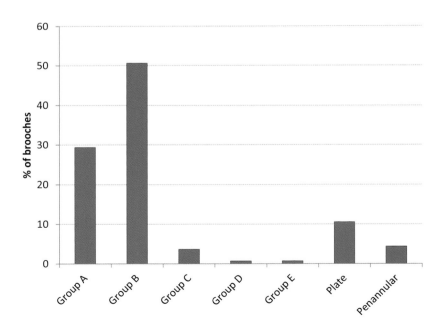

FIG. 2.16. Percentages of brooches from each group in the East region (total no. brooches=1280)

and 55 per cent of enclosed farmsteads. This might indicate wider access to material culture in general in the East, as well as a greater degree of cultural homogeneity for those occupying farmsteads of all types, reflected through broad similarities in the ways that people dressed.

A further striking aspect of the rural brooch assemblages in the East is the near total absence of brooches of Groups C, D and E at all types of farmsteads and villas. Roadside settlements, however, are far better represented by brooches of

Group C (predominantly Trumpet brooches and Headstuds), which occur at just over a quarter of these sites, although they nevertheless make up only a very small proportion of the total assemblages. The later Roman types – Groups D and E – are also exceptionally rare at these sites.

As with villas, roadside settlements stand out as being notably better represented by plate brooches than most other rural sites, and although they are far fewer in number than the late Iron Age and early Roman bow brooches, they have been

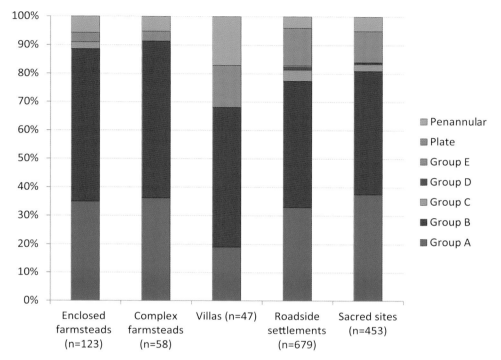

FIG. 2.17. Percentages of each brooch group from main site types in the East region (n=no. brooches from site type)

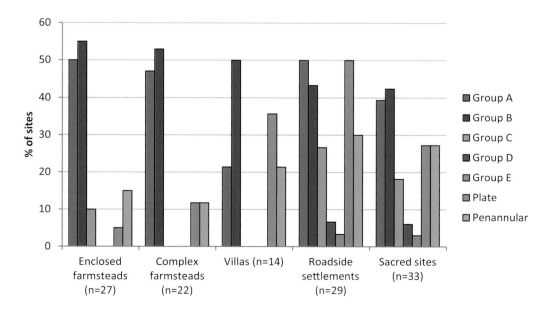

FIG. 2.18. Representation of brooch groups from main site types in the East region (n=no. of sites)

recovered from 50 per cent of these sites. This is likely to reflect several factors. First, roadside settlements, which by their very nature were situated on the major communications network, were no doubt visited by a wider range of people from different geographical areas and different social and cultural backgrounds to those occupying most farmsteads, as people passed through these settlements and stayed in them as they moved through the province. This in itself may account for the loss of a wider range of brooch types at these settlements, although, as a result, the permanent inhabitants of the roadside settlements themselves had a greater degree of exposure to both objects and ideas about how to dress in different ways. Some of the occupants of these settlements may have had the opportunity to acquire wealth through the provision of services to passing road-users by offering food, beverages and lodgings at taverns and inns, and may have chosen to display this through wearing more elaborate and colourful brooches.

A further factor is that several of the roadside settlements also acted as foci for religious activities, with a number containing shrines or Romano-Celtic temples and, as discussed above (p. 8), brooches were sometimes used as votive offerings. At the roadside settlement and shrine at Hockwold cum Wilton, Leylands Farm, Norfolk, for instance, the brooch assemblage was overwhelmingly dominated by plate brooches, and those from the shrine in particular were very distinctive, including circular plate brooches, a raptor clutching a hare and eight Horse-and-Rider brooches (Mackreth 1986, 61–7). At Hacheston, Suffolk, a roadside settlement without any clear structural evidence for a religious focus, the large brooch assemblage

(predominantly unstratified finds recovered by metal-detector users) included many plate brooches, a number of which were of zoomorphic and skeuomorphic form, suggesting ritual activity nearby, as noted in the brooch report for the site by Plouviez (2004, 107). Such roadside settlements evidently could serve as religious foci (see Ch. 5), and the use of brooches for particular religious purposes, whether deposited as votive offerings or worn as badges to declare an association with a particular divinity (or both), has the potential to have a strong influence on the brooch assemblage from a site.

PERSONAL ADORNMENT IN THE CENTRAL BELT REGION

The social distribution of dress accessories and personal grooming equipment in the Central Belt follows a similar pattern to the previous two regions, with nucleated sites (roadside settlements and villages) the best represented by all five groups of personal equipment (FIG. 2.19). Roadside settlements appear somewhat better represented by hairpins than villages, with some sites producing hundreds of examples (e.g. Wanborough, Wiltshire; Anderson et al. 2001), likely reflecting the role that some of these sites played as central places in the landscape, where people gathered. The profiles for complex farmsteads and villas are similar, although the former are quite substantially better represented by brooches, again reflecting differences in the chronology of many of these site types, with several villas developing only late in the Roman period (see Smith 2016d, 157–60), well beyond the peak period of brooch-use in the region (see below).

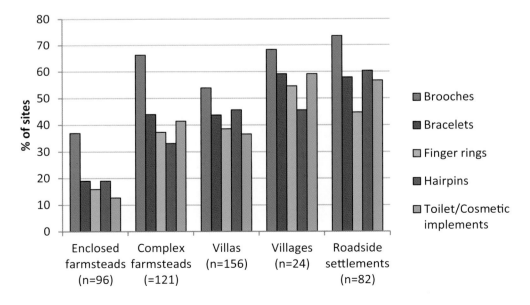

FIG. 2.19. Representation of personal display equipment in the Central Belt region by site type (n=no. of sites)

As in the South, villas are notably better represented by hairpins than complex farmsteads (46 per cent of sites compared with 33 per cent) – again, an indication of the status of the female occupants of these sites, as well as the possibility that they may have been served by personal female attendants. The generally low frequency of objects associated with personal display, apart from brooches, at enclosed (and open) farmsteads represents evidence that the occupants of these sites engaged with new market centres to a lesser extent than those occupying complex farmsteads or villas.

BROOCH USE IN THE CENTRAL BELT

A total of *c.* 40 per cent of sites in the project database for the Central Belt region had brooches, placing it between the East and the South in terms of brooch prevalence. Again, Groups A and B dominate, particularly Group B (FIG. 2.20), though the merging of Colchesters and Colchester Derivatives must bias against Group A, meaning that there is likely to have been less of a difference between the two groups than is suggested in the charts. This all indicates a peak in brooch use towards the end of the first century A.D., which is broadly in keeping with Cool and Baxter's observation (2016, 85), although their regions differed from the ones used here.

In terms of the composition of the two main groups, those of Group A are again dominated by one-piece La Tène III variants, especially Nauheim Derivatives, while one-piece Colchesters are also common. Less common, though nevertheless numerous, are brooches of Langton Down form,

and to a lesser extent Thistle/Rosette brooches and those that developed from them – the Aesica and their derivatives. Where these are found they are concentrated at roadside settlements, complex farmsteads and villas, and seldom at villages or enclosed farmsteads. Other Iron Age brooch types are uncommon. Group B is dominated by Colchester Derivatives (even without the potentially misidentified Colchesters), although in this region several other brooch types in Group B are very numerous, including over 340 Hod Hill brooches and 325 Polden Hills. The latter in particular have a strong focus on the west of the region, especially at nucleated roadside settlements, reflecting the core area of these brooches in the West Midlands (e.g. Bayley and Butcher 2004, 160). Over 100 examples of Aucissa brooches (or derivative strip-bow types such as the Bagendon) have been recorded, while Initial T-shaped brooches are known, but not especially common – where these occur there is an emphasis on the south-west of the region, reflecting the distribution of these types more generally (*ibid.*, 159).

The Central Belt stands out from both the South and the East for being notably better represented by brooches within Group C. These made up just 7 per cent of the brooches from the South and 4 per cent from the East, whereas in the Central Belt brooches in Group C account for 11 per cent of all brooches. The differences are subtle, but nevertheless represent a considerably stronger emphasis on the Central Belt area than in the areas to the south and east. This may indicate not only that their centres of production lay within the

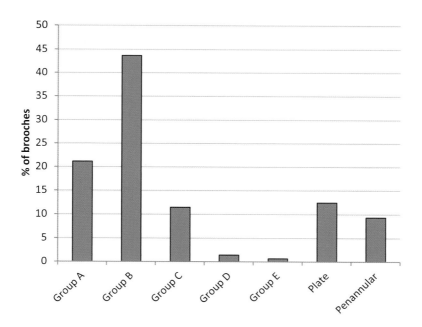

FIG. 2.20. Percentages of brooches from each group in the Central Belt region (total no. brooches=4212)

Central Belt, but also that these brooches were perhaps 'badges' of regional identity. Of the brooches in Group C, varieties of the Trumpet brooch are the most common, with 250 examples, followed by the Developed T-shaped type (which, as with the initial T-shaped type is focused on the south-west of the region), and a reasonably large number of Headstud brooches have been recorded. Other types, such as the Wroxeter, are encountered, though they are less frequent. The later types of bow brooch, Groups D and E, appear to be just as rare at rural sites in the Central Belt as they are in the South and East, although the region is somewhat better represented by both plate brooches and penannulars than either of the previous regions.

Like the South, the settlement pattern of the Central Belt is complex, with a range of different settlement types, and considerable sub-regional variation. Naturally, there is therefore variation in terms of the social distribution of different types of brooch (FIGS 2.21 and 2.22). As in the previous regions, there is a hierarchy that is repeated across each of the groups. For almost all groups sacred sites are the best represented, followed by the roadside settlements (several of which contained religious foci). Villages are, on the whole, better represented by brooches than all types of farmstead, and for the earliest brooch groups they

are also better represented than villas, although villas overtake villages from Group C onwards.

Part of the reason for the difference between site types is, as in the previous regions, chronological. As in the South, there is little doubt that the low incidence of early brooch types at villas, compared with complex farmsteads for instance, reflects the late foundation dates for many villas in the Central Belt, especially those in the Cotswold area (Smith 2016d, 160). Brooches of Group B considerably outnumber those of Group A at roadside settlements (even if all potential one-piece Colchesters were to be included in Group A), reflecting the fact that most of these sites developed in the post-conquest period, with many emerging during the second half of the first century A.D. (*ibid.*, 166). At enclosed farmsteads, Groups A and B are evenly matched, yet at all other site types there is a notable rise in brooches of Group B (and this distinction between enclosed farmsteads and the other site types only becomes *more* marked if Colchesters are placed in Group A rather than B).

As with the South, while the difference between enclosed farmsteads and the other sites may in part be chronological, there seems to be rather more to it. Although there is a 20 per cent reduction in the number of enclosed farmsteads occupied between the late Iron Age and the first

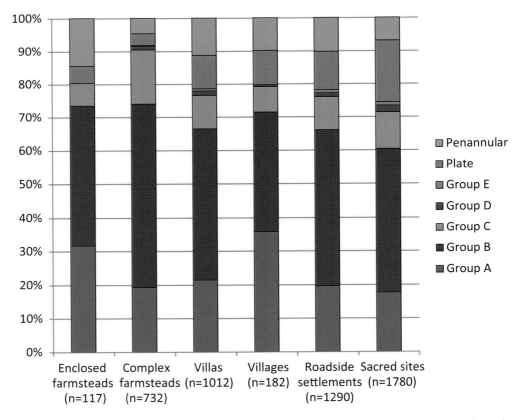

FIG. 2.21. Percentages of each brooch group from main site types in the Central Belt region (n=no. brooches from site type)

part of the second century A.D., the majority of late Iron Age enclosed farmsteads remained in use at this time. Filtering out all enclosed farmsteads that were abandoned prior to the second century, the difference between the enclosed and complex farmsteads is striking (FIG. 2.23). There appears to have been a fundamental difference between the two site types in terms of who was using the different types of brooch (which again does not alter significantly if all potential Colchester

one-piece brooches are included in Group A). As in the South, the rise in the use of the newer brooch types is most evident for those occupying site types that have greater evidence for engagement with markets at towns and nucleated settlements, and this corresponds with the social distribution of dress accessories more generally, shown in FIG. 2.19; it is fair to say that people at many enclosed and complex farmsteads looked different to one another.

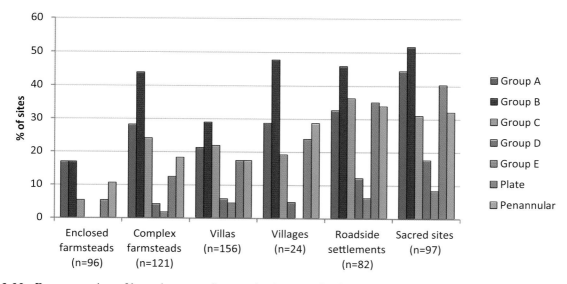

FIG. 2.22. Representation of brooch groups from main site types in the Central Belt region (n=no. of sites)

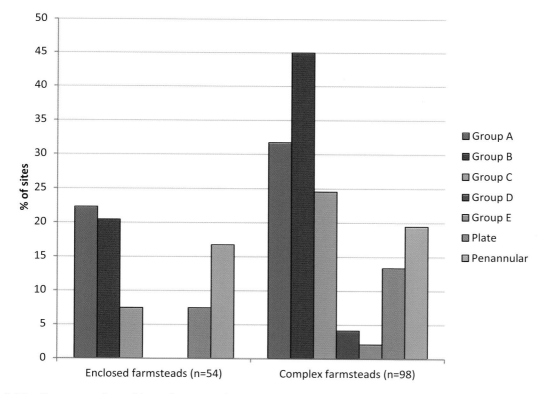

FIG. 2.23. Representation of brooch groups from enclosed and complex farmsteads in the Central Belt region occupied to at least A.D. 150 (n=no. of sites)

That sacred sites stand out above all others in terms of brooch loss in the Central Belt is likely to reflect both their role as hubs on the communication network, where people may have gathered for religious festivals, and that personal objects, including brooches, were often selected as votive offerings. While relatively high numbers of plate brooches are in general a feature of sites with a religious element, skeuomorphic and zoomorphic brooches have an exceptionally strong relationship with these sites – brooches depicting axes, shoes/sandals, daggers, chickens, fishes, ducks, dogs, hares and eagles are all represented, and appear to have had particular religious significance, although association with any particular deity is difficult (e.g. Ferris 2012, 35). As noted above (p. 19), Horse-and-Rider brooches also have a strong association with religious sites, being recovered from the Romano-Celtic temple sites at Woodeaton, Oxfordshire (Harding 1987), and Nettleton Scrubb, Wiltshire (Wedlake 1982), as well as shrines at Haddenham (Evans and Hodder 2006) and Stonea Grange (Jackson and Potter 1996), both in Cambridgeshire. Most noteworthy of all is the site at Bosworth Field, Sutton Cheney, Leicestershire, where around 100 Horse-and-Rider brooches were found (predominantly by metal-detector users), along with other skeuomorphic and zoomorphic plate brooches, many depicting axes, horses and hares, as well as a range of other types (Fillery-Travis 2012).

PERSONAL ADORNMENT IN THE NORTH-EAST REGION

Again, the broad social hierarchy presented in the previous three regions is repeated, although there are some notable distinctions (FIG. 2.24). First, there is a greater difference between villas and both types of farmstead in the North-East than in the South, East or Central Belt, with villas being much better represented by objects associated with personal display than farmsteads in general. This might suggest that a reduced proportion of the rural population in this region adopted new aspects of dress represented by brooches, bracelets, finger rings, hairpins and personal grooming equipment. This is part of a wider pattern here, there being in general a lack of evidence for economic integration between the rural population and those occupying urban and military sites in the region (Allen 2016b, 273–6).

A further striking aspect of the personal display equipment from the North-East is that, while most dress accessories are less widely distributed across rural sites than in other regions, objects in the bracelet category (which includes bracelets, armlets and bangles in a range of materials) occur at around the same frequency here as they do in the South, East or Central Belt. This may partly reflect the fact that, whereas objects such as finger rings and hairpins were for the most part introduced following the Roman conquest, arm jewellery had a long tradition in British prehistory (Johns 1996a, 108). In the North-East, jet or shale bangles were a form of object used during the late Iron Age, present at sites such as Great Chilton, Ferryhill (Jenkins 2013), and West House, Coxhoe (Haselgrove and Allon 1982), both County Durham, and Percy Rigg, Kildale, North Yorkshire (Close 1972), and it is possible that similar objects of wood, bone and antler were also more common, but are less likely to survive. Shale and jet arm jewellery continued in use into the Roman period, and is found at a number of rural sites in the region.

However, following the conquest there emerged in the region a new type of object, which was not widespread in the late Iron Age. While the types of

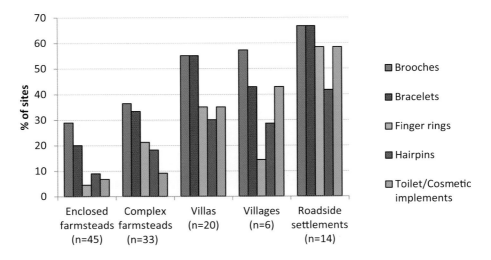

FIG. 2.24. Representation of personal display equipment in the North-East region by site type (n=no. of sites)

later Roman copper-alloy bracelet, which are far more common in the regions to the south, do sometimes occur, the North-East is especially well represented by glass bangles – a form of object that appears only to have developed in Britain from the time of the conquest (Kilbride-Jones 1938a; Stevenson 1956; 1976; Johns 1996a, 121; Price 1988; 2003, 91; Hunter 2016). Rare evidence for the manufacture of such glass bangles has been found at Thearne, near Beverley, East Riding of Yorkshire (Campbell 2008; Halkon 2013, 55). These objects are very rare at non-nucleated rural settlements in all regions other than the North-East and the North (discussed below). The function of glass bangles has been debated, and it is not clear that all were worn on the arms, or whether they were necessarily even worn by humans (Stevenson 1976, 53). Indeed, some have very small diameters, and Stevenson suggested that these may have been used as hair-rings or even horse fittings (*ibid.*, 50, 53). A ritual, apotropaic or magical function is also possible, as suggested by a group of objects including bangles from Cairnhill, Aberdeenshire (*ibid.*, 50), though this, of course does not preclude their use also as personal ornaments. Several glass bangles were recovered from Victoria Cave, Settle, North Yorkshire (Dearne and Lord 1998), a site that has produced a finds assemblage suggestive of a distinct religious focus (see below, p. 31). Whatever their true function(s), glass bangles represent a distinctive type of object recovered at rural (as well as urban and military) settlements in the North-East, and in northern Britain more generally. Indeed, they are the single most commonly found type of object included in the bracelet category at farmsteads in the North-East, accounting for 38 per cent of all such artefacts from these sites. For comparison, in the Central Belt the project has recorded only two glass bangles from farmsteads (one from the unusually rich settlement at Claydon Pike, Gloucestershire (Miles *et al.* 2007), and the other from Sturton le Steeple, Nottinghamshire: Elliot 2004), representing just 0.4 per cent of the objects in the bracelet category recorded from farmsteads there.

The sub-regional distribution of farmsteads with glass bangles in the North-East is of particular note, focused as it is so clearly on the area to the north of the Humber (FIG. 2.25) – a distribution that continues into the North region and beyond into Scotland (Hunter 2016). This is indicative of

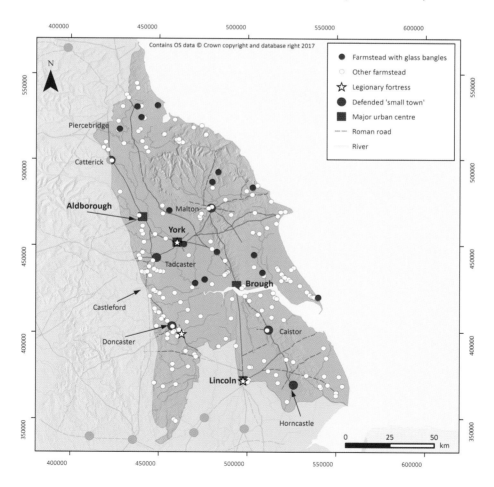

FIG. 2.25. Distribution of farmsteads with glass bangles in the North-East region

the regional development of a very distinctive type of object following the conquest, perhaps derived from the similar jet and shale objects used during the prehistoric period (Stevenson 1976, 50). The emphasis on the area north of the Humber may suggest that the river served as a boundary between groups of people with distinctive cultural identities. Traditionally, the rivers Humber and Ouse have been regarded as a boundary between the Parisi, who are thought to have occupied the area of the East Riding of Yorkshire, and the Corieltauvi, to the South (e.g. Halkon 2013). The distribution of glass bangles at rural sites may possibly be associated with 'tribal' differences in personal display (or other aspects of social practice that differed from the area south of the Humber), though, if so, their occurrence at rural sites across much of northern England and Scotland is suggestive of broad cultural affinities that transcend the hypothesised territories of different tribes in the north (e.g. Rivet 1958). Given that pre-Roman bracelets appear predominantly to have been of shale/jet in the region, it may have been that the newly abundant glass (brought in as vessels and other objects to supply the military sites) had particular qualities that made it an appropriate material for the construction of these objects, assuming, that is, that glass bangles and jet/shale bracelets were used for similar purposes. The importance that texture and colour had in terms of giving objects special status has increasingly been recognised (e.g. Eckardt 2014, 95). Given that jet and shale are believed to have held magical or apotropaic properties for many people in the ancient world (*ibid.*, 112, 124), the creation of similar types of objects from glass might be connected with the feel and appearance of glass objects, as well as the specialist knowledge required to work with the material, which may have imbued glass bangles with special, perhaps magical, properties.

BROOCH USE IN THE NORTH-EAST

Brooch use in the North-East was quite substantially lower than in the preceding regions, with brooches present at 24 per cent of sites, although it is still substantially higher than in regions further north and west, discussed below. The region is therefore an interface between areas where brooches were used most widely in the countryside and those where they were much less frequently worn.

The issue with the potentially misidentified Colchester/Colchester Derivative brooches is far less of a problem in this region, for the simple reason that there are so few examples of the former – placing the five Colchester brooches in with the Colchester Derivative group makes little

difference to the overall number of brooches in Groups A and B. Indeed, brooches in Groups A and B both make up a considerably lower proportion of brooches in the North-East than in any of the regions considered so far (FIG. 2.26), accounting for just 18 per cent and 17 per cent respectively. In the North-East the most common brooches are those in Group C (particularly Trumpet brooches, along with fewer Headstuds) and the penannulars, which both account for around 22 per cent of the total brooch assemblage. However, it is important to point out that while Group C bow brooches and penannular brooches are *relatively* more frequent in the North-East, this must be recognised as being a product of the general scarcity of brooches in Groups A and B. For instance, while Group C brooches are distributed across more settlements in the North-East than in the South and East, they occur at the same frequency as in the Central Belt – found at around 10 per cent of sites. Penannular brooches have a similar distribution across sites in the North-East (8 per cent of sites) as the South, East and Central Belt regions (6 to 10 per cent of sites). It is therefore the general dearth (but not total absence) of the brooch types that are so abundant in the south and east of the province – in particular the Nauheim Derivatives, Colchesters and Colchester Derivatives – which make the Group C brooches and penannulars seem so important in the North-East. The obvious implication here is that wearing brooches was not a fundamental part of dress for most people occupying the region during the late Iron Age. Based upon the date range of the brooches in Group C, brooch use appears to have become increasingly widespread during the late first to second century A.D., indicating that it was fundamentally a post-conquest phenomenon in this region. There are, however, exceptional sites, such as Dragonby, North Lincolnshire, which has all the hallmarks of an important power centre during the late Iron Age, and where late Iron Age types are very well represented (May 1996).

Whereas brooches, at least those in Groups A and B, were fairly widespread across all rural sites in the South, East and Central Belt, there is a far starker contrast in the North-East in terms of the sorts of sites where brooches occur (FIG. 2.27). When they are found they are chiefly recovered – in order of frequency – from military *vici* (not included in the charts in FIG. 2.27 as only four are in the project database), sacred sites, roadside settlements, villas and complex farmsteads, but hardly ever at enclosed farmsteads. Brooches of Group C (predominantly Trumpets) are rare at all types of farmstead, but much more common at the *vici*, villas, roadside settlements and sacred sites. The implication is that, while those living at forts and their extramural settlements, towns and other nucleated settlements were adopting the new fashions of clothing that required brooch use, those in the wider countryside – except for those who occupied villas – were not. This is likely to correspond with the general lack of evidence for economic integration between those in the countryside and nucleated settlements on the road network (Allen 2016b, 274). It suggests that while military *vici*, towns and other nucleated settlements may have been, in relative terms, cosmopolitan, multi-cultural centres with occupants from a variety of backgrounds that encouraged new ways of dressing, those occupying farmsteads in the wider countryside remained far more culturally conservative. It is important to note, however, that those occupying the military *vici*, towns and nucleated settlements, where brooches began to be used, were not merely adopting a new 'Roman' object. The Trumpet (and most other) brooches

that are most common in the region are fundamentally a native type of artefact, incorporating decorative motifs, and often enamelling, which are of Celtic and not classical design (Johns 1996a, 182–5; Hunter 2008, 138–9). The use of these objects at the sites where they are most commonly found was undoubtedly a native response to the changed social fabric created by the Roman conquest, which forged new opportunities for social interaction, leading to the development of new ways of dressing that likely fused pre-existing elements with those imported from the Continent, and indeed, from further south within the province.

It is worth noting here that the farmsteads best represented by brooches are also typically those at which the above-discussed glass bangles occur – of the fifteen farmsteads with glass bangles, ten (67 per cent) yielded brooches (compared with just 23 per cent of farmsteads generally). This indicates that the farmsteads which acquired and used glass

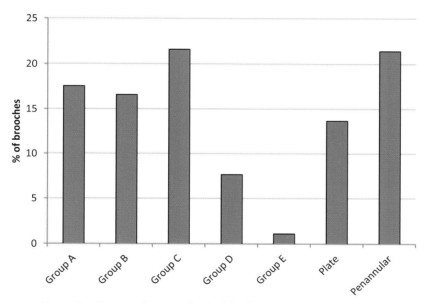

FIG. 2.26. Percentages of brooches from each group in the North-East region (total no. brooches=517)

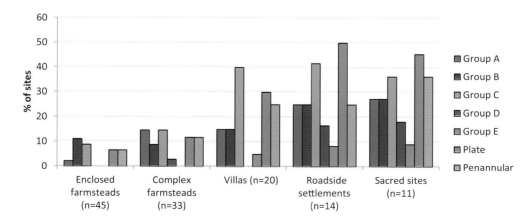

FIG. 2.27. Representation of brooch groups from main site types in the North-East region (n=no. of sites)

bangles were those that appear to have been most closely integrated with the populations at towns and military sites (i.e. complex farmsteads), where both brooches and glass bangles are found more widely, and were thus most likely to engage with this new form of post-conquest material culture.

Because brooches of Groups A and B are scarce in the region, plate brooches make up a greater proportion of all brooches recorded in the North-East than in the previous regions, though they are on the whole less widely distributed. While a range of types is represented, one type – the Dragonesque brooch – merits particular attention, as it is such a distinctive regional type. Although it is fairly widely distributed, and has been found in small numbers across the whole of the province, there is a distinctive clustering in the North-East, with Yorkshire being recognised as their homeland (Hunter 2010, 95; Mackreth 2011, 186–8; 2012). These brooches are not common on excavated rural settlements in the region, with single examples recovered from just eight sites (2 per cent), though this is still substantially higher than in most other regions, with just one example from 1509 sites in the Central Belt (0.06 per cent).

Indeed, when one looks at the distribution of these brooches recorded by the Portable Antiquities Scheme (PAS), the North-East focus is very stark (FIG. 2.28; see Hunter 2010, 95, fig. 2, for a map combining PAS and other finds). While the type is without doubt a predominantly North-Eastern family of brooch, consideration of sub-types has enabled Hunter to propose some other areas of manufacture, south of the Humber and in southern Scotland (ibid., 100).

Although there are many examples of Dragonesque brooches recorded by PAS, there is of course usually very little in the way of contextual information about them. As with all brooch types in the North-East, those from excavated sites are unevenly socially distributed, favouring sites on the road network. The sites include a military vicus (Piercebridge, County Durham), roadside settlements (Winteringham, North Lincolnshire; Hayton, East Riding of Yorkshire; Bainesse, North Yorkshire), a villa (Rudston, East Riding of Yorkshire), two complex farmsteads (Faverdale, Darlington, County Durham; Crossgates, Seamer, North Yorkshire), and a single enclosed farmstead (Hall Quarry, Stainton, South Yorkshire). Many of

FIG. 2.28. Distribution of Dragonesque brooches recorded by the Roman Rural Settlement Project (RRSP) and Portable Antiquities Scheme (PAS)

those recorded by Mackreth are from towns and military sites (Mackreth 2011, 186–8). These brooches have generated considerable academic interest in the past, chiefly because they are such attractive objects, and because their appearance is so unique. There has been much discussion of the social significance of their development, especially as, although they appear ultimately to be derived from a distinctly regional Iron Age S-shaped brooch (Hunter 2010, 95), they are a post-conquest type that employs distinctively Iron Age British 'Celtic' design (Feachem 1951; 1968; Johns 1996a, 183–4; Jundi and Hill 1998; Hunter 2008, 139–41; 2010). The social distribution of these brooches, together with a general lack of evidence for brooch use in the wider countryside during the pre-Roman period, might suggest that the development of these brooches was a very particular regional response to new social circumstances at sites on the major road network, which meant that brooches (or badges) became a new and important means for expressing regional cultural ideas. Mackreth went so far as to suggest that the type may have been a badge used exclusively by members of the Brigantes tribe (Mackreth 2012, 12). Linking a type of material culture with a particular tribe is problematic given our imperfect understanding of the tribes of Roman Britain and their territories (cf. Smith and Fulford 2016, 402–3), and it fails to consider how objects may have been viewed, adopted and treated differently by people in different circumstances and at different times. Eckardt has also shown how the distribution of particular brooch types is arguably more likely to reflect localised workshops, and the consequent marketing network for brooches, than tribal areas of use (cf. Eckardt 2014, 128–32).

Nevertheless, the North-East focus for Dragonesque brooches is a striking example of regionality and the development of a particular form of material culture, which, when worn, may have carried subconscious messages about belonging to a local area. It may be no coincidence that these brooches appear to have been considerably more common at sites on the major communications network, where engagement with people from different backgrounds was a regular occurrence. Indeed Hodder's work on the distribution of material culture items in western Kenya suggested, in this instance, that the importance of the symbolic nature of artefacts was stressed at boundaries and in places of contact between different identity groups (Hodder 1977). If this was the case, then there would have been less need to reinforce and display group identity at settlements more removed from the main foci of social interaction; for example, at more 'remote' farmsteads in the North Yorkshire Moors, everyone would have known the occupants belonged to a certain 'tribal' group, and they would not have needed any 'badges' to display this fact.

The social distribution of the few Dragonesque brooches found outside of the North-East is again focused on nucleated settlements, particularly forts and their *vici* and roadside settlements, with only very occasional examples from farmsteads. The pattern is suggestive of occasional movement along the major communications network, and much of the northern distribution of these brooches is perhaps a result of the general flow of traffic as supplies from the south of the province made their way through the roadside sites in the North-East to the northern military frontier. However, Hunter's (2010, 100) observation that there appear to be at least two other areas of manufacture, with sub-types produced in Scotland and south of the Humber, indicates that there was imitation in other regions.

If many plate brooches carried ideological messages, as suggested by Allason-Jones (2014), we should question whether Dragonesque brooches manufactured in different areas were necessarily viewed in the same way. That such brooches may have had some ideological significance is hinted at by some of the findspots from which they have been recovered. An association with caves has previously been noted (Jundi and Hill 1998, 131–4; Eckardt 2014, 132), and, given their general rarity at rural sites, it may be of significance that examples were recovered from Thirst House Cave, Deepdale, Derbyshire (Branigan and Dearne 1991b), and Victoria Cave, Settle, North Yorkshire (Dearne and Lord 1998), which may both have been foci for ritual activity (see Ch. 5, p. 146). The latter produced five Dragonesque brooches, along with a number of other plate brooches. Other potentially ritually deposited examples include one from Borness Cave, in Scotland (Feachem 1968), and another included in a hoard of metalwork deposited in a bog at Lamberton Moor, Scotland (*ibid.*). Their selection as possible votive objects in some instances of course does not mean that any ideological meaning was necessarily shared by all those who wore or deposited them – different people may not have viewed them in the same way, depending on the period and context (cf. Hill 2001, 14; Eckardt 2014, 26).

PERSONAL ADORNMENT IN THE NORTH REGION

As illustrated in Volume 1, the settlement pattern in the North region was considerably less varied than in many other parts of the province, with the principal settlement types being the enclosed farmstead and the military forts along with their *vici* (Brindle 2016a). FIGURE 2.29 shows the representation of the five major types of dress accessory in the region by these site types (the two sites classified as roadside settlements, Walton-le-Dale, Lancashire, and Chester-le-Street, County Durham, have been included with the military *vici* as they also had probable military origins, and were themselves perhaps *vici*, a known fort being located *c.* 0.5 km south of the latter site; Platell 2014). The social distribution of dress accessories and personal grooming equipment, as would be expected, is entirely orientated towards the *vici* and roadside settlements. Farmsteads are exceptionally poorly represented by almost all the groups of objects, though, as in the North-East, the bracelet category stands out as a result of the fairly widespread distribution of glass bangles (discussed above, pp. 27–8), recovered from 22 per cent of farmsteads, especially those in the very north and east of the region. Unlike in the North-East, however, the presence of glass bangles at farmsteads in the North does not generally correspond with increased evidence for brooch use, although often there is evidence for other dress accessories, especially jet or shale bracelets/armlets and glass beads. While the relatively widespread distribution of glass bangles indicates there may have been cultural affinities among people occupying the North and North-East regions, there are also differences in the material culture from the settlements in the two regions,

which suggests that there were distinctions, and it would be wrong to suggest cultural homogeneity within the native populations of northern Britain as a whole. The particular contexts of deposition in some instances hint that glass bangles may have been considered to be particularly appropriate for structured deposition. At Glencoyne, Ullswater, Cumbria, for instance, glass bangles, along with samian, other fine pottery and glass beads, were believed by the excavators to have been deliberately deposited inside a roundhouse (Hoaen and Loney 2010), and the group of glass bangles from Victoria Cave, Settle, North Yorkshire (referred to above, p. 31) are also within this region. The potential magical or apotropaic qualities of glass have been discussed above (p. 28), and it is noteworthy that, despite the general lack of finger rings and other classically derived dress accessories from farmsteads in the North, at two sites in Northumberland intaglios were found, one of glass (at Hartburn; Jobey 1973), the other of cornelian (at Gowenburn River Camp; Jobey and Jobey 1988). Both were engraved, one depicting Achilles dragging Hector around the walls of Troy, yet perhaps the material these objects were made from gave them new importance at these native sites, possibly altered now that they were divorced from their original settings.

There is in the North region currently no evidence for any sort of high-status native settlement with preferential access to Roman material culture, as at Traprain Law, in East

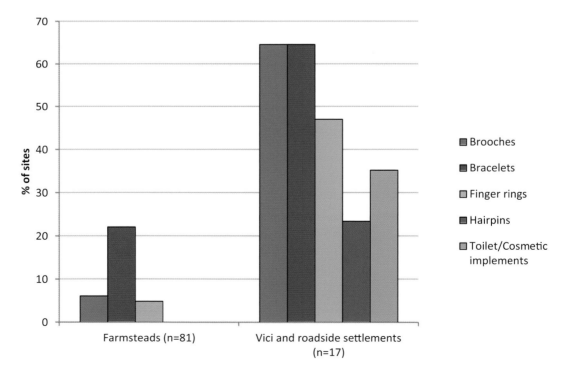

FIG. 2.29. Representation of personal display equipment in the North region by site type (n=no. of sites)

Lothian, Scotland (Hunter 2009; 2016), and most rural settlements produce very little in the way of material culture generally. Indeed, there is considerably greater evidence for Roman material culture from rural sites further north, in south-east Scotland, which may suggest that the presence of Hadrian's Wall and the military zone had a profound effect on local societies, restricting opportunities to develop power and wealth (Hunter 2016, 192). This may be related to the evidence for marked settlement abandonment in the area to the north of Hadrian's Wall in the second century A.D. (Hodgson *et al.* 2013; Brindle 2016a, 315; and see conclusions, below, p. 44).

BROOCH USE IN THE NORTH

As in the North-East, brooch use among the rural population of the North was low. Of all sites in the North, only 17 per cent yielded brooches. Again, Groups A and B are scarcely represented, apparently reflecting a lack of brooch-use by the population in the Iron Age, and the most commonly recovered types are those of Groups C and D, of early and mid-Roman date, along with plate brooches and penannulars (FIG. 2.30). Where brooches were recovered, these were almost exclusively from military *vici* or other sites associated with the military. They are almost completely absent from farmsteads, with a few exceptions. At Bank Newton, North Yorkshire (Casswell and Daniel 2010), a penannular brooch was found; this site was also notable for being one of the few rural sites in the region with coins.

At Doubstead, Scremerston, Northumberland (Jobey 1982), a Nauheim Derivative brooch was deposited in a ditch terminal along with other finds of metalwork, and may have been part of a structured deposit (see Ch. 5); it was not only unusual in terms of its recovery from a farmstead in this region, but also in terms of its early date and its distribution, these types being more typically found much further south, as noted above (p. 23). At a farmstead at West Gunnar Peak, Northumberland (Hogg 1942), a Trumpet brooch and a possible penannular brooch were both recovered, while at Old Brampton, Cumbria (Blake 1960), a Crossbow brooch was found at an apparently high-status site, which may have had military associations. Finally, at Milking Gap, Northumberland (Kilbride-Jones 1938b), a single Dragonesque brooch was recovered from an enclosed farmstead that may have been abandoned during the construction of Hadrian's Wall.

As in the North-East, by far the most common type of brooch is the Trumpet, which accounts for nearly 80 per cent of the Group C brooches. A number of penannular brooches have been recorded, and there are several Headstud and knee brooches, but other types are rare. The relatively large proportion of Group D brooches at military sites in the North (at least compared with areas such as the Central Belt and the South), of which the most common are knee brooches, is no doubt part of the reason for the tendency to see them as being of military type, although, as Cool and Baxter (2016, 86) and Eckardt (2005, 154–6) have noted, they are found on non-military sites

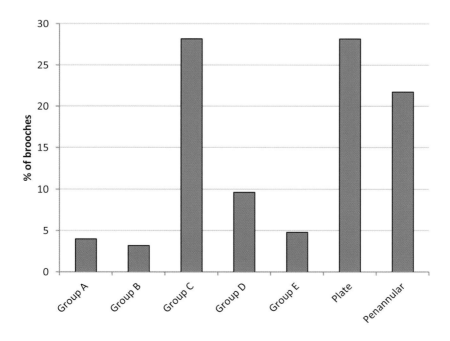

FIG. 2.30. Percentages of brooches from each group in the North region (total no. brooches=124)

elsewhere, and their scarcity at rural sites in the North is merely reflective of non-brooch use by the wider population of the region, along with the absence of the earlier brooch types. The lack of brooches at rural sites suggests that traditional clothing remained uninfluenced by the new fashions that arrived with the Roman army and its followers, representing further evidence for the strong impression of an only marginal relationship between the native inhabitants of northern rural settlements and those occupying the forts and their associated *vici* (Brindle 2016a, 325).

Given that brooch use in the North appears to be restricted in the main to sites directly associated with the military, it is unsurprising that there is, in general, little evidence for their use as votive offerings in the wider countryside. An exception, however, is the potential shrine at Victoria Cave, Settle, North Yorkshire, discussed above (p. 31; see also Ch. 5), which yielded a range of brooches, including several Dragonesque types, along with many other artefacts, some of which appear to have particularly close associations with caves in general (Eckardt 2014, 146–8). Evidence for metalworking at Victoria Cave suggests that brooches may have been made at the site, and it has been suggested that the cave may have had a dual industrial/ritual focus (Dearne and Lord 1998).

PERSONAL ADORNMENT IN THE CENTRAL WEST REGION

Objects associated with personal adornment and grooming in the Central West are socially distributed in a similar way to the other regions, with roadside settlements, military *vici* and villas substantially better represented than farmsteads

(FIG. 2.31). The categories of object other than brooches are somewhat less well represented here than in some other regions, even at roadside settlements and *vici*, though here that seems likely to be a product of the small sample sizes rather than any genuine social distinction between these types of settlements in the different areas. What is striking, however, is that farmsteads are so poorly represented by all types of dress accessory, especially those other than brooches. As enclosed sites make up the overwhelming majority of classified farmsteads in this region (Brindle 2016b, 292), all farmsteads have been grouped together here, yet when compared with enclosed farmsteads in, for instance, the Central Belt or the South, brooches are distinctly less widespread, and the other types of object are barely present at all, recovered, in all cases, from less than 5 per cent of sites. The geographical distribution of the farmsteads that have yielded brooches and other dress accessories is also of interest. While such finds are rare at all farmsteads in the region, there is a notable lack of brooches from farmsteads in the area surrounding the *civitas* capital at Wroxeter, compared with the area to the north, near Chester. This is part of a wider pattern presented in Volume 1, where some farmsteads in the Chester area appear to have been more integrated into the market-based economy than those nearer Wroxeter, with more evidence for coin use and the wider adoption of ceramics (Brindle 2016b, 302–3).

When finds of brooches recorded by the Portable Antiquities Scheme (PAS) are plotted on a map it seems hard to reconcile the dearth of brooches at farmsteads in much of the region with those recorded by PAS, as they appear to be very numerous, occurring across much of the lowlands

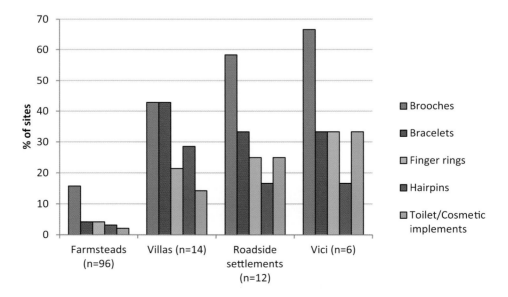

FIG. 2.31. Representation of personal display equipment in the Central West region by site type (n=no. of sites)

of the region. However, a kernel density plot of the PAS brooches indicates that, as with the results from excavated sites, they are considerably more common finds in the landscape surrounding Chester than around Wroxeter (FIG. 2.32). This is likely to reflect differing cultural values in the two areas, with those in the countryside surrounding Wroxeter continuing to favour traditional tribal dress, and, given the lack of ceramic evidence in the countryside of this area, traditional ways of eating and drinking (Gaffney *et al.* 2007, 280; Brindle 2016b, 302–3). Particular clusters of brooches occur in the immediate vicinity of the roadside 'walled towns' at Wall, Staffordshire, and Alcester, Warwickshire, yet there are also clusters of finds recorded by PAS in other areas, away from known Roman towns, especially to the south-west of Water Eaton and the north of Rocester. Given the general lack of finds at farmsteads, the usual social distribution of brooches and other dress accessories has important implications for our understanding of findspots that have produced unusually large groups of such objects, but whose character remain unknown. At, Worfield, Shropshire, adjacent to the River Severn, the

quality and nature of the PAS finds, including large numbers of Polden Hill and Trumpet brooches, as well as instances of personal grooming equipment, are suggestive of a well-integrated riverside nucleated settlement, and the proximity of both the Severn and a Roman road running east–west, slightly to the south of the main PAS distribution are likely to be the reasons for the site's importance. In the area near Ilam, in the Staffordshire Peak District, hundreds of finds have been reported by metal-detector users, including many brooches, dominated by Polden Hill and Trumpet types, as well as finger rings and toilet equipment. The reporting of many early Roman silver *denarii* from the area is suggestive of a military association (see Brindle 2017a), and the recovery of the remarkable Staffordshire Moorlands patera (an enamelled bowl that lists four forts at the western end of Hadrian's Wall; PAS reference WMID-3FE965) from nearby represents strong evidence for a military connection. The finds evidence around Ilam is suggestive of an important nucleated settlement with likely military origins, and given that such sites are usually on the road network, one might

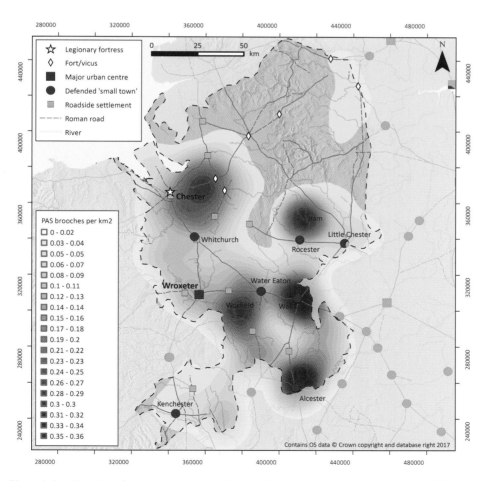

FIG. 2.32. Kernel density plot of brooches recorded by the Portable Antiquities Scheme (PAS) in the Central West region

hypothesise a Roman road running through the area, perhaps connecting the site with Little Chester to the south-east and Rocester to the south. Our increasing understanding of the social distribution of brooches and other objects in the region allows us to attempt to characterise such findspots, in broad terms, with increasing confidence.

BROOCH USE IN THE CENTRAL WEST

As we have seen above, brooches appear to have been used much less widely in the countryside of the Central West than in some other regions, with such artefacts being recovered from just a quarter of sites. As in the North and North-East, the emphasis is overwhelmingly on the nucleated sites – the roadside settlements and military *vici*. Just 16 per cent of farmsteads yielded brooches, with villas being better represented, at 43 per cent, though with just fourteen excavated villas from the region, the sample is small.

Groups of Type A are scarcely represented in the region, accounting for just 8 per cent of all brooches (FIG. 2.33). As only a single Colchester brooch was recorded from the region, incorporating this type with the Colchester Derivatives in Group B has had little impact. Where early brooch types were recovered they were predominantly found at sites that appear to have been high status during the late Iron Age and/or early Roman period, or are unusual in some way. Examples include the hillforts at Midsummer Hill, Herefordshire (Stanford 1981), and the Berth, Shropshire (Morris and Gelling 1991), and the likely port at Meols on the Wirral peninsula (Griffiths *et al.* 2007). In addition, early brooches were recovered from Grimstock Hill, Coleshill, Warwickshire

(Magilton 2006), a site that developed into a Romano-Celtic temple complex in the second century A.D., and also from certain caves with a possible ritual focus, as at Poole's Cavern, Buxton (Smithson and Branigan 1991) and Thirst House Cave, Deepdale (Branigan and Dearne 1991b), both Derbyshire. The remaining brooches are from military *vici* at Castleford, West Yorkshire (Cool and Philo 1998), and Greensforge, Staffordshire (Webster 1981; Jones 1999). Apart from such high-status, religious or military sites, there is little evidence for early brooch-use in the wider countryside.

Brooches in Group B are somewhat more common, accounting for 24 per cent of the total number of brooches. Most Group B brooches are of Polden Hill type, accounting for 64 per cent of the group, reflecting the general distribution of the type, which centres on the region (e.g. Bayley and Butcher 2004, 160).

Group C brooches are the most abundant type in the region, accounting for 36 per cent of all those recorded. As in the North and North-East, the group is dominated by those of Trumpet type (67 per cent), though Headstud brooches are also numerous (22 per cent), and Developed T-shaped brooches, enamelled bow brooches and Wroxeter brooches are sometimes found. While Group C brooches have been recovered from nearly a third of the region's villas and almost half of the nucleated sites (*vici* and roadside settlements combined), even these brooches remain uncommon at farmsteads, recovered from only six sites (6 per cent) (FIG. 2.34). Where such brooches have been recovered from sites defined as farmsteads, there is often evidence to suggest that these settlements were atypical in some way.

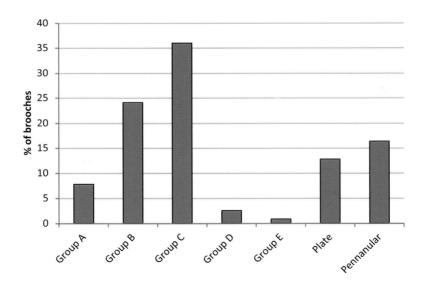

FIG. 2.33. Percentages of brooches from each group in the Central West region (total no. brooches=362)

The finds assemblage from Plas Coch, Wrexham (Jones 2011), is suggestive of an unusually high-status site, and the possibility exists that it may have been a villa. The extensive but poorly understood settlement at Rainster Rocks, Derbyshire (Makepeace 1998), has a relatively rich finds assemblage (Dool 1978), including high numbers of coins, suggesting that it was not a typical farmstead.

As with Dragonesque brooches in the North-East, there is a particular brooch type in the Central West that merits some discussion. The Wirral brooch is a fairly recently recognised, distinctive type of brooch from the area around the Wirral peninsula, Cheshire and North-East Wales, but which has been shown to have further concentrations at military sites in the North, and in Scotland (Philpott 1999; McIntosh and Ponting 2014; cf. Eckardt 2014, 130). Known primarily from metal-detector finds, the type has been regarded as a rural type by McIntosh (McIntosh and Ponting 2014, 127), although, much like Dragonesque brooches in the North-East, the type is scarcely represented at rural sites in the project database. This may partly be explained by the fact that the type has only recently been recognised as a distinct form of brooch, and has often been classed as a Trumpet type (e.g. Williams and Reid 2008), and, indeed, it has sometimes been viewed as developing from it (Philpott 1999). However, the scarcity of brooches in general at excavated rural sites in the region may suggest that the type, as with others, was far more commonly used at military sites, towns and other nucleated sites on the major communications network than by most of the wider rural population. Certainly, of the few excavated examples identified by McIntosh, most are from military sites, with a very small number of examples from rural sites, the exceptions being Acton Trussel villa in Staffordshire, Beeston in Cheshire West and Chester, and the unusual open farmstead at Halewood, Merseyside (McIntosh and Ponting 2014, 116–20, table 1).

While the lack of such brooches from farmsteads may be a result of a relatively small sample of excavated sites in the region, together with sometimes small-scale excavations, comparisons with farmsteads in the South, East and Central Belt regions suggest that it is a genuine pattern. There may be several reasons for the apparently rural distribution of the Wirral brooches recorded by PAS. The distribution is concentrated across a broad area that may be regarded as the hinterland of the legionary fortress at Chester, and there is a notable emphasis on the major roads and rivers. The prevalence of this regional type of brooch in the landscape surrounding Chester may be related to intensive production in a landscape that is likely to have been controlled by the military, and may have been used to generate supplies for the army (Carrington 2012; Brindle 2016b, 300–6). It is possible that some of the rural losses reflect stray finds in the landscape associated with periodic but significant movements of people (for example, troop movements from the legionary fortress at Chester). Another very likely reason is that there are currently a number of sites awaiting identification which, if they were excavated, would probably be characterised in the same way as the sorts of sites that *do* yield brooches and other types of material culture – military and industrial sites, roadside settlements and villas.

Although the single finds of Wirral brooches may be casual losses, an examination of the distribution of findspots with multiple stray Wirral brooches shows that there is a distinct focus on the

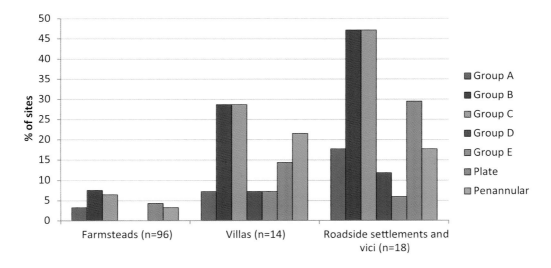

FIG. 2.34. Representation of brooch groups from main site types in the Central West region (n=no. of sites)

road network and the rivers (FIG. 2.35). There is, for instance, a notable cluster at Farndon, on the opposite side of the River Dee to the well-known Roman industrial site at Holt (Ward 1998), and it seems quite possible that the distribution is linked in some way with the military tile production site. There is an example from the excavated roadside settlement at Middlewich (Williams and Reid 2008; Garner and Reid 2012), along with a further example recorded by the PAS. There is a distinct cluster at Weaverham, on the River Weaver, and at this location a Roman road has long been postulated to have run through the modern village, with traces supposedly discovered in the late nineteenth century (Waddelove and Waddelove 1985). The group of Wirral brooches, along with a large number of brooches, coins and other objects recorded on the PAS database, may relate to a previously unrecognised roadside industrial settlement. The two examples on the PAS database from Aston also occur alongside a range of other objects, including other types of brooches and coins, suggesting some sort of nucleated settlement, perhaps associated with industrial supply.

The overall impression is that, as Philpott (1999) and McIntosh and Ponting (2014) have both argued, this brooch is a regionally distinctive type, but not one that can be said to be evenly distributed across all types of rural settlement. It does not appear to be a universally 'rural' type; the general lack of brooches of all types at farmsteads in this area suggests that most of the rural population may not have worn brooches. Rather, there seems to be a likely association with sites linked to provisioning the military in the north, as excavated examples from the sites at Wilderspool and Middlewich suggest. This would help account for the distribution of brooches at military sites in the north, and, indeed, would be an explanation for the means by which such brooches entered Scotland, where they appear to have been selected for use by some members of native society (McIntosh and Ponting 2014, 132–3). This is not, of course, to suggest that the brooches themselves were a 'military' type, if such a thing can even be said to exist, but that they developed and became popular among the communities who lived in and worked at the types of site that were bound up with supplying the military machine. These people are likely to have been exposed to a wide range of material culture and ideas, and the populations may have been made up of people from diverse

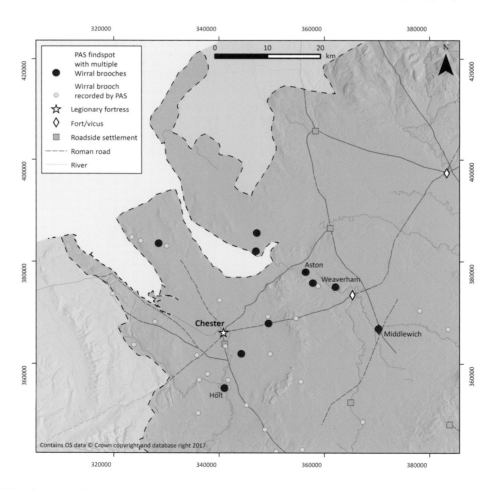

FIG. 2.35. Distribution of Wirral brooches recorded by Portable Antiquities Scheme (PAS) in the Chester area

backgrounds. The inhabitants of these sites may therefore have had a very different relationship with material culture, and perhaps attitudes towards dress, to those occupying low-status farmsteads in the wider countryside, as appears also to have been the case in some other parts of the province.

PERSONAL ADORNMENT IN THE UPLAND WALES AND MARCHES REGION

As with other regions, brooches are the dominant form of dress accessory in Uplands Wales and the Marches, with other types of artefact associated with personal display mostly limited to the military *vici* and roadside settlements. Owing to the small numbers involved, *vici* and roadside settlements have been grouped together within FIG. 2.36, while villas have been omitted as so few have been excavated from the region, and full finds data are not available from all of these. Farmsteads of all types have been grouped together, although these are dominated by those of enclosed form (see Brindle 2016c for the striking morphological differences in different areas).

Finger rings, hairpins and personal grooming equipment are rare finds at farmsteads, although objects in the bracelet category are somewhat more frequently found, especially at farmsteads in North Wales. Indeed, they are the only one of the groups of dress accessories more commonly found

at farmsteads than at military *vici* or roadside settlements. The reason for this seems clearly to be linked to the typically early dates of military *vici* in the region, with many being abandoned by the mid-second century (e.g. Burnham and Davies 2010, 48–60; Brindle 2016c, 364); these sites were not always in existence long enough to see the widespread use of the copper-alloy bracelets, which became most common during the late Roman period. While copper-alloy bracelets are present at some rural sites, the objects in this category most often recovered from farmsteads are typically made of stone, jet or shale and glass. The greater prevalence at farmsteads here is therefore likely to reflect the native origins of these types of object (Johns 1996a, 108), and their popularity among the native rural population. At the single *vicus* where bracelets were recovered, Caersws, in Powys (Britnell 1989), they were also of shale/jet or glass, which is perhaps suggestive of a native presence at some military *vici*. Where other types of dress accessory are found at farmsteads, they tend to be from north Wales rather than south-west Wales, and such finds are also better represented in the Portable Antiquities Scheme data from north of the region. Coygan Camp, in south-west Wales (Wainwright 1967), is somewhat anomalous, being represented by numbers of finger rings, hairpins, bracelets and toilet equipment (but not brooches), amid an unusually rich finds assemblage in general for the region; this site appears to have been of particularly high status.

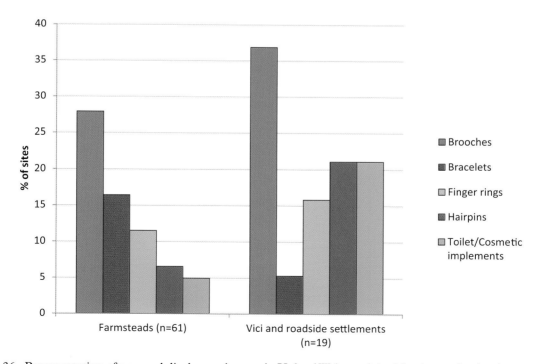

FIG. 2.36. Representation of personal display equipment in Upland Wales and the Marches region by site type (n=no. of sites)

BROOCH USE IN UPLAND WALES AND THE MARCHES

Brooches are again rare in Upland Wales and the Marches, recovered from just 28 per cent of sites recorded on the project database. Brooches of Group A are very uncommon, with those of Groups B and C making up the majority (FIG. 2.37). Group B brooches are dominated by those of Polden Hill type (accounting for 67 per cent), reflecting the main distribution of the type in the West Midlands and into north and east Wales. Although these brooches have an origin in the early years following the conquest, most of the examples are likely to be late first to second century in date, and are thus broadly contemporary with those in Group C, which are dominated by Trumpets and their derivatives (60 per cent), with some Headstuds, but few other types. The Wirral-type brooches discussed in the previous section occur in north Wales (McIntosh and Ponting 2014), and though there are none on the project database, this is possibly because some have been classified as either Trumpet derivatives or Headstud types in reports. The overall chronological impression for the region is that brooch-use took off from the end of the first century A.D., and there is little evidence for widespread use of brooches by the rural pre-Roman native populations.

While brooch use appears to have been generally uncommon across the region as a whole, there is not a substantial difference between the two main settlement types in the region, farmsteads and military *vici*, with brooches identified at 28 per cent of farmsteads and 37 per cent of *vici*. Given how widespread brooches are at military sites elsewhere, the relatively low proportion of *vici* with brooches in this region is somewhat anomalous, and may reflect the small-scale interventions undertaken at many of the *vici* that have seen archaeological investigation. The relatively high number of farmsteads with brooches (especially compared with the Central West, where it was just 16 per cent) requires some consideration.

The uneven geographical distribution of brooches at farmsteads is shown in FIG. 2.38, with those in the north and east of the region appearing far more likely to have used brooches than those in the south. This is likely to reflect what seem to have been very distinctive differences in the settlement pattern between these different areas, as highlighted in Volume 1 (Brindle 2016c). The distribution of brooches recorded by the PAS is also strongly focused on north and east Wales, and while this may reflect variation in levels of metal detecting, taken together with the data from excavated sites, it is suggestive of greater levels of brooch-use in these areas, which, in turn, suggests differences in the way people dressed. The military interest in the mineral resources available in the mountainous area of north Wales meant that there was a long-lived military presence in some areas (Mattingly 2006, 418), with the fort at Caernarfon (*Segontium*), for instance, occupied until the end

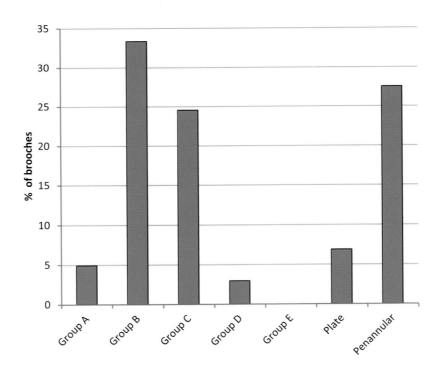

FIG. 2.37. Percentages of brooches from each group in Upland Wales and Marches region (total no. brooches=102)

of the Roman period. The route between the legionary fortress at Chester and the auxiliary fort at Caernarfon is likely to have been an important conduit for both material culture and ideas to enter the region, as evidenced by the distribution of Wirral brooches in north Wales (McIntosh and Ponting 2014), and although few are known, we might envisage the development of some nucleated roadside settlements along this route, where such material perhaps circulated widely.

Hillforts are a key site type in the archaeology of Upland Wales and the Marches, although only seven have been excavated that have yielded evidence for late Iron Age or Roman activity. The sample is therefore small, although five of the seven have yielded brooches, suggesting that brooch use at these sites (as in the Central West region) may have been somewhat different from farmsteads. Only one of these sites (Braich-y-Dinas, Conwy; Hughes 1923) had a brooch of Iron Age date, while the others were represented mainly by brooches in Groups B (Colchester Derivatives and Polden Hills) and C (Trumpet brooches and Headstuds), and some penannulars. It therefore

seems that the brooches were in the main post-conquest arrivals, and that brooch-use was not widespread at these site types in the Iron Age. In some cases the presence of brooches at hillforts may reflect a change in use during the Roman period. At Croft Ambrey, Herefordshire (Stanford 1974), for example, a number of brooches were recovered from an area that became the focus for a shrine during the early Roman period.

PERSONAL ADORNMENT IN THE SOUTH-WEST REGION

As demonstrated in Volume 1 (Brindle 2016d), the settlement pattern in the South-West is dominated by enclosed farmsteads (of many different forms), and there are too few types of other settlement to allow graphical comparison of object types. The two villas from the region are poorly represented by dress accessories, although this is likely to be more reflective of the very limited archaeological intervention at Crediton, Devon (Griffith 1988), and the lack of a full finds report for Magor Farm, Illogan, Cornwall (O'Neill

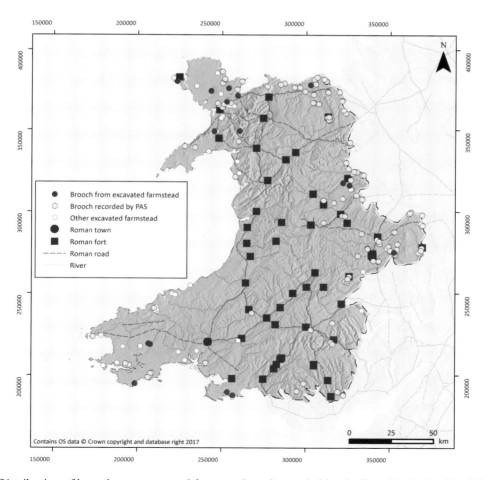

FIG. 2.38. Distribution of brooches at excavated farmsteads and recorded by the Portable Antiquities Scheme (PAS) in the Upland Wales and Marches region

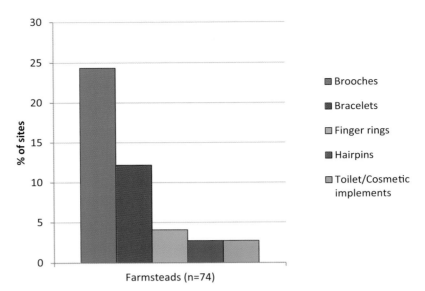

FIG. 2.39. Representation of personal display equipment at farmsteads in the South-West region (n=no. of sites)

1933), than any real lack of objects. The few roadside settlements in the region have also seen fairly limited intervention, though, as might be expected given the pattern in other regions, brooches and toilet equipment have been found at some. The farmsteads of the region are, for the most part, not particularly well represented by dress accessories or personal grooming equipment (FIG. 2.39). There is, however, a very important geographic distinction within the region, with 15 per cent of the sites from Devon and Somerset having brooches, compared with 34 per cent with those from Cornwall. There can be little doubt that this is associated with the striking differences observed within the settlement patterns of the region, discussed in Volume 1 (Brindle 2016d), and what appear to have been very different cultural expressions in the two areas. As in the other regional case studies discussed above, bracelets are typically more common than the other types of dress accessory at farmsteads, other than brooches, again reflecting a prehistoric native and not classical tradition, though all farmsteads with bracelets are located in Cornwall. While a small number were of copper alloy, those of shale are most common within the region, with fragments from nine bracelets recovered from Trethurgy (Quinnell 2004). Dress accessories are similarly rare at the region's hillforts and promontory forts, though, where recovered, shale bracelets are most common. However, the finds from Cadbury Castle hillfort in Devon are of note, where what seems to have been a votive deposit including a large number of bracelets (of copper alloy and shale), as well as other personal objects, was placed in what may have been a well in the centre of the Iron Age hillfort, probably during the late Roman period (Fox 1952; see Ch. 5).

BROOCH USE IN THE SOUTH-WEST

Before considering the composition of the brooch assemblages from the region, it is important first to point out that of the 438 brooches from rural sites in the South-West, 330 (76 per cent) come from just one site. This exceptionally large number of brooches was recovered from a site on Nornour, a remote islet in the eastern Isles of Scilly, and the number of brooches, along with the range of types represented, as well as a number of other objects typically recovered from ritual sites, indicate that the site was an important shrine (Butcher 2004a; though see Fulford 1989a for an alternative explanation). The brooches from this site will be discussed in more detail below, but because the site is so exceptional, and the large number of brooches skews the regional profile so considerably, it has been removed for the purposes of the following regional overview.

Of the remaining 108 brooches in the South-West, 70 were classified, and the apparent distribution of these may be affected by the fact that very few rural sites have been excavated in Devon. Those brooches in Group A were rare, recovered from just seven sites (FIG. 2.40), some of them being found within Iron Age graves, such as Trethellan Farm, Newquay, in Cornwall (Nowakowski 1991) and Bryher in the Isles of Scilly (Johns 2006). Of the three excavated sites in Devon with early brooches, two are very atypical rural settlements. The nature of activity at the cave at Kent's Cavern, Torquay (Silvester 1986), is uncertain, but religious activity of some sort is a possibility. Mount Batten, Plymouth (Cunliffe 1988a), appears to have been an important port with trading contacts with the Mediterranean, at least during the late Iron Age,

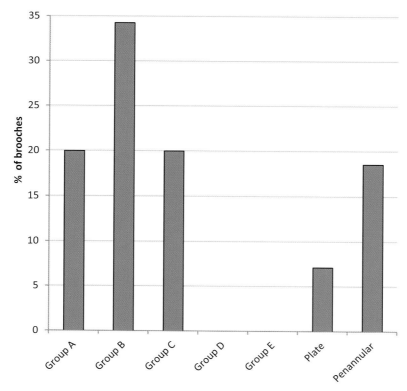

FIG. 2.40. Percentages of brooches from each group in the South-West region (excluding Nornour) (total no. brooches=70)

and the brooch assemblage includes types with possible continental influences, even if some were perhaps made locally (Boudet 1988, 62; S. Adams 2013, 71–2). A recently identified variant of the Aucissa brooch has been recognised as having a predominantly Cornish distribution, leading to the suggestion that they may have been manufactured in the area (Tyacke *et al.* 2011; Thomas 2016, 117).

The fact that some sites in Cornwall produced early brooches, and that they have been recovered from Iron Age burials, may be of significance, as it suggests that at least certain members of society wore brooches during the pre-conquest period. This may be part of the explanation for the far greater prevalence of brooches in Cornwall during the Roman period – the inhabitants of this part of the South-West were familiar with brooches, and the types of clothing that they were used to fasten, and were thus open to the continued use of brooches during the Roman period.

Brooches of Group B are substantially better represented in the South-West, though they have been recovered from Cornish sites far more frequently than from those in the east of the region. Indeed, the only eastern sites with Group B brooches are the aforementioned port at Mount Batten, Plymouth, as well as an enclosed farmstead at Lower Well Farm, Stoke Gabriel (Masson Phillips 1966), which has a finds assemblage

somewhat richer than is usual for farmsteads in much of Devon.

In Cornwall, Group B brooches have been recovered from a number of sites. A range of types is represented, but most common are initial T-shaped types, with some appearing to be a distinctively South-Western type. Thomas (2016) has noted how the increased evidence for brooch use in Cornwall following the Roman conquest, and the increased range of decorative forms, may have been important in the process of renegotiating identities during the early Roman period.

Where brooches occur, they are usually found in small numbers, although some sites have produced unusually large assemblages. At Carvossa in Cornwall (Carlyon 1987), eighteen brooches were recovered, part of a particularly rich finds assemblage for the region, which is suggestive of Roman military activity at the site. The enclosed 'round' at St Mawgan-in-Pydar in North Cornwall yielded seventeen brooches, alongside a fairly large assemblage of other artefacts (for the region), which might be related to the site's role in smelting tin (Threipland 1956). Several cist graves from the first century A.D. cemetery at Porth Cressa, St Mary's, Isles of Scilly, contained brooches that may have had continental influences (Ashbee 1954; 1979). The two brooches found at Trethurgy serve as an important example of the potentially long use-lives of brooches, as two late first-century

A.D. brooches were recovered from late fourth-century contexts (Butcher 2004b; see also Thomas 2016 for a discussion of the long life of brooches in Cornwall more generally). These brooches may, perhaps, have been acquired through different means, and were possibly treated differently from those recovered from some other sites.

Group C brooches are restricted to Cornwall. A striking feature of the South-West Group C brooches is that Trumpet brooches, which dominate the group in other regions, are infrequent finds (recovered from one site other than Nornour; St Mawgan-in-Pydar; Threipland 1956), whereas Developed T-Shaped types are much more common. This is indicative of the emergence of a distinctive regional group during the later first and second centuries A.D., and the general lack of Trumpet brooches may suggest that markets in the South-West did not have a close relationship with those that operated in, for instance, the North or the Central West, where such brooches are far more common.

Aside from penannular brooches, which occur at a number of sites in Cornwall (yet rarely in Devon), most other brooch types are rare across the South-West region. Plate brooches are occasionally found, but only at four sites in Cornwall, and only at the roadside settlement at Topsham in Devon (Dyer 1999). Group D brooches are absent from sites apart from Nornour, and Group E brooches, the Crossbows, are absent, even at Nornour.

Nornour has already been singled out as an exceptional site for the region, and indeed, for the province. Located in the eastern Isles of Scilly, the site had Bronze Age origins, and was a focus for ritual activity throughout the Roman period, with figurines, miniature pots, coins, brooches and an array of other finds recovered from in and around the Bronze Age houses. The huge brooch assemblage from the site has very few brooches from Group A, yet hundreds of brooches in Groups B and C – consistent with its use from the early Roman period onwards. It is dominated especially by T-shaped brooches, particularly those of developed form, and there are also well over 100 plate brooches. Some of these have strong religious associations, with types including the Horse-and-Rider, skeuomorphic shoe sole and dagger brooches, zoomorphic brooches depicting hippocamps, horses and birds, and others depicting wheels and stars.

DISCUSSION

This chapter has presented a broad overview of the evidence for the appearance of people in the countryside of Roman Britain through a study of five of the most commonly found categories of object associated with dress and personal display – brooches, bracelets, finger rings, hairpins and personal grooming equipment. What is abundantly clear is that the rural population encompassed a great diversity of peoples, with very different appearances. At the broad geographical level this is evidenced by major differences in the extent to which objects such as brooches and other objects were adopted at settlements in the countryside.

Many of those occupying farmsteads in the south and east of the province wore clothes that required the use of brooches to fasten them, whereas those inhabiting rural sites in the north and west did so to a significantly lesser degree. Bayley and Butcher have previously suggested that during the first 150 years of Roman occupation brooches were a standard part of everyday costume, and that most individuals would have had at least one (Bayley and Butcher 2004, 206). While this may have been the case at many types of settlement in the south and east of the province, it seems almost certainly not to have been true for most of the rural populations of the north and west, who must have had very different ways of fastening their clothes, and indeed, of dressing generally. This is clearly demonstrated by the kernel density plot shown in FIG. 2.41, which shows the density of brooches at farmsteads (of all types), with brooches quantified according to the area excavated. This uneven distribution of brooches (and most other dress accessories at sites in the countryside) occurs despite the fact that dress accessories such as brooches occur widely at Roman military sites and towns in the north and west. The reduced evidence for their use across most of the rural sites in these areas is therefore suggestive of a general lack of integration of the rural population, who seem likely to have adhered to traditional, and for the most part archaeologically invisible, ways of dressing. The development and use of new types of object, however, such as the glass bangles that are common finds at rural sites in the North and North-East regions, indicate that, even in these areas, contact with Rome resulted in some changes to people's appearance (if, that is, glass bangles were a form of dress accessory), which may reflect the construction of new group identities in the face of a changing world (Eckardt 2014, 27; Derks and Roymans 2009). It is notable that the areas that have produced the least evidence for brooches at farmsteads, most notably the uplands of Wales and much of the North, correspond in broad terms with the main distribution of Roman-period beaded torcs, mapped by Hunter (2008; 2010), which have a core area running from the Forth to the Severn–Wash line (Hunter 2008, 134). These

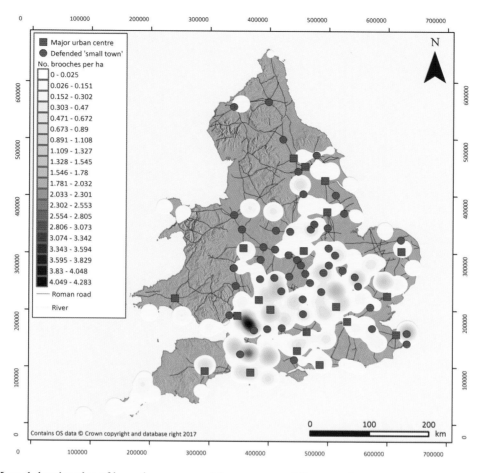

FIG. 2.41. Kernel density plot of brooches recovered from excavated farmsteads

torcs were now increasingly manufactured from base metal, rather than gold or silver as they had been in the Iron Age, indicating that they were being used by a wider social base within parts of northern and western Britain (*ibid.*, 133). Although these objects are rarely recovered from excavated rural sites, the distribution is suggestive of the development of a particular 'native' form of display, with Iron Age origins. This may have been part of a broad cultural response – the revival or reinvention of a tradition (Eckardt 2014, 29) – to the increasing use of classically influenced ways of dressing, which required the use of objects such as brooches, finger rings and hairpins, at what were predominantly military sites in these areas. As just noted, the lack of brooches and most other dress accessories at sites in the countryside in much of the north and west of the province is suggestive of a relative lack of interaction between the rural population and the military sites. Whether this represents a deliberate cultural reaction resulting in an emphasis on traditional values on the part of the native populations and an active rejection of what may have been perceived as alien influences (e.g. Bennett 1983, 217), or, rather, a general lack of opportunities for the occupants of native rural

settlements to acquire material in a tightly controlled militarised landscape, remains for the time being unclear, though the subject has attracted considerable academic discussion (e.g. Allason-Jones 1991; Ferris 2012, 19–21). It is, however, notable that in some parts of northern Britain, beyond the frontier, objects such as brooches were evidently desirable, at least for some people, as the rich finds evidence from some lowland Scottish brochs, and of course, Traprain Law, demonstrates (Hunter 2016, 190–2). The general lack of such objects from most farmsteads in the North may therefore reflect tight military control of the settlement hierarchy, and restricted opportunities for groups to gain preferential access to such material, even if they desired it (e.g. Higham 1989, 169). This may be related to the evidence for changes in the social hierarchy at native sites in some parts of the North following the conquest, where what had been monumental settlement enclosures, suggestive of power and status, had gone out of use by the end of the first or during the second century A.D. (Hodgson *et al.* 2013, 193–4, 213; Brindle 2016a, 324–5).

While the evidence for different appearances in the countryside is at its most stark when viewed in broad geographical terms, the evidence for the social distribution of dress accessories demonstrates quite clearly how, even in the areas where objects such as brooches, finger rings, hairpins and personal grooming equipment were most widespread, these were not used by everyone. While many of those who occupied the towns, nucleated roadside settlements, villages, villas and complex farmsteads, which were well integrated into the Roman market economy, were influenced by new ways of dressing following the conquest, those occupying enclosed farmsteads did so to a much reduced extent. As we have seen, this has important implications for our understanding of the social context of regional brooch types, which are more often recovered by metal-detector users than during excavation, such as the Wirral Brooch or the Dragonesque. Sometimes regarded as being 'rural' brooch types, owing to their distribution in the countryside outside major towns and military sites, we are able to offer a more nuanced understanding of the sorts of rural sites at which they circulated most widely. In both cases these are most likely to have been nucleated roadside settlements, sometimes associated with military industrial production, and not the sorts of low-status farmsteads occupied by most of the rural population, who are likely to have dressed in ways that did not involve wearing brooches, finger rings and other such items of personal adornment.

Indeed, it seems very likely that, when they came into contact, many of the occupants of a town, villa or a complex farmstead in the Central Belt or South, for instance, would be able to distinguish themselves from the occupants of an enclosed farmstead, based upon their appearance. The wearing of clothes fastened by shiny brooches, finger rings, and, for women, the creation of fashionable and sometimes elaborate hairstyles, must have set individuals apart from those who seem to have adopted very few of these aspects of personal display.

Yet how did those who did adopt the use of classical objects such as finger rings perceive themselves? The increasingly visible influence that classical traditions had on some people in the countryside of Roman Britain, in much of the south and east of the province, need not necessarily be viewed in traditional terms as evidence of the 'Romanization' of a certain element of the population (e.g. Haverfield 1912). While influenced by classical fashions imported by the Roman administration, the army and its followers, the quick emergence of insular forms of classical objects such as hairpins (Cool 1990), and the development of distinctively British (regional) types of brooch – disseminated into the countryside through markets at towns and roadside nucleated

settlements – indicates that new types of object were often adopted and developed in accordance with the social and cultural milieus of the native inhabitants of the province. The concept of creolisation (Webster 2001; Carr 2003; 2006; 2007) – a merging of aspects of different cultures, as well as the use of objects in new ways – is probably a more useful way of seeking to understand changes that took place in the appearance of *some* people in *some* parts of the countryside of Roman Britain.

Certainly, the usefulness of the simplistic, polarised distinction between 'Roman' and 'native' has for some time been called into question (e.g. Hill 2001, 13; Eckardt 2014, 20), and the increasing evidence for social stratification and what may have been distinctive, visible cultural values among the native rural populations of Britain, even within fairly closely defined geographical areas, indicates the presence of myriad, and perhaps conflicting, identities within native populations, which in some cases may have led to social tension. It seems inconceivable that such differences in personal appearance would not have been made manifest in the way that individuals and groups perceived and treated one another. Did the occupants of enclosed farmsteads view the wealthy elite in their villas with envy? Indeed, did a caste system develop, where the occupants of some enclosed farmsteads who may have farmed at the subsistence level, were persecuted and treated with disdain for being uncultured, uneducated, as well, perhaps, as being regarded as dirty and smelly? Might these differences in personal appearance even provide insights into the extent to which people at different classes of rural sites had the *freedom* to engage with the market economy and the access to objects this provided? Enslaved peoples are distinctly difficult groups to recognise in the archaeological record, yet private ownership of land and the freedom of movement are exceedingly unlikely to have been universal rights throughout the province (see Ch. 8). The evidence discussed above for differences in personal appearance may reflect distinctive social identities based upon perceptions of class (whether wealthy vs poor; free vs enslaved; or entirely different notions altogether), which may have transcended broader group identities that were perhaps based on shared membership of a tribe. The evidence for diversity across different types of site in some parts of the countryside of Roman Britain may be regarded as evidence for a complex interplay of personal and group identities, which operated at various levels (e.g. Eckardt 2014, 4–6).

It is important to recognise that this chapter has aimed to present broad regional and social trends in the distribution of artefacts associated with personal adornment and display throughout the countryside, in order for us to recognise some of the regional and social variation in terms of broad group appearances. In all societies, across all regions, appearances are likely to have differed based on clothes and accessories, which carried messages about an individual's social position, including, but not limited to, age, gender, experience and their role within society.

Furthermore, little attention has been paid here to the identification of 'other' at rural sites, although as is well recognised, Roman Britain was a diverse place with frequent movement of people to, from and around the province (e.g. Ferris 2012, 144–9; Eckardt 2010; 2014, 35, 50, 59). It is clear that the most diverse places within the province would have been the major urban centres and military sites, and there is a range of epigraphic, artefactual and scientific evidence for mixed populations at many such sites. There is substantially less evidence from the countryside for the movement of people from different areas. In all regions, however, there are sites that have produced unusual groups of artefacts that differ from those in the surrounding areas (see also evidence from burials in Ch. 6 and wider discussion in Ch. 8).

What, for instance, does the presence of an unusually large group of brooches, of wide ranging and regionally unusual types, from the farmstead at St Mawgan-in-Pydar, Cornwall (Threipland 1956), tell us about the movement of people and contact with the wider province? This site is the only excavated farmstead in Cornwall to have produced a Trumpet brooch, a type which, as we have seen, was far more common in other areas, and few have been recorded by the PAS (though many are known from Nornour; see above, p. 44).

Intriguingly, the site is also currently the only farmstead from mainland Cornwall from which a Roman-style finger ring has been recorded, and a range of imported pottery was also recovered. The form of the settlement is fairly typical of rural sites in this part of the region generally, and we cannot know whether the occurrence of these objects represents the presence of outsiders at this site. It does, at the very least, suggest that the occupants of the settlement had a greater level of access to, and an interest in acquiring and wearing, 'exotic' dress accessories that did not circulate widely at other settlements in the region. This may be related to the evidence for tin smelting identified at the site; did engagement in tin production mean that the occupants of this site had considerably wider networks than those at many other settlements in Cornwall? Did the availability of such mineral resources attract others to the area, who engaged with and perhaps intermixed with the locals? Occasional, unusual finds assemblages such as these occur at rural sites across the province, and examples could have been selected from any region. Such unexpected finds at rural settlements are testimony to the mobility of people and objects around the province, as well, of course, from outside it. While we are now able to recognise some broad regional differences in terms of the ways that people may have looked, there must always have been groups and individuals whose appearance differed. The introduction of new types of object from other areas, and the ways in which they were used and displayed, meant that regional styles of dress and appearance must have been constantly developing and being renegotiated, as people were exposed to the new and changing appearances of others.

CHAPTER 3

LIFESTYLE AND THE SOCIAL ENVIRONMENT

By Alexander Smith, with Tom Brindle, Michael Fulford and Lisa Lodwick

INTRODUCTION

Cultural identities and social strategies could be manipulated not only through personal appearance, but also through a wide variety of lifestyle choices and the active creation and control of the surrounding physical environment. These may relate to differences in eating and drinking habits, leisure pursuits, forms of communication, levels of education, and a host of other variables, alongside variations in architectural form and embellishment, and outside space (cf. Gardner 2007, 99). This chapter will explore some of these themes as they relate to the peoples of rural Roman Britain, highlighting their regional and social diversity. Given the lack of contemporary written accounts relating to most of these aspects in Roman Britain, especially outside of urban and military contexts, the evidence typically takes the form of portable material culture, environmental remains and the archaeological remains of buildings and other features, all of which inevitably present a very incomplete picture. Nevertheless, they do conclusively demonstrate that many of the existing accounts of 'life in Roman Britain' (e.g. Alcock 2006) are only relevant to a relatively small proportion of the population, a fact that has on occasion been duly acknowledged (cf. de la Bédoyère 2015, xiv).

RURAL HOMES AND GARDENS

The artificially constructed environment, particularly as expressed through architecture, has long been viewed as a microcosm of society and therefore a tool in understanding social structure (e.g. Rapoport 1969, 50; S. Foster 1989; Reid 1989; Hingley 1990; Sanders 1990, 43; Grahame 2000). Furthermore, recent work has highlighted that architecture is not only reflective of the social, political and economic realities, but can also be an active agent in enabling these realities (Taylor 2013; Bille and Sørensen 2016, 3). The wide variety of excavated buildings within the countryside of Roman Britain has already been discussed at length in Volume 1 (Smith 2016b), where a complex continuum of architectural expression was revealed (FIG. 3.1). This work will be drawn upon and combined with selected elements of portable material culture to assess the heterogeneous domestic environment of peoples across the rural landscapes of the Roman province.

First and foremost, it must be reiterated that those rural settlements classed architecturally as villas would have formed only a very small percentage of overall settlement in the Romano-British countryside, and yet, alongside urban houses, they continue to dominate in many discussions of domestic life in Roman Britain (e.g. Perring 2002; Allason-Jones 2005, 78–103; Alcock 2006, 115–25). Despite the considerable variety in form and scale (cf. Smith 2016b, 71–4), villa buildings can be regarded as representing a particular form of cultural aspiration and would have required considerable expenditure (Millett 2016, 703). At the uppermost end of the scale were the lavish courtyard-villa complexes, mostly dating to the later Roman period, such as at Woodchester in Gloucestershire, which have been viewed as the centres of social exhibitionism for the 'super-elite' of Roman Britain, providing stages for the competitive display of wealth and culture (Scott 2004, 43). However, villas at all levels could have fulfilled such roles within their contemporary social groups, and would have been strikingly different architectural settings to the 'typical', modest, rural farmhouse buildings. They have, by their very definition, relatively high levels of investment in architectural elaboration such as painted plaster walls, tiled roofs, window glass, hypocaust heating systems and mosaic floors, while there is also much greater evidence from portable material culture for internal furnishings, lighting, security and the like. With all these highly visible forms of evidence, it is hardly surprising that they have formed the dominant backdrop for pictures of 'typical' Roman rural lifestyles over many years. That is not to say that other lifestyles within different architectural settings have not been acknowledged, but this often comprises little more than a brief discussion of social activities within roundhouses, thus perpetuating the simple Roman–native dichotomy. Yet, it is now abundantly clear that from the most palatial of villas to the simplest of single-roomed dwellings, there is a very broad spectrum of domestic architecture, representing a mix of cultural traditions, socio-economic aspirations and individual choice, with clear geographic and chronological variation.

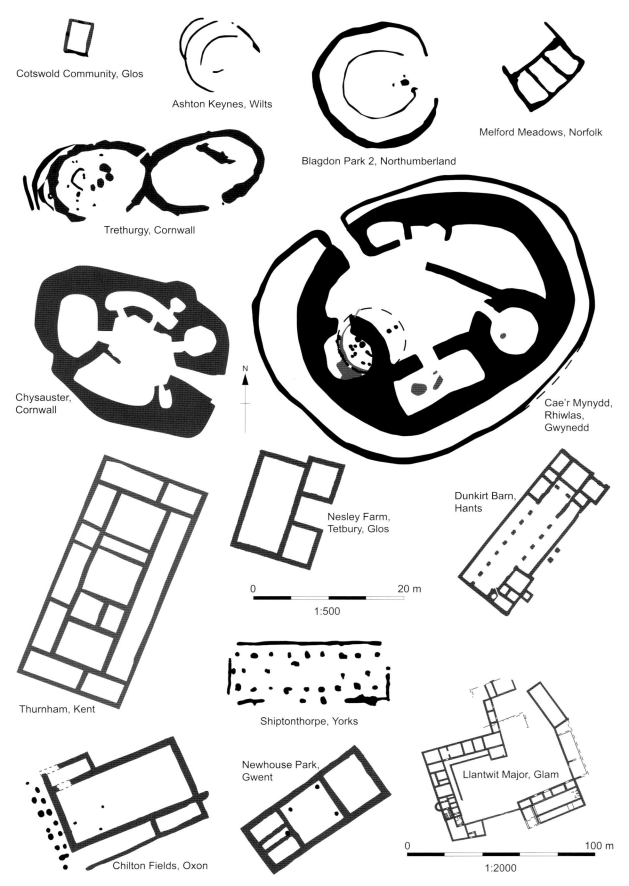

FIG. 3.1. Selection of domestic building plans from across rural Roman Britain (all 1:500 except Llantwit Major at 1:2000)

The excavated evidence suggests that the majority of vernacular architecture in the countryside of Roman Britain probably comprised relatively simple single-roomed buildings, of circular and/or rectangular form (Smith 2016b, 64–5). Nevertheless, these could still house quite complex divisions of internal space, as demonstrated by Taylor (2001) for open aisled buildings in the East Midlands, where various parts of the structure were consistently used for cooking and eating, agricultural processing and/or craft activities, storage and possible areas of assembly. These were, however, usually quite large buildings and probably associated with those of relatively high status, many of them developing into more complex architectural forms with 'villa' attributes such as mosaic floors, hypocausts and bath suites. Yet, even within smaller buildings, it is likely that there was often a mix of 'domestic' (cooking, eating, sleeping) and 'non-domestic' (storage, craftworking, agricultural processing, livestock shelter) practices operating within a singular or minimally divided space (e.g. Nesley Farm, Glos.; see below p. 54, FIG. 3.6), even if some of the latter was on a temporary basis, perhaps structured by the agricultural year.

The scale, form, materials and construction techniques of rural domestic housing exhibit great variation across different parts of England and Wales, even beyond those classified as villas, and there are certain distinctive regional architectural traditions, noted in Chapters 4 to 11 of Volume 1 (Smith *et al.* 2016). Most of the 'non-villa' domestic buildings in all areas have no evidence for any elaboration, though 12 per cent of 881 farmsteads with structural evidence appear to have had at least one building with a tiled (as opposed to, for example, thatch, turf or shingle) roof, while 7 per cent had indications of painted plaster walls, though sometimes this only comprised whitewash. Although it is generally acknowledged that painted plaster was mainly found in urban and villa buildings, there is still a tendency for analyses of Romano-British domestic environments to focus almost exclusively upon these site types, and it is clear that the interiors of most houses would have been far less colourful than those belonging to the upper end of the social spectrum. Glazed windows seem equally rare outside of villa contexts, with window glass being recovered at 38 per cent of roadside settlements (but by no means in every building) and just 6 per cent of farmsteads. It is not possible to ascertain just how common windows would have been in domestic buildings, though it is generally thought that, where they existed, most would have been shuttered (Mould 2011, 156). Evidence for flooring of any form is also rare within 'non-villa'

domestic buildings, with assumptions based upon a few survivals that most must have comprised mortar, timber planks or just beaten earth, such as the chalk and clay floors defining buildings within the roadside settlement at Scole, Norfolk (Ashwin and Tester 2014, 219).

The farmsteads that do exhibit more of the elaborate structural elements tend to lie in the Central Belt region, where the architectural boundary between villas and other buildings is at its most blurred (Smith 2016d, 171–2), possibly reflecting, and in turn helping to create, a more complex social stratification. A suite of architectural embellishments may have been actively used to help elevate and maintain social standing in local society, and seems to have been particularly important in this part of the province during the mid- to late Roman period. One example is that at Stonebridge Cross near Droitwich in Worcestershire, where a series of mid- to late Roman, stone-footed, multi-roomed buildings were identified within enclosures, at least one of which was thought to be domestic, with fragmentary evidence for a stone-tiled floor, tiled roof, glazed windows and at least one painted wall (Miller *et al.* 2004). Although not categorised in this project as a villa, the building would have appeared strikingly different from those on most other farmsteads in the local area, many of which have left little archaeological trace other than the occasional post pad (e.g. Areley Kings; Buteux and Hemmingway 1992) or cobbled surface (e.g. Hindlip; Wainwright 2010).

The variation apparent in architectural form, material and elaboration within rural homes is matched by the mixed evidence for internal furnishings and fixtures. A full consideration of the wide range of household object types is beyond the scope of the current project (see Cool 2006, Mould 2011, Eckardt 2014 and Swift 2017 for recent works on this subject), but the social and geographic variation is demonstrated through brief analyses of objects and features associated with security, lighting and heating.

SECURITY

Locks and keys are persistent, if uncommon, finds from excavated Roman sites across much of the province, though they were not always associated with domestic contexts. A few were clearly part of what are termed 'structured deposits', such as the key found within an early Roman 'votive' pit near to the river at Billingford in Norfolk, alongside a copper-alloy torque, glass beads and a ring (Wallis 2011; see Ch. 5 for definition and discussion of structured deposits). They have also been recorded as grave goods at a number of sites, for instance at Higham Ferrers in Northamptonshire, where one adult inhumation burial had a group of three keys placed on the chest (Lawrence and Smith 2009; see Ch. 6). These examples suggest that such objects may have held some symbolic value, though it is obviously as functional objects relating to security where their importance mostly lies.

There were two major types of lock – mounted locks and padlocks – and four main types of key – latch-lifters, lift-keys, slide keys and rotary keys – in use during the Roman period (Mould 2011, 176; Swift 2017, 114). They would have been used on a variety of doors, furniture and other contexts, including slave manacles, and had differing levels of security, with latch-lifters just being used to raise unspecific single bolts or tumblers. The prevalence of such security devices within the Roman period has been well noted, with suggestions that it related to the increased affluence of a section of society – those with more materials to protect – as well as to increasing concerns about personal security, particularly within urban environments that had a more transient population (Mould 2011, 177). Such insecurity correlates with the increased incidence of lead tablets from temples such as Bath, north-east Somerset, and Uley, Gloucestershire, cursing the theft of objects (e.g. clothing) or animals (see Ch. 5, p. 178). Swift (2017, 120) has also argued that as certain types of keys and locks were relatively new introductions, and implied the possession of wealth, they may have been seen as potent status symbols, possibly accounting for the number of finger rings with keys attached.

A total of 438 different sites included in the current project had some evidence for security objects, including at least 101 with simple latch-lifters and 284 with more complex keys. As can be seen from FIG. 3.2, they are more likely to be found within nucleated settlements and villas, correlating with the above-suggested associations with wealth, status and increased insecurities of larger population centres. The pattern is repeated in terms of the average numbers of objects found at sites where they do occur, which ranges from over eight at defended 'small towns' to under two at farmsteads, though this presumably relates to differences in population size. Villas, though, have almost as many security objects per site as nucleated settlements, these also comprising the broadest mix of key and lock types, suggesting either a particular concern with security at many of these sites, or else, as just stated, a greater emphasis on locks and keys as objects of status.

The distribution of the site types with security objects is shown in FIG. 3.3, overall being far more common in the Central Belt and parts of the South region. Farmsteads in particular are more likely to have security objects within the Central Belt landscapes, most of these being the complex farmsteads of the major river valleys, which have been shown to be more integrated into the socio-economic networks of the province than smaller, enclosed farmsteads (Smith 2016d, 186–7; see also Ch. 2 and below, p. 74). Some farmsteads display an increasing preoccupation with security objects over time, which is clearly seen at Claydon Pike in the Upper Thames Valley. Major changes occurred at this site during the fourth century A.D., including the creation of a substantial ditched and walled enclosure around the multi-roomed farmstead building, while at the same time there was a much higher number of tumbler and lever

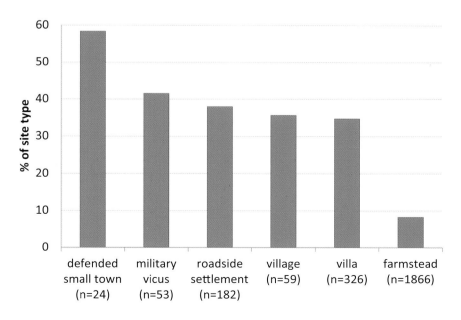

FIG. 3.2. Proportion of settlement types with evidence for security objects (n=no. sites)

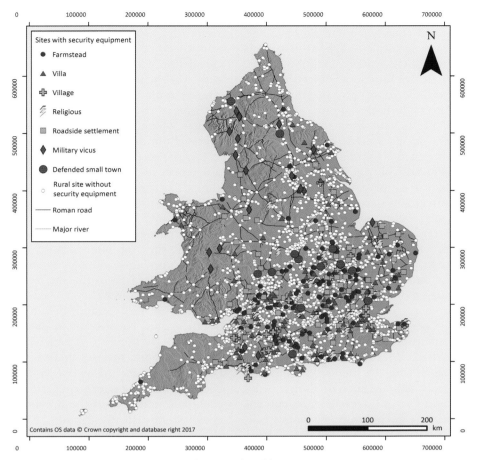

FIG. 3.3. Distribution of site types with evidence for security objects

locks and padlocks, compared with the few lower security latch-lifters of the previous phase (Cool 2007, 190). Ultimately, whether this represented a genuinely increased threat to security, an increased paranoia or a shift towards greater use of security measures as status symbols remains uncertain.

LIGHTING AND HEATING

Artificial lighting of some sort would have been required in most homes in Roman Britain, and yet evidence for associated material culture is very scarce, particularly outside of certain major urban centres and large military sites (Eckardt 2002; 2011, 192). Just 149 sites in the current project had evidence for lighting equipment, these mostly comprising ceramic and metal oil lamps, of open and closed types, and candlesticks. Such lighting equipment was introduced to Britain after the Roman conquest, with lamps only being prevalent at certain sites during the first century, and candlesticks becoming more common during the later Roman period (Eckardt 2011, 187). FIGURE 3.4 shows the social distribution of all lighting equipment by site type, with much higher proportions of defended 'small towns' and military *vici* being equipped with such items than other

settlements. They are found in only *c.* 1 per cent of farmsteads, almost all of complex type, and these are far more dispersed across the province than was the case with those farmsteads associated with security items, which, as noted above, were more concentrated in the Central Belt region (FIG. 3.5). Most of the 22 farmsteads just have the odd fragment of an iron tripod candlestick or ceramic lamp, though a copper-alloy vine leaf-shaped lamp reflector from the complex farmstead at Claydon Pike in Gloucestershire suggests a higher degree of affluence (Cool 2007, 134). An unparalleled seven ceramic lamps were recovered during excavations of a complex farmstead at Langdale Hale on the Cambridgeshire Fen edge, though this site is thought to have been associated with state supply networks (Evans 2013a, 169), and so the presence of the lamps may result from possible military connections.

Villas may be expected to have considerably more evidence for lighting equipment, yet it was only found on 11 per cent of those included in this project, mostly, like farmsteads, in very small numbers. Just five villas had five or more items of lighting equipment, and most of these had some possible 'official' connection, such as the early to

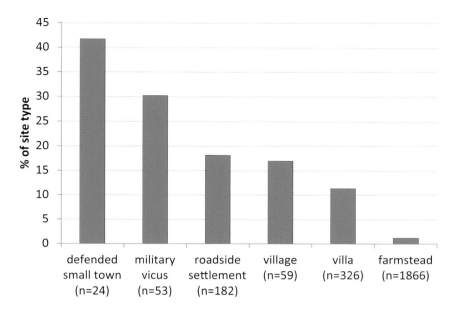

FIG. 3.4. Proportion of settlement types with evidence for lighting objects (n=no. sites)

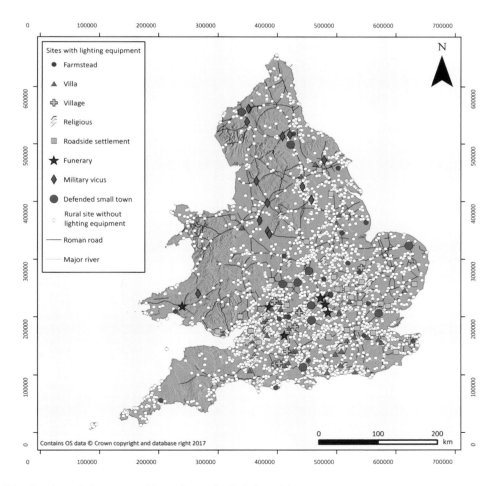

FIG. 3.5. Distribution of site types with evidence for lighting objects

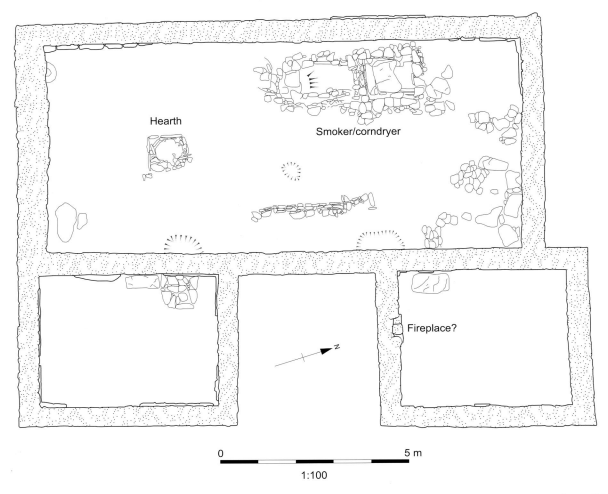

FIG. 3.6.   Masonry building at Nesley Farm, Gloucestershire, showing central hearth in main room and possible fireplace in northern annexe (Roberts 2013)

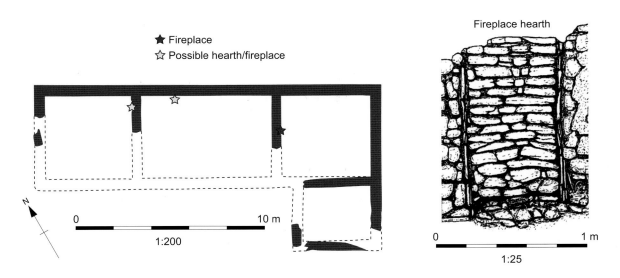

FIG. 3.7.   Masonry building at Vineyards Farm, Charlton Kings, Gloucestershire, with example of recessed fireplace (after Rawes 1991, fig. 8)

mid-Roman palatial villa at Fishbourne in West Sussex (Cunliffe 1971) and the villa lying very close to the nucleated settlements at Bays Meadow Villa, Droitwich in Worcestershire, which has been suggested as the official residence of a 'junior procurator' responsible for managing the local salt industry (Shotter 2005, 43; Barfield 2006).

Some of the lamps from farmsteads and villas were found as grave goods within burials, and there are a further six 'isolated' funerary sites with burials being accompanied by lamps, mostly iron types of open form (cf. Eckardt 2011, 190). Previous research by Eckardt (2002, 154) has shown that the use of lamps as grave goods generally follows that of the overall consumption of these items, in being far more common within burials at military and urban sites. However, it is clear that they were not always simply selected for interment due to their availability, as Cool has pointed out that at Chichester in West Sussex, lamps are relatively common finds in graves, yet extremely rare discoveries from excavations within the Roman town itself, with implications that they were seen as more suitable for the dead than the living (Cool 2011, 307). The ritual significance of lamps and other lighting equipment can also be seen with their occurrence on fifteen rural religious sites, including two parts of a candlestick and a ceramic 'votive lamp' from the temple complex at Nettleton Scrubb in Wiltshire (Wedlake 1982). The manipulation of lighting, as well as sounds and smells, was probably an important part of the 'religious experience' at these sites (see Ch. 5).

Ritual associations aside, the question arises as to why did apparently so few rural settlements take up the use of lamps and candles? Eckardt (2011, 192) has suggested that the adoption of lamps was closely related to an urban and Mediterranean lifestyle, and their use never spread far beyond the larger towns and forts because most people in the countryside had no need or desire for them. They would have been relatively labour-intensive to use, requiring constant trimming of the wick and filling with oil, as well as creating a great deal of soot. For the majority of the rural population, especially those living in single-roomed dwellings, lighting provision probably consisted of nothing more than the focal hearth, which would also have acted as the major source of heat, and, in what were predominantly illiterate societies, probably the focus for important cultural and social activities such as storytelling (see below, p. 69). The possible cultural associations of the hearth fire may have been another reason why other lighting equipment was not adopted more widely.

Hearths have been noted at 346 sites in the project database, mostly lying within the centre of rooms or buildings. A later Roman masonry farmhouse building at Nesley Farm in Gloucestershire, for example, had clear evidence for a substantial, long-lived hearth in the centre of the southern half of the main room, constructed of layers of sandstone roofing tiles and kerbed by upright stones (Roberts 2013; FIG. 3.6). This was probably the main domestic zone of the house, with the northern half being used for agricultural purposes, as indicated by the presence of a substantial smoker or corndryer. The two small annexes were later additions and may have been bedchambers, with painted plaster walls and a possible fireplace in the wall of the northern annexe, though there was no evidence of associated burning (ibid., 21). Fireplaces recessed into walls are occasionally attested elsewhere, usually in villas or 'upmarket' farmhouses of the later Roman period such as at Vineyards Farm, Gloucestershire (Rawes 1991, 36–9; FIG. 3.7). In addition, it is likely that torches and iron braziers with wood, coal or charcoal were used in some of the larger houses, though there is little direct evidence for this in Britain.

Of course the best-known form of Roman domestic heating is the hypocaust system, where hot air from a furnace, usually stoked from the exterior of the building, passes under the floor in open channels and up through hollow (box) tiles in the walls. In terms of domestic housing, such heating systems are largely unknown except within villas and high-status urban dwellings, and, even with these, examples are often found in just one or two rooms at most, with the likelihood that many were fired up only on occasion (Eckardt 2011, 180). Nevertheless, the provision of such heating would undoubtedly have been expected within the houses of the upper echelons of society, alongside the package of other decorative elements noted above, such as painted plaster walls and mosaic floors. Although the evidence is not always as clear, such elements were probably also to be found outside such high-status dwellings, in the form of formal gardens.

ORNAMENTAL GARDENS AND PLANTS

By Lisa Lodwick

Across the Roman world, there is abundant evidence for the creation of ornamental gardens featuring fish ponds, swimming pools, hedges, pathways and trees, based on literary and artistic evidence, as well as exceptionally well-preserved garden layouts in Pompeii (Jashemski 1981; Farrar 2011). Ornamental plant layouts were a feature of public gardens, funerary gardens, public parks and villa portico gardens (Farrar 2011). Literary evidence describes the translocation of new plant

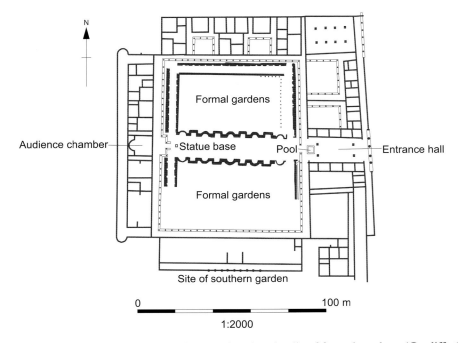

FIG. 3.8. Plan of Fishbourne Palace, West Sussex, showing details of formal gardens (Cunliffe 1981)

species from the Middle East to Italy and beyond, including balsam, citrus and cherry, for use in military triumphs, private housing and dining (Macaulay-Lewis 2008; Marzano 2014). However, in Britain literary and artistic evidence for ornamental gardens is largely lacking, with the stylised flowers, plants and trees featuring on mosaics not as yet having been approached from a botanical perspective. Instead, the study of ornamental gardens and plants relies on the exceptional preservation of garden layouts, or on archaeobotanical samples, as outlined in previous reviews (Cunliffe 1981; Zeepvat 1991).

Formal garden layouts have been recorded at six villas in southern Britain, in both the South and Central Belt regions, but are, as yet, unknown outside such high-status rural dwellings. At Frocester Court, Gloucestershire, a walled front courtyard and fourth-century A.D. formal garden were recorded including a gravel path and planting beds containing midden material (Price 2000, 105–9). Antiquarian excavations at Darenth villa, Kent, revealed walled gardens with a swimming pool and ornamental fish pool (Philp 1973). Similarly, at Bancroft villa, Milton Keynes, a large walled formal garden contained a fishpond and an artificial pond or lake to supply a mill (Williams and Zeepvat 1994). The most detailed villa-garden plan derives from Fishbourne, where four areas of ornamental gardens were recorded attached to the Flavian palace; the peristyle gardens, the central formal garden (FIG. 3.8), the kitchen garden in the north-west, and a possible 'natural' area on the southern terrace. Alongside tree-planting holes

and ceramic water pipes, distinctive bedding trenches were recorded around the perimeter of the central courtyard and adjacent to the main pathway. The trenches were cut into the gravel and clay soil, and filled with calcareous loam, interpreted as an indicator that a shrub, such as box, was grown in them (Cunliffe 1981). Areas of ornamental gardens have also been postulated at Keynsham villa, Somerset, on the basis of an extensive cultivation layer (Cox 1998) and, at Dunkirt Barn, Hampshire, a garden enclosure was identified by the villa building, within which was a hexagonal structure thought to have been a shrine (Cunliffe and Poole 2008b).

Alternative evidence for the creation of new landscapes derives from the plants themselves. However, the preservation of garden plants relies largely on the presence of waterlogged conditions (Murphy and Scaife 1991), which is mostly limited to the major river valleys and urban areas. A range of plants is attested to have been used in Roman gardens in Italy, including acanthus, bay-laurel and myrtle (Farrar 2011), primarily evidenced by literary and artistic sources. Of course any plant can be used ornamentally, but definitive evidence for the use of plants to create managed gardens comes from the presence of introduced plant species, such as *Buxus sempervirens* (box), *Pinus pinea* (stone pine) and *Picea abies* (Norway spruce). Box was favoured in Roman gardens for its use in topiary (Lodwick 2017b). There was a small-scale presence of this evergreen shrub before the Roman period, but leaves have been recovered from numerous Roman settlement sites, as well as in association with burials (see Ch. 6, p. 271). Box leaves have been recovered from many sites in London, but in rural Roman Britain it is primarily at villas where box appears to have been grown. These include Rectory Field, Godmanchester, Cambridgeshire (Murphy 1998), Chew Park, Somerset (Stant and Metcalfe 1977), Winterton villa, North Lincolnshire (Dimbleby 1978), and Stanwick villa, Northamptonshire (Campbell pers. comm.). However, box leaves have also been recorded at farmsteads, including at late third/fourth century A.D. Marsh Leys, Kempston, Bedfordshire (Robinson 2011a), a fourth-century farmstead at Farmoor, Oxfordshire (Lambrick and Robinson 1979, 127) and at a mid- to late Roman farmstead at Claydon Pike, Gloucestershire (Robinson 2007). The majority of sites are not in calcareous regions, the natural habitat of box, and therefore suggest the purposeful cultivation of box plants. The burial evidence shows that box leaves may have been used partly for wreaths, while the wood also provides a raw material for combs and writing tablets (Pugsley 2003). However, the strong association with villas suggests that these plants were being purposefully grown for their ornamental value, inducing different sensory experiences and temporalities (Lodwick 2017b; see also Ch. 4, p. 98 for introduction of 'exotic' animal species).

Norway spruce is a much less common occurrence in rural Roman Britain. Definitive evidence for a nearby tree was recorded from several ponds associated with a villa at Rectory Field, Godmanchester, Cambridgeshire, in the form of wood, leaves, twigs, cones and seeds (Murphy 1998). The ponds and wells at Godmanchester also produced evidence for yew, opium poppy, fennel, fig, marigold and beet, suggesting the presence of a Mediterranean-style garden. A *Picea abies* cone has also been confirmed from the nucleated settlement at Stonea Grange in the Cambridgeshire Fens (Murphy 2001, 17). Stone pine has been recorded from numerous rural settlements, albeit only as cones and nutshells, and not leaves or wood. Given the evidence for the widespread trade in stone-pine cones across the Roman world (Lodwick 2015), it is likely that these finds all derive from trade. At Bancroft villa, a stone-pine cone, which was recorded from a ditch fill to the south of an enclosure and rectangular structure (Pearson and Robinson 1994), provides the closest indication of a growing stone pine.

There is very limited archaeobotanical evidence for other ornamental plants. Dickson (1994) highlighted records of *Aquilegia* cf. *vulgaris* (cf. columbine) at Alcester, *Lavatera* cf. *arborea* (tree mallow) at Caerwent, *Rosa* sp. (rose) at Farmoor and Nantwich, and *Aegopodium podagraria* (ground elder) at York, but it cannot be proven that these were grown ornamentally. A record of *Prunus lusitanica* (Portuguese laurel) at Silchester has been identified as *Prunus* sp. (Lodwick 2017a), and no other occurrence of *P. lusitanica* has been recorded. Native plants may also have been grown ornamentally, such as *Ilex aquifolium* – holly, which has been recorded alongside box leaves at York (Hall and Kenward 1990, 359) and Silchester, Insula IX (Robinson 2011b).

Overall, the evidence suggests that the creation of ornamental gardens and landscapes did occur at certain higher status rural sites in Roman Britain, but definitive evidence for the character of these is limited. The only sites where archaeobotanical evidence for ornamental plants co-occurs with a garden layout are at Frocester and Bancroft villas. At the former, boxwood charcoal was identified, and at the latter was a single stone-pine cone, which may well have been imported. The reliance on waterlogged preservation for any garden plants being preserved means it is very difficult to evaluate the extent of ornamental plant landscapes in rural Roman Britain, with the only definitive archaeobotanical evidence for a range of Mediterranean trees limited to the villa at Rectory Farm, Godmanchester, which is awaiting full publication. As imported plants were used to articulate elite status in the Mediterranean (Marzano 2014), a smaller range of plants was probably used similarly in Roman Britain. These areas of vegetation would have been just as important for the creation of the lived environment and articulation of elite status as built architecture, perhaps being used for occasional dining, recreational pursuits and other types of social interaction. This review thus firmly highlights the importance of future investigation of open areas associated with villa buildings, using a suite of palaeoenvironmental techniques. The widespread presence of box also indicates that these plants were being cultivated at a range of settlement types (Lodwick 2017b), though whether primarily as a strategy to articulate social status, or to provide raw materials for wood-working, remains uncertain.

FOOD AND DRINK

By Michael Fulford

The consumption of food and drink was clearly an important element in the construction and maintenance of social identities (Twiss 2007; 2012; Van der Veen 2007b). Variations in the types of food and drink, the methods of preparation, and the etiquette and context of consumption can all contribute towards social and cultural differentiation.

The evidence for eating and drinking in Roman Britain, including its social context, has recently been well and extensively treated by Hilary Cool (2006). She used material from a select range of rural sites, including a limited number of case studies that exploited data from three settlements with comparatively good environmental data (Claydon Pike, Gloucestershire, Orton Hall Farm, Cambridgeshire and Parlington Hollins, West Yorkshire) (*ibid.*, 189–92, 203–7), from the temple at Uley, Gloucestershire (*ibid.*, 210–13), and from burials at Foxton and Bartlow Hills, both Cambridgeshire, as well as Stansted, Essex (*ibid.*, 101–2, 193–6). Since 2006 there have been important reviews of fish, seed and plant remains from Roman Britain (Locker 2007; Van der Veen *et al.* 2007; 2008). There have also been important contributions to our understanding of diet in the province from the analysis of stable isotopes both from human remains, which concluded, albeit from a predominantly urban sample, that diet had improved for the better compared with the Iron Age (Müldner 2013), and from the lipids preserved in pottery vessels, notably mortaria and cooking pots, which showed a strong presence of animal (ruminant) adipose as well as plant-derived fats (Cramp *et al.* 2011).

In this section we have the opportunity to look across the whole of rural Roman Britain and assess variation in patterns of consumption, both regionally and across the settlement hierarchy, drawing on the evidence from the *c.* 2500 sites that form the basis of the Roman Rural Settlement Project. Nevertheless, given the importance of subsistence to everyday life, even taking account of the increased amount of data since the publication of *Eating and Drinking in Roman Britain* (Cool 2006), it is perhaps surprising how little can yet be said about what the rural population of Britain actually ate and drank, as opposed to the plants and animals that they exploited and the wild resources potentially at their disposal. Although the countryside produced the great majority of the food and drink consumed in Roman Britain, it should not be assumed that all its inhabitants had equal and unfettered access to it.

A starting point for considering what was eaten and drunk is very much the corollary of what was set out in *The Rural Economy of Roman Britain*, namely the products of arable farming, horticulture and viticulture, and of pastoral farming (Allen 2017; Lodwick 2017c). In addition, in the next chapter of this volume Martyn Allen sets out the evidence for the exploitation of wild animals, including fish and shellfish. Importantly, some of the impacts on health of what was or was not eaten and drunk can be seen in Rohnbogner's study of the skeletal evidence from rural settlements in Chapter 7 of this volume.

Although the Romans regarded cereals as their staple, or the most important part of their diet (Cool 2006, 69), it is animal bone that figures most prominently in the archaeological record. It has previously been observed that, where soil conditions allow for their preservation (cf. Allen 2017, fig. 3.1), the great majority of rural settlements were engaged to some degree in raising the principal domesticates, cattle, sheep and pig, and that a proportion of the animals that died or were slaughtered were consumed on site. Indeed, the sampling of the organic residues from a sizeable sample of cooking vessels from two sites, the farmstead at Faverdale, County Durham, and the villa and nucleated settlement at Stanwick, Northamptonshire, showed a consistent presence of ruminant, i.e. cattle and sheep/goat, adipose animal fats (Cramp *et al.* 2011).

While we can see regional patterning, such as the increased presence of cattle on northern settlements, or the greater occurrence of sheep on chalkland settlements in the South region, what the evidence does not allow is any estimation of how frequently meat, from whatever type of animal, was eaten, and thus how important it was in rural diets. However, the implication of the greater frequency of cattle at villa sites in the Central Belt and South regions is that villa owners had greater access to beef, and of better-quality meat, than other people in the countryside, where the mortality profiles show animals being kept longer to meet the demands of traction rather than to provide prime beef (Allen 2017, 112–13, figs 3.5, 3.10, 3.15, 3.34–6). The situation with sheep is a little different, with a tendency for slaughter at sub-adult ages, thus emphasising meat production (*ibid.*, 114–16, figs 3.39–41). In the future, one way by which we might gain further insight into the contribution of meat to the diet is to assess, where conditions of preservation allow, the results of estimating the quantities of the meat potentially consumed relative to the different species and the parts of the animal skeleton recovered in relation to the amount of soil excavated and the length of occupation of the site in question. This would then provide the basis for comparing the incidence of meat consumption by type of site and by region. Such a task will become easier when volumes of excavated soil are systematically recorded.

In the case of milk and cheese, while there is some evidence from the mortality profiles to support dairying in the countryside associated with sheep, this is not so with cattle, except perhaps on a very small-scale basis, and in proximity to some towns and military *vici* (Allen 2017, 113–14). Analysis of the lipids preserved in the cooking vessels analysed at the villa and nucleated settlement at Stanwick, Northamptonshire, showed a significant presence (<40 per cent) of dairy fats (Cramp *et al.* 2011, 1347).

Even if we cannot easily estimate the importance of different animal and plant foods in the diet of the rural population, we can see a greater variety of food types over the Roman period and, to differing degrees, at all types of settlement, particularly in the Central Belt and South regions. Although never forming more than a very small percentage (<5 per cent) of the animal and bird bone recovered from different types of settlement, chicken becomes more prevalent over time, its presence recorded at over 60 per cent of rural settlements by the fourth century. However, although the proportions are small, chicken is relatively more abundant at defended small towns, villas, military *vici* and roadside settlements than it is at villages and all other types of farmstead (Allen 2017, 134–8, figs 3.54–8). Differential access to certain food types can also be seen with wild animals, fish and shellfish (see Ch. 4, pp. 103–18). It is notable, for example, that, although the bones of wild mammal species are present across the spectrum of rural settlements, if only to a very small extent, never exceeding 2 per cent of total mammal assemblages, there is an appreciably higher representation of the post-cranial, meat-bearing bones of red and roe deer at villas than at other rural settlements, where these animals are better represented by their shed antler than their meat-bearing bones. Differential access is also a feature of wildfowl which, like wild mammals, are slightly more common in the late Roman period. While these are documented in almost two-thirds of villa assemblages, elsewhere, in all other types of farmstead and in villages, the proportion of assemblages where they are found hovers around 40 per cent (see Ch. 4, FIGS 4.20–21). A very similar pattern of differential access occurs with fish, also more commonly found in the later Roman period, and with the largest assemblages from villas (see Ch. 4, FIGS 4.22–25) (cf. Müldner 2013). Greater popularity in the third and fourth centuries also appears to be the case with marine molluscs, particularly oyster, though detailed analysis has so far been confined to the south-west counties of England (see Ch. 4, FIGS 4.26–30). Although they probably only made a very minor contribution to the diet, oysters and other marine molluscs are widely distributed across the Central Belt, North-East and South Regions, as FIG. 4.26 shows, distance from the coast being no barrier to where they were consumed. The detailed study of the incidence of oyster in the south-west shows a wide distribution across rural settlements in Dorset, Gloucestershire, Somerset and Wiltshire, but an almost complete absence in Cornwall and Devon. In those counties, however, it is clear that marine resources in general contributed more to the diet of coastal communities than that of settlements inland. Although the data have not been analysed for all the regions, we can predict that the same, or a similar, pattern to that of fish of differential access will be presented by the consumption of marine shellfish, particularly the most abundant, oyster.

Whereas cost, including of transport, will have been a factor in the consumption of marine fish and molluscs away from the coast, this need not have been the case for chicken or wild animals, all of which *could* have been available on the farm or in the local environment. There could be a variety of explanations to explain their rarity on farmsteads other than villas, ranging from cultural choice or a lack of resources to establishing viable, breeding flocks in the case of chicken, to estate owners prohibiting access to the game on their estates by the peasantry. It is clear from the above that, even if we do not know how frequently or in what quantities meat, fish and shellfish were eaten, villas in particular had access to a greater variety of these foods than other rural settlements. In times of poor harvests or famine the estate owners had more to fall back on than other country dwellers.

As the incidence of burial of their articulated remains suggests, dog and horse meat were not particularly favoured by the people of Roman Britain, but in both cases there is more evidence for their butchery and consumption among the rural than the urban population. This may have been a response to shortages of food more generally, but, as the example of mortality profiles from certain sites suggests, horse may have partly been raised for eating (Ch. 4, p. 90; Allen 2017, 127–8).

Turning to the staple crops we can also see that, where the evidence survives, principally in the form of cereals and cereal by-products charred in the course of being processed, the incidence of the different types of wheat, barley and other cereals has been recorded (Lodwick 2017c). Other crops or plant foods that were consumed, but which did not require charring to process them, may only be preserved in waterlogged or mineralising conditions. Even so, as with the animals, what we do not know is the relative importance of cereals and other plant foods in rural diets. Nor do we know much about how cereals were consumed, whether as porridge or bread, although the presence of querns and mills indicates the processing of some of the harvest into flour, presumably for local consumption. As the principal crops of Roman Britain, it is reasonable to assume that wheat and barley did form a staple part of the diet, but hard evidence is lacking. In addition two pulse crops, pea and Celtic bean, under-represented in charred assemblages as they do not require direct heating as part of food preparation, are also widely recorded, but with a lower incidence or absence in the North and Upland Wales and the Marches (Lodwick 2017c, 33–6, figs 2.22–23).

It is only with the recovery of deposits of mineralised cereals and other plant foods that we have direct evidence of the food that has passed through the human gut, but such deposits are extraordinarily rare on rural settlements. However, they do broaden the range of foods that we know were eaten to include fruits, pulses and vegetables and flavourings. Although mineralised pulses (pea and Celtic bean) have only been recorded from a single site, the late Roman roadside settlement of Baldock in Hertfordshire (Rackham 1998), the picture is better for horticultural crops. From the twenty assemblages with mineralised or waterlogged deposits containing three or more horticultural crops (Lodwick 2017c, 78–9, table 2.23) we can see that damson/plum has the highest incidence among the fruits recorded, which also include apple/pear, cherry, grape and walnut. In addition, mulberry has been recorded at the temple at Uley, Gloucestershire, and blackberry, sloe and sweet cherry at the late Roman villa at Monk Sherborne, Hampshire (Girling and Straker 1993; Higgins 2005). Among the flavourings coriander is the most common, followed by celery and dill, then fennel and summer savory, while there are single records of beet and lentil. The types of sites where these assemblages have been found range from military *vici* to roadside settlements, villas and complex farmsteads. In addition, there are two examples of enclosed settlement, Farmoor, Oxfordshire, and the late Roman phase at Claydon Pike, Gloucestershire, but no records from any village. Exotic foods, such as imported or potentially imported plant foods are generally confined to military *vici* and roadside settlements, but fig, grape, and olive have been reported from villas, such as Bucknowle, Dorset, and Castle Copse, Wiltshire (Green *et al.* 2009, 168; Clapham and Gleason 1997, 351), but not from farmsteads (cf. Lodwick 2017c, 77; Van der Veen *et al.* 2007; 2008).

As with plant foods, meat, fish, etc., similar issues prevail with understanding the role of liquid foods in rural diets. It is likely that brewed beverages, such as ale, were frequently consumed and archaeobotanical records suggestive of malting, as well as the recognition of cisterns and ovens used in this process rather than for corndrying, show a distribution concentrated in the Central Belt, where they have been found in <20 per cent of settlements, in the East, and in the South Region, where they have been noted in over 40 per cent of villas. However, there is a steep decline in incidence to a representation of less than 5 per cent

among enclosed and complex farmsteads in the South (Lodwick 2017c, 64, fig. 2.49). Drinking vessels, such as pottery beakers and tankards, are consistently present in small percentages, commonly about 5–6 per cent, among rural settlements through the Roman period in the west of the Central Belt (Timby 2017, figs 7.34–36).

Although wine was imported in wooden barrels, these do not survive well in the archaeological record (cf. Boon 1975) and ceramic evidence in the form of amphorae remains our best proxy for wine consumption, particularly in the early Roman period, but it is rare in the countryside. Timby notes that in her study area of the western Central Belt (Gloucestershire, South Gloucestershire and Bristol) amphorae account for less than 5 per cent of pottery assemblages at most rural sites, but, of these, the great majority were Baetican Dressel 20 vessels used to transport olive oil. Gallic wine amphorae are the second most frequent but have been recorded in only about one-third of the rural assemblages (Timby 2017, 332, table 7.11). These observations chime with Brindle's survey where he noted that amphora sherds were recorded from only about one-third of rural sites overall (Brindle 2017b). Individual types were not recorded in the database, but, as in Timby's study area, the likelihood is that the majority are Baetican olive oil amphorae. Apart from military *vici*, sherds of such vessels accounted for less than 2 per cent of the assemblages in question (*ibid.*, figs 7.2–4). When such data are conceived in terms of the possible volume of wine or olive oil consumed per annum, the likely quantities are minute – this also assumes that such vessels reached their final destination carrying their original contents, and not some other commodity, or even as empty containers to be used for storage. However, the data do allow us to see differential access, with significantly greater representation at military *vici*, and very slightly more at roadside settlements compared with other rural settlements, including villas.

The preference for olive oil, almost certainly driven by its supply to the military, which had uses in the bathhouse and as a fuel for lighting as well as for cooking, raises the question how far approaches to the preparation and cooking of food changed during the Roman period in the countryside. We have noted above that flavourings such as coriander and dill became more common in rural contexts and this, with the evidence of the residue analysis of the distinctive, specialised vessel, the mortarium, suggests a degree of change in the preparation of food, but not one that maps on to perceptions of Mediterranean-based practices (Cramp *et al.* 2011). In any case mortaria are not very common, though more so in the late period, as Timby's case study of assemblages in the west of the Central Belt region has shown (2017, figs 7.31–2). Overall, the question is difficult to answer without more analysis of organic residues in rural pottery assemblages, but recent analysis of a large sample of late Iron Age and early Roman cooking vessels from Silchester provides further evidence of a move to a more meat-based diet compared with the earlier Iron Age (Colonese *et al.* in press). Whether this trend extended to the countryside, particularly to the non-elite, remains to be determined.

The overall lack of evidence for wine consumption in rural settlements seems surprising, not least among the late Roman villas of the elite. Mid- and late Roman wine amphorae are rare and none is recorded in Timby's (2017) study area (cf. Bidwell 2017, fig. 7.13, for third-century Campanian amphorae in the north of Britain). The failure of wooden barrels to survive in the archaeological record is a likely explanation for the lack of evidence for wine consumption, otherwise what were those delicate, late Roman, glass drinking vessels for (Cool 2006, 224–6)? Definite evidence for wine production in Britain is so far limited to one site at Wollaston in the Nene Valley, but bedding trenches appropriate for the planting of vineyards have been recognised more widely, particularly in the east of the Central Belt (Lodwick 2017c, 73–7, fig. 2.51).

To conclude, the majority of the rural population had access to a limited range of food types with a comparatively poorer nutritional value compared with the Roman army, town dwellers and the rural, estate-owning elite. This is further supported by Rohnbogner's study of the skeletal evidence from predominantly non-villa settlements in the countryside, which shows widespread, direct and indirect evidence of malnutrition through all age groups across the Central Belt, East and South regions (below, Chapter 7).

RECREATION

In most contemporary western societies, leisure time is viewed as an essential part of existence, ensuring what is typically described as *quality of life* (Henderson 2010, 12), while at the same time having the potential to significantly advance cultural development (cf. Pieper 2009). The societies of ancient Greece and Rome are thought to have been crucial in the nascent development of many different forms of recreation, leisure and sport, which have influenced modern understanding of social entertainment in many parts of the world (El-Harami 2015, 168). Most accounts of Mediterranean Roman society include discussions of well-known, public, leisure activities such as gladiatorial games in the amphitheatre,

horse racing at the circus and social interactions at urban bathhouses (e.g. Coleman 2011; Fagan 2011). These are not only evidenced by significant extant monuments, such as the Colosseum in Rome, the circus at Merida in Spain and the public bathhouses of Pompeii, but also by graphic contemporary accounts by the likes of Juvenal, Pliny, Ovid and Horace writing in the early imperial period. Pliny the Younger, for example, displayed his incredulity that 'so many thousands of grown men should be possessed again and again with a childish passion to look at galloping horses, and men standing upright in their chariots' (*Ep.* 9.6; Toner 2009, 115), while Ovid portrayed the public baths as meeting places for furtive lovers (*Ars am.* 3.638–40; Fagan 1999, 51).

The evidence from Britain is far patchier, though there is no doubt that its incorporation into the Roman Empire brought with it gradual, piecemeal, but fundamental changes to many of the indigenous societies, and these included increasing opportunities for some to dedicate time to leisure and recreation. However, for the most part these are likely to have been restricted to elements of the military and urban populations, alongside higher status rural dwellers in central, southern and eastern parts of the province, i.e. those who also had a stake in urban society. For rural peoples living in much of the north and west, and at the lower end of the social scale across the province, it is doubtful whether there was ever much 'free' time to devote to recreation, at least not of the 'Roman' types noted above.

PUBLIC ENTERTAINMENT

Public recreational activities in particular were very much an urban and military phenomenon. The only definite circus for horse and chariot racing lies outside Colchester (Crummy 2008), though a series of parallel lines revealed by geophysical survey on the edge of the gravel terrace outside Silchester have also been tentatively suggested as such a feature (Creighton with Fry 2016, 424–30). In addition, the well-known but fragmentary inscription from Chedworth villa in Gloucestershire translated as 'The green (company)' (*RIB* 127), is usually taken as referring to a chariot team (cf. Allason-Jones 2011b, 225), suggesting that at least some elite folk with rural residences were versed in the public recreational activities that could be found across the Roman Empire. Amphitheatres have been located outside of at least nine towns in Roman Britain to date, including the legionary fortresses at Chester and Caerleon (Wilmott 2008). Rural amphitheatres are rare, these comprising a possible example from the nucleated lead-mining settlement at Charterhouse-on-Mendip in Somerset, revealed by earthwork survey, aerial photographs and LiDAR analysis (Fradley 2009; Smith 2017, 193–4) and another possible example defined by earthworks at Winterslow, Wiltshire (Vatcher 1963; cf. Deniger 1997, 150–73). In addition, what has been termed a 'semi-amphitheatre' has been excavated within the religious complex at Marcham/Frilford in Oxfordshire, somewhat analogous with structures in northern and central Gaul, often located within large rural sanctuaries (Kamash *et al.* 2010, 115; see Ch. 5, p. 165). Such 'semi-amphitheatres' have some design elements of theatres and serve to highlight the close associations between aspects of what we may regard as recreation and the religious experience. This is seen even more explicitly with 'true' theatres.

Just four definite theatres are known from Roman Britain, three within urban contexts, located next to temples at Canterbury, Colchester and Verulamium, with the fourth being part of a rural religious complex at Gosbecks, near Colchester. In addition, a monumental structure near to the temple/baths complex at Bath has also been suggested as a theatre (Cunliffe 1969, 149; La Trobe-Bateman and Niblett 2016, 101), while another theatre has been postulated recently at 'Blacklands', Faversham, in Kent (11 km from Canterbury), landscaped out of a hillside, within what was thought to have been an extensive religious site, dating from the second to early fourth century A.D. (Wilkinson 2013; see Ch. 5, p. 165). Further investigation is required to substantiate the nature of this site. Such theatrical settings, linked as they were to sanctuaries, may have staged regular public performances at specific festival times, when large numbers of people may have attended, drawn from the urban and rural populace. However, the evidence suggests that such large theatres were very rare, and are as yet unknown beyond south-east England (with the possible exception noted at Bath), with the vast majority of the rural population probably never experiencing them. This is not to say that drama on a smaller scale would not have occurred, though this would leave no tangible archaeological evidence, except, perhaps, in the form of the occasional ceramic or metal face mask used for performances, as has been noted on eleven sites in the current dataset, all of them villas, military *vici* and other nucleated settlement.

BATHING

Public bathing was another very important social and recreational activity throughout much of the Roman Empire (Fagan 2011), though again it is doubtful how much, if at all, it would have figured in the lives of the vast majority of the rural population in Britain, with most of the excavated settlements included in this study having no obvious provision for bathing (FIG. 3.9). Bathhouses were revealed within 7 of the 24 defended 'small towns' (*c.* 30 per cent) and 18 of the 182 roadside settlements (*c.* 10 per cent) included in the project, although some of these only appeared to have operated for relatively brief periods, such as that at Braughing in Hertfordshire, which was established by the River Rib in the later first century and abandoned by the mid-second century (Partridge 1977). The bathhouse within the roadside settlement at Cowbridge in South Wales only seems to have been used during the early second century, possibly associated with the site's postulated military origins (Parkhouse and Evans 1996), suggesting that provision for public bathing was no longer required after the cessation of military use. There is doubt over whether some of the bath buildings at nucleated sites were ever intended to be used as public bathing facilities, as opposed to more restricted use by private individuals or groups. At Bitterne in Hampshire, for example, a small bathhouse or sauna (see below, p. 66), 5.2 m square with four rooms, was built in the later second century, and then re-modelled into a two-roomed building during the early third century, the function of which is not entirely clear (Cotton and Gathercole 1958).

Baths attached to *mansiones*, official resting places on the Roman road network, are known at a number of nucleated settlements, and some of these could be quite extensive, such as at Godmanchester in Cambridgeshire, where a large (*c.* 37 × 15 m) bathhouse was located to the south of the *mansio* (Green 1975; FIG. 3.10). This building had a colonnaded portico with numerous rooms, and evidence for glazed windows, tessellated floors, mosaics, marble and painted wall plaster, potentially accommodating reasonable numbers of people, though how restrictive access would have been remains uncertain. Recent excavations of a large bathhouse by the River Thames in an extensive late Roman settlement just 1.2 km to the east of the walls of London at Shadwell produced a rich finds assemblage, including a gold earring and necklace, suggesting a wealthy, possibly official clientele, and there were perhaps limited or no opportunities, at Shadwell and possibly at bathhouses more generally, for other sections of society (Douglas *et al.* 2011).

It would seem standard practice for Roman forts to have been provisioned with bathhouses outside of the defences (Johnson 1983, 220), and many of the military *vici* included in this project have evidence for such buildings. Excavations of well-preserved military bathhouses, such as the legionary baths at Caerleon in South Wales, have indicated that they would have been 'public' to

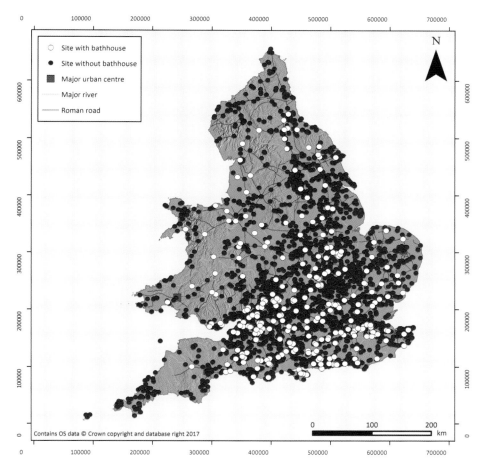

FIG. 3.9. Map showing the restricted distribution of bathhouses within the countryside of Roman Britain

some extent, with objects suggesting men, women and children used the facilities (Zienkiewicz 1986; Allason-Jones 2011b, 240). These are, however, likely to have been limited to the inhabitants of the *canabae* or *vicus*, rather than the surrounding rural populations, which generally display little obvious interaction with the military communities (e.g. Brindle 2016a, 330; but see below, p. 68).

Away from nucleated centres on the road network, there is limited evidence for public bathing, with, as yet, no bathhouses from settlements defined as 'villages'. At least six religious sites are thought to have contained bathhouses (Wood End Lane, Herts; Lydney Park, Glos; Coleshill, Warks; Bath, north-east Somerset; Gosbecks, Essex; Springhead, Kent), though aside from the great temple-spa complex at Bath (and possibly at Buxton in Derbyshire, recorded as *Aquae Arnemetiae* on the Ravenna Cosmology; see Ch. 5, p. 165), these were mostly quite small, and it remains uncertain if they were for public use or perhaps, as suggested by Derks for Ribemont-sur-Ancre in Gaul, restricted for use by cult officials and/or wealthy patrons (Derks 1998, 194). Six primarily industrial sites had evidence for bathing establishments, with notable

examples in north Wales, primarily associated with tile production and the lead industry, and in Sussex (East and West), associated with the iron industry. The sites in Wales at Holt, Wrexham (tile-production), Pentre Farm, Flintshire (lead industry) and Prestatyn, Denbighshire (metal-working), would all appear to have developed into nucleated settlements with official military involvement, while another likely bathhouse associated with official mineral extraction was found at Risca in South Wales (cf. Burnham and Davies 2010, 309). At the Sussex sites of Wiggonholt (pottery production and metal-working), Beauport Park and Hartfield (both iron industry), activity was more dispersed, though Beauport Park at least would appear to have been closely connected with the Roman military in the form of the *Classis Britannica* (Brodribb and Cleere 1988). This bathhouse developed to a substantial size with ten rooms, and was thought to have been used by the military unit, at least until abandonment of the site in the third century A.D. (*ibid.*, 242–4).

The occasional, 'isolated' rural bathhouse has also been excavated and usually assumed, quite reasonably, to belong to a villa estate. These are

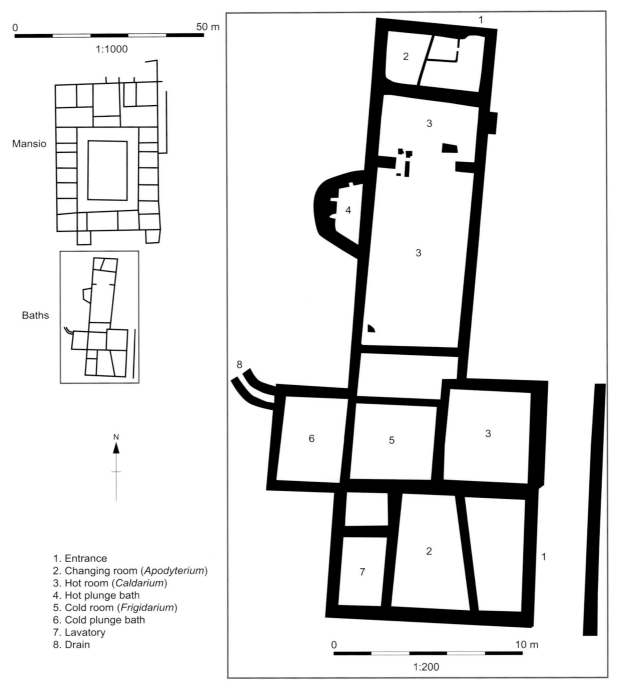

1. Entrance
2. Changing room (*Apodyterium*)
3. Hot room (*Caldarium*)
4. Hot plunge bath
5. Cold room (*Frigidarium*)
6. Cold plunge bath
7. Lavatory
8. Drain

FIG. 3.10. Plan of the *mansio* and bathhouse at Godmanchester, Cambridgeshire (Green 1975)

largely restricted to eastern and south-eastern parts of England, although such bathhouses have occasionally been found much further north, such as that at Old Durham in County Durham, which is thought to be associated with an as yet undiscovered villa (Wright and Gillam 1953). Most of these bathhouses are not of a size that suggests use by large numbers of estate workers, as for example at Haddon, Peterborough, Cambridgeshire, where a small (6 × 3 m) late Roman two-roomed bathhouse with painted plaster walls was excavated *c*. 700 m south of two

aisled buildings interpreted as a working farmyard within a wider estate (Upex 1994; Hinman 2003; see below, p. 66). The occasional larger and more elaborate 'isolated' rural bathhouse is encountered, including the remarkable late Roman octagonal building (*c*. 14.5 m across) at Bax Farm in North Kent, located on a raised area surrounded by intertidal marsh and 2–3 km from a number of known villas, though this example may have had specific religious associations, and further investigation of its immediate context is required to establish its precise nature (Wilkinson 2009).

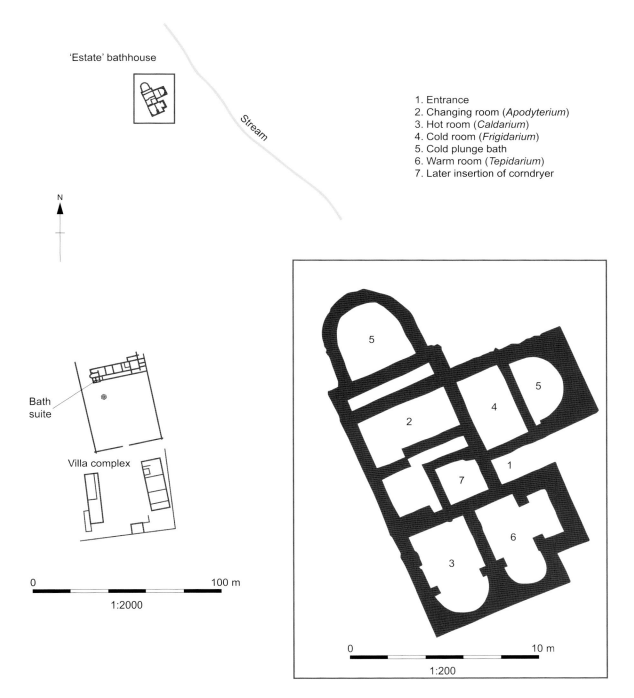

'Estate' bathhouse

Stream

1. Entrance
2. Changing room (*Apodyterium*)
3. Hot room (*Caldarium*)
4. Cold room (*Frigidarium*)
5. Cold plunge bath
6. Warm room (*Tepidarium*)
7. Later insertion of corndryer

N

Bath suite

Villa complex

0   100 m

1:2000

0   10 m

1:200

FIG. 3.11. Plan of the villa and bathhouse at North Wraxall, Wilts (Andrews 2009a)

Perhaps a more likely example of a possible villa estate bathhouse is the large building found at Truckle Hill, North Wraxall, Wiltshire, 150 m north of a courtyard villa, probably part of a complex of buildings and other features thought to be associated with the estate (Andrews 2009a; FIG. 3.11). The main villa contained a substantial integrated bath suite, presumably for use by the villa's occupants, and there is every chance that the detached bathhouse, which was situated closer to a main water source, was utilised by at least elements of the estate's workforce, at least until the fourth century when it was robbed and a corndryer then inserted into the abandoned shell (*ibid.*).

While much of the rural population probably had little or no access to 'Roman' bathing facilities, the same was not true for most people of higher social status, at least in the southern and eastern parts of the province. Bathing facilities were noted in 201 of the 326 villas recorded in the project, while their absence in many others is probably due to the lack of extensive excavation. Bath suites were often integrated within the main villa building, as at Truckle Hill noted above, but in many cases were later structural additions, such as at Little Oakley in Essex, where a stone-founded corridor villa built in the mid-second century, was altered 100 years later with baths inserted (Barford 2002). While these would have been expensive additions, they would have surely have added a degree of social prestige to the inhabitants of the villa. Some of the larger villas developed two or more bathing establishments, as at North Leigh in Oxfordshire, where three bath suites were identified in different wings of the courtyard complex, though not all strictly contemporary (Wilson 2004). As with public bathhouses, it is likely that such bath suites were not just a means of personal cleanliness and relaxation, but were important social settings for business and pleasure among social contemporaries, and were thus also markers of status.

It is the very presence of bathhouses within smaller rural settlements that is a major factor in our definition of them as villas (cf. Allen and Smith 2016, 17), and yet there are also a few sites where 'bathing' facilities existed, but where other architectural aspects fall short of this categorisation. A recently published example comes from Newnham in Bedfordshire, where part of an elaborate stone-founded bathhouse dating to the third century A.D. was revealed within what otherwise is interpreted as a modestly wealthy farmstead, without the more luxurious domestic elements of a villa (Ingham *et al.* 2016). The settlement appears to occupy the increasingly blurred boundary between what may be classified as 'villa' and 'non-villa', which is particularly marked in the Central Belt region (cf. Smith 2016b, 69–70). A more unusual discovery of bathing facilities within what appears to be a 'typical' farmstead is at Cedars Park, Stowmarket, Suffolk, where what has been suggested as two bathhouses were built between the mid-second and mid-third century A.D., alongside a rectangular stone-founded building, rectangular timber structures and two roundhouses (Nicholson and Woolhouse 2016). The buildings were clearly part of an agricultural set-up, being surrounded by paddocks, droveways and fields, indicating that at least some farming communities thought it pertinent to invest in bathing establishments, perhaps in order raise their social standing.

As may be expected, most of the bathhouses within these smaller rural settlements were relatively modest structures. One example from a complex farmstead at Faverdale, County Durham, comprised a small two-roomed stone building (6 × 3.5 m) with a hypocaust system and painted-plaster walls, considered as a small bathhouse or *caldarium* (hot room), though there were no other obvious masonry buildings within the main enclosure (Proctor 2012). Another settlement at Chilton Fields, Oxfordshire, had a small two-room hypocausted structure lying over 25 m from a relatively simple rectangular masonry building with a tiled roof and at least one painted plaster wall (Pine and Preston 2015; see FIG. 3.1). It was suggested to have contained a heated pool, though it was probably another *caldarium*. To these buildings could be added other small 'bathhouses', such as the two-roomed example at Haddon, Peterborough, in Cambridgeshire noted above, which did not necessarily utilise heated water, but instead acted as saunas. Some could have even ended up having more prosaic functions such as smokeries, as has been suggested for the two-roomed heated building within the farmstead at Claydon Pike, Gloucestershire (Miles *et al.* 2007, 173–5; see Allen 2017, 123). However, the painted plaster walls of most of these structures suggest the occupants of these sites had the resources and cultural and social aspirations to create small 'heated' establishments for leisure purposes. Such 'leisure' environments would not have been experienced by the vast majority of the rural population of Roman Britain.

RECREATIONAL ACTIVITIES

If the physical infrastructure of social and recreational space (e.g. theatres, baths etc.) can be seen to have been quite limited in a rural context, then what of other evidence for leisure activities? Here, material culture and to a certain extent environmental remains come to the fore, with the recovery of objects relating to hunting, gaming and music providing some measure as to how certain people in society may have spent their leisure time (cf. Allason-Jones 2011b). The importance of hunting is explored in Chapter 4, while the social and geographic distribution of certain other types of artefact associated with recreation will be addressed here.

There are a total of 2634 objects recorded under the category of 'recreation' in the project database, 90 per cent of these coming from 306 settlements, with the remainder from cemeteries, religious sites, industrial sites and field systems. The vast majority of these comprise gaming counters, usually made of pottery, bone, glass and/or stone, and sometimes other materials such as the jet counters recovered from the small town of Baldock in Hertfordshire (Stead and Rigby 1986). Although far less numerous, dice were recorded at 50 sites and were nearly always made of bone, though the occasional ivory example was noted, such as at Claydon Pike in Gloucestershire (Miles *et al.* 2007). Swift's recent study of bone dice has highlighted their varied use, being linked not only with gaming and gambling but also divination – interpreting the will of the gods (Swift 2017, 123). Gambling was certainly linked with divine fate and fortune and had a long tradition in the Roman world, probably being widespread in public and private areas, though seemingly with more of an urban emphasis (*ibid.*, 126; Toner 1995, 90–5).

Although there is no way of knowing for certain, most of the gaming counters and many of the dice found in excavations of Romano-British sites would probably have been used to play board games. Some of these are well known through contemporary Roman literature and the occasional recovery of a gaming board, including backgammon-like games played with dice such as *XII Scripta (Ludus Duodecim Scriptorum)* and *Alea/Tabula*, and games of skill such as *Ludus Latrunculorum (latrones)*, a game of military strategy (Allason-Jones 2011b, 235). Such board games were played throughout the Roman world and their enduring appeal in some areas is illustrated by two examples from North Kent.

At Northumberland Bottom on the North Kent Plain, a high-status early Roman cremation burial was interred with 23 gaming pieces, a gaming board and two bone dice (Allen *et al.* 2012). Meanwhile, over 200 years later at Lullingstone, *c.* 20 km to the south-west, a late Roman inhumation burial of a young adult male in the villa mausoleum was also buried with what must have been one of his favourite possessions – a complete set of 30 glass counters and a probable folded wooden gaming board, which had been placed upon the coffin (Meates 1987). The association of gaming boards with high-status burials is also seen within two of the remarkable conquest-period cremation graves at Stanway, Colchester, one where the board had been laid out with thirteen white glass counters on one side and thirteen blue glass counters on the other, arranged in what may have been the first stages of play (Schädler 2007).

The social distribution of objects associated with recreation is shown in FIG. 3.12. Unsurprisingly, nucleated settlements are most

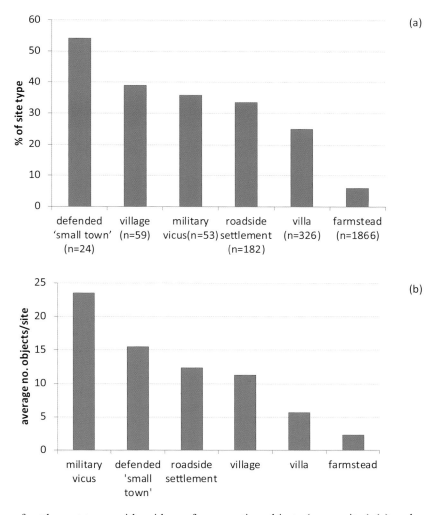

FIG. 3.12. Proportion of settlement types with evidence for recreation objects (n=no. sites) (a) and average number of recreation objects per site type (b)

likely to have evidence for such artefacts, and they are particularly plentiful within certain military *vici*, such as Piercebridge in County Durham, Castleford in West Yorkshire, Old Penrith in Cumbria, and Caersws in Powys. These would have been used not just by the soldiers, but also the wider military community (cf. Haynes 2014), though for the most part their use does not seem to have spread into the surrounding rural settlements. One possible exception is in north-west Wales (Gwynedd and Isle of Anglesey), where alongside the fort at Caernarfon (*Segontium*), eleven rural settlements had some evidence for objects associated with gaming or gambling (FIG. 3.13). One of these was the villa at Glasfryn, Tremadoc, where stone gaming counters were found within the bathhouse (Breese and Anwyl 1909), while the others were all farmsteads or industrial sites, with a particular concentration in Anglesey. Most of these objects were gaming counters, though the remains of two gaming boards and stone pieces were recovered from the ironworking site at Bryn y Castell (Mighall and Chambers 1989), and pieces of patterned tufa, suggested to be part of a gaming board, were

found in the farmstead at Graeanog (Fasham *et al.* 1998). It was argued in Volume 1 that the military presence in this area appears to have had more of an impact on the local rural settlement pattern compared with many other parts of the north and west (Brindle 2016c, 384), perhaps because of this region's mineral resources (cf. Smith 2017, 191), and this may account for the increase in such objects associated with recreation. However, this impact was clearly not uniform across all aspects of lifestyle, as these gaming counters and boards appear far more widespread here than other items such as security and lighting equipment, or artefacts associated with literacy (see below, p. 69).

Elsewhere, only a very small proportion of farmsteads has any evidence for recreation-associated objects, suggesting that most of the rural population were not spending any leisure time that they may have had playing games like *XII Scripta* or *latrones*, though of course there could have been plenty of other games and social activities that leave no recognisable trace in the archaeological record. Very little is known about music in Roman Britain, aside from occasional representations of musicians in mosaics and other

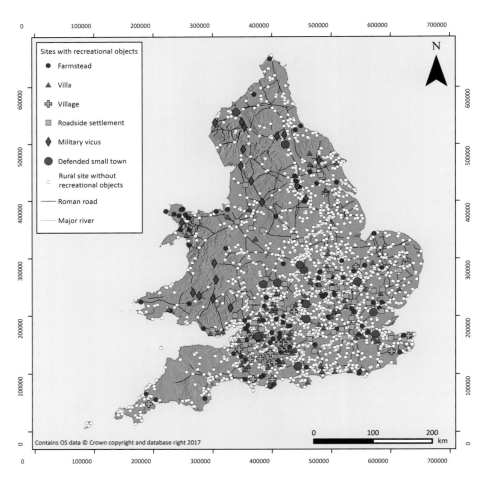

FIG. 3.13. Distribution of site types with recreational objects

art forms, and the rare recovery of what are interpreted as instrument parts (Liversidge 1968, 352–63; Allason-Jones 2011b, 236). Much of our information for musicians in the Roman world comes from military contexts, with several military musicians represented on funerary monuments, and fragments of wind instruments such as the *tuba* (signal trumpet) and *cornu* (horn) being recovered, including one from a military camp at Strageath in eastern Scotland (Summer and D'Amato 2009, 175). Probable instrument parts have been recorded at just twelve sites in the current database, these a mixture of farmsteads, villas, nucleated settlements and shrines/temples. Most of these comprise parts of wind instruments, often mouthpieces such as the metal examples from the religious sites at Muntham Court in West Sussex (Burstow and Hollyman 1957) and Lydney Park in Gloucestershire (Wheeler and Wheeler 1932, 81), though what are thought to be tuning pegs for a stringed music instrument were found in the *vicus* at Piercebridge, County Durham (Cool and Mason 2008) and bone mounts from the yoke of a lyre were found in a fifth-century grave in the nucleated settlement at Abingdon, Oxfordshire (Bruce-Mitford and Bruce-Mitford 1970, 8).

Ultimately, what was regarded as entertainment within most rural communities of Roman Britain may have had little to do with mainstream perceptions of recreation in the Roman period, but instead been rooted in long-standing traditions perhaps including song, dance and story-telling (see above discussion of social activities around hearth fires, p. 55). The oral telling of 'histories' in particular would probably have been an important social practice within communities of pre-Roman Britain, helping to create and maintain perceptions of their past (cf. Bradley 2002, 8). Maintaining these traditions was arguably even more crucial in the turbulent post-conquest period, though without being written down these 'histories' or 'stories' are unlikely to have remained static (*ibid.*). Of course, one of the major changes within certain parts of society over the course of the Roman period is the development of literacy, and it is to this that we now turn.

LITERACY AND LATIN IN THE COUNTRYSIDE OF ROMAN BRITAIN

By Tom Brindle

The issue of how widespread literacy was in Britain during the Roman period has received a considerable amount of recent attention (e.g. Hanson and Conolly 2002; Pearce 2004; Tomlin 2011; Ferris 2012, 100–8; Eckardt 2014, 177–207; Mullen 2016). Our body of evidence for reading and writing in the province has increased substantially, especially through the discovery of the now well-known collections of lead curse tablets from major religious sites such as Uley and Bath (Tomlin 1988; 1993; 2002), and from the survival of groups of wooden writing tablets at Vindolanda, Carlisle and London (Bowman 1994; Pearce 2004); London has very recently produced a large number of well-preserved texts (Tomlin 2016). These survivals not only provide us with valuable insights into the lives of the inhabitants of military and urban sites, as well as information on the daily concerns of those who visited temples to seek divine intervention (see Ch. 5, 178), but also give indications as to the adoption of Latin as a spoken language, and the development of the skills of reading and writing (cf. Mullen 2016). Ultimately, however, what this evidence really tells us is that some people at urban and military sites spoke Latin and could read and write the language (soldiers in particular would have needed to understand, if not write it), and that some of the people who visited major religious sites were similarly literate. The finds from these sites provide us with little information regarding levels of literacy or spoken Latin among the wider rural populations of Roman Britain; this section will consider the archaeological evidence for Latin and literacy in the Romano-British countryside.

It is widely accepted that there was very little tradition of writing in Britain prior to the Roman conquest, and although occasional finds of writing equipment are found in late Iron Age contexts, the evidence suggests that literacy was restricted to a select elite in the south-east of Britain (Hanson and Conolly 2002, 156, 159; Tomlin 2011, 133; Eckardt 2014, 178; Mullen 2016, 576). Even when reading and writing appear to have become more commonplace after the Roman conquest, it would not seem to have been widespread everywhere. Furthermore, as most inscriptions are in Latin (though see Hope 2016, 297, for inscriptions in Greek and Mullen 2016, 580–1, for the evidence for some Celtic writing), and not the indigenous Celtic languages, it has been taken to indicate that Latin itself was spoken (alongside Celtic) only among the elite, the army and by some of those occupying towns (Jackson 1953, 105).

Nevertheless, analysis of the growing body of archaeological finds associated with literacy (Hanson and Conolly 2002; Pearce 2004), as well as recent research in sociolinguistics (e.g. Mullen 2016), suggests that bilingualism may have been more widespread within the province than hitherto presumed. While Latin is unlikely to have ever replaced the native British Celtic as the primary spoken language (cf. Parsons 2011), it has become increasingly clear that it would have been spoken by people occupying many different levels of society though at widely varying levels of competence, depending on a range of factors including social background and status, occupation, education, geographical location, age and gender (J. Adams 2007; 2013; Mullen 2016, 577). Similarly, where people could read and write at all, their ability will have been very variable, ranging from being able to mark one's own name to writing fluent Latin (Eckardt 2014, 177; Tomlin 2011, 134). Yet, even if Latin was more widespread as a spoken language than has previously been recognised, it seems likely that high-level literacy was not widespread among the rural population.

EVIDENCE FOR LITERACY

The archaeological evidence for literacy is available to us in several forms. Tomlin (2011), Ferris (2012, 100–8) and Eckardt (2014, 177–202) have recently presented useful overviews of this evidence, although a brief summary of the main types is presented here. Epigraphy – inscriptions on stone and other materials – represents our largest and most important body of data for the province, with tombstones and altars forming the bulk of this evidence. However, they are considerably less common in Britain than in many other parts of the Roman Empire (Blagg 1990, 28; Hope 2016, 288), and they tend to be recovered mainly from military, and, to a lesser extent, urban and religious sites (Raybould 1999; Tomlin 2011, 140; Ferris 2012, 101; Eckardt 2014, 179; Hope 2016). Wooden leaf-tablets, written on in ink, are rare survivals, but have been found in numbers at some, again predominantly military, sites (Bowman 1994; Pearce 2004). Inkwells, used to contain the ink for writing on wooden tablets, occur in a range of forms and materials, and these are the focus of ongoing work by Eckardt (2014, 177–207; 2017). Other artefactual evidence for writing include spatulae and styli, mainly of iron or copper alloy though occasionally in bone, used respectively for applying wax (and deleting text) to wooden tablets prior to inscription, and then inscribing the wax. Styli are fairly widespread at some types of site, though iron examples in particular are often difficult to recognise, especially without the metalwork being X-rayed (see below, p. 72). Very occasionally the wooden wax tablets themselves are found, where waterlogged conditions allow. Seal boxes, traditionally believed to have been used for protecting seals on private documents, are often found, and, being predominantly of copper alloy, are common finds reported to the Portable Antiquities Scheme. However, recent work has suggested that they may have been used to protect the contents of important consignments

other than documents, such as bags of valuables (Andrews 2012, 80–92), and need not always be associated with literacy. There is also evidence from many sites for graffiti; words, names or letters inscribed onto pots, which presumably in most cases were intended to denote ownership. Not all graffiti are literate, however, and there are examples from many sites where symbols and not letters were used, which may indicate that the owner was illiterate (Tomlin 2011, 144; Ferris 2012, 103). Furthermore, graffiti appear to be far less common on rural than urban or military sites (cf. Evans 1987 and analysis in Frere and Tomlin 1995b, 16–29; *RIB* II.8).

SOCIAL CONTEXT OF LITERACY

Previous work into the social distribution of writing equipment (Hanson and Conolly 2002; Mattingly 2006, 461; Eckardt 2014, 177–207) in Roman Britain has suggested that the extent and levels of literacy probably varied considerably, both geographically and over time. The large body of data collected by the Rural Settlement Project allows us to explore this in a little more detail.

It is, of course, important to recognise the limitations of our data. It was not possible to verify every artefact, and, for instance, it is possible that some objects identified as styli are misidentifications. It is, however, also likely that some iron styli have gone unrecognised due to corrosion, and may have been misidentified and recorded as nails or unidentified iron objects (Tomlin 2011, 149). Nevertheless, given the large sample of sites in the database, the broad patterns in the social and geographical distribution of these objects are likely to be meaningful. Given the generally low quantities of writing equipment recovered from rural sites, the approach adopted here, as with objects associated with lighting, security and recreation discussed above, has been to consider their distribution (and other proxy indicators of literacy) at different classes of rural settlements by a simple assessment of presence versus absence.

Before going into detail, it is worth noting that potential evidence for literacy was found at just 490 sites on the project database. While this seems like a reasonably large number, it only represents around 13 per cent of all recorded sites. By comparison, some form of evidence for literacy was recovered at 15 of the 24 sites (63 per cent) recorded on the supplementary database of defended 'small towns', indicating a focus, perhaps unsurprising, on the larger nucleated settlements on the road network. Similarly, of the sites in the main database that have produced such evidence, the undefended nucleated roadside settlements are by far the best represented site type, with nearly 50 per cent having produced objects suggestive of some literacy among the inhabitants. This reduces to 26 per cent for villas and just 6 per cent of farmsteads. This resonates with observations by Tomlin (2011, 144) and Wilkes (2005), that the imperial road network was of critical importance for the spread of literacy and, we can assume, bilingualism, discussed further below.

Given that there have been several recent suggestions that bilingualism and literacy may have been more widespread among the population of Roman Britain than had hitherto been recognised, it is worth considering the distribution of the various types of evidence in slightly more detail. The charts in FIGS 3.14 to 3.18 respectively present the distribution of graffiti on ceramics, inscriptions, styli and wax spatulae, seal boxes, and inkwells across the main domestic settlement types recorded by the project.

The social distribution of all forms of evidence for literacy is for the most part quite similar; the defended 'small towns', roadside settlements and military *vici* consistently stand out as being the best represented for most classes of object. This is particularly the case with the evidence for graffiti on ceramics (FIG. 3.14), which is indicative of several things. First, it suggests a higher degree of literacy at these site types; while not all graffiti are literate, the widespread use of personal names indicates some reading and writing ability, although whether, for many people, this went beyond being able to mark their own name is a question difficult to answer. Second, the higher incidences of graffiti at nucleated settlements are also likely to be reflective of their relatively large population sizes, and the need to mark ownership

on one's possessions within environments where some people were strangers and not everyone could necessarily be trusted. This correlates with the social distribution of objects associated with security, discussed above (p. 50). Furthermore, Evans (1987, 202) has illustrated a preference for inscribing marks of ownership on finewares, especially samian, and as samian vessels are substantially more common at military sites, defended 'small towns' and roadside settlements than other rural site types (Frere and Tomlin 1995a, 1–14 (*RIB* II.7); Willis 1998; 2011; 2013a; Brindle 2017a), this also reflects the social distribution of these desirable forms of material culture. While the relative dearth of graffiti at other site types is likely to reflect in part lower levels of literacy in the wider countryside, the occupants of these sites may also have had a relatively higher degree of perceived security and many (except the occupants of some villas) are also likely to have had fewer highly desirable objects, which appear to have been less widely accessible for most people in rural communities.

In terms of the social distribution of inscriptions, military *vici* are substantially better represented than any of the other settlement types (FIG. 3.15). This reflects the aforementioned military focus for inscriptions on stone, with soldiers and their associates being the most likely to erect tombstones and dedicate altars; this 'epigraphic habit' was not one that was widely adopted among most other sectors of society in Britain (Eckardt 2014, 169; Hope 2016). While inscriptions (of a range of types, not necessarily 'monumental') have been identified at a reasonably high proportion of

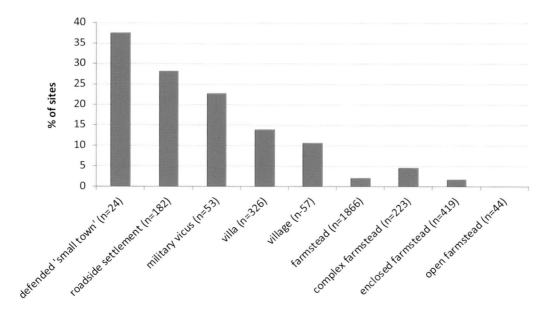

FIG. 3.14. Proportion of settlement types with evidence for graffiti on ceramics (n=no. sites)

defended 'small towns' and roadside settlements, they are exceptionally rare at all other settlements in the wider countryside.

The social distribution of styli and wax spatulae (and seal boxes, if we are to associate them with seals attached to written correspondence) generally follows that of graffiti, in being similarly present at a reasonably high proportion of defended 'small towns' and roadside settlements (FIGS 3.16 and 3.17), furthering suggestions that literacy was relatively widespread at settlements on the road

network. This does appear to be at odds with the traditional, minimalist, interpretation of the spread of bilingualism and literacy, which was seen as restricted to the elite, the army and urban dwellers (Jackson 1953, 105). Although most nucleated settlements along the main road network should not be regarded as urban centres, usually lacking the sorts of monumental buildings and street grids that characterise larger towns, the new road network appears to have been vitally important for the transmission of ideas regarding new ways of

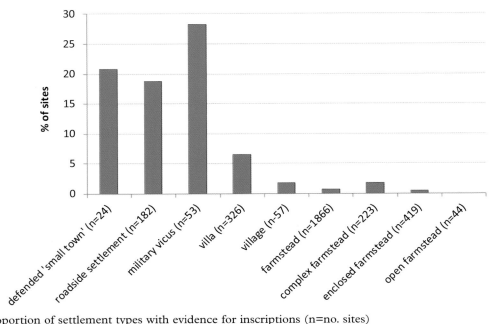

FIG. 3.15. Proportion of settlement types with evidence for inscriptions (n=no. sites)

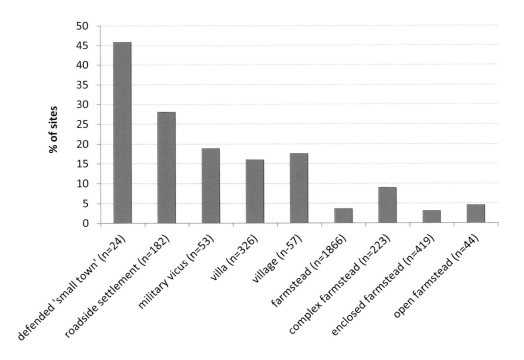

FIG. 3.16. Proportion of settlement types with evidence for styli and wax spatulae (n=no. sites)

doing things. Settlements that developed alongside the roads were places where, for instance, new forms of personal display were being adopted most widely (see Ch. 2). Many roadside settlements are also likely to have performed local administrative and small-scale market functions, suggested by the distribution of objects such as coins and weighing equipment (Brindle 2017b). If many of these settlements increasingly acted as markets for traded goods, including imports, this may have facilitated both the spread of Latin and the writing equipment

needed to record transactions. After major urban centres and military sites, this category of roadside nucleated settlements is also the type of site at which we might expect to see incomers to the province settling most widely; not all of those using writing equipment at these ostensibly 'native' sites need necessarily have been Britons.

Inkwells, one of the rarer types of artefact associated with literacy, have recently been given attention by Willis (2005) and Eckardt (2014, 193–207; 2017). Ceramic inkwells of samian are

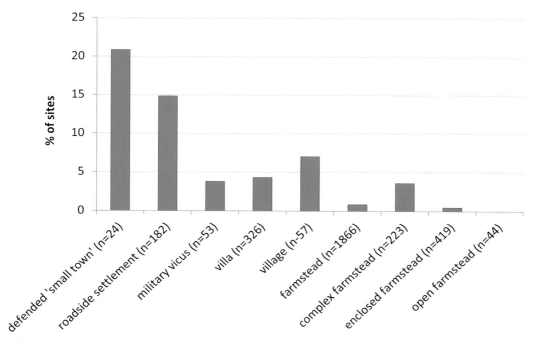

FIG. 3.17. Proportion of settlement types with evidence for seal boxes (n=no. sites)

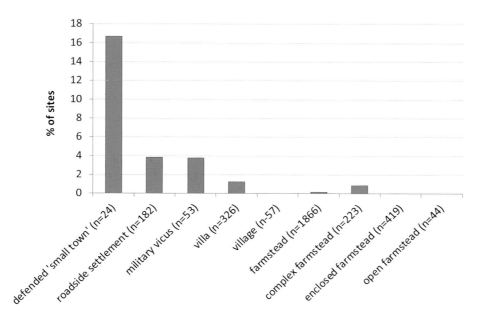

FIG. 3.18. Proportion of settlement types with evidence for inkwells (n=no. sites)

the most commonly found, although their social distribution is overwhelmingly biased towards military sites and major urban centres, with far fewer recovered from smaller nucleated sites and rural settlements (Willis 2005, 103–7). Non-ceramic inkwells are very rare even at urban sites in Britain (and indeed, across the empire generally; Eckardt 2014, 195–6), although London stands out as being fairly well represented. Inkwells are very rare at all sites in the project database, and are only really significant at the defended 'small towns', although they have been identified at a very small number of roadside settlements, military *vici*, villas and complex farmsteads (FIG. 3.18).

The broad hierarchical distribution of the objects discussed above is repeated across almost all types of artefacts associated with literacy, including the small number of writing tablets and curse tablets, and is a continuation of the social hierarchy presented for writing tablets by Pearce (2004, 48, table II), where there is an emphasis on military and urban sites. It is possible that the apparent distinction between the defended 'small towns' and other nucleated roadside settlements might tell us something about differences in terms of the status and function of some of these sites on the road network; for instance, writing in ink has been recognised as being most closely associated with official business and administration (e.g. Willis 2005, 113). Our sample of defended 'small towns' is very small, and we are discussing only four sites with inkwells and two with writing tablets, yet the apparently greater prevalence of evidence for writing at these sites might support the suggestion that some of these settlements became important economic and/or administrative centres; indeed this may be part of the reason that they were provided with defences in the mid- and late Roman periods, while others on the road network were not (cf. Burnham and Wacher 1990, 315).

While the evidence for literacy at settlements in the wider countryside is extremely limited, it is worth considering some of the settlements that have produced archaeological evidence for reading and writing in a little detail, in order for us to consider why these sites might have such evidence while most others do not. As the charts in FIGS 3.14 to 3.18 show, apart from the sites on the road network, settlements characterised as villas tend to be those best represented by evidence for literacy. Indeed, of the 120 sites classified as farmsteads with some form of writing evidence, 12 per cent had features that led to them being regarded as of possible 'villa status' for the purposes of the project database; this emphasises the association between high-status rural sites and evidence for literacy. Sites classified as villas (or possible villas) are not considered in any further detail here; these sites,

although immensely variable in terms of their form, scale and levels of opulence (see Smith 2016b, 71–4), may be regarded for the most part as the settlements of the elite, and therefore those that might reasonably be expected to have occupants who were bilingual and could read and write.

Of the remaining 105 farmsteads with evidence for literacy, there is a strong emphasis on those of complex form; these account for 32 per cent of the sites, enclosed farmsteads 16 per cent, open farmsteads 2 per cent, while the remaining 50 per cent were unclassified morphologically. The most widespread form of evidence at complex farmsteads was the stylus, identified at 19 sites. The settlements with such evidence are sometimes unusual, often appearing to be of relatively high status, and therefore potentially not that different from many villas. Others seem to have been particularly geared up for production, with a number having corndryers. The highly unusual site at Orton Hall Farm, in Cambridgeshire (Mackreth 1996), for instance, had a number of corndryers as well as evidence for large-scale brewing, and this site is notable for having produced not only styli but also a samian inkwell. Some other complex farmsteads with styli have finds assemblages that are unusually large and varied with certain objects suggestive of a religious emphasis, for example at Neigh Bridge, Somerford Keynes, Gloucestershire (Miles *et al.* 2007).

Of the five farmsteads where writing tablets have been recognised, four were morphologically of complex form, while one was unclassified. While the recovery of most tablets from wells/ shafts may simply reflect there being a considerably better chance of wood surviving in waterlogged well-deposits, Pearce (2004, 50) has noted how several of these contexts contained other material, such as complete pots and skeletal remains which, together, might indicate votive activity. We may be seeing, at some of these rural settlements, the power of the written word used for ritual purposes at what were ostensibly domestic settlements. Several farmsteads, particularly those of complex form, have also produced possible curse tablets. However, these finds are rare outside religious contexts (see Ch. 5) and many of those identified at farmsteads are tentative identifications, with few containing clear text.

As with complex farmsteads, several of the enclosed farmsteads that have produced objects associated with literacy may also be regarded as unusual in some way, often with features or finds assemblages that distinguish them from other, usually low-status, sites in the same broad morphological class. Plas Coch, Wrexham (Jones 2011), which produced two styli, has already been referred to in Chapter 2 (p. 37) as being unusually well represented by brooches as well as other finds, and there are a number of indications that the settlement was of atypically high status for the region, with rectangular masonry buildings and evidence for a tiled roof. Likewise at Coygan Camp, Carmarthenshire (Wainwright 1967), a stylus was part of a rich finds assemblage that included objects associated with personal display, which were regionally very unusual, and again this coincided with the presence of a masonry building. At Boxfield Farm in Hertfordshire (Going and Hunn 1999), a site characterised by the project as an enclosed farmstead, a stylus was found, and this was part of a rich finds assemblage that included many coins, brooches and other personal equipment, including mirror fragments, which are exceptionally rare finds at rural settlements. At Ochre Brook, Merseyside (Philpott 2000; Cowell 2009), an iron stylus was recovered from a site that produced evidence for tile production, with tile stamps indicating that they were being produced for the twentieth legion at Chester. In all these instances (and further examples could be listed), styli were elements of generally rich or atypical finds assemblages that mark the sites out as different; the association such finds have with

rich groups of personal dress accessories or other material correlates with wealth/status or links with the military, and is compelling evidence for a strong connection between literacy and the elite in the countryside, even at sites that, morphologically speaking, would not appear to be of especially high status.

The geographical distribution of settlements with archaeological evidence for literacy is shown in FIG. 3.19, with a firm focus on the south and east of the province, generally reflecting the known spread of non-military 'small towns', roadside settlements, villas and complex farmsteads (see Allen and Smith 2016). It is perhaps an obvious point, although one worth making explicitly, that the areas where bilingualism and literacy appear to have become most widespread are also the areas where we witness the greatest evidence for engagement with new ways of dressing following the Roman conquest (see Ch. 2). In parts of the north and the west of the province especially, where there is considerably less evidence for classically influenced ways of dressing, it seems very unlikely that Latin would have been spoken very widely at all except within the forts and their associated extramural settlements.

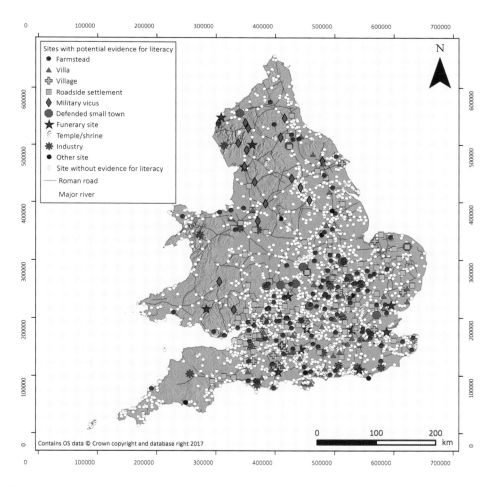

FIG. 3.19. Distribution of sites with possible evidence for literacy

Given the lack of evidence for literacy at the vast majority of rural settlements across the province as a whole, we need to reconsider some of the recently published evidence that suggests literacy may have been reasonably widespread in some areas. For example, analysis of the handwriting on lead curse tablets from the sacred sites at Bath and Uley has indicated that the tablets were inscribed by many different people, and not professional scribes, suggesting that those depositing the curses were largely responsible for writing their own texts (Tomlin 2002). Given the very restricted evidence for literacy in the wider countryside, we might surmise that those who deposited curses at these sites were not in general the typical inhabitants of low-status rural settlements, but rather those who occupied surrounding villas and particularly nucleated settlements on the road network, where the evidence for reading and writing is most concentrated. The fact that most curse tablets are primarily concerned with requesting divine retribution for a theft (*ibid*.) might also suggest that those leaving the curses were from settlements with reasonably large populations, where, as suggested above (p. 71), people's personal possessions may have been at increased risk from the attentions of nimble-fingered individuals. Even at Bath and Uley, however, not all curse tablets are necessarily evidence for literacy; some bear illiterate marks, intended to look like writing (Tomlin 1988, 84–94; 2011, 134), and some from Uley are blank (Tomlin 2011, 134). We should not assume, by any stretch, that even in roadside settlements all of the occupants were literate individuals.

Overall, given the evidence available to us, it seems likely that both the speaking of Latin and the ability to read and write it were in the main confined to military sites, urban centres and the larger nucleated settlements on the major communications routes. While some villas have produced objects that suggest the presence of educated elites, who were perhaps engaged in administration at some of the roadside centres we have discussed, the evidence from other probable agricultural sites in the wider countryside is restricted to an extremely small number of farmsteads, primarily those that appear to be of particularly high status, or of unusual function. The ability to speak, read and write Latin at rural settlements away from the main communications routes, was probably for the most part restricted to a few rural elite. For these members of society, reading and writing Latin was one element of a broader engagement with and connection to what may be regarded as an elite 'pan-Roman' culture, also expressed through factors such as personal appearances, architectural settings and demonstrations of 'classical' knowledge through the display of mythological scenes on mosaics and wall paintings (e.g. Scott 2000, 168; 2004, 51; Mattingly 2006, 463–9). The distribution of the evidence for literacy suggests two things. Firstly, in agreement with general current academic opinion, speaking Latin and the ability to read and write (at varying degrees of competency) were probably more widespread in Roman Britain than has traditionally been allowed for. Secondly, however, the spread of Latin and literacy appears to have been largely dictated by the presence of the road network, along with access to elite education. The vast majority of those who lived in the countryside are unlikely to have spoken any Latin, and almost certainly could not read or write the language.

CONCLUSIONS

There is no single concept of a 'rural Romano-British lifestyle'. Yet many previous syntheses have equated 'country dwellers' with 'villa owners' (e.g. Birley 1979, 137), which is rather like assessing the lives of nineteenth-century rural folk across England and Wales through the lens of those inhabiting grand country houses in the Cotswolds. There are of course many examples of large, elaborate country villas, where the lifestyles of the elite could be played out against a backdrop of brightly painted rooms with mosaic floors depicting classical scenes, perhaps surrounded by formal gardens. In some landscapes, such environments may even have been commonplace and closely interconnected, as seen for example with the two probably inter-visible courtyard villas at Spoonley Wood and Wadfield, lying 2 km apart on either side of a valley to the south of Winchcombe in Gloucestershire. But, even within the upper echelons of society, there was still considerable heterogeneity, with 'elite' families operating within a wide social hierarchy. When all social, cultural and economic variables are taken into account, we can start to appreciate the great diversity of life in the countryside of Roman Britain. This chapter has highlighted just a few selective aspects of lifestyle in order to appreciate some of this diversity.

The many different domestic environments of rural Roman Britain have been assessed previously in Volume 1 (Smith 2016b), though it is fair to say that most people continued to live in fairly simple, but probably multi-functional, dwellings with minimal architectural embellishment. In fact, although there were certainly significant developments in people's domestic arrangements in large areas of the country during the course of the Roman period, including a greater tendency for rectangular buildings, it would seem that many aspects of lifestyle remained largely unaltered, at least as far as can be discerned in the archaeological record. Aside from villas and some of the more atypical farmsteads, it was principally in the newly developing nucleated roadside settlements that the extent and pace of lifestyle change can best be observed. Here, for example, there is evidence for the greatest use of locks and keys, suggesting both greater affluence and also a greater need for security, perhaps linked to the transient element of the population. Likewise, it is such sites and particularly the defended 'small towns' that tend to produce more evidence for lighting equipment, perhaps impacting upon aspects such as the length of the working day and social activities like reading and dining (Eckardt 2011, 182). Eating and drinking are perhaps the most important social activities at all levels of society, though we have surprisingly little direct evidence for the diets of rural inhabitants of Roman Britain. Nevertheless, there would appear to have been differential access to certain foods across different site types, with sections of the populations of roadside settlements and villas in particular seeming to have much broader diets than those living in most farmsteads. This fits in with palaeopathological observations of restricted rural diets outlined by Rohnbogner in Chapter 7.

The social disparity in diet is matched in other areas of lifestyle, such as bathing. While the majority of villas would appear to have had bathing establishments for the principal residents, public bathing facilities are rare except in military and larger urban centres, and, where they did exist, were perhaps restricted to certain elements of the population. Large-scale public entertainment was probably almost entirely lacking in rural areas, except in the hinterlands of cities and a few of the larger rural religious complexes. Nevertheless, there is better evidence for personal leisure activities in the form of gaming counters, dice and gaming boards, though again mostly recovered from nucleated settlements on the road system, military sites and villas. The relative paucity of such objects from most farmsteads need not imply a lack of provision for any entertainment, though presumably there would not have been much in the way of 'leisure' time, but perhaps more of an emphasis on traditional activities such as music and story-telling rather than 'Roman' games.

The extent of Latin and literacy in the countryside of Roman Britain was the final aspect to be considered in this chapter, and perhaps more than any other highlights the influence of the road system and its associated settlements on the extent of lifestyle innovation. Many of these settlements were clearly dynamic places with flows of people from the local countryside, other parts of the province and from across the empire, and where the use of Latin in some form was probably expected to a certain degree. Of course there was still a great deal of variation in the scale and form of these types of site, and no doubt in the lifestyles of the people who inhabited them. But at the same time this high degree of connectivity appears to have enabled a greater propensity for social and cultural change.

CHAPTER 4

THE SOCIAL CONTEXT OF ANIMALS AND EXPLOITATION OF WILD RESOURCES

By Martyn Allen

INTRODUCTION

Humans exist within ecosystems – they are constantly interacting with other species and are well versed at adapting and manipulating their environment to suit their needs. Animals, in particular, are a key source of evidence for understanding how people engaged with the world around them, as has been demonstrated by a wide range of historical, philosophical, anthropological and geographical studies (Wolch and Emel 1998; Mullin 1999; Ingold 2000; Philo and Wilbert 2000; Fudge 2013). Human–animal interactions are mutual exchanges, which not only represent economic exploitation but also reflect patterns of human social behaviour and identity (Mullin 1999; Armstrong Oma 2010; Sykes 2014, 5). However, zooarchaeologists have been comparatively slow to engage in discourse that considers animals beyond their productive capabilities. While zooarchaeological evidence is often used to explore ancient economics, as we have done in Allen *et al.* 2017, it can also provide opportunities for studying the cultural importance of animals (e.g. Russell 2012; Sykes 2014).

In late Iron Age and Roman Britain, as in most other periods, the manner in which animals were treated reflects specific attitudes to farming, food consumption, trade and exchange, landscape, and social status, as well as expressions of group ideology and religious belief (Grant 1984; Sykes 2009; Morris 2011). Ritual exploitation of animals is, of course, key to our understanding of the cultural or symbolic significance of animals and, although there is some overlap in this chapter, this issue will be covered in more detail in Chapter 5. This section focuses on the social context of human–animal relationships by considering five main themes: livestock farming, the social role of horses, companion animals, the introduction of new species, and wild animal exploitation.

While evidence for differing agricultural strategies was previously considered in economic terms (Allen and Lodwick 2017), differences in farming regimes can also help account for significant variations in social practice and lifestyle. The ubiquity of farm animals in late Iron Age and Roman Britain means that they would have fulfilled a range of social customs – their value as living animals extended well beyond their productive capabilities (Ducos 1978, 54). Drawing upon these data, this section discusses how different methods of farming were related to changing social attitudes towards livestock.

While farmed livestock would have been of major importance to all communities in Roman Britain, interactions with other species would also have shaped human behaviour and experience. The changing role of horses as prestige, religious symbolic and companion animals will be considered here in this context. The role of dogs and cats as companion animals has yet to be fully explored by zooarchaeologists working on Roman Britain. MacKinnon (2010) has reviewed the evidence for dog-keeping in the Mediterranean during this period, concluding that, in general, dogs were fairly well kept and cared for by people. In many societies dogs often form close social relationships with humans, which are manifested in their roles in pastoral farming, as vermin controllers, as guardians, and as household pets. Cats, too, have long and complex histories of living with people. This section will consider the evidence for the treatment of both of these animals.

It is now known that a number of new animal (and plant) species were introduced during the Iron Age and Roman periods (Yalden 1999, 122–9; Van der Veen *et al.* 2008; Sykes 2009; Allen and Sykes 2011; Witcher 2013). Some of these animals may have been completely alien to the native Iron Age population and their introduction probably contributed to ecological changes, which impacted on the existing landscape. The variety of species introduced differed in terms of how, when and why they came to Britain, ranging from deliberately imported exotica to commensal animals that travelled alongside people to exploit human environments. The evidence for certain introduced species and their potential impact on society and the landscape of Roman Britain will be reviewed.

In contrast to farmed livestock, companion animals and imported exotica, wild native animal exploitation has quite different social implications. As Sykes (2014, 51) points out, some of the most important changes in human history have been characterised by the interactions between people and wild animals. Of course, wild animals only became 'wild' once people had domesticated certain types of animal. In farming societies, the killing of wild animals takes on a different meaning because meat is no longer required from hunted sources (*ibid.*). Nonetheless, hunting, fowling and fishing have continued to be important human pursuits in many cultures, including the Roman world, as evidenced by historical and iconographic evidence (Anderson 1985; Tuck 2005). Part of this section focuses upon the analysis of zoo-archaeological data concerning wild mammals, birds, fish and shellfish, but it also incorporates relevant literary and iconographic evidence for wild animal exploitation in order to broaden the context of these activities and to provide a window into human perceptions of nature, and how people perceived their place within it.

LIFE ON THE FARM: THE SOCIAL CONTEXT OF LIVESTOCK HUSBANDRY

Farming underpinned the everyday lives of the vast majority of the population of late Iron Age and Roman Britain (Allen *et al.* 2017). Individual and group identities were formed around life on the farm, through working relationships with livestock and the cultivation of crops. Yet despite the importance of agriculture in Roman Britain, precious little has been said about the ways in which farming – the exploitation of land, animals and plants for food – was central to social

organisation and identity. Taylor (2013) is one of the few to have broached the subject of 'agricultural identities'. Drawing upon evidence for material culture consumption and the use of buildings, Taylor stressed the importance of kinship, agricultural occupation and settlement locality as being of greater concern to local communities than the idea of 'being Roman', which may have been of little consequence to most people (*ibid.*, 186–7). For the majority of people in Roman Britain, rural life would have encapsulated a wide range of activities, the primary goal of which would have been to provide food, and their success depended on overcoming several obstacles. Every farmer would have been responsive to the environment, while economic pressures would have impacted on farming practice. Changing patterns of land tenure after the Roman conquest may also have had a significant effect.

Most late Iron Age and Romano-British farmers engaged in a mixture of cereal and livestock husbandry (Allen and Lodwick 2017). However, it is evident that there was much regional variation in the relative abundance of different livestock and crops across the country. This is shown in FIGS 4.1 and 4.2, which highlight the relative proportions of major livestock and cereal taxa. It is important to note these patterns can be affected by differences in recovery strategies and variations in soil acidity, and are not simply reflections of Romano-British

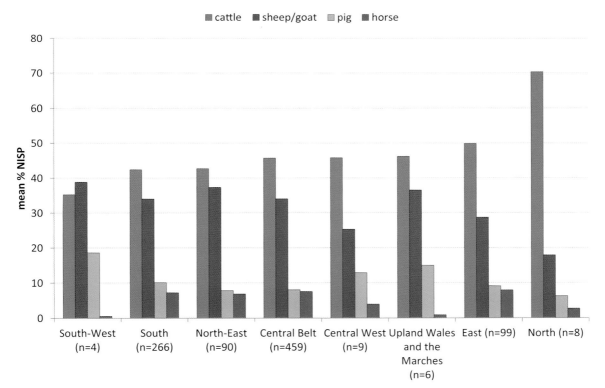

FIG. 4.1. Relative frequency of cattle, sheep/goat, pig and horse bones from rural sites in the eight project regions (n=no. of sites with at least 100 identified specimens (NISP)

farming strategies and consumption patterns (cf. Smith and Fulford 2016, 398). Small sample sizes, particularly in animal bone assemblages, mean that some patterns are not representative of whole regions. Sites in the North, for example, appear to be overwhelmingly dominated by cattle bones. This can be explained by the fact that most faunal assemblages in this region derive from military *vici*, which tend to show evidence for large-scale processing of cattle carcasses (Allen 2017, 122). Many of these animals were probably imported from other sites and were potentially driven over long distances to supply the army (Stallibrass 2009). This observation is important in social terms, as it would suggest that people living in military *vici*, and the associated army garrison, would have had little direct engagement with the livestock being supplied to the settlement, unlike the farmsteads where they were being raised.

In the south and east of England, bio-archaeological data are present in quantities that make it possible to identify individual farming

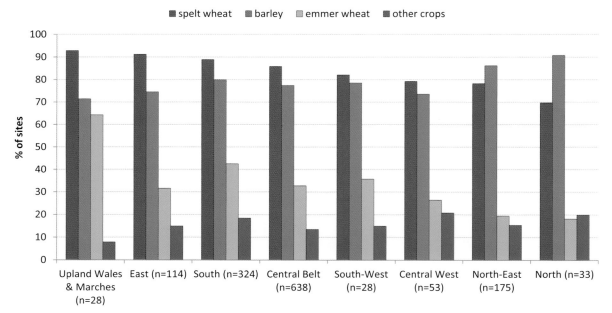

FIG. 4.2. Proportions of sites with evidence for major crops in the eight project regions (n=no. of sites with archaeobotanical evidence)

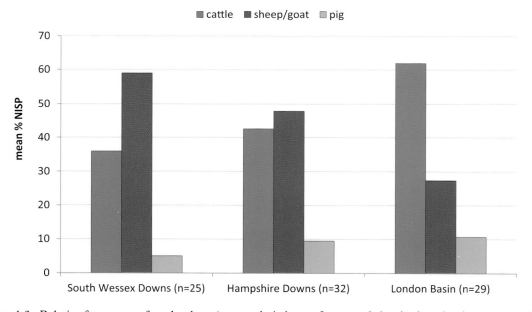

FIG. 4.3. Relative frequency of cattle, sheep/goat and pig bones from rural sites in three landscape zones in the South region

landscape zones. For example, notable differences in the relative frequencies of major livestock species were observed between rural settlements on the chalk downs of South Wessex and Hampshire, and those on the heavy clays and gravel terraces of the London Basin (Allen 2016a, 125–6). FIGURE 4.3 shows the dominance of sheep bones recovered from sites on the South Wessex Downs, with more equal proportions of sheep and cattle bones on the Hampshire Downs, and cattle overwhelmingly dominant in the London Basin. There are also notable differences in cattle slaughter patterns from rural sites in these landscape zones (FIG. 4.4). High proportions of neonates and juveniles have been recovered at rural sites on the South Wessex and Hampshire Downs, whereas they are rare at settlements in the London Basin, where a higher frequency of cattle appear to survive to older ages. Taken together, these livestock frequencies and ageing data indicate that very different strategies of pastoral farming took place in these landscape zones. Furthermore, settlement and landscape evidence in these regions strongly suggest that the Wessex Downs was predominantly exploited for arable, while pastoral farming appears to have been more common in the Middle Thames Valley (Allen 2016a, 129–39). The different ways in which communities in each area farmed the land and treated their livestock may be reflective of strong and perhaps conflicting group identities (Sykes 2014, 12–13).

In Volume 2, the dominant farming strategies of four landscape zones – the West Anglian Plain, the Upper Thames Valley, Kent and the Thames Estuary, and the chalk downland of Wessex – were analysed through the zooarchaeological and archaeobotanical data (Allen and Lodwick 2017). These were supplemented by a fifth case study from Gwynedd in north-west Wales, a region with a distinctive settlement pattern, few environmental data, but with an abundance of landscape and material culture evidence, which shed light on farming practices. In each of these areas it was evident that animal husbandry and arable farming were co-dependent activities. Livestock were essential for maintaining soil fertility through manuring, while cattle appear to have been important as plough animals. Equally, a proportion of cereal produce would no doubt have been utilised as fodder to sustain livestock, particularly through the winter months when fewer resources would have been available. Evidence for hay production in the Roman period also highlights the importance of foddering and the need to maintain herd numbers (Lodwick 2017c, 80–1). In each of the four main case studies, the representation of certain types of livestock was related to specific cereal crops. For example, sheep were notably better represented on the Wessex Downs, where barley also occurs relatively frequently. This was in contrast to the West Anglian Plain, where proportions of cattle increased in tandem with a shift towards spelt wheat cultivation (almost to the exclusion of other cereal crops). It was argued that these variations related to differences in agricultural strategy. The influence of other regional factors also needed to be considered, such as pre-existing Iron Age traditions, local environmental conditions, regional infrastructural developments (e.g. roads), and state demands for agricultural produce.

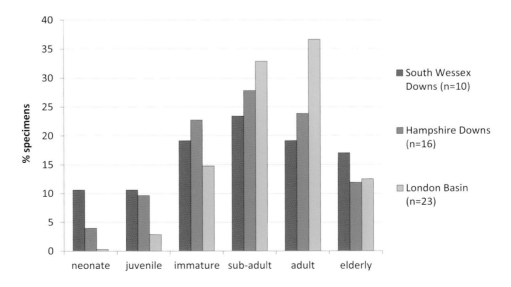

FIG. 4.4. Cattle ageing data from rural sites in three landscape zones in the South region

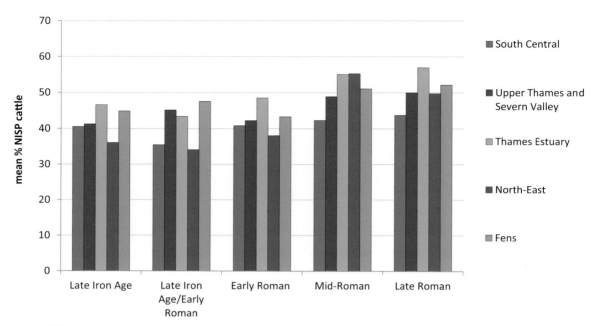

FIG. 4.5. Mean percentages of cattle over time by region (see Volume 2 for definitions of regions and data)

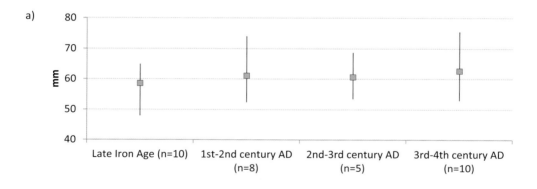

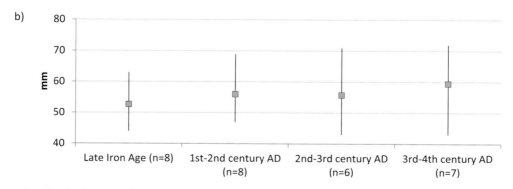

FIG. 4.6. Cattle size over time, shown as (a) mean greatest length of astragalus and (b) mean breadth of distal tibia (n= no. of sites)

THE EXPLOITATION OF CATTLE IN EXTENSIVE ARABLE FARMING REGIMES

In several case study areas of southern and central England, spelt wheat cultivation and cattle husbandry were found to be common and, together, these were argued to reflect extensive arable farming patterns (see Allen and Lodwick 2017, 177). Increased proportions of cattle were observed in many areas, which have largely been attributed to an increased reliance on animal-drawn tillage (Allen 2017, 112). Mean cattle percentages rose from 36–46 per cent in the late Iron Age to 44–57 per cent in the late Roman period (FIG. 4.5). This trend has previously been identified and argued to reflect a widespread response to arable expansion (e.g. Dobney 2001; Albarella 2007).

At the same, there is also good evidence that livestock increased in size. Using data from a range of sites from across England and Wales, FIG. 4.6 shows the average body size increase in cattle (in both height and breadth) from the late Iron Age to the late Roman period (see Allen 2017 for a more detailed overview of these data). Size increases were particularly marked in eastern England, where notably large cattle have been identified at Great Holts Farm, Essex (Murphy et al. 2000), Wavendon Gate, Milton Keynes (Dobney and Jacques 1996), Haddon (Baxter 2003) and Orton Hall Farm, Cambridgeshire (King 1996). The importation of breeding cattle from the Continent also appears likely, as evidenced by significant size changes occurring as early as the late first century A.D. at Elms Farm, Heybridge, Essex (Albarella et al. 2008). These cattle broadly mirror the sizes of contemporary livestock found in the Netherlands, and it seems likely that they were imported for cross-breeding with native types to produce improved traction animals.

One of the key aspects of extensive arable farming is that it needs a relatively low labour input per unit area of land compared with intensive farming, but increased workforces in busy periods. During ploughing and harvesting seasons, it is possible that households may have needed to co-operate in order to mobilise larger labour forces of people and livestock (Halstead 1996; 2014, 298–9). On the Salisbury Plain, where there is also evidence for arable expansion, the development of extensive village settlements may have been facilitated by co-operative farming strategies on the surrounding chalk downland (McOmish et al. 2002; Fulford et al. 2006). Given the increasing pressures of land availability under extensive arable regimes, particularly in relatively highly populated areas such as the West Anglian Plain (Smith 2016d), the sharing of resources may

have been a viable option for farmers. This is likely to have been important considering the lack of evidence for large granaries on Romano-British settlements, which means that it would have been necessary to move bulk quantities of surplus grain to their intended markets fairly quickly (Smith 2016b, 59; Lodwick 2017c, 68). Labour-sharing also provides opportunities for uneven distributions of wealth. It is possible that, in some areas, the expansion of private estates seeking to maximise profits through arable production utilised coerced labour or even slave labour (Hingley 1989, 128), though clear evidence for this is currently lacking (see discussion Ch. 8, p. 355).

Further evidence for the increasing use of cattle for traction can be found in the apparent rising incidence of trauma and pathological lesions found on foot and toe bones (Albarella et al. 2008, 1836; Allen 2017, 112–13). While these lesions may be associated with old age, they are often a sign of increased burden being placed on plough cattle. Such pathologies may also suggest a lack of welfare being afforded to these animals. Where expansive arable regimes were undertaken, cattle would have been economically valuable, but were probably viewed more as 'commodities'. This has also been suggested by Sykes (2014, 15) who argues that, where livestock improvements occur, animals tend to be seen as 'products' that can be manipulated by people according to their own desires.

PASTORALISM AND LARGE-SCALE HERDING

Pastoralism, defined here as the large-scale herding of livestock, as opposed to household herding, is known to have been an important farming strategy throughout prehistory (Halstead 1996). Communities that practise pastoralism tend to exhibit distinctive cultural identities (e.g. Burton 1981; Abbink 2003; Ivarsdotter 2004). In Roman Britain, arable agriculture was the mainstay of the agrarian economy, and the extent to which pastoralism occurred is uncertain. It is possible that communities in the north and west of the province practised traditional pastoral regimes, perhaps using the upland regions on a seasonal basis to rotate grazing – some of these areas are certainly better suited to livestock husbandry than arable cultivation (Stallibrass 2009, 103). However, without additional higher quality environmental data, agricultural regimes in these regions remain largely invisible.

Evidence for pastoral farming may be identified by cropmarks, where long-distance droveways and associated enclosure systems have been identified. One of the best examples of this type of landscape can be found on the Yorkshire Wolds, where aerial photography has revealed land-use patterns that

FIG. 4.7. Three droveway complexes on the Yorkshire Wolds at Kilham parish (a), Langtoft parish (b) and Rudston parish (c) (Giles 2007, 241, fig. 4, after Stoertz 1997)

appear to be suited to large-scale herding (Stoertz 1997, 52–4; Giles 2007, 237). Domestic sites in this landscape are often referred to as 'ladder settlements' owing to their morphological layout, but most have not been extensively excavated (FIG. 4.7). Small-scale excavations at Burton Fleming (Tabor 2009) and Heslerton (Powlesland *et al.* 2006) suggest that some originated in the later Iron Age and were used throughout the Roman period. The site at Burton Fleming is notable because of a trackway that runs for well over a kilometre, curving around the valley slope following the topography of the hillside (Allen 2016b, 261, fig. 7.26). Cropmarks show many of the droveways linking settlements together, and it seems likely that there was a great deal of movement between communities. In pastoral communities, exchanges of livestock and other goods are facilitated through shared customs and are used to invest in kinship ties (Banks 2001; Barfield 2011). These exchanges would have been essential for establishing how the land would have been managed, perhaps requiring inter-communal co-operation.

Environmental evidence indicates that the slopes of the Wolds began to be cultivated in the later Iron Age (Powlesland 2003), and Giles (2007, 246–7) has argued that the evidence for short-fallow cultivation within enclosed plots by the first century A.D. suggests that systems of land tenure began to change over this period. She suggests that increasing land divisions could be taken as evidence of communities becoming more tightly drawn and less inclined to co-operate with regard to the care and maintenance of the wider landscape. This theory is difficult to substantiate, though an increase in cattle may reflect changes in local farming practice. Unfortunately, there are few large animal bone assemblages from rural settlements on the Yorkshire Wolds, though evidence from High Wold, Bridlington, and Melton A63, suggest that sheep were dominant in the early phases of occupation, but with a distinct shift towards cattle in the mid-Roman period, perhaps reflecting an increased emphasis on arable agriculture (Roberts 2009; Fenton-Thomas 2011). The appearance of a few villas on the periphery of the Wolds, such as at Welton Wold, Langton and Rudston, may also indicate a shift towards arable farming (Allen 2016b, 255–6). There is, for example, considerable evidence for bulk-processing of cereal grain at Welton Wold. It is possible that regional changes in land-use disrupted traditional farming patterns and inter-communal relationships (e.g. Giles 2007), though further evidence is required to substantiate this.

While upland areas tend to be suited to extensive sheep husbandry, river floodplains are generally exploited for cattle grazing, particularly as cattle are less susceptible to parasites such as liver fluke. In the Upper Thames Valley, livestock husbandry was central to the agricultural economy throughout later prehistory and the Roman periods (Allen 2017, 91–4; Hambleton 2008, 58; Hesse 2011). Environmental evidence of dung-enriched grasslands and a relative absence of arable weed flora at sites in middle–late Iron Age deposits at Thornhill Farm and Claydon Pike suggest that livestock husbandry may have been fairly intensive prior to the Roman conquest (Robinson 2004, 141; Booth *et al.* 2007, 278). Some innovations in husbandry occurred in the early Roman period at Barton Court Farm, where larger cattle have been identified in second-century A.D. deposits alongside hornless types of sheep (Wilson 1986; see Allen 2017, 104–7, for a review of the significance of polled livestock). It is also notable that Roman settlements in low-lying areas have tended to produce higher proportions of barley than those on the upper terraces, which may be linked to livestock foddering, while hay production appears to have been fairly prevalent (Lodwick 2017c, 80–1).

A major reorganisation of the settlement landscape in the Upper Thames Valley during the early second century A.D. has been suggested to represent changing patterns of land tenure (Booth *et al.* 2007, 374; Smith 2016d, 148). New complex farming settlements became established within a network of droveways and field systems, which may have impacted upon existing patterns of livestock husbandry. Areas of extensive grazing may have been increasingly defined by ditches and trackways, which suggest that access to certain areas of land became more restricted (Booth 2011a). One possible explanation for these changes is an increasing control over agricultural resources. In the Upper Thames Valley, this would almost certainly have been livestock rather than arable surplus (Allen 2017; Lodwick 2017c). Long-term excavations over 75 ha at Gill Mill, Ducklington, Oxfordshire, have revealed the remains of a nucleated settlement, complete with continuous lines of large, rectilinear enclosures running alongside metalled trackways (Booth and Simmonds 2018). The faunal assemblage from the site is overwhelmingly dominated by cattle bone, despite an extensive sieving programme that usually mitigates for biases in the recovery of bones from smaller animals such as sheep and goats (*ibid.*). Halstead (1996, 24) has suggested that faunal assemblages dominated by one domestic species could indicate large-scale herding. Set within its regional context the proportion of cattle bone against other major livestock taxa is among the highest for settlements

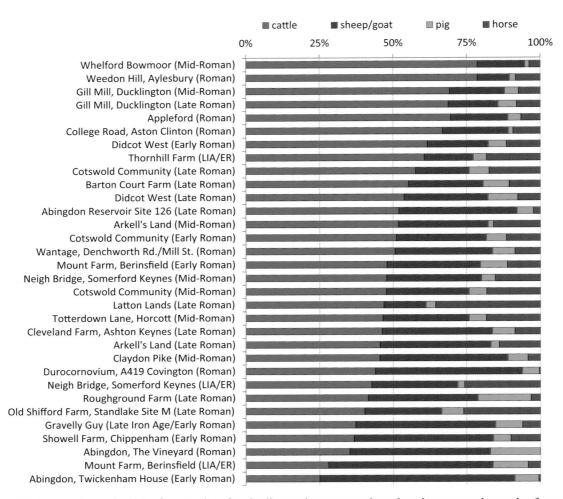

FIG. 4.8. Comparison of relative frequencies of major livestock taxa at nucleated settlements and complex farmsteads in the Upper Thames Valley

in the region. FIGURE 4.8 shows the relative frequency of livestock remains from nucleated settlements and complex farmsteads in the Upper Thames Valley with over 100 identified specimens. Only the farmsteads at Whelford Bowmoor and Weedon Hill, Aylesbury, produced higher frequencies of cattle bone. Gill Mill also produced almost no evidence for cereal processing, which strongly hints that livestock husbandry underpinned the economy of the settlement. Using the available evidence, it has been suggested that the site functioned as a cattle-corralling centre, perhaps as part of a wider estate (Booth 2016, 259–60). This is one of a number of possible interpretations, though the evidence for changing land tenure in this region may indicate that livestock herding was being centralised, possibly for export to towns such as Cirencester, or even further afield to the army (Allen and Lodwick 2017, 174–7).

Organised cattle herding on this scale potentially required the presence of professional drovers, whose job it was to collect livestock from farmsteads and move them between collection points on their way to their intended markets. It is well known that faunal assemblages excavated at the outskirts of towns and at military *vici* are normally dominated by cattle remains, reflecting the regular supply, slaughter and processing of livestock (Dobney 2001; Maltby 2015). Stallibrass (2009) has suggested that cattle were being moved to forts in the north of England, including on Hadrian's Wall, from pastoralists living north of the wall. A contrasting explanation is that cattle were being driven over long distances along the main roads from the Central Belt region, particularly landscapes like the Thames Valley (Allen 2017, 91–4). Cattle may have been moved as part of large collection drives from areas where retired plough cattle were no longer required. The organisation of cattle droving in Roman Britain is poorly understood, though strontium isotope evidence is beginning to show that cattle were being moved around with increasing frequency (Minniti *et al.* 2014), and it is the appearance of professional drovers acting as middle men between rural estates and the army that could have facilitated it.

LIVESTOCK IN TOWNS

While rural communities undoubtedly had close relationships with livestock, it is also worth considering the social importance of animals in urban contexts. As places of relatively dense human populations, towns required regular supplies of livestock for meat and raw materials for product manufacturing (hides, horn and bone). Numerous urban excavations have produced bulk quantities of animal bones, usually far in excess of what is normally found at rural sites (Maltby 2010b; 2015). However, as briefly discussed in the section above, the organisation of urban livestock supply is poorly understood.

In the first instance, the impact of urban demands on the countryside is uncertain and it is not clear how far livestock were driven. The prevailing view of most zooarchaeologists is that cattle were predominantly kept by farmers for traction purposes, for pulling ploughs and carts and producing dung (e.g. Maltby 1984; Dobney 2001; Albarella *et al.* 2008; Allen 2017). There is little evidence that livestock were specifically raised for meat on farmsteads, and it seems likely that urban beef provisioning occurred as a by-product of arable farming. However, the proportions of cattle and sheep bones recovered from rural sites located in the economic hinterlands of Dorchester (Dorset), Winchester, Chichester and Silchester broadly reflect the assemblages that have been excavated from the towns (Allen 2017, 88). It is well known that urban faunal assemblages vary considerably within the same settlement, though it appears that livestock supply to these towns was influenced by local patterns of pastoral farming (Maltby 2010b, 255–63). The high proportion of sheep bones found at Dorchester and at nearby rural settlements is especially notable (see also Maltby 1994, 94–7).

Second, it is uncertain how much of a direct relationship rural farmers had with urban consumers. While it is possible that some rural producers would have been able to exploit free-market trade, it has been argued that such opportunities would have been limited (Allen and Lodwick 2017; Fulford 2017). Instead, agricultural resources may have been aggregated and redistributed at the estate-level, rather than by individual small-holders. O'Connor (1992) has similarly pointed out that urban provisioning in Roman and medieval Britain would have been more complicated than a simple market exchange system. Although a coinage-based economy may have been in place in towns by the second century A.D., facilitating the local redistribution of animals and animal products (e.g. Maltby 1984; O'Connor 1988, 118–19), the mechanism of urban livestock supply remains unclear.

Although it is difficult to understand fully how livestock got from fields to towns, the evidence indicates that urban inhabitants may have had little contact with many of the animals they consumed before they died. Professional butchers may have acted as a buffer between rural producers and the urban consumers. Their presence in towns is indicated by the regular patterns of cleaver marks found on bones, mainly from cattle. These have been excavated in bulk quantities from urban sites, indicating that large numbers of carcasses were being processed rapidly and systematically (Seetah 2004; Maltby 2007). Sykes (2014, 14) suggests that the establishment of towns in Roman Britain may have signalled a complete overhaul in human–animal relationships. In later prehistoric communities, cattle were important as multi-purpose animals reared for dairy and traction and were probably rarely killed primarily for their meat (Seetah 2005, 5). This appears to have been replaced by a value system that focused on meat, hides, horn, bone and marrow, one where livestock were viewed as commodities rather than individuals (Maltby 2007, 72; Sykes 2014, 15).

The establishment of urban environments may have changed the attitudes of some people towards livestock and meat consumption. Symons (2002, 443) suggests many town citizens may never have known where much of the meat they consumed came from. However, urban communities were probably not completely ignorant of all the animals they ate. While the commodification of meat is indicated by the large numbers of heavily butchered carcasses deposited at the outskirts of many towns (Maltby 2010b, 283–7), much would have depended on where individual animals were raised and how they ended up in urban deposits. Towns were undoubtedly net consumers of livestock, yet a certain amount of stock-keeping took place within towns and some animal husbandry may have occurred on land around their periphery (Maltby 1994, 94). There is now increasing evidence of neonatal livestock being found in urban contexts (Ingrem 2012; Maltby 2015, 183–4), as well as signs of herbivore dung (Banerjea 2011, 72–3, 92–3; Robinson 2006, 214). O'Connor (1992, 102) suggests that intensive livestock exploitation is an adaptive strategy, and it is possible that some people saw this as a response to new social and economic conditions brought about by the establishment of towns. Based upon the analysis of biometric and ageing data, Maltby (1994, 94–7; 2010b, 146–52) has forwarded the idea that Winchester was supplied with retired dairy cows. If so, these livestock were probably locally reared under fairly intensive conditions, since milk and cheese are unlikely to have been bulk-produced far from consumer markets.

In much of rural Roman Britain, there is very little zooarchaeological evidence for cattle dairying (Allen 2017, 113), though exploitation closer to towns may have made it more viable.

Signs of tuberculosis appear more frequently in adult human skeletons in the South than in other regions during the Roman period (see Ch. 7). Modern studies of African populations have shown a correlation between *Mycobacterium bovis* infection in cattle and the presence of the disease in the human population (Cosivi *et al.* 1998), and there is some evidence to suggest that inter-species transmission rates are directly related to different husbandry regimes and cross-breeding (Oloya *et al.* 2007; Munyeme *et al.* 2008). Tuberculosis is usually transferred between cattle and people through the consumption of unpasteurised milk. It can also be transmitted through beef consumption, though this is generally less common because of cooking practices. There are no systematic zooarchaeological studies of animal pathologies from Roman Britain, and the prevalence of bovine tuberculosis is poorly understood. However, if the human bone evidence can be taken as a proxy for the distribution of bovine tuberculosis in Roman Britain, this may reflect a higher incidence of cattle dairy consumption in southern Britain, perhaps related to more intensive husbandry practices occurring closer to towns.

A high proportion of juvenile sheep bones has been observed in several major towns and it has been suggested that lamb was considered to be a luxury meat by urban inhabitants (Gidney 2000; Liddle *et al.* 2009; Maltby 2015, 183). While this may be true, such high proportions of young sheep suggest that regular supplies were probably deriving from local flocks being managed under intensive conditions fairly close to the town. Based upon cut and chop-mark evidence, Maltby (2015, 183) has suggested that not all sheep consumed in towns would have been processed by professional butchers; some may have been acquired by individual households, then butchered and eaten on their properties. Whether some of these animals were raised by those people as well is difficult to answer, though some urban sites have produced anomalously high proportions of neonatal sheep bones (Maltby 2010b, 290, fig. 2.228).

Pig-keeping was almost certainly a feature of town life. The identification of neonatal pig bones in several towns attests to pig breeding and rearing in urban environments (Maltby 2015, 184), while preliminary micromorphological data suggest the presence of slurry at Leicester, *Ratae Corieltavorum* (Morris *et al.* 2011, 29). Maltby's (2010b, 203) observation that town pigs tended to be larger than their rural compatriots may be indicative of improved nutrition from stall-feeding; though this

may also be accounted for by a preference for male pigs with greater carcass weights (cf. Maltby 1993a, 337; Ingrem 2011, 266). Several studies of urban material of Roman date have shown that evidence for trauma and disease on pig bones is rare (Dobney *et al.* 1996, 45; Maltby 1979, 59; Strid 2011, 11). Where the occasional example has been found it tends to indicate periods of healing (Ingrem 2011, 259, fig. 123). This may suggest that pigs were fairly well kept and cared for in towns, though until more systematic studies of pathologies are undertaken it is uncertain whether the urban pattern differs from that in rural assemblages.

Chickens are another animal that were undoubtedly kept in towns, as attested by the relatively high proportions of domestic fowl bones recovered from urban deposits (Maltby 1997). While they were clearly husbanded for meat and eggs, chicken imagery from Roman contexts suggests that they also performed other roles as religious icons, animal sacrifices, and were kept for cock-fighting (Henig 1993, 92–4; Sykes 2012; see Ch. 5). Since chickens are non-native to Britain, having been imported in the Iron Age, these animals will be assessed in more detail below (p. 99), in the discussion of introduced fauna.

DISCUSSION: THE SOCIAL CONTEXT OF LIVESTOCK HUSBANDRY

The identification of agricultural strategies can increase our understanding of local and regional economies, but it can also provide evidence for social attitudes and group identity. During the Iron Age in southern England, cattle were multipurpose animals, generally kept under non-intensive conditions for traction, breeding and dairy (Hambleton 2008, 65). Overall, cattle do not appear to have been kept primarily for meat, and their slaughter probably only occurred in exceptional circumstances. The care and attention afforded to cattle in this period is also evidenced in the way that their carcasses were butchered, predominantly with knives used for careful dismemberment (*ibid.*, 62). This evidence mirrors anthropological studies of modern agro-pastoral societies where livestock are respected as part of human communities, and are central to many of the social exchanges that take place (Zohary *et al.* 1998; Abbink 2003).

After the Roman conquest, southern England witnessed an expansion of arable cultivation, a change that may have begun in the late Iron Age in some areas (M. Jones 1996). The increasing use of cattle for traction is indicated by the evidence for older and larger animals (Albarella *et al.* 2008; Allen 2017, 100). Based on the controlling and servile nature of plough equipment and the heightened stress placed on the body, Sykes (2014, 42) argued that the intensive use of cattle for traction highlights a human perception that these animals were effectively thought of as no more than slaves. The apparent increase in cattle foot pathologies seen in Romano-British faunal material (Albarella *et al.* 2008, 1836) also suggests that working animals were treated in a way that caused discomfort. However, this is not to say that herdsmen on the West Anglian Plain or the Wessex Downs did not care for their cattle. On the contrary, their success, indeed their survival, was based on their ability to work together, and it is worth noting that although cattle were probably feeling the pain of increased workloads, the same may have been true of some of the human population. Incidences of spinal and joint degeneration caused by exposure to physical activity have been shown to have been relatively high in Roman Britain compared to earlier periods (Roberts and Cox 2003). Rohnbogner (Ch. 7) has found pathological evidence in adult males that is consistent with accidents related to agricultural labour and working with traction animals. Spinal traumas sustained through falls are common in the East region, while rib fractures caused by blunt force impacts were more prevalent in the South and Central Belt. It would seem that people and cattle began to suffer more from the agrarian changes occurring in the Roman period.

The greater numbers of plough cattle needed for arable expansion would have required increased maintenance, particularly since they were living for longer. It is suggested above that, for this to work, cattle may have become a shared resource. Co-operative livestock management could reduce the pressures of animal maintenance on individual households. It is possible that cattle were being increasingly managed at the estate (villa?) level rather than from individual farmsteads. Evidence for large-scale livestock management at Gill Mill, Oxfordshire, may suggest that cattle were being removed from farmsteads to be trafficked and sold on. Strontium isotope evidence is also beginning to show that cattle were being moved around the landscape with increasing frequency in the Roman period (Minniti *et al.* 2014). The large numbers of cattle bones found in towns and military sites show that there was a great demand for livestock (Seetah 2005; Maltby 2007), and at these consumer settlements we begin to see the commodification of livestock. Butchery patterns clearly change to reflect the rapid and systematic dismemberment of carcasses. There appears to be very little consideration for the individual animal, and it is worth highlighting the discovery of cattle skulls at Vindolanda with numerous square holes made by ballista bolts (Birley 2009, fig. 62).

It would appear that Roman soldiers in northern England used livestock as target practice. Regardless of whether these animals were slaughtered prior to being shot, it is inconceivable that such brutal acts would be carried out by a farmer who raised livestock. Clearly, different social groups treated and cared for animals in very different ways.

The agricultural changes in the Roman period may not have been restricted to arable farming and cattle management, but possibly affected other livestock species as well. At Elms Farm, Heybridge, in Essex, Albarella *et al.* (2008) showed quite clearly that sheep, pigs, horses and even chickens all increased in body size after the Roman conquest. While the increase in cattle body size might be related to an emphasis on traction, this cannot explain why other animals also got bigger, though horse breeding may have been related to transport requirements (see below, p. 91). It is notable that when significant changes in livestock husbandry regimes occur in other places and periods, they are usually also associated with social and demographic changes (Albarella 1997; Thomas 2005). Sykes (2014, 48–9) points out that it is worth considering these shifts in terms of cultural ideology. For example, in early modern England, the intensive breeding of larger livestock served to represent the status and social standing of their owners, and many breeds were regularly displayed at markets and in shows (Ritvo 1987). This is not to say that Romano-British animal 'breeds' were sent around the countryside for public display, but it is possible that the appearance of new livestock types was also related to changing social structures and attitudes towards agricultural resources.

While changes in farming practice were occurring in the south and east of England, it is worth considering the situation in the north and west regions of the province. In the South-West, Upland Wales and the Marches, and the North, most people in rural communities lived in fairly small enclosed farmsteads, with little sign of change in settlement types or building styles (Brindle 2016a–c). Although zooarchaeological evidence is sparse in these areas, phosphate analysis from areas within several farmsteads in Gwynedd suggests that people and livestock were living in close proximity. Whether these were cattle, sheep, goats or pigs is uncertain. However, the evidence for close living arrangements strikes a chord with Armstrong Oma's (2010, 181–5) study of Scandinavian longhouse communities in the Bronze Age, where people and livestock also shared internal living spaces. Here, the daily routines of milking, feeding and grooming could be undertaken, with mutual trust being developed between person and animal. Armstrong Oma (*ibid.*, 182) highlights the fact that milking requires 'a calm and comfortable atmosphere to encourage the animals to relax and let down their milk', and presumably similar conditions are required for other activities, such as wool shearing, breeding and birthing. Shepherds, for example, require intimate knowledge of their flock, knowing when ewes come into heat and when to allow (and encourage) the ram's access to them (*ibid.*, 183).

Overall, it is clear that a better understanding of agricultural strategies can inform upon some aspects of lifestyle and social practices. In many areas of Roman Britain, livestock may have been considered as little more than commodities to be exploited and sold off when their economic value had reduced. This certainly seems to have been the case once livestock had entered urban and military environments, to be unceremoniously slaughtered and butchered, though this is likely to have differed from farming communities themselves, where people and livestock spent their whole lives together, building up mutual trust and emotional connections. It is argued here that such differences would have contributed to the various agrarian identities present in the countryside of Roman Britain.

THE SOCIAL ROLES OF HORSES

Horses were exploited for a range of activities in late Iron Age and Roman Britain, enhancing travel and transport and performing vital roles on the farm. They were also a key element of the *cursus publicus*, ensuring the functioning of state administration and communication across and beyond the province. While the economic importance of horses throughout this period is not in doubt (Allen 2017, 124–31), the considerable time, resources and care that are involved in their upkeep means that they would have formed close social relationships with the people who bred, reared and rode them. Horses would have been used for social recreation, particularly as rides for hunting, and some may have been involved in aspects of public entertainment. The circus at Colchester appears to have hosted chariot-racing (Crummy 2008), while Fulford (1989b, 187–9) has suggested that the high number of horse bones found in the Silchester amphitheatre perhaps represents equestrian spectacles. Clearly horses fulfilled a variety of roles in everyday life, yet there is evidence that the status and perception of the horse altered between the late Iron Age and the Roman period as the province underwent social, political and economic change.

THE HORSE IN THE LATE IRON AGE: SYMBOLS AND STATUS

The frequent depiction of these animals on late Iron Age coins provides some insight into how much they were revered as icons worthy of incorporation into elite imagery. Green (1993, 8–14) has highlighted the common depiction of horses alongside the sun and chariot wheels on many coins, and has interpreted these as representing mythological histories, perhaps involving a solar cult or sun god (see also Green 1992, 46). Creighton (2000, 65–6) has also pointed out the frequent horse imagery on Iron Age coins, and suggests that the animal reflected high-status notions of power. Although horses were primarily used for transportation, they would also have played a central role in warfare, and the use of horses to pull chariots during this period may have provided a context for their association with elite activity (Cross 2011, 191). If, as it seems, the horse was an important cultural icon during this period, it may have been its physical attributes that elite groups were seeking to highlight and associate themselves with; the ability to travel at speed would have been essential for maintaining power and communication over large territories.

At Bury Hill, Hampshire, a middle to late Iron Age hillfort in the Test Valley, horse bones accounted for about 50 per cent of the overall faunal assemblage, becoming comparatively more abundant in the later phase (Hamilton 2000a). The significance of this assemblage is brought into sharper focus when considering the quantity and array of horse fittings and riding gear that were also recovered from the site (Cunliffe and Poole 2000, 62–3). The focus on horses at Bury Hill may have a ritual element, but it suggests a link between riding and high-status groups during this period. It is also notable that these animals were from local stock, as indicated by strontium isotope analysis of horse teeth from the site, though the presence of a non-local animal from a nearby site at Rooksdown suggests that some horses may have travelled over considerable distances during this period (Bendrey *et al.* 2009, 148).

The evidence just outlined provides an impression that the use of horses was elite-controlled to some degree, although there is some debate surrounding the logistics of horse-breeding during the Iron Age. Previously, a lack of reported neonatal horse remains on Iron Age sites led Harcourt (1979) to suggest that horses were not deliberately bred by people, but instead were seasonally rounded up from feral herds and managed from these sites. This view continued to find some support, most notably from Grant (1984), who interpreted the apparent prominence of male horses at Danebury as evidence for a lack of controlled breeding. More recent finds of perinatal horse remains on Iron Age sites, however, indicates that controlled breeding may have taken place in some areas (e.g. Powell and Clarke 1996; Mulville and Levitan 2004, 472). The dataset from the current project shows that around 15 per cent of late Iron Age sites with evidence for neonatal livestock include bones from immature horses (Allen 2017, 127, fig. 3.50). While these data show that horses probably were deliberately bred at settlements in the Iron Age, the proportion of sites with immature horse bones doubles into the Roman period, featuring on around a third of early Roman and late Roman sites. This suggests that horse-breeding was a comparatively restricted activity during the later Iron Age, which perhaps reflects the special status of the horse during this period.

THE CHANGING STATUS OF THE HORSE IN ROMAN BRITAIN

It is difficult to assess the impact of the Roman conquest on the use of horses. Horse bones are found on the vast majority of rural settlements, and usually contribute between 5 and 10 per cent of most faunal assemblages relative to cattle, sheep/goats and pigs. There are notable regional and chronological differences in the relative proportions of horse bones, which become less abundant on rural settlements after the late Iron Age in the Central Southern and the North-East case study areas, while the opposite is true in the Fens and the Thames Estuary and London Basin areas (Allen 2017, 124, fig. 3.47; see also fig. 3.1 for case study areas in question). The reasons behind these changes are not easy to explain, but are probably complicated by a variety of regional factors.

King (2001, 216–17) has suggested that the Roman conquest brought about an end to the eating of horse meat in Britain. The Romans are thought to have detested its consumption (Pascal 1981, 268), which perhaps provides a context for the lack of evidence for horses being eaten during the Roman period (Cross 2011, 194). However, there is no strong zooarchaeological evidence that horses were consumed before or after the conquest, or that there was a change in cultural attitudes in this regard. Often, cut and chop marks on horse bones are not systematically recorded and quantified, so it is difficult to assess the prevalence of horse butchery over time or the reasons why their carcasses were processed (e.g. skinning, etc.). A few Romano-British rural sites have produced horse bones with filleting marks indicating that the meat may have been eaten (Buckland-Wright 1987; Strid 2015), and Maltby (1989a) has

suggested that horses could have been raised for their meat at the early Roman settlement at Easton Lane, Hampshire. Certainly, horse bones are often relatively abundant on rural sites compared with urban settlements (Allen 2017, 124–5; Maltby 2016). However, instances of horse butchery cannot be taken as evidence that horse meat was a common element of the Romano-British diet, and in some cases a ritual or sacrificial explanation for its consumption may be apparent (Cross 2011, 197–200).

The increase in the proportion of Roman-period sites with immature horse bones perhaps indicates that the rearing of young horses became more widespread in the countryside. Not all sites with immature horse bones were necessarily engaged in horse-breeding, owing to the fact that some long bones do not fuse until the animal reaches four years old. However, perinatal horse bones have been identified at several rural settlements (Allen 2017, 126). Horse breeding and rearing requires stabling, though there is remarkably little evidence for such buildings on rural settlements (Smith 2016b, 57). This no doubt owes much to difficulties in interpreting the function of buildings, though there are increasing signs that environmental evidence for stable manure can illuminate the subject further (Hall and Huntley 2007, 54; Large et al. 2009, 52–3). The arrival of the Roman army would also have created a demand for horses, perhaps requisitioning or purchasing young animals from rural settlements. That the military trained and broke their own horses is indicated by the discovery of the *gyrus* at the Lunt Fort, Warwickshire, which is the only known cavalry training arena in Britain (Hobley 1975).

The expansion of arable and pastoral farming in Roman Britain may have increased the need for more horses at some rural settlements, particularly in southern, central and eastern regions. The increase in the relative abundance of horse bones at rural sites in the Thames Estuary and London Basin region is notable (Allen 2017, 124, fig. 3.27), and may reflect the development of cattle-droving in lowland areas (e.g. Allen 2016a, 130–5). The fact that horse bones outnumbered pig bones at the probable cattle-corralling centre at Gill Mill, Oxfordshire (Booth 2016, 258), may be a testament to the role that horses had in moving herds over longer distances, as the marketing and supply of livestock to towns and military sites developed. The expansion of larger, complex farmsteads from the second century A.D. may also have required an increased contribution from horses as working animals; in most areas, horse remains were relatively abundant on complex farmsteads compared with enclosed farmsteads

(Allen 2017, 125, fig. 3.49). Horses were undoubtedly important for transporting people, but their use as pack and traction animals in Roman Britain is not well understood. Cattle are thought to have been the predominant draught animal (*ibid.* 112–13), though horses may have had a minor role in moving goods and produce around settlements and on the road.

Hipposandals may be one indicator for the use of horses on the harder surfaces of metalled roads and potentially on the plough (though it is possible that ox-sandals were worn by cattle). Hipposandals are a distinctive type of Roman horseshoe consisting of an iron plate with side wings, a narrowed, hooked back and a raised looped front, which allows the shoe to be tied to the foot of the animal (Manning 1985, 63–6). The iron underside undoubtedly protected the hoof against hardstanding surfaces, but the fact that some horseshoes also had grooved undersides suggests that they were made to help prevent slipping on wet and/or muddy ground (Crummy 2011, 61). It is perhaps unsurprising that hipposandals are most common at military *vici*, being recovered from 7.5 per cent of sites, compared to 6.8 per cent of villages, 2.5 per cent of roadside settlements, 1.2 per cent of villas and 0.3 per cent of farmsteads. The importance of equids (including donkey and mules) to the military is in little doubt, though these protective implements were important enough for their use to spread to other types of settlements in the countryside.

As noted above, horses probably played a role in hunting activities, though direct evidence for this in Britain is lacking. Hunting on horseback is depicted in classical imagery including mosaics, such as those at Piazza Amerina in Sicily, wall paintings and sarcophagi motifs, which show the rural elite chasing and spearing deer, wild boars and other wild animals (Tuck 2005). Evidence for a hunting element involving horses in some cult practices in Roman Britain has previously been suggested by King (2005, 347–8), who highlighted an association of the bones of horse, dog and red deer in ritual deposits at Bancroft villa, Milton Keynes, and horse and dog bones at Folly Lane, Verulamium, Hertfordshire. At Fishbourne, West Sussex, the second-century A.D. burial of a horse with the skull and foot bones from a red deer (presumably representing the skin of the animal) possibly signifies the interment of a horse used for hunting (Allen 2011, 238–9).

SUMMARY: THE HORSE

Horses were evidently important in Roman Britain for their role supporting the local and provincial economies, but it is clear that they also fulfilled a range of social roles. Their status as symbols of power and high-status identity in the late Iron Age is demonstrated by their frequent depiction on coins. The Roman conquest brought about a change to the political status quo, and with it an end to the use of the horse as an icon of elite culture. This appears to coincide with the more widespread evidence for horse breeding and rearing, perhaps reflecting the possibility this activity was not as controlled as it once was. Economic demands for horses may also have influenced this change, particularly in the use of the horse on the farm and for travel between settlements, but also to supply a growing demand from the state, for the *cursus publicus* and the army, and, on a much smaller scale, for performances in the amphitheatre and the circus.

There is very little evidence for the consumption of horsemeat, and the dataset is not currently able to show whether a change in attitudes towards hippophagy occurred between the late Iron Age and the Roman period as has been previously suggested. Butchery marks on horse bones have been found at some sites, though this does not necessarily indicate that the meat was being eaten, and in cases where it was, this may have been undertaken under special circumstances. Future work requires greater attention from zooarchaeologists to record and report butchery marks on horse bones using standard protocol. Evidence of pathologies will also go a long way to understanding how horses were treated (both positively and negatively) by the people in different parts of the province, in different types of settlement, and whether attitudes to horse-care changed over time.

PETS OR PESTS? DOGS AND CATS IN ROMAN BRITAIN

Perhaps more than any other animals, dogs and cats are seen today by western society as the most quintessential companion animals. Our attitudes to pet-keeping can often be seen as a barometer for wider social and cultural attitudes (Serpell 1996, 125–43; Sykes 2014, 139–46). However, the social relationships between people and dogs and cats have not always been as close as they are today. The role of both species in late Iron Age and Roman Britain would have formed part of a much longer and complex history of living with people. This is not only glimpsed through the study of faunal remains, but also, in the Roman period at least, through representative artwork and even the imprints of cat and especially dog paw prints on wet ceramic tiles, which are a persistent, if uncommon, find among Roman artefact assemblages (cf. Cram and Fulford 1979).

DOGS IN LATE IRON AGE AND ROMAN BRITAIN

People and dogs are particularly suited for co-habitation, especially with regards to food acquisition, though it may not always have been the case that dogs in Roman Britain were considered as companion animals. Dogs can be bred or exploited for economic activities such as livestock herding, hunting or vermin control, though they are also able to exploit human environments, for example, in scavenging food from settlements (Morey 2010, 81–5; Russell 2012, 211). The full range of contexts must be considered when examining dog remains.

Compared to the major domestic livestock mammals, dog remains are scarce. Where they have been identified, dog bones average between 2 and 4 per cent in faunal assemblages dating between the late Iron Age and the late Roman period (FIG. 4.9). However, the fact that dog bones occur in over 80 per cent of assemblages across

the same period shows that they were fairly common animals and would have been present on most rural settlements. The disparity between the high proportion of sites with dogs and their low relative frequency relates to the fact they were not regularly eaten. It should be pointed out that butchered dog bones are more frequently encountered at rural sites (Clark 2012, 173–4), though this need not imply that dog meat was being consumed (see below). There is little variation in the proportion of sites with dog bones between different settlement types (FIG. 4.10a). It is also worth pointing out here that there is very little regional variation in the proportion of sites with dog remains, though they appear to be most common in the South region and become less common further north.

However, simply treating all dogs as a single, homogeneous group of animals is misleading (cf. Clark 2012). These animals fulfilled a variety of roles on human settlements, and people's attitudes

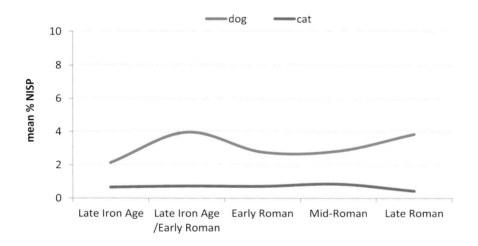

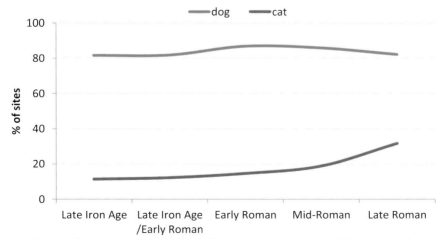

FIG. 4.9. Proportions of dog and cat remains over time: mean percentages of dog and cat bones against cattle, sheep/goat, pig and horse (only assemblages with dog or cat bones present in assemblages with a total of 100 NISP), and the percentage of sites with dog and cat bones present (only assemblages with over 100 NISP)

towards them differed accordingly. Biometric analysis of remains from a late Iron Age/early Roman settlement at Selhurst Park, West Sussex, showed that two distinct dog sizes were present, perhaps representing different types (Allen forthcoming). It was noticeable that some of the bones from the larger type were butchered, while bones from the smaller dogs did not exhibit cut marks, suggesting that the two were treated in very different ways. It is possible that the larger bones derived from wolves or hybrids, though the bone measurements fell within the range of large Romano-British dogs (Clark pers. comm.). Similarly, a large canid humerus from an early Roman feature at Nettlebank Copse, Hampshire, has fine cut marks suggestive of defleshing and perhaps skinning (Hamilton 2000b).

It is now widely accepted that dog-breeding intensified in the Roman period. This is based upon biometrical evidence showing that dogs increasingly varied in size in several provinces, including Britain, after being subsumed by the Roman Empire (Harcourt 1974; Clark 1995; 2000; Bartosiewicz 2000; Cram 2000; De Grozzi Mazorin and Tagliacozzo 2000; Bennett and Timm 2016; MacKinnon 2010). The appearance of both large 'fighting' dogs and small 'lap' dogs is often cited in the literature as evidence for the appearance of specific dog breeds (e.g. Clutton-Brock 1999, 60). As Sykes (2014, 142–4) points out, however, in most cases it is difficult to appreciate how these animals were exploited, considered and treated by people. There is increasing evidence for very small dogs in Roman Britain, particularly at rural sites such as Camp Ground (Higbee 2013) and Longstanton site XX (Evans *et al.* 2006) in Cambridgeshire, and Dicket Mead in Hertfordshire (Rook 1986). Most zooarchaeologists refer to these as pet 'lapdogs', though they may just as easily have been working ratters (Clark 2012, 165–8; Sykes 2014, 143). However, does this mean that the animal was any less cared for by its human companions? Burial contexts sometimes provide useful information.

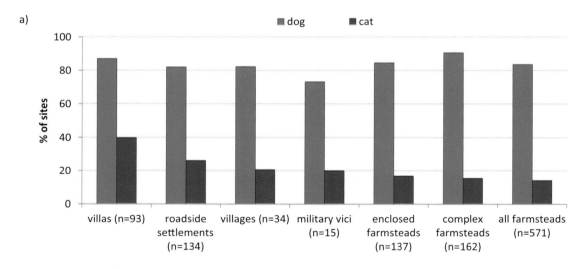

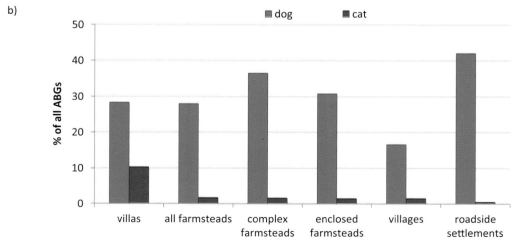

FIG. 4.10. Percentage of sites with dog and cat remains by site type (a) (only assemblages with over 100 NISP) and percentage of dog and cat Associated Bone Groups found at different site types (b)

For example, a very small dog was placed in a fourth-century A.D. human-sized grave at Leicester (Baxter 2002), while another example at Stanwick, Northamptonshire, was buried within its own cist grave (Crosby pers. comm.). In contrast, at Keston villa, Kent, the remains of two cremated lapdogs had been placed in a 'ritual shaft', a deposit claimed by the excavator to have had chthonic associations (Fox 1967; Philp *et al.* 1999).

One area of study that is increasing our understanding of human-dog relationships is isotope analysis. Dogs are often sampled to provide baseline data by researchers hoping to examine human diets, but Sykes (2014, 141–2, fig. 7.2) has shown that these data are also useful for showing linkages between people and dogs. By aggregating nitrogen isotope data from human and canid bones dating between the Mesolithic and the medieval period, the closest average values in both species occurred during the Roman period. While there is a considerable amount of variation within these data, human and dog diets appear to have been more similar in Roman Britain than at any point previously, both apparently being high in protein. While it could be argued that Roman dogs were able to access more meat and bone at human settlements, it is also possible that a degree of food-sharing was occurring.

Comparing animal burials provides some indication of human attitudes towards different species. FIGURE 4.11 shows the proportion of rural sites with evidence for articulated remains or associated bone groups (ABGs) of dogs, cats and sheep/goats, where these taxa have been identified. These data indicate that when dog bones are

present at late Iron Age and Romano-British rural settlements, they are found as articulated deposits twice as often as when cats are found. It is possible these data are affected by poor recovery, which would bias against the generally smaller and more fragile bones of cats. However, it is also possible that dogs were more often interred in discrete burial contexts, reflecting an element of human emotional consideration, which would help to preserve their skeletons in articulation. Animals that were, perhaps, less ceremoniously deposited in open ditches, seemingly along with other domestic waste, are far less likely to be recovered as associated bone groups.

Morris (2011, 67–71) has shown that dog burials were the most common type in the Roman period, marking a change from the Iron Age when other species tended to be favoured. However, this pattern is heavily influenced by deposits in urban settlements, such as Dorchester in Dorset, where large numbers of dogs were found to have been placed in shafts or wells (*ibid.*, 86–90). As Sykes (2014, 142–3) points out, many of these burials are unlikely to have been animals that were cherished pets (see below). At rural settlements, dog burials are slightly less common immediately after the Roman conquest, and then they gradually increase into the late Roman period (FIG. 4.12). However, these data vary when different settlement types are considered. Dog burials form a high proportion of ABGs at roadside settlements, showing similarities to the urban pattern (FIG. 4.10b).

That some dogs were kept as working animals on farmsteads is implied from the evidence for pathologies. A brief survey of pathology data from the South region shows that evidence for trauma, mostly healed fractures in dogs, outnumbers other types of pathologies on farmsteads, whereas the distribution is more equal on other types of settlement (FIG. 4.13). It is also notable that evidence for healed fractures is comparatively rare at villas, where dogs may have been less exposed to the rigorous daily routine of farm life.

It is possible that dogs living in urban environments would have been treated differently from those in the countryside. As noted above, many dogs have been recovered from abandoned wells and pits in towns (Fulford 2001), and some of these have been interpreted as sacrifices associated with foundation deposits (Woodward and Woodward 2004). This may be true, but it is worth considering other evidence from the skeletal remains to highlight what life might have been like for dogs living in towns. Of 23 dog skeletons excavated from *Noviomagus Reginorum*, the *civitas* capital at Chichester, West Sussex, 12 showed signs of pathology and trauma, with some exhibiting signs of multiple fractures (Levitan

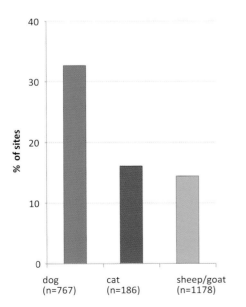

FIG. 4.11. Percentage of sites with dog, cat and sheep/goat Associated Bone Groups (only assemblages with over 100 NISP)

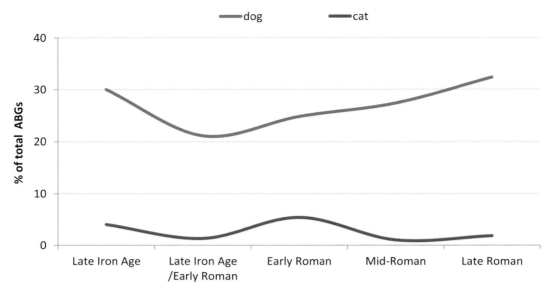

FIG. 4.12. Proportions of dog and cat Associated Bone Groups at rural settlements over time

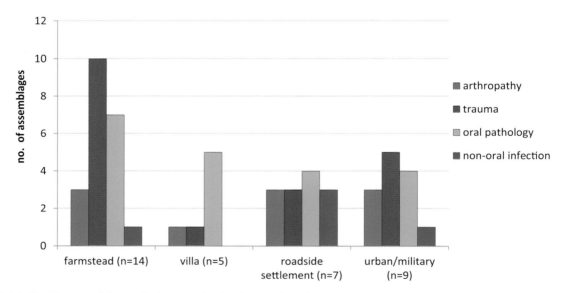

FIG. 4.13. Incidences of dog pathology at sites in the South region

1989, 265–6). One animal appears to have completely lost the lower end of its front leg, while it also received a blow to the head that resulted in it losing several teeth. All the individuals in this sample were adults, some living to comparatively old age and none appear to have been butchered. It seems unlikely (though not implausible) that the Chichester dogs had been deliberately killed. With a high proportion showing signs of trauma and healing, the evidence suggests that they were part of a stray population that were poorly treated, their bodies perhaps being removed from the streets and deposited after death. Evidence of malnutrition in dogs may explain the identification of several bowed-leg dog bones at Staines (*Pontibus*), Surrey (Chapman and Smith 1988), and perhaps supports the idea of a poorly treated

stray population. Maltby (2010a; 2010b, 246–7) has argued that the large number of dogs, including puppies and elderly individuals, deposited in wells and shafts at Winchester were put there as a result of deliberate culling in order to manage the stray population.

However, other explanations for dog burials in towns should be considered. Some dogs were found buried with complete pottery vessels at Winchester, which may imply a ritual context (*ibid.*), and at some religious sites, dogs have been argued to have been associated with healing cults (see Ch. 5, p. 192). At Silchester, in contrast, the presence of butchery marks on dog bones found in wells indicates that some carcasses were skinned prior to burial, which perhaps provides a more utilitarian context for their deaths (Clark 2011,

477; 2012, 174–6). It would thus appear that towns and roadside settlements probably attracted communities of stray dogs that were drawn to these places by opportunities for food, and perhaps were a nuisance to local people. However, there are several explanations for their eventual deaths and for the context of their burials, and these must be appreciated when examining dog remains in urban contexts.

CATS IN LATE IRON AGE AND ROMAN BRITAIN

Cats were first domesticated in the Near East, much later than dogs, around 4,000 years ago (Russell 2012, 208, table 6.1). However, the process of cat domestication appears to have been largely due to developments in the social behaviour of their wild progenitor: the wildcat. The common view is that wildcats began to scavenge food sources at larger, nucleated human settlements, where easy pickings at middens could be had, and where they had access to rodent populations that were drawn to grain stores (Todd 1978). Eventually, cats became tolerated by people and, most importantly, by other cats – a key behavioural change – and were able to exploit an abundant food source. In effect, cats were 'self-domesticating' rather than deliberately selected and tamed by people (Kitchener and O'Connor 2010, 88).

Two wild relatives of domestic cats – the lynx and the wildcat – have been resident in Britain since the end of the last Ice Age, though the former is now extinct from these shores and the latter is restricted to a small breeding population in Scotland (Hetherington 2010; Kitchener and O'Connor 2010). It was not always this way – the history of the domestic cat in Britain appears to have been strongly linked with these two species, firstly because they would have competed within the same environments for food, and secondly because wildcats and domestic cats can inter-breed (Kitchener *et al.* 2005). This also causes zooarchaeologists a problem in determining the emergence of domestic cats in Britain. It seems likely that they were present in the Iron Age, as seen by discoveries at Gussage All Saints in Dorset (Harcourt 1979) and Owslebury in Hampshire (Maltby 1987), though their identification as 'domestic' animals rests upon our understanding of their behaviour and relationship with people and this requires an understanding of the context of cat deposition. The comparative rarity of cat remains from Romano-British sites means that there is a lack of biometric data and isotope analysis to investigate feline populations in the same way as dogs. For the most part, we are reliant upon relative frequencies of cat bones, contextual evidence, and signs of pathology and butchery.

Cat remains are present in far fewer assemblages than dogs (FIG. 4.9). This may be partly due to poor recovery or rapid excavation, which can bias against the smaller bones of cats (Kitchener and O'Connor 2010, 91), though the difference between the proportion of sites with dogs and cats is great enough to suggest that the latter simply were not as common on rural settlements. Interestingly, a higher proportion of late Roman sites has produced cat bones than earlier settlements; the ratio increases from around one in ten of late Iron Age and early Roman rural sites to around one in three late Roman sites. This may in part be due to differences between site types. Around 40 per cent of villas produce cat bones, which compares to 20–26 per cent of nucleated settlements and 14–17 per cent of farmsteads (FIG. 4.10a). This pattern is also reflected in the proportions of Associated Bone Groups. Over 10 per cent of partial or whole animal burials at villas are of cats, though the species accounts for less than 2 per cent at all other settlement types (FIG. 4.10b). The association between cats and villas could reflect residents more often keeping cats as pets, or that villa settlements provided more suitable environments for cats to feed. Corndryers and storage buildings at villas (though not limited to villas) may have increased the number of rodents at these sites, giving cats more opportunities to hunt. The arrival of the house mouse in the Iron Age (O'Connor 2010) and the black rat in the first century A.D. (Rielly 2010) must have provided cats with extra incentive to exploit human settlements. Fish-keeping may also have been a factor at some villas, and, though there is less direct evidence for this activity (see below), the lure of easy fish and frogs may also have been tempting to cats.

There is some evidence that cats were cared for by people. The remains of an adult cat recovered from a well at Dalton-on-Tees villa, North Yorkshire, showed signs of a severe fracture of the hip joint, as well as further breakages to the left fore and hind limbs (Buglass and West 2014). These traumatic injuries had largely healed by the time the cat died. However, they surely would have stopped the animal from hunting while it was alive and it seems very likely that it managed to survive through human intervention. The fact that it was deposited in a well indicates that this method of burial may not have been a simple method of waste disposal.

Cats have been recovered from wells at several rural settlements, such as Welton villa in the East Riding of Yorkshire, where the remains of at least 28 cats of varying ages were buried (Mackey 1999). Some cats appear to have been afforded burial in other contexts on rural settlements, though the evidence is sparse. At Mansfield Woodhouse, Nottinghamshire, a cat was found to have been placed in a wooden coffin and buried during the late first/early second century A.D. (Oswald 1949). The excavator's suggestion that the skeleton could be a polecat is less convincing but raises some doubt over the identification of the skeleton. At Latimer villa, Buckinghamshire, a cat was laid in the foundations of a villa corridor during a period of modification in the early fourth century A.D., and it may well have been of ritual significance related to the development of the house (Hamilton 1971, 163).

At several sites, there are deposits of kitten litters or juvenile cats that appear to have been rounded up and killed. The late Iron Age burial of five kittens at Gussage All Saints, Dorset, is often highlighted as one of the first examples of domestic cat in Britain (Harcourt 1979, 154; Kitchener and O'Connor 2010, 92; Morris 2011, 42). These were argued to have been domestic cats on the basis that it would have been unusual for the inhabitants to capture a litter of wildcat kittens and then bury them at the settlement. The identification of house mouse at Gussage All Saints was also thought to have been an indication that the cats were domestic (Harcourt 1979, 150). At Whitcombe, Dorset, two newborn kittens and five immature cats were placed together in a single pit (Buckland-Wright 1990). The absence of butchery marks on many of these examples and the fact that they were still so young would argue against them being exploited for their fur. Otherwise, it is possible that while domestic cats may have been present on human settlements, not everybody was yet willing to accept them as companion animals; the discovery of cat litters at some sites may not have been a welcome sight.

Cats appear to have been exploited for their fur at some rural sites. At Houghton Down, Hampshire, the body of a skinned cat was placed down a well (Hammon 2008a), while at Royal Manor Arts College, Portland, Dorset, a coastal site involved in shale manufacturing, four discrete groups of cat bones were recovered, one of which included the remains of a hind leg with several cut marks on the bones (Maltby 2009). It is possible that all the specimens at Portland were the result of skinning, though a skilled butcher may not have left any trace of cutting on the bones. This raises some doubt over how many other cats found on Roman rural sites might also have been skinned.

SUMMARY: DOGS AND CATS

It is probably inappropriate to consider dogs and cats in Roman Britain as 'pets' in the modern, western sense of the term. The zooarchaeological and contextual evidence strongly suggests that both animals were treated in a variety of ways. Dogs appear to have been deliberately bred, most likely for different roles, ranging between hunting, livestock management, pest control, and household companions. There is less evidence for the controlled breeding of cats, though kitten litters have been found at some sites. These may not always have been welcomed by people, though the evidence for cats with healed fractures shows that some were cared for, and the fact that certain dogs and cats were buried in ways similar to humans suggests that some were considered in a like vein to people. In towns and other nucleated settlements, stray dogs were probably fairly common sights, perhaps taking advantage of domestic household waste. These animals appear to have been tolerated, if not treated quite so well. There is a growing body of evidence to show that dogs and cats were sacrificed and buried as part of ritual practices, with some perhaps being imbued with medicinal or magical properties (Sykes 2014, 147), and this topic will be considered further in Chapter 5.

NEW ANIMALS, NEW LANDSCAPES: THE SOCIAL CONTEXT OF INTRODUCED SPECIES

It is becoming increasingly recognised that the Roman period witnessed a considerable amount of movement and trade in animals and plants around the empire, and Britain was no exception (Van der Veen et al. 2008; Sykes 2009; Witcher 2013). Furthermore, these introductions are likely to have been more than simply an elite desire for exotic fauna and flora. Several studies have shown that, regardless of place or time, the movement of species into new habitats can have profound effects on the environment, giving rise to ecological changes with often dramatic implications for landscapes, identity and diet (Allen and Sykes 2011; Pluskowski et al. 2011).

Witcher (2013, 7–9, table 1) lists 47 plants and animal species that are often assumed (correctly or incorrectly) to be Roman introductions. Of the fourteen animals listed, several are now known to have been native, introductions from other periods, or were never introduced at all. Elephants and the edible dormouse (*Glis glis*) are two examples of the last, since no remains of either species have been found in Roman contexts. Rabbits (*Oryctolagus cuniculus*) are popularly thought to have been a Roman introduction (Witcher 2013, 18). Though rabbit bones certainly occur on many Roman sites, most (perhaps all) are from modern intrusions of burrowing animals. The recovery of butchered rabbit bones from an apparently sealed Roman pit at Lynford, Norfolk, has caused much excitement, with a similar find at Beddingham villa, East Sussex also being rumoured (Sykes and Curl 2010, 120), though without radiocarbon dating, these examples must be viewed with caution.

Some animals, however, were deliberately imported as status symbols. For example, the enigmatic discovery of a Barbary macaque (*Macaca silvanus*) skull at Catterick, North Yorkshire, highlights an animal brought to these shores from north Africa (Stallibrass 2002). The rarity of this species suggests that this may have been a single oddity, reflecting the wealth and status of the owner, or it may have been imported as a skull and kept as a curio. In other instances, animals were imported to enhance the splendour of private residences, such as fallow deer (*Dama dama*) and some exotic bird species, while the importation of the chicken in the later Iron Age may have been associated with several social activities such as cock-fighting and ritual sacrifice. This section examines these species, as they were deliberately imported to reflect attitudes to wealth, landscape and the natural world. Other animals were imported for economic reasons, such as donkeys and mules (see Allen 2017), or were not deliberate introductions, such as the black rat (*Rattus rattus*), which undoubtedly impacted on the lives of many people (Yalden 1999, 125; Rielly 2010).

CHICKENS

Chickens (*Gallus gallus*) were not a Roman introduction, but were imported in the Iron Age (Poole 2010). As with black rats, the chicken seems to have fared particularly well in Romano-British towns, though it also appears to have flourished in the countryside after the conquest (see Maltby 1997 and Allen 2017 for extensive analyses of the abundance and distribution of chickens). While chickens were certainly around prior to the conquest, their rarity in the Iron Age may indicate that they were comparatively 'alien' to much of the population. It is generally thought that chickens were not often eaten by Iron Age communities, an assumption based primarily upon Caesar's comments about fowl, geese and hares being the focus of pleasure and amusement instead of food, though some justification for this idea may be found in the fact that chicken remains from this period tend to be commonly recovered as whole carcasses, rather than as dismembered remains (Sykes 2014, 84). Some chicken burials may reflect religious activity. For example, Morris (2008) relates that chickens have been found with late Iron Age inhumation burials, perhaps suggesting a close social connection existed between some people and their birds. This does

not, however, mean that chickens were not eaten in Iron Age Britain, as the numbers of chicken bones from late Iron Age *oppida* at Braughing, Hertfordshire (Ashdown 1981), Fishbourne, West Sussex (Allen and Sykes 2011), and Silchester, Hampshire (Grant 2000), all suggest that the bird was consumed by high-status groups, perhaps as part of feasts.

An important reason for their initial establishment and spread through Britain in the late Iron Age and early Roman period may have been the increasing popularity of cock-fighting. Sykes (2014, 84–5) has highlighted a number of cases where chickens have been introduced to new places, but were rarely exploited for meat and eggs. As discussed in Volume 2 (Allen 2017), chicken remains in several Roman towns have high male to female ratios, suggesting a preference for cockerels. This has been argued to reflect both cock-fighting and ritual sacrifice (Serjeantson 2000, 499). Serjeantson (2009, 326–30) has suggested that the Roman taste for cock-fighting was adopted from Greek culture, though there is comparatively little evidence for it, save for some depictions in late Roman mosaics (e.g. Sykes 2012, 161, fig. 2).

Based upon contemporary human skeletal evidence from southern Britain, Sykes (2012, 164–5) argued that cock-fighting may have coincided with a reduction in interpersonal violence. Citing anthropological evidence from societies where cock-fighting is common, she suggested that cock-fighting in Roman Britain may have been a mechanism for diffusing male–male violence. Of course, there may be many reasons why changes in interpersonal violence occurred during this time, though cock-fighting in towns is apparent from the finds of artificial cock spurs at Silchester (Serjeantson 2000) and Braughing (Hingley 2006, 231). Studies have shown that close social relationships exist between fighting cocks and their handlers (Dundes 1994), and it seems unlikely that these chickens would have been eaten.

EUROPEAN FALLOW DEER

The European fallow deer (*Dama dama*) was previously thought to have been a Norman introduction to Britain. Over the past fifteen years, however, zooarchaeological evidence for Roman introductions of fallow deer have increasingly come to light (Bendrey 2003; Sykes 2004; 2010). Prior to this, a few records of fallow deer bones on Romano-British sites had been made, but were largely dismissed either because of the possibility of misidentification, since fallow deer bones can be confused with red or roe deer bones, or because of the likelihood of fallow deer bones dating to a later period being intrusive in Roman contexts. In the 1970s, Grant (1975) identified several specimens of fallow deer from late Roman pit deposits at Portchester Castle, Hampshire. However, a later reanalysis of the specimens by Sykes (2004, 77–8) indicated that these were in fact bones of roe deer. Another example, a calcaneus from Redlands Farm villa, Northamptonshire, was later radiocarbon dated to the eleventh or twelfth centuries A.D. (Davis 1997). This left the remaining few purportedly Romano-British fallow deer specimens in some doubt.

Despite the lack of conclusive evidence in Britain, historical and zooarchaeological evidence on the Continent had long suggested that fallow deer were being traded and maintained by elite groups. Pliny the Elder (*Nat. Hist.* VIII, 78.211), Columella (*Rust.* IX, I.4) and Varro (*Res Rust.* 3.12.1–2), each discuss the management of fallow deer on private estates in Italy and other provinces from the late Republican era onwards, while faunal remains have demonstrated the presence of fallow deer (an animal native to modern Turkey) at Roman sites in Portugal (Davis 2005), Sicily (Wilson 1990) and Italy (MacKinnon 2004). Back in Britain, fallow deer finds have tended to be of antler or foot bones (Sykes 2010, 53–5). These are not necessarily evidence for the importation of live animals, as it is possible that these represent trade in deer antler and feet, perhaps from the trafficking of furs or possibly items considered to have amuletic properties (Sykes 2004, 78–9). Pliny the Elder (*Nat. Hist.* XXVII) noted how deer antlers were thought by some to have had healing properties, while the smell of burning antlers was considered to combat epilepsy. This may have been the case with the large fallow deer antler recovered from the roadside settlement at Scole Dickleburgh, Norfolk, which clearly shows signs of being shaven (Sykes 2010, 54, fig. 12). It is worth noting, however, that antler and foot bones are the easiest deer elements to identify, which may partly explain why they are well represented. Nonetheless, examples of 'live' fallow deer populations in Roman Britain have proved difficult to substantiate.

Excavations of the rural 'village' settlement at Monkton on the Isle of Thanet, Kent, produced several fallow deer remains, including both antler and post-cranial bones, from sealed deposits dating from the late second to early fifth century A.D. (Bendrey 2003). Since this discovery, further excavations on the Isle of Thanet at Tothill Street, Minster (Cotton n.d.), and East Kent Access Road (Strid 2015) have added to the number of Roman-period fallow deer specimens known from the area. The finds on the Isle of Thanet are interesting given that, in the Roman period, it was

separated from the mainland by the Wantsum Channel, which later silted up. If live fallow deer were being imported to Britain by elite groups it seems very likely that they would have been intended for enclosure on private land, so that they could be viewed for pleasure by land-owners and their guests. *Vivaria* were game parks specifically set up for managing deer, and, according to Roman historians, these landscape features appear to have become common in Italy and other provinces (Anderson 1985, 86; Starr 1992, 436; Allen 2014, 179–81). Of course, many parks would not have been restricted to one type of animal, and it may be that the Roman linguistic terms for parks were referring to specific areas where animals might be kept separate for feeding or other purposes. For example, Columella (*Rust.* IX, I.1) states that, 'wild creatures, such as roe deer, chamois and also scimitar-horned oryx, fallow deer and wild boars sometimes serve to enhance the splendour and pleasure of their owners'. It is possible that each animal being maintained in parks was well managed and looked after by keepers. Considering that herds of fallow deer may have been trafficked over long distances, presumably at significant cost, their value to their owners would have warranted further investment. The use of the Isle of Thanet for emparkment may have been particularly useful since it was naturally enclosed, and it may also be relevant that the port at Richborough lies to the south of Thanet at the mouth of the Wantsum Channel.

That herds of fallow deer were being imported over long distances for emparkment at high-status residences has also been demonstrated by radiocarbon and strontium isotope analysis of two fallow deer mandibles at Fishbourne, West Sussex (Sykes *et al.* 2006). One dated to A.D. 60 (± 40 years) while the second dated to A.D. 90 (± 40 years). These are currently the earliest, conclusively dated fallow deer remains from Britain (Sykes 2010, 55). Strontium isotope analysis of an early erupting tooth in the A.D. 60 specimen (i.e. within its first eight months of life) gave a non-local signature, and although its precise origin could not be ascertained, it almost certainly lived on the Continent while it was a fawn. Analysis of a later-erupting tooth in the same mandible gave a local signature, which demonstrated that it had been trafficked over some distance before dying at Fishbourne (Sykes *et al.* 2006, 951–3). Significantly, all the teeth analysed from the A.D. 90 specimens gave local signatures, indicating that they derived from a resident breeding population, perhaps one that had been established at Fishbourne 30 or 40 years earlier. Since this study was undertaken, a much larger collection of fallow deer bones has been identified from Fishbourne (Allen 2011).

Any understanding of how these animals were managed in parks is limited due to the relative paucity of known specimens. Elevated nitrogen isotope values (δ^{15}N) from the Fishbourne specimens indicate that they may have been grazing on the salt marshes around Chichester Harbour to the south of Fishbourne (Madgwick *et al.* 2013, 121). Osteometric data suggest that both males and females were kept at Fishbourne and Monkton and there is little evidence for specific selection of either sex (Sykes *et al.* 2011, 162–3). However, the Monkton deer appear to have been particularly small, which prompted Sykes *et al.* (*idem*) to suggest that they were imported from translocated herds in Europe rather than being first-generation animals from Turkey or Greece. This argument is supported by genetic data from the same study. As more fallow deer remains come to light from Roman sites in Britain and beyond, their scientific analysis will undoubtedly improve understanding of how these exotic animals were managed, and will further elucidate patterns in their trade around the empire.

EXOTIC BIRDS

The bones of pheasants (*Phasianus colchius*) and peacocks (*Pavo cristatus*) have been found on Romano-British rural settlements, and are almost certainly imported fauna (Witcher 2013, 9). Pheasants have a natural habitat range stretching from the Pacific Ocean to the Black Sea. They are known in Greece from the fifth century B.C., and are mentioned by Roman writers during the first century A.D. (Poole 2010, 159). It seems likely that, as with fallow deer, pheasants were moved around the empire to furnish private estates. Unfortunately, pheasant bones are exceptionally difficult to distinguish from those of domestic fowl. The surveys of Yalden and Albarella (2009, 107) and Poole (2010) have highlighted eleven Romano-British sites with purported pheasant remains, the majority of which appear to be high-status or urban settlements. None is known from pre-Roman sites. Peacock finds (blue peafowl) are even rarer than pheasants. Toynbee (1973, 250) suggests that the bird was extensively reared in Roman Italy during the late Republic and early Imperial periods. In other provinces, however, peacock bones are exceptionally rare, with Poole (2010, 161, table 10) noting three examples each from Roman Gaul and Britain. Throughout history, peacocks have been kept for the visual splendour of their bright, expansive plumage, and it is possible that this was the reason for their remains being recovered from the villas at Winterton, North Lincolnshire, and Great Stoughton, Cambridgeshire (*ibid.*).

THE CONTEXT OF ANIMAL INTRODUCTIONS

The deliberate introduction of some animals was almost certainly a demonstration of wealth and social power. The sourcing, movement and maintenance of these animals would have required considerable financial investment, with the animals needing to be carefully managed, cared for and fed during their transportation, particularly as some species are sensitive to changes in their local environment.

Once in Britain, animals such as fallow deer and peacocks would have been kept in parks or enclosures from where they could be viewed and enjoyed as spectacles in their own right. The value and expense of their importation suggests that it is very unlikely that these animals would have been simply left to roam the countryside, or used as meat for the table, though some may have been eaten as 'exotic delicacies' at banquets. Perhaps most importantly, the introduction of these new species would have altered the environments and landscapes where they came to reside (Allen and Sykes 2011). These may have been deliberate attempts to demonstrate control and power over the natural world. In this sense, animal introductions should be considered alongside the evidence for wild animal exploitation, a subject to which we now turn.

PEOPLE AND NATURE: THE SOCIAL ROLE OF WILD ANIMALS

Evidence for the exploitation of wild animals in Roman Britain has often been overlooked. The abundance of cattle, sheep, pig and horse remains in most animal bone assemblages usually far outweighs those from non-domestic species, which can give the impression that hunted fauna were of little consequence to Romano-British society (cf. Maltby 2015, 185–6). Traditionally, archaeologists have tended to think about wild animal exploitation as a means of producing meat for the table, with some considering wild resources as a risk-buffering strategy used mostly in times of agricultural stress (e.g. Grant 1981; O'Shea 1989). On the other hand, social anthropologists have often highlighted the cultural and political importance of wild animals, particularly in agricultural societies, where very little food is taken from wild sources (Cartmill 1993; Marvin 2000; Kowalski 2010). In the light of these perspectives, archaeologists are becoming increasingly aware of the potential for understanding past attitudes towards landscapes and social identity through the study of wild animals (Hill 1995a; Hamilakis 2003; Pluskowski 2006; Willis 2007; Sykes 2009; 2014, 51–75; Allen and Sykes 2011; Russell 2012, 144–75; Crummy 2013; Allen 2014).

It is important to recognise that wild animal exploitation can come in a variety of forms. Strictly speaking, hunting is a highly ritualised, symbolic practice, which involves only truly wild animals that are free to run away (i.e. not tame or captive animals), but are killed in a very specific, violent manner (Cartmill 1993, 197; Sykes 2014, 52). This is very different to animal trapping, for example, where the hunter need not be present at the kill. However, if the definition of hunting is restricted to these specific criteria, it arguably accounts for very little animal killing, and does not incorporate the wide range of other activities where animals that are perceived to be wild are caught and slaughtered by people. The problem for archaeologists is that the context of the kill is usually not known. This section examines the evidence for wild animals that would seem to have been hunted, but also considers other activities such as trapping, wildfowling and fishing. As with hunting, these practices would also have had important social and cultural implications.

PERCEPTIONS OF WILD ANIMALS IN THE IRON AGE

Previous studies have highlighted a general lack of wild animal bones on British Iron Age sites (Sykes 2009; Allen and Sykes 2011). This is not restricted to mammals and birds, as a widespread absence of fish bones and marine molluscs has also been noted (Dobney and Ervynck 2007; Willis 2007). In addition, it may be significant that wild plant remains are also comparatively rare, being more often encountered in 'ritual' deposits (Van der Veen et al. 2008; see Lodwick Ch. 5). It is possible that this lack of exploitation reflects an Iron Age, cultural attitude towards nature. That pre-Roman communities perceived wild animals differently from farm animals is evidenced by Caesar's often quoted comment that the Britons abstained from eating hare (as well as fowl and geese), believing that it was 'unlawful' to do so, and that instead they reared them purely for 'pleasure and amusement' (BGall., V. 12). Interestingly, this may point to the possibility that hares were coursed with dogs, but not necessarily eaten, and it was Strabo (Geog. IV.5.3) who famously mentions the export of British hunting dogs to the Continent. The placement of whole or partial skeletons of wild animals in so-called 'structured deposits' has prompted the suggestion that the consumption of wild fauna may have been prohibited or restricted to special events and gatherings (Hill 1995a, 104), while under 'normal' circumstances it may have been considered taboo (King 1991, 17). However, the treatment of different types of wild animals varies. Corvids, such as crows and ravens, and buzzards are more often found in deposits as associated bone groups, a pattern that led Serjeantson and Morris (2011, 101) to suggest that, as scavengers, these birds may have been associated with death and the transition to other realms, particularly if they were commonly witnessed feeding from human bodies left exposed during excarnation rituals (see Ch. 6).

The association of the wilderness with other realms or unfamiliar landscapes is not such a far-fetched idea. It is widely accepted among social anthropologists and cultural geographers that the wilderness is considered by many (non-western) cultures to be a place beyond the domestic sphere, where the 'normal' rules and rhythms of everyday life do not apply (Helms 1993, 153–7; Ingold 2000; Hamilakis 2003, 240). People with the ability to transcend these boundaries are often imbued with special status, with shamans perhaps being the best-known examples of people with supernatural powers, most notably the ability to change shape and to take on the appearance of wild animals (Helms 1993, 211; Willerslev 2004). This takes place when shamans are in the wild. Hunters may also fall into this category and in some societies there may be little difference between them and shamans.

It is, of course, difficult to simply superimpose the ideology of traditional cultures onto British Iron Age society, though there are some clues that suggest similarities existed. Numerous deposits of metalwork, such as coinage and weaponry, were placed in landscape features that may have been considered liminal to the domestic sphere, particularly rivers, bogs and lakes (Creighton 1995, 297–8; Bradley 2000, 159–60; see Ch. 5, p. 130). Similarly, discoveries of Iron Age human remains in watery contexts appear to follow a long-held, later prehistoric tradition of marking boundary points with deposits of human and animal body parts and high-value items (Bradley 2000, 149–50; Madgwick 2008). The idea that watery places were sacred during this period, owing to their association with the dead, may partly explain why fish were largely avoided during this period (Sykes 2014, 65).

This 'mixing' of humans and animals in liminal contexts is also reflected in Iron Age iconography. Aldhouse-Green (2001b) has traced this artistic tradition across Britain and north-western Europe. Perhaps the most famous example comes from the Danish Gundestrup Cauldron, which dates to the second/first century B.C. and depicts an antler-headed man sat cross-legged, holding a snake in one hand and a torc in the other, while being surrounded by a menagerie of wild beasts (Green 1992, 146, fig. 3.3a). Aldhouse-Green (2001b, 225) argues that images of human–animal hybrids were symbolic of boundary-crossing and shamanic practices, involving death, warfare, hunting and healing. Hybridised human/animal iconography continued to be a feature of Romano-British and Gallo-Roman society and there is some evidence that offerings continued to be made in watery contexts (Willis 2007; Rogers 2007; Ch. 5, pp. 162, 186). However, contact with the Roman world brought about certain changes. Examples of ritual iconography begin to be found in cult centres, such as the human-faced dog figurine found at the late Roman healing sanctuary at Lydney Park, Gloucestershire (Wheeler and Wheeler 1932, 45, 89, pl. XXVI, no. 119) rather than in natural settings more often used in the Iron Age. An increase in long-distance trade and exchange in the late Iron Age and early Roman period may have changed some people's concept of distance and geography, while cultural exchange no doubt had some effect on religious attitudes.

PERCEPTIONS OF WILD ANIMALS IN THE ROMAN WORLD

Evidence for hunting and attitudes to wild animals in the Roman Mediterranean is supplemented by classical literature, which traces its roots back to ancient Greek culture (Anderson 1985, 115–25; Lane-Fox 1996). Here, hunting is thought of as a form of military training, where the quarry is representative of a human enemy and the hunting landscape is perceived as a foreign land (Cartmill 1993, 32). A military context was pursued by the Trajanic–Hadrianic emperors, who used hunting as a means of displaying *virtus* (virtue). Domitian, in particular, can be seen in numerous reliefs and carvings slaying many wild beasts (Tuck 2005, 239). Suetonius (*Dom.* 19) also notes that Domitian spent much time in his game park outside Rome, where wild animals were hunted. This imperial hunting imagery was no doubt affiliated with the popularity of the beast hunt in the arena, the *venatio*, where the mass slaughter of wild and exotic animals was carried out for the pleasure of citizens across the empire (Lindstrøm 2010).

Of course, very little of this animal killing can really be defined as hunting under the criteria set out above. This is perhaps best exemplified by Pliny the Younger, who derided many of his contemporaries by claiming that they captured animals, not with spear and lance, but with pen and notebook in hand (*Ep.* 1.6, after Anderson 1985, 100). However, it does appear that imperial hunting was used as a device to demonstrate the mastery of Roman culture over the natural world, and, by implication, over the barbarian world. It is quite different to the Iron Age worldview seen across much of northern Europe prior to and during this period. The expansion of the Roman

Empire into north-west Europe is likely to have witnessed a clash of these varying attitudes towards nature and wild animals. For example, Sykes (2014, 66) notes that changes in burial traditions for some elements of the population from probable excarnation and deposition in watery contexts to cremation and inhumation (see Ch. 6) would have ensured that the dead were no longer accessible to wild animals, an idea that may have been completely abhorrent to a Roman mind-set. A second point worth mentioning is that while some shamanic iconography continued to be produced and viewed in Roman Britain and in Gaul, Roman deities were regarded as dominant over wild animals and were rarely depicted as hybrids (*ibid.*). Indeed, sexual encounters between people and animals, and human–animal transformations were often described as particularly bad for those involved (Gilhus 2006).

As with the Iron Age, wild animal remains generally make up very small proportions of animal bone assemblages from Roman-period sites in Britain (see below). This was picked up by Cool (2006, 116–18), who noted a discrepancy between the lack of wild fauna in the zooarchaeological record and the regular depictions of hunting in Romano-British artwork. Various hunting scenes of horsemen capturing deer, hares and boars, hunters on foot spearing game, and dogs chasing hares are known from ceramics, glass bowls and metalwork. Cool (*ibid.*) argues that these images tend, on the whole, to be late Roman and overtly religious in nature. Certainly, wild animals are commonplace in Orphic imagery, where Orpheus controlled the animals with music (Allen 2014, 183). The context of these images has been argued to have been used as a theatrical element for social encounters in villas and other high-status buildings (Scott 2004, 47–8). Overall, the Romano-British imagery is quite different to the zoomorphic, Iron Age tradition, stressing instead the division between human and animal (Sykes 2014, 66–7).

HUNTING AND TRAPPING

Wild mammal remains commonly represent between 0.5 per cent and 2 per cent of most animal bone assemblages. Overall, there is an increase in the mean percentage of wild mammal bones recovered from rural sites over time, accounting for 0.8 per cent of the mammalian assemblages dating to the late Iron Age compared with 1.3 per cent in the late Roman period (FIG. 4.14a). This is a fairly minimal rise overall, but it can be partly accounted for by the establishment of villas in Britain after the conquest and their increased number during the later Roman period. On average, wild mammal remains from villa sites account for over 3 per cent of faunal assemblages, around three times higher than on most other types of rural settlement (FIG. 4.14b).

Red deer were increasingly exploited over time, accounting for less than 1 per cent on late Iron Age sites, but rising to 1.7 per cent on late Roman sites (FIG. 4.15). In contrast, roe deer bones are recovered in similar quantities over the same period of time, usually around 0.5–0.7 per cent of assemblages. Again, this can be largely put down to the increasing number of villas in the landscape, of which over 75 per cent produce red deer remains (FIG. 4.16). Although roe deer remains do not appear to increase in abundance over time, they also occur more frequently at villas than other types of rural settlement.

Analysis of deer body parts from different settlement types appears to confirm an interest in deer hunting by villa inhabitants (cf. Liversidge 1968, 363–7). Post-cranial bones of red and roe deer are, on average, three times as common as antlers at villas (FIG. 4.17). Comparatively high

numbers of butchered deer bones at some villas, such as Fishbourne, West Sussex (Allen 2011), Shakenoak, Oxfordshire (Cram 2005), and Keston, Kent (Locker 1991), attest to the fact that venison was fairly regularly consumed. Evidence from Fishbourne, in particular, suggests that large stags were especially targeted, perhaps indicating that hunts were well organised and managed (Allen 2014, 176). At most other types of settlement, post-cranial bones and antlers occur in equal quantities, and it is notable that post-cranial bones are generally poorly represented. At farmsteads and villages, antlers tend to outnumber deer bones. Antlers may, of course, derive from hunted deer, but since stags and bucks shed their antlers every year after the rut (the mating season), they can be collected from the countryside for manufacturing into tools and other useful items.

Although deer were the most prolific wild mammal in the majority of faunal assemblages from rural sites in Roman Britain, there is a range of other species represented. Two species of hare

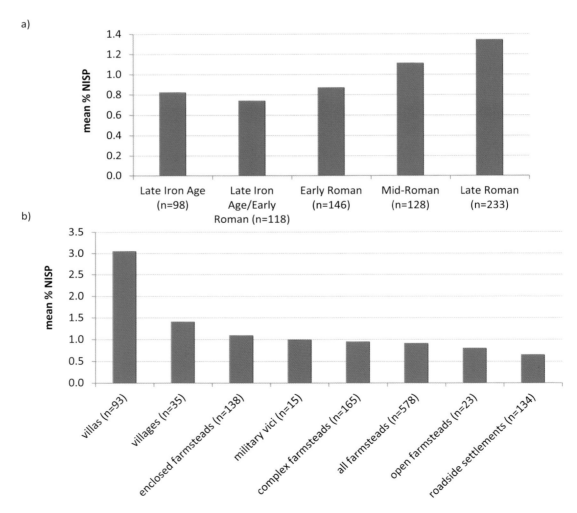

FIG. 4.14. Proportions of wild mammals over time (a) and on different site types (b) (values calculated as the mean percentage of the total mammal assemblage)

were known to the Romans, alongside rabbits: the brown hare *Lepus europaeus* and the mountain hare *Lepus capensis* (Crummy 2013, 111). Although rabbits are often thought to have been introduced during the Roman period (Sykes and Curl 2010), there are as yet no credible examples that have been securely dated (see above, p. 98). Brown hares were probably deliberately imported, and this is now supported by recent DNA evidence, which suggests the establishment of a fairly small, initial group (Stamatis *et al.* 2009). Exactly when

this occurred is not known, but they appear to have been widespread by the Iron Age (Sykes 2014, 56, table 3.1). Mountain hares are native to Britain, though their modern ecological distribution suggests that their primary habitat is largely restricted to colder, upland regions (Yalden 1999, 127). If this was also the case in the past, it is likely that many of the bones found on archaeological sites from the Neolithic onwards are probably from brown hares. As noted above, Caesar's comments suggest that hares may have

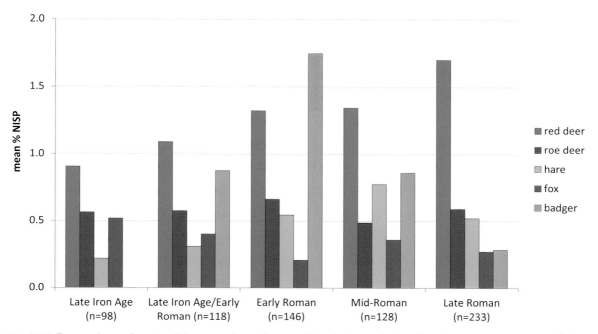

FIG. 4.15. Proportions of main wild mammal species over time (values calculated as the mean percentage of the total mammal assemblage)

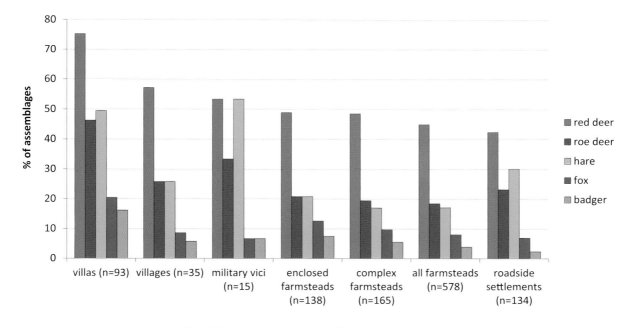

FIG. 4.16. Representation of main wild mammal species at different site types

been revered by late Iron Age communities (Crummy 2013), and it is possible that hare-coursing was a fairly popular pastime during this period, though direct evidence for this is lacking.

Hare bones are fairly frequently found in faunal assemblages throughout the period being examined here, and, as with red deer, they appear to increase in abundance over time. Hare may be under-represented as their bones are small and gracile and fairly fragile. They are morphologically similar to rabbit bones and some misidentification may occur, though hares tend to be much larger, similar in size to domestic cat bones. Again, hares are often found in villa assemblages, though interestingly they are slightly better represented at military *vici*, where they have been identified in over 50 per cent of assemblages, occurring as frequently as red deer, though these data may be partly skewed by a smaller sample size (FIG. 4.16). Hare bones are also better represented at roadside

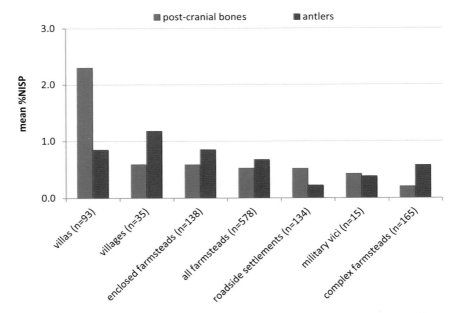

FIG. 4.17. Proportions of red deer and roe deer post-cranial bones and antler specimens at different site types

FIG. 4.18. Mandible from a domestic pig from Roman Chichester, West Sussex (top) and a wild boar mandible from first century A.D. Fishbourne (below) (photo by M. Allen)

settlements compared to farmsteads, where there is a greater disparity between red deer and hare. This general pattern has been observed by Crummy (2013, 115, fig. 7.4) who also noted that hare bones are even more common in major towns, which she put down to continental, dietary influences (*ibid.*, 124).

The high representation of red deer, roe deer and hare at military *vici* may have been partly associated with the activities of the army. King (1999b) has shown that wild animals are particularly well represented at many forts, notably in areas such as north Wales, where their populations may have been more abundant (see also Cool 2006, 112). The Vindolanda tablets provide details of orders for roe venison, destined for the *praetorium* (Bowman 1994, 157), and it appears that Caesar preferred roe deer meat over that from other wild animals (Dalby 2000, 248). The remains of red deer and roe deer haunches and bones of hare and wild boar were recovered from deposits associated with a tribune's house at Caerleon (Hamilton-Dyer 1993, 133). While some army garrisons are known to have kept specialist teams of hunters (*venatores immunes*) and trackers (*vestigiatores*) (Epplett 2001, 217), it is possible that a military desire for meat from hunted mammals created a market for their capture among the local civilian populations linked to the forts.

Epigraphic evidence demonstrates the presence of wild boar in Roman Britain, and that that they were hunted by members of some communities, particularly the military (*RIB* 1041). Zooarchaeologically, however, wild boars are notoriously difficult to distinguish from domestic pigs. Although they tend to be larger, there is considerable variation in the size of the bones from animals from different breeding populations (Albarella *et al.* 2009). Eighteen Romano-British sites report the presence of wild boar, which is typically identified from noticeably large *Sus* bones. The reliability of these identifications may be questionable, though some are more secure than others. FIGURE 4.18 shows a large mandible specimen from Fishbourne, West Sussex, which is almost certainly from a wild boar. The width of the mandible is excessively broad, while the third molar is significantly longer than all other examples found at Fishbourne and nearby Chichester.

Remains of fox and badger are also fairly well represented on Romano-British settlements, being most common at villas (FIG. 4.16). Both of these animals burrow and some finds may be the result of later intrusions. Many remains, however, are found in secure contexts. In some cases, there is clear evidence that these animals were exploited for their fur. A badger skull with cut marks made during skinning was recovered from a Roman well

at Northfleet, Kent (FIG. 4.19), while at Quinton, Northamptonshire, the skeleton of a decapitated badger from a fourth-century A.D. well may also have been killed for its pelt (Friendship-Taylor 1999).

A range of other mustelid species is known from several late Iron Age and Romano-British contexts, including weasels, polecats, pine martens and stoats. As with foxes and badgers, these are generally found in wells and some may also have been exploited for their pelts. Otters and beavers may have been of some economic importance around the Fens, in particular, with beavers appearing to have been intensively exploited at Haddenham V, Cambridgeshire, during the late Iron Age, Serjeantson (2006, 216–17) noting an abundance of hind leg bones, with many exhibiting cut marks. The butchery evidence suggests that the animals may have been eaten as well as exploited for pelts. Otter bones were fairly common in mid-Roman and late Roman features at the Fenland port at Camp Ground, Cambridgeshire, which Higbee (2013), again attributed to a desire for pelts.

Bones from wolves and bears are exceptionally rare from late Iron Age and Roman sites. Though some may have been exploited for their fur, the dangers involved in hunting these animals would have been considerable. Very little is known of the geographic distributions of wolves and bears during this period, though both were almost certainly present in the British Isles (Yalden 1999, 115, 146–7). Wolves became extinct in England by the beginning of the fifteenth century (Pluskowski 2010), while the date of extinction of bears is

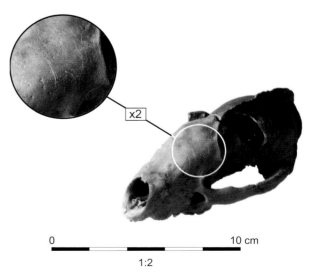

0   10 cm

1:2

FIG. 4.19 Badger skull with cut marks made during skinning from a Roman well at Northfleet villa, Kent (Grimm and Worley 2011, 49, plate 6). Reproduced with permission HS1, © HS1

unknown (Hammon 2010). As with foxes, wolf bones are also difficult to differentiate on the basis of size from those of large domestic dog types, though the length of the lower carnassial tooth tends to separate north European populations rather well (Yalden 1999, 99, fig. 4.6). Animal bone reports that highlight the possible presence of wolf remains draw attention to the identification of particularly large canid bones (e.g. Hamilton 2000b; Clark 2012, 168–9; Higbee 2013).

Bear bones are better represented than those of wolf. At Fullerton villa, Hampshire, three brown bear upper limb bones (a scapula, humerus and ulna) were recovered from a late Roman ditch (Hammon 2008b), while a single bear phalanx, or toe bone, was recovered from an early Roman ditch at Westward House, close to Fishbourne, West Sussex (Allen 2011). Cut marks were present on the bone suggesting that the animal had been skinned, and it is possible that this example was brought to the site as part of a pelt rather than coming from a local animal. Bear claws are fairly common in late Iron Age, high-status burials in northern Europe, suggesting that bear furs were sometimes worn by elites (Meniel 2002), and contemporary examples have been found at Welwyn Garden City and Baldock, Hertfordshire (Hammon 2010, 98). Elsewhere, a bear tibia was recovered from Catterick, North Yorkshire (Stallibrass 2002), and a mandible from Sheepen, Essex (Luff 1985). These are examples that may have been associated with urban or military populations, including a brown bear skull found in a late fourth/early fifth century drain at Drapers Gardens, London (Rielly 2008), and a possible bear humerus found outside the London amphitheatre, which may hint at the use of bears in staged hunts (Bateman 1997, 58). Specialist military bear-trappers, known as *Ursarii*, would have been utilised in some provinces to capture bears and transport them around the empire for amphitheatre displays (Epplett 2001, 214); the appearance of a Caledonian bear in the arena in Rome during Domitian's reign (A.D. 81–96), suggests that *Ursarii* were at work in the British Isles (Mart., *Spect.* 7). It is also worth pointing out that bears had a ritual significance for some Romano-British communities. Deposits of bear amulets made from jet have been found in a number of child burials in Colchester, York and Malton, which Crummy (2010) interpreted as reflecting protective rituals, aimed at guarding the children into the afterlife.

WILD FOWLING AND HAWKING

Wildfowl remains are comparatively rare in most faunal assemblages, although, as with wild mammals, there is a noticeable rise in their relative frequency over time, increasing from 0.2 per cent to 0.7 per cent between the late Iron Age and the late Roman period (FIG. 4.20a). Typically, higher proportions of wildfowl are found at villas, where they occur in nearly two-thirds of assemblages (FIG. 4.20b). At other types of settlements, wildfowl remains are found in 38–46 per cent of faunal assemblages, and in only 20 per cent of military *vici*, though this figure may be affected by a low sample size.

Although wildfowl are exceptionally rare at late Iron Age sites, some sites have produced a large number of corvids, particularly ravens and crows/ rooks (bones of crows and rooks are morphologically indistinct). At Danebury, Hampshire, around one-third of pits containing 'special animal deposits' also produced skeletons of ravens or crows/rooks (Grant 1991, table 6). The special animal deposits tended to contain remains of domestic mammals, usually articulating limbs or other carcass parts, with butchery evidence showing that the meat had been prepared for consumption. Careful reanalysis of the corvid bones, however, showed no evidence of butchery, indicating that none had been eaten by people but, based upon contextual evidence and associated finds, it was argued convincingly that these birds were deliberately placed in the pits (Serjeantson and Morris 2011, 87–9). Danebury appears not to have been an isolated example of this practice, which seems to have occurred across a number of hillforts, *oppida*, and other settlements (*ibid.*, table 4). Interestingly, the practice does not die out with the Roman conquest, and can even be found in several major towns, including Silchester and Dorchester (Dorset), indicating the continuation of an Iron Age tradition in a Romano-British context.

Remains of other wildfowl species are rare in the late Iron Age, and their consumption certainly appears to have been exceptional. The Fen edge, late Iron Age settlement at Haddenham V, Cambridgeshire, produced a high proportion of wildfowl remains from a wide range of species (Serjeantson 2006). Over 40 per cent of all the animal bones at Haddenham V derived from birds, which is much higher than other late Iron Age settlements with notable avian assemblages, including Dragonby, North Lincolnshire (7 per cent; Harman 1996), Danebury, Hampshire (4 per cent; Serjeantson 1991), and Silchester, Hampshire (2 per cent; Serjeantson 2000). This is all the more exceptional given that chicken bones were completely absent. Instead, bones of swan and mallard were particularly abundant and other large birds, such as common crane and pelicans, were also exploited.

Parker's (1988) review of birds in Roman Britain shows the wide variety of species that were

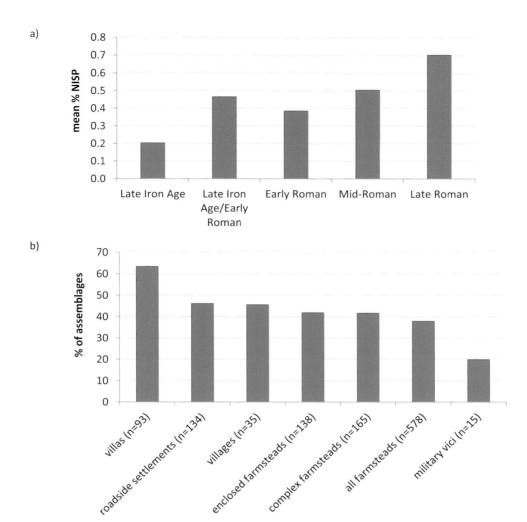

FIG. 4.20. Proportions of wildfowl over time (a) and representation of wildfowl on different site types (b) (graph (a) values calculated as the mean percentage of the total NISP of mammals and birds)

exploited. Ducks and geese were two of the most commonly occurring types of bird found in faunal assemblages (FIG. 4.21). Albarella (2005), however, argues that the low relative frequencies of duck and goose bones found on Roman sites (particularly compared with medieval sites) demonstrates that these birds were not domesticated until well after the Roman period. Woodcock bones have been identified in nearly 12 per cent of assemblages and are fairly common at villas, suggesting that this bird was favoured by some high-status groups. The woodcock is a wader but is frequently found on farmland, particularly where there is hedgerow cover to keep it safe during the day. Today, wildfowlers use beaters to flush woodcocks into the open where they can be shot. Woodcock populations increase in the winter when many migrate from the east to breed. Golden plovers and snipe are also fairly common on Roman sites (Parker 1988, 210–13), and their numbers also increase due to winter migrations. Serjeantson (1998) notes that winter is a traditional time for

wildfowling, and it may be that it became more commonplace within certain sections of Romano-British society.

Parker (1988, 203) notes that a range of wildfowling equipment, including nets, snares and baited traps, could have been used to catch birds. The Vindolanda tablets list a number of snares for swans and nets for ducks and thrushes left by one of the garrisons (Bowman et al. 2003, 47). Presumably, both large and small birds were targeted, including some species not thought acceptable for consumption today. Bow hunting may also have been undertaken. The recovery of a second-century A.D. 'hunting kit' at Turner's Hall Farm, near St Albans in Hertfordshire, included numerous arrowheads of differing sizes and shapes, which presumably were meant for different types of quarry, including small birds (the find is not published, though see Allen 2011, 329–30, fig. 204). It seems likely that elites were wildfowling on their estates, as indicated by the range and quantity of bird bones found at Fishbourne. Wing

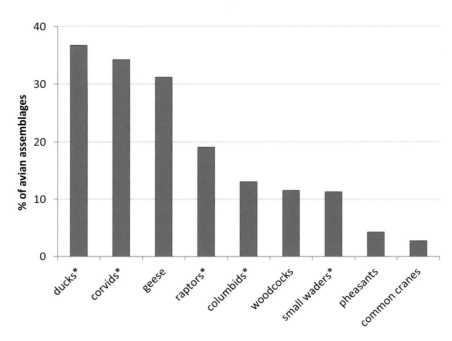

*ducks include mallards, teals, wigeons, pochards, shelducks and tufted ducks
*corvids include crows, rooks, ravens, magpies, choughs and jackdaws
*raptors include buzzards, white-tailed eagles, red kites, peregrine falcons, goshawks, sparrowhawks and kestrels
*columbids include pigeons and dove species
*waders include plovers, coots, lapwings, moorhens, godwits, curlews and snipes

FIG. 4.21. Proportions of different wildfowl taxa found in avian assemblages

TABLE 4.1: NUMBER OF ASSEMBLAGES WITH RAPTOR BONES BY PERIOD

Taxon	mid–late Iron Age	late Iron Age/early Roman	late Roman
Buzzard	16	12	17
White-Tailed Eagle	6	12	5
Red Kite	6	5	6
Peregrine Falcon	1	3	1
Goshawk	2	3	0
Kestrel	2	0	3
Sparrowhawk	0	0	3
Golden Eagle	0	0	1

bones of common crane have been found with numerous butchery marks showing that the meat had been consumed.

Bones from birds of prey (raptors) have also been identified in nearly 20 per cent of bird bone assemblages (FIG. 4.21). Buzzards are the most common bird found on sites between the later Iron Age and the end of the Roman period, followed by white-tailed eagles and red kites (TABLE 4.1). As mentioned above, buzzards were found in many pits at Danebury, and it is possible they too were deliberately deposited in the same way as crows and ravens (Serjeantson and Morris 2011, 101). There is very little evidence that raptors were eaten, though a butchered buzzard bone from Piercebridge and several eagle wing bones with cut marks at Binchester, suggest that consumption may have occurred occasionally (Cool 2006, 115). The use of their feathers may also have been important. The willingness of buzzards and white-tailed eagles to scavenge probably brought them into closer proximity with human settlements, both in rural and urban contexts (Mulkeen and O'Connor 1997, 441–2). It is possible that some bones identified as white-tailed eagle may, in fact, be of its close relative, the golden eagle. The two species can be distinguished on morphological grounds (Yalden and Albarella

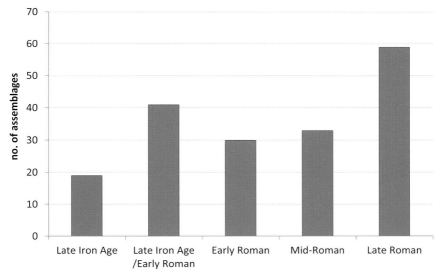

FIG. 4.22. Number of fish bone assemblages over time

2009, 12), though the only known example of the latter comes from the roadside settlement at Bainesse, North Yorkshire (Meddens 2002, 420). Of course, the eagle is often depicted in Roman imagery and sometimes found associated with Jupiter (Durham 2013, 96–100).

There is little evidence that raptors were used for hawking in Roman Britain. However, sparrowhawk remains were found deposited in a third to fourth century A.D. well at Great Holts Farm villa, Essex, alongside bones from numerous thrushes (Murphy *et al.* 2000, 40). Since thrushes are one of the most common prey animals of sparrowhawks, the find raises the possibility that hawking was undertaken here during the late Roman period. Sparrowhawks are certainly very rare in Roman contexts, with the only other known examples coming from the late Roman villa at Barton Court Farm, Oxfordshire (Wilson 1986), and a second-century context at Holme House villa, North Yorkshire (Gidney 2008). There are too few examples to make a conclusive interpretation on the use of sparrowhawks, but their restriction to villas hints at the possibility that they may have been kept by wealthier individuals. The earliest evidence for hawking in Europe comes from the fourth/fifth century A.D. (Prummel 1997). The fourth-century 'small hunt' mosaic at Piazza Armerina in Sicily depicts the use of a raptor as a decoy bird, perhaps used for hare coursing or for driving small birds, rather than conventional falconry (Parker 1988, 205). Certainly, sparrowhawks are not known to scavenge and there is no evidence that they were eaten, so the idea that they were used for hawking as part of late Roman elite practices is not unreasonable.

FISHING

Dobney and Ervynck's (2007) study of late Iron Age fish exploitation in England, Belgium and the Netherlands highlighted a genuine lack of evidence for marine and riverine exploitation in the North Sea region. They point to issues of poor preservation, of shallow contexts on rural settlements, and inconsistent sampling of features having an effect on this pattern. It is true that fish remains suffer from retrieval bias far more than mammal and bird bones. On sites where environmental flotation has been employed, one in three have produced fish bones, which compares to less than one in ten where wet-sieving is absent. Nonetheless, a substantial number of fish bone assemblages are now available from late Iron Age and Romano-British sites that invite further analysis. Although there have been studies of Iron Age and Roman fish remains (Dobney and Ervynck 2007; Locker 2007), rarely have changing patterns of fish exploitation and consumption between the two periods been considered.

The number of rural fish assemblages increases over time, from less than 20 in the late Iron Age to nearly 60 in the late Roman period (FIG. 4.22). This chronological shift is brought into sharper focus when the average number of fish bones per site is considered (FIG. 4.23). Although nearly 20 late Iron Age sites have produced fish bones, these generally only amount to a few isolated fragments, which supports Dobney and Ervynck's (2007, 409) assertion that this was a period when 'fish, it would seem, were hardly exploited'. In the Roman period, there is a greater abundance of fish remains on rural settlements, and, by the third/fourth century, average numbers exceed 100 specimens. Considerable quantities of freshwater fish were recovered from the Fen edge inland port at Camp Ground, Cambridgeshire, while small marine fish were also recovered from the nearby farmstead at Langdale Hale; at both sites, large-scale sampling of contexts was undertaken (Higbee 2013).

The data would suggest that changing attitudes to the consumption of fish were occurring soon after the Roman conquest. By the late Roman period, fish-eating may have been considered fairly normal in some areas, if perhaps only irregularly. Cool (2006, 105) notes that fish would have formed a comparatively small part of the diet in towns, and may have been considered a luxury. The range of species found includes both marine and freshwater taxa. This observation is also supported by Locker's (2007) more wide-ranging study of fish in Roman Britain, which is notably dominated by data from towns, particularly London, where large numbers of bones from sieved samples have been examined. In London there is evidence that fish sauce, or *garum*, was being produced, not necessarily from imported fish, such as Spanish mackerel, but from species caught locally, perhaps from the Thames Estuary (*ibid.*, 152). Dobney *et al.* (1999) note the abundance of bones of sand eels and small clupeids (herring sp.) in late Roman contexts at Lincoln waterfront, and in York at St Mary Bishophill, finds that they attribute to local *garum* production, while there is also evidence for fish sauce production from Dorchester, Dorset (Trevarthen 2008).

Fish-hooks have been found at Fishbourne (Allen 2011, 329, fig. 203), Chichester (Down 1979, 200–1) and Portchester (Cunliffe 1975,

212–13), suggesting that the coastal estuaries of Hampshire and West Sussex were being exploited. However, evidence for fish-processing is far less common in the countryside. Considerable quantities of bones from small marine fish retrieved from a well in a complex farmstead at Langdale Hale, Cambridgeshire, were suggested to be the result of *garum* production (Ingrem 2013, 133), as was a mass of small fish bones from a single deposit in the late Roman salt-making site at Stanford Wharf, Essex, on the Thames Estuary (Biddulph *et al.* 2012, 171). At the early Roman salt-making site at Scotney Court, Kent, a large number of halibut and haddock bones were recovered from a single pit, with many including knife-filleting marks suggesting that the fish were being strung for salting (Barber 1998). A wicker-work basket found in a clay-lined 'tank' at Claydon Pike, Gloucestershire, contained the remains of several species of beetle (Elmidae sp.) that are known to frequent fast-flowing freshwater (Robinson 2007, 206). The basket had presumably been placed in a local stream, perhaps as a fish-trap, where the beetles were able to clamber inside, and, once fish had been caught, they were taken back to the settlement to be retained in the tank where the basket was found. The excavators went further, suggesting that a small hypocaust room at the site was used as a smoke-house for preserving fish (finds of pierced cattle scapulae suggest that shoulders of beef were being smoked at the site) (Miles *et al.* 2007, 175; Sykes 2007, 204; Allen 2017, 121).

The frequency of faunal assemblages with fish bones varies markedly between different regions (FIG. 4.24). Fish exploitation appears to have been most common in the South and South-West,

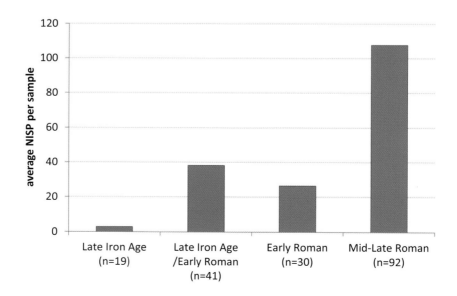

FIG. 4.23 Average number of fish bones per site over time

becoming less frequent further north and into Wales. This pattern may be partly due to soil acidity in the north and in Wales. The South-West region is poorly represented by animal bone assemblages but has a high proportion of sites with fish bones. This may partly reflect a small sample size. Sites with fish bones in this region are, perhaps unsurprisingly, coastal. Particularly high numbers of fish have been recovered from two sites on the Isles of Scilly at Bryher (Johns 2006) and Halangy Down, St Mary's (Ashbee 1996). Both sites also produced exceptional numbers of marine molluscs and bones of sea birds, indicating fairly intensive exploitation of coastal resources. Similar evidence derives from coastal sites on the mainland in Cornwall, Devon and Dorset. At Royal Manor Arts College, Portland, Dorset, excavations over 0.1 ha with very little environmental sampling produced almost 800 fish bones. A wide range of species was identified from the site, including bream, cod, pollock, bass, scad, wrasses, and conger eel, among others (Maltby 2009; Maltby and Hamilton-Dyer 2012). That marine fish were traded to sites further inland, however, is indicated by the recovery of flatfish (plaice or flounder), sea bream and scad in excavations in the suburbs of the walled town at Ilchester in Somerset (Locker 1999).

In the North region, fish bones derive almost exclusively from military *vici*. This could be due to the comparatively deeper stratigraphy at these sites, which may have aided preservation, though it could also relate to links to the military supply network, if fish were being brought in for the army as a food source. However, Locker (2007, 147–8) notes that forts generally produce very little fish bone, even where sampling has been carried out. It is possible, therefore, that fish was reserved for higher-ranking officers.

Variation in the size of fish bone samples between different site types suggests that consumption may have been related to social status and dietary fashions. Villas consistently produce larger fish-bone assemblages than other rural settlements (FIG. 4.25). Imported Spanish mackerel were identified from first/second-century A.D. deposits at Gorhambury villa, Hertfordshire, and probably represent Mediterranean tastes (Locker 1990). At Fishbourne, over 160 fish bones were recovered from a single, late first/early second-century ditch fill (Allen 2011, 97). Most of these could have been caught in the local estuary, though there is good evidence that flatfish were targeted, while eel, bass and mullet were also fairly well represented. The deposit appears to represent the remains of a feast. Of the 487 fish bones recovered at Tarrant Hinton villa, Dorset, 97 per cent were from late Roman deposits, while the remaining 3 per cent were early Roman (Graham 2006). Both Ballan wrasse and sea bream were identified, species that can be found in southern British waters between April and July, and may have been brought up from fisheries in Poole Harbour around 20 km to the south. The same

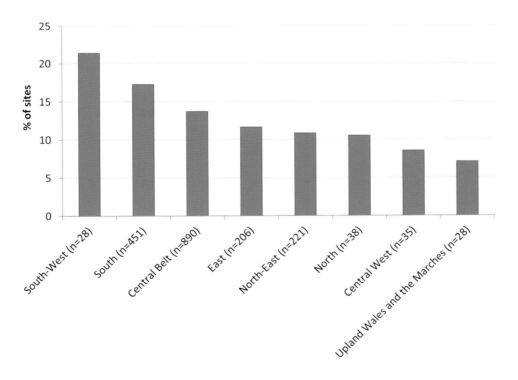

FIG. 4.24. Percentage of sites with fish bones present in faunal assemblages by region

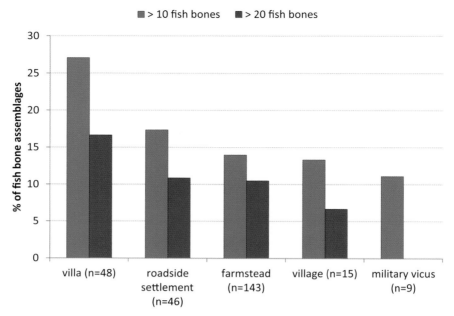

FIG. 4.25. Percentage of assemblages with more than 10 and 20 fish specimens from different site types

fisheries may have supplied the nearby villa at Bucknowle, where sampling produced over 400 late Roman fish bones, with lower quantities coming from early deposits (Light and Ellis 2009).

Excavations at another Dorset villa at Halstock produced evidence for managed water-systems, utilising a local natural spring, which was modified in the third century A.D. to supply an ornamental pond and 'control' tanks within the main courtyard (Lucas 1993). Unfortunately, no environmental sampling was undertaken to recover fish bones, though the structural evidence indicates that fish may have been kept in the garden. A similar water-management system was also identified in the purported 'southern garden' at Fishbourne, though whether this was to supply ponds or other ornamental garden features with water is uncertain (Cunliffe et al. 1996; Allen and Sykes 2011, 19). Other possible ponds associated with fish-keeping have been identified at the villas at Shakenoak, Oxfordshire (Cram 2005), Claydon Pike, Gloucestershire (see above), and Bancroft, Milton Keynes (Williams and Zeepvat 1994). Hurst (2016) has recently surveyed the evidence for ponds in Roman Britain, though very few have been interpreted as being used for fish.

While the evidence for fish-keeping in Britain is sparse, it is worth noting its popularity as an elite past-time in Roman Italy. The construction of fishponds on villa estates was common at continental villas dating to the first centuries B.C. and A.D., in which a number of species are known to have been kept (Bergmann 1994, 50). Varro (Res Rust. 3.17.2–3) also notes that saltwater pisciculture was the reserve of the elite, perhaps due to the

investment required for constructing water channels from the sea or estuaries. Thomas and Wilson (1994, 166–7) detail the logistics involved in these ancient practices. Garden ponds were deliberately flooded in order to support saltwater fish: '...while he was building he became so enthused that he allowed the architect to run a tunnel from his ponds to the sea so that the tide might run to the pond and back to the sea twice a day and cool off the ponds' (Varro, Res Rust. 3.17.9). According to Columella (Rust. 8.16–7), the piscinarii of the late Republic are not to be seen as simply fanciful features but a deliberate elaboration of villa fashions, and the development of coastal fishponds was integrated into the philosophy of the elite pastoral villa (Purcell 1994, 158).

SHELLFISH EXPLOITATION

Oysters are often thought of as one of the most quintessential of Roman foods. Although they are frequently found in large quantities on Roman sites, rarely are they examined and reported in sufficient detail (see FIG. 4.26 for distribution of all marine shell, but mostly oyster, on rural sites from current project). It is thus very difficult to assess their distribution and quantity accurately on a regional or chronological basis. Cool (2006, 106–8) similarly lambasts the situation as frustrating. She highlights the work of Winder (1992), whose studies have shown that much can be gained from more detailed analysis, most notably in detecting the locations of oyster beds. Some specialists have been able to provide insights into the movement of oysters from their tidal beds to major towns (Cool 2006, 107), such as shellfish

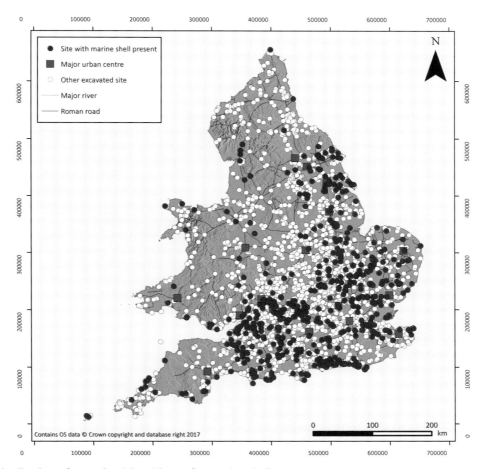

FIG. 4.26. Distribution of records with evidence for marine shell

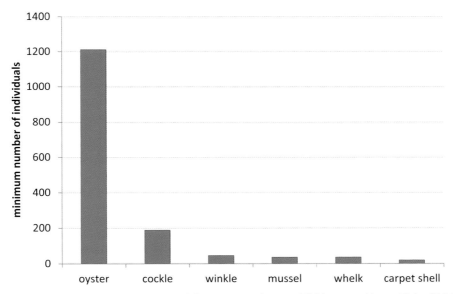

FIG. 4.27. Quantities of marine molluscs recovered from excavations at Fishbourne (Area C) in 2002 (all phases – data from Somerville and Bonell 2006, 95, table 6)

at Silchester, which came from the south coast (Somerville 1997, 135–9), while those eaten at Leicester travelled over longer distances from the Thames Estuary (Monckton 1999, 340). Unfortunately, the lack of consideration given to oysters by archaeologists is true of all marine molluscs; if oyster exploitation and its role in the Romano-British diet is to be fully understood it must be compared to other taxa via quantitative analysis.

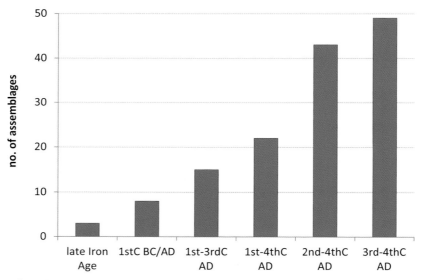

FIG. 4.28. Number of marine mollusc assemblages over time in south-west England

Shellfish no doubt flourished around the British coastline during the Iron Age and could have been a very useful food source during certain times of the year. In this period, however, marine molluscs only tend to be found at coastal sites, and are comparatively sparse inland. Willis (2007, 111–12) notes that even at coastal settlements shellfish would have provided only a small contribution to the Iron Age diet. There appears to have been little evidence for the selection of particular mollusc species in Iron Age assemblages. Excavations at Rookery Hill, Bishopstone, East Sussex, for example, produced large quantities of mussels, limpets and periwinkles among other species, including a crab claw from a late Iron Age ditch (Bell 1977). Oysters were recovered, but did not become more common until the Roman phase of occupation, and this also appears to have been the case at other Iron Age sites that continued to be occupied post-conquest.

Early traces of a cultural ('Romanised') preference for oysters over other species are detectable in an assemblage recovered from a pre-conquest ditch at Fishbourne, West Sussex (Somerville 2005, 91; Sykes 2005, 84). Shellfish continued to be eaten at the site over the next 350 years and it is clear that oysters were selected over other species (FIG. 4.27; see also Somerville and Bonell 2005). Analysis of the morphology of the Fishbourne oyster shells suggests that they were being managed locally in shallow waters, so that the beds could be exploited on a regular basis (Somerville and Bonell 2006, 96).

Using the south-west of England as a case study area, it is possible to detect the increasing exploitation of marine molluscs over time, both in terms of the regional distribution of shellfish and the growing discrimination in favour of oyster over

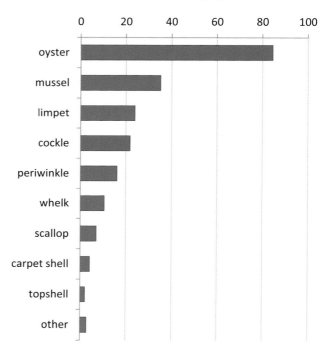

FIG. 4.29. Frequency of different marine mollusc taxa in south-west England

other species. The case study area extends beyond the project's South-West region of Cornwall and Devon to include the counties of Dorset, Somerset, Wiltshire and Gloucestershire. Based only on the number of dated marine shell assemblages recovered from the area, it is clear that the exploitation of shellfish as a food source increased over time (FIG. 4.28). Oysters were by far the most common species identified, being found in nearly 85 per cent of mollusc assemblages (FIG. 4.29). Mussels were the next best-represented species,

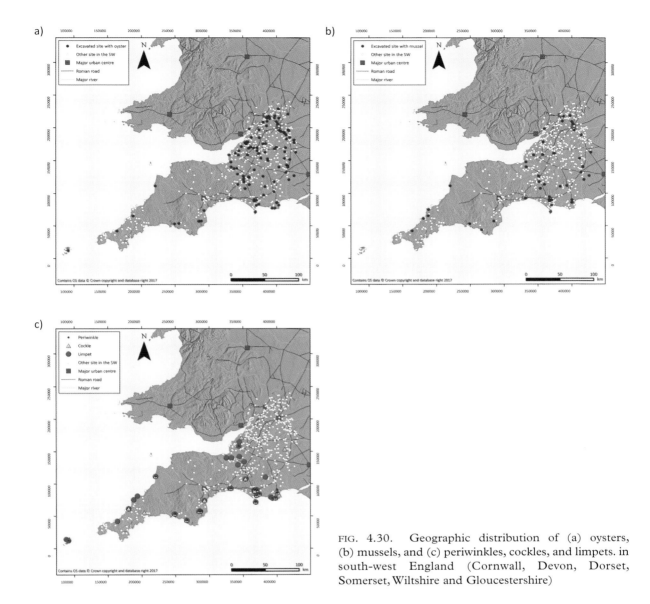

FIG. 4.30. Geographic distribution of (a) oysters, (b) mussels, and (c) periwinkles, cockles, and limpets. in south-west England (Cornwall, Devon, Dorset, Somerset, Wiltshire and Gloucestershire)

occurring in 35 per cent of assemblages, and these were followed by limpet, cockle and periwinkle, which occurred in 16–24 per cent of assemblages. Other species included scallops, whelks and carpet shells, all of which are edible. Unfortunately, it was not possible to quantify individual assemblages for comparative analysis, though the available data suggest that oysters become more frequently targeted after the Roman conquest. It is notable that sites with oysters are fairly evenly distributed between coastal and inland areas in the region (FIG. 4.30). It is important to consider the increased soil acidity of Devon and Cornwall, which provides unfavourable conditions for shell preservation and undoubtedly biases their distribution towards the eastern half of the case study area. Nonetheless, it is instructive to compare the distribution of different mollusc species. Mussels are also found at inland sites, but not to the same extent as oysters. Cockles and winkles are found at coastal sites and

at a few inland sites, notably between Ilchester, Somerset, and Dorchester, Dorset, while periwinkles are completely restricted to the coast. The varied distribution of different mollusc species suggests that most taxa were being exploited close to the coast, though only oysters and, to a lesser extent, mussels appear to have been desired by the inhabitants of inland settlements, with all the transport costs that this would bring.

Compared to molluscs, there is a notable lack of evidence for the consumption of crustacea. Crab remains are recorded at three sites, including the late Iron Age phase at Rookery Hill, Bishopstone, East Sussex (Bell 1977), Atlantic Road, Newquay, Cornwall (Reynolds 2001) and Holme House villa, North Yorkshire (Harding 2008). Only one site in the database, the villa at Magor Farm, Illogan, Cornwall, records the presence of lobster claws (O'Neill 1933), which may reflect the consumption of a locally caught delicacy.

The synthesis presented above is restricted by the available data. However, evidence for the exploitation of marine and estuarine resources will benefit from standardised sampling strategies and an increasing recognition of the potential for the analysis and quantification of mollusc remains. Only with an improved dataset can the importance of marine resources be more fully considered in terms of the Romano-British economy and social attitudes to the consumption of shellfish.

CONCLUSIONS

Human–animal relationships in Roman Britain were wide-ranging. People certainly came into contact with a considerable number of animal species, far more than could be covered here, and it is clear that these interactions extended far beyond the simple need to produce food. As stated at the beginning of this chapter, zooarchaeological studies that focus solely on the productive capabilities of animals restrict us to a very small part of the human–animal relationship. By drawing upon a range of zooarchaeological data, alongside material culture, iconographic and documentary evidence, it is possible to move discussion beyond the economy to consider people's attitudes to animals, reflecting the cultural diversity of Roman Britain.

Cattle are an interesting case study for understanding aspects of late Iron Age and Romano-British society. By far the most important animal in the Romano-British economy, cattle became steadily more common than other livestock species, at least from the second century A.D. onwards, and their remains are found in large quantities at towns and military sites. The growth in cattle numbers was in response to a widespread expansion of arable agriculture across southern and central England, as indicated by changing patterns of cattle slaughter. In the late Iron Age, a relatively high proportion of immature cattle were slaughtered at rural sites, whereas in the Roman period cattle more often lived to adult and elderly ages (Allen 2017, 110, fig. 3.34). Older cattle are often a sign of an increased emphasis on traction, but it also reflects a change in the way that people and cattle were living together. It is possible that the culling of young cattle in the Iron Age was due to feasting, where livestock are utilised as a form of wealth, only to be slaughtered during social exchanges, such as bridewealth, to settle differences, or to cement client–patron relations. There is a wide range of anthropological literature that discusses these phenomena in many societies where animals are kept as stores of wealth (cf. Russell 2012, 297–357). That this was the case in the Iron Age finds some support from Tacitus (*Germ.* 5) who talks of the Celts of northern Europe keeping large numbers of cattle as a reflection of their wealth and status (Green 1992, 14). Animals of such value are unlikely to be slaughtered frequently, and such an event may only be reserved for gatherings and seen as a sacrifice.

After the conquest, it seems likely that socio-political changes concerning matters such as land tenure, urbanisation, and military supply, affected the way that rural communities were organised and how they engaged with each other. The lack of evidence for immature cattle slaughter may be a sign of such change. By switching to 'beasts of burden' in areas where arable expansion was occurring, cattle may have become less important as stores of social wealth. It has been hypothesised in this chapter that cattle became a shared resource between Romano-British households in order to undertake the work needed to produce enough grain to supply the estate and eventually the army (see also Allen and Lodwick 2017). Signs of foot pathologies appear to reflect the increasing pressures being placed on plough cattle. However, this should not necessarily be seen as a reduction in animal welfare, as the human bone evidence also indicates that some rural folk had to work harder and suffered alongside their cattle (see Ch. 7). In the Roman period, cattle were generally living longer and were probably spending more time toiling in the fields with people. Armstrong Oma (2010, 181) argues that plough animals and their handlers build up years of trust through the mutual rhythms of their daily movements. Rather than thinking of cattle as commodities in these contexts, it is perhaps more likely that farmers and cattle were able to build up stronger social bonds. It is only when cattle reached the end of their productive life that they were sent to urban or military markets, and it is here that the evidence for intensive butchery patterns has become evident, reflecting the commodification of meat and a lack of mutual respect between people and domestic animals. It is in the towns, forts and villas where attitudes toward livestock, including sheep, goats, pigs and horse, may have been quite different to elsewhere in the countryside.

The symbolism of animals is an important element of human–animal relationships. The frequent use of horse imagery by late Iron Age elites is testament to the social role this animal played in demonstrating power and political identity. It seems likely that the physical attributes of the animal, its speed and strength, contributed to its position as an icon, and horse images may have played a significant role in the creation of mythologies. However, the Roman conquest brought about changes in human–equid relationships. Zooarchaeological evidence has demonstrated that horses increased in size during the Roman period (Allen 2017, 129–30), perhaps reflecting variously a demand of the military and the *cursus publicus* for larger horses, a need for animals that could withstand harder workloads on the farm, and, perhaps, for larger, faster animals for the arena. Horses may have become particularly revered in some urban quarters as chariot-racers, and these animals were probably afforded higher quality care and maintenance than many of those on rural settlements.

Differences between rural and urban environments may have influenced perceptions of dogs and cats. As with other animals, there is good evidence for more intensive breeding of dogs after the Roman conquest. This development may have been undertaken for a variety of reasons, though it is difficult to establish the specific reasons why dogs were kept by people. The appearance of small 'lapdogs' is often cited as representing pampered pets, though small working animals may also have been important on farmsteads and no less cared for, as suggested by the ceremonious burials afforded to some dogs on rural settlements. Greater incidences of pathologies in dog skeletons found in urban deposits suggests that stray populations were probably fairly widespread in towns. Instances of broken bones and cracked skulls suggest that these animals came in for some particularly tough treatment at the hands of townspeople.

Changing perceptions of the natural world are also hinted at through the zooarchaeological evidence for animal introductions and the exploitation of wild fauna. The importation of fallow deer and exotic birds certainly points to the establishment and maintenance of parks and gardens. Deer hunting and wildfowling appear to have become more common in the Roman period, alongside an increase in fishing and in the consumption of shellfish. In other societies, where increased exploitation of wild resources is seen, it is usually consistent with political changes where there is an increased emphasis on landed wealth (e.g. Wickham 1994). Under Roman law, hunting of wild animals was restricted on private land (McLeod 1989), and it may be that deer hunting became a means of expressing land rights. At sites of exceptional high status, the introduction of exotic species, such as fallow deer, and the establishment of parks, only served to further articulate notions of status and wealth. This marks a very clear change in ideology from the Iron Age worldview, where wild animals appear to have been viewed with reverence. Iron Age iconography suggests that the wilderness was cosmologically separate from the domestic sphere, and only those with supernatural powers were able to cross such boundaries and engage with animals on the other side (Aldhouse-Green 2001b). The introduction of wild animal enclosures, fish ponds and, indeed, formal gardens in the Roman period, marks a very different attitude to the way in which the natural world could be approached and treated (Allen and Sykes 2011, 20).

CHAPTER 5

RELIGION AND THE RURAL POPULATION

By Alexander Smith

With contributions by Martyn Allen, Tom Brindle and Lisa Lodwick

INTRODUCTION

First sprinkle the ground with water, and sweep it, and decorate the sheepfold with leaves and branches, and hide the festive door with a trailing garland. Make dark smoke with pure burning sulphur, and let the sheep bleat, in contact with the smoke. Burn male-olive wood, and pine, and juniper fronds, and let scorched laurel crackle in the hearth. Let a basket of millet keep the millet cakes company: The rural goddess particularly loves that food. Ovid, *Fasti*, book 4

That religious thoughts and practices pervaded all aspects of rural life in the Roman world is demonstrated by a number of ancient poets and authors, including Ovid's account of the *Paralia* festival, excerpted above, and Seneca's description of caves, springs, rivers and woods imbued with a divine presence (cf. Rives 2007, 89–92). However, it remains very difficult to attempt any reconstruction of the religious experiences of those residing in the countryside (North 2005), and, of course, the accounts of classical authors are firmly rooted in the Mediterranean, with perhaps minimal relevance to the situation in Roman Britain. Nevertheless, the wealth of archaeological evidence from this province does enable some considerable insight to be gained into ritual practices, even if the motivations and beliefs behind these actions remain more elusive. Furthermore, as Hingley has recently reiterated (2011), the use of archaeology enables us to draw away from a study of religion that is focused upon the elite perspectives of classical writings, and instead focus on the religious activities of a broader section of society.

This chapter presents a review of the archaeological evidence for religious practice in the late Iron Age and Romano-British countryside, including the different sites and structures interpreted as being sacred in nature, the varied material culture, animal remains and plant remains associated with ritual activities, and the nature of ritual deposition in both ostensibly 'sacred' and 'secular' contexts, as far as these can be differentiated. Throughout these analyses, the geographical and chronological variations in cult practice will be highlighted, in order to assess the degree of continuity and regionality in religious expression, subjects that have been repeatedly highlighted in recent literature on the subject (e.g.

Derks 1998, 181–2; Ghey 2007, 19; King 2007a; Revell 2007, 226; Adams 2009, 115; Hingley 2011; Garland 2013, 195; Atkinson and Preston 2015, 91; Rose 2016).

The nature of this archaeological evidence, discussed in more detail below, is such that the emphasis of analysis remains firmly on the practice and context of religious acts, as opposed to beliefs and doctrines. Indeed, such a 'practice-centred' approach to religion seems entirely appropriate to the Roman world, where orthopraxy – ensuring the 'correct' religious actions such as sacrifice and offering – appears to have been more important to ensure civic and cosmic stability than orthodoxy – ensuring 'correct' beliefs – at least until the rise of Christianity in the fourth century A.D. (Frankfurter 2006, 557; though see below, p. 182).

ARCHAEOLOGICAL EVIDENCE FOR RELIGIOUS PRACTICE

With only the occasional ancient written source touching upon religious aspects (cf. Ireland 2008, 167–204), and relatively few religious inscriptions away from military zones (with some stark exceptions; see below p. 180), we are left with an extensive and often bewildering array of archaeological evidence with which to reconstruct ritual practices in late Iron Age and Roman Britain. The well-known difficulties of identifying religious ritual in the archaeological record have been discussed at length elsewhere (e.g. Renfrew 1994; Hill 1995a; Whitehouse 1996; Morris 2011; Chadwick 2012; 2015; Garrow 2012), and are touched upon in all of the sections below. Even in cases where the interpretation of ritual activity and/ or locations does seem more unequivocal, there will still be many aspects of the 'religious experience' that remain largely unknown, including specific sights, sounds and smells, that, from analysis of contemporary religions, are certain to have played crucial roles in peoples' perceptions of cult and the divine (Chryssides and Geaves 2014, 58). As Rives (2007, 1) has lamented with regard to an overview of Roman religion in the empire, it is like putting together a jigsaw when most of the pieces are missing, and the pieces we do have can fit together in many ways. Nevertheless, there are new approaches developing to the archaeology of religion, notably highlighted in Raja and Rüpke's edited volume, *A Companion to the Archaeology of Religion in the Ancient World* (2015), where the concept of *Lived Religion*, a contemporary, ethnographic framework for understanding people's religious beliefs, practices, and experiences, is being utilised to study aspects of ancient religions.

Perhaps the most consistently studied aspect of religion in the archaeological record is that of sacred space – the shrines, temples and other places in the landscape where there appears to have been a close connection with the supernatural (cf. Carmichael *et al.* 1994). Such sacred sites have been the subject of much academic attention, both in the wider Roman world (e.g. Orlin 2002; Stamper 2005) and in Roman Britain (e.g. Lewis 1966; Woodward 1992; Smith 2001; King 2007a), though the present study has demonstrated that the range of sites appears far more diverse than most previous accounts have indicated, notwithstanding the major problems of interpretation (see below).

In many cases, the interpretation of sacred sites relies upon a recognition of religious qualities in the associated material culture, either intrinsically (e.g. religious figurines or inscriptions; see Bird 2011) or in the quantities, types and contexts of objects recovered. Analyses of these artefacts can inform on the nature of rituals and other activities within sacred sites, and, on rare occasions, provide a glimpse into the types of gods worshipped, the religious attendants, and even the aspirations and concerns of the religious supplicants. Perhaps even more important, analysis of 'ritual' material culture away from shrines and temples can reveal crucial insights into the levels of religiosity inherent in peoples' everyday lives, in the fields, farms, and nucleated settlements of Roman Britain.

It is, of course, not just material culture that aids in our understanding of religious ritual. The extract from Ovid's account of the *Paralia* festival presented at the start of this chapter provides a striking demonstration of the role that plants and animals could play in Roman religious life. The mass of developer-funded excavation data of the past 25 years in England and Wales has led to a greatly increased corpus of environmental remains that appear to have been associated with ritual activity, and brings with it the potential to enhance further our understanding of Iron Age and Romano-British religious practices. This is particularly the case with faunal remains, with large assemblages from some temple sites representing both ritual feasting and selective deposition (King 2005), and animal bones from settlement contexts forming prominent elements within many 'structured deposits' (Maltby 2010a; Morris 2011; see below pp. 192 and 199).

Overall, the evidence from archaeological features, material culture and environmental remains, occasionally supplemented by epigraphy, can provide considerable insights into certain types of religious ritual, and the contexts within which they were performed. This evidence appears to cover a broad social spectrum, from those residing in modest farmsteads to elaborate villa complexes, though geographically it is heavily biased towards the south and east. Any understanding of religious ritual further north and west in the province is hampered by the relative lack of material culture and poor survival of plant and animal remains, but there were also undoubtedly genuine regional differences in the mechanisms of religious expression.

DEFINITIONS AND INTERPRETATIONS

Throughout this chapter a range of terms will be used to describe various aspects of religion in Iron Age and Roman Britain, and it is worth noting here how some of these are being defined, along with an account of the main issues involved with their interpretation in the archaeological record.

Sacred space

Sacred space in general can cover a very broad spectrum of structures and places, and the present author has previously used the wide definition of 'a place subject to a range of regulations regarding people's behaviour to it, based upon a set of beliefs in a supernatural identity' (Smith 2001, 6). In the Roman Rural Settlement Project database, sacred sites have been divided into 'Romano-Celtic temple' and 'shrine'. The characteristics of the former will be outlined below (p. 132), while the latter covers a very broad range of sites and structures, and should not be viewed as homogeneous; it is essentially a 'catch-all' term for all rural sacred sites, or at least those interpreted as such, that are not defined as Romano-Celtic temples.

It is in the interpretation of the 'shrine' category that most ambiguity arises, and so this will now be examined in more detail. There has been a large increase in the incidence of structures or places suggested as Roman shrines within archaeological publications in recent years, with *c.* 80 per cent of the 224 records from the current project dating after 1990. Much of this is simply due to the general upsurge in archaeological activity from this time, with many more Roman rural sites being excavated (see Smith *et al.* 2016, 2, fig. 1.1), but there also appears to have been a genuine increased appreciation of the broad range of features that could have functioned as shrines when examined in a fully contextualised manner. Of course the degree of certainty with regard to the religious interpretation of these sites varies tremendously, with a recently published example from Mucking in Essex (Lucy and Evans 2016) providing a prime example. Here, a rectangular gully, 4 × 4.6 m, enclosed (and was partially cut by) a penannular gully, 3.3 m in diameter, with both entrances aligned (FIG. 5.1). There was no obvious function for this arrangement, and the authors of the report suggested, 'it is possible that together these constitute some kind of minor shrine setting' (*ibid.*, 99). Although such an interpretation is perfectly feasible, the lack of any other corroborating evidence necessitates caution, and there are many other similar examples across England and Wales, of late Iron Age and Roman date.

In order to obtain a more robust interpretative platform for analysis in this volume, those structures or places suggested as shrines have been divided into three categories, based upon four criteria that have been used in reports as positive indicators of a religious nature. The first of these criteria is an association with finds of a particular type (e.g. religious object; see below), or quantity, such as an unusual concentration of coins and/or brooches. Second is the association with one or

more structured or placed deposits, although, as discussed below (pp. 123 and 182), such deposits are also relatively widespread in general settlement contexts. Third is an interpretation based upon morphology or characteristics of the structure, either the fact that it appears 'unusual' within a contemporary domestic context, or that it resembles another place/structure that has a more robust interpretation as a shrine. The dangers of using purely morphological criteria to identify religious sites have been previously expressed (Smith 2001, 15–16), yet, as discussed below, the fact that a site or feature looks 'a bit out of place' remains a relatively common parameter in the identification of shrines. The final criterion is concerned with the general context of the 'shrine', with factors including a direct stratigraphic/spatial relationship with more certain sacred sites (usually an Iron Age feature underlying a later Roman temple), position within an otherwise open area of the settlement, and association with a prominent landscape feature (hill, spring, rock outcrop etc.) or earlier monument.

Each of these criteria by themselves may leave a great deal of room for uncertainty, though when found in combination they provide stronger levels of interpretation. FIGURE 5.2 presents the three different categories of shrine according to the four criteria just outlined. Category 1 shrines generally conform to three or more of the criteria, with almost all containing a significant associated finds signature and over 80 per cent having one or more structured deposits. An example from Haddenham in Cambridgeshire, near the junction of the River Great Ouse and the peat Fens, originated in the second century A.D. as an octagonal masonry-footed building and another associated building on the site of an earlier Bronze Age barrow, set within a ditched enclosure (Evans and Hodder 2006).

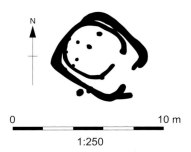

N

0   10 m

1:250

FIG. 5.1. Plan of possible shrine within Romano-British village at Mucking, Essex (Lucy and Evans 2016)

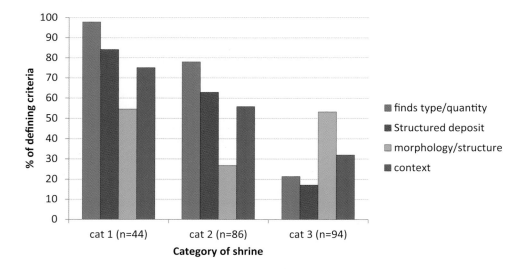

FIG. 5.2. The three categories of shrine against their defining criteria

A large animal bone assemblage included structured deposits of sheep, alongside coins and pottery vessels (*ibid.*, 352–8). In category 2 the shrines generally have two associated criteria, though in the same order as category 1. A recently examined example includes a site at Llanddowror in Carmarthenshire, where a pipeline excavation revealed an early/mid-Roman rectangular structure built within a former Neolithic henge ditch, with a contemporary pit cut into the henge terminal containing the burnt bones from up to two sheep/goats, a neonatal sheep/goat, and cereal remains, and suggested as a possible structured deposit (Barber and Hart 2014). The 'shrines' with the least robust level of interpretation (category 3) typically rely on just a single criterion, which, in over 50 per cent of cases, is morphology, such as the Mucking example provided above. These category 3 'shrines' form *c.* 40 per cent of all those recorded in the current project, highlighting the need for some level of caution when reviewing the results of analyses presented below.

Religious objects

The 'religious object' category of the project database covers a wide range of artefact types that could have been used for many different purposes. As Whitehouse (1996, 11–12) has demonstrated, defining the term 'ritual object' (used in this sense to denote religious ritual) is problematic in that there can be a continuum of values attached to artefacts, from mostly practical to mostly symbolic, with some objects having shifting biographies (i.e. changes in function and perceived value). Furthermore, it is sometimes only when objects are found in specific archaeological contexts (e.g. as grave goods or within temples) that their religious symbolism may become apparent to us. Nevertheless, Whitehouse (*ibid.*, 13) has identified six different categories of ritual object: *sacra* (objects of worship), votaries (representations of people making offerings), offerings, objects used in rites (including furnishings and priestly equipment), grave goods and amulets. While all of these categories are examined at some level below, or in the case of grave goods in Chapter 6, the artefacts defined as 'religious objects' are here limited to those objects that appear to have been specifically manufactured for religious use, or at least have frequent associations with religious contexts, as recently summarised by Bird (2011).

Structured deposits

As just stated, it is often only when objects are found in certain archaeological contexts that any possible religious associations may become apparent, and, notably, this includes those found within what have been termed 'structured' or 'placed' deposits. This project has collected data on a considerable number of these structured deposits, included mostly on the basis of their explicit interpretation as such within the excavation report. The problems with interpreting such deposits are manifold, and a particular issue to be noted from the start, which has been recently highlighted by Garrow (2012, 94), is that there are no consistent parameters used in their definition. Following Garrow (*ibid.*), therefore, a two-fold categorisation can be advanced that covers the multitudinous definitions of structured deposits. Firstly are *odd deposits*, which seem 'out of place' compared to contemporaneous patterns of discard. Examples include complete horse burials at Marsh Leys, Kempston, Bedford (Luke and Preece 2011) and Horcott Quarry, Glos (Hayden *et al.* 2017), an inverted cattle skull placed in a small pit in the centre of a doorway in an aisled hall at Thruxton, Hants (Cunliffe and Poole 2008a), and an unusual three pronged iron object that lay on the base of an enclosure ditch terminal at Love's Farm, Cambs, which was argued as 'representing the community's respect for iron as a source of social and cultural power' (Hinman and Zant forthcoming). The second category comprises *material culture patterning*, whereby the nature of deposits seems to have been governed by intentional, clear-cut spatial and/or temporal patterning. Examples recorded within the current project include the sequence of animal, human and plant deposits in a ritual shaft at Springhead, Kent (Andrews *et al.* 2011, 80, fig. 2.55), the differential spatial patterning of animals and pottery within the rubble banks of the settlement at Thornwell Farm, Chepstow (Hughes 1996, 97), and clear spatial selectivity of different animal species within the temple site at Chanctonbury, West Sussex, with a mass of pig bones in the polygonal shrine and sheep and cattle skulls in the surrounding ditch (Rudling 2001). Most examples of structured deposits recorded within excavation reports and analysed below would seem to lie within the *odd deposits* category, rather than *material culture patterning*, presumably because such types are easier to recognise in the archaeological record.

Of course, as Garrow and others (notably Chadwick 2012) have noted, such categorisation disguises a broad continuum of depositional practices, making it very difficult in most cases to isolate religious and secular motivations for such acts. It is most unlikely that all instances of structured deposition relate to some form of dialogue with an otherworld (cf. Morris 2011, 182–5; Chadwick 2015, 53), and even when they occur within defined religious locations they may still represent the final stages of a wide range of different rituals associated with a variety of beliefs (Smith 2016a, 643–4). The heterogeneity evident in structured deposits clearly represents the varied motivations of the actors engaged with their creation, which highlights the need to assess their meaning on an individual basis (Hingley 2006, 239; Roskams *et al.* 2013). However, collective analyses of the *c.* 1400 examples from 599 sites collated for this project do enable broad regional and chronological patterns to be observed in the character and context of these deposits, which appear to have been a widespread form of ritual expression throughout the Iron Age and Roman periods.

THE ARCHAEOLOGY OF RELIGIOUS PRACTICE IN THE LATE IRON AGE

In order to assess the impact of Roman conquest and administration on religious practice, some account must be provided of the situation in the preceding Iron Age. Here, classical sources along with early medieval Welsh and Irish literature have been used in the past to describe a world of druids, human sacrifice and sacred groves (e.g. Ross 1967; Green 1986; Webster 1986). In reality, very few of these texts specifically relate to Britain, and the tendency to produce accounts of a static, pan-European 'Celtic' religious culture has now received its fair share of critical attention (e.g. Fitzpatrick 1991, 126; 2007; Webster 1992, 312; 1995a; Smith 2001; Joy 2011). Although, if used critically, the literary accounts undoubtedly do contain much useful information on certain aspects of religion in the Iron Age, it is only when integrated with archaeology that the variety of pre-Roman ritual practices becomes slightly more apparent. A brief summary of this archaeological evidence will now be provided, focusing upon religious objects, sacred sites and landscapes, and patterns of deposition. An account of late Iron Age burial is presented in Chapter 6, although there is no *a priori* reason why 'religious' and 'burial' rituals should be viewed as separate constructs at this time, as clearly evidenced below.

RELIGIOUS OBJECTS IN THE IRON AGE

Unlike the relative wealth of evidence for religious objects in the Roman period, the late Iron Age, in Britain at least, has very few identifiable artefacts that may be related clearly to divine beliefs or cult practice. This is not to say that much of the imagery seen, for example, on Iron Age coinage (Creighton 2000, 191) or the occasional anthropomorphic bucket handle (e.g. Baldock; Stead and Rigby 1986, 51–61), would not have had any religious reference, but that objects specifically created as cult images (*sacra*), amulets or as 'priestly equipment' appear extremely rare. A notable exception is the concentration of chalk figurines depicting sword-bearing warriors (some decapitated) from the East Riding of Yorkshire, part of a very distinct regional ritual tradition of Iron Age date, alongside square-ditched funerary barrows and chariot burials (Stead 1988; Halkon 2013, 117–18). Fitzpatrick (2007) has further identified a number of objects that he suggested may have been associated with a class of religious specialists, including a small number of what are called spoons (shallow, oval-shaped, bowls) found across Britain, thought to date from the mid- to late Iron Age and to have had lunar symbolism. Other, mostly antiquarian finds, included probable Iron Age headdresses at Newnham Croft, Cambridgeshire, Old Castle Down, Vale of Glamorgan, Cerrig-y-Drudion, Clwyd, and Hounslow, Middlesex, as well as one from an excavated inhumation burial at Mill Hill, Deal, Kent, which was dated later third or early second century B.C. (*ibid.*, 299–302; Parfitt 1995).

Religious objects of late Iron Age date have only been recorded on a handful of excavated sites within the current project database. A crude sandstone figurine was noted in association with the shrine at Stansted, Essex, found in a pit alongside pottery of the mid-first century A.D. (Havis and Brooks 2004), while a chalk figurine was found in a possible subterranean shrine at Mill Hill, Deal, Kent, though this could be early Roman in date (Parfitt and Green 1987). Miniature objects, assumed to have had some ritual significance, are somewhat more numerous, being recorded from excavated late Iron Age contexts at Harlow, Essex (Smith 2001, 39), South Witham Quarry, Lincolnshire (Nicholson 2006a), and Meare lake village, Somerset, the latter site also having a copper-alloy figurine of a boar (Foster 1977, 6–7). The miniaturisation of objects, typically wheels, axes and weapons, has a widespread tradition across the Mediterranean and north-west Europe, and is particularly prevalent during the Roman period in Britain and Gaul (Kiernan 2009; see below p. 178). They are much rarer within British Iron Age contexts, though a well-known hoard from near Salisbury contained 24 miniature shields, 46 miniature cauldrons and two miniature socketed axes (Stead 1998). A group of 22 miniature shields, six spears, four swords, and two model axes was found by a metal detectorist in Lincolnshire in the 1970s, recently discussed by Farley (2011) in the context of other Iron Age miniature objects from Lincolnshire. The site, at Nettleton Top, lay at the highest point in the Lincolnshire Wolds, where excavations over many years have revealed a multi-period ritual complex and settlement (Willis 2013b). It was thus a suitable context for the concentration of these miniature weapons, which were regarded as a late Iron Age 'innovation' (notwithstanding the existence of late Bronze Age miniature socketed axes) developed from earlier traditions of offering full-size weapons at non-settlement sites like Fiskerton (Field and Parker Pearson 2003), the miniaturisation allowing 'these powerful symbols to be deployed in a 'safer' and more controlled form, appropriate to occupational sites' (Farley 2011, 45).

IRON AGE SACRED SPACE

The extent to which Iron Age peoples in Britain made use of specific sacred sites in the landscape, or at least sacred sites that were modified by human agency, has long been debated (e.g. Lewis 1966; Wait 1985; Woodward 1992; Webster 1995b; Smith 2001; King 2007a). There can be little doubt, however, that there were some shrines in use at this time, being identified at 49 sites in the current project database, although 34 per cent of these occupy the lowest level of interpretational confidence (category 3; see above, p. 122). These have been broken down by type within FIG. 5.3. A few were clearly purpose-built structures, although these types do not appear to have been particularly numerous, and despite traditional assumptions that have equated rectilinear buildings of this date with shrines, the current study has provided a far more mixed picture with regard to morphology (see also Moore 2003 and Smith 2016b, 50). In a review of constructed sacred space conducted in the late 1990s, the present author identified only eight convincing shrines of late Iron Age date, with

their nascent development suggested as being associated with increasing socio-political complexity and ideologies derived from Gaul (Smith 2001, 162; see Garland 2013 for recent discussion of ritual connections between Gaul and pre-Roman Britain). While the dismissal of some sites interpreted as shrines may have been a little over-zealous (e.g. Danebury and Heathrow, included here as category 3 shrines), it remains striking how few additional excavated structures of late Iron Age date have been suggested as shrines in the past two decades, despite the massive increase in the volume of archaeological fieldwork. One of these newly discovered built 'shrines', at Duxford in Cambridgeshire, was closely associated with funerary activity (Lyons 2011), while another at Marsh Leys, Kempston, Bedford, was interpreted largely on the basis of its morphology – a rectangular timber building defined by a gully (Luke and Preece 2011) (FIG. 5.4). Based upon slightly firmer interpretative ground was a rectangular timber structure at Sigwells, Charlton Horethorne, in Somerset, which lay immediately west of pits and ditches containing whole and partial animal and human burials, pottery vessels and Iron Age metalwork deposits (Tabor 2002). This site lay near to a late Iron Age shrine with similar characteristics within the hillfort at South Cadbury, Somerset (Barrett *et al.* 2000; Smith 2001, 44–50). None of these, however, has quite the same surety of evidence as at Hayling Island in Hampshire, which, despite being excavated between 1976 and 1981, remains as the stand-out example of a late Iron Age shrine in Britain (King and Soffe 2013; FIG. 5.4). This site, which awaits final full publication, is thought

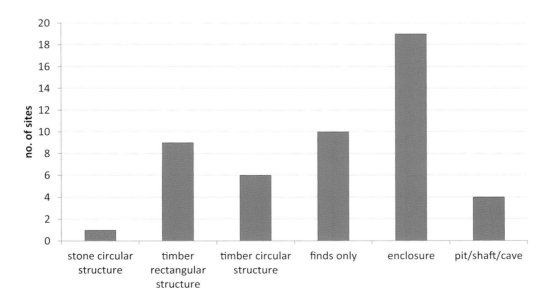

FIG. 5.3.   Characteristics of late Iron Age shrines

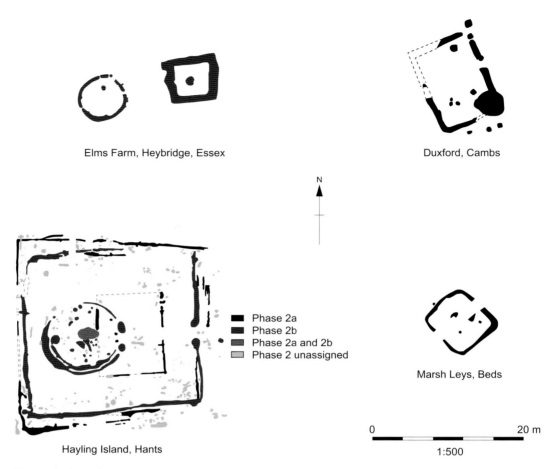

FIG. 5.4.   Plans of selected Iron Age built shrines (Atkinson and Preston 2015; Lyons 2011; Luke and Preece 2011; King and Soffe 2013)

to have had two main phases during the late Iron Age – the first, of early to mid-first century B.C. date, comprised inner and outer palisaded enclosures with a central pit, while in the second phase the inner enclosure was demolished to make way for a circular timber shrine, which resembled a typical domestic roundhouse (*ibid.*, 5–6). The spatial organisation and substantial finds assemblage demonstrated clear links with Gaul, where such shrines are far more commonplace.

Although relatively few shrine structures of Iron Age date have been excavated, there are an increasing number of other sites where sacred space of this date has been postulated. The earliest phase of Hayling Island provides some indication that, for the most part, it was an enclosed, separated space that was the most important feature of religious sites, and furthermore, as Webster (1995b, 459) has previously pointed out, 'an enclosure ditch was not simply a delimiter of sacred space; it was itself a primary focus of cult activity'. This is borne out by the nineteen sites of Iron Age date where an enclosure remained the principal component of the shrine (see FIG. 5.3). Most of these sites did have other associated features, however, which often provided the

evidence to make the interpretative leap towards a religious function. At Irchester, Victoria Park, Northants, for example, a small late Iron Age sub-rectangular enclosure contained a tree-throw hole in the centre, suggested as a possible ritual focus, while deliberately deposited globular jars came from the fill of the ditch (Morris and Meadows 2012). A more impressive site at Hallaton, Leics, spanned the very late Iron Age to early Roman period, and comprised a possible polygonal enclosure on a hilltop associated with intense deposition of a mass of animal bone (mostly pig), alongside coins and other metalwork (Score 2011). Together, these ritual enclosures make up almost 40 percent of postulated late Iron Age shrines, while others appear to consist of finds concentrations only, or else apparently isolated pits or shafts containing structured deposits (FIG. 5.3). At Springhead in Kent, there are suggestions of a ritual landscape of late Iron Age date, focused around the source of the Ebbsfleet River (Andrews *et al.* 2011, 190–2; FIG. 5.5). Features include a 'processional way', leading to a terrace above the springs, several pits with structured deposits and a rectilinear enclosure, extended on two occasions, which was associated with cremation burials,

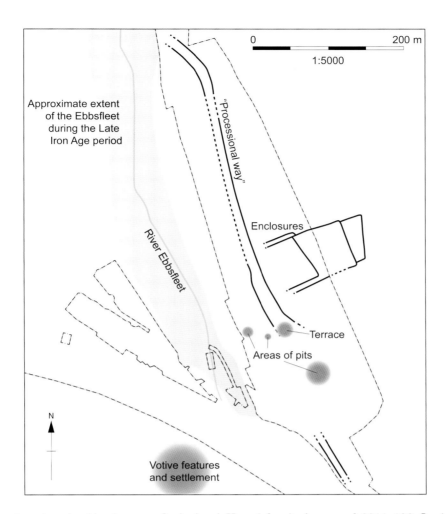

FIG. 5.5. A late Iron Age ritual landscape at Springhead, Kent (after Andrews *et al.* 2011, 190, fig. 4.1). Reproduced with permission HS1, © HS1

discrete deposits of pottery and possible free-standing posts. Around 100 Iron Age coins were also recovered from the springs, and the site later developed into a major Romano-British religious complex (see below, p. 163).

Sites where late Iron Age shrines have been interpreted are almost exclusively concentrated in parts of southern and eastern England (FIG. 5.6). Those incorporating built structures have an even narrower distribution in the south, though with some western outliers as far as Uley in Gloucestershire (Woodward and Leach 1993) and South Cadbury in Somerset (Barrett *et al.* 2000). A particular grouping of built shrines is noted in parts of Essex/south Cambridgeshire, including that at Elms Farm in Heybridge, which has recently been published (Atkinson and Preston 2015). The earliest shrines here comprised adjacent small square and circular buildings dating to the second half of the first century B.C., with three other post-built structures in the vicinity thought to have been further parts of an apparently unenclosed sacred complex (*ibid.*, 87). To the north of this grouping of sacred structures, in East

Anglia and around the Fens, all postulated shrines comprise enclosures or finds concentrations devoid of any structural component, such as the potential late Iron Age/early Roman ceremonial enclosure at Love's Farm in the Ouse Valley, represented by two concentric ring ditches, 55 m in diameter externally, on a ridge overlooking the main agricultural focus, some distance from the contemporary settlement foci (Hinman and Zant forthcoming). If genuine, this pattern of non-structural shrines may reflect a tradition that continues into the Roman period, when this region generally had less of an architectural emphasis than other areas further south and west, with status seemingly reflected more in portable wealth (Smith and Fulford 2016, 396).

The overall concentration of shrines in south and east England may be a consequence of the relative lack of objects and faunal remains from many areas further north and west, as these are so often used in the interpretation of sacred space (see above, p. 122). However, this does not explain the apparent lack of late Iron Age shrines in the north-east, where faunal remains and material culture are generally well attested (Allen 2016b, 273–80). There is some indirect evidence for the veneration of sites in this area, as seen with the remarkable sequence excavated at Ferry Fryston in West Yorkshire (Brown *et al.* 2007). This landscape, lying by a crossing of the River Ouse between the Pennines and Vale of York, had clearly been of ritual significance since the Neolithic, with a variety of monuments and burials, and was the location of a square-ditched chariot burial, radio-carbon dated to the early second century B.C. Some cattle bones in the primary ditch fills of the barrow were contemporary with the burial, but the vast majority, which represented a total of 162 cattle, were radiocarbon dated to the later first to fourth centuries A.D., with a definite emphasis on the later Roman period. Isotope analysis indicated the cattle derived from a wide geographical area, and it seems that at least some of the bones were curated over many years before being eventually deposited in the ditch during the late Roman period (*ibid.*; Orton 2006). While it cannot be proven that there was any continuity of ritual activity at the monument from the middle Iron Age to the late Roman period, it seems quite likely that some sense of sanctity persisted, as is also suggested

by the deposition of a bent Iron Age sword scabbard in the nearby henge ditch (Halkon 2013, 79).

Elsewhere in the north and west there is very little evidence for the definition of sacred space in the late Iron Age, though the association of possible Roman-period shrines with earlier prehistoric features at places like Capel Eithin, Gaerwen (White and Smith 1999) and Cefn Cwmwd, Rhostrehwfa (Cuttler *et al.* 2012), in Gwynedd, may hint that, like Ferrybridge, some persistence of sacredness was maintained from earlier times (see below, p. 160, for discussion of Roman ritual re-use of prehistoric monuments). There are also a number of sites where what would appear to have been ritual deposits have been found in watery contexts, highlighting the significance of natural sacred space, and particularly water, in pre-Roman religious practice (Green 1994; Bradley 1998). Of these sites, by far the best known is Llyn Cerrig Bach in Anglesey, where 181 items of iron and copper alloy, including swords, spears and slave chains, as well as animal bone (and possibly human bone) were deposited in a lake, probably intermittently, between the third century B.C. and the end of the first century A.D. (MacDonald 2007; Steele 2012).

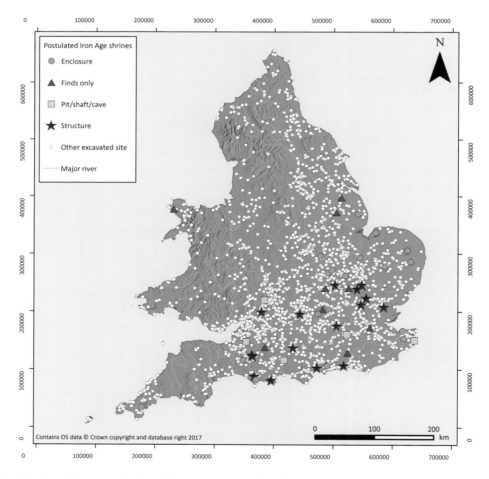

FIG. 5.6. Distribution of excavated sites where one or more late Iron Age shrines have been postulated

The overall picture of sacred space in the late Iron Age, as far as can be ascertained from the archaeological evidence, is one of relative scarcity and general diversity. There were places in the landscape that appear to have been imbued with particular sanctity, though rarely were they elaborated structurally to any great degree. Where dating evidence is refined enough, most shrines appear to have been established *de novo* at this time, many during the later first century B.C. to early first century A.D., possibly as part of a more centralised, focused approach to religious practice, as has been suggested by regional studies of ritual practice in late Iron Age Norfolk and Lincolnshire (Hutcheson 2004, 92; Farley 2011, 42). Their appearance should in turn be linked with other widespread changes of the late Iron Age in central and southern Britain, including the relatively widespread use of coinage, adoption in some areas of cremation burials, and significant increases in the overall number of settlements (Creighton 2000; Smith and Fulford 2016, 408). The distribution of shrines is strikingly similar to that of Iron Age coinage (Creighton 2000, 223, fig. A.2), and there is indeed a strong association between the two, these coins being present in 24 of the 30

late Iron Age shrines with recorded finds assemblages, sometimes in considerable numbers (e.g. Harlow, Essex and Hallaton, Leics; see Haselgrove 2005). There is also a close connection between at least eight Iron Age shrines and another late Iron Age phenomenon in south-eastern Britain – cremation burial – with structures/enclosures thought to have been associated with mortuary rituals (e.g. Westhampnett, West Sussex; Fitzpatrick 1997; see Ch. 6). As with the changing burial traditions, use of coinage, and increasing numbers of settlements, the emergence of specialised shrines in parts of southern Britain at this time appears to have been linked with major upheavals in the socio-political system, at least in the upper echelons of society, and certainly had a profound effect upon aspects of ritual expression during the Roman period, which is discussed further below.

RITUAL DEPOSITION IN THE IRON AGE

Iron Age studies have long recognised that structured deposition of objects and bones within pits and ditches were seemingly regular expressions of religious propitiation (e.g. Cunliffe 1992; Hill 1995a; Wilson 1999; Pitts 2005), with Tracey

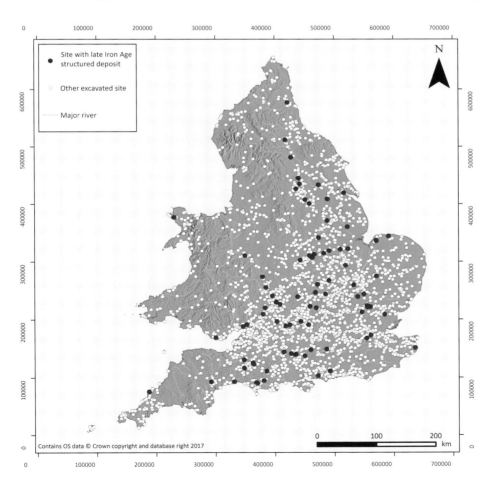

FIG. 5.7. Distribution of excavated sites where one or more late Iron Age structured deposits have been postulated

(2012) recently highlighting the variability of such rituals, even within relatively close geographic proximities. Within the current project, *c.* 194 structured deposits of certain late Iron Age date have been identified on 84 sites, spread over a wide area, though still largely absent from much of the north and west (FIG. 5.7). Ten of these sites have been interpreted as shrines, while the rest comprise farmsteads (58), hillforts (6), funerary sites (3), villages/*oppida* (3), field systems (3) and an ironworking site. As discussed in Chapter 1, for pragmatic reasons it has not been possible to systematically catalogue each individual structured deposit found on every site, but instead the amalgamated features of such deposits were recorded by site and phase. Although this may disguise a great deal of individual variation, there are wider patterns that can be observed in the character of these deposits, patterns that provide the basis for an examination of change from the late Iron Age to the late Roman period, discussed in detail below (p. 182).

The general character of late Iron Age structured deposits is shown in FIG. 5.8, in terms of their broad composition and the types of features with which they are associated. Overall, the deposition of material in pits appears most commonplace, followed by ditches and then structures, with water deposits only being recorded in the lake at Llyn Cerrig Bach and springs at Springhead, both discussed above, alongside Cotswold Community in the Upper Thames Valley, where a rare complete Gaulish Unguiforme brooch in the upper fill of a later Iron Age waterhole was very tentatively suggested as a ritual deposit (Powell *et al.* 2010, 106–9). Of course, as this project is only dealing with sites that have had some element of excavation, it has not recorded the many examples of Iron Age (and Roman) objects found, mainly dredged up from river beds (e.g. River Thames; Booth *et al.* 2007, 217), which may suggest that watery deposition was actually a much more common occurrence than the excavated evidence suggests (see Bradley 2000, 47–63). Furthermore, it remains possible that some of the pits that received structured deposits may have functioned as waterholes, or at least may have been periodically inundated.

Although, overall, pits were clearly a favoured context for this type of deposition, there are notable geographic differences. Pits are a feature at 70 per cent of sites with structured deposits in the East region, and 85 per cent in the South region, being particularly prominent within the Wessex chalk downlands (see Cunliffe 1995, 87–8). This compares to just 44 and 33 per cent of sites in the Central Belt and North-East respectively. In these latter areas, it seems that

deposits were much more likely to have been made within ditches (58 and 55 per cent of sites as opposed to 24 per cent in the South), with a particular concentration in and around the Fenlands, where perhaps drainage ditches may have taken on a greater spiritual significance as protection against flooding. One example is a group of three cattle skulls placed in a mid- to late Iron Age ditch terminus in a settlement close to the Fen edge at Mill Drove, Bourne, Lincolnshire (Jarvis 1995). Deposition within ditch termini, such as the example observed here, is a well-noted phenomenon (e.g. Rees 2008; Chadwick 2010, 397; 2012, 301), and has been recorded at 42 per cent of all late Iron Age sites with ditch deposits in the current project. Such apparent traditions seem to be widespread but disguise variations in the exact patterning of deposits and, of course, in the types of objects that were being placed.

As shown in FIG. 5.8, pottery vessels and animal remains are the two most common items forming parts of structured deposits of late Iron Age date, though only twenty sites (23 per cent) have records of both found in contemporary deposits. Deposits of animal bone, usually articulated (Associated Bone Groups = ABGs; see Allen below, p. 192), are the most ubiquitous across all regions, although unfortunately the poor survival of bone from much of the north and west precludes any real understanding of how widespread they were across the country as a whole. Nevertheless, the rare survival of cattle skulls in an inner enclosure ditch terminal at Blagdon Park on the Northumberland Coastal Plain (Hodgson *et al.* 2013), together with the animal bone in the Iron Age lake deposit at Llyn Cerrig Bach, hint that such deposits were to be found in all areas. Cattle are the most numerous of the animal species represented by ABGs in these deposits, found at 27 per cent of sites, followed by horse (24 per cent) then dog (18 per cent). Sheep/goat occur at just 15 per cent of sites, though this rises to 38 per cent of those sites in the South region, with a corresponding near absence from sites in the North-East (with the exception of late Iron Age/ early Roman examples from Wattle Syke, West Yorkshire; Martin *et al.* 2013), despite their relatively good representation within general faunal assemblages of this date in this region (Allen 2016b, 277). The distribution of pottery vessels (and possibly their contents) in structured deposits is almost as widespread as that of animal bone, though they rarely occur at sites lying to the north of South and West Yorkshire.

Aside from animal bone and pottery there is a range of other items occasionally found within structured deposits, including items of metalwork, quernstones and textile-processing objects. Much

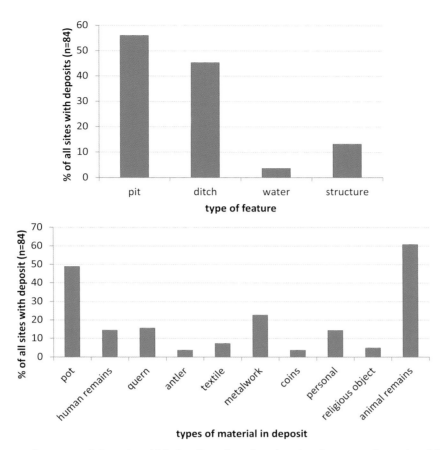

FIG. 5.8. Character of structured deposits within late Iron Age sites showing the types of associated features and types of material incorporated into deposits

of the metalwork, which includes brooches, tools, currency bars and items of a martial nature, is found in deposits from southern Britain, often alongside other objects and animal bone. For example, at Runfold Farm, Farnham Quarry in Surrey, deposits from opposing entrance ditch terminals to the farmstead included animal bone, pottery, fossils, an intact quernstone, and a brooch (Lambert 2009). Quernstones also feature in late Iron Age deposits at twelve other sites (c. 16 per cent of the total), indicating a particular symbolic role for this artefact. Peacock has recently highlighted the religious significance of querns and mills throughout many past and contemporary cultures, suggesting that they may be representative of the cycle of death, regeneration and new life (2013, 166). Such associations are strengthened by the discovery of Roman millstones with phallic symbols found near Winchester and Rochester (*ibid.*, 168–9).

Human remains are specifically recorded in late Iron Age structured deposits at twelve sites, these mostly comprising fragments of adult skeletons in features, often deliberately placed with animal bone and artefacts. For example, salvage excavations during construction work at Rushey

Mead, Leicester, revealed a pit containing the torso and head of an adult male along with a deposit of charred clean grain, sawn antler and a range of ceramic artefacts, including fragments of at least two loomweights (Pollard 2001). This feature well demonstrates the highly blurred boundary between what we now term 'structured deposits' and 'regular' graves, which are of course among the most structured deposits of all. The large number of infants found buried within and around buildings, and sometimes interpreted as foundation deposits (e.g. two burials associated with a late Iron Age roundhouse at Middle Barn, Selhurst Park, West Sussex; Anelay 2010) are another prime example of this blurred boundary. Where they are complete burials, these have generally not been included under the 'structured deposit' category (see instead discussion in Ch. 6), but they demonstrate the important role human remains could take in matters of religious observance (cf. Smith 2001, 69).

Overall, it seems clear that the placing of 'unusual' deposits within pits, ditches and structures of settlements was a fairly widespread phenomenon across much of England and Wales during the late Iron Age and, unlike the nascent development of shrines, was seemingly part of a much longer tradition of religious propitiation (Garrow 2012). However, although geographically widespread, they have still only been revealed (or recognised) in *c.* 12 per cent of all excavated settlements of this date, and may have been created quite sporadically on an *ad hoc* basis in particular or unusual circumstances. On the sites where we do have evidence, most (60 per cent) have just one deposit recorded, and so these are unlikely to have been regularly performed rituals that may, for example, have structured the agricultural year (cf. Roskams *et al.* 2013; Chadwick 2015, 52). Of course there may well have been many more examples of this behaviour involving the use of perishable materials such as plants and wooden objects, or perhaps just involving the deposition of single items such as a brooch or coin, that would simply not be recognised archaeologically as having had a ritual motivation. In the absence of clearer evidence we are still left with only faint, ill-understood traces of the rituals and beliefs of those in Britain prior to the Claudian conquest.

RELIGION IN THE COUNTRYSIDE OF ROMAN BRITAIN: SACRED SITES

ROMANO-CELTIC TEMPLES

Since Lewis's iconic and influential national survey of Romano-British temples published in 1966, *Temples in Roman Britain*, there have been a number of more or less detailed accounts of sacred space within the province (e.g. Wilson 1975; Rodwell 1980; Blagg 1986; Henig and King 1986; Woodward 1992; Smith 2001; King 2007a; Adams 2009). Classical temples, of the type generally seen in the city of Rome, were rare in Britain, and largely unknown outside urban or military contexts, and so with a few exceptions (e.g. Bird 2004a; Ghey 2005), the focus of these studies has been primarily centred upon the most widely recognised of all religious structures in the north-west provinces, the Romano-Celtic (or Gallo-Roman) temple. These temples are defined by their element of concentricity, with an inner cella, generally believed to house the main cult focus (in most cases probably a statue of the deity), surrounded on at least three sides by a walkway, or ambulatory. Although other religious structures certainly share an element of concentricity and have quite reasonably been termed Romano-Celtic temples on this basis (e.g. Hayling Island: King and Soffe 2013, 24; Heybridge: Atkinson and Preston 2015, 96), here the term is reserved more strictly for those buildings with an architecturally integral cella and

ambulatory, although there are still many variations on this arrangement. Some of these variations can be seen in FIG. 5.9 (see also Smith 2001, 152–3). Although the majority were relatively substantial masonry-footed rectilinear structures (typically *c.* 150–200 m² though with examples up to 500 m²), a smaller number were circular or polygonal (e.g. Chelmsford), while some had annexes to the front, sides or rear (e.g. Marcham/Frilford) or comprised two conjoined temples (e.g. Friars Wash). A recently published example from within a roadside settlement at Scole on the Norfolk/Suffolk border had the basic concentric elements of a Romano-Celtic temple, but was much smaller than most (76.5 m²), comprising an insubstantial masonry outer-sill-footing with an inner cella defined by postholes (Ashwin and Tester 2014, 207–8). Many of these temples were sited within sacred precincts, usually described as the temenos (though see Killock *et al.* 2015 251–2, for a recent discussion of terminology within Roman temple sites), and, where excavation was extensive enough, there was sometimes a variety of other associated features in the vicinity including ancillary structures (some possibly additional shrines), ovens and pits, all of which served the functioning of the temple cult to some degree (Smith 2001, 152, fig. 5.12).

The dominance of the Romano-Celtic temple in previous studies has led to the acceptance that such buildings were the 'standardised' form of religious architecture in Roman Britain (King 2007a, 13; Wintle 2013, 67). Given their easily recognised morphology and often (though not always; see below, p. 168) rich assemblages of material culture, this is perhaps not that surprising, yet this dominance comes at the expense of attempts to understand other forms of sacred space. Hingley (2011, 754) has recently commented, in relation to sacred sites across the Roman Empire, that 'archaeological attention has focused on the most monumental and impressive temple complexes, while less monumental and open-air cult places have been comparatively ignored'. In many ways this recalls the domination of villas vis-à-vis farmsteads in previous studies of Roman rural settlement and architecture, discussed in Volume 1 (Smith 2016b, 44). Although Romano-Celtic temples are clearly very important to our understanding of Romano-British religion and society, they are, as with villas, quite restricted in their numbers and geographic spread, and by themselves provide only a limited understanding of religious practice in Roman Britain

The mass of mainly developer-funded archaeological excavation that has taken place since 1990 has led to a huge corresponding increase in the number of interpreted sacred sites of non-Romano-Celtic form, here initially all

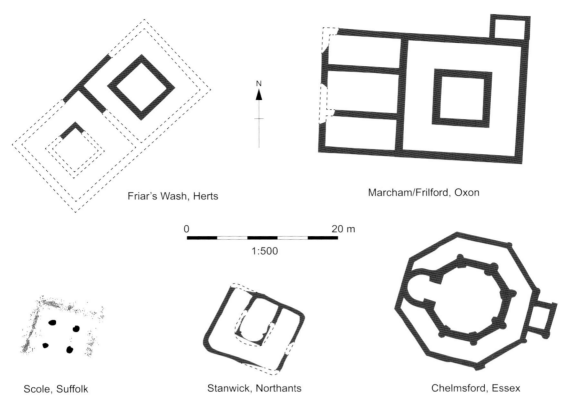

FIG. 5.9. Site plans of Romano-Celtic temples at Scole, Suffolk (Ashwin and Tester 2014), Marcham/Frilford, Oxon (Bradford and Goodchild 1939), Stanwick, Northants, Chelmsford, Essex (Wickenden 1992) and Friars Wash, Herts (Birbeck 2009)

grouped together under the umbrella term 'shrine' (see definitions above, p. 121) and discussed by type below. A total of 207 sites in the project database have had one or more structures or places dating to the Roman period interpreted as shrines, almost 80 per cent of which have only been reported (via published or grey literature) since 1990. As with the upsurge in excavated and reported farmsteads discussed in Volume 1 (Smith *et al.* 2016), this ensures that the wide range of different enclosures, shafts, open spaces and structures grouped as shrines can now take on more of a central role in our understanding of Romano-British religious practice.

DISTRIBUTION AND CHRONOLOGY OF RELIGIOUS SITES

The distribution of all excavated rural sites with shrines and Romano-Celtic temples is shown on FIG. 5.10. It is immediately apparent that the 54 sites with Romano-Celtic temples have a much more restricted spread than the wider, heterogeneous group of shrines, with all but two found to the south of the line approximately from the Wash to the Severn Estuary, notwithstanding a few others known from urban (e.g. possible examples near the classical temple in Wroxeter; White and Barker 2000, 95–6; White *et al.* 2013,

191) and military contexts (Vindolanda) further north. In contrast, religious sites of a different form are to be found within all major regions, from a possible rock shrine north of Hadrian's Wall at Yardhope, Northumberland (Charlton and Mitcheson 1983), to Nornour on the Isles of Scilly, where prehistoric circular buildings appear to have been the focus for ritual deposition throughout much of the Roman period (Butcher 2004a; though see Fulford 1989a for an alternative interpretation). Despite their general ubiquity, there are still some areas such as South Wales, much of the South-West and large parts of the Central West region where there remain very few interpreted shrines; as there are many sites with evidence for structured deposits in these areas (see below), this perhaps suggests a different emphasis of cult practice, without the need for obviously defined sacred sites.

FIGURES 5.11 and 5.12 show the steady increase in the number of sacred sites in use over time, reaching a peak, at 141 sites, during the late Roman period. The apparent growing need for the definition of sacred space, particularly in much of central and eastern England, is probably related to the major changes in rural life witnessed here. The rituals performed within shrines and temples may have been actively utilised to create and maintain

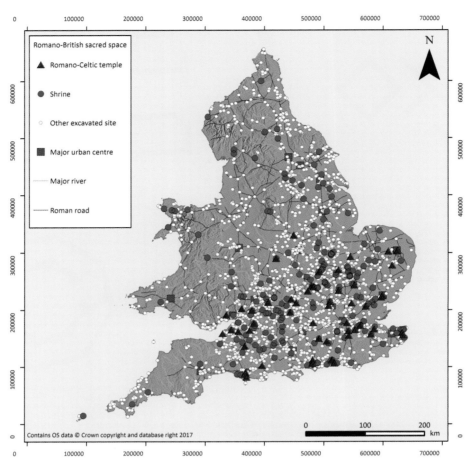

FIG. 5.10. Distribution of excavated Romano-British sites where one or more sacred sites have been postulated

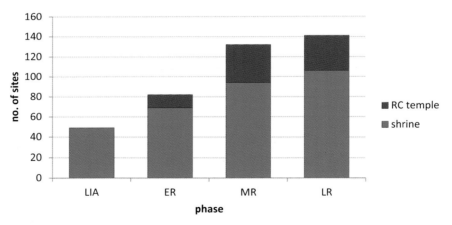

FIG. 5.11. Number of sacred sites in use over time

community identities, which would have become increasingly important in an ever-changing world.

The overall chronological pattern of sacred sites is, however, far from uniform across the province, with the numbers in active use appearing to decline in the South region during the late third and fourth centuries, especially in the south-east, much in line with the wider settlement evidence (Allen 2016a, 81, fig. 4.6). In the North-East, meanwhile, not only do the number of sacred sites increase during the late Roman period, but these shrines are now more likely to comprise built structures, such as the masonry, sub-rectangular building (15 × 11.5 m) at West Heslerton, which was part of a larger rural sanctuary in a dry valley at the foot of the Yorkshire Wolds (Powlesland 1998).

As highlighted above, one of the major points of discussion with regard to Roman-period sacred

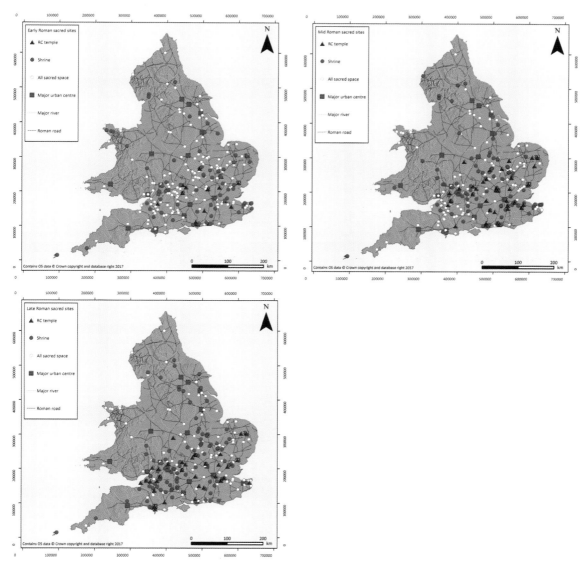

FIG. 5.12. Distribution of sacred sites in use over time (red = Romano-Celtic temple; blue = shrine)

sites is the degree of continuity with cult sites of Iron Age date. It has just been established that the 49 Iron Age sacred sites were a diverse and diffuse group that developed in parts of southern and eastern Britain, mostly within the 100 years or so preceding the Claudian conquest. Of the 82 rural sites with shrines or temples belonging to the early Roman period, 37 (45 per cent) had some evidence for previous ritual activity, including almost 60 per cent of the early Romano-Celtic temples. Indeed, the overall distribution of Romano-Celtic temples, even at their maximum extent in the mid- to late Roman period, closely follows that of late Iron Age shrines (see FIG. 5.6 above) in being restricted to parts of central and southern Britain. The origin of this temple form has long been debated, with some arguing for an indigenous development (e.g. Wilson 1975, 15; King 2007a), largely on the basis of parallels with a single concentric structure from

Heathrow, which was very loosely dated to the mid- to late Iron Age (Grimes and Close-Brooks 1993, 336). The Gallo-Roman temple became well established in parts of northern Gaul from the Claudio-Neronian period (Derks 1998, 183), and it remains most likely that the concept came to Britain from there alongside new forms of high-status domestic architecture (i.e. villas), with both building forms maintaining a close relationship in central and southern Britain into the late Roman period (Smith 2001, 114; Adams 2009, 115–16; see below, p. 152). Nevertheless, the lack of Romano-Celtic temples in the North-East, where there are many examples of villas, suggests that their distribution was not just mirroring the extent of 'Roman' style domestic architecture, but was linked to underlying traditions of constructed sacred space. This indicates how the late Iron Age development of sacred sites had a fundamental impact on the religious landscape of the Roman period.

At least twenty sites show evidence for continued use from the late Iron Age right through to the late or even post-Roman period, including Harlow in Essex (France and Gobel 1985) and Farley Heath in Surrey (Poulton and Bird 2007). Perhaps the best known of these is Uley in Gloucestershire, which developed from a late Iron Age shrine, utilising earlier prehistoric features, to become a major Romano-British religious complex with a Romano-Celtic temple, and a possible post-Roman Christian chapel, though the evidence for the latter is somewhat tenuous (Woodward and Leach 1993; cf. Heighway 2003, 59). In many other cases there is evidence for decline within the Roman period, although continuity of cult may still be apparent at sites even where there is evidence for dereliction of shrine/temple buildings, such as at Springhead in Kent, where deposits of coins were found above the rubble of one of the shrine buildings (Penn 1962, 116). Structural alterations and decline in temples dating to the fourth century have sometimes been attributed to a conflict with Christianity (Watts 1998; see below, p. 203). Ultimately, however, the fortunes of most sacred sites appear more likely to have been tied up with those of the surrounding settlements, and there is little evidence that specific late Roman 'anti-pagan' imperial policies from Christian emperors had any effect upon the fate of these cults (Smith 2008).

Of the 141 sacred sites recorded in the current project that show evidence of use in the late Roman period, 110 (78 per cent) are thought to have continued in use at least until the end of the fourth century. In most cases, the exact end of activity from this time remains uncertain, as is often the case with settlements of this date (see Smith and Fulford 2016, 414–16), though sixteen are argued to have continued at least into the early fifth century, usually on the basis of a very strong late Roman finds signature or associated dated features. One example comprises the late Roman shrine/mausoleum at Cannington in Somerset, which is thought to have acted as a focus for the surrounding cemetery that continued in use until the seventh or eighth century A.D. (Rahtz et al. 2000).

Overall, it remains very hard to gauge the 'end' of use of most of these late Roman religious sites, and although there have been suggestions that many became the focus for subsequent Christian churches (e.g. Henig 2008), unequivocal evidence is usually lacking. It is quite likely that most continued to exhibit an aura of sanctity in the minds of local people for a considerable period, even if the specific rituals and practices undertaken during the Roman period had long since ceased.

SHRINES: FORM AND DEVELOPMENT

The analysis of late Iron Age shrines above demonstrated a variety in physical characteristics, from apparently open sites with concentrations of finds, to pits, shafts, enclosures and different types of built structure. All of these forms of sacred space are found in the Roman period, though with the increase in numbers came an even greater variation in their attributes. The form and development of Romano-Celtic temples has been touched upon above, and here all of the other sacred sites falling into the category of 'shrine' will be dealt with. The problems relating to the interpretation of shrines have already been outlined (p. 122), and 40 per cent of the examples here lie within the weakest interpretative category (3), many of these comprising structures that seem unusual within their local context, such as that at Mucking in Essex cited above (see FIG. 5.1). Such interpretational fragility must be kept in mind when considering the patterns revealed in the analysis below.

FIGURE 5.13 shows the principal characteristics of all 207 sites interpreted as having Roman-period shrines in the current dataset, including those that developed from Iron Age sites. The broad categories disguise a wealth of variation in individual form and development, and these will now be examined in more detail.

Constructed shrines

Just over half of all shrines shown in FIG. 5.13 comprise some type of structure. As discussed above, during the late Iron Age the concept of constructed sacred space appears to have been in its infancy, with, in particular, relatively few examples of actual roofed buildings used as cult houses. Nevertheless it is clear that the incidence of constructed shrines increases significantly over time, from accounting for 32 per cent of shrines in the late Iron Age to over 60 per cent by the mid- and late Roman periods (FIG. 5.14). If Romano-Celtic temples were to be included, then the proportion of built structures would increase to 70 per cent of all sacred sites by the late Roman period.

Variation within the 'built shrine' category is enormous. A few were clearly small household shrines sited internally within villas, and these will be examined below when looking at the wider context and use of sacred space (p. 147). The graph and map on FIG. 5.15 break the remaining constructed shrines down into basic form and construction material, but there are still many differences in scale, levels of embellishment and in the type and extent of surrounding features. Rectangular masonry (or at least masonry-footed) buildings are the most commonly defined shrine structures, being interpreted as such on 37 sites, mainly across parts of central, southern and eastern areas of the province. At one end of the spectrum these buildings include a small classical-type temple lying within a sacred precinct alongside a circular shrine in the military *vicus* at Maryport, Cumbria (FIG. 5.16), the only certain example of its type known outside of urban contexts in Britain and recently excavated by Newcastle University (http://www. senhousemuseum.co.uk/excavation). At the other end lies a number of small structures usually

interpreted as shrines by association with certain objects or structured deposits such as at Monkston Park, Milton Keynes, where a small stone-footed structure (2 × 3 m) produced much animal bone including a near-complete dog skeleton along with eight later fourth-century coins (Bull and Davis 2006). Further articulated remains of horse and cattle lay in a nearby ditch, and the site lay within an enclosure group on a valley slope overlooking the main farmstead. Aside from their basic form and construction material, there is no real cohesive element to any of these structures,

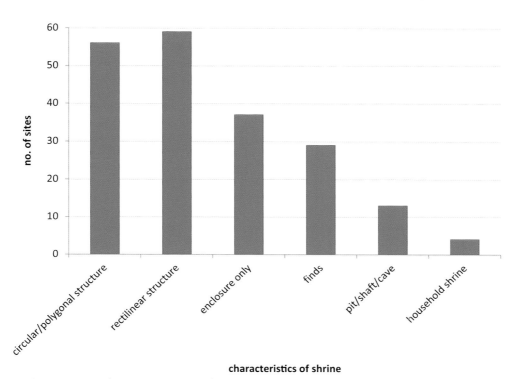

FIG. 5.13. Characteristics of rural Roman shrines

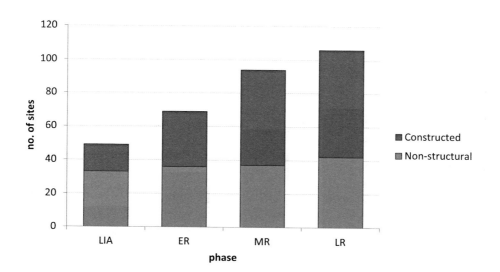

FIG. 5.14. Development of constructed shrines

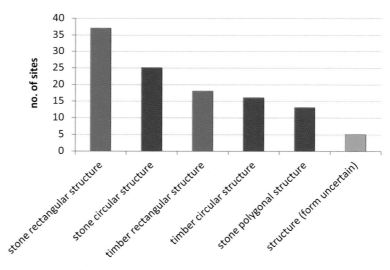

FIG. 5.15. Distribution and forms of constructed shrines

although most were on a somewhat larger scale than that of Monkston Park, and were sometimes surrounded by a defined enclosure, assumed to demarcate the temenos or sacred area. Some may have performed a similar role in 'public cult' to that of most Romano-Celtic temples, discussed below, the variations in building form highlighting the fact that such religious architecture need not be standardised, which is somewhat at variance with the rigorous formulaic approach taken to orthopraxy.

In total, 25 sites contained one or more circular masonry buildings interpreted as shrines, while a further 13 sites produced polygonal masonry shrines. They are fairly widespread, but with a definite concentration in the West Anglian Plain to

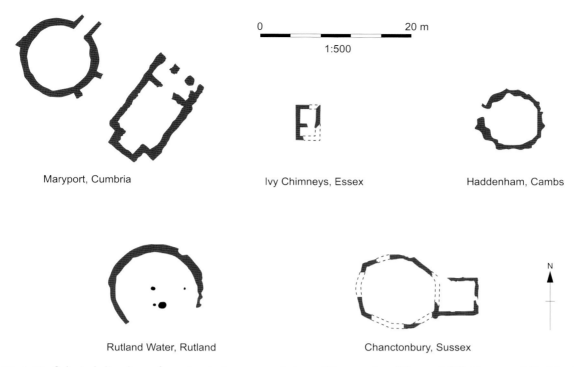

0   20 m

1:500

Maryport, Cumbria   Ivy Chimneys, Essex   Haddenham, Cambs

Rutland Water, Rutland   Chanctonbury, Sussex   N

FIG. 5.16. Selected site plans of constructed masonry shrines of Roman date (Turner 1999; Evans and Hodder 2006; Carlyle 2011; Rudling 2001)

the west of the Fens, as well as in and around the Upper Thames Valley (FIG. 5.15), the former relating to an area that had a strong tradition of circular architecture continuing right through the Roman period (Smith 2016b, 47–51). On occasion such buildings are found in association with Romano-Celtic temples, such as at Marcham/Frilford in Oxfordshire (Kamash *et al.* 2010), Chanctonbury in West Sussex (Rudling 2001) and the religious complex at Friars Wash, Redbourn, Herts (Birbeck 2009), where they are usually argued to have served as subsidiary shrines. In other cases the circular shrine is seen to be replaced by a Romano-Celtic temple, as at Wanborough in Surrey (O'Connell and Bird 1994) or Nettleton Scrubb in Wiltshire (Wedlake 1982). At the latter site a circular temple built on a raised knoll later had an octagonal platform built around it, perhaps functioning as an ambulatory, before being completely replaced with a rather more elaborate octagonal Romano-Celtic temple in the mid-third century A.D. (*ibid.*). On most sites, the circular/polygonal shrine represented the primary religious structure, which could be quite a substantial building, certainly in the range of most Romano-Celtic type temples, such as the polygonal structure, 15–17 m in diameter, partially revealed during an evaluation adjacent to Ermine Street in a roadside settlement at Navenby, Lincs, and suggested as a possible shrine (Allen and Palmer-Brown 2001, 5). The economic investment required to build masonry shrines of this scale would have been considerable, and certainly no

less than for most Romano-Celtic temples. Furthermore, as with some of the rectangular masonry shrines, the material culture assemblages from many of these circular/polygonal shrines matches that recovered from many Romano-Celtic temples (see below, p. 174), with the indication that all building types could be used as settings for the performance of public religious rituals, the differences perhaps relating to local traditions and preferences of those responsible for funding the construction of the religious site.

Timber structures interpreted as shrines are found in lower numbers but cover the same broad distribution as masonry shrines. They do, nevertheless, form a slightly higher proportion of sacred sites in parts of eastern England, an area noted for generally high concentrations of timber and/or mass-walled (i.e. made of turf or cob) buildings during the Roman period, partly due to the relative lack of good building stone (Smith 2016b, 52, fig. 3.8). The less substantial nature of such buildings probably ensures that they remain relatively under-represented, while many may be hard to differentiate from domestic dwellings or other more utilitarian structures. For example, a circular timber or mass-walled building within the late Roman village at Butterfield Down, Amesbury, on the Wessex chalk, was suggested as a shrine largely owing to the presence of a sceptre head on the floor surface and an infant burial in one of the drip gully terminals (Rawlings and Fitzpatrick 1996). Without the fortuitous survival of the

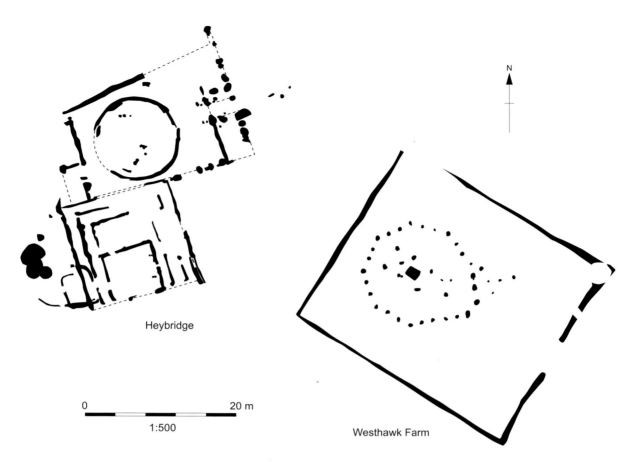

Heybridge

0 ———————————— 20 m

1:500

Westhawk Farm

FIG. 5.17. Site plans of Roman-period constructed timber shrines at Heybridge (Atkinson and Preston 2015) and Westhawk Farm (Booth *et al.* 2008)

sceptre head (which still may not necessarily have been used in religious ritual), it is doubtful whether such an interpretation would have been advanced, although it was the only circular structure noted during the excavations. Likewise, a four-post structure (2 × 2.5 m) built into the footprint of a henge ditch at Land East of Vaynor Farm, Llanddowror, in Carmarthenshire, was only suggested as a possible shrine, with the alternative being a storage structure, on the basis of its context and the presence of a nearby pit containing a structured deposit (Barber and Hart 2014).

Not all timber structures interpreted as shrines are necessarily that modest, however, with some representing important cult centres within their local and wider landscapes. One such site is Heybridge in Essex, which has already been discussed in terms of its Iron Age cult site. The religious focus of this growing nucleated settlement clearly became more important during the early post-conquest period, with significant architectural changes to the shrine site, including a large timber building with internal labyrinthine sub-division, and an 11 m diameter circular timber shrine, possibly un-roofed, set within a trapezoidal enclosure just to the north (Atkinson and Preston

2015, 89; FIG. 5.17). It was suggested that the sacred precinct was used for large congregations, and further conjectured that it was a place for pilgrimage (*ibid.*, 99). Another quite striking example of a fairly elaborate timber shrine, also situated within a nucleated settlement, was at Westhawk Farm in Kent (Booth *et al.* 2008, 94–102; FIG. 5.17). Here, a polygonal shrine defined by postholes lay within a rectangular-ditched enclosure, which was located within a large area of seemingly open space on the south side of the road from the Weald to Canterbury. As with Heybridge, whether the shrine was roofed remains uncertain, though on balance the excavators considered it unlikely, with the polygonal arrangement of postholes instead either representing screens or free-standing posts surrounding a large, central post (*ibid.*, 379). Sites such as Heybridge and Westhawk Farm seem to blur the boundaries between constructed shrines as buildings and shrines defined by enclosures alone.

Religious enclosures

The importance of enclosure in the morphology of sacred space is well demonstrated, (e.g. Parker Pearson and Richards 1994, 24; Smith 2001, 17),

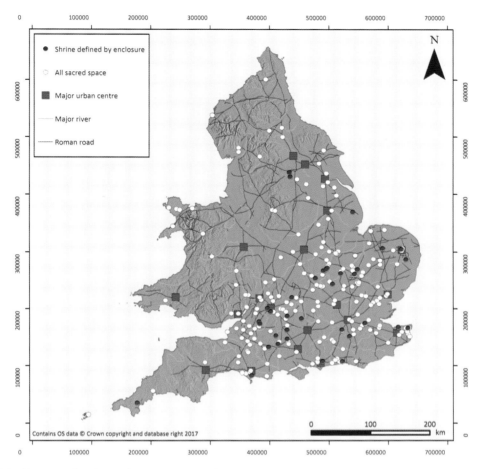

FIG. 5.18. Distribution of shrines of Roman date defined by enclosures only

and has been commented upon above (p. 126) with regard to Iron Age cult sites (cf. Rees 2008). Many Gallo-Roman temple sites originated as enclosures and pits without any major structural element (Smith 2001, 70–1; Ghey 2007, 19), and there are a few examples that suggest similar developments in Britain, such as at Nettleton Scrubb, Wilts (Wedlake 1982), Jordan Hill, Dorset (Drew 1932) and Folly Lane, Herts (Niblett 1999). In addition there is evidence from the recently excavated Roman religious site at Tabard Square in Southwark, London, to suggest that the area was enclosed as a sacred precinct prior to the construction of the two Romano-Celtic temples (Killock *et al.* 2015, 243). In many of the other 79 cases where a religious structure is demonstrably surrounded by an enclosure, it is unfortunately not possible to determine which element – structure or enclosure – came first, though there are cases where the enclosure certainly appears to have been the most impressive feature of the site, notably at the conquest-period shrine at Fison Way, Thetford, in Norfolk (Gregory 1991). In addition, it is certainly not the case that all or even most shrines progressed in a sequence from enclosure to constructed shrine, as there are a

total of 37 shrines of Roman date that would seem to have been defined solely by an enclosure, and which did not develop any obvious internal structure. The distribution of these sites is shown on FIG. 5.18, appearing largely concentrated in a band from the Wessex chalk through to the West Anglian Plain (Nene and Ouse Valleys) and parts of East Anglia, though with other examples in the south-east and further north.

A high proportion (75 per cent) of these sacred enclosures had ditched boundaries, though others utilised timber palisades and masonry walls. The majority were relatively small, with all but six below 0.3 ha, and most falling in the region of 500–2500 m². Given that there were often very few other features within the enclosure, many would still have been able to hold reasonably large numbers of people, assuming that they were designed for such 'congregational' type rituals, which is far from certain. Nine (24 per cent) of the enclosures had two or more concentric boundaries, perhaps reflecting the concentricity found in Romano-Celtic temples. However, there is a danger of interpreting every 'unusual' double or triple enclosure in the Romano-British countryside as religious in nature, as analysis for this project has shown that there are many examples of such enclosures that appear to be farmsteads, the arrangements possibly reflecting differences in social status and/or the control of movements of livestock (Allen and Smith 2016, 26–8). As ever, it is only in the contextual analysis of the site and associated features and finds that any religious function may be postulated.

FIGURE 5.19 shows the main characteristics of these enclosures that have enabled them to be interpreted as shrines. Over 50 per cent have some kind of structured deposit, either in the enclosure ditch or in one or more 'ritual' pits/ shafts, similar to certain rectilinear enclosures from the Continent termed *Viereckschanzen*, which have often been viewed as pre-Roman cult sites, though with increasing debate over any homogeneity of religious function (Brunaux 1989; Venclova 1993; Webster 1992, 35). Sometimes the presence of one or more structured deposits may be the only indication of the religious nature of the site, as at Luton Road, Wilstead, Bedford, where a late Roman enclosure contained minimal evidence for domestic occupation, but was associated with a hollow containing three sheep skulls, all apparently carefully positioned on their sides facing different directions (Luke and Preece 2010). Whether this was a dedicated shrine or else a stock pen containing a dedicatory deposit is of course uncertain and once more highlights the blurred boundaries between secular and religious use of space. The somewhat more elaborate structured deposits within some enclosures may provide greater clarity of dedicated sacred space, such as at Rothwell Haigh, Leeds, where almost the only feature within a square ditched enclosure (0.27 ha) was a 12.3 m deep, unlined well containing a sequence of deposits suggested as a closure event, including complete pottery vessels,

a yew bucket, ash spade, ash drinking vessels, querns, hobnailed shoes, articulated animal bone and a human adult skull (Cool and Richardson 2013; FIG. 5.20). Yet even here the excavators, although proposing ritual activity, have not actively interpreted the whole site as a shrine (*ibid.*).

Specific religious objects (see definition above) have been found at twelve of the enclosure sites, including possible sceptre bindings at Stratton Farm, Godstone in Surrey (Hall 2007) and Slonk Hill in West Sussex (Hartridge 1978), tazze (incense burners) at Claydon Pike, Glos (Miles *et al.* 2007), and representations of Mercury at Lee's Rest, Charlbury in Oxfordshire (Bagnall-Smith 1995, 201), and Great Bedwyn/Shalbourne in Wiltshire (Brindle *et al.* 2013). A copper-alloy hairpin from the 'ceremonial' enclosure ditch at Love's Farm St Neots in Cambridgeshire was modified, seemingly to represent a model spear (Hinman and Zant forthcoming).

The wider contexts of shrine sites will be discussed below, but it is worth noting here that seven of the proposed ritual enclosures appear to be related to funerary activity, and may have been used for quite different purposes from shrines, including possibly as places for excarnation of human remains. In some cases, the association seems more connected with possible ancestral cults, such as is suggested at Thruxton in Hampshire, where a late Roman fenced enclosure was built around a late Iron Age grave and ritual shaft, which was thought to have still been open to some level (Cunliffe and Poole 2008a). An undated square post-hole structure/enclosure (20 m²) lying near to the middle Iron Age chariot burial at Ferry Fryston, West Yorks, discussed above (p. 128), is thought by the excavators to have been a possible shrine contemporary with the mass deposition of

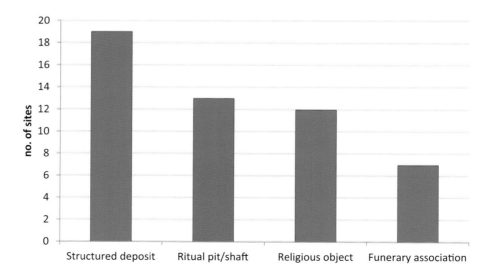

FIG. 5.19. Characteristics of religious enclosures of Roman date

cattle bones in the barrow ditch, and may represent part of a similar ancestral cult.

Aside from subterranean features such as pits, shafts and wells, there are usually few other features associated with the sacred enclosures. At least five were associated with prehistoric monuments, with those at Slonk Hill, West Sussex (Hartridge 1978), Uffington, Oxfordshire (Miles *et al.* 2003), and within the roadside settlement at Stanwick, Northamptonshire (Crosby and Muldowney 2011), actually encompassing Bronze Age barrows, part of a more widespread association between prehistoric features and Roman ritual discussed below (p. 160). The last site initially took the form of a narrow ditch dug around the barrow with a sand and gravel path encircling it, during the late Iron Age/early Roman period. The temenos underwent elaboration in later first century A.D. with a limestone surface replacing the old path and a possible pier base set up to the west. A pit was cut into the centre of the burial mound during the second century A.D. to hold a post/column, and the whole area was re-metalled in the third century, with another pier added to

form an entrance on the approach road. A stone-footed building by this path may have served in a cult ancillary role. Final major alterations occurred in the late third to mid-fourth century when an encircling wall was built and some kind of water feature was associated with the entrance into the temenos.

The increasing elaboration of the entrance zone is seen in an even more spectacular fashion at an enclosure shrine just a few kilometres away in the Nene Valley at Higham Ferrers (Lawrence and Smith 2009; FIG. 5.20). Here, a shrine of second–third century date was located on the western periphery of a roadside settlement, adjacent to a single Bronze Age cremation burial, although it remains uncertain if a burial mound was still visible and therefore acted as a marker for the Roman sacred site. It was defined on three sides by a masonry wall and left open to the west near the steep break of slope leading down to the River Nene. There appear to have been two separate 'precincts', with the outer south-facing entranceway comprising a huge pitched-limestone foundation over 20 m long and 3.6 m wide, with colonnette

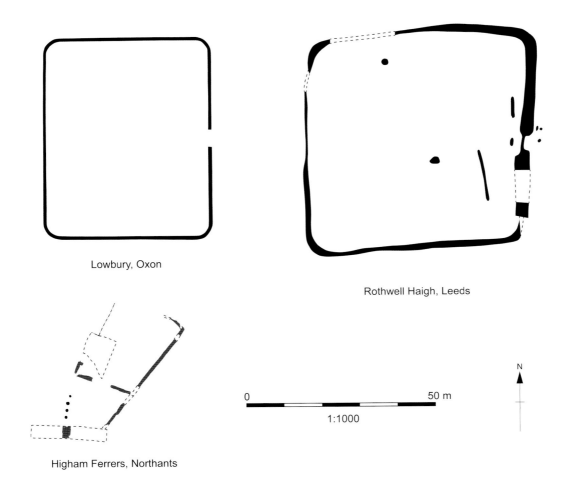

Lowbury, Oxon

Rothwell Haigh, Leeds

Higham Ferrers, Northants

0   50 m

1:1000

N

FIG. 5.20. Selected site plans of religious enclosures of Roman date (Lawrence and Smith 2009; Atkinson 1916; Cool and Richardson 2013)

fragments and concentrations of tile suggesting some level of embellishment. The only other feature of the shrine with any hint of monumentality was the entrance to the inner precinct, within which was a mass of votive deposits but no evidence for any central focus aside from a cleared area of space devoid of any finds, which may have contained an altar or statue. Shrines like Higham and Stanwick ably demonstrate that, even within nucleated roadside settlements with all the trappings of 'Roman' architecture and material culture, religious sites did not have to include a central, covered building, but that a bounded space was deemed more important, with the emphasis being firmly placed on marking the transition from profane to sacred.

Shrines as shafts, wells and caves

The deposition of what would appear to be ritually motivated structured deposits in wells, pits and shafts of Iron Age and Roman date has long been recognised (e.g. Piggott 1968; Webster 1997; Black 2008, 1–8), usually thought to be propitiatory offerings to chthonic deities. Yet such features are typically found within and around settlements (see above, p. 129, for Iron Age discussion and below, p. 182, for Roman discussion), or associated with more readily defined ritual contexts, such as those described above, and are rarely seen as 'shrines' in their own right (though note Ross 1968 and Rudling 2008b, 118–19). There is, however, a small group of otherwise apparently isolated (or at least clearly separated from any nearby settlement) wells and shafts containing 'unusual' deposits, which may mark out the loci as sacred space. There may have been a distinction between 'dry' shafts, dug specifically to allow communication with chthonic deities/the underworld, and wells, which could have originally been dug for a more practical function as a water source, before 'attaining' a more overt religious significance. Both shafts and wells, however, produced a similar range of structured material (see below, p. 189), and the distinction may not ultimately have been that significant.

The distribution of sacred sites principally defined by wells and/or shafts is shown in FIG. 5.21, with a clear grouping across the south of England, which is corroborated by a similar concentration of shafts/wells with structured deposits from certain farmsteads (e.g. Oakridge, Hants; Oliver 1992; see discussion below, p. 194), villas (e.g. Keston, Kent; Philp et al. 1991; 1999) and larger religious sites (e.g. Springhead, Kent; Andrews et al. 2011). At Deal in Kent a 2.5 m deep shaft was located between two cemeteries of Iron Age–early Roman date, and gave access to an underground chamber (Parfitt and Green 1987;

Parfitt 1995, 156). This was filled in during the second century A.D., and was suggested as a shrine partly on the basis of the recovery of a small carved chalk figurine. Elsewhere in the south-east a possible Roman shaft with animal bone, pottery and oyster shell lay within an Iron Age hillfort at Mount Caburn near Lewes (Hamilton 1998, 33), while a number of late Iron Age Age/early Roman pits and deep shafts on the dip slope of the North Downs near Ewell, overlooking the nearby roadside settlement, produced a wide range of finds, including rotary querns, loomweights, spindlewhorls and articulated animal bone (Cotton 2001; see discussion below, p. 195). Further west were possible ritual wells containing votive material at Armsley, Godshill, in Hampshire, at a spring located near the confluence of the River Avon and the Millersford Brook (Musty 1977), and another possible ritual well, of late Roman date, lay within a hillfort at Cadbury Castle, Devon (Fox 1952). The site at Godshill is ill understood and may have been part of a larger settlement, though the well from Cadbury Castle appears to have been the only feature of this date in the vicinity. As with Mount Caburn, and other shrines/temples within hillforts, the outer ramparts of the fort may have acted as a sacred boundary, and so these two sites may be better viewed as religious enclosures.

The only 'isolated' ritual shaft to be included in the current dataset further north was that recently excavated at Bretton Way, Peterborough in the Central Belt region (Pickstone and Drummond-Murray 2013). Here, a late Roman shaft/well (construction cut 6.5 × 3.5m, 2.5m deep) was lined with 36 re-used limestone blocks from a monumental building, and contained a large finds assemblage, probably of ritual origin, including 14–16 leather shoes, iron bucket handles, bone sledge runners, articulated animal remains (including a drilled cattle skull) and three folded strips of some fibrous material, probably birch bark, tentatively suggested as organic curse tablets (ibid.). The feature lay near to an agricultural aisled building within a field system, and possibly represented a small field shrine within a larger (villa?) estate.

In addition to sacred shafts and wells, there is evidence that some natural subterranean features were imbued with a certain sanctity, including the Alveston fissure (remnants of a cave system) in South Gloucestershire, which contained the remains of many dog and human skeletons, including one with evidence for cannibalism, radiocarbon dated to around the time of the Roman conquest (Aldhouse-Green 2004a, 196–7). The ritual use of caves in particular is very well attested across many cultures and periods (Moyes

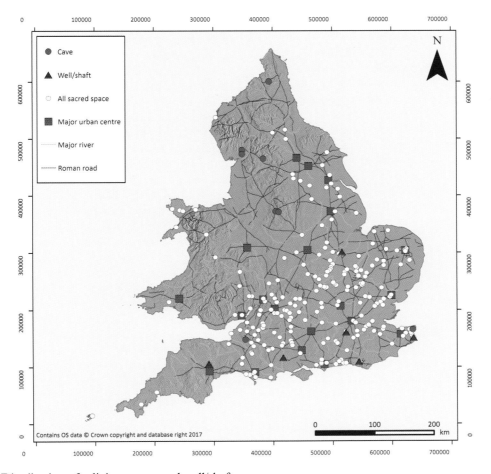

FIG. 5.21. Distribution of religious caves and well/shafts

2012a), being particularly associated with the worship of Pan within the Greco-Roman world (Orlin 2015, 690). These were dark, mysterious places, surely perceived as the junction between different worlds, with Moyes (2012b, 9) recently suggesting that 'the very nature of the cave as a natural, chthonic, immovable cavity, carved in stone, can represent the earth itself, its associated deities, and its enduring presence'.

Roman artefacts alongside human remains and animal remains have been found within many cave systems in Britain, though they have not always been systematically excavated and reported (Branigan 1992). It is usually very difficult to ascertain the nature of Roman activity in these caves, although some certainly appeared to have had at least temporary domestic use, while industrial use is also attested at sites such as White Woman's Hole in Somerset, where there is evidence for late Roman coin counterfeiting (Barrett and Boon 1972). However, it does seem that certain caves were used for ritual purposes, including for human burial and possibly as subterranean shrines, or indeed as both (Branigan 1992, 15–16). This project has not included all

caves where a possible religious use has been suggested, but instead has incorporated a selection of excavated cave sites where use as a shrine seems quite possible, these being shown on FIG. 5.21. As would be expected, almost all are concentrated in the main limestone cave areas in the west and north of England, though a cave exposed by chalk quarrying at Spratling Court Farm, Manston, in 1996 contained deposits of animal bone radiocarbon dated to the second century A.D. (Baker 2006). It was suggested that this seemingly isolated and still-wooded part of the Thanet ridge was the site of a possible early Roman pit/cave shrine (*ibid.*).

Further west, there are a great many caves in the Mendip Hills with evidence for Iron Age and Roman activity, though the largest cave system utilised was at Wookey Hole on the southern edge of this landscape (Branigan and Dearne 1991a). Here, activity of second to fourth century A.D. date was recovered from four chambers, including a cemetery of at least 28 individuals within the furthest chamber, and a large quantity of objects found elsewhere, though mostly from the entrance area. Although in a re-appraisal of the finds

Branigan and Dearne suggested likely domestic occupation (*ibid.*, 77), the quantity of objects, including over 130 coins, 17 brooches and almost 100 hairpins, was far in excess of the assemblage from most local non-nucleated settlements, with a composition more in line with many temple sites (see below, p. 169). It is perhaps more likely to have functioned as liminal, sacred space, also suitable for human burial, associated with the settlement known *c.* 100 m from the cave entrance (Ashworth and Crampton 1964).

Other possible Romano-British cave shrines lie to the north, including Poole's Cavern (Smithson and Branigan 1991) and Thirst House Cave (Branigan and Dearne 1991b) in the Peak District, both of which contained artefacts of unusual quantity and quality compared to local domestic settlements. A religious interpretation for these sites has generally been disregarded in favour of metalwork manufacture, though they are of course not mutually exclusive. Victoria Cave, near Settle in North Yorkshire, is one of many caves in this area with evidence for Roman activity, and, as with the other sites just discussed, had what seems to be an exceptionally large volume of finds for the area, including almost 60 brooches and 118 coins (Dearne and Lord 1998). Unusual finds included 23 perforated spoons of uncertain function, of which more examples were found in other local caves, altogether accounting for *c.* 60 per cent of all such objects found in the country (Eckardt 2014, 127). Possible cave shrines are also known outside of the Roman province in Britain, such as at High Pasture Cave on the Isle of Skye in Scotland. Here, investigations revealed a steep flight of stone steps leading to a natural limestone cave, in which was found human remains of Iron Age date and a wide range of unusual artefacts and ecofacts (http://www.high-pasture-cave.org/; Aldhouse-Green 2010, 199).

Ultimately it is the nature and scale of the finds assemblages in these caves that mark them out as possible shrines, though there is one example, a natural rock chamber rather than a cave, that contained no finds, but was interpreted as a shrine on the basis of a figure carved on the rock face (Charlton and Mitcheson 1983). The site, at Yardhope in Northumberland, lay immediately below the summit of a long ridge, and the figure was identified with the god Cocidius, known from inscriptions on Hadrian's Wall (*ibid.*). Other features in the 2 m² chamber comprised a posthole cut into rock by the doorway and a hearth. It remains uncertain whether there are other similarly modified natural contexts that were used as shrines, but its presence is surely a reminder of the extremely varied nature of Romano-British cult sites.

Shrines identified by finds alone

This category of 29 'shrines' (FIG. 5.22) represents a very heterogeneous group that in many ways could be conflated with those just outlined, in that their religious interpretation relies upon the presence of finds concentrations of unusual character and/or quantity. At nine sites, nearly all of them nucleated settlements, the presence of shrines has only been tentatively suggested owing to the generally high quantities of religious objects recovered during excavations. One such site, at Gill Mill in Oxfordshire, had items including a stone Mater-type goddess figure, an incomplete altar to a Genius, a small stone-relief panel of a horse and rider, a stone miniature altar, three 'pipeclay' figurines and two unusual lead and copper-alloy dodecahedrons (Booth and Simmonds 2018; see below). The actual location and form of any shrine remain unknown, though it was suspected to lie at the heart of the settlement where excavation was not possible (*ibid.*). At five other settlements, a shrine was proposed due to the concentration of religious objects in a particular area, though no associated features or structures were noted. At a farmstead in Devizes, Wiltshire, for example, there was an extensive late Roman midden deposit containing an inscribed lead curse tablet, a crushed copper-alloy garment collar, suggested as priestly regalia, alongside coins and personal items (Valentin and Robinson 2002).

All of the remaining fifteen sites represent possible shrines where there may genuinely have been no man-made focal or defining features. Four of them comprise concentrations of objects found in relation to prehistoric monuments, discussed further below (p. 160), while four others relate to objects deposited in watery contexts, such as the large numbers of artefacts found in the river bed by the bridge crossing the River Tees at Piercebridge, County Durham, to the south of the military *vicus*. These include personal items, large amounts of military equipment and many religious objects such as copper-alloy and pipeclay figurines, votive plaques, miniature objects and fragments of rolled lead sheets, possibly curse tablets (Walton 2016). The final seven sites in this category are represented by concentrations of finds in otherwise 'rural' settings, such as the many coins, brooches and other objects found within a Roman field system at Leaze Farm in the Upper Thames Valley, near to the confluence of the Rivers Thames and Leach (Miles *et al.* 2007, 311–13) (see also discussion of coin hoards below, p. 191). At Frensham on the Surrey/Hampshire border, metal-detector survey and excavation near the top of a hill revealed over 400 coins associated with small pits and over 60 miniature pots, the preliminary testing of which indicated the presence

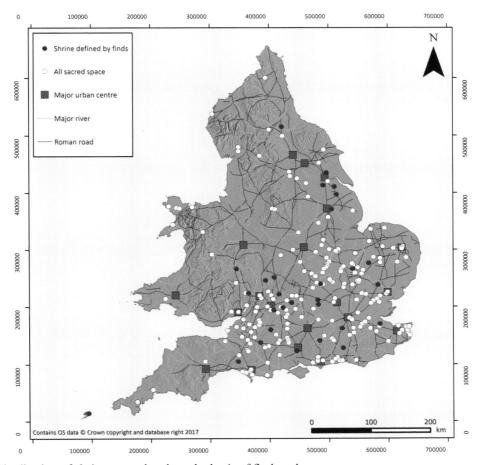

FIG. 5.22. Distribution of shrines postulated on the basis of finds only

of cannabis (Graham 2001). Further evidence for religious activity from this site comprised fragments of iron sceptre binding and parts of a copper-alloy vessel, though the only features, aside from the pits, comprised parts of a possible field system (Bird 2008, 70).

The sites discussed here and above illustrate how, ultimately, it was the place itself rather than any specific form of man-made feature that was the most important element of any sacred site. The reasons that certain sites were chosen as places of veneration may seem fairly clear to us on one level, such as an association with an extant prehistoric monument, or landscape feature like a cave or spring. In most other cases any reasoning is far harder to discern, and of course the specific cosmological rationale behind a place being deemed sacred – the site of a mythological event, the home of a local supernatural being, a place associated with ancestors, etc. – is largely recondite without contemporary records. Archaeological evidence can, however, provide some evidence for patterning in the settlement and landscape contexts of sacred sites, as well as providing a limited understanding of how at least some of these religious loci may have functioned.

THE WIDER CONTEXT AND USE OF SACRED SITES

Archaeological evidence for sacred space can be found across all regions and within all settlement types to some extent. Although it is clear that ritual practices were also tightly interwoven with everyday domestic life (see below, p. 182), this suggests that there was a need for specific religious space within many communities, perhaps facilitating family and wider public gatherings with the performance of rituals in order to bind people together. Some sites may also have attracted religious visitors, or pilgrims, from far afield, as has been attested elsewhere in the Greco-Roman world (Gray 1999; Elsner 2008). As has just been shown, the form that this sacred space could take varied markedly, with some evidence for spatial patterning of different types across different landscapes. There are also some notable patterns relating to sacred sites within different settlement and landscape contexts, some of which may relate to the type and scale of rituals and other activities performed there. FIGURE 5.23 provides a breakdown of the broad contexts for Romano-Celtic temples and all of the other many forms of

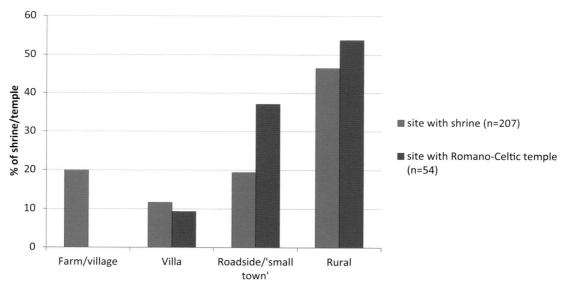

FIG. 5.23. Contexts of shrines and Romano-Celtic temples

Sacred sites on farmsteads

sacred space grouped together as 'shrines', which will now be discussed in turn.

Despite the fact that farmsteads are by far the most numerous type of settlement in Roman Britain, and have benefited particularly from the recent upsurge in developer-funded excavation, there are very few that have been directly associated with any sacred space. Just 33 farmsteads of Roman date have been suggested as containing defined religious space, representing less than 2 per cent of all excavated examples, and with a slight emphasis on those of the later Roman period. None of these have buildings of Romano-Celtic form; instead the evidence comprises a variety of generally small timber and masonry structures, alongside enclosures and concentrations of finds (FIG. 5.24). Some examples, such as the small masonry building at Monkston Park, Milton Keynes, have been highlighted above, while another comprised two circular structures/gullies found within an enclosure in the midst of a farmstead at Topham Farm, Sykehouse, South Yorkshire, which were suggested as superimposed shrines on the basis of the unusual nature of construction and possible structured deposits of complete pottery vessels (Roberts 2003; FIG. 5.25). Many of the shrines lay on the periphery of the farmstead, such as at Little Paxton Quarry in Cambridgeshire, where a circular foundation trench (15 m dia.) at the southern end of a rectangular enclosure lay close to Bronze Age barrows on the north-western edge of a farmstead. Its religious interpretation was suggested on the basis of its form, location, concentration of coins and the presence of three votive letters (Jones 2001; FIG. 5.25). At Broughton, Milton Keynes, a

pentagonal enclosure containing a smaller sub-rectangular enclosure/structure and a posthole structure was located to the south-west of the main settlement (Atkins *et al.* 2014). It lay in the vicinity of a late Iron Age/early Roman cemetery, and the fact that the smaller enclosure surrounded a mid-second century A.D. cremation burial indicates that the function of this 'shrine' was closely interwoven with funerary ritual, an association more readily found in villa and non-settlement 'rural' settings (see below and Ch. 6).

At Claydon Pike in Gloucestershire, a probable double-ditched enclosure-shrine of second to third century A.D. date lay at the heart of the complex farmstead, overlooking a central area of cleared space (Miles *et al.* 2007; FIG. 5.26). Among the radical changes made at this settlement during the late Roman period was a complete change in its religious focus, with the central enclosure shrine no longer being used and a new circular masonry shrine built *c.* 50 m to the east on the edge of marshy ground, with a metalled path leading around the building and into the marsh (*ibid.*). Such a momentous shift in the location and form of the sacred space may have marked changes in the rituals and ideologies of the inhabitants, going from a central, perhaps communal, enclosed space with evidence from the ceramic and glass assemblages for feasting and the burning of incense, to a more distant, private devotion characterised by the offering of coins and personal votives. This may be a direct reflection of the transformation of the nature of the settlement, arguably from an estate centre with a relatively large and diverse community focused in part on a centrally placed religious enclosure, to a much smaller community with a different focus.

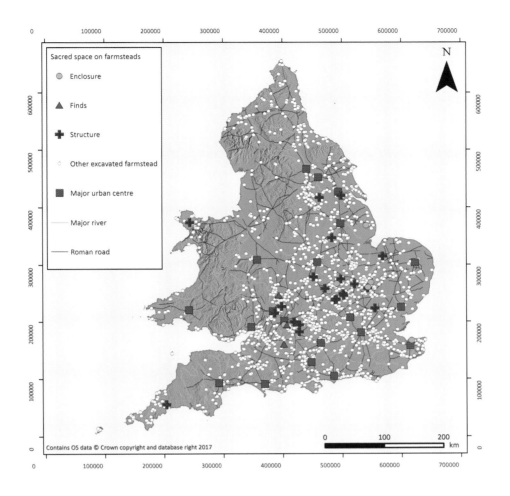

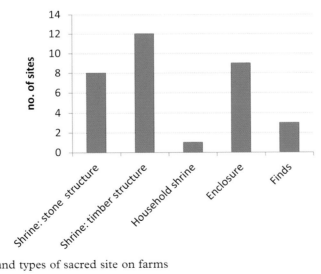

FIG. 5.24. Distribution and types of sacred site on farms

The distribution of farmsteads with suggested shrines shown in FIG. 5.24 highlights their marked concentration in the Central Belt region, which has 24 of the 33 sites. Most of these (sixteen examples) are complex farmsteads, mainly lying in the principal river valleys of the Nene, Ouse, Thames and Severn. Such farmsteads are characterised by their physical differentiation of space (Allen and Smith 2016, 28), with particular zones being utilised for a variety of domestic, agricultural and industrial activities. It is therefore hardly surprising that this type of farmstead is more likely to have had separated and distinct provision for certain forms of religious expression.

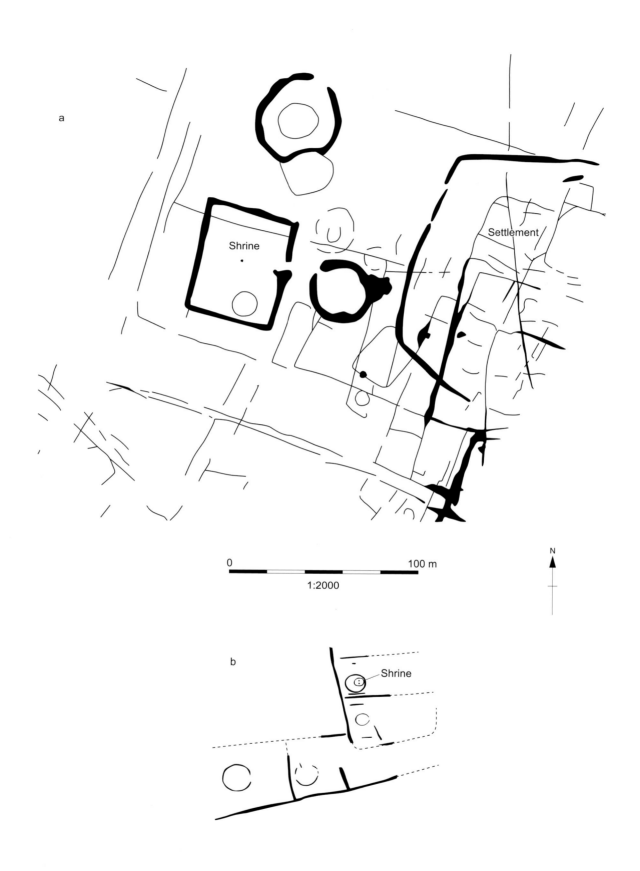

FIG. 5.25. Site plans of farmsteads at (a) Little Paxton Quarry, Cambs (Jones 2001) and (b) Topham Farm, Sykehouse, S Yorks (Roberts 2003) showing location of shrines

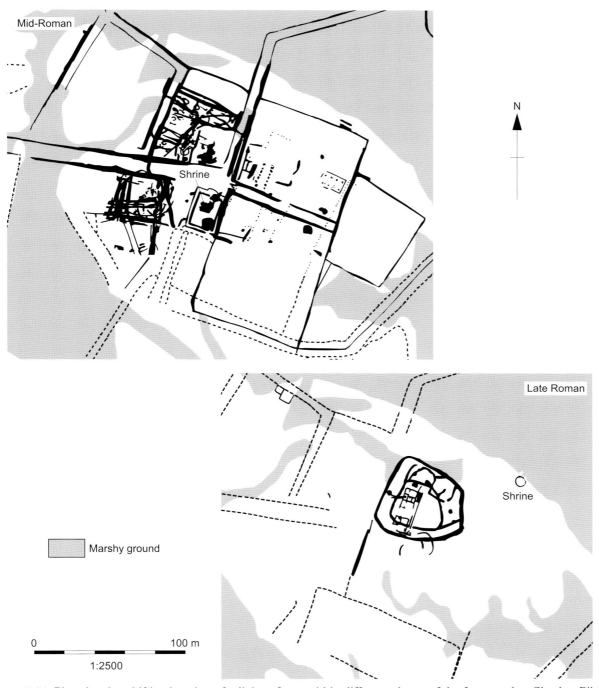

FIG. 5.26. Plan showing shifting location of religious focus within different phases of the farmstead at Claydon Pike, Glos. (Miles *et al.* 2007)

This is not to say, however, that there was necessarily any greater division between sacred and profane at these sites than in any other settlement, as indicated by the many instances of structured deposits found in all parts of the settlements, discussed below. The differences may lie partly in larger population sizes within certain complex farmsteads, with some perhaps comprising multiple family units of the same kin-group, and others, like Claydon Pike, seemingly incorporating different zones of more socially

distinct occupation, including those of higher status and general agricultural workers of the farming estate (see also discussion of villas below). In these cases, the provision of dedicated sacred space within or in close proximity to the settlement may have provided one means of maintaining some level of immediate social cohesiveness, perhaps even reinforcing social hierarchies, with certain members of the community acting in a priestly capacity to perform public ritual actions, as is likely to have been the case within larger nucleated settlements (see below, p. 155). However, it must be remembered that the proportion of even complex farmsteads with evidence for shrines remains very small, and it is likely that most 'public' ritual would have taken place either within local nucleated settlements or else in other special places in the surrounding countryside.

Sacred sites on villas

A total of 28 villa sites had some form of postulated sacred space directly associated with the main settlement, representing just under 10 per cent of all excavated villas. These included five with Romano-Celtic temples, which in three cases, Lullingstone and Keston in Kent and Bancroft in Milton Keynes, were believed to have functioned as funerary monuments, essentially being used as mausolea. The remaining two comprised a substantial but ill-understood temple at Chedworth, on a hill terrace overlooking the River Coln, *c.* 800 m from the large multi-courtyard villa (Baddeley 1930), and a possible early/mid-Roman Romano-Celtic variant within the villa complex at Thurnham in Kent (Booth and Lawrence 2006), although a religious interpretation of the latter is now thought unlikely (Booth 2011b, 283–6). A further Romano-Celtic temple lay within the villa complex at Cosgrove, Northants, though by the time of its construction in the late second century A.D. (succeeding an earlier timber shrine), the main villa building appears to have gone out of use, with a more simple house remaining the only domestic structure (Quinnell 1991).

The remaining sacred sites on villas comprise other freestanding masonry structures, alongside a few internal rooms/features grouped under the term 'household shrines', a fenced 'ritual enclosure' at Thruxton, Hants, discussed above (p. 142), and two sites, Gestingthorpe in Essex (Draper 1985) and Salford Priors in Warwickshire (Palmer 2000), where shrines were suggested on the basis of the quantity, type and distribution of finds (FIG. 5.27). Two of the household shrines comprised sunken rooms within the main villa building, including the well-known cult room at Lullingstone in Kent (FIG. 5.28), which had a small well or cistern in the middle of the floor and wall paintings including three water nymphs in a niche in the wall (Meates 1979). The cellar in the villa at Wortley in Gloucestershire had painted plaster walls and an underfloor drain, suggested as being connected with a possible lead tank in the middle of the room (Wilson *et al.* 2014). Perring (1989) has argued that a series of common characteristics in cellar location and design within other Roman-British buildings (mostly villas) is indicative of a general

association with cult practice, though more definitive evidence is usually lacking. The importance of water at both Lullingstone and Wortley is found repeated in many other freestanding villa shrines, including possible nymphaea (water shrines) suggested at Chedworth in Gloucestershire, Box and Groundwell Ridge in Wiltshire, Darenth in Kent, Whatley Combe in Somerset and Swainshill in Herefordshire, to which can probably be added a hexagonal building enclosing a well-shaft with possible structured deposits close to the main villa building at Truckle Hill, North Wraxall, Wiltshire (Andrews 2009a).

Most of the external, freestanding villa shrines, including the possible nymphaea, were relatively modest structures, sometimes interpreted on no stronger a basis than unusual morphology, such as the octagonal building near the villa at Bancroft, Milton Keynes (Williams and Zeepvat 1994; FIG. 5.28), and the apsed building at Preston Court Farm, Beddingham, West Sussex (Rudling 1998). Larger and more unusual buildings do occasionally occur, however, such as the substantial Y-shaped building near to the modest corridor villa south of the Roman town of Caistor-by-Norwich, which was suggested as either a temple or summer triclinium (Bowden 2011). A possible classical-style temple has also been suggested at Castor in Cambridgeshire, on the site of a monumental Roman building complex near the town of Durobrivae, which may have had an administrative function (Upex 2011). For the most part, however, dedicated sacred space within villa complexes appears either to have been for specialised funerary purposes (temple/mausolea) or else to have been on a very modest scale, some probably used solely by the villa owners and family for the worship of household deities, and others by the immediate estate workers.

The veneration of household gods had a very strong tradition within Mediterranean Roman culture, with two particular groups of deities, the Lares and Penates, featuring in many literary accounts (e.g. *Aulularia* of Plautus, 1–36), although their nature remains quite ill understood (Rives 2007, 118). The hearth was the typical focus for domestic rituals, though specialised shrines called lararia also existed, with many varied examples being found within Roman houses in Italy (*ibid.*, 119). Such household shrines are far rarer in Gaul (Fauduet 2014, 79) and in Britain are only really visible in villas such as Lullingstone and Wortley just mentioned, alongside another suggested example comprising an arrangement of ceramic tiles set into a corner wall in a modest villa/farmstead building at Alfred's Castle in Oxfordshire (Gosden and Lock 2013), and further possible examples in urban houses (cf. Boon

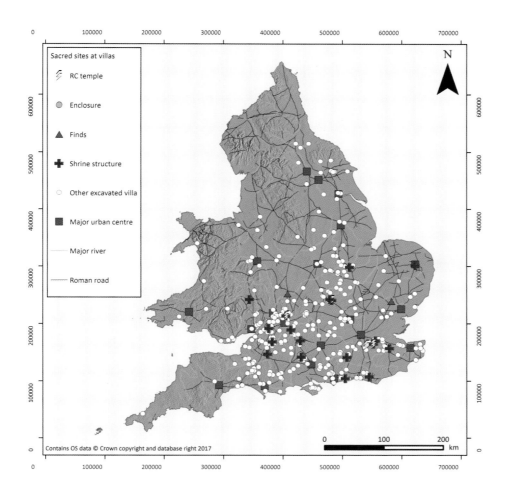

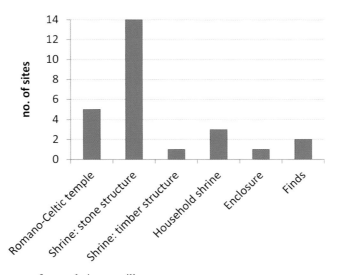

FIG. 5.27. Distribution and types of sacred site on villas

1983; Perring 2002, 197). How far any of the other small shrine structures on villas may have been used for the worship of household deities remains uncertain; some may have been erected for the *genius* or divine alter-ego of the head of the household, which was not uncommon in central parts of the empire, and used to help reinforce social hierarchy within the household (Rives 2007, 119). There may, of course, have been a variety of sacred spaces within villa complexes, each serving a different function and/or related to different social groups, as was possibly the case at Lullingstone, where a Romano-Celtic temple/ mausoleum, circular shrine and internal cult room have all been identified in relatively close proximity (FIG. 5.28). The temple may have originally served a purely religious function, before later being used as a mausoleum for two adult individuals (Meates 1979). During the late Roman phase of the villa at Bancroft, there were two possible shrines, an octagonal building lying close to the main villa, which was devoid of diagnostic finds, and a circular building lying *c.* 350 m to the west on a hill overlooking the complex (near to an earlier temple-mausoleum), containing structured deposits of coins, iron spear tips/heads and a complete articulated pig (FIG. 5.28). Assuming the octagonal building was used in a religious capacity, the shrines were clearly being used for variable ritual strategies, perhaps relating to differences in

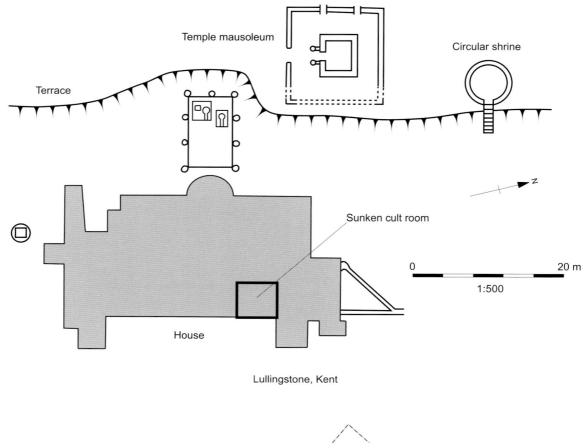

Lullingstone, Kent

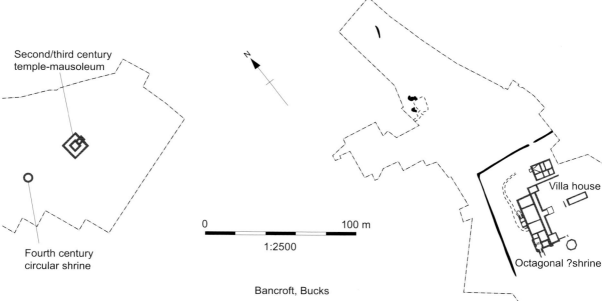

Bancroft, Bucks

FIG. 5.28. Site plans of villa complexes at Lullingstone, Kent (Meates 1979), and Bancroft, Milton Keynes (Williams and Zeepvat 1994) showing location of defined sacred space

the deities worshipped, and/or to the social groups participating in the rituals. On a wider geographic scale it is likely that many of the apparently isolated rural shrines and temples in parts of central and southern Britain, discussed below, lay on villa estates, and may represent a further element in the complex organisation of religious expression that seems apparent in the Romano-British countryside.

Sacred sites in nucleated settlements

Nucleated settlements with larger populations have, unsurprisingly, much more evidence for sacred space than smaller farms and villas. These 58 sites comprise defended small towns (8), roadside settlements (37), military *vici* (4) and villages (9), while an additional five sites have been included in this contextual category as 'semi-urban' on the basis that they lie less than 1 km from a town and are clearly associated. Sacred sites lying within or immediately outside of major towns (e.g. London, Colchester, Verulamium, Canterbury, Caerwent etc.) have not been included, nor have temples in small towns that are known only from aerial photographs, such as the

Romano-Celtic temples from Alchester in Oxfordshire. A number of these sites are, however, referred to for comparative purposes.

The distribution of nucleated settlements with sacred sites is shown in FIG. 5.29, along with an account of their variable type. There is a much stronger association between Romano-Celtic temples and nucleated centres than with other settlement types, although this connection appears largely concentrated in the east of England. Here, such temples have been found in association with nucleated settlements at Crownthorpe and Scole in Norfolk, Stonea Grange and Godmanchester in Cambridgeshire, Irchester in Northamptonshire and Chelmsford in Essex, while also being found in 'semi-urban' locations outside of Great Chesterford, Verulamium (Folly Lane), Colchester (Sheepen) and Caistor-by-Norwich (FIG. 5.30). These latter sites were all located within substantial precincts that may well have been designed to congregate large numbers of people from the urban centres, perhaps in seasonal festivals, with processions leading from the towns (cf. Esmonde Cleary 2005; see also Perring 2011 for discussion of ritual processions within Roman London). The two recently published Romano-Celtic temples

FIG. 5.29. Distribution and types of sacred site on nucleated settlements

from Tabard Square, Southwark, on the periphery of a suburb of Roman London, were also set within a large precinct, and were argued to have been designed by the town's authorities 'to satisfy the religious needs of the population of *Londinium*' (Killock *et al.* 2015, 254; FIG. 5.30). Such large, religious public cult complexes would have been relatively costly to build and maintain, and would undoubtedly have relied upon civic patronage, perhaps with local magistrates acting as priests (Rives 2000, 253; see below, p. 178).

The Romano-Celtic temple was clearly deemed a suitable form of religious architecture for the performance of public ritual in these cases, and indeed, in much of the east of England their use is largely confined to larger settlements and urban centres. Further west the situation was more mixed, with the majority of such temples being found in rural contexts. Examples within nucleated settlements have been revealed by aerial photographs within the walled town at Alchester (M. Foster 1989, 147) and the roadside settlement

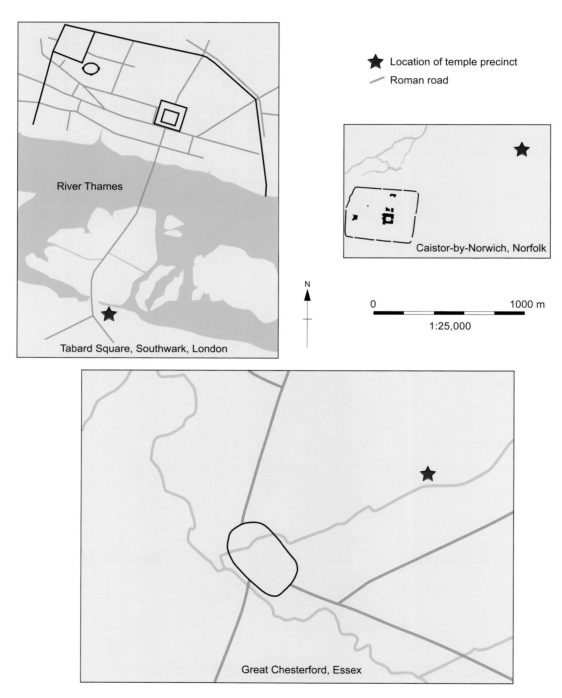

FIG. 5.30. Locations of 'semi-urban' temple precincts at Tabard Square, Southwark, London (Killock *et al.* 2015), Caistor, Norfolk (Gurney 1986a), and Great Chesterford, Essex (Medlycott 2011)

at Sansom's Platt, both in Oxfordshire (Winton 2001, 306). In addition, there is a possible Romano-Celtic temple revealed by geophysical survey in a roadside settlement at Great Bulmore near Caerleon, Newport, in South Wales (Yates 2000), and nearby is the well-known excavated example in the centre of the *civitas* capital at Caerwent (Ashby *et al*. 1910). The remaining three nucleated settlements with recognised Romano-Celtic temples within the west of Britain – Marcham/ Frilford, Bath and Nettleton Scrubb – are perhaps best described as large rural religious complexes rather than 'typical' nucleated roadside settlements. As such, these sites will be discussed further below, along with the religious complex/roadside settlement at Springhead in Kent (p. 163).

While Romano-Celtic temples are more readily associated with nucleated settlements than with farms and villas, especially in the east of England, they are still outnumbered by other types of sacred space in these contexts. Most of these comprised different forms of masonry or timber buildings, some contained within enclosures or at least set within an area of cleared space. On occasion they could be quite monumental in scale, such as the shrine complex at Elms Farm in Essex noted above (p. 140), and a large late Roman basilican temple almost 20 m by 14 m in size, which replaced an earlier circular shrine within an ill-defined roadside settlement/religious complex at

Thistleton in Rutland (Smith 2001, 257). More often, however, the shrines identified within nucleated settlements were the usual array of smaller rectangular, circular and polygonal structures, along with the occasional enclosure, such as those at Higham Ferrers and Stanwick in the Nene Valley discussed above (p. 143). The variety in scale was considerable and some are likely to have been little more than wayside shrines, such as the rectangular arrangement of chalk footings, just *c*. 3 x 4 m in size, with coin deposits by the junction of two roads in the roadside settlement at Springhead in Kent (Andrews *et al*. 2011, 89; FIG. 5.31).

The shrines interpreted within the nine village settlements were all either fairly small timber structures or else enclosures or finds concentrations, and would seem more akin to the range of sacred sites found on farmsteads. A small rectangular timber building adjacent to a trackway on the western fringes of the settlement at Monkton in Thanet, Kent, has been interpreted as a roadside shrine (Bennett *et al*. 2008), while in the Roman village at Longstanton site XIX in Cambridgeshire, sacred space was only suggested on the basis of a concentration of 'votive' material in one evaluation trench, possibly associated with inhumation burials from the same trench (Evans *et al*. 2006). The fairly modest architectural nature of these village shrines befits the status of their parent sites as essentially

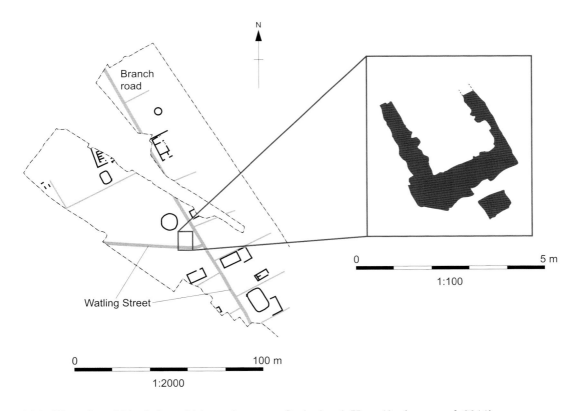

FIG. 5.31. Plan of roadside shrine within settlement at Springhead, Kent (Andrews *et al*. 2011)

large, aggregated farmsteads, though the fact that they were interpreted in over 15 per cent of excavated examples suggests that they may have been important parts of these larger communities.

Just four of the military *vici* included in this study (i.e. excluding those from the Hadrian's Wall/ Stanegate area) contained evidence for religious structures, including a square building enclosed by a palisade at Caersws in Powys (N.W. Jones 1996), and the small rectangular classical temple and adjacent circular shrine within the military *vicus* at Maryport in Cumbria, noted above (p. 139). However, additional *vici* in the area of Hadrian's Wall and the Stanegate include sacred sites, such as at Vindolanda, which contained the northernmost example of a Romano-Celtic temple, probably dating to the early second century A.D. (Birley 2009). Elsewhere there is the remarkable situation of three sacred sites outside of the fort at Carrawburgh – a mithraeum, a nymphaeum and a shrine dedicated to a local goddess Coventina, which comprised a stone-lined well within a precinct wall, associated with thousands of coins and other finds (Allason-Jones and McKay 1985). It is possible that these shrines were components of a larger religious site sited in the valley leading out of Coventina's Well, though further landscape study is needed to support such an idea. Whether or not it was only soldiers who frequented these shrines is not easy to tell, but work on the finds from a sanctuary within the *colonia* at Apulum in Dacia indicated quite firmly that here at least, soldiers and civilians were using the cult place contemporaneously over long periods (Haynes 2014).

The evidence overall indicates that nucleated sites were more likely to have had some provision for sacred space than any other form of settlement, as is also suggested by the type and quantity of religious objects, discussed below (p. 168). Some of these shrines/temples could be quite substantial, and undoubtedly provided for the formal religious requirements of the inhabitants and probably people from other settlements in the vicinity. In places like the east of England, where nucleated settlements appear particularly common and few farmsteads would have lain more than a day's journey away (Smith 2016c, 222), they may have catered for the wider population. Elsewhere, the distance to such centres would often have been too far, and instead a network of large and small rural sanctuaries is likely to have fulfilled these religious needs.

Sacred sites in rural 'non-settlement' contexts

Around half of all excavated sites with evidence for sacred space do not seem to be associated with any specific settlement, instead being found in general 'rural' environments. These, however, cover an extremely broad range of sacred sites, from what would appear to have been major rural sanctuaries with many associated buildings, to minor and perhaps infrequently visited places in the landscape, such as some of the cave sites discussed above, whose remoteness and sense of danger may be relevant and important reasons why such loci were chosen. Questions then arise as to why so many sacred places were located away from settlement contexts, why specific sites were 'chosen' as being worthy of devotion, and what connections did they have with surrounding landscape features, other sacred sites and the settlements where most people lived?

All of these questions are very hard to address, given the lack of historical sources and vagaries of the archaeological evidence. The distribution and form of these rural sites is shown in FIG. 5.32, well spread across much of England and Wales, though with caves/rock shelters being the only type known in the far north and north-west of England, with the exception of circular and rectangular masonry shrines at Scargill Moor in County Durham, which were clearly related to the fort at Bowes, 3 km to the north (Richmond and Wright 1948). Elsewhere a slight concentration of ritual enclosures is seen in parts of East Anglia, continuing the trend seen in the late Iron Age (see above p. 128), while rural Romano-Celtic temples are largely confined to central southern England. The proportion of sacred sites located in settlement and rural 'non-settlement' contexts in the South, East and Central Belt regions is shown in FIG. 5.33, and clearly demonstrates the greater dominance of rural sites in the South. This is largely because of the increased number of farmsteads in the Central Belt with evidence for shrines, as noted above, while there is also a higher percentage of postulated sacred space located in nucleated sites in the East and Central Belt (*c.* 34 per cent) than is the case in the South (*c.* 22 per cent). Nevertheless, the higher number of rural sacred sites in the South may also reflect the higher numbers of shrines in this region during the late Iron Age and the fact that many of these places seem to have retained some level of sanctity into the Roman period, even though no associated settlement was ever established. One example located on a distinctive hilltop at Farley Heath in Surrey appears, on the basis of the quantity and type of finds, to have been a late Iron Age ritual site, which then developed into a Romano-Celtic temple within an unusual polygonal enclosure during the Roman period (Poulton and Bird 2007). While there is evidence for some Roman-period activity outside the temenos, it does seem that the site remained an essentially rural sanctuary right up until the end of the Roman period or even beyond (*ibid.*).

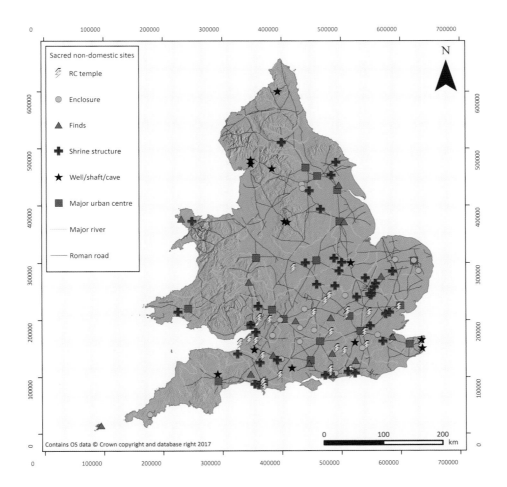

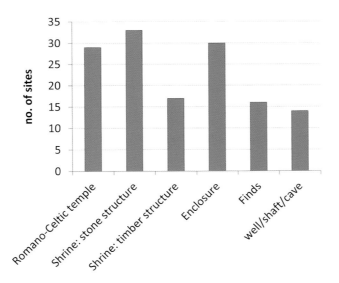

FIG. 5.32. Distribution and types of sacred site on rural 'non-settlement' sites

The location of many of these rural sacred sites – and indeed those in other contexts – may have been governed in a large part by the existence and manipulation of collective memories within communities regarding specific places in the landscape. In a recent assessment of the role and processes of memory in Roman Britain, Kamash (2016) has highlighted how communities may have created 'legendary topographies' around extant monuments such as Neolithic and Bronze Age barrows, with sacred sites in particular being established in relation to such features in order to direct collective memories towards a much earlier, more idealised, past. The association between Roman-period sacred space and prehistoric monuments is now well established, both in Britain (Williams 1998; Smith 2001, 150; Hutton 2011), and in other parts of the empire (García Sanjuán *et al.* 2008). Of the 35 examples of such

association explicitly noted in this project, 80 per cent were located in non-settlement rural contexts, with features ranging from Bronze Age cairns to Neolithic henge monuments. Sometimes this involved the construction of substantial religious buildings, such as the Romano-Celtic temples close to prehistoric barrows at Uley in Gloucestershire (Woodward and Leach 1993) and Brean Down in Somerset (Apsimon 1965). In other cases the evidence for religious appropriation of earlier monuments is far slighter, such as the small rectangular building found next to a large Bronze Age circular ditch surrounding a natural chalk outcrop at Red Lodge, Suffolk; the building contained pits with structured deposits of pig skulls facing east with coins placed on their forehead, while further Roman objects were recovered from the ditch fill (*Current Arch.* 2017). Sometimes, indications of possible religious use

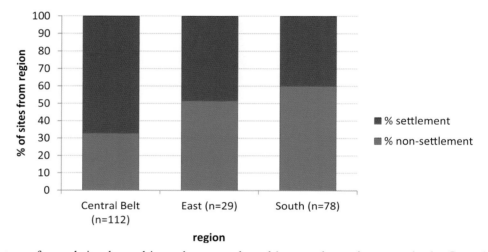

FIG. 5.33. Percentage of sacred sites located in settlement and rural 'non-settlement' contexts in the Central Belt, East and South regions

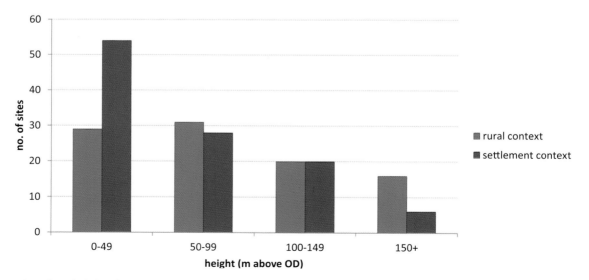

FIG. 5.34. Spot height of all sacred sites in Central Belt and South regions showing difference between those in rural and settlement contexts

are limited to objects alone, such as the Roman artefacts, including a copper-alloy votive leaf, placed in and around a Neolithic oval barrow on a prominent chalk ridge on the Chiltern escarpment at Whiteleaf Hill, Buckinghamshire (Hey *et al.* 2007). As Hutton has reiterated, it remains difficult in these instances to gain any measure of how such sites were used, in particular 'whether it was formal or informal, or private, involved individuals, families or larger groups, or was dedicated to specific deities, to spirits specific to the location concerned, or to dead humans, or to any mix of these' (Hutton 2011, 14).

The creation of 'legendary topographies' need not, of course, be limited to observable prehistoric monuments. Specific natural landscape features may well have been imbued with special religious significance, perhaps as a way of anchoring communities to their local environment. Specific context details were not systematically collected for all rural sacred sites in this study, though at least 40 were described as being situated on a hill top or upper slope, with an emphasis on visibility. Spot height analysis for the South and Central Belt regions, where most excavated examples lie, indicates that overall they have a greater preference for higher ground than sacred space located within settlements, or indeed than settlements in general (FIG. 5.34; see spot height analysis in Smith *et al.* 2016, 114, 175). A particularly notable group of possible religious enclosures lie in prominent positions on the chalk downs of central southern England, including Lowbury Hill (Atkinson 1916; Fulford and Rippon 1994; see FIG. 5.20 above) and Uffington (Miles *et al.* 2003) along the line of the Ridgeway, and Great Bedwyn/Shalbourne on the western slope of Carvers Hill (Brindle *et al.* 2013). The preference for late Iron Age and Roman rural sacred sites to be situated on elevated positions in the landscape has been commented on before (Smith 2001, 150; Bird 2004a, 83; Ghey 2005, 112; Garland 2013, 193), with certain landscapes having a number of inter-visible sacred loci. These may have acted as fixed spiritual points in the landscape, creating sacred or pilgrimage pathways, and maintaining linkages between communities.

Most rural sacred sites are likely to have had strong associations with settlements in their localities. Of the 132 'rural' sacred sites, almost 85 per cent lay within 5 km of an excavated settlement (farmstead, villa or nucleated site), suggesting a high level of connectivity. As just outlined, rural Romano-Celtic temples were largely restricted to parts of central southern Britain, and 23 of the 26 examples (88 per cent) lay within 5 km of a contemporary settlement, 15 lying in the near vicinity of a villa. Most of these temples developed

in the mid- to late Roman period at around the same time as the majority of villas in this area (see Smith *et al.* 2016, 92, 158) and their similar chronology, close geographic proximity and in many case similar construction methods suggest that many of them were integral parts of wider villa estates. A Romano-Celtic temple at Wood End Lane, Herts, was built on a plateau *c.* 5 km west of Verulamium and *c.* 3.5 km from two villas lying on either side, at Gorhambury and Gadebridge (Neal 1984; FIG. 5.35). It was interpreted as a mausoleum on the basis of a sunken chamber in the cella, but the monumental nature of the complex, set around a walled temenos of 0.8 ha, with ancillary buildings including possible subsidiary shrines and a bathhouse, suggests a more important religious site, despite the relative lack of finds. The meagre dating evidence suggested activity in the second and third centuries A.D., contemporary with major architectural developments in the nearby villas, and it is not hard to suppose that it lay within the estate of one of the villas, or perhaps upon their common boundary, and was used periodically for festivals by the inhabitants of the estates, including those in the three contemporary excavated farmsteads that lay within 2 km of the site.

Located just 7 km north of Wood End Lane was another religious complex at Friars Wash, with two conjoined Romano-Celtic temples and two possible subsidiary shrines set within a ditched temenos enclosure (Birbeck 2009). Unlike Wood End Lane it is located on lower ground, 60 m east of the River Ver and *c.* 400 m from the major Roman road of Watling Street, at approximately the point where it changes direction (FIG. 5.35). The complex probably owed its architectural elaboration, if not its actual existence, to the regular traffic along Watling Street, and may have catered largely for a more transient group of supplicants. The overall context of the site, together with the quantity of coins recovered from the small area excavated, suggests a different type of cult place from Wood End Lane; Burleigh (2015, 110) has argued that it marked the boundary between the territories of *Durocobrivae* (Dunstable) and Verulamium.

Most excavated examples of rural religious sites did not comprise Romano-Celtic temples, but a variety of other masonry and timber structures, along with enclosures, finds concentrations, wells, shafts and caves (see FIG. 5.32). At least sixteen of these had wider associations with funerary ritual, such as the late Roman shrine/mausoleum on the highest part of the hill at Cannington in Somerset, which was represented by a circular rock-cut trench with traces of a red sandstone revetment, and probably formed the focus of a major late/

post-Roman cemetery (Rahtz *et al.* 2000). At most other sites this association was on a smaller scale, as at Gallows Hill, Swaffham Prior in Cambridgeshire, where an early Roman ritual site on a chalk hill near the Fen edge comprised enclosures and structures, including a single small masonry shrine/mausoleum containing an adult burial, belonging to the final phase of use (Malim 2006).

The location of the Gallows Hill site overlooking the Fen edge can be viewed as part of the well-noted wider religious fascination with water in Roman Britain (Rogers 2007; 2013; Kamash 2008), with shrines often lying close to springs, water courses, or marshy areas. Another example

nearby is the octagonal masonry-founded shrine within a rectangular enclosure at Haddenham, Cambridgeshire, which lay near the junction of the river Great Ouse and the peat Fens (Evans and Hodder 2006). Further afield, the probable enclosure shrine at Hailey Wood Camp, Sapperton in Gloucestershire, lies close to a spring that may have been viewed as the source of the River Thames (Moore 2001), while a shrine at Wycomb in Gloucestershire lies close to the source of the River Coln, a tributary of the Thames (Timby 1998). At Bawtry, South Yorkshire, archaeological monitoring of a wetland area produced late Roman coins, pottery and a number of possible lead curse tablets, along with *in situ* column bases, positioned

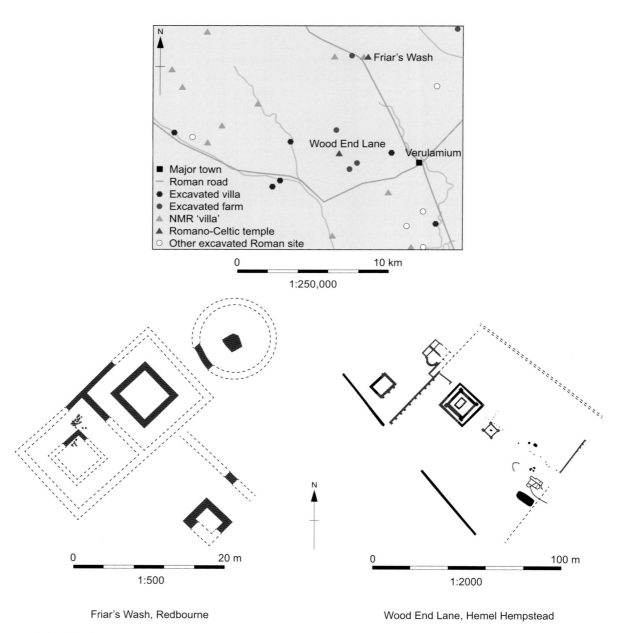

Friar's Wash, Redbourne   Wood End Lane, Hemel Hempstead

FIG. 5.35. Landscape context around rural Romano-Celtic temples near Verulamium and plans of temple complexes at Friars Wash (Birbeck 2009) and Wood End Lane (Neal 1984)

near to where a Roman road crossed the River Idle (Berg and Major 2006). This was probably a riverside shrine, located *c.* 5.5 km south-east of the known villa at Stancil.

There are a number of exceptional rural religious complexes in central and southern Britain that nearly all have some association with water, and often with roles connected with healing. The scale and context of some of these sites has led to debates regarding whether they should be viewed as nucleated settlements with a major religious focus, or else as large rural religious complexes with associated domestic, commercial, social and industrial infrastructure that catered for the needs of the cult and its attendants. Ultimately this may be a meaningless distinction, but, as outlined above (p. 157), for the purposes of this study such sites are discussed in this section as 'rural' religious complexes.

One of the most extensive of the known rural religious complexes is at Springhead in Kent, lying at the head of the Ebbsfleet Valley around the source of the river (Andrews *et al.* 2011; FIG. 5.36). The late Iron Age ritual activity at this site has already been discussed (p. 127), and post-conquest it appears that religious activity continued

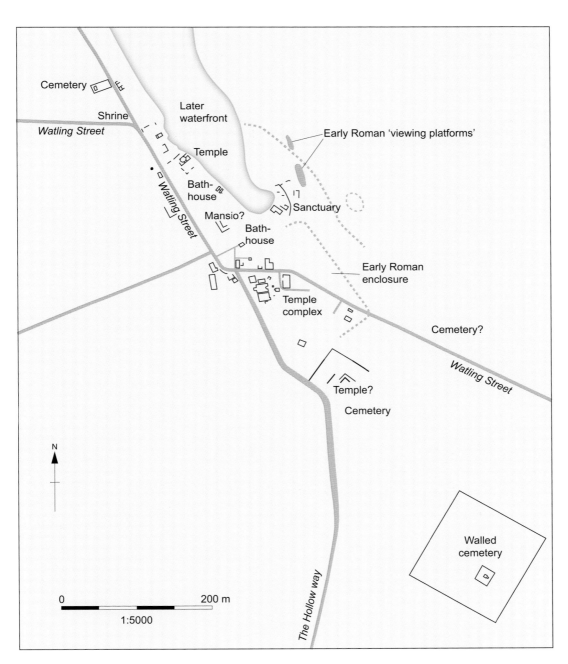

FIG. 5.36. Roman roadside settlement/religious complex at Springhead in Kent (after Andrews *et al.* 2011, fig. 4.2). Reproduced with permission HS1, © HS1

around the springs, while settlement soon developed further west along Watling Street, which was probably in place by A.D. 50. During the later first and particularly the second century there is clear evidence for a monumentalisation of religious expression, with a complex of five temples – three of Romano-Celtic form – built within the heart of the site at the point where Watling Street changed its course. In addition, a 'sanctuary' was created around the springs, and at least two other large temples were built in the near vicinity (*ibid.*, 209). Of the many objects associated with the religious complex were some that suggested an association with healing (see below, p. 171). There is evidence for decline from the later third century, in line with much of the settlement in Kent (Allen 2016a, 82), and by the mid-fourth century the main temple complex was falling into decay, a group of

faded and crumbling buildings situated within what was by then probably a sparsely populated and dispersed rural settlement. Votive deposits were still being made within ruinous temples right through the fourth century, however, while the small late Roman roadside shrine noted above (p. 157; FIG. 5.31) also points to some level of continued sanctity.

One exceptional Romano-British cult site that was also focused upon sacred springs and had some association with healing is of course Bath (*Aquae Sulis*). Here, the earliest phase of this massive temple-baths complex around the thermal springs, constructed *c.* A.D. 70–80, seems to have occupied a largely open setting surrounded by trees and shrubs, with no evidence for any other monumental buildings (FIG. 5.37), although there was significant occupation revealed *c.* 1 km to the

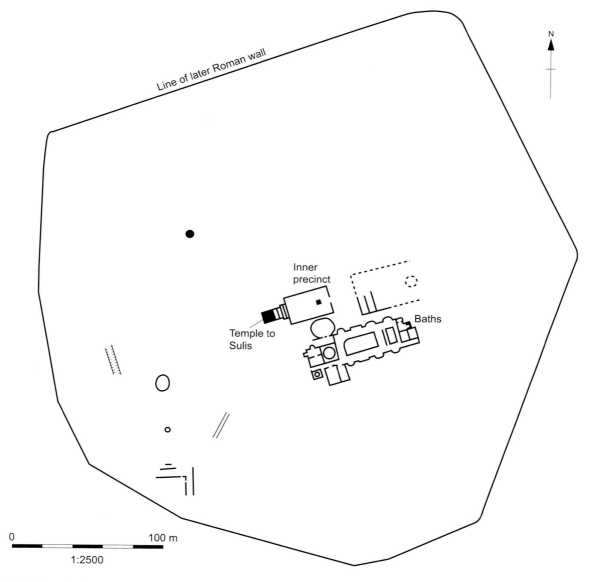

FIG. 5.37. Late first/early second century A.D. Bath within the later walled area (after La Trobe-Bateman and Niblett 2016, fig. 2.31)

north at Walcot, which seems, at some point at least, to have become part of a continuous suburban development along the road outside of the walled precinct (Davenport 2000; La Trobe-Bateman and Niblett 2016, 98–9). The temple at Bath is well known for being one of the few examples of a classical-style temple known from Britain, though, from the late second or early third century A.D., the addition of an ambulatory around the temple appears to change it into more of a hybrid Romano-Celtic form, perhaps indicating more fundamental changes in religious practices and beliefs. This period also saw a gradual increase in the number of buildings around the expanded temple/baths complex, although these could all have been associated with the public cult, including pilgrim hostels, shops and accommodation for workers, while the earth rampart along the line of the later walls probably defined the temenos boundary (La Trobe-Bateman and Niblett 2016, 101). The fourth century saw major changes within the walled area, with increasing numbers of high-status domestic dwellings and, from the middle part of the century in particular, a rise in the number of workshops; it would seem by this time that the religious significance of the site had waned and it may possibly have taken on more of an administrative role, similar to other walled late Roman towns.

Other major rural religious complexes connected with water include what is likely to have been an additional thermal bathing complex at Buxton in Derbyshire, recorded as *Aquae Arnemetiae* on the Ravenna Cosmology, a list of all the towns and road-stations throughout the Roman Empire recorded during the seventh century A.D. (Haverfield 1905, 222; Rivet and Smith 1979, 254–5). However, although Roman buildings, including a possible temple and baths, are known at this location, no systematic excavation has taken place.

At Marcham/Frilford by the River Ock in Oxfordshire, many years of excavation by the University of Oxford have revealed an extensive area of activity to the west of a walled temple compound. This includes what appears to be a 'semi-amphitheatre', *c.* 40 m in diameter, at the head of a relict stream channel, deliberately positioned to harness its relationship with water (Kamash *et al.* 2010, 115). This association is furthered by the deposition of large numbers of artefacts within a marshy area on the edge of the palaeochannel near where the drain came out of the semi-amphitheatre (*ibid.*, 116). Other excavated parts of this religious complex, which lay close to a Roman road crossing the Vale of the White Horse, included additional shrines, pathways, workshops and possible dining areas,

while a major cemetery was located further to the north. At Nettleton Scrubb in Wiltshire, a large religious complex developed on the Fosse Way road, *c.* 14 km north of Bath, with the temple positioned next to a specially canalised water course, which seems to have been a focus for deposition (Wedlake 1982; Smith 2001, 94). Another religious complex further west at Lydney Park, Glos, may not have been sited immediately on a water source, though a possible spring could have fed the tank that supplied the bathhouse, but nevertheless had definite aquatic associations, as shown by the images of fish and monsters on the mosaic floor in the temple cella (Wheeler and Wheeler 1932; Smith 2001, 134–5). Furthermore, it was sited on a hillfort spur overlooking the River Severn (and possibly inter-visible with the temple complex at Uley, *c.* 17 km to the east; FIG. 5.38), with which it may have been connected, perhaps being associated with the Severn bore, a spectacular natural phenomena in the form of a surge wave, which develops in the estuary at about this point (Boon 1989, 212). The Lydney temple was also associated with healing, with votive objects including a copper-alloy model arm showing possible evidence for iron deficiency – particularly appropriate for a site that had associations with iron mining (Hart 1970).

The distribution of all these larger excavated Roman rural sanctuaries in southern Britain is shown in FIG. 5.39; the only possibly comparable example outside of this area is at West Heslerton, in a dry valley at the foot of the Yorkshire Wolds (Powlesland 1998). These sanctuaries are defined as those places where in addition to the main temple there are at least two other buildings and/or shrines, and include the sites just discussed where the division between nucleated settlement/religious complex is more blurred. A possible religious complex recently investigated at 'Blacklands', Faversham, in Kent incorporated what is thought to be a theatre dug into the hillside and two probable bathhouses, with other buildings revealed by geophysical and aerial survey over an area of up to 8 ha (Wilkinson 2013; see Ch. 3). The full physical extent of most of these sites, however, remains uncertain, as often little investigation has taken place beyond the immediate area of the temple, and so there are probably other apparently 'isolated' rural temples that may well have been part of larger complexes. The apparent lack of larger rural religious complexes in much of the East of England may simply be because of the more developed network of nucleated centres here, which, as noted above, often had provision for sacred space that may have fulfilled much of the public religious needs of surrounding communities. There were, in addition, many

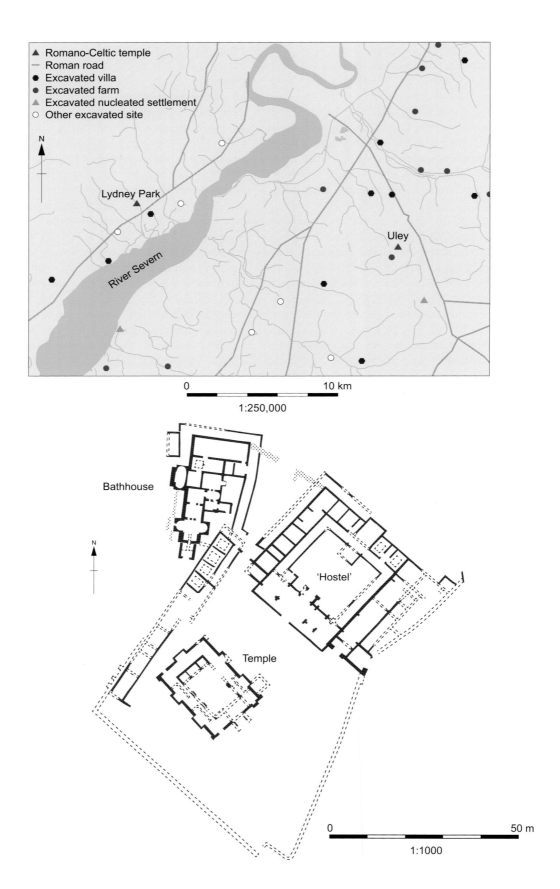

FIG. 5.38. Site plan and landscape context of the rural temple complex at Lydney Park, Glos (Wheeler and Wheeler 1932)

smaller scale rural religious sites, both in the East and elsewhere in the South and Central Belt (see FIG. 5.32).

The large rural religious complexes are comparable to many sites in Roman Gaul such as at Ribemont-sur-Ancre, Orrouy-Champlieu, Sanxay and *Fontes Sequanae*, which Derks (1998, 191) has proposed as public sanctuaries of the *pagi*, the local administrative districts within the *civitates*. These Gallic sanctuaries sometimes covered vast areas, *c*. 35–40 ha at Ribemont, and votive inscriptions occasionally record the financial contributions of local families to the construction and maintenance of cult buildings (*ibid.*, table 4.3). No such inscriptions come from rural sanctuaries in Britain, though it is likely that a similar situation existed here, at least for some temples. The well-known letters of Pliny dating from the late first/early second centuries A.D. certainly suggest that in other parts of the empire the local wealthy elite funded and maintained temples on their estates for the benefit of the surrounding population (*Ep.* 9.39; see below p. 168). Pliny also mentions a town/community at Hispellum (Spello) in Umbria owning a rural spring sanctuary, and providing amenities including a baths complex and 'entertainment' (*Ep.* 8.8). The scale of the largest rural sanctuaries in Britain would suggest that ownership is likely to have been on a civic level, with Bath, for example, being suggested as being established by the client king Togidubnus and subsequently belonging to the *civitas Belgarum* on the basis of an attribution by Ptolemy (Henig 1999). A more plausible scenario here is perhaps an early association with the military, as suggested by the epigraphic evidence (La Trobe-Bateman and Niblett 2016, 100; see below, p. 181). It remains possible, however, that some of these large sanctuaries may have been independent cult communities, or at least had some measure of financial autonomy, perhaps based on rental income from temple estates, including in some cases, as suggested by Fulford and Allen (1992, 204) for the temple at Lydney Park in the Forest of Dean, Gloucestershire, revenue from the control of mineral resources. Elsewhere in the classical world it is known that temple cults could gain revenue from a number of different sources – private benefactions, civic funds, fees of worshippers and the incomes from leased land (Kvium 2008; Horster 2010; 2016). Determining how far this may have been the case

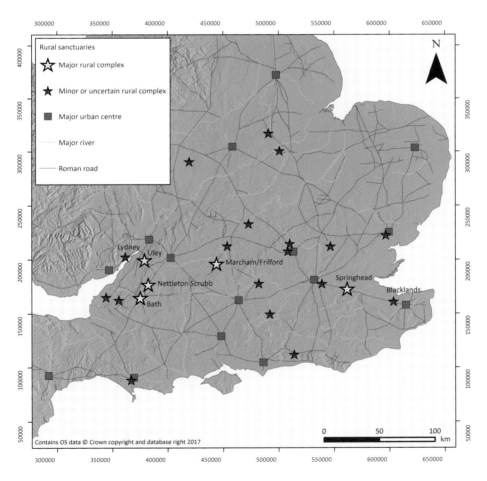

FIG. 5.39. Distribution of rural Roman sanctuary complexes in southern Britain

at rural Roman sanctuaries in Britain is highly problematic and would need detailed archaeological examination of the wider use of space around temple complexes. King (2016) has, however, recently argued that the enclosures seen on the periphery of some rural temples may have been used to hold sacred flocks or herds, which has potential implications for them as landowners (see also King 2005, 334, and below p. 195).

ROMANO-BRITISH SACRED SITES:
A SUMMARY

The provision of dedicated sacred space was a fundamental part of religious expression in many areas of Roman Britain, with evidence suggesting that overall its importance increased over time. The rituals performed at such places may have helped bind communities together and reinforce social hierarchies, providing a framework of surety in an increasingly changing world. In this sense, the major recurrent associations of sacred sites with certain places – water, hills, caves and extant earlier monuments – may have helped to create and maintain bonds with the landscape and perhaps between peoples. The form that sacred space took was in many ways less important than the place itself, and is more likely to reflect the type and scale of cult practice. Romano-Celtic temples were but one form of religious architecture – one that was relatively restricted numerically and geographically. They were largely confined to the larger population centres in the East region, while being found more often in rural contexts elsewhere in central southern Britain. In all areas they would seem to have been important elements in most of the larger civic public sanctuaries, which often developed from pre-Roman ritual sites, some becoming particularly extensive with evidence for associated subsidiary shrines, baths, guesthouses and other amenities. These may have held important social and commercial roles, particularly during festival periods when people could have been attracted from considerable distances. Aside from such large religious complexes there was an array of smaller religious sites, though this is not to say that these were any less important in the religious lives of the local communities. Indeed, some may still have attracted considerable numbers of people on festival days, as, for example, with the small, old temple of Ceres mentioned by Pliny on his estates in Italy, which was said to be 'very crowded on a particular day. For, on the ides of September, a large assemblage is gathered there from the whole district, much business is transacted, many vows are undertaken and many are paid, yet there is no refuge near at hand against the rain and sun' (Pliny, *Ep.* 39). Notwithstanding the many problems of interpretation, these religious structures, enclosures, shafts, caves or just particular places in the landscape, would have fulfilled a variety of spiritual roles, whether they lay within settlements or in the wider countryside. Patterns in their social and geographic distribution demonstrate the great variation in religious traditions across different parts of the Roman province, matching other differences previously noted within rural settlements (Smith *et al.* 2016), and the economy (Allen *et al.* 2017). These differences are further noted in the material culture associated with religious expression, which will now be examined in more detail.

THE MATERIAL CULTURE OF RURAL ROMANO-BRITISH RELIGIOUS PRACTICE

In any account of religion based primarily upon archaeological evidence, it is the material culture along with animal and plant remains that play a pivotal role in our interpretation and understanding (cf. Houlbrook and Armitage 2015). Objects given to the gods may tell us something of the concerns of the supplicant or the nature of the deity, while temple furnishings and priestly regalia can provide a glimpse into the organisation of the cult. Occasionally cult images and written dedications survive to provide some evidence for the range of gods worshipped, and changes over time. With regard to 'Roman' and 'native' divinities, the precise nature of any syncretism will remain largely unknown (cf. Zoll 2016). This section will discuss in broad terms the variety of material culture found on many of the shrines and temples discussed above, as well as providing more detailed accounts of specific 'religious' artefacts (see definition above, p. 123) in terms of their association with various types of excavated site. The two other important components within ritual assemblages – animal and plant remains – will be discussed in the following section as part of a wider discussion on ritual practices in the Romano-British countryside.

MATERIAL CULTURE FROM SACRED SITES

Roman religious sites are well known for having lots of 'stuff' (Woodward 1992; Smith 2001; Bird 2011; Ferris 2012, ch. 2). The very fact that unusually large numbers of objects are found in a particular place is often one of the primary criteria for identifying sacred sites in the first place (see above p. 122). However, it is not the case that all sites proposed as sacred space produced lots of objects, or even any at all, and the quantity and type of finds is as variable as the physical form of

TABLE 5.1: DIFFERENT CATEGORIES OF OBJECTS RECORDED FROM SACRED SITES DIVIDED INTO
'VOTIVE' AND 'NON-VOTIVE' ASSEMBLAGES

'Votive' assemblage	*Other finds from sacred sites*
Coins	Tools
Brooches	Textile processing (spindlewhorls, loomweights, needles)
Other personal objects (hairpins, bracelets, finger rings etc.)	Cereal processing (querns, millstones)
Religious objects of stone, metal, pottery, wood (altars, sculpture, figurines, miniature objects etc.; see below)	Security (locks, keys)
Martial objects (spearheads, other weapons, armour etc.; miniature weapons included under religious object category)	Recreation (dice, counters)
	Writing (styli, seal boxes)
Toilet objects (tweezers, probes etc.)	Weighing (weights, steelyard)
Specialist pottery (face pots, tazze, miniature pots etc.)	Craftworking debris (slag, hammerscale, boneworking debris etc.)

the sites in question. The objects from sacred sites discussed here have been broadly divided into two groups (TABLE 5.1): first, the artefacts which – for the most part – appear to have been offered to the deity or deities at the cult site, presumably as 'ex votos', that is given in fulfilment of a vow (see *rites and practices* below); second is the much broader group of items, which may relate to other practices occurring within the environment of the sacred site.

'There are many problems in trying to separate 'votive' assemblages from more prosaic objects on sacred sites, with explicitly religious objects such as altars or figurines of deities being comparatively rare, and many other object types often having a great deal of interpretational ambiguity. In these cases, the identification of 'votive' assemblages is only possible through a detailed contextual consideration of the finds. In this study, only the object types most commonly interpreted as offerings in excavation reports have been included in the 'votive' dataset, though this is not to say that all of these were used in such a way, with, for example, coins probably having various uses within ritual, social and commercial spheres (see below, p. 173). Similarly, it is quite possible that any of the other finds types, such as writing equipment, tools and objects associated with weighing and recreation, may have been used as ex votos. In some case they most demonstrably were, such as at Elms Farm, Heybridge, where a series of ritual pits in the shrine precinct contained animal bone, personal objects and religious objects alongside styli, tools, spindlewhorls and needles (Atkinson and Preston 2015, 101–5). Nevertheless, by restricting the 'votive' assemblages to the more commonly identified finds categories, broad patterns may be recognised in the material culture

according to the type, context and chronology of the cult sites. An additional significant problem, however, is that for many of the sacred sites lying within settlement contexts, it was not possible to firmly differentiate and quantify the finds assemblage from the shrine/temple separately from that of the remainder of the site. Where this is the case, such sites have been excluded from the more detailed analyses presented here.

'Votive' assemblages from sacred sites

The above discussion of Iron Age shrines noted a number of sites such as Hayling Island and Hallaton where large numbers of objects were recovered and assumed to have been offerings made to a divine presence. During the Roman period there was a similar proportion (*c.* 65–70 per cent) of sacred sites with evidence for a 'votive' assemblage, though in general the quantity and variety of objects found was much greater. Perhaps the biggest variable with regard to the presence of such assemblages is the context of the sacred site, as shown in FIG. 5.40. Most of the structures or places interpreted as sacred at farmsteads and, in particular, villas, do not have evidence for votive offerings, save for the occasional object, usually within a structured deposit, such as a complete pottery vessel or the articulated remains of an animal. Assuming of course that the features in question were actually shrines (see above, p. 121), this has significant implications for our understanding of ritual practices at these sites, suggesting either that the supplicants were more likely to have offered perishable objects such as organic matter (flowers, fruit etc.), or that different types of rituals occurred here, without the need for any regular offering of artefacts. Some of these sites were associated with funerary ritual, such as

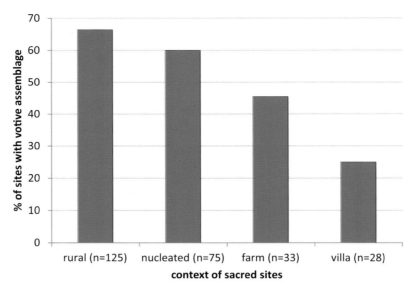

FIG. 5.40. Proportion of sacred sites from different types of rural settlement with evidence for 'votive' assemblages

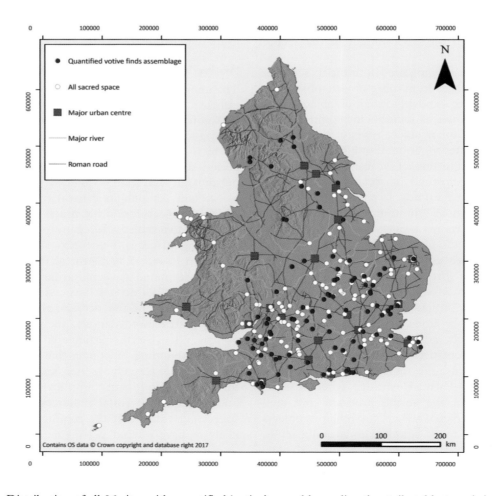

FIG. 5.41. Distribution of all 96 sites with quantified 'votive' assemblages directly attributable to a shrine or temple

the Romano-Celtic temple-mausoleum on a hillside above the villa at Bancroft (Williams and Zeepvat 1994), while most would seem to have been relatively simple shrines used by families or small communities, seemingly without the same need for regular offerings as seen at most larger sacred sites. Yet even within a few of these larger sites, such as that within the nucleated roadside settlement at Westhawk Farm, the number of possible votive objects was minimal, here including a fragment of stone pine and some coins from a waterhole on the opposite side of the road to the shrine (Booth *et al.* 2008).

The distribution of all 96 Roman period sacred sites with quantified 'votive' assemblages is shown in FIG. 5.41. These include 33 Romano-Celtic temples, which, as has been discussed above, are the most prominent form of religious building within larger sanctuaries. With their generally more impressive architectural presence and increased association with public cults, it is hardly surprisingly that a higher proportion of Romano-Celtic temples had evidence for the regular offering of ex votos than other sacred sites (FIG. 5.42). Nevertheless, the overall range of ex votos and their relative frequency is comparable across religious assemblages from all types of sacred site,

with coins generally being the most favoured object, followed by items of personal adornment and toilet artefacts. The religious significance of brooches, particularly horse-and-rider and plate types, is well noted (e.g. Ferris 2012, 35–9) and has already been commented upon in Chapter 2. It remains unproven whether different types of brooch can be associated with particular deities (*ibid.*), but it is clear that many appear to have been carefully chosen as offerings to the deity, and were not simply a generic 'token' personal offering. Further work would be required to ascertain whether specific types of other personal item were selected as ex votos, though in a review of the ritual significance of jewellery in Roman Britain, Puttock (2002, 115) suggested that the shapes, colours, motifs and materials were all specifically chosen and were at least as important as the object type itself. It is notable, however, that hairpins are quite well represented in many cult sites, and are thought to be particularly associated with women and linked with aspects such as childbirth and fertility (*ibid.*). As such their particular proliferation within known healing sanctuaries such as Lydney Park (over 300 examples) and Springhead (over 100 examples) is perhaps to be expected. Glass bangles, which are particularly notable in the

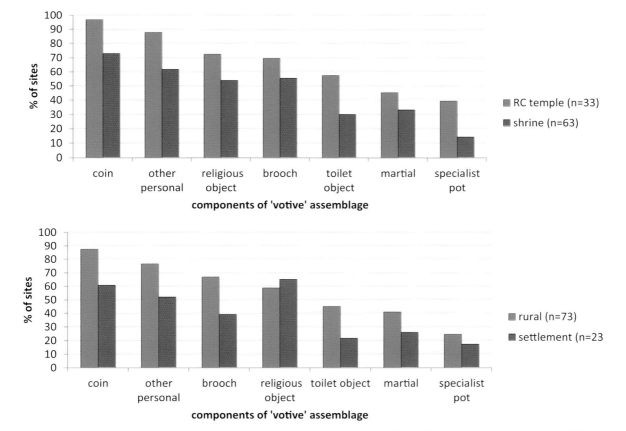

FIG. 5.42. Relative frequency of 'votive' assemblage components within different forms of sacred space, and different contexts of sacred space (Note: The rural category comprises all those sites with no associated settlement and the major 'rural' religious complexes; see FIG. 5.39)

north of England, have also been suggested in Chapter 2 as having possible apotropaic/magical properties, and are found in a number of votive assemblages, including that at Victoria Cave in Settle, North Yorkshire.

Objects specifically manufactured to be used as ritual offerings or in cult ritual were, unsurprisingly, common, occurring in over 70 per cent of votive assemblages from Romano-Celtic temples, and *c.* 50 per cent from other shrines; indeed many of those from the latter formed key elements in their religious interpretation. The specific nature of some of these religious objects is examined below. The final type of object found recurrently as part of 'votive' assemblages comprises artefacts of a martial nature. Aside from assemblages within shrines intimately connected with military sites, such as the river deposits from Piercebridge in County Durham, which included a range of different military equipment (Walton 2016), these martial items invariably comprise spear and other projectile heads. At Bancroft in Milton Keynes, for example there were four spearheads and fourteen miniature spearheads or bolt heads in the late Roman circular shrine (Williams and Zeepvat 1994), while ten spearheads were found among a significant votive assemblage within the ritual enclosure at Lowbury Hill in Oxfordshire, some with unusual features that suggest ceremonial use (Atkinson 1916; Fulford and Rippon 1994). Further indications of the ritual significance of weaponry come from large numbers of miniature weapons found both on and at a distance from sacred sites (see below p. 178).

Keeping in mind that many of the objects recovered from religious sites in settlements were not able to be separately quantified, it appears that, in general, the votive assemblages from rural sacred sites (i.e. those without any associated settlement and major religious complexes) have higher frequencies of most types of finds (FIG. 5.42). Coins, for example, are found in 87 per cent of rural assemblages, as opposed to 60 per cent of those from settlements. Assuming that not all of the coins from rural shrines were used as votive offerings, then this might reflect a wider market function at some of these sites – perhaps periodic country fairs based around certain religious festivals. The only component to counter this overall trend is religious objects, found in over 65 per cent of settlement votive assemblages, against 58 per cent in rural contexts, although the difference is not that marked. Most of these objects came from shrines in military *vici* and roadside settlements, which follows the correlation noted below in terms of the reasonably widespread occurrence of religious artefacts within larger settlements, possibly in part because it was in these places where much of this material was probably manufactured.

Assessment of chronological changes in the character and individual components of votive assemblages is difficult, as generally finds are not phased within excavation reports and so consequently were not recorded in phase groups within the project database, unlike, for example, the plant or animal remains. To attempt any meaningful analysis of change over time, it has been necessary to break down the votive assemblage dataset into those sites where all activity was confined to the early to mid-Roman period (first to early third century A.D.) and those of the late Roman period only (later third to end of fourth century). This has necessarily restricted the

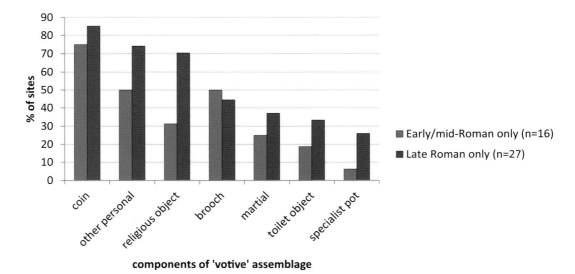

FIG. 5.43. Relative frequency of 'votive' assemblage components within sacred sites of early to mid-Roman (first to early third century A.D.) and later Roman (later third to end of fourth century) date

number of sites that can be considered, but nevertheless has brought out some trends in chronological patterning (FIG. 5.43). Some of these patterns make sense in terms of the wider proliferation of different object types, with brooches, for example, being more common in assemblages from earlier Roman sites, and other personal items being more prevalent in the later Roman period, when items such as bracelets and hairpins are more commonplace. The chronological difference in coinage is much less marked than may have been expected, given the huge imbalance in rural coin use pre- and post- the mid-third century A.D. (Brindle 2017a). This suggests that coins (possibly to be regarded as 'discs with images' rather than money) have always had a strong religious significance, as has been argued on a number of previous occasions (e.g. Haselgrove 2005; King 2007b; Wythe 2007). However, the possible motivations and beliefs behind this association and the many ways that coins could be used in ritual are subjects that are only just starting to be addressed, as seen in the 2015 conference at the University of Tübingen, *Money and Ritual in the Greco-Roman World*.

Religious objects are particularly prevalent in late Roman votive assemblages when compared with those of earlier date, although not all of these may have been fabricated at this time, as for example the pipeclay Venus figurine from the late Roman shrine at Hockwold, Norfolk (Gurney 1986b), which was probably manufactured in central Gaul or Cologne during the first or second century A.D. (see below, p. 180). The greater prevalence of religious objects at late Roman shrines may simply reflect their survival after the eventual demise of cult activity. Some objects may have been selectively retrieved from sacred sites that had been abandoned earlier in the Roman period.

The analyses above highlight patterns in the broad range of object types present within votive assemblages, but do not indicate the quantities in which some of these objects were recovered. At twelve sites, for example, over 1,000 coins were recovered, numbers far above those found in the majority of rural settlements, even with the benefit of metal-detecting. Brooches are also recorded in their hundreds at six sites, including the remarkable collection of 236 from the shrine at Bosworth Field, Sutton Cheney in Leicestershire, with up to 101 horse-and-rider examples (Ray and Farley 2012). Most of the sites with substantial quantities of one type of find also have significant assemblages of other probable votive objects. These invariably comprise sacred loci in rural contexts, particularly if the large 'rural' religious complexes such as Springhead, Bath and Nettleton Scrubb are included (e.g. such religious complexes make up 31 of the 35 sacred sites with 150 or more coins). The generally large votive finds assemblages from these rural sanctuaries contrast with those from many of the shrines and temples in nucleated settlements, suggesting either that the objects from the latter were more likely to be disturbed and/or removed, or that there were inherent differences in their organisation and ritual behaviours. The larger rural complexes in particular may have been operating as independent communities, as discussed above, and this is also suggested by the type and scale of other finds recovered from these sites.

Other finds from sacred sites

Most of the attention on material culture from sacred sites is usually focused on the inherently religious objects, or at least those artefacts deemed to have been used within cult rituals. However, it has been noted in a previous study by the present author that on some sites the finds suggest that a variety of other activities were taking place (Smith 2001, 158). As stated above, it can be difficult to determine the final use of an object prior to deposition; it may have served an essentially utilitarian function for most of its 'life', but then ultimately have been deposited in a ritually motivated manner (cf. Gosden and Marshall 1999). For example, it has been highlighted in this chapter (p. 131) how quernstones often form part of structured deposits, but their presence need not necessarily imply that there was grain processing occurring in the immediate vicinity. Nevertheless, many sacred sites contained a variety of artefacts that do not appear on the face of it to have been used in religious ritual, and were probably associated with wider industrial, commercial and social activities, or were related to the physical infrastructure of the site.

FIGURE 5.44 presents the frequency of occurrence of some of the main 'non-votive' object types recovered from Romano-British religious sites. They have been divided by broad context and it is immediately apparent that, even more so than with the votive assemblages, this material generally occurs more frequently on 'rural' shrines and sanctuaries (including the major religious complexes), as opposed to those directly associated with settlements. Tools of all different types are particularly common, with, for example, iron chisels and a farrier's comb coming from the complex at Uley, a variety of horticultural tools and an animal shackle from the Springhead Sanctuary area, and cleavers, an axe blade, a chisel and a reaping hook from the temple at Farley Heath, Surrey. Some of these may relate to the construction and general maintenance of buildings, though others suggest that certain sites may have

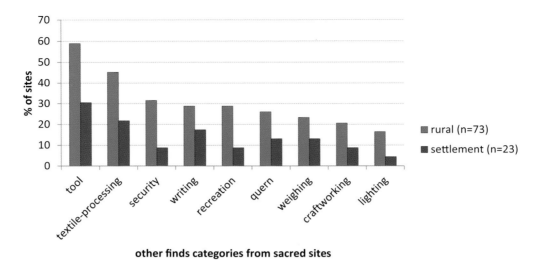

FIG. 5.44. Relative frequency of other 'non-votive' finds categories from sacred sites, according to site context

been keeping their own animals and growing their own food. A rural temple complex at Grimstock Hill, Coleshill in Warwickshire, contained a large number of tools including a saw blade, drill bit, chisel, punches, a smith's hammer and a cobbler's anvil, indicating smithing and other craftworking facilities, which was also suggested by plentiful slags and furnace bottoms (Magilton 2006). General craftworking debris, usually comprising concentrations of slag, but also with occasional boneworking waste, was also found in sixteen other sites, almost all in rural contexts.

The overall evidence of the material culture suggests that many of the larger rural sanctuaries in particular may have had at least some permanent resident population – cult attendants, craftsmen, shop/innkeepers and labourers – that was no doubt swelled significantly at times of festivals. Some of these complexes may even have been run like businesses, either independently or as part of the public religious cult of the wider *civitas*, perhaps in order to help control areas well-removed from the principal centres of civic administration (cf. Haeussler 2013, 269). At the smaller rural shrines, where the financial requirements of the cult may have been relatively minimal, it is more likely that they were run by local communities or within villa estates, catering for a population mostly living in dispersed small rural farmsteads, and probably only utilised at certain times of the year. There is little evidence from the finds that these sites were engaging in any significant commercial, industrial or agricultural practices. Shrines and temples associated with nucleated population centres would have had ready access to the facilities of the settlements, which perhaps explains the relative paucity of some categories of 'non-votive' finds (e.g. craftworking and textile-processing objects)

from the specific area of the cult site. These sacred sites would have been components of their associated settlement, rather than being 'self-contained' cult communities as was probably the case with many of the larger rural sanctuaries.

RELIGIOUS OBJECTS

There has been a great deal written recently about religious objects and imagery from Roman Britain (e.g. Aldhouse-Green 2004b; 2012; Bagnall-Smith 2008; Bird 2011; Ferris 2012; Durham 2012; Fittock 2015; Esposito 2016), and it is not the intention here to discuss the various types at any great length (for definition of religious object, see above, p. 123). Instead, the emphasis will be placed on examining these objects in their excavated contexts, and looking at broad social and geographic patterns.

Context and distribution of religious objects

A total of 1931 religious objects were recorded from 427 separate excavated sites. FIGURE 5.45 shows the frequency of occurrence of these objects on different types of site, while FIG. 5.46 shows the distribution of these sites across England and Wales. Such objects occur on over 50 per cent of military sites, mostly military *vici*, but including some supply depots, and are also prevalent on nucleated settlements and, unsurprisingly, rural religious sites. Over a quarter of excavated villas had evidence for religious artefacts, but this falls to just 5 per cent of farmsteads, this latter proportion barely changing throughout all the regions. However, complex farmsteads were considerably more likely to have these objects (present on *c.* 14 per cent) than enclosed types (present on *c.* 3 per cent), which reflects their generally more diverse range of material culture, and their greater provision for sacred space noted above.

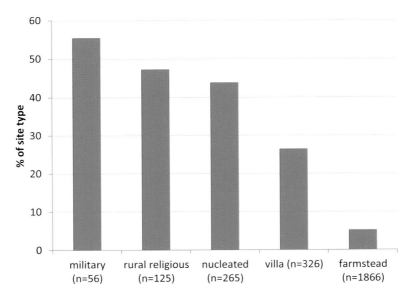

FIG. 5.45. Percentage of site type with evidence for religious objects

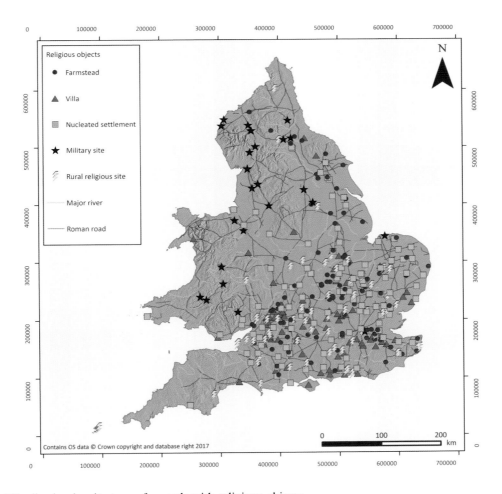

FIG. 5.46 Distribution by site type of records with religious objects

TABLE 5.2: CATEGORIES OF RELIGIOUS OBJECTS BY TYPE OF SITE

* includes 13 farmsteads, 10 villas and 40 nucleated sites with evidence for sacred space
+ includes major 'rural' religious complexes at Bath, Marcham/Frilford, Nettleton Scrubb and Springhead
++ includes 20 possible curse tablets from Piercebridge

Context	No. sites with religious objects	Total no. of objects (selected 'religious' categories)										
		figurine	sculpture	other image of deity	miniature object	votive leaf/ plaque	priestly regalia	curse tablet	votive letter	altar	amulet	inscription
farmstead	95*	29	9	7	23	2	4	24	1	5	7	2
funerary	14		1	1			1					
industry	18	8		5								
military	31	29	6	8	11			21++		38	2	30
nucleated	116*	132	67	37	69	45	6	18	11	24	6	14
rural (field system & 'isolated' rural context)	8			1			2	2			1	
rural religious	59+	95	47	36	114	96	76	299	62	22	5	32
villa	86*	54	39	12	11	5	1	2	5	5	11	1
Total	**427**	**347**	**169**	**107**	**228**	**148**	**90**	**366**	**79**	**95**	**32**	**79**

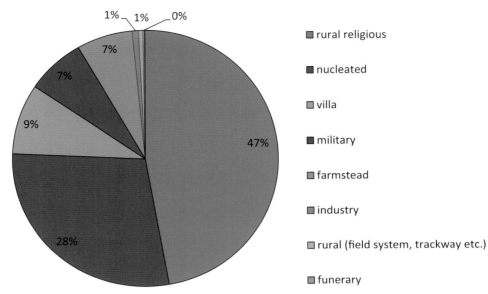

FIG. 5.47. Percentages of total number of religious objects (n=1931) from different types of site

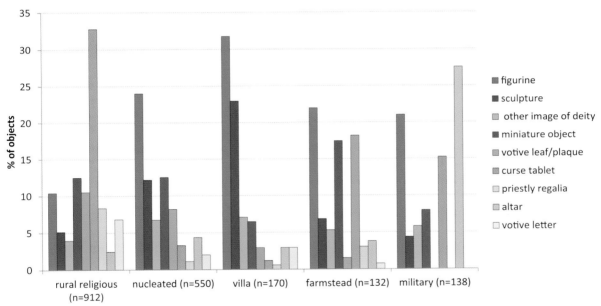

FIG. 5.48. Selected categories of religious object from different types of site (n=total number of religious objects from site type)

In terms of the actual numbers of religious objects, 'rural' religious sites are very much dominant, primarily because of the major complexes like Lydney Park, Uley and Bath (FIG. 5.47). However, not all large rural sanctuaries necessarily had many religious objects, as shown at Marcham/Frilford in Oxfordshire, where despite comprehensive excavations over many years producing large volumes of finds, very few explicitly cult items were recovered, one of the few being a fragmented fired clay representation of a bull. This is in stark contrast to another rural sanctuary in Oxfordshire at Woodeaton, which, with the except of Bath and Uley, produced one of

the largest collections of religious objects in the country, with over 75 artefacts including copper-alloy letters, miniature weapons and representations of Mars, Venus, Minerva and Cupid (Bagnall-Smith 1995; 1999). Away from some of these larger rural sanctuaries the numbers of religious artefacts from individual rural religious sites are generally quite small, particularly those categorised as 'shrines'. As ever, there are notable exceptions, including the newly discovered shrine at Ashwell End, near Baldock, where a hoard of 'temple treasure', was found by a metal detectorist in 2002, and subsequent excavations revealed further objects, these including a silver gilt figurine and decorated votive leaf plaques, many of which contained images of Minerva and dedications to a local goddess named Senuna, who may have been depicted as the Roman goddess (Burleigh 2015, 94–9; Jackson and Burleigh 2017).

The next largest group of religious objects comprises the 550 items from nucleated sites, 63 per cent of these coming from settlements that also had evidence for sacred space, though the objects did not necessarily derive from such areas. The remaining objects are split fairly evenly between farmsteads, villas and military sites, although, as just discussed, a very small percentage of the first contained such artefacts.

Combining all religious objects together of course disguises an extremely heterogeneous group of artefacts. The only thing they have in common is that they were explicitly manufactured to have some association with the divine, whether as ex votos, cult images, priestly regalia, temple furnishings or as talismanic items. TABLE 5.2 and FIG. 5.48 show that different types of site can have very different 'suites' of cult artefact. This in part reflects the individuality of religious expression, though it may also be associated with broader variances in social structure, identity and the types of ritual practices carried out in these different environments.

As just stated, the substantial number of religious objects from rural religious sites is dominated by those of a few large sanctuaries, with the curse tablets from Uley and Bath in particular forming a very high proportion of the overall number of cult artefacts from these sites. The curse tablets, or *defixiones*, were messages, usually inscribed on lead, which would be written by an individual or dictated to a scribe in order to ask the deities to act on their behalf against another, usually in the case of a perceived wrong-doing (see http://curses.csad.ox.ac.uk/index.shtml for many translated examples from Britain). They can often be quite dark and vengeful and are part of a widespread tradition found across the Roman Empire, the curses occasionally being accompanied by figurines fashioned from wax, lead and clay, linked to 'magic' practices, which bound victims to the practitioner's desires (Bailliot 2015). Although these were in effect private rituals, the great majority of curse tablets from Britain come from major rural religious complexes, over 70 per cent from the sacred spring at Bath and from within and around the temple building at Uley. The extent to which professional scribes were used remains uncertain (see Ch. 3, p. 76), although there is a 'scribal' link between Bath and Uley, as seen in the style and formulae of curses from both sanctuaries. Whatever the situation, the likelihood is that provision was made for the manufacture

and purchase of such curse tablets on the temple site, indicating that, here at least, they were a part of mainstream religious practice and not some secretive superstitious activity. However, away from Bath and Uley, the practice does not seem that widespread, with *defixiones* – some only probable examples – being found on just ten other rural religious sites.

Aside from curse tablets, rural religious sites have the broadest mix of other types of religious objects, including figurines, cult statues and other sculpture, altars, miniature objects and votive copper-alloy letters, which may have been attached to a wooden plaque for a dedicatory inscription that could be re-used as necessary (cf. Hassall 1980, 85) (FIG. 5.49). Miniature objects are particularly well represented on rural shrines and temples, most probably used as ex votos, though, as Kiernan (2009, 211–13) has suggested, with a wide variety of underlying meanings. Unlike their representation at sacred sites within settlements (nucleated sites, villas and farmsteads), axes were not the most common form of miniature object, with martial/hunting items – notably spears – being more numerous, correlating with, but outnumbering, the incidence of full-size items on cult sites highlighted above. Most of the small numbers of miniature anatomic objects (forming part of Whitehouse's (1996) 'votaries' category of ritual object; see above p. 123) were also found on rural religious sites, with heads, legs, arms, feet, toes, thumbs, eyes, breasts and even possible hearts all being recorded. The sites in which these objects were found, such as Lydney Park and Springhead, are likely to have been healing sanctuaries, with the body parts reflecting the various ailments of the supplicants who came there asking for divine intervention.

Most of the religious objects highlighted above are likely to have been offerings or votives given to the temple deities, or else the actual images of deities that were worshipped (*sacra*) at the cult loci. However, rural sacred sites also provide the only excavated contexts where there is any reasonable artefactual evidence for the priests themselves, though there are indications that some of these items may also have been ultimately deposited as votive offerings (Esposito 2016). Eighteen rural shrines/temples contained 76 objects that may have formed parts of priestly headdresses, sceptres/staves, or possible sacrificial implements, such as the jet knife handle with silver binding from Gestingthorpe in Essex (Draper 1985). These are all located in the Central Belt, East and South regions, with a notable concentration in parts of Surrey and West Sussex, though other, largely unstratified, examples are mostly found in rural landscape contexts in the east of England (Esposito

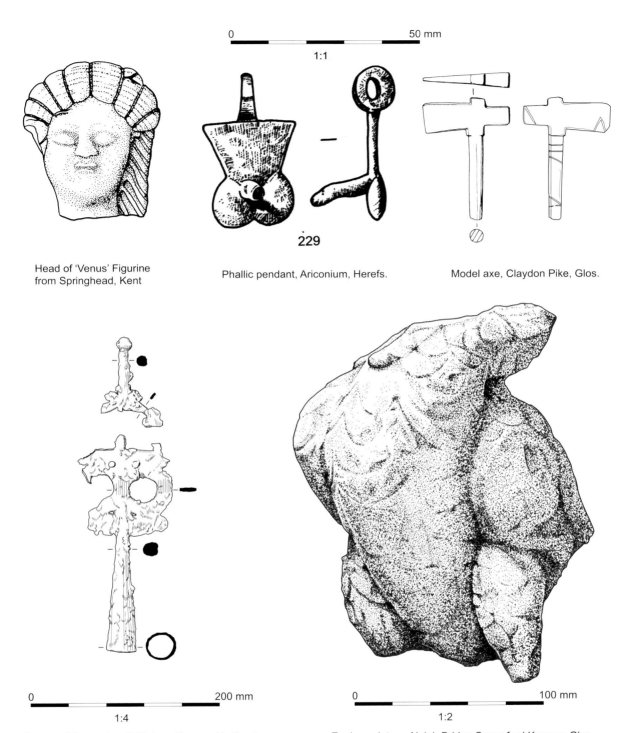

0   50 mm

1:1

229

Head of 'Venus' Figurine
from Springhead, Kent

Phallic pendant, Ariconium, Herefs.

Model axe, Claydon Pike, Glos.

0   200 mm

1:4

0   100 mm

1:2

Ceremonial spearhead, Higham Ferrers, Northants.

Eagle sculpture, Neigh Bridge Somerford Keynes, Glos.

FIG. 5.49. Illustrations of selected types of Romano-British religious object (Biddulph *et al.* 2011, fig. 147 (Reproduced with permission HS1, © HS1); Jackson 2012, fig. 440; Miles *et al.* 2007, figs 6.19 and 9.19; Lawrence and Smith 2009, fig. 5.27)

2016, 106, fig. 2). The most extensive excavated assemblage of priestly regalia comes from Wanborough in Surrey, where parts of five priestly headdresses and at least 22 sceptres were recovered, some of the crowns carrying a wheel symbol, thought to be a 'Celtic' manifestation of Jupiter (O'Connell and Bird 1994; Bird 1996).

The overwhelming preponderance of priestly regalia at certain rural temple sites needs some consideration. Were these just chance survivals providing glimpses of religious specialists that were officiating across all types of cult site, or was it only certain, larger, religious complexes that had such specialists, or at least specialists that required such paraphernalia? Public priestly offices in the Roman world were usually drawn from the ranks of the elite who may have actively competed for them to enhance their social prestige (Frankfurter 2006, 550; Hingley 2011, 749). There is well-known epigraphic evidence for priests from the sanctuary at Bath, where Calpurnius Receptus (*RIB* 155), a priest of Sulis, and Memor, the *haruspex*, each left a 'footprint' (Cunliffe and Davenport 1985, 65, 130). How far religious specialists convened rituals on smaller, local cult sites is less certain, though the presence of fragments of sceptre binding and a 'special' bronze vessel at the open air hilltop shrine at Frensham, Surrey (Graham 2001), suggests that they may have existed, perhaps as peripatetics, able to serve a number of communities within an area. The paucity of evidence for priestly regalia from within settlement contexts may be partly because such items were dispersed away from any shrines and temples, and so were perhaps not as readily identified as such. There are some examples of these objects, particularly from nucleated settlements, such as the iron 'cult spearhead' from the roadside shrine in the settlement at Higham Ferrers, Northants, which may have been used by specialists within the religious site for rituals and/or processions (Lawrence and Smith 2009, 220). Nevertheless, it is notable that items interpreted as priestly regalia make up less than 2 per cent of all 550 religious objects from nucleated settlements.

The overall corpus of religious artefacts from nucleated settlements – as with all other domestic contexts – was dominated by figurines, with 132 examples from 61 sites, most of them probably used in personal worship (Durham 2012). Within nucleated sites the numbers were equally divided into pipeclay and metal (usually copper alloy) examples. Pipeclay figurines were made in parts of Gaul during the first and second centuries A.D., with the divinities represented mostly comprising Venus, along with Dea Nutrix, Apollo, Mercury and Minerva. Recent work on the large corpus of pipeclay figurines from Roman London has suggested that many may have been deliberately broken into different recognisable body parts prior to deposition, perhaps used as ex votos linked with divine pleas for healing, as would appear to be the case with model votive body parts just discussed (Fittock 2015, 128). A study of the metal figurines of Roman Britain by Durham (2012) noted over 1000 examples, with multiple and widespread representations of the most popular gods, such as Mercury, Hercules and Jupiter, as well as many other divinities, including limited numbers depicting some of the household deities – *Genius paterfamilias* and the Lares – which may have been

kept in small household shrines as discussed above (p. 152). Of the 579 metal figurines in Durham's study that came from known Roman sites, most were from urban and military contexts, with London in particular having a very large number; just 155 were from rural contexts with most of these coming from a small number of religious sites (*ibid.*, table 11).

In addition to figurines, roadside settlements and villages also had relatively high quantities of miniature objects (primarily axes) and 'religious' stone sculpture, the latter being even more common than in rural religious sites. This may be partly because some of these sculptured pieces actually derived from funerary monuments on the periphery of the settlement, such as the fragments of two statues – one of a lion and one of a human torso, two-thirds life size – found in early excavations at Girton College in north-west Cambridge near to a number of Roman burials (Evans and Newman 2010, 148). Other sculpture may have come from public shrines or temples (or funerary monuments) within the nucleated settlements, though much of this material appears to have been removed from its original context, such as the 30 or more items of highly accomplished figured sculpture re-used in later features at the roadside settlement at Stanwick, Northants; these depicted subjects from classical mythology, including life-size figures of Hercules, Minerva and a river god (Neal 1989).

The emphasis on divine imagery is seen most clearly in the corpus of religious objects from villas, where over 60 per cent of all such artefacts comprise either figurines, sculpture or other depictions of the deity, such as a lead plaque of the goddess Isis from the villa at Groundwell Ridge, Swindon (Brickstock *et al.* 2006). These may be combined with the many images of gods, goddesses and mythological creatures and events seen in the figurative mosaics within many villa buildings in Britain (cf. Neal and Cosh 2009), to suggest the overall importance of display. These villas, particularly the large later Roman examples from the west of England such as Chedworth in Gloucestershire (Esmonde Cleary 2013), appear actively to use religious imagery, usually in its most 'Roman' form, to help define the status of their occupants, as part of the wider suite of cultural indicators, including architecture, landscaping, personal appearance and culinary tastes (see Chs 2 to 4). This is not to say that the underlying beliefs of the villa occupiers were necessarily superficial, but just, perhaps, that it was important that their peers would perceive their piety to be of the 'correct' kind. How far any of the divine images were actively used in cult ritual is largely uncertain, though many were no doubt placed in the various lararia, nymphaea and other shrines within and around the villa as noted above (p. 152).

The relatively limited numbers of religious artefacts from the small proportion of farmsteads to have such items are, like villas, most likely to comprise figurines, with sculpture and other divine representations being very scarce. Most of these figurines were of copper alloy, though wooden examples may have been more common, with rare survivals found in other contexts, such as at Ickham in Kent (Bennett et al. 2010, 215). As with those on other settlement types, the figurines were probably used in personal worship, which is corroborated by the fact just three of the 23 farmsteads with figurines also had possible evidence for sacred space. Many of these figurines were fragmentary and some may even have been furniture or cart fittings rather than free-standing statuettes, such as the rather crudely modelled left hand and hip of a draped female figure from a Romano-British farmstead in the Stour Valley near Wixoe in Suffolk (Atkins 2014). Twenty-three miniature objects were also found at sixteen farmsteads, these mostly comprising axes, such as that found near to a late Roman shrine on the edge of the farmstead at Claydon Pike in Gloucestershire (Miles et al. 2007). The copper-alloy model of a human leg found at Waste Management Park, Waterbeach, Cambridge, may have been an ex voto related to the shrine tentatively identified in the vicinity (Ranson 2008), though most of these objects probably functioned as personal religious tokens/amulets, albeit reflecting a variety of underlying beliefs and concerns. Up to 24 possible lead curse tablets were recovered from seven farmsteads, hinting that these highly personal rituals were not always confined to the larger religious sites. However, in most cases this attribution remains uncertain as there was either no writing or any script remained undecipherable, and small pieces of rolled up sheet lead could also, for example, have functioned as net weights (Dütting and Hoss 2014). The possibility remains, nevertheless, that these represent 'verbal curses', as may have been the case for the eight rolled lead sheets found within the shrine at Higham Ferrers, Northants, which were all blank except one, which had illegible 'pseudo-text' (Tomlin 2009). The only legible curse tablet from a farmstead came from a late Roman settlement at Nursteed Road, Devizes, Wiltshire, which was largely undecipherable, but included the line 'the person who stole this' (Valentin and Robinson 2002). It was found in a large midden along with other possible religious objects, all of which may have originally derived from a nearby shrine.

Military vici and possible supply depots represent the last major context type within which religious objects have been recorded, and here we are limited by the fact that data were not collected from the region of Hadrian's Wall. Nevertheless, although objects such as figurines are still well represented across many sites, it is immediately noticeable that altars form a distinctly larger proportion of the overall corpus than in any other context. In part this is influenced by the large number of altars found in pits in the vicus at Maryport, most dedicated to Jupiter Optimus Maximus, that were re-used as footings for a large timber building (Haynes and Wilmott 2012). Yet even without this it would appear that altars are generally more frequent on such sites, at least in the north of England, when compared with settlements or even religious loci further south, with the exception of places like Bath, where numerous altars and altar fragments have been found. The altars from this site include those with dedications by military personnel, such as that by Forianus of the Sixth Legion Vitrix to the Genius Loci (RIB 139), suggesting that the development of this religious complex had close connections with the army (see above, p. 167). Inscribed altars have long been noted to have been concentrated in military zones, both in Britain and in Gaul, all generally dating to the second and early third centuries A.D. (Derks 1998, 82; Zoll 1995; 2016). This north–south, or 'military–civilian', division in the provisions of inscribed altars has been argued to relate to wider variances in the articulation of social and spiritual identities within differing communities (Zoll 2016, 636).

RELIGIOUS MATERIAL CULTURE: A SUMMARY

Despite presenting a very incomplete picture, material culture associated with religious beliefs remains a very important evidential base for attempting any understanding of the range of divinities worshipped and rituals practiced, as well as how the various cults were organised in rural Roman Britain. The excavated objects form a key element in interpreting the nature and function of sacred sites, and also in assessing variations in the way that different communities and social groups articulated religious expression and identity.

It has been established that the physical form of sacred space could vary widely across rural Roman Britain, and the associated material culture is just as varied. What have been termed 'votive' assemblages – primarily the physical remains of offerings to the gods – may be relatively consistent in terms of the range of object types (coins, personal objects etc.), but are largely absent, or present in very small quantities, from shrines situated in farmsteads and villas, suggesting either different types of offerings (e.g. perishable remains) or divergent forms of rituals. Further differences lie between religious sites associated with most nucleated settlements and those in rural, non-settlement contexts, with the latter generally having much larger assemblages of both 'votive' and 'non-votive' finds. Many of the more extensive rural sanctuaries in parts of central and southern Britain in particular have quantities and types of artefacts that suggest they had at least some permanent resident population, possibly acting as largely independent cult communities, or as outposts of the public religious cult of the wider *civitas*, with associated industrial, commercial, and agricultural practices.

Away from defined sacred sites, we are left with fairly limited evidence for religious belief and ritual behaviour, but these include the range of intrinsically religious objects found across different settlement and landscape contexts. It is clear that the types of religious object recovered varied across these contexts, partly reflecting differences in the way that religious beliefs were articulated within their social environments, as seen with the emphasis on divine imagery and display within villa settlements. This analysis has focused upon the context of religious finds from excavated sites, but other work using primarily unstratified data can provide complementary evidence for the regional variance in religious expression, as seen for example in Daubney's (2010) analysis of inscribed 'Tot' rings, referring to the god Toutatis, which are found almost exclusively in eastern parts of the Central Belt region.

Clearly the type, quantity, distribution and broad context of material culture are of significance for our wider understanding of religious expression in rural Roman Britain, but just as important is an understanding of how such objects were actually used, alongside animal and plant remains, within religious rituals in the countryside.

COMMUNICATING WITH THE GODS: RELIGIOUS RITUAL WITHIN THE COUNTRYSIDE OF ROMAN BRITAIN

The complex, shifting, multifarious range of divinities and spirits encountered across the Roman world would all have required some form of dialogue with their supplicants, whether as grand spectacles of public ritual and sacrifice for the well-being of the state, or private prayers beseeching help for personal concerns. Individuals and communities may have interacted with numerous deities, and the details of such divine dialogue would have varied tremendously, both geographically and chronologically, and across different cults. Nevertheless, there were a number of key ritual practices thought appropriate for communication with the divine realms that would appear more widespread across the Roman Empire, notably prayer, sacrifice and divination (Rives 2007, 24–7).

The importance of using 'correct' procedures for these religious rites and practices is often seen as paramount within Roman religion, or at least in terms of the public cult, in order to provide civic and cosmic stability, these two worlds being completely entwined (Whittaker 1997). Such public religious rituals were organised through large numbers of festivals detailed in official calendars, and comprehensive literary articulations of 'traditional' Roman religious practices were set out by the likes of Varro and Cicero in the late Republic (Ando 2007; MacRae 2016, 141). Central to these rituals was the sacrifice of animals by a priest or official upon an altar within a temple complex, often followed by divination of the entrails by a specialist, and subsequent feasting – sacrifices essentially being 'meals that the human community shared with gods' (Frankfurter 2006, 557; see discussion on the ritual use of animals and plants below, pp. 192, 199).

While the overall emphasis on orthopraxy – ensuring the correct ritual behaviour – in Roman religion is important, it does potentially obscure the multiplicity of beliefs behind Roman ritual behaviours, as recently demonstrated by Hunt (2016) in her study of the use and symbolism of trees in Roman ritual practices. It is also not necessarily the case that such a rigid adherence to certain ritual behaviour was always followed in Britain, even within civic cult sites, let alone in the wide range of other sacred loci discussed above. Nevertheless, it does seem that all of the key rituals noted above were practised in this province, and were no doubt used to help create and maintain shared identities at a number of different levels – family, wider community and even a sense of 'Roman-ness' (cf. Revell 2007, 211).

Archaeological evidence for these rituals is occasionally glimpsed from inscriptions, as for example the curse tablets discussed above, or dedications found on objects such as those to the goddess Senuna revealed on some of the votive plaques from the shrine at Ashwell End, Hertfordshire, including one reading 'To the goddess Senua[.....] Firmanus [.....] willingly fulfilled his vow' (Tomlin 2008). Most of our archaeological evidence for ritual, however, does not come from inscriptions, but from observation of depositional patterning in objects, animal and plant remains. The majority of artefacts within the 'votive' assemblages recovered from sacred sites discussed above would likely have been offerings to the deities, possibly deposited in such loci as part of formal vows (ex votos), an established and formulaic method of communication with the deity within the Roman world (Derks 1995; Bagnall-Smith 2008, 153–4; Smith 2016a). The *solutio* part of this ritual relates to the paying of the vow by the supplicant, and is directly attested on numerous inscribed altars mainly from military frontier zones (Zoll 2016), as well as on other objects such as the votive plaques at Ashwell End just noted. Quite how many of the other coins, brooches, figurines, animal remains, etc. found on sacred sites would also have been deposited as part of the same formulaic ritual is uncertain, but it would seem likely that the same basic principle of paying the divine debt was in operation, even if the mechanics of the overall ritual were more varied.

It is clear that not all artefacts, and animal and plant remains from sacred sites, were treated in the same way, with some material being specifically deposited in sub-surface features such as pits, wells and ditches, while others were recovered from floors within buildings or across exterior surface layers. In most cases this surface material has been truncated and re-deposited and so any 'formal' spatial patterning that might relate to religious ritual or another function is largely lost or difficult to ascertain (cf. Smith 2001, 20). One of the few exceptions is the distribution of artefacts, including hobnails, brooches and hairpins, on the ground surface of the inner shrine enclosure at

Higham Ferrers in Northants, many of which were arranged around a central cleared space, presumed to have been the location of the main cult focus (Lawrence and Smith 2009). The inclusion of so many hobnails is unusual and, rather than representing shoes, it was suggested that some may have been used alongside other nails as fixings to attach objects (offerings?) to the focal feature (*ibid.*, 331; FIG. 5.50).

The material from pits, ditches, wells and shafts within sacred sites includes that which can reasonably be defined as being part of structured deposits (see definition and discussion above, p. 123). This may have been material that was originally displayed in the temple or shrine structure – if such a feature existed – before being carefully collected and deposited, perhaps in formally orchestrated ceremonies. Animal remains from the shrine at Haddenham in Cambridgeshire were divided into those from surface deposits, which were thought to have been used in divination (examining the entrails), and those deposited in pits, which were suggested as representing sacrifices used in asking divine favour or paying off divine debt (Evans and Hodder 2006, 358). As will be discussed below, many sacred sites appear to have no evidence for any structured deposit, while at others the practice appears commonplace, again pointing to the variability of ritual practice across different religious loci, even within those with similar chronologies and architectural arrangements.

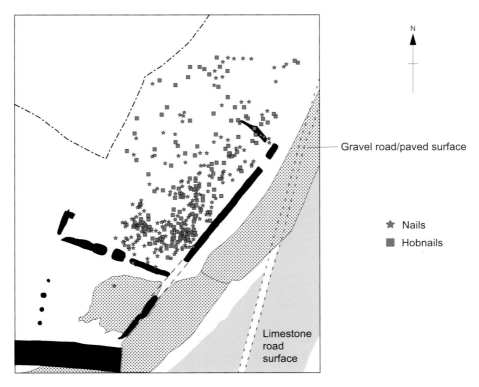

FIG. 5.50. Distribution of nails and hobnails within the shrine at Higham Ferrers, Northants (Lawrence and Smith 2009)

While the occurrence and significance of these 'special' deposits within Romano-British sacred sites has long been appreciated, it is only fairly recently that attention has been drawn to other instances of seemingly 'unusual' or 'patterned' deposits in Roman-period contexts located away from dedicated sacred space (e.g. Fulford 2001; Hingley 2006; Chadwick 2012; Smith 2016a). Such deposits have a longer history of investigation within Iron Age studies, and the brief analysis of late Iron Age ritual presented above (p. 129) has revealed broad geographic patterns in their materials and contexts. This will now be taken forward into the Roman period, when it appears that the concept of communicating with the otherworld through such acts of deposition continued in strength.

STRUCTURED OR PLACED DEPOSITS

There has been a large increase over recent years in the incidence of structured deposits being reported from Romano-British sites. Over 60 per cent of the 516 Roman sites, accounting for *c.* 1200 examples included in this project's database, were identified in reports produced after 2001,

which is, in large part, due to the much greater recognition of the significance of these unusual or 'patterned' deposits, following on from work such as Fulford's 'Pervasive "ritual" behaviour in Roman Britain' (2001). Of course, as discussed above (p. 123) not all of these articulated animal skeletons, complete pottery vessels and other 'odd' arrangements of artefacts and ecofacts may necessarily have been deposited as part of religious rituals, and even of those that were, the motivations behind such actions were undoubtedly complex and varied. But nevertheless, as highlighted above with the late Iron Age examples, there are certain broad characteristics and patterns that can be drawn out of the necessarily rudimentary data collected on these deposits as part of this project.

The Roman sites with structured deposits are spread throughout much of the province (FIG. 5.51), covering more of the north and west than was the case with the late Iron Age examples (see FIG. 5.7). Chronologically, both in terms of numbers of sites and deposits, there was an increase in occurrence during the late Iron Age–early Roman period (deposits dating to the first century A.D.) and another, much larger, spike

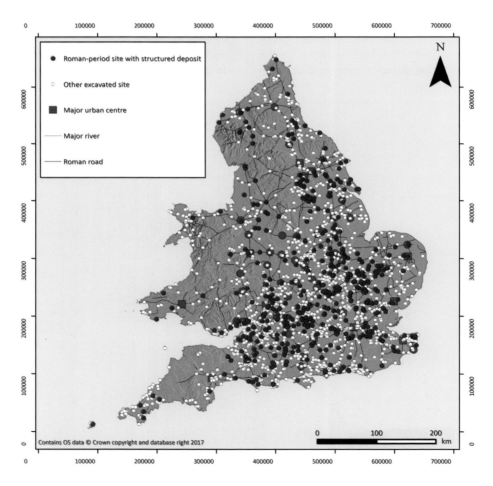

FIG. 5.51. Distribution of excavated Roman-period sites with evidence for structured deposits

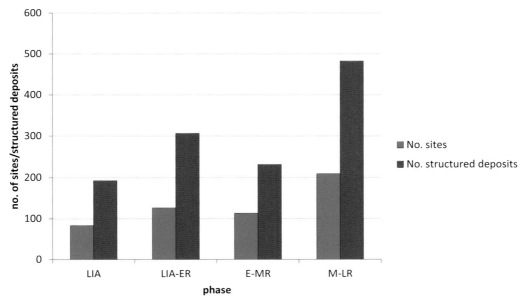

FIG. 5.52. Occurrence of structured deposits over time

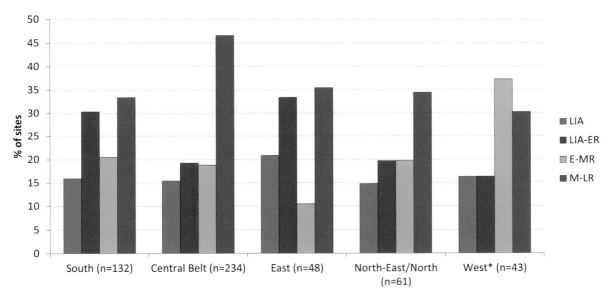

FIG. 5.53. Regional variation in occurrence of structured deposits over time (*West includes Central West, Upland Wales and the Marches and South-West regions)

during the mid- to late Roman period (third to fourth century A.D.) (FIG. 5.52). This pattern does not simply follow the overall chronological trajectory of settlements in use, as these peak during the second century A.D. (Smith and Fulford 2016, 405), a period where there appears to have been a reduction in the number of structured deposits. One possibility is that the peaks in the numbers of such deposits are related to periods of greater stress and upheaval. Kamash (2016, 688) has highlighted the major role that religion can play in social renegotiation in times of stress, with other possible examples being the revival of activity at certain prehistoric sites in the south of

England at the start of the Roman period, and particularly from the late third century A.D. onwards, as shown by Hutton (2011, 15–16). FIGURE 5.53 shows the incidence of structured deposits over time across different regions, and it is clear that the major spikes during the late Iron Age to early Roman (LIA–ER) period only occur in the South and East – arguably the areas most affected by the early aftermath of the Claudian invasion and particularly the Boudican revolt. Elsewhere, the west of England and Wales is the only 'region' to have the greatest rise in deposits during the early to mid-Roman period (later first to early third century A.D.), which corresponds with the period of greatest Roman military expansion in these areas. Meanwhile the Central Belt and North-East are marked by major spikes during the mid- to late Roman period, perhaps affected by the many changes in settlement form, landscape character and agricultural regimes witnessed in these parts at this time (Smith *et al.* 2016; Allen *et al.* 2017). Of course these are only broad regional and chronological trends and there are undoubtedly many individual and local circumstances that may have contributed towards a rise in the incidence of ritual deposits.

As mentioned above, the occurrence of structured deposits is not limited to sacred sites; they can be found across all types of settlement, as well as in wider parts of the landscape, including field and trackway ditches, and in rural cemeteries and industrial sites (TABLE 5.3). Most have been identified within farmsteads, though this is both a product of the sheer number of these sites, and the fact that many more have been excavated in recent years (cf. Allen and Smith 2016, 20). As a proportion of the total number of sites in each category, farmsteads actually have the lowest incidence of structured deposits (at 13 per cent), followed by villas (16 per cent), with much greater representation at nucleated settlements (*c.* 52 per cent). Interestingly, rural religious sites are not any more prolific in terms of evidence for these deposits than nucleated settlements, and both have a similar average number of deposits within sites where they do occur. The incidence still remains fairly low at between three and four examples per site, although, unsurprisingly, this is higher than at farmsteads, villas, and wider rural landscape features. There are of course many individual exceptions, with, for example, 24 deliberate deposits within pits in the shrine precinct at Elms Farm, Heybridge, Essex, and over 40 further examples in ditches, pits, wells and structures within the main settlement (Atkinson and Preston 2015, 105–15). For the most part, however, there are relatively few recognised examples of these ritual deposits at any site type, especially given the duration of use of many of the sites, and – as suggested for the late Iron Age above – it is debatable how far they were ever regular acts of propitiation. It is perhaps more likely that many of the archaeologically detectable examples of structured deposits highlighted here were specific responses to certain circumstances, perhaps in times of particular celebration or stress. Of course we have to accept that there may well have been many other less 'unusual' deposits of objects, plant remains or animal parts that could have been ritually motivated, but would be impossible to distinguish within the archaeological record (cf. Chadwick 2015, 50–2).

TABLE 5.3: TYPES OF SITE WITH STRUCTURED DEPOSITS DATING TO THE ROMAN PERIOD

	No. sites	No. deposits	Average no. of deposits
farm	245	443	1.81
villa	53	104	1.96
nucleated settlement	95	313	3.29
military	15	52	3.47
religious	66	257	3.89
rural/field system	24	26	1.08
Other (industrial, funerary)	18	20	1.11

It was highlighted above how, in the late Iron Age, most structured deposits were found in pits or ditches, with a particular emphasis on the terminals of the latter features. While this largely continued into the earlier post-conquest period, the pattern appears to change from the end of the first century A.D. onwards, with a greater variety of other features being utilised (FIG. 5.54). The deposition of material in wells and waterholes in particular appears to increase, some with fairly simple deposits such as the complete Savernake jar placed upright on the base of a waterhole in a farmstead at South Marston Industrial Park, Swindon, Wiltshire (Askew *et al.* 2014). Others were more complex, for example a late second/early third century A.D. well in the roadside settlement at Staines, with deposits of whole pots, including two Rhineland hunt cups, at least sixteen dogs, two rotary querns and a complete red deer antler (Jones 2010, 182; FIG. 5.55). The existence of 'sacred wells' has long been recognised in many cultures, often suggested as being places of healing, fertility and life (Varner 2009, 1), and the structured deposition of material in such places would seem to have been part of the wider religious association with water noted above (pp. 144, 162). Certainly there are many instances of what may have been ritually deposited objects of Roman date in rivers, lakes and wetlands (e.g. Rogers 2007; 2013, 124), with pewter in particular having a strong association (Poulton and Scott 1993). Lee (2009, 103) noted a distinction between deposits of pewter jugs in the Fenlands and more mixed assemblages from the Rivers Thames, Walbrook (in London), and Ver in Hertfordshire. Pewter vessels were also placed within the sacred spring at Bath (Cunliffe 1988b).

Many of the well/waterhole deposits recorded in this project were interpreted as 'closure events', at the end of the feature's practical life (cf. Chadwick 2015, 41). This does not necessarily mean that these features were not already imbued with some level of sanctity while being used as a water supply,

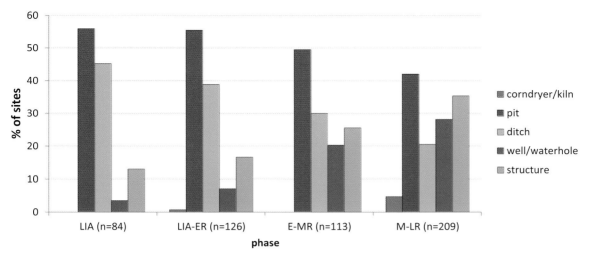

FIG. 5.54. Chronological variation in the contexts of structured deposits

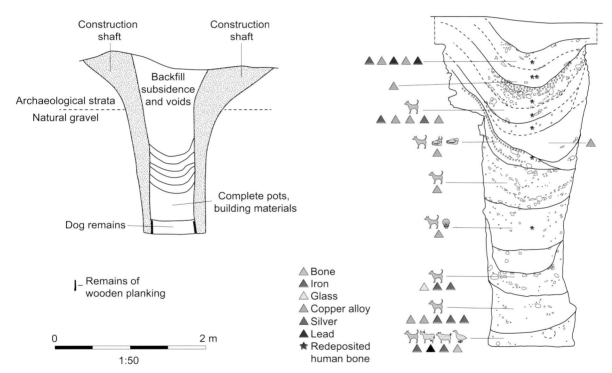

FIG. 5.55. Section of well with structured deposits from County Sports Ground, Staines (after Jones 2010, fig. 3.14), and section of ritual shaft at Springhead (after Andrews *et al.* 2011, fig. 2.55; Reproduced with permission HS1, © HS1)

with most of the small number of villa nymphaea discussed above (p. 152), such as that at Chedworth, probably combining roles as water sources and shrines. It is also possible that some of these wells never had any practical function. Some of the ritual shafts discussed above could have functioned as wells, or at least have been periodically inundated, but probably did not act as primary water sources, as for example the 4.5 m deep ritual shaft at Springhead Sanctuary, where deposits, primarily of animal remains, were made periodically throughout the life of the feature (Andrews *et al.* 2011, 80–2; FIG. 5.55).

In addition to the increase in structured deposition within wells and waterholes, there was a marked rise in the number of deposits within structures, including corndryers, kilns and larger buildings, particularly during the late Roman period (FIG. 5.54). Eight sites had corndryers of third to fourth century date with 'unusual' deposits, such as neonatal puppies found alongside millstone fragments in a dryer at Leadenham Quarry, Lincs (WYAS 2001), and a group of nine coins found close together in the flue of a corndryer at Burnby Lane, Hayton, East Riding of Yorkshire, four of them in association with partial skeletons of two dogs and a neonatal pig (Halkon *et al.* 2015). Alongside the ritual use of cereal remains discussed by Lodwick below (p. 199), this serves to highlight the significance of arable farming in the Central Belt and North-East regions. Those deposits within buildings are often interpreted as foundation offerings, such as the inverted cattle skull placed in a small pit in the centre of a doorway in the west wall of the aisled hall at Thruxton, Hampshire (Cunliffe and Poole 2008a). Others were associated with the end of the building's life, as with the almost complete domestic fowl skeleton that was placed in a feature

seemingly linked with the demolition of the villa at Blacksmith's Corner, Walberton, West Sussex (Robertson 2008). As discussed above, it seems likely that such deposits were not regular offerings, but instead marked specific, important episodes in the life of the building.

The changing pattern in the context of structured deposition is in part due to the types of site that these features were associated with. Villas in particular were more numerous in the mid- to late Roman period, and had much higher incidences of deposits within buildings and wells than other sites (FIG. 5.56). Elsewhere pits

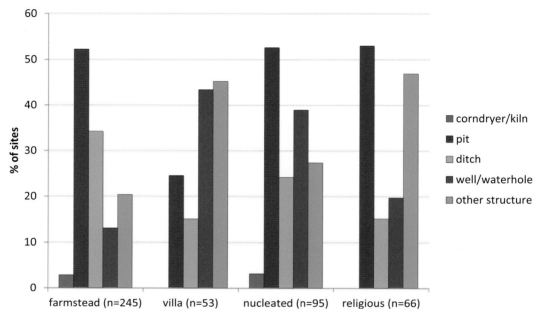

FIG. 5.56. Variation in the contexts of structured deposits of Roman date by site type

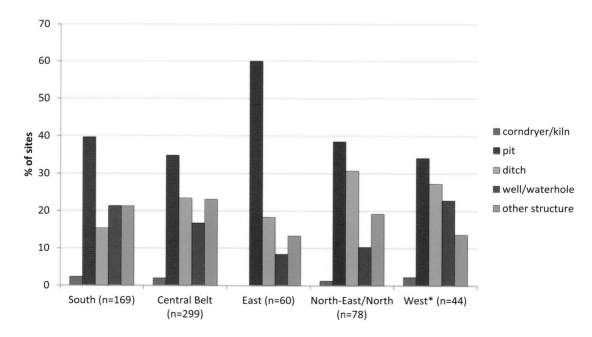

FIG. 5.57. Regional variation in the contexts of structured deposits of Roman date

remained the most common context for structured deposits, though wells were also well represented in nucleated settlements (e.g. the Staines well noted above), and there are many incidences of deposits associated with shrine or temple buildings, such as the three small fourth-century cups buried in pits within the circular shrine at Rutland Water (Carlyle 2011). All of these types of site were at their most numerous during the mid- to late Roman period.

The analysis of structured deposits from late Iron Age contexts above (p. 122) noted major regional differences in the types of associated features, with pits being particularly prevalent in the South and East regions, and ditches being better represented further north and west.

Although the pattern is not quite as stark for the Roman period, the evidence does generally suggest that such traditions continued (FIG. 5.57). The East in particular is very much dominated by pit deposits, and had a low incidence of deposition associated with buildings compared with the South and Central Belt, this probably reflecting the limited evidence for buildings as whole in this region (Smith 2016c, 225–7).

In general, the major types of material incorporated into structured deposits of the Roman period differed little from the late Iron Age, with complete pottery vessels and, in particular, animal remains being dominant (FIG. 5.58; see FIG. 5.8 above). Noticeable differences in the minor categories include a reduction in the

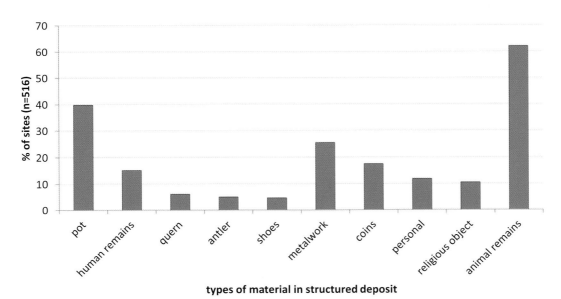

FIG. 5.58. Incidence of the principal types of material within structured deposits of Roman date

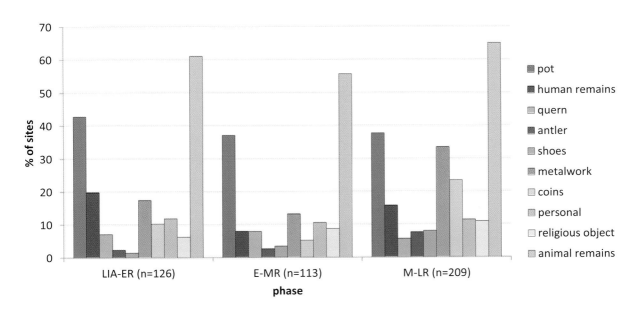

FIG. 5.59. Chronological variation in the principal types of material within structured deposits

proportion of deposits with quernstones, and increases in those with coins and religious objects, this reflecting their much greater abundance in the Roman period. Likewise, the incorporation of shoes in deposits at 25 sites remains a post-conquest phenomenon. There were some broad changes in composition within the Roman period, most notably an increase in coins and other metalwork during the third and fourth centuries A.D., the former reflecting the major increase in coin loss in the countryside at this time (FIG. 5.59; see also discussion of coin hoards below, p. 191). The inclusion of human remains (other than burials as reported in Ch. 6) peaks at *c.* 20 per cent and *c.* 16 per cent of deposits during the late Iron Age to early Roman (LIA–ER) and mid- to late Roman (M–LR) phases, with an intervening fall to just *c.* 7 per cent in the early to mid-Roman (E–MR) period. The use of human bone within these deposits, such as the fragment of human skull placed with a pottery vessel and animal bone in a LIA–ER pit at Stone Castle, Kent (Haslam 2009), probably held great symbolic value, and may have been reserved for particular periods of societal stress, as has been suggested for the occasional practice of human sacrifice (Aldhouse-Green 2001a, 169; see also Ch. 6, p. 275).

The relative prevalence of different materials within structured deposits varied according to the type of site they were associated with (FIG. 5.60). Deposits within farmsteads generally contained few materials apart from pottery vessels and animal remains, though, as highlighted by Lodwick below, plant remains are occasionally recorded on

such sites, and were probably far more common than current evidence suggests. Villas and nucleated settlements had a similar prevalence of pot/animal deposits, though with much higher incidences of other finds, particularly metalwork and coins. This reflects the generally greater range and higher quantities of artefacts recovered from these types of settlement, and there is nothing at this level of analysis to suggest that occupants of villas and nucleated sites were choosing radically different assemblages to incorporate into these 'special' deposits. As ever, it is only when analysis is scaled down to the level of the individual site that the full variety in the composition, context and form of deposits can be appreciated.

Religious sites exhibit the most variation in terms of the composition of their structured deposits. Although animal remains and pottery vessels are still commonly incorporated (see discussion of animal remains below, p. 192), metalwork is just as frequently found, including many coins, personal items and specifically religious objects. Antler is found in far fewer deposits, though it is relatively common compared with other site types. Some of these objects no doubt entered the ground as the result of larger scale public ritual, such as the mass of mainly young lambs, oyster shell and pottery from large pits in the corner of the temenos at Great Chesterford, which surely represents the remnants of ritual feasting (Medlycott 2011, 84). In other cases, however, the structured deposits may have arisen from smaller scale personal devotions within the cult site, more akin to the deposits seen within settlements and

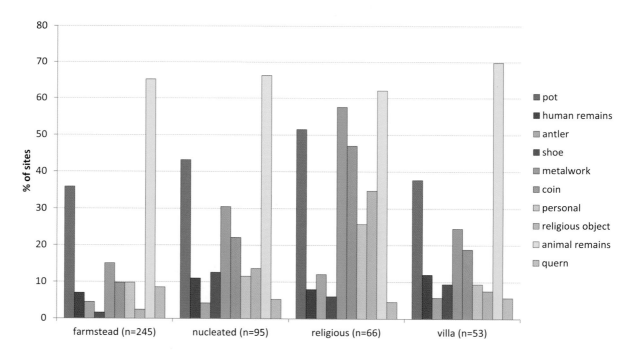

FIG. 5.60. Incidence by site type of the principal types of material within structured deposits

field systems, though presumably in most cases sanctioned by any attending cult personnel.

The analyses presented here on the chronological, contextual and compositional elements of structured deposits in the Roman period disguise a huge degree of individual variation. Furthermore, the ritual use of different material elements of these deposits has the potential to be studied in much greater detail than is possible in this publication; indeed this has been done for a number of types such as metal objects (e.g. Hobbs 2006; Lee 2009; Lundock 2015), coins (King 2007b; Wythe 2007), shoes (van Driel-Murray 1999) and animal bone (e.g. Maltby 2010a; Morris 2011). In this context, some wider consideration of the ritual significance of certain materials/categories will now be presented, namely coin hoards, animal remains and plant remains.

COIN HOARDS

By Tom Brindle

While Roman coin hoards are often seen in economic and/or political terms, as stores of wealth hidden with the intention of recovery, particularly in times of political or social instability, there has also been a long-held recognition that not all groups of coins were necessarily deposited for such reasons (e.g. Aitchison 1988; Reece 1988; 2002; Johns 1994; Millett 1994; Hobbs 2006; Bland 2013). This section presents a brief discussion of the potential ritual significance of some coin hoards. First, however, it is important to emphasise that the Roman Rural Settlement Project focused primarily on the excavated evidence for Romano-British settlements. Relatively few coin hoards have been recovered from excavated settlement sites (indeed, only 201 coin hoards were identified, recovered from 136 sites – just 4 per cent of sites on the project database), and they are far more often discovered by metal-detector users. A recent major collaborative project between the University of Leicester and the British Museum has sought to explore the various reasons for the hoarding of coins during the Roman period (see Bland 2013). That project has shown how, where the contexts of such coin hoards have been explored, they are often recovered from outside core settlement areas, frequently in the landscapes surrounding domestic sites, a pattern previously recognised for hoards generally (e.g. Johns 1996b, 8–9); this largely explains the scarcity of coin hoards in the current RRSP database. Readers are therefore directed towards the University of Leicester/British Museum forthcoming monograph for a detailed and nuanced discussion of coin hoarding during the Roman period, as well as for an overview of the extensive literature associated with the study of hoarding, and how our perceptions of them have changed, and, indeed, continue to do so.

By using the term hoard in this section, there is an intention to differentiate between coins deposited at known, formalised, religious sites (temples and shrines, discussed above, p. 132), and those buried in the wider landscape, where the ritual significance of the location is not always clearly obvious, and which, before the greater awareness of the potential votive nature of some coin hoards, were usually considered in purely economic terms. It is important to emphasise, however, that groups of coins were evidently buried for a wide range of reasons, which are usually unknowable. Some, without any doubt, must have been stores of wealth, buried for safekeeping, as references in ancient textual sources tell us (see Johns 1994 for examples). We should therefore be wary of unquestioning assumptions that coins were buried for any particular reason, whether as stores of savings, emergency deposits or votive offerings, but open to a range of possibilities, guided by the specific context within which an individual coin hoard is found. A further point to make concerns the definition of the term 'hoard'; while coin hoards, by their very nature, tend to be defined by the deposition of multiple coins together, single gold coins often represent more value than finds of multiple coins of base metal, and in this sense, as stores of value, ought not automatically to be considered as distinct from groups of lower denominations (Haselgrove 1993, 50; Hobbs 2006, 7; Bland 2013).

Although often difficult to establish archaeologically, the difference between a hoard hidden for safe keeping and that deposited for votive purposes has often been seen as the distinction between a group of objects that were hidden with the intention of recovery, and that which was dedicated for religious purposes, where no recovery was anticipated (e.g. Reece 1988, 262). However, Johns (1994; 1996b) has made the point that the votive dedication of a hoard need not necessarily have meant its permanent removal from circulation; 'safekeeping' and 'votive' are not mutually exclusive categories (Johns 1996b, 6). Coins (or other objects) dedicated at temples, for instance, were not necessarily permanently removed from circulation; they may have been used by priests for temple expenditure, thus re-entering circulation (*ibid.*, 10), or else have been deposited temporarily at the cult site to be guarded by the gods until needed (no doubt for a fee), as was the case at certain Greek sanctuaries (Tomlinson 1976, 64–71). Coins deposited at temples were not therefore necessarily 'ritually abandoned'.

There are also concerns over the unquestioning and uncritical use of the term 'votive' (Johns 1996b). Even where a coin hoard may have been deposited for 'ritual' purposes, 'votive' practices are likely to have been dynamic, with cultural, geographical and temporal differences. Seeking to interpret coin hoards in a normative fashion does an injustice to what may have been important distinctions in terms of the meaning and ways in which hoards were buried. As with other 'structured' deposits noted above, there may have been many religious reasons for depositing coin hoards in the ground, in wells, rivers or other places, and they need not all have been similar. The landscape context of hoarding has been given a great deal of recent attention, and the choice of where to deposit a hoard has often been seen as an indicator as to its potential meaning. The ancient meanings of any landscape are, however, impossible to reconstruct through modern viewpoints, and meanings are likely to have varied over time and between individuals. Such issues are discussed at considerable length in the forthcoming publication by the 'Hoarding in Iron Age and Roman Britain' project (Ghey pers. comm.).

While the complex nature of coin hoards and the difficulties surrounding their interpretation require considerable caution to be exercised, the remainder of this section discusses some particular instances of coin hoards recorded by the Roman Rural Settlement Project which, potentially, may be regarded in some way as being of ritual significance. For instance, at Ilchester Mead in Somerset a group of 56 dispersed late third-century A.D. radiate coins were recovered from one of the rooms of the villa (Hayward 1982). The dispersed nature of the hoard only makes interpretation all the more difficult, yet it is striking that this site had a number of features that might be regarded as being of particular ritual significance. These include the burial of an infant in a lead coffin outside the paved entrance to the northern range of buildings, as well as stone-lined pits that contained what may be interpreted as 'special' deposits, including a late third-century coin in a jar and animal bone in another. The presence of these other features at the site do not, of course, necessarily mean that the dispersed hoard was originally buried with any particular ritual significance, but they are evidence for behaviours at the site that make little sense from a modern perspective, and which suggest that a form of religious observance should at least be considered a possibility.

At West Park, Rockbourne, Hampshire, a hoard of late third/fourth century A.D. coins, placed in a pot, was deposited in a shallow pit outside a building, accompanied by 'sprigs of spice' within the vessel (RCHME 1983). We do not know whether these 'spices' were considered valuable, and were therefore hidden with the coins for safekeeping, or whether they had a religious votive significance. It is notable that this villa also had an infant burial placed outside the building where the coin hoard was found.

At Bradley Hill, Somerset, one building contained a group of six third-century A.D. radiate coins and three *nummi*, found together with a pot and a sheep's skull (Leech 1981). Within the corner of the same building there lay an infant burial. There is an analogous example from Wint Hill, Banwell, in North Somerset (Cottrell *et al.* 1996). Whether or not there is any firm association between coin hoards and infant burials, and, if so, whether these are related to ritual practices of some sort, are topics for future research.

The above examples demonstrate how important it is to consider the precise archaeological context, not only of large coin hoards but also of single and small groups of coins, in order to better understand how they may have been used. It is, however, important to reiterate a point made in Volume 2. In such cases we witness only the final deposition of the coins, and the particular use of them at only one moment. Such instances tell us nothing about the circulation of these objects prior to their selection for that specific process (Brindle 2017a, 240; Johns 1996b, 5).

RITUAL USE OF ANIMALS

By Martyn Allen

Animals played a central role in religious practices and beliefs throughout Britain and Europe during the Iron Age and Roman periods (Green 1992, 92–127). Many Celtic and Roman gods were themselves imbued with the ability to take on animal forms and the iconography of the period is littered with examples of human–animal hybrids (Aldhouse-Green 2001b; Gilhus 2006). Historical literary sources depict priests as being able to observe and interpret animal behaviour, entrails, and other omens as divine messages (Green 1992, 97; Papaioannou 2016). Animals were representatives of the gods on earth, and their sacrifice was a principal method of communication between humans and deities.

Iconographic and historical evidence suggest that animal sacrifices were commonplace in the Roman world. Livestock may even have been bred specifically for this purpose, with size and colour, for example, being important factors in the choice of animal (MacKinnon 2004). Pliny's description of two white bulls being chosen for sacrifice by druids during the mistletoe festival on the sixth day of the moon in Gaul suggests that animal selection may have been just as important in Iron Age cultures (*Hist. Nat.* XVI, 95). Such literary evidence relating specifically to Britain is lacking, and for direct evidence of animal sacrifice we must turn to zooarchaeological remains. However, this is less than straightforward. Although animal bones are one of the commonest classes of find on archaeological sites, they are comparatively rare as articulated body parts or complete skeletons. Even where articulated remains have been recovered, the cause of death is almost always unknown, because practices such as throat-slitting tend to leave little or no trace on the skeleton (Allen 2017, 119). Therefore, it is difficult to be certain about what remains were the results of sacrifices. Coupled with this problem is the fact that a distinction between 'ritual' and 'mundane' or 'everyday' killing of animals is a modern concept (Symons 2002). In many modern, non-western societies, the slaughter and consumption of domestic livestock could, in most cases, be considered as sacrifice, involving a range of ritual connotations (e.g. Mooketsi 2001; Abbink 2003; Lokuruka 2006). A similar intimate relationship between meat-eating and sacrifice is found in ancient Greece (Detienne 1989, 3).

Animal burials have been discovered on archaeological sites since the late nineteenth century. However, the possibility that they may have represented ritual activities did not receive much attention until the 1980s and 1990s when zooarchaeology was developing as a discipline in its own right (Morris 2011, 1–11). Grant's (1984; 1991) study of the animal bones at Danebury, Hampshire, highlighted a considerable number of whole and partial animal carcasses. These were described as 'special animal deposits', and, rather than simply being the remains of food detritus, they were thought to have formed an important part of the ritual framework of Iron Age society at Danebury. Hill (1995a) built upon Grant's study by considering a wider range of Iron Age sites in southern England, though he was careful to use the term 'Associated Bone Groups' or 'ABGs' in order to remove the assumption that all articulated animal remains should be thought of as being ritual in nature. Importantly, Hill examined animal remains alongside other forms of material culture, with the co-occurrence of animal carcasses with particular artefacts sometimes termed 'structured deposits' (*ibid.*, 84–95; see above, p. 123). As archaeologists increasingly came to recognise the importance of animals in structured deposits it became clear that this was not an Iron Age phenomenon, but one that had continued from the early prehistoric to the later medieval period (Morris 2011, 149–66), and, as already discussed in this chapter, it was clearly an important form of

ritual expression during the Roman period (Fulford 2001; Smith 2016a).

While the study of animal remains in this context is useful for understanding belief systems and ritual practices, it is important to bear in mind that terms such as 'ritual' and 'sacrifice' may be too simplistic with regard to animal remains. The motivations that lay behind many of these deposits would have been wide-ranging (Morris 2012, 16–18). Some may have been interred as part of burial rites (see Allen in Ch. 6), while others may have been foundation deposits, signifying the importance of a new settlement or construction (Woodward and Woodward 2004; Maltby 2012), or were perhaps the remains of ritual feasting associated with festivals or gatherings (King 2005). Notwithstanding the difficulties of recognising and interpreting animal remains in structured deposits, the following section examines the evidence for the possible use of animals in ritual activities across rural Roman Britain.

Animals in structured deposits

As discussed above (p. 190, FIG. 5.60), animal remains are a common component of structured deposits, being found on between 60 and 70 per cent of most types of rural sites where such deposits have been found. The fact that overtly religious sites – temples and shrines – show little difference from domestic sites in terms of the proportion that include animal bones in structured deposits, reveals not only how endemic animal sacrifice was throughout society, but that it is a mistake to try and distinguish between ritual practices and mundane everyday behaviour.

In terms of species representation, horses, dogs and cattle are most commonly deposited in structured deposits at complex farmsteads, while cattle dominate at enclosed farmsteads (FIG. 5.61). These patterns appear to differ from those at villas and roadside settlements, where dogs are most frequently chosen for deposition. The overall patterns belie the typical structure of animal exploitation, where the remains of cattle and sheep, followed by pigs, tend to dominate most faunal assemblages (Allen 2017), although this may partly be explained by the preference not to eat horse and dog, hence the burial of complete/ near complete animals. These patterns are, however, also influenced by regional differences, as shown in FIG. 5.62 (see also above discussion of regional differences during the late Iron Age, p. 129). Cattle tend to be most common in structured deposits on sites in the Central West and the North-East. Horses are most frequently encountered in the Central Belt, closely followed by cattle and dogs. Dogs are the commonest animal in the East, while the pattern from the

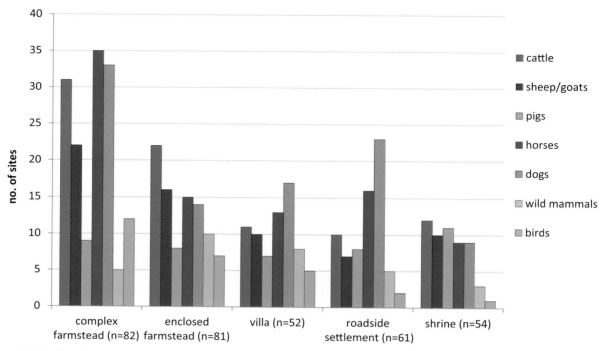

FIG. 5.61. Species representation in structured deposits at different site types

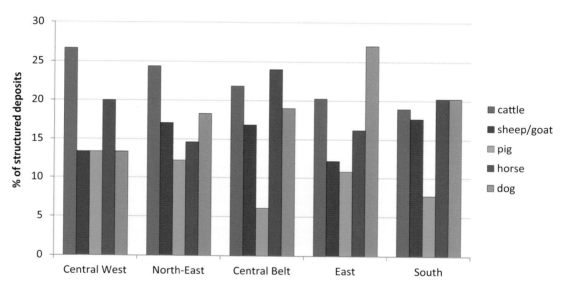

FIG. 5.62. Percentage of structured deposits with different animal species in different regions

South region shows a more equal distribution between cattle, horse, dog and sheep, with only pigs being less frequently found. While there is clearly a great deal of variation between different types of settlements and different regions, it is difficult to appreciate these data without considering the context of animal deposits.

Shafts and wells

The placement of animals in shafts and wells is a common trait associated with the Roman period. The excavation of the well at Oakridge, Hampshire, is perhaps one of the most notable examples

(Maltby 1993b). This feature was excavated to a considerable depth of over 26 m in the 1980s, showing that it began to backfill in the middle Iron Age and was almost completely filled by the end of the Roman period. The feature is distinctive for containing something in the region of 170 to 180 associated bone groups from a wide range of species, including both domestic and wild varieties of mammals and birds. This is the largest number of ABGs known from a single feature and is only surpassed by Owslebury, Hampshire, for having the greatest number from a single settlement (Morris 2011, 70). The total number of animals buried in the well was difficult to estimate, largely due to post-depositional slumping of the fills which caused many of the skeletal remains to become mixed (Maltby 1993b, 55). Maltby was reluctant to interpret any of the faunal remains recovered from the Oakridge well as deriving from ritual practices. For example, large numbers of puppies were considered to have reflected attempts at controlling the dog population, a group of swallows were thought to have been nesting within the disused well, while a raven may have been deliberately killed if it represented a threat to livestock (*ibid.*, 59). Much of the domestic livestock remains found in the well had clearly been butchered and eaten. Despite this, several complete ceramic vessels dating from the first to the fourth century A.D. were also recovered, which were thought to have been deliberate offerings, alongside the disarticulated remains from at least 27 people (Oliver 1992, 74–6). Morris (2011, 95–7) highlighted the apparent difficulties the excavator had in reconciling ritual explanations for the human bones and the pottery with the more functional interpretations for the animal remains. Less prosaic explanations for some of the Oakridge faunal remains include the raven being killed and placed there because its wing feathers were utilised for headdresses (Serjeantson and Morris 2011).

Oakridge is by no means an isolated example as there are many other rural sites where animal carcasses have been deposited in wells, such as Brislington, Bristol (Branigan 1972), Rudston, East Riding of Yorkshire (Chaplin and Barnetson 1980), Barton Court Farm, Oxfordshire (Wilson 1986), and Bays Meadow, Droitwich, Worcestershire (Noddle 2006). The fact that animal carcasses were present in these features almost certainly shows that they had already ceased to function as clean water sources, and yet many remained open and used for other purposes for a considerable period of time; in the case of Oakridge, the well was filled over a period of several centuries (Oliver 1992). The question remains whether these provided convenient receptacles for the disposal of domestic waste or represented ritualised spaces where the placement of animals and other artefacts held more significant meanings. Such meanings are in most cases very unclear. The remains of large quantities of butchered livestock remains at Oakridge may not have had any overtly religious connotations, but they must represent the production of considerable quantities of meat, which may have been consumed by large numbers of people.

Other deposits from wells are equally difficult to explain. At Beddington, Greater London, a stone-lined well contained several complete and semi-complete third-century A.D. pots, numerous leather shoes, and a horse skull from the lower fills. It was suggested that these remains reflected a ritualised response to the well running dry (Howell 2005).

At larger, nucleated settlements, denser populations required more wells to satisfy demand for fresh water. Here too, the placement of animal carcasses in disused features appears to have been relatively commonplace. At Baldock, Hertfordshire, the remains of four dogs were found in one early Roman well, while parts of at least thirteen horses were placed in two late Roman wells (Stead and Rigby 1986). Wild animals also appear in some of these features. One late fourth/early fifth century well contained the partial skeletons of two young (*c.* 6 months old) red deer, together with two hares and a fox. A large number of arrow and spearheads in several wells may indicate a symbolic importance of hunting, particularly when these are deliberately associated with horses, dogs and wild animals.

Numerous excavations and finds have identified the presence of a probable roadside settlement on Stane Street at Ewell, Surrey, though the size and character of this settlement is poorly understood (Bird 2004b, 60–2). It is, however, notable for the number of supposedly ritual shafts that have been discovered in the vicinity. These were first encountered in the mid-nineteenth century by Diamond (1847), though more have been found during more recent excavations. The nearby site at Hatch Furlong, situated on an elevated spur of the North Downs, included three shafts cut deep into the chalk (*c.* 12 feet deep) during the late second century A.D. (Cotton and Sheldon 2006). The shafts contained the remains of several young dogs, which were placed in the features between the second and the fourth centuries. Two of the shafts appeared to have been bounded to the north by a shallow linear ditch, the fill of which also contained a number of dog skulls. Further Roman shafts with whole and partial animal skeletons have been discovered at the King William IV and Reigate Road sites (Orton 1997; Cotton 2001). The animal bones were poorly reported at both of these sites though dog burials, pig burials, a horse burial, and an interesting deposit of several horse skulls were recorded at the former. The repeated nature of the evidence at Ewell suggests that the Roman settlement incorporated a significant ritual element, perhaps including one or more shrines used by the inhabitants or travellers along Stane Street.

Animals at religious sites

Animal remains are commonly encountered within Iron Age and Roman religious contexts, no doubt relating to a variety of different practices (Smith 2001, 29–30, 156–7; 2016a; King 2005). Many would have been associated with sacrifice and feasting, though others could have been kept at the religious site for other reasons, such as the dogs from the temple at Lydney Park, Gloucestershire, who may have been brought to the site for the supposed healing properties of their saliva (Boon 1989, 214–15). Here, a broad distinction will be made between faunal remains from Romano-Celtic temples and other rural shrines, with, as discussed above (p. 132) the former being more likely to relate to larger religious complexes in the South, East and Central Belt regions.

Rural shrines

The relative frequency of the main animal taxa from selected late Iron Age and Roman shrines is shown in FIG. 5.63. The principal observation is that animal bone assemblages vary greatly at different shrines. Cattle remains dominate in all the phases at Ivy Chimneys, Witham, and at Bulls Lodge, Boreham, both in Essex. The exceptional assemblage of cattle bones deposited during the Roman period in the ditch surrounding an Iron Age chariot burial at Ferry Fryston, West Yorkshire, has been noted above (p. 128). At least 162 animals were represented, with clear evidence for body-part selection as the remains were mostly skulls and articulated right forelimbs (Brown *et al.* 2007). Ageing data also showed that most cattle were slaughtered at either one-and-a-half or

two-and-a-half years old, which suggested that culling was seasonal, occurring during the late summer/autumn months. Strontium isotope analysis, a scientific provenancing technique that examines isotopic ratios in teeth to identify geological sources of origin, showed that most cattle had not been raised on the Magnesian Limestone where the site is located. It is possible the cattle used in the rituals at the site had either been traded in from a wide range of sources, had been brought in by people travelling over long distances for gatherings/festivals, or that the cattle had already been slaughtered and were brought in from a distance as dressed carcasses. Despite the Roman date of most of the animal bones, the site is notable for the complete absence of Roman material culture, which may suggest that the patrons of the site were disconnected from Roman provincial culture (Hodgson 2012, 52).

In contrast to Ferry Fryston, the shrine at Hallaton, Leicestershire, produced a faunal assemblage completely dominated by pig, which were thought to represent the remains from feasting episodes during the later first century A.D. (Score 2011). Clear evidence for age selection was noted here, with the vast majority of the pigs being slaughtered within their first two years of age, and a significant number being killed around six months. This pattern may also suggest a seasonal pattern to the rituals. Spatial patterning of the

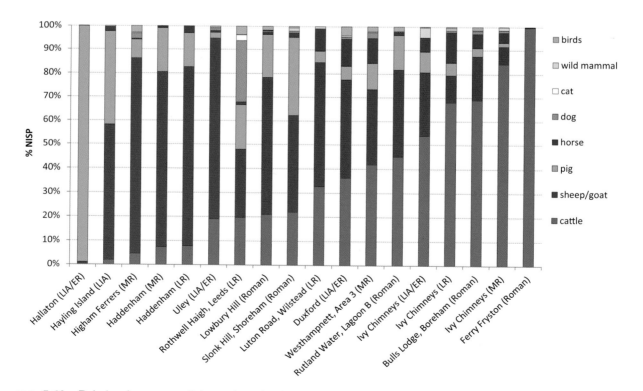

FIG. 5.63. Relative frequency of the main animal taxa found at late Iron Age and Romano-British rural shrines (assemblages with over 100 NISP)

bones showed strong evidence for not only species selection but also deposition within particular zones inside the main shrine area. These data show distinct similarities with the late Iron Age shrine at Hayling Island, Hampshire, where the faunal assemblage was more evenly divided between pig and sheep bones (King 2005). Evidence for the zonation of deposits, including coinage, metalwork and faunal remains, demonstrated the ritual character of the activities undertaken at the site. In particular, sheep were largely represented by upper limb bones and mandibles, while pig remains mostly consisted of mandibles and maxillae followed by upper limb bones. The Hayling Island shrine also had horse bones, found in association with horse equipment and vehicle fittings. Horse bones are fairly often found on shrine sites, though rarely in large quantities. They tend to be recovered in higher quantities on sites where cattle are better represented, though it is possible that this is due to differential preservation. Horse remains are notably better represented in late Roman contexts at Ivy Chimneys, Witham, with cranial bones being particularly common (Luff 1999). Numerous equid bones were also found with butchery marks, and it has been suggested that horse exploitation at Ivy Chimneys may have represented the presence of a local Trinovantian cult, though worship of the more widespread cult of Epona cannot be ruled out (cf. Green 1999, 255).

In general, dogs do not make up a significant proportion of the animal remains at most shrines, other than at Rothwell Haigh, West Yorkshire, where a stone-lined well was positioned within an enclosure. At this site, a well-preserved animal bone assemblage, including a high proportion of dogs and goats, was recovered alongside other objects, including complete pottery vessels and an adult human skull (Cool and Richardson 2013; see above p. 143). This is similar to the c. 80 m deep well near to the Roman shrine at Muntham Court, West Sussex, which contained at least sixteen dog skeletons (Burstow and Hollyman 1957). The association of dogs with wells/shafts may highlight a relationship with water. This has been previously suggested by Green (1992, 112) who proposed a possible chthonic aspect to dog symbolism. The watery location of Salt Hill Saltings in Kent may have been significant when a group of seven pots, each containing puppy bones from single individuals and quantities of charcoal, was placed in an exposed location within the Upchurch Marshes (Noel Hume 1956).

Rural temples

In some respects, the distinction between rural shrines and Romano-Celtic temples is an arbitrary one. Several temples developed from earlier shrines, but evidence suggests that the pattern of animal exploitation continued much the same. Animals appear to have been an important element at the large religious complex at Springhead, Kent, from the late Iron Age to the start of the fourth century A.D. The late Iron Age phase witnessed a horse being buried in a pit close to the elevated platform, while early Roman deposits included the skeleton of a cockerel placed above that of a puppy, the nearly complete skeletons of an adult ewe, a piglet, and a raven (Grimm and Worley 2011). The mid-Roman phase saw the construction of several shafts and deep pits, similar to those found at Ewell (see above, p. 195). One particular shaft located in the Sanctuary area by the springs, dug 4.5 m deep, included the articulated remains of nineteen dogs (one recovered with an iron chain), along with a horse skull, the neck of a young cow, three cattle skulls, the skeletons of a calf, a pig, a chicken, a goose, and a raven, and an adult human skull and infant skeletons (ibid.; see FIG. 5.55).

The rural religious complex at Uley in Gloucestershire is another site that shows a long history of animal exploitation in religious rituals (Woodward and Leach 1993). A huge faunal assemblage of over 230,000 fragments was recovered from this site, dominated by sheep and goat bones, with clear evidence for the predominance of the latter (Levitan 1993). This pattern began during the late Iron Age, associated with a timber shrine and enclosure, and continued through into the Roman period, when the shrine was replaced by a substantial masonry Romano-Celtic temple complex during the early to mid-second century A.D. Bones of sheep and goat constituted over 70 per cent of the late Iron Age/early Roman assemblage, a proportion that rose steadily over time to nearly 95 per cent by the early to middle fourth century. Uley is also one of the few temples with a relatively high proportion of chicken bones, and the analysis of these remains showed that cockerels were far more common than hens (ibid., 260, 300). The sacrifice of cockerels and goats at Uley has often been associated with the evidence for the worship of Mercury, signified by a statue that depicts both animals alongside the deity, as well as copper-alloy figurines and an altar (Woodward 1992, 79; Henig 1993, 88–95).

King's (2005, 357–62) survey of animal bone assemblages from temples in Roman Britain, which include those located at towns, identified five characteristic groups, though some sites may fall within more than one category. According to King's criteria, Group A sites include large faunal assemblages often with clear evidence for species selection and seasonal slaughter patterns. These sites may have been locations for periodic gatherings at certain times of the year and may have focused on the worship of particular deities. Uley in Gloucestershire, Harlow and Great Chesterford in Essex, Hayling Island in Hampshire, and Chanctonbury in West Sussex are examples of Group A sites. Group B sites are similar to those of Group A but are distinguished by the specific deposition of partially or completely articulated skeletal remains, often within temple buildings. The remains, King (*ibid.*, 359) suggests, represent 'individual acts of votive deposition, presumably following personal offerings and sacrifices'. Group B sites include Bancroft in Milton Keynes, Brigstock in Northamptonshire, Springhead in Kent, and Henley Wood and Lamyatt Beacon in Somerset. Group C sites are characterised by high proportions of horse bones. King (*ibid.*, 360) discusses examples at Folly Lane, Hertfordshire, and Bancroft, where the remains were found at temple-mausolea. He suggests that the association of horses with dogs at both sites, and the presence of wild animal remains at the latter, may have been linked to hunting cults, perhaps with a chthonic element. The assemblage from Ivy Chimneys, Witham, Essex, was also included in this group. As discussed above, there is some debate over

whether these remains reflected worship of Epona or a local Trinovantian cult. Group D sites are ones where animal exploitation does not appear to have been a significant element of the site's rituals. These include Nettleton Scrubb in Wiltshire, Bath in north-east Somerset, and Lydney in Gloucestershire. The remains from Bath, for example, do not derive from the main period of temple activity. King (*ibid.*, 361) highlights the possibility that the healing cults associated with these sites were of more importance than animal sacrifice and feasting. Finally, Group E includes non-Romano-Celtic sites, most notably Mithraea and classical temples associated with towns and military sites.

King's assessment clearly shows the variation in animal remains found at temples in Roman Britain. This variation is highlighted again in FIG. 5.64, though it should be pointed out that King's data included sites that have been classified here as shrines. In comparison with shrines, assemblages from temples tend to lack cattle remains, while chickens appear to be more common. These differences may reflect cultural decisions regarding which animals were more appropriate for sacrifice and ritual consumption. In many cases, the rituals associated with the animal remains are unclear, and the different contexts in which they were

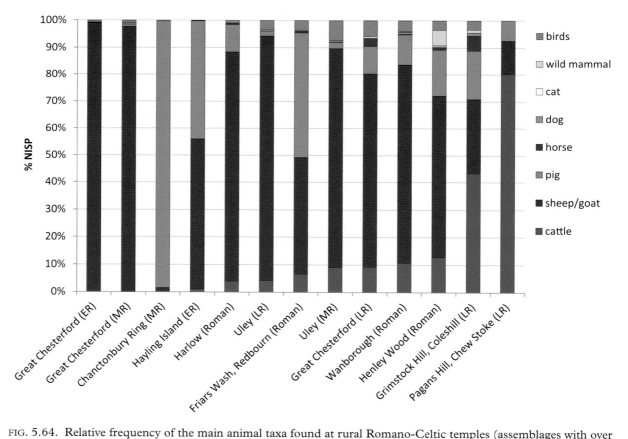

FIG. 5.64. Relative frequency of the main animal taxa found at rural Romano-Celtic temples (assemblages with over 100 NISP)

deposited and the character of their deposition (i.e. whether they were articulated or focused upon particular body parts) need to be considered on a site-by-site basis. This is true of faunal remains in ritual contexts from temples, shrines, and rural settlements.

The exploitation of animals

The animal remains found on religious sites or in structured deposits represent the final act of the ritual activities they were involved in. Yet we know very little about how these animals were managed and sourced for ritual events. King (2005, 334) highlights the identification of hay and coprolites at Uley as evidence that livestock were being kept at the site, at least periodically. This might suggest that many of the goats and sheep that were slaughtered were locally managed, though whether they were husbanded specifically for sacrifices is uncertain. Iconographic and historical evidence from other provinces clearly show that livestock destined for sacrifice were very carefully managed and specifically selected (MacKinnon 2004).

The question of whether 'ritual flocks' were managed on site or were imported from rural settlements is open to question. As mentioned above, strontium isotope analysis of cattle teeth recovered from the ritual ditch at Ferry Fryston shows that the majority were raised some distance from the site (Orton 2006). The selection of specific cattle limb-bones and skulls for deposition suggests that the animals were brought in as livestock which were slaughtered and butchered at the site, with the rest of the carcass removed afterwards, or that body parts were brought to the site as dressed carcasses. Orton (*ibid.*) even suggests that the remains may have been curated for some time prior to being deposited in a single episode.

A similar pattern where specific body parts were deposited was found at Hayling Island. It is not known whether pigs and sheep were kept on the island or ferried across at particular times of the year for festivals. It is also possible that the animals entered the site as dressed carcasses. Future work on animal remains from religious sites needs to focus on geochemical provenancing techniques, such as strontium isotope analysis, alongside dental microwear analysis, which can be compared with remains from local rural settlements to demonstrate variations in feeding patterns (e.g. Mainland and Halstead 2004).

RITUAL USE OF PLANTS

By Lisa Lodwick

Plants have often been overlooked in studies of Roman ritual and religion in Britain, both in terms of structured deposition, and offerings within temples and shrines (Lodwick 2015). In part, this is due to the limited consideration of plant offerings in Roman literary evidence (e.g. North 2000, 44–5), although it is now recognised that there was a greater diversity in the range of materials included in Roman religious sacrifice beyond animals, including incense, libations and plant foods (Elsner 2012; Schultz 2016). The lack of recognition of the role of plants in ritual is also linked to preservation. Generally, plants will only survive if they become charred, and they would only be recovered by archaeologists if sampling was undertaken during excavation. Many temples and shrines were excavated in rural Roman Britain before the advent of sampling in the late 1970s. Hence, sites where the ritual use of animals is well attested do not have any evidence for the use of plants, although this may be because of a lack of sampling. The role of plants in ritualised deposition has, however, been recognised where large imported plant foods, primarily *Pinus pinea* (stone pine) cones, were recovered by hand collection, at sites such as the Triangular Temple, Verulamium (Wheeler and Wheeler 1936, 119), the Carrawburgh Mithraeum (Richmond and Gillam 1951) and the London Mithraeum (Grimes 1968). More recently, the recognition of structured deposition at Roman sites has occasionally included the plant remains present, such as the poisonous plant *Atropa belladonna* in wells at Silchester (Fulford 2001, 206). Plant foods have also been recorded from cremations and inhumation burials, and will be discussed in Chapter 6.

It is considered here that the ritual use of plant remains can be identified using similar methods by which ritualised deposition of any material culture or animals is recognised, that is through taphonomic indications of specific use (charring, fragmentation), a high density of plant items and spatial co-occurrences or avoidances with artefacts (Lodwick 2015, 59–60). Certain categories of plant remains will be under-represented or absent from such assemblages, namely delicate remains such as flowers and leaves. Given the relatively late onset of sampling, and the hesitation of archaeologists to incorporate plant remains within studies of structured deposition and religious offerings, the instances discussed here can be considered as just a small representation of the ritual uses of plants in rural Roman Britain. Plant remains were identified as components of structured deposits at thirteen sites in the project database, and are complemented by further sites previously collated by the author (Lodwick 2015). The ritual use of plants is first discussed by the type of plant items used, before the context in which these offerings have been recorded is considered.

The first category of plants are imported plant foods, mainly intact or fragmented cones of *Pinus pinea* – Mediterranean stone pine (Kislev 1988; Lodwick 2015) and *Phoenix dactylifera* – date (Livarda 2013). Stone pine nut-shell fragments were recovered from early to mid-Roman contexts at Westhawk Farm shrine and the Springhead religious complex in Kent, with a bract also being found at the latter site. The small number of items, present at low densities, most likely indicates remnants of offerings (Pelling 2008; Stevens 2011). At Great Holts Farm villa, cone fragments and nutshells were recorded from a late Roman well, possibly in an instance of structured deposition (Murphy *et al.* 2000), while waterlogged nuts and bracts were recovered from a late second-century A.D. well at Lullingstone villa (Doherty 1987). Intact stone-pine cones have also occasionally been recorded from cut features, for example from a waterhole at the complex, mid–late Roman farmstead at Claydon Pike (Robinson 2007), and the later third-century Clatterford villa on the Isle of Wight (Busby *et al.* 2001). A possible domestic offering of stone pine, burnt pottery and jewellery was also recorded from a Flavian deposit in the west wing of Fishbourne Palace (Reynolds 1996), while charred remains of pine cones, dates and grapes were recovered alongside lamps and intact pots from an enclosure at a military annexe at Orton's Pasture, Rocester, Staffordshire (Ferris *et al.* 2000, 77). Imported cherry/plum/bullace fruits have also been suggested as elements of a structured deposit within a tannage pit at Lullingstone villa, alongside suckling pig and sandals (Meates 1979, 107).

The second major category of plant offerings is charred cereal grain, occurring in ditches or buried pots. Many charred grains were recovered from an enclosure ditch alongside a horse skull and quernstone within a mid- to late Roman complex farmstead at the proposed Abingdon Reservoir, Oxfordshire (Hall 1994). At an industrial site at Grendon Underwood, Bucks, a Black-Burnished ware vessel containing charred grains, chaff and pea was placed next to a wall (Thatcher *et al.* 2014), while spelt and barley grains (density 13.3 items/L) were interpreted as part of a ritual deposit alongside an iron anvil, spindlewhorl and vessel glass, all recovered from a ditch terminal in a late Roman farmstead at Hillyfields, Taunton, Somerset (Leach 2003).

Deposits of cereal chaff have also been recorded among distinctive material culture assemblages. At Thurnham villa, Kent, a storage jar in a pit contained charred spelt wheat chaff (Booth and Lawrence 2006), and likewise at Wilcote roadside settlement, a pot containing a large amount of spelt chaff was recovered from a second-century

A.D. quarry pit, alongside copper-alloy and iron objects (Hands 2004). Other plant-derived substances that appear to have been involved in ritualised deposition include three strips of birch bark, found in a fourth-century A.D. well at Bretton Way, Peterborough. These were suggested as a form of curse tablet, although preservation was not sufficient to reveal details (Cartwright 2013). The pollen spectrum from a late Roman well at nearby Love's Farm, St Neots, was suggested as containing taxa with culinary or medicinal use (Green and Boreham forthcoming), although as observed in Volume 2 (Lodwick 2017c), the majority of plant taxa have some form of medicinal use, and a ritual origin cannot be substantiated. The presence of mistletoe pollen is rarer, however, and perhaps significant (Hinman and Zant forthcoming). Further indications of mistletoe occurring alongside holly in wells have been highlighted within certain late Iron Age/early Roman sites in Cheshire (Chadwick 2015, 41).

The contexts associated with the ritual deposition of plants in rural Roman Britain are much broader than has previously been realised. Taking into account the limited dataset available, these include wells, pits, cesspits and enclosure ditches, and both religious and wider settlement/landscape sites. Stone pines often occur in watery contexts, with representations of the stone-pine tree being associated with water and regeneration, occurring, for instance, at fountains and on fountain jets in Rome and Pompeii (Lodwick 2017b). Although deposits of charred cereal grain are recorded as buried in the ground, within pots, pits or ditches, such small deposits would of course have become dispersed and perhaps unrecognisable in watery contexts. The burnt offering of imported stone pine is limited to shrines and villas, although there are indications that deposition in watery contexts at farmsteads and villas may also be significant.

Acknowledging the limitations of this dataset, we can make two observations. First, that the deposition of charred cereals in the Roman period may be a continuation of Iron Age practices, as charred grain in storage pits has been suggested as having ritual associations (Williams 2003; Thurston 2009). Definitive evidence for the structured deposition of charred cereals derives from a number of Iron Age sites, including Alfred's Castle, Oxon, where the charred remains of whole sheaves of cereals were recorded from six early Iron Age pits (Pelling 2013). Second, the spatial distribution of plant offerings is limited to the Central Belt and the South regions. Doubtless, this is a result of the higher intensity of fieldwork in these regions, although the possibility must be raised that cereal offerings were made by social groups where arable farming was vitally important, signalling the continued centrality of the agricultural cycle from later prehistory (Williams 2003). Furthermore, the instance of structured deposition in corndryers (see above, p. 187) also indicates the significance of arable farming in society. In contrast, the majority of plants used in ritual within towns and military sites are imported plant foods, such as stone pine, lentil and date (Livarda 2013; Lodwick 2015).

CONCLUSIONS

It seems quite likely that all aspects of rural life in Roman Britain were intimately connected with a belief in the supernatural. From the ploughing of the fields and the building of houses to merely travelling through the landscape, all areas of existence may have involved some level of dialogue with the otherworld, though the articulation of this dialogue appears to have varied markedly across time and space. With an almost complete lack of contemporary written accounts concerning religious matters, archaeological evidence, patchy as it is, provides our primary insight into this world of multifarious gods and spirits. This chapter has focused upon analyses of sacred space – those places with a particular cosmological significance – alongside the material culture, plant and animal remains that either formed part of ritual practices, or else had some other connections with religious spheres. The problems and limitations of the data have been duly acknowledged, though they have clearly demonstrated the wide variety and complexity of religious expression in the countryside of late Iron Age and Roman Britain.

Analyses of religion in this chapter have centred upon variations in geographic patterning and social context, based around a chronological framework in order to assess changes over time. The emergence of specialised shrines, for example, was shown to have been a late Iron Age phenomenon in parts of southern Britain, probably linked with significant upheavals in the socio-political system. Yet this was far from uniform, and there were still clear local and regional traditions in terms of the types of sacred site. Similar regional distinctions were noted with the form and content of so called 'structured deposits', the unusual or patterned placement of artefacts and ecofacts in features, which may have been governed by superstitious and/or religious beliefs. Although there were clearly major changes in the quantity, form and nature of structured deposits and particularly sacred space during the Roman period, many of the pre-conquest regional traditions persisted or at least had some influence on later patterns, such as the distribution of Romano-Celtic temples, which generally followed that of late Iron Age sacred space.

The eight regions outlined in Volume 1 (Smith et al. 2016; see Ch. 1, FIG. 1.1), which were largely based upon settlement patterns, have been used here to assess the regional diversity of religious practice. In broad terms, these regions do appear to correlate with differences in religious expression, most strikingly between those regions to the north and west (North, Wales and the Marches, South-West), and those to the south and east (South, East, North-East and Central Belt). In the former areas, there are very few places or structures that have been interpreted as shrines or have evidence for religious objects, apart from military contexts, though there is far more evidence for structured deposition. On the face of it, this suggests fundamental differences in the ways that people interacted with their gods, which matches similar differences in settlements, buildings, farming practices and use of material culture (Smith et al. 2016; Allen et al. 2017). However, this was not just a simple divide between the north/west and south/east, as there is still significant variation within the much greater body of evidence from the central, southern and eastern regions. In the East, for example, there appears to have been a preference for religious enclosures without architectural embellishment, particularly in rural 'non-settlement' locations, while there is also a relative lack of large rural religious sanctuaries compared with parts of the South and Central Belt. Instead there are higher numbers of shrines and particularly Romano-Celtic temples within or immediately outside the many nucleated settlements in this region, which may have fulfilled the larger-scale, 'public' religious requirements of the local populations. In the Central Belt, there is more evidence for sacred space within farmsteads, mostly complex farmsteads of the river valleys, while this is also the area where most rural sanctuary complexes developed. A few of these grew to a considerable size and no doubt attracted worshippers from some distance, some people perhaps undergoing sacralised journeys, or pilgrimages, perhaps to seek cures for an illness, as suggested for the Gallo-Roman religious complex at Fontes Sequana by the source of the River Seine (Aldhouse-Green 1999). Many of these large rural sanctuaries were located on or close to the main road system, and effectively became nucleated settlements in their own right, possibly under some level of *civitas* control or even operating as independent cult communities.

Ultimately, the religious experiences of the peoples of Roman Britain were not only governed by local and regional traditions, but also by variations in their social context. Even within a

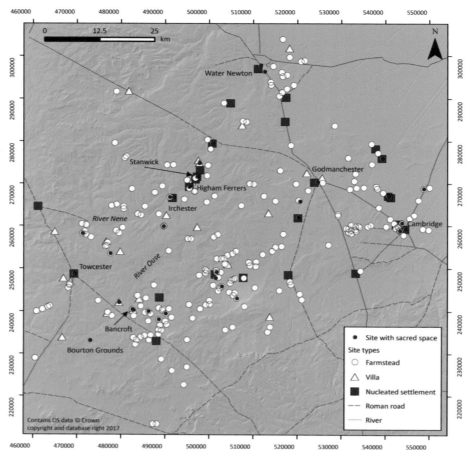

FIG. 5.65. Distribution of Roman period settlements in the West Anglian Plain, highlighting those sites with sacred space

single landscape, at least some aspects of the religious lives of peoples living in simple enclosed farmsteads, larger complex farmsteads, high-status villas and nucleated roadside settlements could have been quite different. This can be illustrated within the West Anglian Plain, a landscape in the east of the Central Belt region incorporating the Nene and Ouse Valleys and an intervening area of boulder clay plateau, where there has been much recent excavation (Smith 2016d, 142–4; FIG. 5.65). Of the 212 excavated farmsteads from this landscape, just 11 (*c.* 5 per cent) had any evidence for sacred space, these being a mixture of enclosures, masonry structures (mostly circular) and timber structures. Almost all of these were complex farmsteads such as at Little Paxton Quarry, Cambridgeshire (see FIG. 5.25), suggesting that the provision of sacred space within or close to the settlement was more important to the inhabitants of such sites than at other, generally smaller, farmsteads. Likewise, of the seventeen farmsteads in this landscape to have evidence for religious objects (pipeclay and metal figurines, miniature objects and various other 'personal' artefacts), nine were complex, just one enclosed

and the remainder unclassified. This all suggests a far greater emphasis on certain visual aspects of religious expression at complex farmsteads, in both the creation of dedicated shrines and use of specific religious objects. However, this is not to say that enclosed farmsteads were lacking any trace of ritual activity, as the distribution of structured deposits is much more evenly spread between different farmstead types. Enclosed farmsteads in this landscape zone tend to be more common on the higher boulder claylands, rather than in the river valleys (Smith 2016d, 175), which seem to have formed the major communications routes. It is this lack of connectivity, together with a chronological bias towards the earlier Roman period, which has probably influenced the differences in religious expression between these farming settlements.

Most of the twenty villas from this landscape have seen very little excavation beyond the main domestic building and so our knowledge of the religious lives of their inhabitants remains quite poor. The best example is Bancroft in Milton Keynes, which, as noted above (p. 154), had two probable shrines, possibly intended for different social uses, along with a Romano-Celtic temple-mausoleum. Religious objects came from eight villas, including stone sculpture, metal figurines and copper-alloy leaves/plaques, but just four sites had evidence for structured deposits, including a near-complete Nene Valley beaker, goose bone and waterlogged wood placed beneath limestone slabs close to a spring by the villa at Manton Lane, Bedford (Luke *et al.* 2015).

For the inhabitants of the landscape's 23 nucleated settlements there was much more likelihood of there being a religious focus on-site, from the enclosure shrines at Higham Ferrers and Stanwick to the Romano-Celtic temples at the defended 'small towns' of Irchester and Godmanchester. Equally, religious objects are much more common in such contexts, from figurines and monumental sculpture, to the occasional altar, curse tablets, and items of priestly regalia. As with villas, there is slightly less evidence for structured deposition, though these do include the thirteen deep ritual shafts with infant burials, dogs and other items from the walled 'small town' at Cambridge (Alexander and Pullinger 2000, 53). Overall, the archaeological evidence from many of these nucleated settlements demonstrates a fairly active and organised religious element, with some of the larger shrines and temples possibly under some level of civic patronage. These sacred sites may not only have been used by the settlement's inhabitants, but also, on occasion, by those from the outlying farmsteads and villas, nearly all of which lay within 20 km (an approximate day's walk) of such sites. Religious festivals held at these sacred sites, and possibly at the single rural religious complex in the south-western part of the landscape zone at Bourton Grounds, might even have been used to help create and maintain some level of community identity.

Yet this was not a single, organised religion. The evidence from the West Anglian Plain and elsewhere in the province indicates a huge amount of individual variation in matters of religious expression. It all suggests that persons and local groups could take control of their own religious lives, or at least most aspects of it, perhaps just occasionally congregating at certain special places for larger scale ritual activities designed to ensure the welfare of the wider community. At the highest level this could have included rituals designed to foster a sense of 'Roman-ness', for example through the imperial cult (cf. Fishwick 1961; 1995), though it is debateable how widespread or common this would have been, with the exception of some military and urban contexts.

Of course one religion that did eventually come to be defined by the Roman state, and which has not yet been discussed, is that of Christianity.

Christianity spread throughout much of the Roman Empire during the first to third century A.D., though it was not until the Edict of Milan in A.D. 313 that it was fully recognised by the State, and only in A.D. 380 did it become the official state religion. Evidence for Christianity in Roman Britain has been discussed at length by various authors, notably Petts (2003; 2016), who argued that in this province it was in the small towns and among rural communities where the religion was strongest (Petts 2003, 163–5). It is not the intention here to assess the evidence for Christianity in any depth, though the data collected for this project does suggest that the Christian faith was never particularly widespread in the late Roman countryside. That rural Christian communities existed, however, is not in doubt, with evidence in the form of chi-rho symbols (the first two letters of the Greek word for Christ, *Christos*), lead tanks (ostensibly used for baptism), and other Christian imagery on objects, mosaics and wall-paintings, coming from over 40 different sites (see also discussion of possible evidence for Christianity from cemeteries in Chapter 6, p. 279). These sites were nearly all located across parts of the East, South and Central Belt regions, though with different regional expressions, such as the concentrations of lead tanks and chi-rho symbols in parts of the east and mosaic imagery further west (cf. Petts 2016, 675). In terms of settlement context, most of these were villas and nucleated roadside settlements (including defended 'small towns'), with just one farmstead, at Heathrow Terminal 5, where a lead tank was recovered from a waterhole to the west of the settlement (Lewis *et al.* 2010, 311–12). A few other Christian objects did come from 'isolated' rural locations, such as the inscribed lead tank from Flawborough in Nottinghamshire, though stone scatters and Romano-British pottery and metalwork found in the vicinity suggest that there was a settlement in the area (Elliott and Malone 2005).

Christianity can therefore be viewed as just one of a number of religious cults in existence within the late Roman countryside in Britain, one that was seemingly more readily adopted by those higher up the social scale as well as in some of the larger nucleated settlements of the south and east (Petts 2016, 676). The adoption of Christianity by certain individuals of rank may have been useful in maintaining political advantages within upper social circles, with the developing church framework becoming increasingly important in the imperial administration, though this is not necessarily to doubt the sincerity of their religious piety. Despite its increased adoption by people of power and status, there were still clearly people of great wealth who held pagan beliefs, as shown by the Thetford treasure (Johns and Potter 1983), and it is very likely that the vast majority of the rural population of Roman Britain continued to worship and respect the large pantheon of pagan deities and spirits. It has been shown in this chapter (p. 134, FIG. 5.11) that the late Roman period was when most shrines and temples were in use, and there were new sacred sites being constructed even in urban contexts, such as the (admittedly short-lived) mid-fourth century timber polygonal shrine set within a ditched temenos outside the walls of Canterbury at Augustine House. This was positioned upon a late Iron Age burial, and thought to commemorate a remembered ancestor (Helm 2014, 140). However, the decline of some religious sites during the fourth century has sometimes been taken as indicating increased competition from Christianity,

and even a destructive zeal in destroying certain shrines, albeit with a 'pagan revival' from A.D. 361, following the two-year reign of the pagan emperor Julian (Watts 1998). A more contextual approach indicates that the fortunes of most sacred sites were closely entwined with that of their associated settlement or with those in the surrounding landscape, with many built temples and shrines falling into decay at approximately the same time as surrounding buildings; there is certainly little conclusive evidence for any widespread friction between paganism and Christianity (Smith 2008). The basis of the Church's structure and organisation in Britain may have remained largely intact at the start of the fifth century (Petts 2003), but it would take some time before it would become the dominant faith of those inhabiting the countryside.

CHAPTER 6

DEATH IN THE COUNTRYSIDE: RURAL BURIAL PRACTICES

By Alexander Smith

with contributions by Martyn Allen and Lisa Lodwick

INTRODUCTION

At some point during the later third or fourth century A.D., the cremated remains of a mature adult were placed within a wooden box in a grave dug along the path of a major droveway on the eastern edge of the River Colne floodplain in the Middle Thames Valley, accompanied by the burnt remains of a sheep or goat and a red deer, possibly intended as sustenance for the afterlife. Lying just over 190 m away, an individual wearing hobnailed shoes was buried within a relict Bronze Age field ditch, probably interred at approximately the same time. These two individuals provide the only evidence for Roman funerary practice within an open-area excavation covering over 70 ha at Heathrow Terminal 5, and both were well removed from the contemporary settlement (Lewis *et al.* 2010, 308–9). They serve to illustrate both the diversity of burial rites apparent during the later Roman period, and, perhaps more importantly, how scarce our evidence can be for the treatment of the dead, even within the heart of south-east England.

Romano-British funerary customs have long attracted academic attention, traditionally focused upon discussion of the more archaeologically obvious cremation and inhumation burials, along with any associated grave goods and containers (e.g. Black 1986; Philpott 1991; Booth 2001). More recently, however, there has been a much greater appreciation of the wider aspects of funerary ritual beyond the final interment, which was of course just one element in what could have been a lengthy and complex process, starting with the death of the individual and ending, perhaps, in repeated acts of commemoration at the grave site (Toynbee 1971; Pearce 2013, 11; Williams 2013; Weekes 2016; Pearce 2017). Much of this focus has been on the cremation process in particular, with examination of pyre sites and other cremation-related deposits leading to a greater understanding of the attendant rituals, though still with the recognition that these features may only represent a fraction of the overall mortuary rites (Weekes 2008; McKinley 2013). Any examination of the wider funerary processes around inhumation burials is hampered by the lack of recognisably associated sub-surface features (cf. Booth 2017),

though recent analysis by Biddulph (2015) has suggested that much of the 'residual' pottery from the backfill of graves and other cemetery features may be associated with funerary-related feasting.

Some studies of Romano-British burials have focused upon the cultural and social identities of the deceased individuals and their wider communities, usually attempted through analysis of grave types and monuments, burial rites and associated material culture (e.g. Philpott 1991; Strück 2000), though occasionally incorporating wider aspects of the ritual sequence (e.g. Pearce 2016; see also Fowler 2013). Variations in social status may also be assessed through detailed osteological analysis, and this is explored at length in Chapter 7.

The corpus of Romano-British burials utilised in most previous 'national' syntheses of funerary ritual has been dominated by the extensive urban cemeteries of London, Canterbury, York, Dorchester (Dorset), Winchester and Cirencester, where mainly developer-funded excavations continue to reveal large numbers of Roman interments, usually sited alongside roads leading from the walled urban core, and primarily dating to the later Roman period (e.g. Booth *et al.* 2010; Weekes 2011; Holbrook *et al.* 2013; Harward *et al.* 2015; Hunter-Mann 2015). In a recent review of the evidence for funerary ritual in the towns of Roman Britain, Pearce (2015, 138) indicated that over *c.* 11,000 burials had been excavated, marking it 'as one of the richest urban burial datasets of any province'. This wealth of evidence has significantly improved our understanding of urban mortuary practice, while isotopic analysis of the skeletal remains has revealed great insights into the cultural and ethnic diversity of populations living within Roman towns (Eckardt *et al.* 2014).

Burial practices within the countryside of Roman Britain have generally received less academic synthesis on a province-wide scale, primarily because the dataset is so vast and diffuse (cf. Esmonde Cleary 2000, 132). Many excavations of Roman farmsteads, villas or fields have encountered the occasional contemporary burial, and – as discussed below – this now equates to over a thousand different sites across England and Wales. The diversity of rural Romano-British funerary practice is already appreciated to some degree (e.g. Pearce 2013, 109–10; Booth 2017), but this current study is the first to collate this mass of data – *c.* 80 per cent of which post-dates PPG16 in 1990 – and provides a more detailed consideration of this heterogeneity, on both a regional and local landscape-based scale.

This chapter presents a broad discussion of rural burial practices in Roman Britain, focusing upon chronological and spatial patterning of different rites, the social contexts of burials, and accounts of grave furnishings and goods, including the use of animals and plants in funerary rituals. Detailed palaeopathological analysis of a select sample of inhumation burials is presented in Chapter 7.

THE BURIALS DATASET

In total, 15,579 human burials were recorded from 1162 excavated sites across England and Wales within the project database. A further 169 sites were thought by the excavators to have had burials, on the basis of 'grave-shaped' pits and possible grave goods, or else had evidence for disarticulated human bone, though no formal burial. Burial is here defined as the disposal of human remains, by inhumation, with complete or near-complete skeleton, or by cremation, into a cut feature in the ground, usually specifically dug for the human interment (i.e. a grave). Although the vast majority of the interments included in the dataset would appear to have been 'formal' burials, mostly carried out with due care and attention, there are some examples where this may not have been the case, such as an adult male skeleton from a cemetery at Dunstable, Central Bedfordshire, which was suggested as having had its face cut off with a sharp weapon and then placed in a re-excavated grave of a young woman (Matthews 1981).

It has not been possible to quantify and analyse each burial individually, and so the dataset comprises burial records, which are burials grouped by site and where possible sub-divided by phase (see chronology below). So, for example, the site at Birchfield Road, Great Barford, Bedford, has two records, one for a cemetery of seven early Roman cremation graves lying on the periphery of the farmstead, and another for a late Roman inhumation cemetery of at least eleven graves established on the by then abandoned settlement (Timby *et al.* 2007b). At some excavated sites there were a number of distinct cemetery groups, which have – where possible – been recorded individually and then further divided by phase, such as at Mucking in Essex, where nine separate records exist for the five main cemeteries and scatters of isolated burials dispersed within the

nucleated settlement (Lucy and Evans 2016). Using this method, there are a total of 1659 burial records.

The distribution of all sites with evidence for human remains is shown in FIG. 6.1, together with the density of 'formal' burials. These are ostensibly sites of 'rural' burials, in that they do not include any evidence from the major towns (*civitas* capitals, *municipium*, *colonia*), although burials from a selected sample of defended 'small towns' (e.g. Cambridge) have been incorporated (see context of burials below, p. 231). Furthermore, there are a small number of burials included that lie within a few kilometres of major urban centres, and whose presence may have been influenced by the town, though most of these lie within field ditches or else are associated with farmsteads lying in proximity to the urban defences.

The overall concentration of burial sites in the Central Belt, North-East, East and South regions is to be expected, given the much greater density of excavation records in these areas, combined with the poor preservation of bone in many areas further north and west, as also seen with distribution of animal bone from excavated sites (cf. Allen 2017, fig. 3.1). Although this bias in the dataset needs to be kept firmly in mind in the analyses below (cf. Pearce 2013, 13–26, for a detailed account of problems with excavated Romano-British burial data), there is sufficient evidence from all regions for it to be possible to take a province-wide approach to the study of variability of funerary customs.

The wide-ranging research aims of the *Roman Rural Settlement Project* necessitated pragmatic limitations on the type and amount of data that could be collected on the human remains. This essentially focused upon basic quantifications of burials, the major rites of cremation and inhumation, certain 'deviant' inhumation rites, broad population demographics (sex and age) and the provision of grave goods and containers. However, as discussed above, most of the evidence for wider funerary processes has not been systematically recorded, as this would have required a much finer level of contextual resolution than was possible here. Nevertheless, on a broader contextual basis, the nature of any associated settlement or landscape feature has been recorded, thus allowing for the social distribution of burial ritual to be analysed.

One issue to be noted with the burials dataset is that many of the excavation records did not contain data on all burials found at the site, either because they were not all fully examined, or because the report was from an interim stage of post-excavation and no further details were forthcoming. Furthermore, while many of the

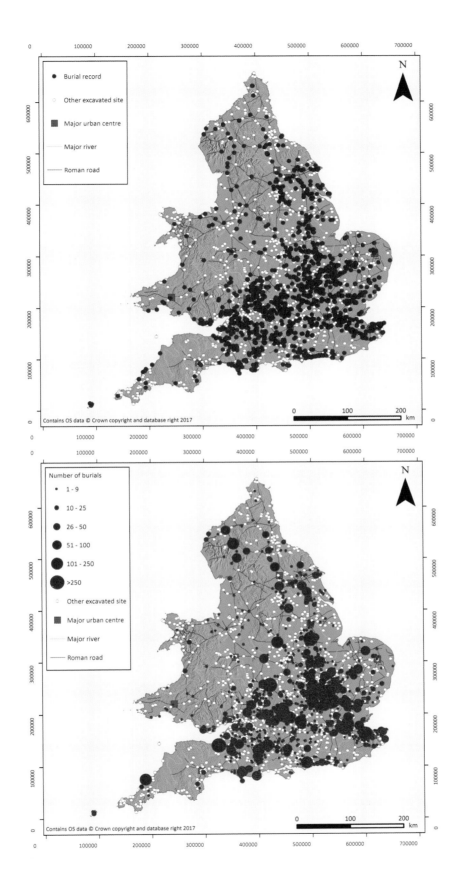

FIG. 6.1. Distribution of all rural site records with indications of human remains and the density of human burials in the countryside

older reports may have an overall quantification of burials, only selective details on other aspects, such as burial rites, grave goods and containers, are included. Nevertheless, as the great majority of reports were produced since 1990, over 90 per cent of the burial records were regarded as 'complete', accounting for 11,760 individual burials. It is this 'complete' dataset that is used in much of the analysis below, unless otherwise specified.

THE CHRONOLOGY, DISTRIBUTION AND FORM OF BURIAL RITUAL

One of the principal concerns of the wider project has been an assessment of change in the countryside over time, from the late Iron Age into the early post-Roman period. Funerary customs are often thought to have been inherently conservative, particularly from the late Iron Age to the second century A.D., though Pearce (2014a) has recently argued for a much higher degree of dynamism, primarily through the evolving symbolism of grave goods, while the analysis presented here suggests distinctly variable forms and rates of change across different regions and landscapes.

Attempts to analyse change in burial customs over time have been hampered by a number of factors. The most crucial of these is the poor chronological resolution of many burials, either through the lack of diagnostic artefacts or lack of scientific dating. Only *c.* 13 per cent of all burial records had any radiocarbon dating (though this is more than with urban burials; Pearce, pers. comm.), this generally being more likely in sites located to the north and west, though the greatest number are in the Central Belt and South regions (FIG. 6.2). Furthermore, this dating often only targeted a very small proportion of the total number of burials found at the site. Where such scientific dating has been widely applied, it has clearly shown the longevity of unaccompanied, extended inhumation burial until well into the post-Roman period, such as at Ipplepen in south Devon, where recent excavation of a Roman roadside settlement revealed a small inhumation cemetery that proved to date from the sixth to eighth century A.D. (http://ipplepen.exeter.ac.uk/).

Most burials are dated through associated ceramics, which have varying degrees of chronological resolution, alongside other datable

FIG. 6.2.   Sites with one or more burials with radiocarbon date

TABLE 6.1: PHASING INFORMATION FOR BURIALS DATASET
(* includes 16 records assigned 'E/MR'; + includes 62 records assigned 'M/LR')

Phase	Date range	No. of records
Late Iron Age (LIA)	First century B.C. to mid-first century A.D.	129
Late Iron Age/early Roman (LIA/ER)	First century B.C. to early second century A.D.	154
Early Roman (ER)	Mid-first century A.D. to later second century A.D.	323
Mid-Roman (MR)	Second to third century A.D.	200*
Late Roman (LR)	Third to fourth century A.D.	484+
Roman (general)	First to fourth century A.D.	196

artefacts such as coins and brooches. As will be shown below, such grave goods are typically encountered in only a small proportion of graves within cemeteries, but it is these that are mainly used as the basis for dating the entire burial group, potentially restricting the overall chronology. Because of these issues, and the fact that some excavated cemeteries had no or only limited internal phasing presented in their reports, it has been necessary to divide burial records into fairly broad chronological groups, as shown in TABLE 6.1. In some cases, particularly within larger cemeteries where no explicit chronological sub-divisions were provided, the phase relates to the main period of burial, but there may well be a few earlier or later outliers. Where the chronological resolution of burial records is particularly poor, they have been assigned a general 'Roman' phase, and are not used in any analysis of change over time.

CHRONOLOGICAL PATTERNS

FIGURE 6.3 shows the total numbers of excavated burials over time, from the late Iron Age to the late Roman period. There is a general recognition that for most of England and Wales there is relatively little evidence for the formal interment of the dead throughout much of the Iron Age, and that the evidence we do have suggests great variability and localisation of burial rites, from the square-ditched barrows of eastern Yorkshire to the pit burials of central Wessex (Whimster 1981; Cunliffe 1995, 552; Joy 2011, 409; Harding 2015). Exposure of the dead and subsequent dispersal of the bones is often assumed to have been the 'normative' rite of this period in most places, occasionally corroborated by the occurrence of disarticulated human bone in archaeological features, including within so-called 'structured deposits' (see Ch. 5, p. 123 and below, p. 275). Alternatively, bodies may have been cremated, with the remains then dispersed across settlements and fields, or scattered in rivers, thus remaining archaeologically invisible (McKinley 2006, 86; Evans 2013b; Harding 2015, 269). Excavations at Elms Farm, Heybridge, in Essex, for instance, revealed nineteen pyre sites of late Iron Age date but just a single contemporary cremation burial (Atkinson and Preston 2015, 117–24). Although it is possible that further graves were located some distance from the pyre sites, this lack of burials may otherwise indicate that the cremated remains were only occasionally interred in the ground. Even in places where there are more substantial cemeteries, such as the 161 cremation burials from Westhampnett in West Sussex (Fitzpatrick 1997), such formal interment is still likely to have been quite selective, or at least only represent the 'typical' mortuary rite for a restricted local community.

The late Iron Age was certainly a period of great change in terms of funerary practices, although these developments varied significantly across different regions. Recent radiocarbon assessments of the east Yorkshire barrow burials suggests that they had largely ceased by the end of the second century B.C. (Jay et al. 2012), while at approximately the same time the earliest cremation cemeteries appear in south-east England. The 'Durotrigan' inhumation burials in the Dorset area generally date from the latest pre-Roman Iron Age (see discussion of burial rites below, p. 216). In terms of the number of burials across England and Wales, the late Iron Age saw a distinct increase, at least beyond the east Yorkshire area, with many cemeteries remaining in use into the early Roman period, when the overall quantity of burials continued to rise (FIG. 6.3). There is a fall in the number of burials assigned to the mid-Roman period only, though this is partly because there were some records that could not be assigned a more refined chronology than 'mid- to late Roman', and these have been included in the latter phase. Nevertheless, there is no doubt that there was a major spike in burial numbers during the late Roman period, when inhumation had replaced cremation as the commoner burial rite. Indeed, it is only at this time that, in some areas at least, the formal interment of the dead, whether in larger cemeteries, small groups or individually, may be considered as even a 'normative' funerary rite. Such a chronological pattern has been well observed in previous studies of Roman burial, being particularly noteworthy in some of the

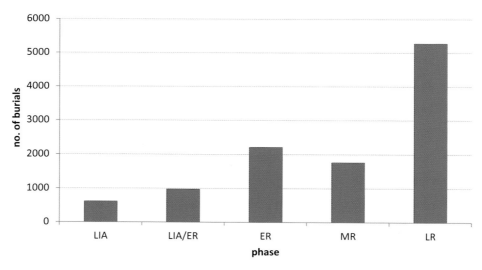

FIG. 6.3. Numbers of recorded burials over time

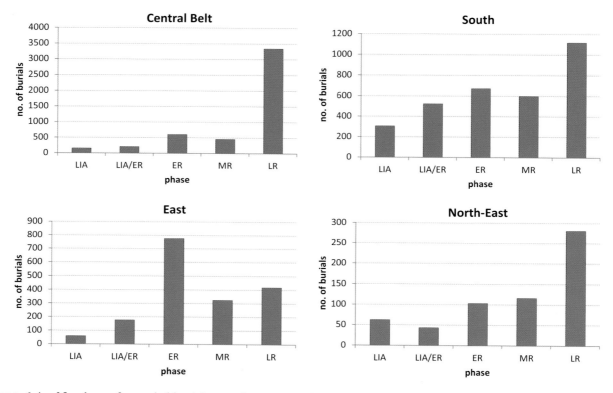

FIG. 6.4. Numbers of recorded burials over time across selected regions

major towns of Roman Britain like Winchester (Booth *et al.* 2010; Ottaway *et al.* 2012), where substantial (primarily inhumation) cemeteries were established during the later third and fourth centuries A.D., usually succeeding more sporadic evidence for burial (cf. Pearce 2015, 143). When discussing this phenomenon at Dorchester in Dorset, Woodward (1993, 237) suggested that the increased size of late Roman cemeteries around the town was due to them incorporating the dead from surrounding rural communities. However, in this case there is equal evidence for an upsurge in

rural burial at this time within Dorset (cf. Redfern *et al.* 2015), suggesting it was more of a widespread shift towards interment of the dead than any increased attraction of the town as a burial location.

The extent of the upsurge in burial during the late Roman period was far from uniform across the province, and indeed there are some regions where this pattern does not appear to have been followed at all (FIG. 6.4). The East region had a significant increase in burial numbers during the early Roman period, particularly in cemeteries

TABLE 6.2: SUMMARY OF BURIAL RITES ACROSS TIME WITHIN EIGHT PROJECT REGIONS
(NB. Only includes 'complete' records)

	Late Iron Age	Late Iron Age/ early Roman	Early Roman	Mid-Roman	Late Roman	Roman (general)	Total
Central Belt							
No. sites with burials	45	47	117	87	250	88	634
No. of burials	151	204	598	452	3341	414	5160
Cremation burials	62	141	396	111	148	28	886
Inhumation burials	89	63	196	340	3192	380	4260
No. cemeteries	6	11	31	14	103	18	183
South							
No. sites with burials	46	63	108	48	106	27	398
No. of burials	305	523	672	599	1118	267	3484
Cremation burials	214	190	374	308	67	25	1178
Inhumation burials	91	333	298	290	1055	241	2308
No. cemeteries	6	24	33	18	33	2	116
East							
No. sites with burials	14	17	39	18	35	17	140
No. of burials	59	176	775	324	418	81	1833
Cremation burials	39	106	733	253	40	8	1179
Inhumation burials	20	70	42	71	378	73	654
No. cemeteries	6	10	14	8	12	1	51
North-East							
No. sites with burials	14	11	19	20	41	16	121
No. of burials	62	43	103	116	281	144	749
Cremation burials		7	66	22	31	16	142
Inhumation burials	62	36	37	94	250	128	607
No. cemeteries	2	1	5	5	12	3	28
North							
No. sites with burials	2	3	6	6	3	3	23
No. of burials	4	8	8	198	27	4	249
Cremation burials		1	7	177	20	3	208
Inhumation burials	3	7	1	21	7	1	40
No. cemeteries		1		3	3		7
Central West							
No. sites with burials		3	8	9	5	3	28
No. of burials		9	18	72	31	4	134
Cremation burials		2	15	48		4	69
Inhumation burials		4	3	23	31		61
No. cemeteries				2	2		4
Upland Wales and Marches							
No. sites with burials	4		8	1	5	3	21
No. of burials	9		35	1	29	10	84
Cremation burials			33			1	34
Inhumation burials	9		2	1	29	9	50
No. cemeteries	1		3		1		5
South-West Peninsula							
No. sites with burials	2	1		1	5		9
No. of burials	22	11		1	31		65
Cremation burials				1	1		2
Inhumation burials	22	11			29		62
No. cemeteries	1	1			2		4

around the expanding roadside settlements at Baldock (Burleigh and Fitzpatrick-Matthews 2010) and Braughing (Anderson *et al.* 2013) in Hertfordshire, and Great Dunmow (ECC 2003) in Essex, and also in many farmsteads such as the 36 cremation burials from Stansted DFS/SCS, Essex (Havis and Brooks 2004). While in most other regions the increase in burials of the early Roman period is followed by a much greater rise during the late Roman period, especially in the Central Belt, this does not appear to have been the case in the East. Whether this was because of a fall in population – the overall settlement pattern of the region does show a steady decline after the second century A.D. (Smith 2016c, 214) – or a change (reversion?) to less visible funerary rites remains uncertain.

The situation further north and west is complicated by the relative lack of burial evidence throughout the Roman period, and shows little consistency (TABLE 6.2). In the North and Central West regions most of the evidence is from military *vici* and roadside settlements, with the numbers of burials here peaking during the middle Roman period, largely because of the excavation of extensive cemeteries near to the *vici* at Lanchester, County Durham (Turner 1990), and Brougham, Cumbria (Cool 2004), together with that sited along the line of Ryknield Street, 0.5 km south of the walled town at Wall in Staffordshire (*Letocetum*) (McKinley 2008). In Upland Wales and the Marches, the peak in early Roman burials is almost entirely a reflection of the presence of military *vici*, while similar numbers of burials assigned to the late Roman phase mostly derive from rural, non-settlement sites, including at least 22 east–west graves arranged in rows at Plas Gogerddan, Ceredigion (Murphy 1993). The only dating evidence from this cemetery was a single radiocarbon date of cal. A.D. 265–640 from a coffin stain, suggesting that the burials could be partially or entirely post-Roman in date, though late Iron Age crouched inhumations were also found, and it was suggested that the site had been the focus for ritual activity since the later Bronze Age (cf. Pollock 2006, 97–9).

Only nine sites with 'complete' burial records were recorded in the South-West region, and even these include a number of cemeteries, such as that at Topsham School, Devon (Sage and Allan 2004), where the bodies were either completely unpreserved or only traced as soil stains. Many of the South-West burial sites were dated mid- to late Roman on fairly minimal evidence, though one preserved inhumation burial of an adult female from Hookhills, Paignton in Devon, had a radiocarbon date of 230–390 cal. A.D. (Chandler 2008). There are also considerable numbers of inhumation burials, mainly flexed, from the South-West, most placed in stone-lined graves or cists (Harding 2015, 78–83) (see below, p. 254). This burial tradition would appear to be of late Iron Age or late Iron Age/early Roman date, though most of the excavated examples from within this project are from sites with incomplete records. There are also further antiquarian investigations of 'cist' cemeteries that have not been included on the basis of the minimal associated information and uncertain dating. One of the largest known cemeteries comprised the approximately 130 burials from Harlyn Bay on the north coast of Cornwall, which, though excavated in the early twentieth century, has limited published information available on most graves (Whimster 1977). Another large cemetery of similar date is known from Mount Batten, Plymouth, but this site has even less information. With the exception of the poorly understood extra-mural burials around Exeter, current evidence suggests that such large cemeteries were not a significant feature of the South-West after the end of the first century A.D., at least until the early medieval period (Petts 2002; Turner 2003, 19–20).

The broad province-wide and regional chronological analyses just presented disguise even greater variation when viewed at a landscape level. The large quantity of burial data from the South, Central Belt and East regions, in particular, allows for these more intricate variations to be highlighted, as shown in FIG. 6.5. Here, the chronological data from nine landscape zones, each with at least 500 burials, are compared, with many revealing strikingly different patterns. From some, such as the London Basin, there is only a slight and gradual rise in the number of burials over time, whereas in others, such as the East Anglian Chalk and East Anglian Plain, there are spikes in numbers during the early Roman period that are either maintained or decline into the late Roman phase. The North Kent Plain has a definite peak in the mid-Roman phase, though this is primarily as a result of the large number of burials from Pepper Hill, Springhead (Biddulph 2006) and Ospringe (Whiting *et al.* 1931) along the line of Watling Street. There is a notable decline in burial numbers in this area during the later Roman period, with the only major cemetery of this date being that at Dartford, further west along Watling Street towards London (Herbert 2011; Trevarthen 2015). This corresponds with an overall significant decline in settlement numbers in this area after the second century A.D. (Allen 2016a, 82).

Four out of the nine landscape zones in FIG. 6.5 have evidence for major increases in burial numbers during the later Roman period. These all lie in the Central Belt or western part of the South region.

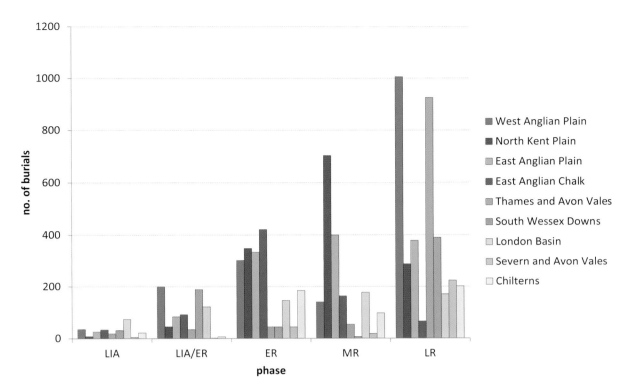

FIG. 6.5. Numbers of recorded rural burials over time across selected landscape zones with at least 500 burials (for details of landscape zones see Smith *et al.* 2016)

This does not correlate with any rise in settlement numbers, as in all of these landscapes except the South Wessex Downs there is a decline in number during the late Roman period, from a second-century peak, albeit not as pronounced as in areas further east (Smith and Fulford 2016, 405). The West Anglian Plain (including the Ouse and Nene Valleys) and Thames and Avon Vales, in particular, have major spikes in burial numbers despite the slight decline in settlement, the 925 burials from the latter representing a *c.* 1750 per cent increase on numbers from the early and mid-Roman periods, when there were 44 and 54 burials respectively. In part this is due to the development of substantial cemeteries, either around nucleated settlements such as the 164 burials from Queenford Mill, Dorchester-on-Thames (Chambers 1987), or from rural sites such as Cassington, Oxfordshire (110+ burials; Booth 2001, 16), and Horcott Quarry, Gloucestershire (58 burials; Hayden *et al.* 2017). There was also a notable increase in sites with smaller cemeteries, such as the 11 inhumations on the periphery of the farmstead at Arkell's Land/ Coln Gravel, Gloucestershire (Stansbie *et al.* 2008), though the number of sites with isolated and scattered burials increased only slightly. This all suggests a shift towards a more communal approach to burial in parts of these central and western areas during the later Roman period. There remain, however, a number of landscape zones in the Central Belt and the west of the

South region (e.g. Midlands Clay Pastures and Dean Plateau and Wye Valley) that continue to have very little evidence for formal burial, in cemeteries or otherwise. This is in part because of differences in bone preservation and the extent of archaeological intervention, although it would also seem to highlight the intricately patterned cultural diversity of the province, as seen through differing attitudes to the disposal of the dead.

The overall distribution and density of excavated burials over time across England and Wales is shown in FIGS 6.6 and 6.7. The late Iron Age and early Roman patterns are broadly consistent, with major concentrations of interments in parts of the south-east and the central southern coast of England, and a more diffuse spread of sites with minimal burial numbers outside these areas (FIG. 6.6). As noted above, most of the early Roman burial evidence from Wales and northern England is associated with military sites, though the occasional burial from a 'native' site is recorded, such as at Haltwhistle in Northumberland, where the partial remains of an adult cremation burial was found in association with samian sherds in a shallow pit at the centre of one of the roundhouses in a late Iron Age to early Roman farmstead (Fraser and Speed 1997). Although there are many developments at a local and sub-regional level, the broader provincial picture does not really change until the late Roman period, when most evidence for burial comes from the Central Belt

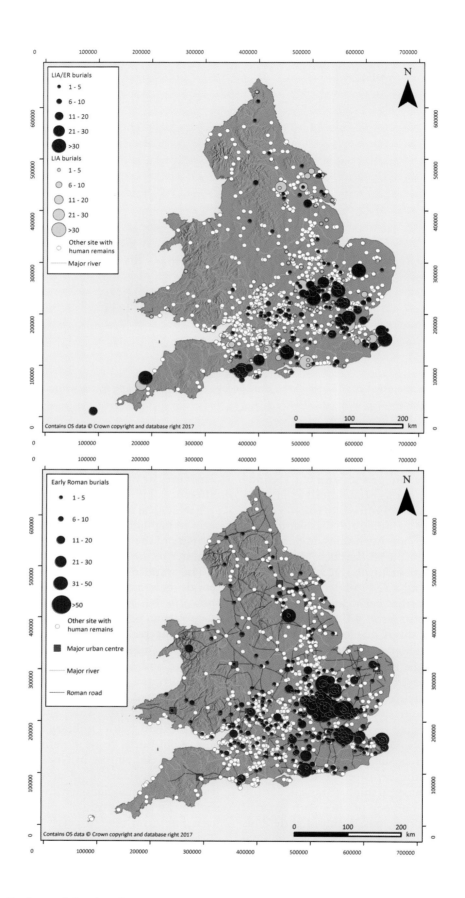

FIG. 6.6. Distribution and density of rural burials in LIA & LIA/ER and ER phase

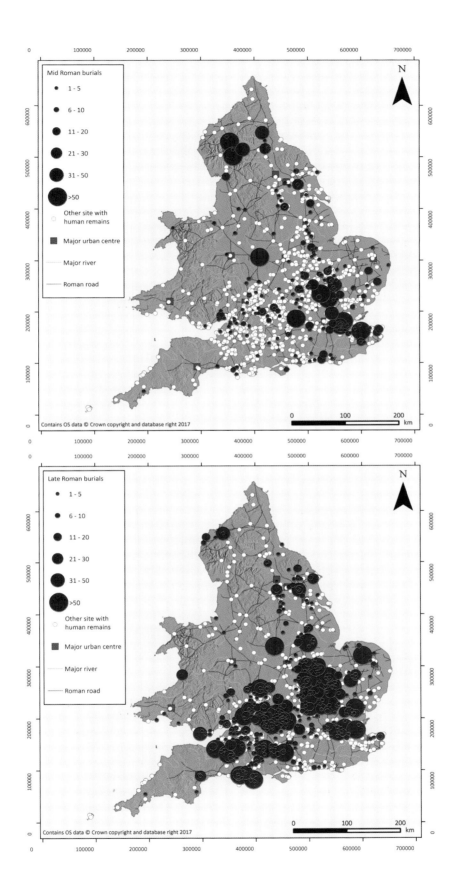

FIG. 6.7. Distribution and density of rural burials in MR and LR phase

region, with continuations up into the North-East and down into parts of Hampshire, Wiltshire and Dorset (FIG. 6.7). This generally follows the same pattern as the relative density of excavated Romano-British settlement in use during the late Roman period, as shown in Volume 1 (Smith and Fulford 2016, 407, fig. 12.19). Although, as stated above, absolute settlement numbers may not have increased in most areas, the late Roman shift in the focus of settlement – and to a certain extent agricultural production (Allen and Lodwick 2017) – to this central zone seems to correspond with major developments in the treatment of the dead.

CREMATION AND INHUMATION BURIAL

Despite considerable local and individual variation, there were two main archaeologically traceable burial rites in late Iron Age and Roman Britain: inhumation, where the deceased was buried, and cremation, where the deceased was burnt on a funeral pyre and at least some of the cremated bone placed in a grave, even if this was on occasion just a 'token' amount (see Andrews and Bello 2006 for a more detailed account of different burial types, and McKinley 2000, 42–3, for discussion on selective retrieval of cremated bone). The act of cremation was, by its very nature, likely to have been more of a visible public spectacle than inhumation burial (Cool 2011, 298), and may have involved considerably more cost and effort (McKinley 2006). This may have helped to restrict the cremation rite to selected individuals within certain communities, although, as discussed below, such selectivity may have been a factor in all burial rites within much of the countryside of late Iron Age and Roman Britain.

Of the excavated burials recorded as part of this project, the inhumation rite (n=10,351) accounts for over twice that of cremation (n=4925). For the most part these burials occur singly within graves, yet in 75 sites there is evidence for multiple individuals within a single grave. These include cremated remains mixed together within a single urn, cremated remains in two separate locations in the grave, inhumed bodies found together in a variety of positions, and very occasionally cremated and inhumed remains interred together (e.g. an urned adult cremation accompanied by a neonate skeleton in a grave at Keston in Kent; Philp et al. 1999). For the most part, such multiple burials comprise an adult and infant or younger child, but multiple adult burials are certainly known, including the highly unusual three adult males from a single grave at Horcott Quarry, Gloucestershire, these having isotope signatures that suggested their origins were different from the rest of the cemetery population (Hayden et al. 2017).

As shown in FIG. 6.8, inhumation and cremation burials are found across all parts of England and Wales, though with clear concentrations in certain areas, notably cremation burial in parts of south-east England, which is a long-observed phenomenon (e.g. Philpott 1991, 217). FIGURE 6.9 highlights this geographical diversity through the proportion of inhumation versus cremation burial in all landscapes with over 100 excavated burials. In some landscapes of the South region, such as the Wealden Greensand in Kent and the South Coast Plain and Hampshire Lowlands, cremation burial accounts for over 85 per cent of all excavated interments, which may be partly for reasons of poor preservation of skeletal remains in certain areas, whereas elsewhere in the region the picture is more mixed. The North Downs, for example, which lie to the north of the Wealden Greensand, has 54 per cent cremation burial, while immediately above this in the North Kent Plain this figure is just 36 per cent. The diversity of burial rites in this landscape is well demonstrated by the major cemetery at Pepper Hill to the south of Springhead, where cremation burial succeeded inhumation as the dominant rite by the later first century A.D., before reverting to an almost complete dominance of inhumation by the start of the third century A.D. (Biddulph 2006; see below, p. 219).

Elsewhere, in the eastern parts of the Central Belt region (West Anglian Plain (Nene and Ouse Valleys), Bedfordshire Greensand Ridge, Chilterns), cremation burials account for between 30 and 40 per cent, while further east in the landscapes of the East Anglian Plain and East Anglian Chalk, this figure lies between 55 and 70 per cent. The only two landscape zones outside of south-east England to have high proportions of cremation burial are the Eden Valley and Solway Basin in Cumbria (96 and 65 per cent), though these are based on a relatively restricted number of sites, including the cemetery associated with the military vicus at Brougham (Cool 2004), and burials around the town at Carlisle (e.g. Giecco et al. 2001). The pattern here is also partly explained by poor survival of non-cremated bone.

Further south, in western parts of Britain, the only landscape to have more than 20 per cent cremation burials is Bristol, Avon Valleys and Ridges in the Central Belt; although the total number of excavated burials from this area is not large (n=103), the cremated remains come from a range of farmsteads, rural cemeteries and roadside settlements. In all other landscapes, cremation burials form a very small percentage of the overall excavated interments, being particularly rare in the South-West region. The recently discovered cremated remains of an elderly female found

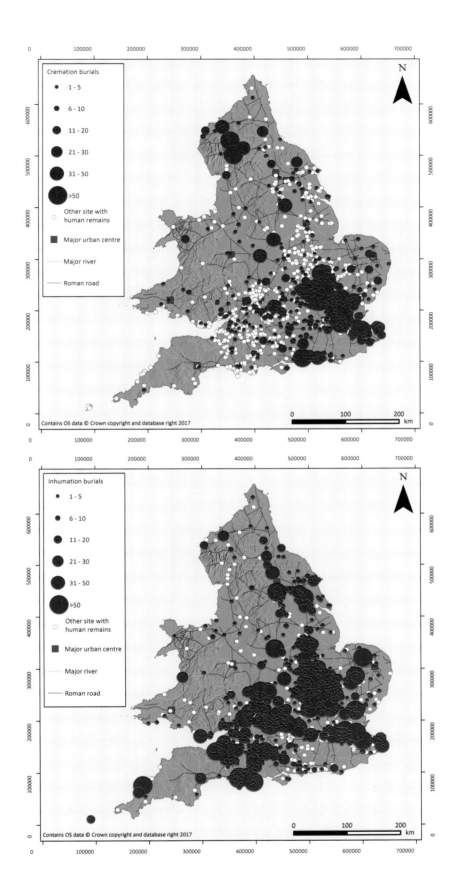

FIG. 6.8. Distribution and density of all rural cremation burials and inhumation burials

within two gabbroic pottery vessels of later second century A.D. date at Penlee House, Tregony in Cornwall, represents the first modern excavation of a Roman-period cremation burial from the county (Taylor 2012). There are slight indications that cremation burial had a longer tradition in the wider region, with, for example, cremated human bone and charcoal radiocarbon dated 480–260 cal. B.C. coming from a pit cutting an enclosure ditch at Aller Cross, Kingskerswell, in Devon (Hughes 2015). However, the vast majority of the evidence, such as it is, indicates that inhumation burial was very much the dominant type of funerary interment rite in the South-West, and remained so over time.

Throughout much of the province, there is evidence for major changes in burial customs over the course of the Roman period, and for

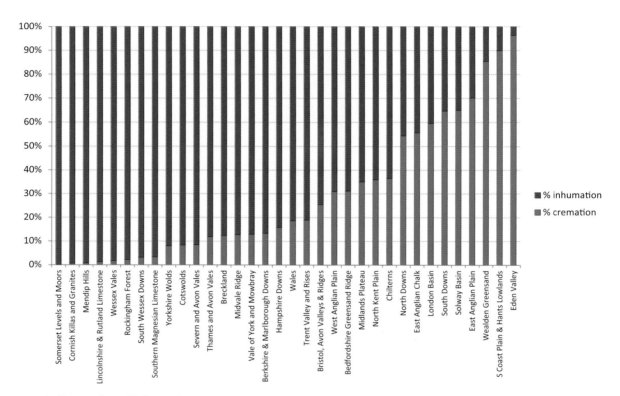

FIG. 6.9. Proportion of inhumation versus cremation burial in all landscape zones with at least 100 excavated burials (note: for purposes of this graph Wales is treated as one zone)

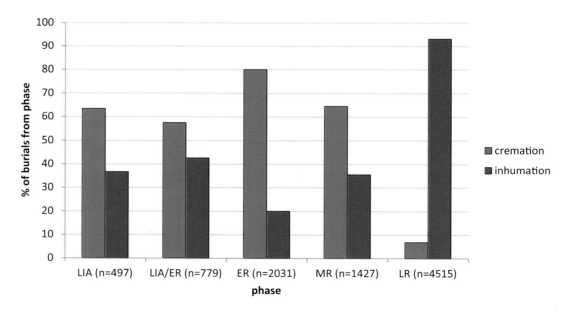

FIG. 6.10. Proportion of cremation and inhumation burials over time (with neonate burials excluded)

south-eastern Britain at least, the general chronological pattern advanced is that inhumation burial superseded cremation burial by the later Roman period (Philpott 1991, 217–27). Although this pattern still holds true in a broad sense, recent analysis has suggested that the sequence is a great deal more complex and variable (Pearce 2013, 145; Booth 2017), and it is not always the case of communities simply switching between these two burial rites. Using as a case study the large Romano-British cemetery at Pepper Hill in Kent, noted above, Biddulph (2012) explained the variable sequence of different burial rituals in terms of Darwinian evolution, with the traditions (types of burial and choice of grave good) at this site probably deriving from northern Gaul, and then diverging to evolve along a different trajectory that proved better adapted to fit their new and changing cultural environments. For example, between the early and middle Roman periods there was an increase in grave goods relative to pyre goods (i.e. objects burnt on the pyre before being placed in the grave), which was suggested as

individuals adapting their funerary practices, those having unburnt items perhaps being better prepared for the afterlife. The decreasing relevance of burnt objects may ultimately have been a factor in the general cessation of the cremation ritual and increase of inhumation at the site (*ibid.*, 84).

FIGURE 6.10 shows the proportion of cremation to inhumation burial within the different phase groups discussed above. Neonatal burials have been excluded, as the great majority of recorded examples are inhumations in all periods. Overall, it is clear that, prior to the late Roman period, there was a mixture of inhumation and cremation rites, though with the latter being numerically superior and particularly prevalent in those burials assigned to an early Roman (ER) phase. In some part this is owing to the large numbers of early Roman cremation burials in the East region, especially at nucleated settlements such as Baldock in Hertfordshire (Westell 1931; Burleigh and Fitzpatrick-Matthews 2010) and Great Dunmow in Essex (ECC 2003) (FIG. 6.11). Baldock is remarkable for its collection of *c.* 2000 burials in

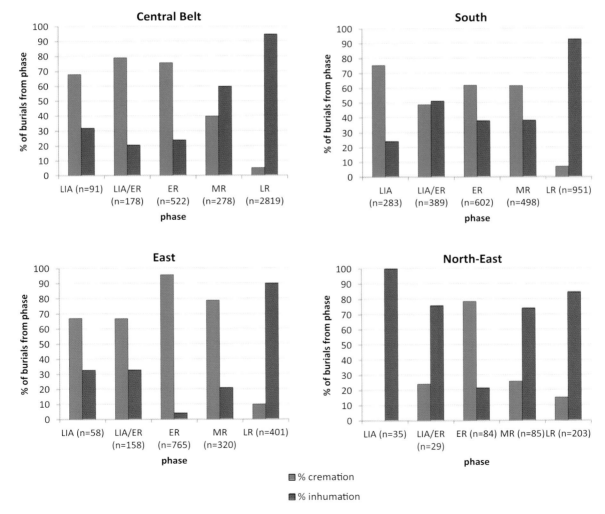

FIG. 6.11. Proportion of cremation and inhumation burials over time within selected regions (with neonate burials excluded)

22 cemeteries, spanning *c.* 100 B.C. to A.D. 550 (Burleigh and Fitzpatrick-Matthews 2010, 31), of which 622 have been included in this project (521 cremation; 101 inhumation), 442 dating from the first century B.C. to the second century A.D.

The East region continued to be dominated by the cremation rite until the later Roman period, when the much smaller number of burials are overwhelmingly inhumations, as is the case across the whole province. In the adjacent Central Belt the relative dominance of inhumation appears to arrive earlier, in the mid-Roman phase, although the overall number of burials from this period is very small compared with the late Roman phase. Burial data from the South are more mixed, as this region encompasses areas with very divergent funerary traditions, particularly in the late Iron Age and early Roman periods, with large numbers of cremation burials to the east and a dominance of 'Durotrigan' inhumation burials further to the west around Dorset and Hampshire (see FIG. 6.12).

The North-East region has many fewer phased excavated burials, but these are dominated by inhumations in all periods except early Roman (ER), when cremations account for almost 80 per cent of the 84 burials, though many of these came from the military *vicus* at Doncaster (Davies 2013). Even with Doncaster omitted, the admittedly very small pool of early Roman burials from the North-East mostly comprises cremations, including two from a ladder-style settlement at Easington, East Riding of Yorkshire; one of the cremations and a single inhumation burial from the same site were radiocarbon dated to cal. A.D. 40–230 (Richardson 2011).

As with the North-East, the chronological patterns in Upland Wales and the Marches and the North regions are heavily influenced by the prevalence of cremation burial on military *vici*, particularly in the early and mid-Roman phases (TABLE 6.2). In the later Roman period, the picture is a little more mixed. In the North, burials of both rites have been excavated in the military *vicus* at Maryport and the town at Carlisle, while the only evidence outside of a military/urban context comes from a small cemetery on the fringes of a farmstead at Skye Road, Wigton, also in Cumbria, where at least five small cremation pits and one possible inhumation burial were revealed; three of the cremations were interred within fourth-century ceramic jars (Giecco 2000). In Upland Wales all of the later Roman evidence comes from farmsteads or rural cemeteries and all comprise inhumation burials. In both regions (and the South-West), the numbers of inhumation burials are almost certainly under-represented given the very poor survival of skeletal material in these parts.

One factor to stress in all of the regional patterns just outlined is that there is not always a simple transitional sequence from cremation burial to inhumation burial as the dominant funerary rite. In particular, it is often the case that burial of one type or another is preceded and/or succeeded by a paucity of evidence for any formal interment. For example, in the Thames and Avon Vales (in the Central Belt region), the substantial number of late Roman inhumation burials followed on from a tradition of rare, sporadic burial, while in the South Coast Plain and Hampshire Lowlands (both in the South region) the reasonable number of late Iron Age and early Roman (mostly cremation) burials were succeeded by a relative absence of evidence in the mid- to late Roman period, with a few exceptions such as the five later second to early third century A.D. cremation graves from Offington Lane, Worthing (Thorne 2009). The shifting patterns of cremation and inhumation burial are made clear through the maps in FIGS 6.12 to 6.15, which show the distribution and density of the two rites across England and Wales over time.

The data for the late Iron Age (LIA) and late Iron Age to early Roman (LIA–ER) phases have been presented together in FIG. 6.12, and show a fairly tight concentration of cremation burial in the south-east of England, from Kent, up through Essex, Hertfordshire, Bedfordshire and into parts of Cambridgeshire and Buckinghamshire, with a more diffuse distribution around this core into Suffolk, Northamptonshire, Oxfordshire, Gloucestershire, Berkshire, Hampshire and Sussex (East and West). Cremation burial, alongside a distinctive range of, usually, wheel-turned pottery, was an integral part of what has been termed the 'Aylesford-Swarling Culture' of south-east Britain, named after two late Iron Age Kentish cemeteries (Cunliffe 2005, 132–41). Although there is little in the wider settlement pattern that directly correlates with this Aylesford-Swarling zone, aside from perhaps a greater tendency for settlement nucleation (Smith and Fulford 2016, 402), the distinctive pottery and focus on cremation burial does suggest a certain level of cultural affinity between communities in these areas (see discussion, Ch. 8). However, from a burials perspective, it must be reiterated that there was still variation at both a local and site-based level, with, for example, the small group of richly furnished late Iron Age 'Welwyn'-type cremation burials being largely restricted to parts of Hertfordshire (Cunliffe 2005, 135–41).

The many burials in and around Baldock in Hertfordshire have already been highlighted, although those specifically assigned to a LIA or LIA–ER phase display a greater mix of inhumations

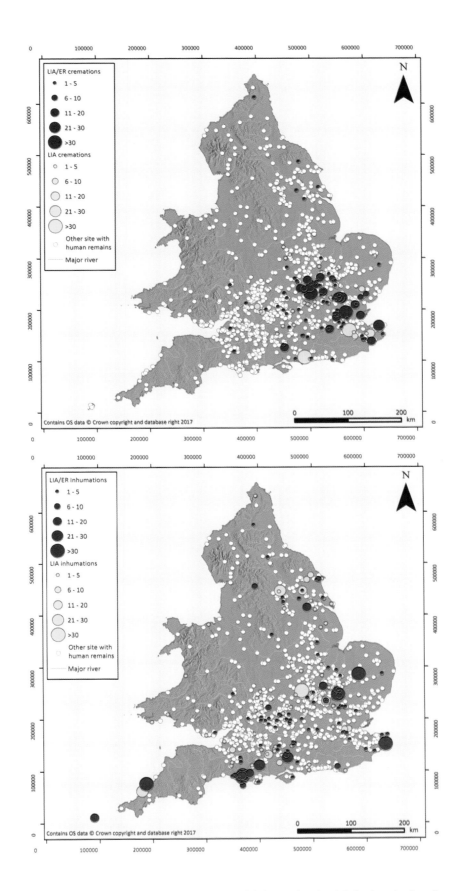

FIG. 6.12. Distribution and density of cremation burial and inhumation burial during the late Iron Age (LIA) and late Iron Age to early Roman (LIA–ER) phases

and cremations than those belonging to a more definite post-conquest (ER) phase, which were almost exclusively cremation, at least in the sample collated for this study. This is a similar sequence to that noted above at Pepper Hill, Springhead, in Kent, and points to the possible effects of conquest on the variable burial traditions of these communities, with greater homogenisation of the cremation ritual. The largest cemetery of late Iron Age to early Roman date, however, at King Harry Lane, St Albans, in Hertfordshire, was completely dominated by cremation burials (455 out of 472 burials) from its start at the beginning of the first century A.D. until it ceased in *c.* A.D. 60 (Stead and Rigby 1989). The site was part of the late Iron Age *oppidum* that developed into the major town of Verulamium, and as such the burial data have not been included in this study.

Another extensive and exclusive late Iron Age cremation cemetery was revealed at Westhampnett on the coastal plain of West Sussex, which included 161 burials, pyre sites and four enclosures, suggested as shrines (Fitzpatrick 1997) (see FIG. 6.34 below). It remains one of the earliest well-dated groups of cremation burials in south-east Britain, starting in *c.* 100 B.C., and ceasing *c.* 40 B.C., with cremation burial resuming in the early Roman period on a more modest scale (*ibid.*; Fitzpatrick *et al.* 2008, 279).

Large late Iron Age cemeteries like King Harry Lane and Westhampnett would seem to contain approximately representative populations (though with a skewed gender ratio at the former and very few infants at the latter; Pearce 1997), and were probably the 'normative' funerary rites for their local communities for most of the 60 years or so that they were in existence. It is perhaps unlikely that this was the case with most of the other, smaller, cemeteries and individual burials of late Iron Age date in the south-east, which instead would have been part of a more selective funerary process. Some communities may have exclusively favoured the cremation of certain individuals or groups, while others may have favoured inhumation (e.g. four mid- to late Iron Age burials from Lower Cambourne, Cambridgeshire; Wright *et al.* 2009), with 28 late Iron Age sites from the south-east having a mixture of both traditions. As Pearce (2013, 147) has pointed out, there does not appear to be a single specific social or cultural reason why different rites were selected, and they probably expressed different identities at a personal and group scale.

Whether the interment of cremated remains or the unburnt individual was favoured, there is little doubt that in most cases large parts of the community, even in the south-east of Britain, were not afforded any visible burial rite upon death at this time. Outside of the south-east such a scenario would appear even more likely, although inhumation traditions did develop in certain areas, such as the Severn Valley (Holbrook 2006, 121), and particularly along the Dorset coast. The Dorset 'Durotrigan' burials are characterised by crouched skeletons usually in shallow graves (though sometimes in cists), often with grave goods, typically Durotrigan (Poole Harbour) pottery, animal remains and occasionally distinctive metalwork (Harding 2015, 83–7). Recently excavated examples include a group of 19 crouched inhumations positioned on South Down Ridge looking towards the English Channel to the south of the Dorset Ridgeway, all interred after the abandonment of a late Iron Age industrial settlement and dating to the first century A.D. (Brown *et al.* 2014). Despite the broad uniformity of Durotrigan burials, there was still considerable variation (cf. Papworth 2008, 82–6), and – as with the south-east – they are more likely to be representative of different distinctive communities, albeit with a level of shared cultural values. Furthermore, even this area is likely to have seen continuation of traditional 'invisible' burial rites.

The only other part of the country with any significant evidence for a burial tradition at this time is the North-East – notably Yorkshire and Lincolnshire – where the evidence comprises mostly inhumations, though with a few cremation burials (e.g. Newbridge Quarry, Pickering; Richardson 2012). The middle Iron Age square-ditched barrow burials of the Yorkshire Wolds have already been referred to above, and this tradition appears to have declined rapidly after the end of the second century B.C. (Jay *et al.* 2012). There is then relatively little evidence for any interment in this landscape, although recently there have been a few excavated sites in the Wolds with burials of late Iron Age/early Roman date, including those within a substantial settlement at Low Caythorpe in the Gypsy Race Valley (Fraser and George 2013). Here, a small middle Iron Age square-barrow cemetery was succeeded by group of seven flexed inhumations in the late Iron Age/early Roman period, with two other burials of similar date in the vicinity (*ibid.*). The relative scarcity of sites with burial evidence at this time, together with the small numbers of interments (Low Caythorpe is among the larger groups), highlights the apparent transformation from the middle Iron Age funerary traditions, when some of the largest cemeteries (e.g. Wetwang Slack) contained over 400 graves, though most were much more modest (cf. Stead 1991; Halkon 2013, fig. 15). This suggests major cultural changes during the late Iron Age, resulting in most communities disposing of the dead in ways that left little trace, similar to most other parts of the country.

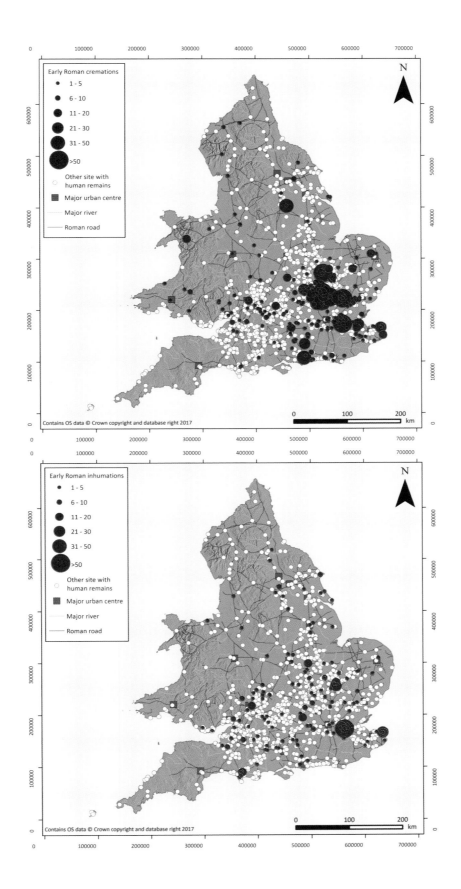

FIG. 6.13. Distribution and density of cremation burial and inhumation burial during the early Roman (ER) phase

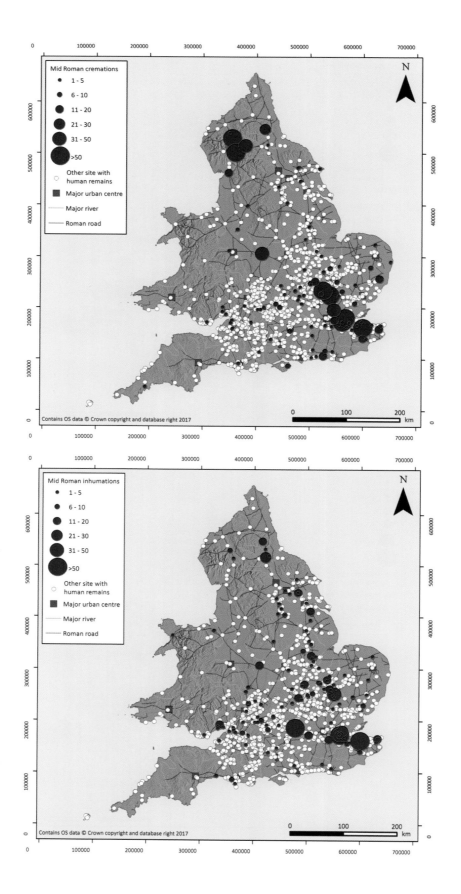

FIG. 6.14. Distribution and density of cremation burial and inhumation burial during the mid-Roman (MR) phase

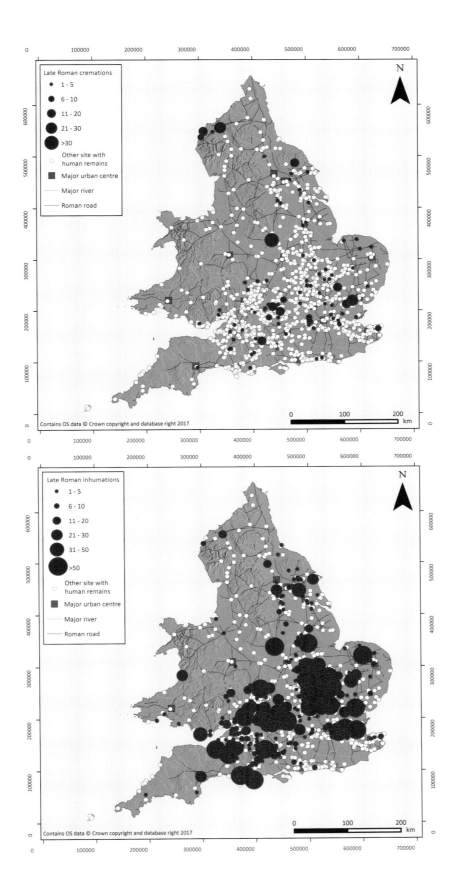

FIG. 6.15. Distribution and density of cremation burial and inhumation burial during the late Roman (LR) phase

The distributions of cremation and inhumation burials assigned to a definite post-conquest early Roman (ER) phase are shown in FIG. 6.13. The core zone of cremation burial in the south-east remains, but by this time the burial rite had spread much further north and west, mostly associated with newly developing nucleated and military sites, such as the *vicus* at Doncaster, discussed above. Very few early Roman cremation burials in these areas occur apart from such contexts, and these tend to be found either individually or in small numbers, such as the two second-century A.D. urned cremation burials found near to field ditches north of an enclosed farmstead at Church Farm, Caldicot in Monmouthshire (Corney 2009). Very occasionally, larger rural cremation cemeteries are encountered beyond the core south-eastern zone, such as the group of around thirteen burials from Gill Mill in the Upper Thames Valley, dating to the later first century A.D. (Booth and Simmonds 2018). For the most part, inhumation burials assigned to a post-conquest early Roman phase also tend to be found in very small numbers within sites spread throughout much of the province. Some of these were clearly important individuals within their communities, which is presumably why they were selected for interment, such as the extended inhumation of an adult male found within a wood-lined chamber surrounded by a ring ditch at Gill Mill, dating to the second century A.D., probably after the nearby cremation cemetery, just noted, had gone out of use (*ibid.*).

During the mid-Roman phase (FIG. 6.14) the pre-existing geographic patterns of cremation and inhumation burials start to break down, with less obvious differences between their distributions. By the late Roman period (FIG. 6.15), despite the overwhelming numerical superiority of inhumation burial, the extent of the coverage of both rites is almost identical, with the exception of a lack of cremation burial throughout most of Wales. Most of the later Roman cremation burials were either single, isolated examples, such as a fourth-century *bustum* burial (cremation that took place over the grave pit) located 500 m north of a farmstead in the Biddenham Loop, Bedford (Luke 2016), or else were minor components of larger inhumation cemeteries. At Cotswold Community on the Gloucestershire/Wiltshire border, for example, a single un-urned cremation burial, radiocarbon dated cal. A.D. 243–384, lay 7 m south of a late Roman inhumation cemetery of 25 burials (Powell *et al.* 2010). Very rarely cremation burial seems to have remained as the dominant rite within a particular community, such as at the farmstead at Newbridge Quarry, Pickering, in North Yorkshire, where, as highlighted above, there was a tradition

of cremation burial stretching back to the late Iron Age (Richardson 2012). Seventeen of these burials were radiocarbon dated *c.* A.D. 170–390, broadly contemporary with two inhumation burials from the same site, both buried in cist graves (*ibid.*).

Ultimately, the merging of the distributions of both burial rites suggests that, if the 'cremation zone' of south-east England had signified an area of particular cultural affinity, this had largely disappeared by the later Roman period. Instead, cremation burial remained as an element within the suite of 'alternative' funerary rites of this time, including certain 'deviant' rites like decapitation, discussed below; all of these may have been used as ways to express different forms of identity. Meanwhile, outside this major zone of late Roman burial, the treatment of the dead in the countryside remains far more enigmatic.

ALTERNATIVE INHUMATION BURIAL RITES

While the 'standard' inhumation burial, especially of the later Roman period, was positioned supine, or face up, and extended within the grave, there does exists a great deal of variation over time, across regions, and between and within individual sites. A particular fascination within studies of Romano-British burial is the existence of alternative or 'deviant' burial rites, with prone (face down) and decapitated burials being especially well noted (e.g. Harman *et al.* 1981; Philpott 1991, 84; Taylor 2008; Tucker 2015; Crerar 2016). Although the wider variations in body position have not been recorded in this study, such prone and decapitated burials have been quantified, primarily as these are readily highlighted within excavation reports, even where minimal osteological information is available. Crouched or flexed burials, while not generally considered as a 'deviant' inhumation rite, have also been recorded and are examined here, as these can be regarded as an 'alternative' to the typical burial position when looked at on a province-wide scale.

FIGURE 6.16 shows the distribution and density of the decapitated, prone and flexed burials from rural contexts and selected defended 'small towns' recorded as part of this project. A total of 250 individual decapitated burials from 101 sites have been included, spread across all site types, but being particularly notable at nucleated settlements, occurring at almost 20 per cent of all 165 recorded examples with burial evidence, as opposed to 7–8 per cent of the 520 farmsteads, 106 villas and 284 'rural' sites with such evidence. The great majority (86 per cent) of decapitated burials lay within defined cemeteries, as opposed to isolated and dispersed interments, which may be one reason why they seem more common within nucleated settlements, which have more evidence for dedicated burial grounds (see *Contexts of burials* below).

A decapitated burial is where the head has been removed from the body, and usually placed by the feet or lower limbs (FIG. 6.17). Within the Roman period, this is a rite largely unknown outside Britain (cf. Tucker 2015, 109–12), although some evidence for varying kinds of post-mortem manipulation of the corpse is now better documented in other provinces (Pearce pers. comm.; cf. Belcastro and Ortalli 2010). The reasons behind the decapitation ritual are widely speculated upon, including human sacrifice, execution, punishing the dead, aiding passage to an afterlife, association with a head cult, witchcraft,

and the fear of ghosts (Taylor 2008). Most of these explanations carry dark undertones of superstition and magic, though in a recent study of decapitation burials around the Cambridgeshire Fen edge, Crerar (2016, 399) has suggested that the rite should be 'viewed as an accepted and "normative" aspect of late Romano-British funerary customs rather than indicative of social exclusion resulting from fear or hostility towards the deceased'. Part of the interpretative problem results from uncertainty over whether the head was removed post-mortem, or was the actual cause of death. Most syntheses indicate that a post-mortem rite was more typical (see Ch. 7, p. 283), though Tucker (2015, 164) has recently argued through further osteological analysis that a much larger proportion of these burials may

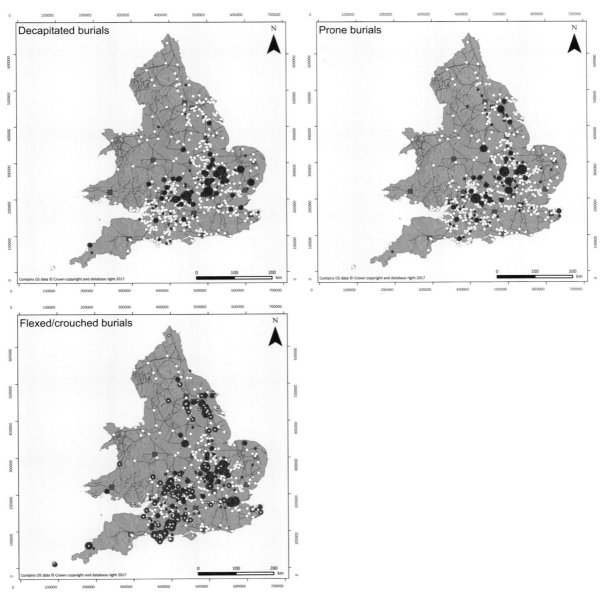

FIG. 6.16. Distribution of sites with decapitated, prone and flexed burials, against a backdrop of all sites with inhumation burial. (Note: in the distribution of flexed burials, sites where burials have been described as 'crouched' have been highlighted)

have been the result of beheading ante-mortem, for example by execution or as sacrifice.

What is more certain is that decapitation was largely restricted to parts of the Central Belt region and peripheral areas, a distribution that has been previously noted (Harman *et al.* 1981; Philpott 1991; Tucker 2015, 48, fig. 6), and which, to some extent, follows the general pattern of late Roman burial discussed above. Another certainty is that the rite occurred in both rural and urban areas, and although traditionally thought to be more prevalent in the countryside, recent analysis by Tucker (2015, 46) has indicated somewhat less of a rural bias. Furthermore, her study has indicated major differences between these two contexts, with rural decapitated burials showing negligible difference from other rural burials in terms of sex, age and grave furnishing, while urban decapitated burials were suggested as being more 'marginalised' individuals, for example in the relative lack of evidence for coffins and grave goods (*ibid.*, 88). Rohnbogner's analysis of palaeopathology in this volume (Ch. 7) has indicated, however, that rural decapitated individuals in the Central Belt generally displayed higher rates of skeletal trauma, enamel hypoplasia and caries than other contemporary burials, providing some indication that many of the people afforded such rites may have been of a lower or 'different' status.

In terms of chronology, decapitation was clearly a late Roman phenomenon, though earlier examples are found, with nine recorded from seven rural sites dating to the late Iron Age or early Roman period (FIG. 6.18). One of these, a late Iron Age example from Barnetby le Wold, North Lincolnshire, was particularly unusual – a decapitated mature woman buried face down in a shallow grave with her hands and ankles apparently tied, and the head placed some metres away in a separate pit (Allen and Rylatt 2002). The incidence of decapitated burial increases into the mid-Roman period, though still only represents 2.3 per cent of inhumation burials (on the *c.* 10 per cent of sites with burial), including a single example within a small informal mixed-rite cemetery in the farmstead at Langdale Hale, Cambridgeshire; the mature adult was placed prone in a wooden coffin with hands behind the back and head placed between the lower legs, and a small mid-second to mid-third century pottery jar placed near to where the head should have been (Evans 2013a, 79).

During the late Roman period, decapitated burials were found on *c.* 18 per cent of sites with burial evidence, though they still only formed 3.7 per cent of inhumation burials, so it clearly remained very much a minority rite. However, there is much individual variation, with cemeteries (of at least ten excavated burials) from seventeen sites having 10 per cent or more decapitated

FIG. 6.17. Photographs of decapitated, prone and semi-flexed burials from Horcott Quarry, Gloucestershire (Hayden *et al.* 2017) © Oxford Archaeology

burials, including fifteen (27 per cent of inhumations) from Knobbs Farm on the Cambridgeshire Fen edge (Evans 2013a, 468–71) and ten (45 per cent of inhumations) from the later fourth-century cemetery at Melford Meadows, Thetford, in Norfolk (Mudd 2002). Such variation can also be seen at some urban cemeteries, with, for example, 5 decapitations revealed among the 29 inhumation burials excavated at Little Keep, Dorchester, Dorset, this representing 17 per cent of the interments, compared with less than 1 per cent at the other cemeteries on the periphery of the *civitas* capital (Dinwiddy 2009, 42).

Alongside decapitation, the interment of individuals face down (prone; FIG. 6.17) is also often associated with negative connotations, this being strengthened further when the two rites are combined. At Cotswold Community, a complex farmstead on the Gloucestershire/Wiltshire border, an adult male lay within a ditch away from the main cemetery, prone and decapitated, with the skull between his legs and hands behind his back; isotope analysis suggested he may have come from a different background to the rest of the community (Powell *et al.* 2010, 163). The wider distribution of the 221 prone burials from 114 sites recorded in this project is very similar to that of decapitated burials, though with somewhat more examples from the North-East (FIG. 6.16).

They also occur in similar proportions across different site types, but with slightly less emphasis on nucleated settlements and with fewer (70 per cent) lying within cemeteries. In fact they are far more likely to be found as isolated interments than decapitated burials (twenty examples compared with six, two of which were also prone), and previous studies have suggested that individuals buried prone may have been socially marginalised to some degree (cf. Philpott 1991, 74–5).

In the current dataset, there are at least seventeen sites where excavators have suggested that the prone burials were treated in such a way as to suggest they occupied the fringes of society, including being isolated from the main burial area (as with Cotswold Community above), having notably fewer grave furnishings, and being treated 'irreverently' in being tipped into graves, pits or ditches. At Heybridge in Essex, for example, a prone adult female inhumation was found in a 'refuse' pit with the detached arm placed in another pit (Atkinson and Preston 2015), while all seven prone burials from the cemetery associated with a roadside settlement at Dunstable, Central Bedfordshire, were found in the enclosure ditch alongside animal burials, rather than in separate graves in the interior (Matthews 1981). Recent excavations of a rural inhumation cemetery at Horcott Quarry in Gloucestershire (Hayden *et al.*

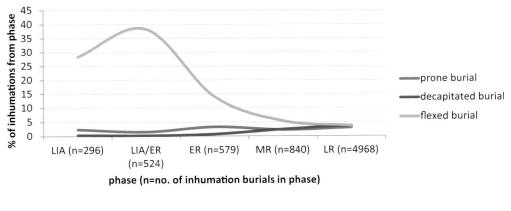

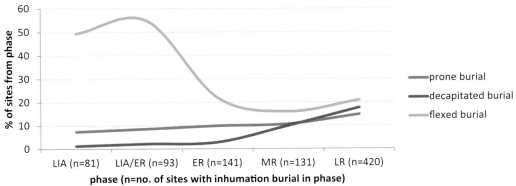

FIG. 6.18. Patterns of decapitated, prone and flexed burials over time

2017; see below, p. 251) revealed twelve prone burials in the main group (*c.* 20 per cent of total), located around the margins of the site, all with a lack of evidence for coffins or grave goods, and with isotope analysis suggesting a less protein-rich diet. Despite this evidence, it is clear that not all prone burials were of marginalised individuals, as most are otherwise no different from other burials. Indeed, some were relatively well furnished, such as at Maddington Farm in Wiltshire, where the only prone burial, of an older adult male, was one of two out of nine burials with evidence for a coffin, and was the only one to have grave goods that were not footwear, comprising the skeleton of a small dog placed under the torso and a coin of A.D. 161–175 placed in the mouth (McKinley and Heaton 1996). Some individuals may even have been buried prone in error, such as one of the six late/post-Roman inhumation burials excavated at Hitchin, Hertfordshire, which was found prone with a small bronze pin underneath, suggesting use of a shroud covering the body (Davies 2005). As with decapitated burials, there was probably a range of reasons and motivations for burying individuals prone, but unlike the former, the rite was not primarily a late Roman phenomenon, forming 2 to 3 per cent of inhumation burials from the late Iron Age to the late Roman period, though with a slight increase in incidence over time (FIG. 6.18).

The final 'alternative' form of inhumation burial to have been systematically recorded is that of flexed burials. Here, there is a problem with conflicting terminologies, explicitly discussed by Sprague (2005, 83–102), between terms such as crouched, contracted, flexed, semi-flexed and others, with the differences usually reflecting the degree of contraction of the body, which is typically, though not always, laid upon its side (FIG. 6.17). Because of the inconsistent use of such terminology within excavation reports, all individuals that have been assigned any of these terms have been grouped under the general label 'flexed', although it is appreciated that there may have been significant differences between those individuals which were tightly crouched, and perhaps bound, and those that may be described as 'semi-flexed'. Because of this, the distribution of these burials in FIG. 6.16 also highlights those sites where burials are described in the reports as 'crouched', although these have not been systematically verified for consistency.

There is a strong tradition of flexed burial in Britain throughout prehistory, so that this must be regarded as the 'normative' position for articulated remains at this time (Whimster 1981, 11; Bradley 2007, 264). The tradition certainly continued in parts of the country into the late Iron Age and

Roman periods, 722 flexed burials being recorded from 241 sites in this project, with notable concentrations in areas to the west and north (FIG. 6.16). Over 50 per cent of these dated to the late Iron Age or early Roman periods, when they accounted for almost 100 per cent of adult inhumation burial in places like Dorset and much of Yorkshire. In the south-east flexed inhumations were far scarcer, particularly during the early Roman period – at Pepper Hill cemetery in Kent for example, just two flexed burials were observed from over 100 early Roman inhumation burials, though the poor preservation of bone here may have masked further examples (Biddulph 2006).

From the second century A.D. onwards, the majority of all inhumations across the province were supine, though there were still 184 examples of flexed burials from 88 sites that date to the third or fourth centuries A.D. (FIG. 6.18). For the most part these late Roman flexed burials were concentrated in areas to the north and west and clearly represented continuing traditions, though even here they rarely comprise over 20 to 30 per cent of all inhumations on sites at this time. There are also perhaps a surprising number of later Roman flexed burials from eastern parts of the Central Belt region, particularly around Cambridgeshire and Bedfordshire, where the overall numbers exceed those of the late Iron Age to early Roman period. At Ruxox in Central Bedfordshire, for instance, there were two flexed burials within the late Roman cemetery, though all of the four second-century A.D. inhumation burials from the same area were supine (Dawson 2004, 312–13). This calls into question whether such flexed burials always represent the continuation of longstanding 'native' burial traditions or else were 're-introduced' rites, or perhaps even reflect the movement of population from areas where such burials were more typical, though this would require extensive isotopic analysis to confirm. In most cases, late Roman flexed burials remain fairly isolated and scattered within settlements and the countryside, or else were very minor components of larger burial grounds, though there were eight examples (12 per cent of burials) from the cemeteries at NIAB near Cambridge (Barker and Meckseper 2015; see below, p. 245) and thirteen examples (16 per cent of burials) from the late Roman cemetery at Kempston, Church End, Bedford (Dawson 2004, 314–34).

By the late Roman period, flexed inhumation burial, including examples of those described as 'crouched', appears to have become part of the wider range of funerary rites employed in the Central Belt region, which included prone and decapitated burial as well as cremation. Yet for the most part these are all still likely to represent selective rites within the wider selective act of formal interment, with both of these being influenced in part by their surrounding contexts, which will now be discussed.

THE CONTEXT OF BURIALS

The countryside of Roman Britain encompassed a mosaic of communities inhabiting a variety of different settlements. It has already been established in Volumes 1 (Smith *et al.* 2016) and 2 (Allen *et al.* 2017), and in this volume, that these farmsteads, villas, villages, roadside settlements and military *vici* often evidenced distinctive socio-economic strategies within their local and regional landscapes, as evidenced through variable types and quantities of material culture, architecture and environmental remains. This section will examine how far these strategies extended to the treatment of the dead by looking at the context of burials. However, before assessing the evidence from site contexts in more detail, some consideration is given to the organisation of burial, notably the differentiation between cemeteries and integrated burials.

CEMETERIES AND INTEGRATED BURIAL

Harding (2015, 269) has recently argued that the crucial distinction in Iron Age mortuary practice was between segregating the dead from the living by means of a separate cemetery, or integrating them into the community through the occasional burial in a pit or field ditch, or by the spread of disarticulated bone through settlement and landscape features, with the latter being the norm. It was further suggested that this situation remained until 'renewed contact with continental "urban" fashion in the late pre-Roman Iron Age brought about progressive and varying degrees of change to more formal cemeteries, notably in the south-east of England...' (*idem.*). While this may have been the case to a large degree, particularly in the developing nucleated centres, the more integrated mortuary practices of the Iron Age continued to be prevalent throughout much of the countryside of the Roman province, even into the later Roman period.

Of the 15,579 burials included in this project, 11,847 (76 per cent) were definitely or probably part of a cemetery. Cemeteries are here defined as groups of burials that were clearly separated from other functional spaces, though in certain cases only a few interments may have been excavated, with other probable graves being located in close vicinity. As discussed below, cemeteries were usually sited on the periphery of settlements or in open countryside, with over a third of examples being at least partially defined by an enclosure; in many other instances the full extent of the cemetery remains unclear and so the provision of an enclosure remains uncertain. The archaeological study of cemeteries provides opportunities to assess funerary customs both on an individual and wider organisational sense, including cemetery planning and aspects relating to the duration of memory for deceased individuals, i.e. the length of time before graves were intercut or disturbed (Duday 2009, 93). They may also provide information on wider cultural values, perhaps relating to sex or age (see Ch. 7) or to the religious beliefs of certain sections of the community (e.g. ostensibly Christian cemeteries at places like Poundbury in Dorset; Sparey-Green 1989).

Although a high proportion of burials were seemingly part of cemeteries, these segregated burial grounds were only a feature of 39 per cent (n=449) of all 1162 sites with evidence for formal interment. For the remaining sites, burials were usually found individually or in small, dispersed numbers, often within or aligned with settlement or outer field ditches, or else in pits, wells, and – particularly in the case of infants – within and around buildings (cf. Moore 2009). Such contexts for burial are not unique to Roman Britain, with, for example, increasing numbers of interments found isolated or in small groups in among field ditches and settlement boundaries in Roman Gaul (e.g. Ancel 2012; cf. Pearce 2017, 2–3). As Esmonde Cleary has argued (2000, 127), it unlikely that these burials were placed at random, although of course the rationale behind the choices of location remains obscure and were undoubtedly manifold. The adult burials in particular clearly represent selected individuals from within their communities, and may have been buried in specific loci in order to reinforce territorial boundaries in terms of land tenure and ownership, or for more cosmological reasons connected with the agricultural cycle (*ibid.*, 138; Chadwick 2010, 432; Pearce 2013, 108). Likewise, Moore (2009, 48) has suggested that the infants found beneath the floors of rooms, around the sides of buildings or even incorporated into the walls were the result of careful decisions based upon spiritual concerns, while Millett and Gowland (2015) have demonstrated the careful disposal of infant remains within the domestic sphere in a study of Roman sites in east Yorkshire.

The preference for either burying the deceased within cemeteries or integrating them within the settlement or landscape was not consistent over time and place. FIGURE 6.19 displays the percentages of burials lying within cemeteries in all the landscape zones with over 100 excavated interments and with at least 10 records. The proportion of cemetery burials ranges from 96 per cent in the Solway Basin in Cumbria, where most of the records are from the town at Carlisle or from military *vici*, to just 47 per cent in the Southern Magnesian Limestone of Yorkshire, where scattered burials are typically found in among farmsteads, villages and field systems. The figures from some of the landscape zones are somewhat skewed by large numbers of burials from one or two cemeteries, such as the late to post-Roman example at Cannington in the Somerset Levels and Moors (Rahtz *et al.* 2000), and the late Iron Age example from Westhampnett in the South Coast Plain and Hampshire Lowlands (Fitzpatrick 1997). In both of these landscapes, most if not all of the remaining records comprise small numbers of dispersed burials, though it is possible that the occupants of some of the contemporary settlements interred their dead within these large rural cemeteries (see below, p. 250).

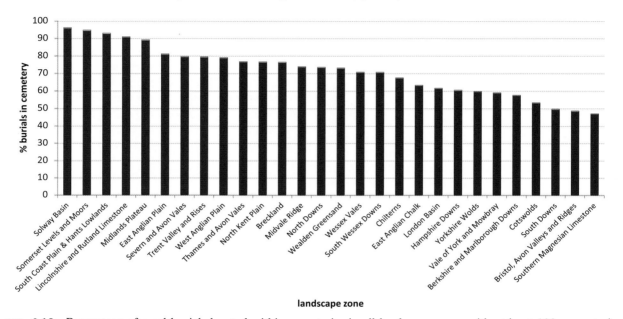

FIG. 6.19. Percentage of rural burials located within cemeteries in all landscape zones with at least 100 excavated burials and 10 records

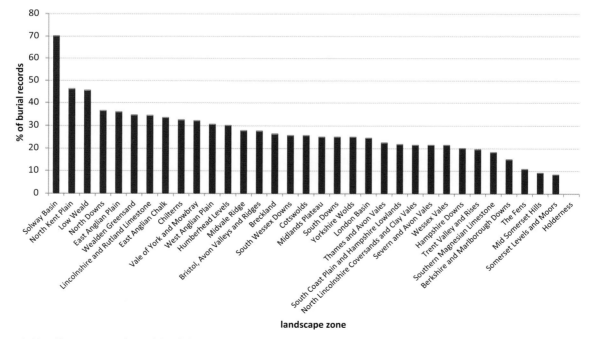

FIG. 6.20. Percentage of rural burial records with evidence for cemeteries in all landscape zones with at least 10 records

The relative prevalence of cemeteries within different landscapes is shown in FIG. 6.20. Aside from the Solway Basin just noted, those landscapes with higher percentages of sites with cemeteries lie in parts of south-east England, particularly in Kent. These not only include the major cemeteries associated with roadside settlements such as at Ospringe (Whiting *et al.* 1931) and Pepper Hill (Biddulph 2006), but also many smaller cemeteries. Some of these had no obvious associated settlement (e.g. Cottington Road; Andrews *et al.* 2009), while others were attached to farmsteads (e.g. East Kent Access (Zone 20); Andrews *et al.* 2015), villas (e.g. Keston; Philp *et al.* 1991; 1999) and ironworking sites (e.g. Jubilee Corner, Ulcombe; Aldridge 2005). In stark contrast, 25 of the 28 burial records from the Fens landscape of East Anglia comprised individuals or small numbers of dispersed burials, such as the crouched prone female inhumation burial from a Roman roadside ditch at King's Dyke West, Whittlesey, Cambridgeshire, which was found not far from the disarticulated remains of another adult (Gibson and Knight 2002). The rare cemeteries from this landscape include 21 cremation and inhumation burials from the periphery of a farmstead at Prickwillow Road, Ely, Cambridgeshire (Atkins and Mudd 2003). This site lay towards the edge of the Fens, where a number of further cemeteries

have been discovered, such as those from Knobbs Farm, Somersham, which spanned much of the Roman period (Evans 2013a, 464–73). Some of the communities within the Fens may have purposefully buried their dead, or at least selected groups, on the margins of the wetlands, while most presumably disposed of them in ways that have left little archaeological evidence.

There was not just variability in the extent of cemetery use across different landscapes, but also over time. Although, as noted above, not all burial records could be phased, the evidence from those that were indicates a marked increase in the use of cemeteries from the late Iron Age into the early Roman period, though thereafter the changes appear fairly minimal (FIG. 6.21a). In terms of the overall numbers of phased burials, the proportion lying within cemeteries rises from *c.* 60 per cent in the late Iron Age to 76–81 per cent during Roman phases (FIG. 6.21b). As ever, these chronological patterns can vary significantly within different parts of the country, as shown by three landscape zones with significant burial evidence located within the South, East and Central Belt regions (FIG. 6.22). The Thames and Avon Vales, on the western side of the Central Belt, have relatively little evidence for formal burial prior to the late Roman period, as discussed above, and for the most part these are fairly scattered examples.

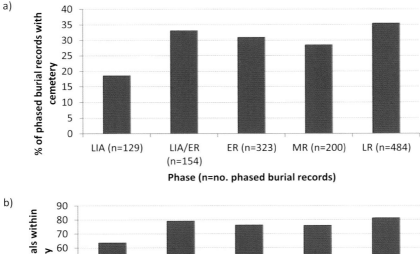

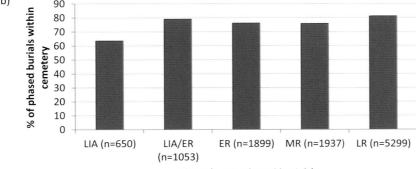

FIG. 6.21. Proportion of phased burial records associated with a cemetery (a) and proportion of phased burials within a cemetery (b)

They could, however, be marking locations of particular importance, as demonstrated by the two second to third century A.D. adult, coffined inhumation burials aligned upon the southern boundary of a farmstead at Cotswold Community south of Cirencester, exactly at the terminus of an earlier Iron Age pit alignment (Powell *et al.* 2010, 136). The only cemetery of any significant size dating to before the late Roman period is the recently excavated group of thirteen cremation burials from Gill Mill, Oxfordshire, which pre-dated the major development of the nucleated settlement in the second century A.D. (Booth and Simmonds 2018). The massive increase in burial numbers during the late Roman period in this landscape is primarily due to the establishment of many large and small cemeteries, though even at this time there were still plentiful examples of burials integrated within settlements. At Gill Mill, for example, there were over 40 burials assigned to the mid- to late Roman period that were found individually or in small clusters (2–6 burials) dispersed throughout the settlement rather than in any discrete cemetery areas (*ibid.*).

In both the North Kent Plain and East Anglian Plain (incorporating parts of Norfolk, Suffolk, Essex and Hertfordshire), cemeteries appear relatively well established by at least the late Iron Age/early Roman period (FIG. 6.22). In the former landscape, this continued through to the later Roman period, with almost the entire late Roman burial contingent deriving from seven cemeteries, including over 230 inhumation burials from East Hill, Dartford, probably associated with a roadside settlement (Herbert 2011; Trevarthen 2015), and 55 inhumation burials excavated along the marshy coastline at Rosecourt Farm, Isle of Grain (Philp 2010). This was a period when both settlement and burial numbers had undergone a significant decline in this landscape (see FIG. 6.5 above), though interment of the deceased within organised cemeteries was clearly still important for many communities. In the East Anglian Plain, the percentage of burials found within cemeteries decreases marginally during the late Roman period, due to both the decreased size of cemeteries around certain nucleated settlements (notably Braughing, Herts), and a slight increase in dispersed burials around particular farmsteads, such as the two inhumation graves aligned on ditch boundaries in the farmstead at Elsenham Quarry, Essex (Hammond and Preston 2010).

If the provision of cemeteries can generally be seen to have increased over time, this does not

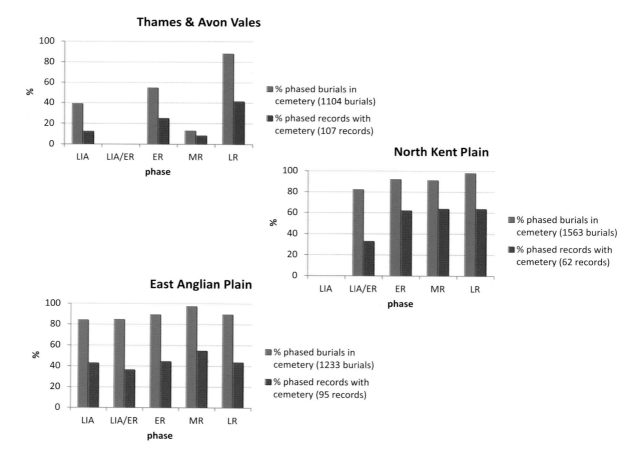

FIG. 6.22.　Cemetery use over time in the Thames and Avon Vales, North Kent Plain and East Anglian Plain

necessarily mean that such burial grounds became a constant feature at settlements. Even accounting for the often poor chronological resolution, in the majority of cases the duration of use of the cemetery does not match that of any associated settlement, often being utilised for a relatively brief period only. A farmstead at Water End East, Central Bedfordshire, for instance, was occupied from the late Iron Age to the fourth century A.D., yet the only associated cemetery, comprising a group of fifteen cremation burials and two infant burials, dated to the second century (Timby *et al.* 2007b, 123). Quite what happened to the dead before or after the period of the cemetery remains uncertain (see discussion of unburied dead below, p. 275).

To conclude, one of the major factors in determining the extent of cemetery use in any given landscape is the site context. Burial evidence from farmsteads and villas, for example, tends to be more dispersed within and around the settlement than at larger, nucleated settlements, where interment within cemeteries is far more common. Thus, landscapes with large numbers of excavated roadside settlements, such as those in parts of the East, Central Belt and South regions, tend to have high proportions of cemetery burials. There is still, however, significant variation in the quantity and nature of the burial evidence, both between and within different site types.

SITE CONTEXTS FOR BURIAL

FIGURE 6.23 and TABLE 6.3 show how the 15,579 excavated burials recorded in this project break down by site context, while FIG. 6.24 maps the distribution of the main site types with burials across England and Wales. There are clearly significant differences in the burial records from each of these contexts, influenced by a multitude of factors; the evidence will now be assessed in turn.

TABLE 6.3: SUMMARY OF BURIALS FROM DIFFERENT SITE TYPES
(*defended small towns, roadside settlements and villages)

Site type	No. sites with burials	No. of burials	Mean no. of burials per record	Cremation burials	Inhumation burials	No. cemeteries
Farmstead (all)	520	3237	5.22	1114	2126	141
Farmstead (complex)	123	1510	12.2	515	996	47
Farmstead (enclosed)	95	481	5.1	158	324	20
Rural	284	3358	11.11	940	2370	125
Nucleated*	165	6662	19.14	2187	4222	170
Villa	106	1326	10.77	164	1160	36
Military *vicus*	38	572	14.3	445	127	18
Religious	20	191	8.3	39	149	2
Industry	17	126	7.66	21	105	1
Hillfort/*oppidum*	12	107	8.23	15	92	2
Total	**1162**	**15579**		**4925**	**10351**	**481**

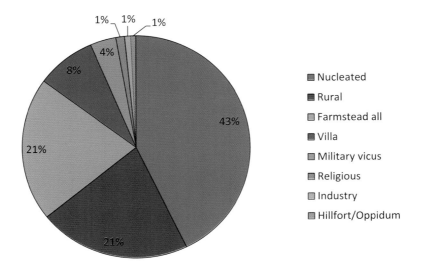

FIG. 6.23. Proportions of total number of burials (n=15,579) by site type

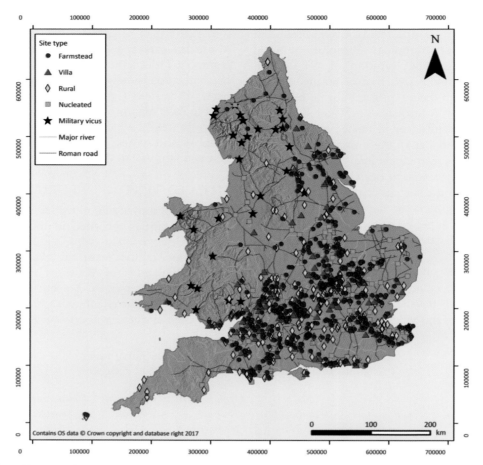

FIG. 6.24. Distribution of burials by site type

Nucleated settlements: defended towns, roadside settlements and villages

By far the greatest proportion (43 per cent) of excavated burials derive from 165 nucleated settlements within central, eastern and southern Britain, comprising 34 villages, 111 roadside settlements and 20 defended 'small towns', these accounting for 57, 60 and 83 per cent of the total numbers of their respective site types included in the project. As larger population centres, it is perhaps unsurprising that these would attract the most evidence for burial, which of course correlates with the large numbers of burials found in cemeteries around certain of the major towns of Roman Britain (Pearce 2015, 138).

Over 94 per cent of burials from these nucleated settlements derived from cemeteries, which inevitably lay on the peripheries of the occupied area, although occasionally some distance further away, such as the mixed-rite cemetery of at least 57 burials situated at a road junction on the line of Ryknield Street, 0.5 km to the south-east of the defended small town at Wall in Staffordshire (*Letocetum*; McKinley 2008). The town had another cemetery located in much closer proximity,

and it remains uncertain if the Ryknield Street burials were exclusively associated with this settlement, or encompassed a wider community; the almost complete lack of burial evidence from elsewhere in the region may suggest the former, with the cemetery representing in effect an 'alien' funerary rite, which was quite divergent from local traditions (cf. Booth 2017). Three other major cemeteries that also seem to have been located some distance from their presumed associated roadside settlements all lay along Watling Street in Kent, at Springhead/Pepper Hill, Dartford and Ospringe; the extensive cemetery at Pepper Hill lay *c.* 1 km south of the town/religious complex at Springhead, with a road leading towards it (Biddulph 2006; see Ch. 5, FIG. 5.36). Such distances may suggest the existence of funerary processions leading from the settlement, and has some resonance with the temple complexes sited outside towns such as London, Verulamium, Caistor and Great Chesterford noted in Chapter 5, which may also have involved processional routes (cf. Esmonde Cleary 2005).

Many nucleated settlements had a number of cemeteries around their periphery, often aligned upon roads, in a similar situation to larger urban

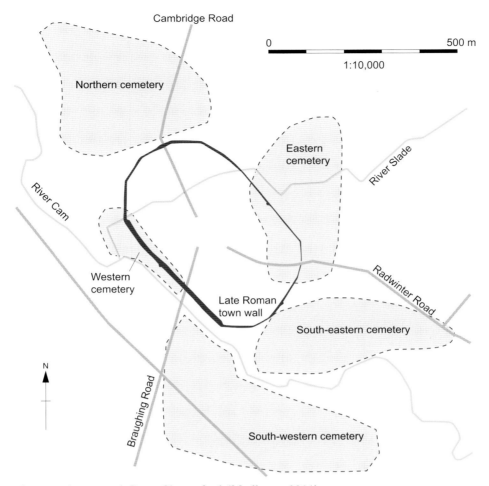

FIG. 6.25. Plan of cemeteries around Great Chesterford (Medlycott 2011)

centres, with at least some having funerary monuments probably used by the civic elite in a form of competitive self-representation (Pearce 2014b), such as the mausolea at Water Newton, Cambs, Great Bulmore in Newport, and Derby racecourse (also note the elaborate sculpture from the roadside settlement at Stanwick, which may have derived from a funerary monument; Crosby and Muldowney 2011). The considerable number of burials in various cemeteries around Baldock in Hertfordshire has already been noted, and the nearby roadside settlement at Braughing also has evidence for many different cemetery groups lying on the periphery of the occupied area, including three areas of cremation burial (245 in total) and two of inhumation burial (64 in total) recently excavated along the Roman roadside at Buntingford Road (Anderson *et al.* 2013). At Great Chesterford in Essex, cemeteries more or less encircled the town, covering approximately 39 ha and overlapping with areas of extra-mural settlement (FIG. 6.25; Medlycott 2011, 94–103). In all of these cases and certain others, it is possible to speculate that a sizeable proportion of the settlement's population may have been interred in the outlying cemeteries,

some people perhaps belonging to funerary guilds, as suggested by a graffito from a ceramic beaker within a grave in a roadside settlement cemetery at Dunstable, Central Bedfordshire, recording a gift possibly made on behalf of a guild to a deceased member (*RIB* II.8.2503, 114; Hassall 1981, 46). In other places such speculation about the relationship between cemeteries and settlement population is more difficult to sustain, largely because relatively small-scale excavation has revealed only limited numbers of burials. At Elms Farm, Heybridge in Essex, however, the overall number of burials remains low despite large-scale excavations (Atkinson and Preston 2015, 125–6). Twenty cremation burials were found scattered around the fields and outer enclosures of the nucleated settlement during the early Roman period, and, though a small group of 7–8 cremation graves dating to the mid-Roman period hints at more formal cemetery arrangements, there is nothing to indicate that such interment was a 'typical' funerary rite of the resident population. There may, of course, have been a cemetery located some distance away from the settlement, as demonstrated for other examples above.

One of the major distinctions within cemeteries attached to defended small towns and roadside settlements in particular is between the large, organised cemeteries that may have had some civic or communal management, and the much smaller graveyard groups, often termed 'family plots' or 'backland' burials (Esmonde Cleary 2000, 129). The former are more akin to the major cemeteries attached to many of the larger Romano-British towns, mostly dating to the later Roman period, though they appear to be relatively rare except for certain settlements in south-east England. To a certain extent this may be following a wider geographic trend, as late Roman managed cemeteries are also apparently absent from the most westerly major towns – Exeter, Caerwent and Carmarthen.

At some of both the larger and smaller towns in the south-east of the province, such as Great Chesterford in Essex or Canterbury in Kent, there was clearly a mix of large, 'managed' cemeteries with burials laid out in neat rows, and smaller, more irregular, burial groups (Medlycott 2011, 99; Weekes 2011, 29–30; cf. Pearce 2015, 143). More typically, these irregular 'family plots' are the only evidence we have for grouped burial, particularly at roadside settlements, such as at Higham Ferrers in Northamptonshire (FIG. 6.26). Here, there were a number of burial groups located in or adjacent to inner field boundary ditches on the periphery of the settlement, with some spatial patterns noted based on age and sex (Lawrence and Smith 2009). These small 'backland' groups blur the boundary between the larger, separate, formal cemeteries and the more integrated burials within and around the settlement; they would seem to have been deliberately placed in specific burial zones, but at the same time they were clearly referencing the 'living' areas of the settlement.

For the most part, these small 'family' burial plots still tend to lie at the edges of nucleated settlements, although there are plentiful examples of individual burials being located both inside and

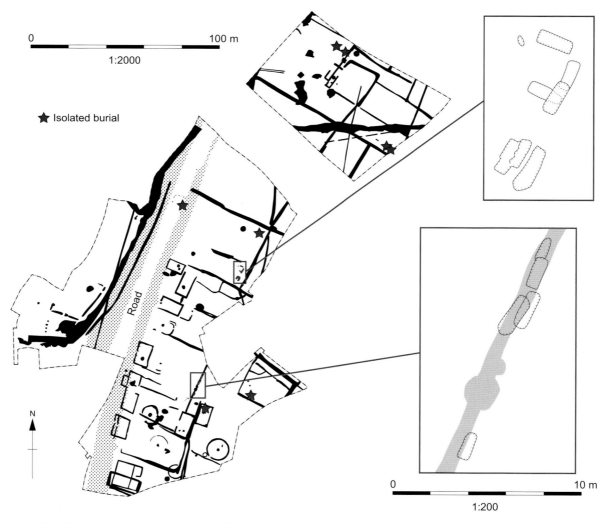

FIG. 6.26. Plan of roadside settlement at Higham Ferrers, Northants, showing location of the 'backland' burial plots (Lawrence and Smith 2009)

outside the settlement core. Despite a large proportion of these comprising neonatal burials, there are at least 70 roadside settlements and defended small towns where individual adult burials have been found dispersed outside cemetery contexts, although this does appear somewhat less common in examples of the latter site type. Many of these settlements also have evidence for more formal cemeteries, but excavations in Baldock, for example, revealed a number of adult inhumations in addition to those in the cemeteries, including four placed in wells and others in ditches and seemingly purpose-dug graves (Stead and Rigby 1986).

Many of the non-cemetery burials within nucleated settlements seem to have been formal interments, such as the isolated decapitated adult female burial accompanied by a neonate, both lying within the same wooden stone-packed coffin within the roadside settlement at Shepton Mallet (Leach and Evans 2001). Some, however, were almost certainly not, one example being the adult male inhumation found within a roadside ditch at Hockwold, Norfolk; here, the body appears to have been left exposed and was covered with alluvium from flooding episodes (Salway 1967). Others are more equivocal, such as the inhumation burial of a young woman wearing an anklet, finger ring and necklace of jet beads found within a system of gullies and soakways outside a bathhouse within the town at Brampton, Norfolk (Knowles 1977). Questions over the 'formality' of burial are also raised from excavations at Dunstable, Central Bedfordshire, where eighteen skeletons (including two infants) were found within four wells adjacent to a defined cemetery on the periphery of the roadside settlement (Matthews 1981). The factors that led to their final disposal in this environment rather in the cemetery proper remain unknown, but could have been linked to social status.

Overall, the evidence suggests that, while burial outside cemetery contexts in nucleated settlements may not have been particularly common in terms of absolute numbers, it was nevertheless fairly widespread, at least within roadside settlements. Such burials have been thought to represent a 'decline of standards' within settlements that may have been contracting (Burnham and Wacher 1990, 31), perhaps indicating a breakdown of societal rules. However, in most cases there is no explicit evidence that these settlements were in decline; instead, such practices are more likely to represent an extension of the wider phenomena of integrated burial seen in many of the smaller farming settlements across the province, and are essentially a continuation of pre-Roman traditions. Crucially, there does not appear to be any noticeable and consistent difference in status between burials within and outside defined cemeteries – the integrated burials would not appear to have been outcasts, excluded from the main burial ground(s).

Burial evidence from the 34 nucleated settlements defined as villages – aggregated agricultural communities located away from the main Roman road network (Allen and Smith 2016, 41–2) – lies somewhere between that of the roadside settlements and that of the larger farmsteads. Only thirteen of these villages (38 per cent) had evidence for defined cemeteries, compared with 62 per cent of roadside settlements and almost all the defended small towns. In all other cases, burials were more dispersed within and around the settlement, such as at Wattle Syke in West Yorkshire, where fourteen neonates, one juvenile and twelve adult burials of late Roman date were found among a group of cellared buildings that appear to have been used for agricultural and craftworking activities (Martin *et al.* 2013).

Nevertheless, in some villages there were clearly separate areas for burials, with five cemeteries of Roman date being revealed in the substantial settlement at Mucking, Essex, ranging from 12 to over 70 graves; a further 16 burials were spread throughout the site (Lucy and Evans 2016; FIG. 6.27). Most of the cemeteries lay on the periphery of the settlement, though one (Cemetery II) was positioned within the main domestic enclosure, sub-divided by a ditched boundary and comprising 11 inhumation burials, 14 cremation burials, and what may have been the remains of a ritual feast (*epulum*), probably for commemoration of the dead (*ibid.*, 324). Many of the graves in this cemetery were relatively well furnished compared with other burials on the site, possibly reflecting the higher social status of those afforded burial near to the heart of the settlement. The remaining cemeteries are believed to have been reserved for different family or household groups, perhaps of varying status within the community (*ibid.*, 430).

The variety of burial practice within village settlements is further illustrated by the site at Amesbury in the chalk downlands of Wiltshire, where a late Roman settlement covering over 10 ha was associated with an area of burials lying *c.* 500 m to the south (Dagless *et al.* 2003; Gibson and Manning 2005; Wessex Archaeology 2008a; FIG. 6.28). The settlement itself included a number of infant burials, while the southern burial zone comprised four separate cemetery groups and a number of isolated burials, totalling over 100 inhumations and 12 cremations. Most of the dated burials belonged to the later fourth century A.D., some time after the establishment of the settlement in the later third century, suggesting some impetus had arisen to stimulate major changes in funerary

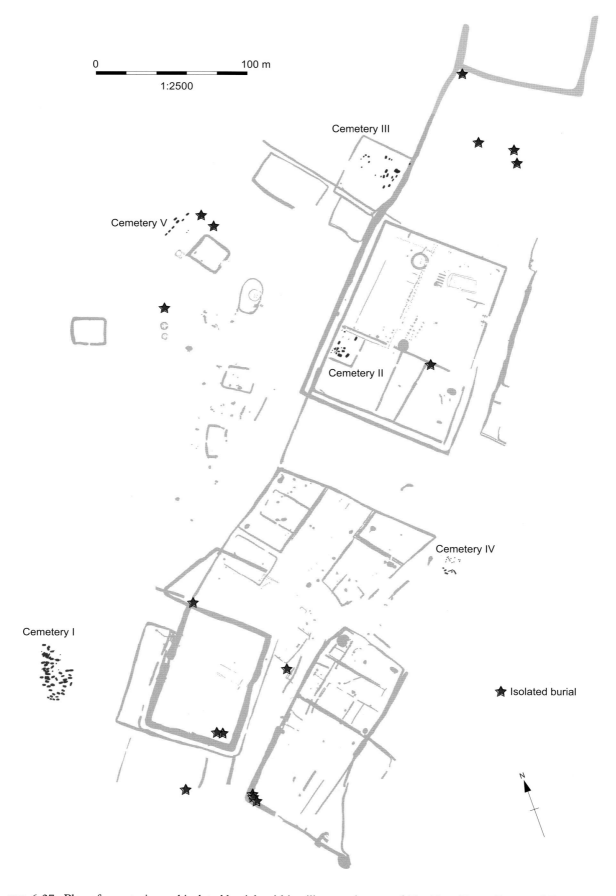

FIG. 6.27. Plan of cemeteries and isolated burials within village settlement of Mucking, Essex (Lucy and Evans 2016)

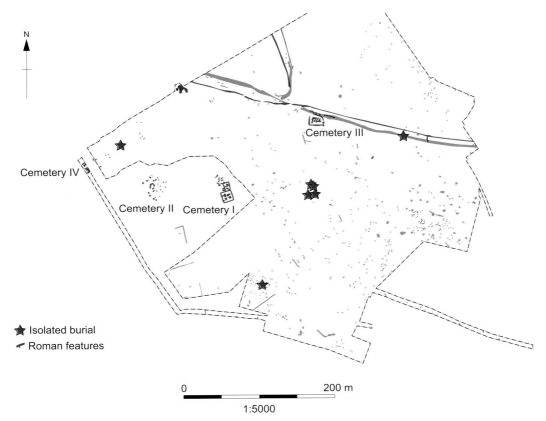

FIG. 6.28. Plan of cemeteries and isolated burials *c.* 500 m south of Roman village settlement at Amesbury, Wiltshire (Gibson and Manning 2005)

practice at this time. As with Mucking, the different cemetery groups had distinct characteristics, with the largest (Cemetery III) comprising sixteen relatively well-furnished north–south coffined-inhumation burials within a ditched enclosure, and with a further 31 burials inserted into a later Bronze Age ditch, these mostly without coffins and with fewer grave goods. Together with the much higher percentage of males in the ditch (61 per cent) than in the enclosure (31 per cent), this suggests some degree of segregation based on sex and/or social status.

The general lack of uniformity of the Mucking and Amesbury burials, in terms of context, burial rites and furnishing, reflects the situation at many other villages, and indeed roadside settlements, and can be regarded as the norm for most rural sites. It is in contrast to most defended small towns and certainly the larger Roman towns, where there is more evidence for some level of municipal control, at least during the later Roman period (e.g. Winchester; Booth *et al.* 2010, 470; Ottaway *et al.* 2012, 367–8). However, even within these late Roman urban cemeteries there can be considerable heterogeneity within the burial rites, as recent excavations at Little Keep, Dorchester (Dorset), have revealed; here, of the 29 inhumation burials excavated, only 38 per cent were supine

and extended, the remainder being a mixture of prone and flexed, with a high proportion of decapitated burials (Dinwiddy 2009).

Military *vici*

Thirty-five of the military *vici* to the north and west of the province had some evidence for associated burial, representing 66 per cent of all the *vici* included in this project. In all areas these largely comprised cremation burials (78 per cent of the 572 burials), in part because of the chronologies of the associated settlements, most being dated early to mid-Roman, and also because of the poor survival of skeletal material, which may have led to fewer inhumation burials being detected. In many cases, inhumation burial is only indicated by grave-shaped pits, some with possible grave goods, while examples of stone-lined cist graves with no or minimal skeletal material have been found associated with at least seven *vici*, including seven graves revealed in recent excavations by the University of Newcastle at Maryport in Cumbria (*Current Arch.* 2014). Despite the evident existence of inhumation burial, it would seem that, for the most part, cremation burial remained the dominant rite at military *vici* through into the late Roman period, suggesting an inherent conservatism with regard to funerary customs, perhaps congruent with the apparent lack of burial tradition in the surrounding native communities.

In fourteen cases the burials were clearly part of cemeteries, typically lying just beyond the *vicus*, 300–500 m from the fort. The largest and best-studied of these cemeteries is that at Brougham in Cumbria, located on a hilltop east of the fort and *vicus* (Cool 2004). Over 140 burials were excavated, mostly cremation burials of third-century date, with evidence of at least two funerary monuments of likely tower form. The cemetery was clearly well ordered, with minimal evidence for intercutting graves, and some indication that the funerary rituals were dictated by the age and sex of the deceased (*ibid.*, 460–1). As with all military *vici*, it is likely that this cemetery was used primarily by the soldiers and their families, and in this case it was suggested that the buried were associated with an army unit that had been transferred from the Danubian region (*ibid.*, 464). The 29 inscribed tombstones from the site suggest a mix of foreigners and native British (Fitzpatrick 2004).

Other excavated *vicus* cemeteries in the north of England include those at Healam Bridge in North Yorkshire (Ambrey *et al.* 2011), Doncaster in South Yorkshire (Davies 2013), Lanchester in County Durham (Turner 1990), and Low Borrowbridge in Cumbria (Hair and Howard-Davis 1996). There are further cemeteries of varying sizes associated with the *vici* along the line of Hadrian's Wall and the Stanegate, though few of these have been investigated; perhaps the best known is at Birdoswald, where a number of cremation burials spanning the mid- to late Roman period (and cist graves of probable fifth-century inhumation burials) have been excavated (Hodgson 2009, 127–31; Wilmott 2010). Military cemeteries may also exist elsewhere in the region, as indicated by a small cemetery at Scorton near the banks of the River Swale, just north of the walled 'small town' of Catterick, North Yorkshire. This comprised fifteen mid- to late Roman inhumation burials, almost exclusively male, with a large proportion buried with crossbow brooches and belt fittings; isotope analysis from nine individuals indicated non-British origins, and it was suggested they may have been members of the late Roman field army (*comitatenses*) (Eckardt *et al.* 2015).

No major cemeteries have yet been comprehensively excavated in any of the military *vici* in Wales, although they are known or suspected around a number of sites, such as the cremation cemetery observed in 1961 south-east of the fort and *vicus* at Llanfair-ar-y-Bryn, Llandovery, in Carmarthenshire (Dyfed HER PRN 4087). A somewhat isolated and exposed Roman fort at Tomen-y-Mur, Gwynedd, had two associated barrow cemeteries lining two of the roads leading from its north-east and south-east gates, respectively; the mounds are assumed to have covered cremation graves on the basis of parallels with similar examples elsewhere (e.g. High Rochester fort, Northumberland; Charlton and Mitcheson 1984), although they have yet to be fully investigated (Pollock 2006, 35). A phenomenon observed by Pollock (*ibid.*, 99) with regard to burial associated with military sites in Wales is that there was a tendency for burials to be placed close to, or within, forts once the army had been reduced in strength or moved on, as seen at Usk, Monmouthshire, and Caerleon, Newport. It was suggested that this may have been either because people wished to be affiliated with visible Roman culture, or else it was a way to reinstate their rights to territory (*ibid.*).

The burials associated with military *vici* were not all found in large, ordered cemeteries. There were many examples of the smaller 'family plots' of the type observed in non-military nucleated settlements further south and discussed above. At Healam Bridge, North Yorkshire, there were a number of small, separate cemeteries, as well as individual burials, mostly lying on the fringes of the *vicus* settlement (Ambrey *et al.* 2011). A range of ages and sexes indicates probable family groups, though one cemetery comprised a single adult, an adolescent, and eight neonate burials, suggesting a more segregated approach. Individual burials have been recorded within fifteen of the *vicus* settlements, some possibly parts of larger cemeteries, but others demonstrably not so, such as the urned cremation of an adult female, which had been placed in a backfilled trench adjacent to the stone colonnade of a building within the *vicus* at Manchester (Gregory 2007). It is possible that some of the individual burials were not 'formal' interments, but the remains of people disposed of by foul play, as graphically demonstrated by the two adult 'murder victims' found during the 1930s, sealed beneath clay in the back room of a building in the *vicus* at Housesteads Roman fort on Hadrian's Wall, one of which had the remains of a knife in his ribs (Birley and Keeney 1935, 236).

Ultimately, aside from the much greater propensity for, and longevity of, cremation burial, funerary practices within military *vici* seem just as varied as in other nucleated settlements, possibly reflecting the diverse range of cultures found within these military outposts (Haynes 1999; James 2001). Nevertheless, the distinctive nature of these communities is highlighted by the complete contrast in funerary customs with those of settlements of the surrounding countryside, where evidence for any form of burial is extremely rare.

Farmsteads

Out of a total population for Roman Britain that may be somewhere in the order of two to three million, it is estimated that 80–90 per cent of people lived in the countryside (Mattingly 2006, 356; Smith and Fulford 2016, 416), with most inhabiting a dense network of relatively small farmsteads. Despite this, only 28 per cent of the excavated farmsteads included in this project have any evidence for burial, these accounting for 21 per cent of the total number of interments (see FIG. 6.23). The 3237 burials from 520 farmsteads are concentrated firmly in central, southern and north-eastern parts of the Roman province, with very few from the north and west, or in much of eastern England, partly for reasons of preservation and different levels of development-led excavation, but also probably owing to cultural factors (cf. FIG. 6.24). As with the general chronological pattern (cf. FIG. 6.3), there is an increase in the numbers of recorded burials at farmsteads over time, from 216 at 69 sites in the late Iron Age to 1155 at 172 sites during the later Roman period, this proliferation being most visible in the farmsteads of the Central Belt.

When analysed in terms of the broad types of farmstead, major differences are observed, with only 18 per cent of enclosed farmsteads having associated burials, compared with 50 per cent of complex farmsteads (TABLE 6.3). This divergence is probably largely the result of the chronological and geographic factors just highlighted, with complex farmsteads being more prevalent during the mid- to late Roman period, particularly in the river valleys of the Central Belt (Smith 2016d, 153). The proportion of these farmsteads (*c.* 38 per cent) with evidence for burials in cemeteries is similar to that of villages discussed above, with both types of settlement characterised by the presence of defined functional zones, which clearly often included burial. As with nucleated settlements, such cemeteries are typically located on the periphery of the main occupied area, though they could still be relatively well integrated, as at Yaxley, Peterborough, located on ground overlooking the Fenland (Brown 2008; Phillips 2014). Here, 23 inhumation burials were revealed along the western side of the mid-Roman settlement enclosure (FIG. 6.29). The burials formed two distinct groups, with the northern group interred either side of the settlement boundary and the southern group all positioned inside and along the settlement boundary; another isolated burial lay to the south (Brown 2008, 17). At other farmsteads, the cemetery was a little further removed, though often located adjacent to or visible from one of the routes into the settlement, such as at Vicar's Farm, west of Cambridge (Lucas 2001). Excavations at this site revealed a small early Roman cremation cemetery of eight graves on the northern periphery of the main settlement, which went out of use by the end of the second

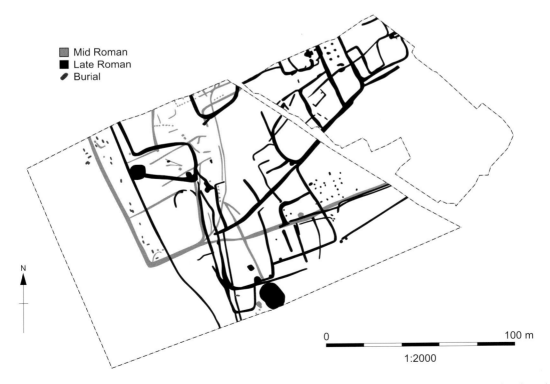

Mid Roman
Late Roman
Burial

N

0   100 m
1:2000

FIG. 6.29. Plan of mid- to late Roman phase of the complex farmstead at Yaxley, Peterborough, showing location of burials (Brown 2008; Phillips 2014)

century A.D. At about the same time, a single cremation urn was interred *c.* 100 m to the south of the farmstead, and this became the focus for a subsequent late Roman enclosed inhumation cemetery of 29 graves, positioned at the corner of a new trackway into the settlement (FIG. 6.30). The cemetery appears to have been an integral part of the radical changes occurring to the main settlement during this period, and similar correlations are found elsewhere; at Claydon Pike in Gloucestershire, for example, a small inhumation cemetery came into existence at approximately the same time as a complete transformation of the farmstead, lying *c.* 100 m to the east, at the start of the fourth century A.D. (Miles *et al.* 2007, 184).

The cemeteries at Yaxley and Vicar's Farm were relatively large in comparison to most of those associated with complex farmsteads, where the number of graves is typically around eight to twelve. Nevertheless, there are ten farmsteads included within the project database with cemeteries of 30 or more graves, including a group of 7 inhumations and 55 urned cremations from Rectory Field, Godmanchester, in Cambridgeshire, all apparently dating to the second century A.D., with minimal evidence for funerary activity after this date (Lyons 2014). At Broughton Manor Farm in Milton Keynes there was an extensive late Iron Age to early Roman (*c.* A.D. 10 to 150) cremation cemetery of 44 graves containing 53 to

FIG. 6.30. Plan of late Roman phase of complex farmstead at Vicar's Farm, Cambridge, showing location of burials (Lucas 2001)

55 individuals mostly grouped within distinct enclosures to the south-west of the main farmstead (Atkins *et al.* 2014). Despite the fact that the settlement continued in use into the late Roman period, albeit somewhat reduced in size, there was minimal evidence for burial at this time, this comprising a single adult inhumation burial found in the former cremation cemetery area (*ibid.*). It is possible that later Roman cemeteries existed outside the excavated areas at both Rectory Field and Broughton Manor Farm, with the dead perhaps being interred within communal rural burial grounds (see below, p. 250). However, it is also possible that funerary rituals at these sites changed from predominantly cremation burial during the earlier Roman period to other practices that left little archaeological trace during the third and fourth centuries A.D. This is somewhat at odds with the wider chronological patterns of the Central Belt region highlighted above, where inhumation burial had become the dominant rite by the late Roman period. However, in the case of Broughton at least, it appears more attuned with local patterns of burial, as later Roman burial of any kind appears relatively uncommon in rural contexts in the Milton Keynes area (*ibid.*, 366).

Among the largest number of burials excavated from any Romano-British farmstead is that recently revealed at NIAB, Huntingdon Road, *c.* 1.4 km north-west of Roman Cambridge (Barker and Meckseper 2015; FIG. 6.31). Two areas of settlement were identified over 400 m apart, linked by a trackway, and both contained burials. The southern settlement contained a small second-century A.D. cremation cemetery of six graves, and three larger mid- to late Roman inhumation cemeteries contained within enclosures, of 27, 12 and 11 graves, with a few other isolated burials outside of these contexts. No cemeteries were found in the northern settlement, but most of the north-western enclosures contained one or two inhumation burials, situated close to the outer boundaries. The differences between the two sites may relate to size, with the southern enclosures thought to represent only the north-western periphery of a larger settlement, possibly even a nucleated village (*ibid.*). If population size was not the main factor, then the differences may reflect diversity in cultural attitudes to disposal of the dead, even within settlements in very close proximity.

Most of the relatively small number of enclosed farmsteads with evidence for burials contained comparatively few interments, with an average of 5.1 burials per record as opposed to 12.2 at complex farmsteads (see TABLE 6.3). Modest-sized cemeteries were found at twenty enclosed farmsteads, fifteen of which dated to the late Iron Age or early Roman period, including one of the largest groups at Boxfield Farm, Hertfordshire, where 25 early Roman cremation graves lay to the north of the settlement (Going and Hunn 1999). The decline in the numbers of enclosed farmsteads over time in the Central Belt and South regions, and the paucity of any burial evidence further north and west where such settlements persisted, together account for the generally poor burial record from such contexts.

In the majority of all farmstead types with evidence for burial, the interments lay not in defined cemeteries, but individually or in small numbers spread throughout the settlement, usually aligned upon ditches, as shown with the northern settlement at NIAB, Cambridge (see FIG. 6.31). Whereas cemeteries typically contained largely adult burials, the integrated interments were far more mixed, with 31 per cent of the 1225 aged burials comprising neonates or infants, and just under 10 per cent being aged as adolescent. At Burnby Lane, Hayton, at the foot of the Yorkshire Wolds, a long-lived late Iron Age to Romano-British farmstead contained 41 neonate/infant and 9 adult burials belonging to the different phases and spread throughout the settlement (Halkon *et al.* 2015). The infant burials at Hayton were specifically placed next to features and walls, and some were thought to have been part of 'structured deposits' (see Ch. 5), such as the infant found in the fill of a late Roman ditch alongside pottery, an immature sheep and a piglet. It has been suggested that such careful deposition here and elsewhere was due to the 'consistent desire to maintain a physical and symbolic connection between the mother (or family) and infant' (Millett and Gowland 2015, 185).

Despite the relatively high incidence of neonatal burials found integrated within and around farmsteads, they are still far outnumbered by adult burials in such contexts; 324 farmsteads (62 per cent of all site types with burials) only have evidence for such adult interments, either within the settlement or more typically dispersed around the periphery, the majority of these with just one or two burials. As with nucleated settlements, most of the integrated burials from farmsteads were probably positioned with great care, some at the junction of ditches (e.g. a cremation burial from Chapel Farm, Wiltshire; Ford *et al.* 2016), others around the entrances to settlement enclosures (e.g. adult female and child inhumations at Coygan Camp, Carmarthenshire; Wainright 1967), but most often aligned upon settlement or inner field boundaries, much the same as with the larger groups of burials.

The individuals chosen for such burial may well have held some special significance among the

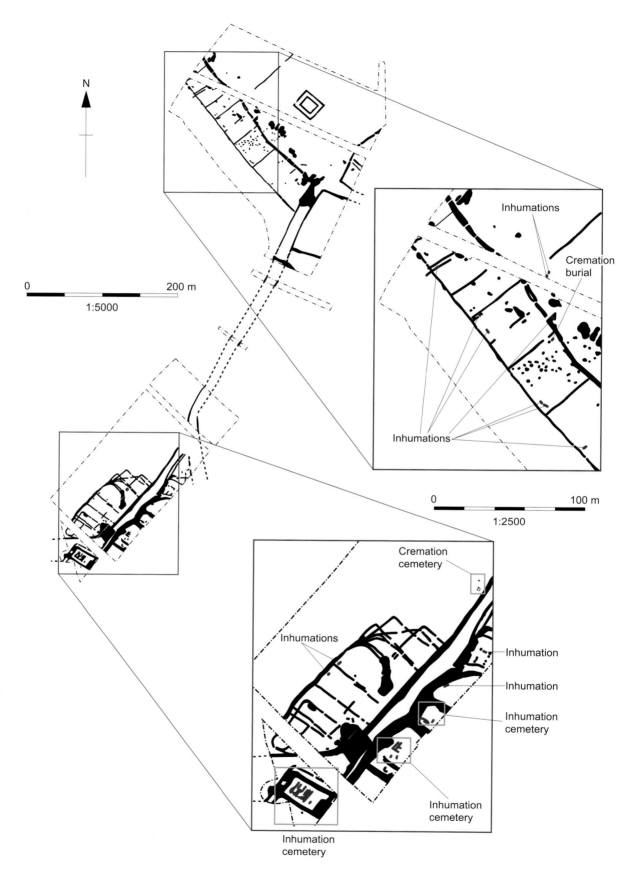

FIG. 6.31. Plan of complex farmsteads at NIAB, Huntingdon Road, Cambridge, showing location of burials (Barker and Meckseper 2015)

occupants of the settlement, as seemingly only a few farmstead communities formally buried their deceased as 'normal' practice. Indeed, in most areas it is those farmsteads that do have more extensive burial evidence that are marked out as special or unusual in some way. As discussed above, these are more often complex farmsteads, which may have had larger resident populations, and, perhaps more importantly, appear to be better integrated within the social and economic fabric of the Roman province (Smith and Fulford 2016, 394). As discussed by Brindle in Chapter 2, the greater connectivity of these farmsteads undoubtedly led to more opportunities for social interaction at a larger scale than was the case at other types of farmstead, and particularly with communities residing in roadside settlements. It may have been this greater social stimulus that led to changes in funerary customs, with cemeteries placed in visible locations around the settlement, perhaps as part of wider mechanisms employed to enhance social standing.

Villas

Villas are only marginally more likely to have associated burials than farmsteads, being recorded at 33 per cent of such sites, though in part this is because of the historical emphasis of archaeological investigation on the main villa building rather than the outlying complex, where cemeteries and other dispersed burials are more likely to be located. This may also at least partly explain the relatively strong association of neonatal burials with villas (54 per cent of the 825 aged burials), these being more often found within the settlement core than in defined cemeteries on the periphery, as discussed above in relation to farmsteads (see also Ch. 7). Nevertheless, there are still many examples of cemeteries attached to villa complexes, some with multiple groups of burials, probably relating to different social/economic groups, as has been suggested in the case of certain nucleated settlements and complex farmsteads discussed above. At Roughground Farm in the Gloucestershire Upper Thames Valley, a large villa complex/estate centre had three small groups of late Roman inhumation burials located on the fringes of the settlement alongside other more dispersed burials; the only example from near to the villa building itself was a single adult female inhumation in a grave cut through the courtyard gravel (Allen *et al.* 1993; FIG. 6.32).

Larger cemeteries were noted in association with some villas, with, for example, 55 inhumation graves of late fourth century date found east of a probable villa at Bletsoe, Bedford (Dawson 1994).

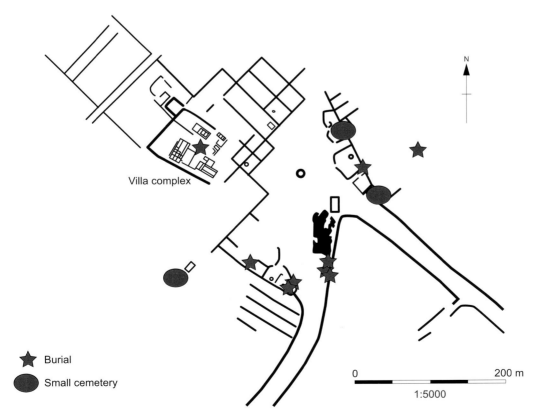

FIG. 6.32. Plan of wider villa estate at Roughground Farm, Gloucestershire, showing location of burials (Allen *et al.* 1993)

These were nearly all adults, and they avoided an earlier group of infant burials from the same area. A similarly late burial ground of 72 inhumation graves at Watersmeet, Cambridgeshire, was thought to relate to a villa lying 200 m to the east; its full extent was not revealed but there appears to have been little of the organisation witnessed at many of the larger contemporary urban cemeteries (Nicholson 2006b). The largest known villa cemetery is at Litlington in Cambridgeshire, where 80 cremation burials and 250 inhumation burials were revealed by antiquarian excavations in 1821, and very limited recent Time Team evaluation (Wessex Archaeology 2010). The burials lay within a walled enclosure 350 m south-east of the villa, though few details are known of the site, except for the existence of possible *in situ* pyres and a buttressed mausoleum containing a stone sarcophagus, which lay to the north of the enclosure.

These larger cemeteries probably encompassed a range of different workers and their families from the villa estate, but there is also evidence for more segregated burial grounds. The most obvious are the infant cemeteries of varying sizes found associated with a small number of villas such as Barton Court Farm, Oxfordshire (Miles 1986), Marshfield in South Gloucestershire (Blockley 1985), Bucknowle in Dorset (Light and Ellis 2009) and Yewden in Buckinghamshire (Eyers 2011; Mays and Eyers 2011). A total of 97 perinatal infant burials were found during excavations at the last site, nearly all in individual graves confined to an area just north of the main villa buildings. These have traditionally been interpreted as the victims of infanticide, either the unwanted children of estate workers, or even of prostitutes in one interpretation of Yewden as a brothel (Cocks 1921, 150; Eyers 2011, 278). Such interpretations have been critiqued (Scott 1999, 110), as has the very idea that infanticide was particularly widespread in the Roman world, with Gowland *et al.* (2014) arguing that it was the abandonment of unwanted infants (i.e. removal and exposure) that was more common, but that this practice was very unlikely to end in any interment, therefore leaving no archaeological trace (see also Millett and Gowland 2015). Certainly at many villas there are indications that infants were treated with just as much respect as older children and adult burials, some receiving grave goods and being buried in coffins; two of the infants from Bucknowle, for example, were buried in cist graves, similar to many adults in the region. Elsewhere, an infant burial was contained in a lead coffin immediately outside the paved entrance to the northern range of the villa at Ilchester Mead in Somerset (Hayward 1982). Infant cemeteries are almost unheard of outside of villa contexts, one of the few examples being the 21 infant inhumation burials (neonate to 3–4 years old) placed within an ancillary building of a late Roman farmstead at Bradley Hill, Somerton in Somerset, all within stone slab cist graves; a separate mostly adult cemetery of 25 graves lay to the south, with individuals radiocarbon dated from the fourth to sixth centuries A.D. (Leech 1981; Gerrard 2005). Although not strictly defined as a villa, the architecture of the two main domestic buildings was clearly more sophisticated than typical farmsteads of the area, and the level of associated material culture suggests a community of some relative wealth. The evidence overall suggests that the social status of rural communities may have had some effect upon the treatment of deceased infants, with those of higher standing being more likely to formally inter them, either within buildings, in graves around the settlement or in dedicated cemeteries. However, as discussed by Rohnbogner in Chapter 7), there is significant variation in the rate and recovery of perinate and infant burials over time and across different regions and individual sites. Whether this was intrinsically linked with variable rates of infant mortality, or else differences in the treatment of the deceased (e.g. either formally buried or exposed) is far harder to tell.

Aside from segregation based on age, it is likely that there was some form of social separation of burials within villa complexes, reflecting the highly stratified nature of Romano-British society, particularly during the later Roman period when social inequalities are thought to be at their greatest (Gerrard 2013, 243). Pearce (2016) has recently highlighted how differing funerary rituals, including the act of burial itself, may have been utilised to express disparate identities, while more direct evidence for the social status of individuals in life may occasionally be obtained from analysis of skeletal material. At Chignal St James villa in Essex, in addition to a few scattered burials, there were several known cemeteries, though only one of these has been comprehensively examined – a group of 24 late Roman inhumation burials located in the corner of an earlier enclosure, *c.* 250 m south of the villa. Rohnbogner's summation (Ch. 7, p. 333) of the pathology of these burials, which comprised twenty adults, an adolescent and an infant, indicated that the group had experienced a particularly strenuous lifestyle, which had led the excavator to suggest that they may have been bonded tenants (*coloni*) of the villa estate (Clarke 1998, 140–1). Whatever the case, they would certainly not seem to have included the family of the villa owners, who were most likely buried in a separate area.

The existence of high-status Roman burials – the likely owners of the villas – has been recognised for some time (cf. Philpott 1991, 229; Strück 2000; Pearce 2014b), primarily through the presence of substantial mausolea and burials with elaborate grave goods. Burials within large barrows have a well-known concentration in areas of south-east England, particularly in parts of Hertfordshire, Cambridgeshire, Essex and Kent, thought to be a continuation of the high-status burial traditions of the late Iron Age (Strück 2000, 88–9, fig. 9.3). Where dated, these mostly belong to the second century A.D., and a number can be directly associated with villa estates, including the seven barrows from Bartlow Hills, Cambridgeshire, which are thought to lie close to a villa investigated in the nineteenth century (Eckardt et al. 2009). In addition to tumuli, stone mausolea have been suggested at eight villas, often located some distance from the villa building in prominent topographic positions, such as at Bancroft in Milton Keynes (Williams and Zeepvat 1994, 89; see Ch. 5, FIG. 5.28). At Truckle Hill, North Wraxall, in Wiltshire, five masonry tombs/mausolea were found 60 m west of the villa complex,

containing inhumation burials in stone or wooden coffins, along with an unurned cremation burial (Andrews 2009a). Such stone mausolea and the barrows would have been very prominent visual reminders of the elite status of the villa owners, though very few can be dated to the later Roman period, when many of the villa buildings were reaching their architectural height. This apparent disparity suggests that other ways were utilised to express the higher status of the deceased and their families, at least at the time of the funeral, perhaps including the greater use of stone and/or lead coffins and an increased emphasis on the personal appearance of the buried individual (Pearce 2016).

Rural landscapes

The relatively low proportion of villas, and particularly of farmsteads, with evidence for burial requires further explanation. One possibility, as noted above, is that many of these smaller rural settlements are more likely to have continued traditional funerary practices that did not involve the formal interment of the dead (cf. Pearce 2013, 145; see below p. 275). This is, perhaps, especially applicable for the generally smaller, enclosed

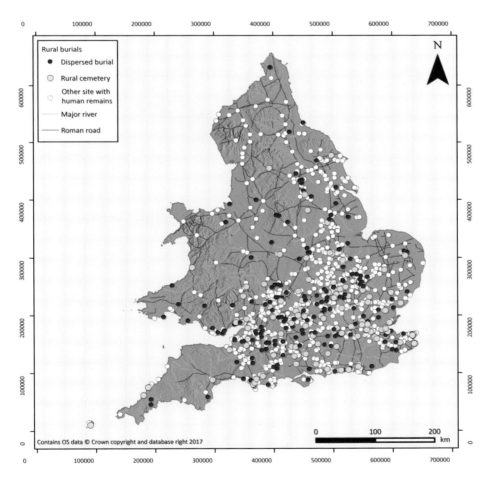

FIG. 6.33. Distribution of burials from rural, non-settlement contexts

farmsteads, which tend to be more numerous during the earlier Roman period and in regions further north and west. Another factor could be that many of the deceased from these settlements may have been buried some distance from the main occupation area, which would account for the large numbers of burials (21 per cent of total) found in ostensibly 'isolated' rural parts of the landscape. These range from one or two burials interspersed among field systems to much larger rural cemeteries, possibly serving a number of different communities.

The distribution of these rural burial sites is shown in FIG. 6.33. Most of the 125 rural cemeteries are concentrated in central and southern England, where some seem to have become established by the late Iron Age or even earlier. At Duxford in Cambridgeshire a hilltop cemetery of *c.* 32 inhumation burials and 2 cremation burials was in use from the middle Iron Age until the early second century A.D. (Lyons 2011), while at Mill Hill, Deal, in Kent, there is a well-known cemetery overlooking the coast, the earliest inhumation burial dating from the early/middle Iron Age, though with most belonging between the second century B.C. and the first century A.D., with a gradual increase in cremation burial over time (Parfitt 1995). Other major cemeteries of late Iron Age date that do not appear to have been associated with any specific settlement include Westhampnett in West Sussex (161 cremation burials) and Harlyn Bay in Cornwall (*c.* 130 inhumation burials), both situated on or near the coast. The extensive cemetery at Westhampnett,

already noted above (p. 222), has helped to transform our understanding of late Iron Age funerary practice in south-east England, with its clearly 'managed' spatial organisation around a central circular area, a large number of pyre sites and associated shrines/mortuary enclosures (Fitzpatrick 1997; FIG. 6.34). A number of contemporary settlements have been found within a few kilometres of the site (e.g. Westhampnett Area 5; Fitzpatrick *et al.* 2008; Copse Farm, Oving; Bedwin and Holgate 1985), with analysis suggesting inter-visibility between them and the cemetery, which lay on a low rise within the coastal plain (Garland 2013, 187). It is not hard to believe that this was the communal burial ground for these communities, though evidence to date suggests that this arrangement was quite unusual at this time, perhaps marking these settlements as 'special' in some way.

There was an increase in the number of rural cemeteries into the early Roman period, although for the most part these remained fairly modest in size, suggesting that, if they were communal burial grounds, communities were being highly selective in the individuals that they interred. One of the larger groups was found on the Isle of Thanet during the recent excavations of the East Kent Access Road (Zone 19; Andrews *et al.* 2015). Here there were two cemeteries, separated by about 120 m, comprising 26 inhumation burials and 26 cremation burials in total, including those burials found in an adjacent earlier excavation. Trackways at the site appeared to lead to the early Roman villa at Minster-in-Thanet, 2 km to the south-west,

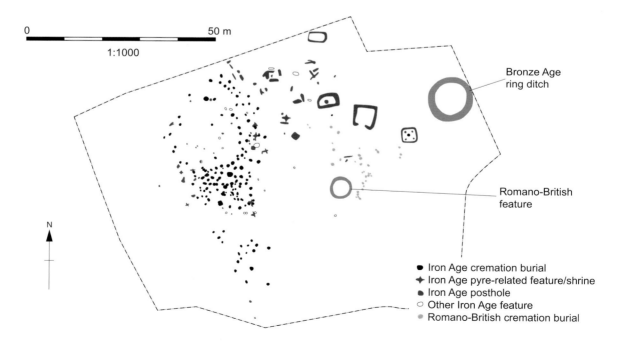

FIG. 6.34. Plan of the extensive late Iron Age rural cemetery at Westhampnett, West Sussex (Fitzpatrick 1997)

with the cemeteries perhaps belonging to this estate, although the trackways also seem to relate to the main east–west road through Thanet, and so the burials may also be associated with settlements along this axis.

Many similar modest-sized rural cemeteries persisted until the late Roman period, when, as with the situation in many settlements, there was a substantial increase in larger burial grounds. Recent excavation of a rural cemetery at Great Ellingham in Norfolk, for example, revealed 96 inhumation burials, with no known associated settlement (Norfolk HER 4257; http://chrisbirksarchaeology.co.uk). This remains one of the largest Roman cemeteries in Norfolk, and is most likely a communal burial ground for a number of dispersed rural communities. Many of the larger late Roman rural cemeteries were located in the Upper Thames Valley, including two separate groups of burials lying 400 m apart at Radley Barrow Hills in Oxfordshire, the larger group (Radley II: Chambers and McAdam 2007) comprising 57 inhumation and 12 cremation burials, and the smaller group (Radley I: Atkinson 1952/3) made up of 35 inhumation burials. These cemeteries were clearly positioned in relation to the surrounding Bronze Age barrows, a phenomenon found at a number of other rural sites, and both may have been laid out along the lines of trackways (Chambers and McAdam 2007, 32, fig. 2.14). A number of settlements are known within 1 km of the cemeteries, including the modest villa with the infant cemetery at Barton Court Farm noted above, and it was suggested that groups of burials differentiated within the cemeteries may well relate to these surrounding settlements (*ibid.*).

Another large inhumation cemetery at Horcott Quarry in Gloucestershire was also separated into two groups, this reflecting a chronological distinction, with 57 graves (with 61 individuals) to the south being dated mid-third to mid-fourth century A.D. and 17 graves to the north (with 14 individuals, mostly sub-adults) dated to the fifth/sixth centuries A.D., all through a series of modelled radiocarbon dates (Hayden *et al.* 2017; FIG. 6.35). A single inhumation burial between the groups was radiocarbon dated cal. A.D. 320–430. The southern burials lay *c.* 200 m east of a small farmstead with a masonry building, partly joined by a trackway but with a small rise restricting visibility between the areas. The settlement had nine burials (7 adults, 1 child, 1 infant) distributed around the building enclosure, radiocarbon dated to the mid-second-to-late third century A.D., contemporary with overall occupation of the farmstead. Therefore, although the earliest burials in the nearby larger cemetery appear to have been

contemporary with the final phase of the farmstead, reflecting a move towards more segregated burial, it is likely that most were interred after the settlement had gone out of use. Although these burials could have been related to an as yet unknown settlement in the vicinity, the overall number of burials is much higher than is typically found among most contemporary farmsteads, such as Claydon Pike (10 burials), Arkell's Land/Coln Gravel (11 burials) and Totterdown Lane (12 burials) (FIG. 6.35). Only at Cotswold Community, 5 km south of Cirencester, was there evidence for a larger cemetery associated with a specific farmstead, this comprising 22 inhumation burials lying on the north-west fringes of the late Roman settlement, with a further three burials found elsewhere (Powell *et al.* 2010). If the Horcott burials did relate to a single settlement, then either it would have been of a more substantial size, or else a much higher proportion of the inhabitants was selected for interment than was typical for the area. The alternative is that it was utilised for selected individuals from a number of communities in this well-populated area, perhaps those incorporated within a larger agricultural estate, as may have been the case at Radley and other rural cemeteries in the region such as Uffington (58 burials; Miles *et al.* 2003) and Cassington (110+ burials; Booth 2001, 16).

The two burial zones within the Horcott cemetery may have been separated by up to *c.* 100 years, with only the single burial between them acting as a possible chronological link. Nevertheless, the place was still clearly perceived as a special place for interment of the dead, and a similar continuity of space was found within the much smaller cemetery at Tubney Wood, Oxfordshire, where a group of eight fourth-century inhumation graves found close to a field boundary lay near to a similarly small post-Roman cemetery with inhumation burials radiocarbon dated A.D. 420–545 (Simmonds *et al.* 2011). There are, however, a number of rural cemeteries where there appears more direct continuity of burial from late to post-Roman, including one of the largest known burial grounds at Cannington in Somerset, on a limestone hill near to the Bristol Channel (Rahtz *et al.* 2000). Excavations here during the 1960s revealed 419 graves (with 542 individuals), part of a major cemetery that may have numbered up to 5000 burials, dating from the fourth (or slightly earlier) to the start of the eighth century A.D., possibly focused upon a late Roman rock-cut shrine/mausoleum. Most of the inhumations appeared well ordered in rows, though there was some variation in grave goods and rites; it was suggested that the cemetery was that of a local Romano-British population that had migrated to the nearby

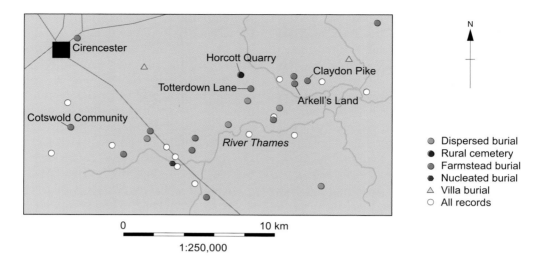

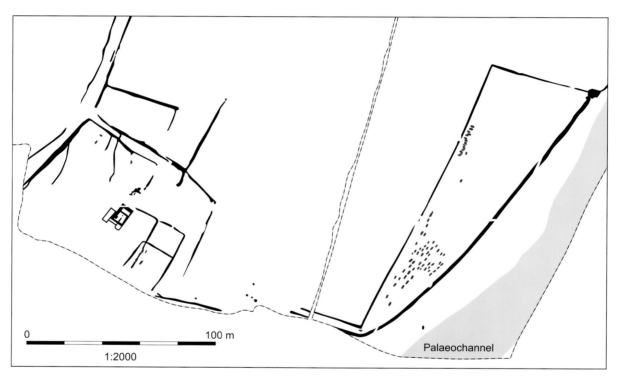

FIG. 6.35. Plan of settlement and cemetery at Horcott Quarry, Gloucestershire, and its location in the landscape (Hayden *et al.* 2017)

hillfort, or else it was a communal graveyard for several local communities (*ibid.*, 421). The scale of this cemetery remains unprecedented within wholly Roman rural contexts, though the relatively extensive burial evidence from the early medieval period suggests that in many places, interment of the dead was becoming more of a normative mortuary practice within the countryside (cf. Williams 2007).

Other site types

Finally, in terms of the broad context of burial, there is a relatively small number of interments that have been excavated within other types of site.

These included 78 inhumation burials from seven hillforts that saw activity into the late Iron Age and early Roman periods, all located in the west of England. Many of these were from the well-known Maiden Castle 'war cemetery' in Dorset, which were untypical of most Durotrigan burials, and seemingly represent combatants or victims of warfare (Wheeler 1943, 62; Sharples 1991, 124; Redfern 2011; Harding 2015, 84). A further 29 cremation and inhumation burials of late Iron Age to very early Roman date came from six sites classed as *oppida*, which were large, high-status, often polyfocal settlements defined by major dyke complexes. Among them are four flexed adult inhumation burials from Stanwick in North Yorkshire, one with a flat slab placed over the body with an inverted horse's head placed on top (Haselgrove 2016), and seven high-status cremation burials from Stanway, Colchester, in Essex, set within extensive funerary enclosures and some accompanied by rich grave goods, including one with a set of surgical instruments (Crummy *et al.* 2007).

There were also 191 burials from 20 sites suggested as being primarily religious in nature, though with varying degrees of certainty (see Ch. 5). These include a possible 60 inhumation burials from the enigmatic early Roman (A.D. 40–70) 'ceremonial' site at Fison Way, Thetford, in Norfolk, though poor bone preservation has ensured that their status remains uncertain (Gregory 1991, 53). Formal burial was not usually associated with Romano-British shrines and temples (Smith 2001, 157), although neonatal burials are slightly more common, particularly at certain sites such as Springhead in Kent, where large numbers of infant burials were associated with the main temple complex and the Sanctuary area around the springs (Andrews and Smith 2011, 208). The main period of interment for the Springhead burials appears relatively restricted, around the mid-second century A.D., suggesting that it may not have been a regular part of cult practice but, instead, a ritualised response to a particular set of circumstances (*ibid.*). Many of the infant burials from sacred sites are likely to have been buried in such places for symbolic reasons, such as the three neonates associated with timber structures in the late Iron Age/early Roman shrine at Uley in Gloucestershire, suggested as possible foundation offerings (Woodward and Leach 1993, 30). The same may have been the case for some of the adult burials, such as the already skeletonised adult male situated under the floor of the temple ambulatory at Bourton Grounds, Buckinghamshire (Green 1966, 358). On at least two occasions, at Brean Down in Somerset (Apsimon 1965) and Rutland Water (Carlyle 2011), burials seem to have been inserted into the temple/shrine at the end of the fourth century or into the early post-Roman period, the burial from the latter being a supine young adult male positioned in the centre of the shrine and radiocarbon dated cal. A.D. 380–550. These may reflect some level of continued sanctity at these sites.

Industrial sites comprise the final category of site type to have any association with burial, although the only place of significance was Laxton Lodge in Northamptonshire (Jackson and Tylecote 1988). This was the site of a major ironworking complex, with 87 graves of a late Roman inhumation cemetery excavated close by, and other burials said to be found further to the west (*ibid.*). Although not on the same scale, there was also some association between burial and ironworking sites in the Weald, with, for example, a late Iron Age cremation cemetery of six graves revealed in close proximity to an iron bloomery furnace at Jubilee Corner, Ulcombe, Kent (Aldridge 2005).

GRAVE FURNISHINGS AND GOODS

The material culture and other remains recovered from the grave can provide a crucial insight into wider funerary practices as well as the beliefs and social structure of the surrounding communities. However, any understanding of the mechanisms by which objects, animal remains or plant remains ended up in or near to the grave can still be very difficult to grasp (Cool 2011; Ekengren 2013). Certainly not all materials found with the burial would necessarily have comprised grave goods or containers for the deceased (e.g. coffins or urns), with Biddulph (2015), for example, suggesting that the miscellaneous sherds of pottery found typically in the backfills of graves and surrounding features may have been related to funerary feasting at the site, either during the burial ceremony or in subsequent visits to the grave (cf. Toynbee 1971, 63–4; see also Sealey 2007, 304–5, for discussion of elite graveside feasting and subsequent smashing of amphorae at Stanway, Essex). Similarly, Booth (1993–4; 2017, 202) has highlighted a particular example from Welford on Avon, in Warwickshire, where the recovery of joining fragments of late Roman glass beakers within a lead-lined coffin and surrounding grave suggested the drinking of 'a valedictory toast', followed by smashing the glasses before the coffin was closed and the grave backfilled. Other objects such as quernstones, ceramic tiles and larger, robust pottery vessels such as amphorae found on or near to the burial may even have acted as grave markers, in the absence of more traditional funerary stelae, which remain very rare outside of military and some urban contexts (Pearce 2011; 2014b; Weekes 2016). Ultimately, determination of an object's possible function in such circumstances depends entirely upon detailed contextual analysis of the grave and its environment. The subject remains beyond the scope of this study, with the data recorded here being limited to the quantification and type of any objects designated in archaeological reports as 'grave containers' or 'grave goods'. The geographic, chronological and wider contextual patterns of these grave containers and goods will now be examined, alongside a more detailed consideration by Lodwick and Allen of the use of plants and animals in burials.

BURIAL CONTAINERS

A basic distinction within all types of burial is whether or not the body, either cremated or whole, was placed within a container before being placed into the grave. In many cases this is impossible to discern in the archaeological record, as cremated remains placed within organic containers would generally appear as loose bone (though see below), and, likewise, wooden boxes or coffins constructed without nails, or in particularly destructive soils, would in most cases leave no trace, though occasionally coffin stains are observed, such as at Pepper Hill in Kent (Biddulph 2006).

Coffins and cists

A total of 1907 inhumation burials within the current dataset had some positive evidence for coffins, 1624 coming from sites with 'complete' records, i.e. those with substantive data on all burials (*c.* 20 per cent of inhumation burials from such records; see above p. 206). In the vast majority of cases these coffins were made of wood, usually oak, where evidence allowed identification, although the form of construction could vary considerably. In most cases evidence for the use of timber coffins comes in the form of iron nails used in their construction, though sometimes the

numbers of nails recovered are insufficient to be completely certain of their use for such purposes, and they may just have been used to secure the lid, or been residual finds in the grave fill. Notwithstanding the issues of preservation just outlined, the seemingly restricted use of coffins may suggest that they were reserved for the deceased of higher social status (cf. Philpott 1991, 53; Russell 2010). This has been shown within the late Roman urban cemetery at Lankhills, Winchester, where isotopic evidence has indicated that those buried without coffins had a less protein-rich diet (Booth *et al.* 2010, 419). Nevertheless, there are over twenty rural cemeteries that have particularly high proportions of burials within coffins (*c.* 60 per cent or over), and it may be that their use was in part due to the choices of individual communities rather than any consistent, province-wide association with higher status. In a late Roman cemetery at Alington Avenue, Dorset, for example, 68 of the 91 inhumation burials (*c.* 75 per cent) appear to have been interred within wooden coffins (one with a stone lid and another with lead lining), including infants (Davies *et al.* 2002), while at the nearby late/post-Roman cemetery at Tolpuddle Ball, none of the 50 graves contained coffin nails, though four of them are

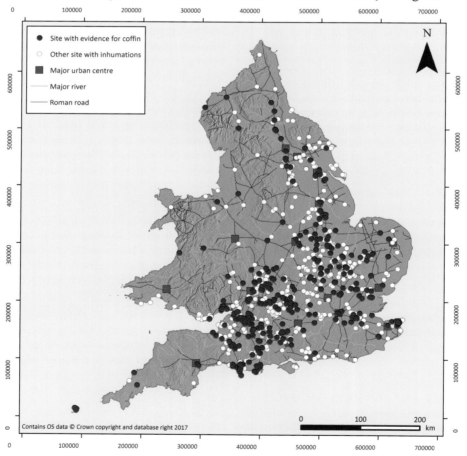

FIG. 6.36. Distribution of all sites with evidence for inhumations buried within coffins

thought to have included coffins based on the position of flint nodules, which may have been used as support packing (Hearne and Birbeck 1999). Only further isotopic work could possibly help to indicate whether or not this distinction was due to the relative status of the individual communities, or wider cultural differences.

The distribution of all sites with coffined inhumation burials is shown in FIG. 6.36. For the most part they cover the same areas as inhumation burials in general, though they seem particularly scarce along the Sussex coastal plain, where burials are in any case dominated by cremation graves (see above, p. 218). In the north-east, coffined burials appear largely restricted to sites along the main road system, where they are mostly, though not exclusively, found in villas, roadside settlements, and a number of military *vici*. One exception was at Garden Lane, Sherburn in Elmet, North Yorkshire, where two late Roman stone sarcophagi were found containing plaster burials in an apparently isolated rural context (MAP Arch. Con. 1997). As discussed below, such burials were clearly exceptional in a rural context, and were probably associated with a nearby villa.

Various studies have noted the overall increase in coffin use over time during the Roman period, albeit using data mostly derived from urban

cemeteries (Philpott 1991, 224; Watts 2005, 70; Russell 2010). The current study, using data from predominantly rural contexts, has indicated a major increase in the use of coffins (or at least the use of nailed coffins) during the early Roman period, but thereafter relatively little change in terms of the proportion of inhumation burials being interred within coffins, notwithstanding the huge increase in the overall number of burials during the late Roman period (FIG. 6.37). Instead, there is more variation between site types (FIG. 6.37), with nucleated settlements being more likely to have coffined interments than any other site type. The low value from military *vici*, where cremation burial is generally dominant, may be because of preservation issues, with iron nails surviving less well in the acidic soils of the north and west, and also because of increased use of cist burials, discussed below. On the face of it, the very low proportion of villa inhumation burials with coffins may seem out of place, especially if such features can be regarded as a measure of status. However, this may be in part because of the high percentage of infant burials associated with villas, which are generally not accorded coffins. There are some notable exceptions to this, including at Keston in Kent, where many neonate and child graves were coffined (Philp *et al.* 1999), while, on

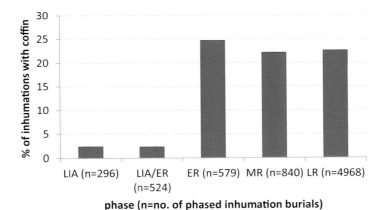

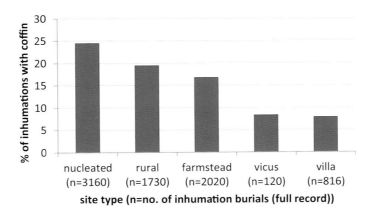

FIG. 6.37. Proportion of inhumation burials within coffins over time and by site type

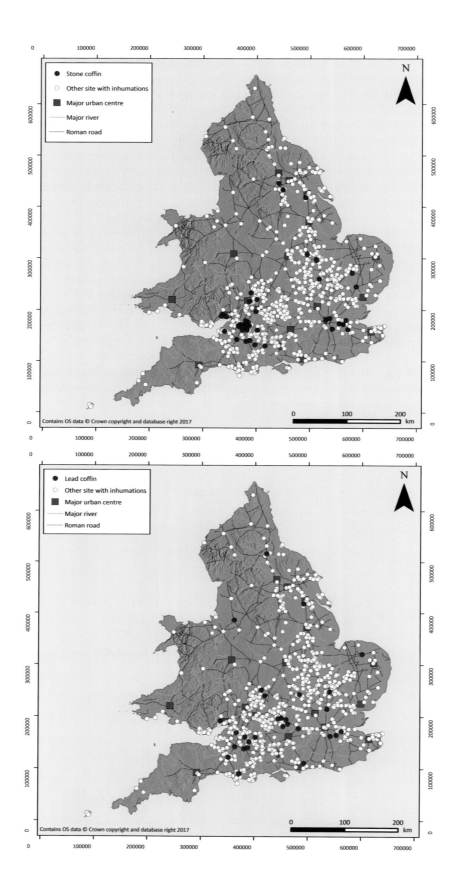

FIG. 6.38. Distribution of all sites with evidence for inhumations buried within stone coffins and lead coffins

rare occasions, infants from villas were even accorded burial within stone (e.g. Budbury, Bradford-on-Avon, Wilts.; Annable 1966) or lead (e.g. Stanton Low, Bucks.; Woodfield and Johnson 1989) coffins, which were certainly indicators of high status (Russell 2010).

The overall distributions of stone and lead coffins recorded in this project are shown in FIG. 6.38. Many of the 49 sites with stone coffins are located in the western Central Belt, an area suggested in Volume 1 (Smith and Fulford 2016, 408) and Volume 2 (Brindle 2017a, 278) as having the greatest concentration of late Roman rural wealth. The concentration around Bath is particularly notable, presumably making use of the good-quality Bath stone, though this is unlikely to have been the only reason for such a marked grouping, as suitable stone can be found in many other locations. Another loose concentration of stone coffins lies on the periphery of London, where there is no local source of suitable stone, with six being found associated with a single settlement at Old Ford, Tower Hamlets (Owen *et al.* 1973). Most of the stone coffins were associated with villas or nucleated settlements, or else were located in ostensibly 'isolated' rural locations, many discovered in the nineteenth and earlier twentieth centuries. One more recently excavated example, at Longbridge Deverill, Wiltshire, comprised a lead coffin, probably encased in timber, with fragmentary evidence of a greensand sarcophagus surviving at one end; the site lay on a low hill overlooking the Upper Wylye Valley, and a coin hoard was found at the same location (Moffatt and Heaton 2003).

The distribution of lead coffins, which are, in effect, linings placed within wooden or stone coffins, is somewhat more dispersed than the stone sarcophagi, though with a slight concentration in the Oxfordshire Upper Thames Valley in the vicinity of Dorchester-on-Thames and Abingdon, and also further west, close to a major source of lead in the Mendip Hills, Somerset. They are generally associated with a similar range of site types, again suggesting that they were used as an expression of status, and yet, as with stone coffins, they would not seem to have been adopted at higher status sites across the whole province.

One rite occasionally associated with the use of stone and lead coffins is the covering of the body with plaster, usually made of lime, chalk or gypsum (a soft sulfate mineral), which seems to have been a fourth-century phenomenon, probably reserved for specific social groups (Philpott 1991, 90–7, 438–9; Sparey-Green 2003). Such burial rites remain extremely rare, particularly in the countryside of Roman Britain, with just four examples noted in the current project, including the Yorkshire burials discussed above and a later fourth-century gypsum burial within the village at Mucking in Essex, on the site of a mid-Roman cremation cemetery (Lucy and Evans 2016, 371).

Overall, it is clear that the provision of stone and lead coffins would have been a major expense, and they remain rare even in urban contexts (Pearce 2015, 148). On the few farmsteads where they do occur, such as the female adult and child in a limestone coffin at Empingham, Rutland (Dean and Gorin 2000), it must have represented an exceptional investment, perhaps indicating

FIG. 6.39. Photograph of late Roman adult burial shown covered by two slanting mud stone/shale slabs, found at Hinckley Point C Somerset (Joyce *et al.* 2012; © Cotswold Archaeology)

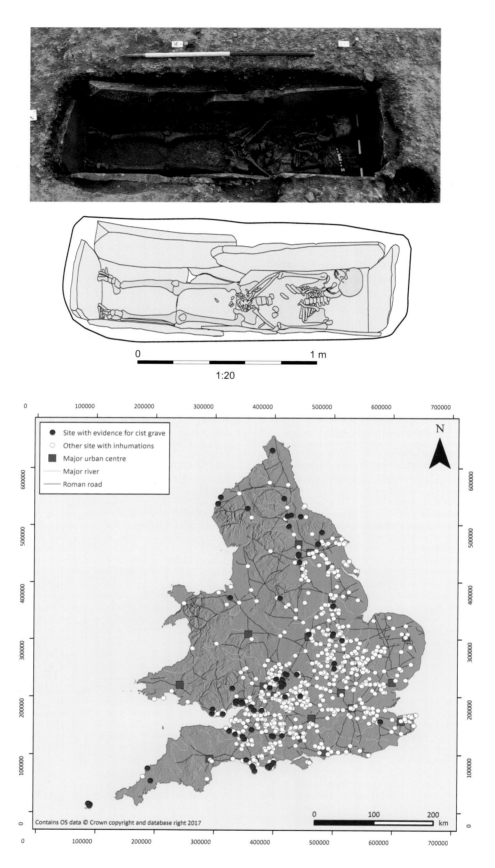

FIG. 6.40. Distribution of all sites with evidence for inhumations buried within stone-lined cist graves, and photograph and plan of late Roman cist grave at Bourton-on-the-Water, Gloucestershire (Hart *et al.* 2017; © Cotswold Archaeology)

exceptional circumstances. There are, however, a number of sites where there appear to have been stone (and much more rarely lead) 'lids' placed over the body, sometimes demonstrably on timber coffins. At Hinckley Point C in Somerset, for instance, a well-preserved decapitated adult burial was covered by two slanting mud stone/shale slabs, which could have acted as a grave marker (Joyce *et al.* 2012; FIG. 6.39). Most of these burials lay in the north and west of the province, and are probably variants of the cist grave tradition.

Cist, or stone-lined, graves have a long tradition, particularly in western and northern parts of Britain, from the prehistoric to the early medieval periods (Philpott 1991, 9–10; Petts 2002; Darvill 2010, 287) (FIG. 6.40). Late Iron Age to early Roman examples recorded within the current project are largely concentrated in the west and south-west. Some of these are clearly associated with high-status individuals, such as the crouched burial at Bryher, Isles of Scilly, where grave goods within the cist included an iron sword and bronze scabbard, shield fittings, a mirror and items of jewellery; the skeleton was dated to the first half of the first century B.C. (Johns 2006). At Harlyn Bay on the north coast of Cornwall, most of the 131 late Iron Age/early Roman inhumation burials appear to have been in cist graves, suggesting more of a 'normative' custom across a wider spectrum of society (cf. Harding 2015, 79–83).

Most of the sites with cist graves recorded in the current dataset date to the later Roman period. The tradition continued in the west and south-west, though they were fewer in number and generally with supine rather than flexed skeletons, but were far more prolific further north, such as the examples at Maryport military *vicus* noted above. A small number of cist graves lay in the eastern part of the Central Belt region, such as an adult female from the farmstead at Biddenham Loop (Luke 2009), and 25 examples from the probable villa cemetery at Bletsoe (Dawson 1994), both in Bedford unitary authority. These burials occur across a similar area to the spread of later Roman flexed burials discussed above (p. 230), again suggesting possible population movement from areas further west or north at this time.

Urns and caskets

Throughout much of England and Wales, it seems to have been customary to inter at least a proportion of the cremated remains of an individual within a container before being placed into the grave, with *c.* 60 per cent of cremation burials being classed as 'urned', although this may be partly because such burials are more easily recognised in the archaeological record than unaccompanied deposits of cremated bone

(McKinley 2013, 151). In some other cases, there is evidence from iron nails and copper-alloy fittings for boxes, or caskets (see below), while there are a few indications for the use of other organic containers, such as one of the burials at East Kent Access Road Zone 11, where the compacted cremated bone within the grave looked to have been contained in a bag (Andrews *et al.* 2015, 270). Unlike coffins, most of the vessels used to contain cremated remains were probably not manufactured specifically for this purpose, but were typically ceramic vessels, particularly jars (Philpott 1991, 35), of a type that may be found across domestic contexts. Romano-British kilns producing specialist 'funerary' pottery have been suggested, for example at Duxford in Cambridgeshire (Anderson *et al.* 2016), and pots occasionally appear to have been altered in some way prior to being used as funerary urns (e.g. perforation or chipping), but for the most part it is likely that 'everyday' pots were selected. However, this is not to say that such vessels held no symbolic value, as argued by Williams (2004), who suggested that as these objects were closely connected to the daily practices of eating and drinking, they represented offerings, much the same as much of the 'domestic' pottery and food remains classified as grave goods (see below, p. 262).

Although pottery vessels are by far the most common type of cinerary urn, there are examples of glass vessels being used, though these remain very rare in rural contexts, no doubt reserved for the wealthiest of individuals, such as the glass urns found within two stone cist burials associated with a villa at Boxmoor House School, Hertfordshire, and the glass cinerary urns from within the early Roman tumuli at Bartlow Hills, Cambridgeshire, all discovered in the nineteenth century (Neal 1976; Gage Rokewode 1842). A more recently discovered example was excavated on the southern slopes of the South Downs at Selhurst Park in West Sussex, where a lead coffin, with the inhumed remains of a juvenile, *c.* 12–17 years, was accompanied by a second-century A.D. glass vessel containing the cremated remains of an adult; a known villa site lay just to the south (Anelay 2010). Other forms of cremation vessel are very occasionally attested in rural contexts, such as a lead container (*ossuarium*) positioned within a stone box on the periphery of a villa at Harnhill in Gloucestershire (Wright 2008), and a similar lead canister interred within a roughly hewn limestone sarcophagus at Wells' Bridge, Barnwood, *c.* 3 km east of Gloucester (Ellis and King 2016; Ellis *et al.* forthcoming). Most examples of *ossuaria* are from urban contexts (Toller 1977, 45–6). Two burials from a cremation cemetery in Dagenham, Essex had fragments of copper-alloy sheet that may have formed parts of vessels or containers, with one of the fragments having burnt human bone attached, though their interpretation as cinerary containers remains uncertain (Biddulph *et al.* 2010).

The distribution of all 2191 urned burials from 'complete' burial records (see p. 206) is shown in FIG. 6.41, against a background of all such records of cremation burial. Although clearly widespread, it indicates that the practice was particularly prevalent in south-east England and in the mostly military sites of the north and west, whereas the situation is more mixed in western parts of the Central Belt, the North-East and the northern part of the East region. For example, urned burials accounted for over 75 per cent of the 637 cremation burials from the East Anglian Chalk landscape, whereas of the 178 cremation burials from the combined Thames, Severn and Avon Vales landscapes, this figure was just 28 per cent. In part this is due to chronological factors. FIGURE 6.42 shows how the practice of burying cremated remains in (mostly) ceramic urns increased from 26 per cent in the late Iron Age to a peak of 64 per cent in the early Roman period, before a decline back to 39 per cent in the later Roman period.

The early Roman peak is well-illustrated by the cemetery at Westhampnett in West Sussex, discussed above; here, just four of the 161 late Iron Age cremation burials were urned (though many had accessory vessels; see below, p. 264), but this increased to 23 of the 31 graves belonging to the early Roman period (Fitzpatrick 1997). Although Westhampnett numerically dominates the overall late Iron Age cremation burial group, even without it there is still a notable increase in the proportion of urned burial into the early Roman period, across the south-east in particular. The apparent decline in urned cremation burial during the late Roman period corresponds with the geographic shift of this now minority rite to the Central Belt, noted above, though other containers such as wooden boxes are still sometimes attested, such as the Heathrow example noted at the start of this chapter. There are also localised exceptions such as in parts of the Upper Thames Valley, where, for instance, just two of the eleven early Roman cremation burials at Gill Mill were urned, compared with at least eight of the twelve late Roman cremation burials from Radley Barrow Hills II.

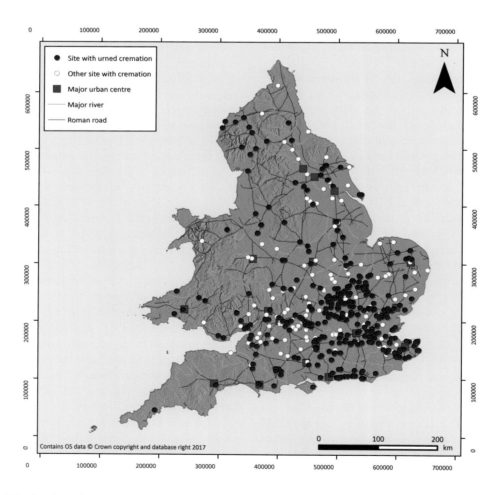

FIG. 6.41. Distribution of all sites with evidence for urned cremation burials

In terms of associated site type, villas stand out as having the highest proportion of urned burials, though with only 48 examples of cremation burials from complete records, the significance of this has to be viewed with a degree of caution (FIG. 6.42). Otherwise, it is clear that the larger population centres – roadside settlements, villages, defended 'small towns' and military *vici* – were more likely to have had cremated remains placed in burial urns than farmsteads or 'isolated' rural burial sites. Aside from military *vici*, this is a similar situation to the use of coffins noted above, and may reflect differences in status and community values.

Most cremation burials, urned or otherwise, were placed directly into an earth-cut grave, although there is evidence that some were contained within stone/tile cists or wooden boxes/caskets. FIGURE 6.43 shows the distribution of all 78 records from the current dataset with evidence for one or more box burials, with most of these being found in parts of Essex, Hertfordshire, Cambridgeshire and Bedfordshire. In some cases funerary urns and grave goods were placed within the wooden casket or chest, though often the cremated remains appear to have been deposited directly on the floor, or possibly within an organic

container. The few examples of box burials further north are all from military *vici*, though there are also a number of stone-lined (cist) cremation graves in this area, mostly notably at Brougham in Cumbria, which has 69 examples made from slabs of sandstone, some appearing to have divisions allowing differential use of internal space within the graves (Cool 2004). Tile cists within cremation graves are more common in southern Britain (Philpott 1991, 9), though few examples have been recorded in the current project, these including a possible example from Langford Rd, Heybridge in Essex (Langton and Holbrook 1997).

Ultimately, the many varied ways in which the inhumed or cremated remains of the deceased could be contained within the grave – coffined or un-coffined, urned or un-urned, and within a box or with a stone or tile lining – were governed by a multitude of different social, cultural and economic factors. The choices may also have been influenced by funerary rituals performed at the graveside, with the likelihood that the open grave would have formed a focal element of display, highlighting certain attributes of the deceased and their family (cf. Pearce 2014a, 235; Weekes 2016, 436). However, by its very nature the number of people

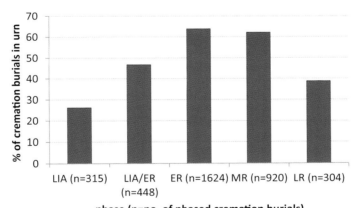

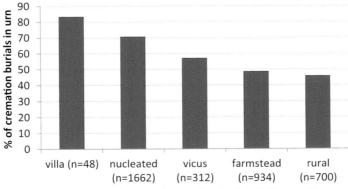

FIG. 6.42. Proportion of urned cremation burials over time and by site type

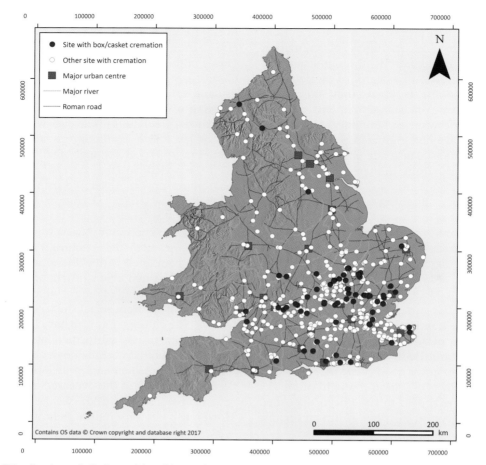

FIG. 6.43. Distribution of all sites with evidence for box/casket cremation burials

who could physically view the grave at any one time would have been restricted and, for cremation burials at least, the pyre itself would probably have formed the most important focus of display (Pearce 2013, 35). Nevertheless, any emphasis on graveside display may also have had an effect upon on the type, quantity and positioning of any associated grave goods.

GRAVE GOODS

As noted above, objects recovered from within and around the grave could have had many different uses and meanings within an extensive suite of funerary rituals. With cremation burials, one of the foremost issues lies in differentiating those items placed upon the funerary pyre with the deceased (pyre goods) from those placed unburnt directly within the grave (grave goods), this difference not always being noted, especially in older excavation reports (Cool 2011, 295; McKinley 2013, 150–1). Pyre goods and other related material (e.g. fittings from funerary biers; Weekes 2008, 152) may well have ended up in the grave, either with the cremated bone or else separated, but these belong to different parts of the mortuary ritual than the laying out of objects around the remains of the

individual within the grave, and may have had very different forms of symbolism. Even within inhumation graves, there could have been a clear symbolic distinction between objects that were worn by the deceased and those that were placed adjacent to them, while there were probably also significant differences between objects placed inside and outside any coffin present (cf. Ekengren 2013, 188).

Artefacts specifically recorded as pyre goods within excavation reports have generally not been included in the current dataset, though, as just highlighted, some of these may have been inadvertently included in the catalogue of objects described as grave goods. In addition, it has not been possible to consider the absolute quantities of grave goods accompanying individual burials, though it is recognised that numbers as well as types of objects interred with the dead can vary significantly, and be an important indicator of relative status within the community. For example at West Thurrock in south Essex, a group of fourteen inhumation and two cremation burials of early Roman date were inserted along a 100 m length of prehistoric ditch; one of the inhumation burials was particularly richly furnished with

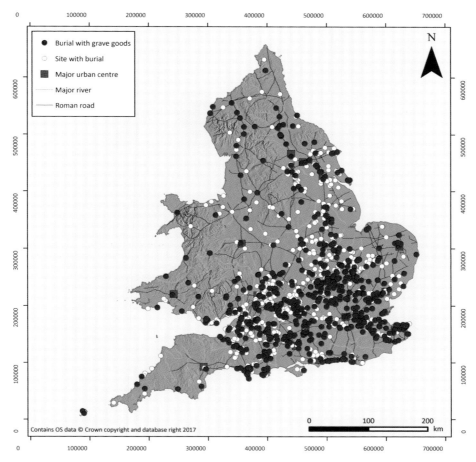

FIG. 6.44. Distribution of all records of burials with grave goods

grave goods, comprising five brooches, four pots, a wooden vessel and a glass unguent vessel (Andrews 2009b).

There has also been no systematic account of the positioning of objects within the graves, though any 'unusual' characteristics were noted, such as with the burial of a young decapitated adult in the roadside settlement at Navenby, Lincolnshire, where the head was placed faced down by the feet and a pottery vessel placed where the head should have been (Allen and Palmer-Brown 2001). Nevertheless, despite the limitations just listed, 'mass' data have been captured on the presence and broad types of object interpreted as grave goods across the whole of the late Iron Age and Romano-British countryside, allowing for general chronological, geographic and contextual trends to be assessed.

FIGURE 6.44 shows the distribution of the 715 'complete' records (i.e. where there is data on all excavated graves) that have evidence for a total of 3773 burials with grave goods. Although well spread across England and Wales, this still leaves approximately half of all complete records and two-thirds of all individual burials having no such evidence. It is clear then, that for the most part the provision of grave goods was only deemed suitable for a minority of individuals, and it can been seen as yet another choice within the overall selective process of physical interment of the deceased. Some of the possible motivations behind the provision of grave goods will be considered below, but first some of the quantifiable relationships between these graves and their broad contextual associations will be assessed.

The proportion of burials containing grave goods was at least partly dictated by geography, as previously highlighted by Philpott (1991). Within the four regions with most burial evidence, for example, the East and South are far more likely to have had furnished burials than the Central Belt and North-East (FIG. 6.45), though as discussed below some of this relates more to chronological factors. The reduced number of burials from regions further north and west have more mixed patterns, with a particularly high proportion (c. 65 per cent) of burials from the north region having grave goods, though this is very much influenced by the major cemetery near the military *vicus* at Brougham in Cumbria, where c. 95 per cent of the 141 burials were provisioned in some way (Cool 2004).

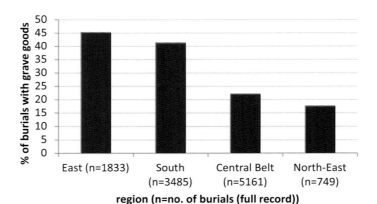

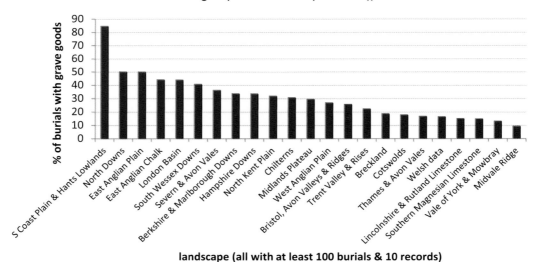

FIG. 6.45. Proportions of burials with grave goods by selected region and landscape zone

The geographic variety can be appreciated more when scaling down to the level of landscape zones. The proportion of furnished graves from all 23 landscapes with at least 100 burials from at least 10 'complete' records is shown in FIG. 6.45. The exceptionally high proportion from the South Coast plain and Hampshire Lowlands (*c.* 85 per cent) can be attributed to the extensive late Iron Age cemetery at Westhampnett, West Sussex, where over 90 per cent of graves were provisioned, usually with a pottery vessel (Fitzpatrick 1997). Elsewhere the proportion of furnished graves ranges from around 50 per cent to under 10 per cent. Most of those in the higher range are located in the East and South regions, though the figure for the Severn and Avon Vales remains relatively high compared with surrounding landscapes, and includes a number of cemeteries where 50 per cent or more of graves were provisioned, such as the small early Roman inhumation cemetery at Hucclecote, Gloucestershire (Thomas *et al.* 2003) and late Roman burials from the extensive cemetery at Wasperton in Warwickshire (Carver *et al.* 2009). Here, in contrast to the burials dated to the fifth century, most of the 23 late Roman graves

had grave goods, including hobnailed shoes (in all but one case seemingly worn by the deceased), bracelets, neck-rings and even two possible lead curse tablets (*ibid.*, 50–1). The site serves to highlight the variation that can be apparent within individual communities in terms of the provision of grave goods.

Many previous studies of Romano-British funerary practice have noted that the use of grave goods decreases over time, albeit mostly using data from urban contexts (e.g. Philpott 1991, 225; Pearce 2013, 141; Weekes 2016, 438). The predominantly rural data collected for the current project indicates the same pattern, from a high point in the early Roman period when almost half of all graves had grave goods, to the late Roman period when this figure lay at just over 20 per cent (FIG. 6.46). There are certainly individual sites that go against this trend, such as Ardleigh in Essex, where six out of the seven late Iron Age/ early Roman cremation burials were provisioned, and the same proportion is found in the seven late Roman inhumation burials (Brown 1999). However, in general, all of the regions follow the same chronological trend, although in the South

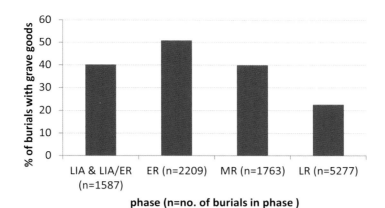

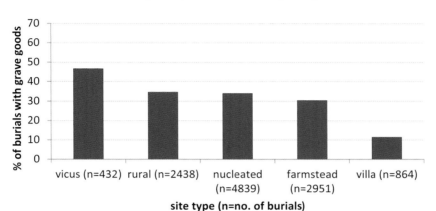

FIG. 6.46. Proportions of burials with grave goods by phase and by site type

the drop is less marked, going from a high of 53 per cent of all graves in the early Roman period, to 36 per cent in the late Roman period; by contrast, in the Central Belt the proportion falls from 43 per cent to 17 per cent across the same time frame. This suggests that the impetus for provisioning graves was always much greater in the South than the Central Belt, and, indeed, in the North-East too, where proportions over time were similar to the Central Belt. In the East there is a substantial fall from almost 60 per cent of burials with grave goods in the early Roman period to just 15 per cent by the third and fourth centuries A.D., though by this time the overall number of burials was relatively low (see above, p. 210).

Another factor that can have some bearing on the levels of grave furnishing is site context (FIG. 6.46). Military *vici* are considerably more likely to have burials with grave goods than other sites, and though this is partly dictated by chronological factors, with a high proportion of burials belonging to the early and mid-Roman periods, it seems probable that cultural factors are also at work. The surprising paucity of burials with grave goods from villas can partly be attributed to the late Roman focus of these sites, and partly, as discussed above (p. 247), to the preponderance of infant

burials, which are less likely to be interred with such items. The proportions of furnished graves from farmsteads, nucleated settlements and 'isolated' rural sites are surprisingly equal, especially given that villages, defended 'small towns' and roadside settlements are generally associated with much higher levels of material culture compared with smaller rural sites (Smith and Fulford 2016, 396). This does, however, correspond with the cemeteries from larger urban centres, where for the most part very few of the burials were accompanied by grave goods (cf. Keegan 2002, 109, table 69; Booth *et al.* 2010, 534, table 8.2).

There is a great deal more variation in terms of the proportion of burials with grave goods between individual sites and even within settlements. The provision of grave goods in the four mid- to late Roman cemeteries at the Romano-British village at Mucking in Essex, for example, ranged from 24 per cent to over 70 per cent, with major differences also noted in the nature of the grave goods between the various burial grounds (Lucy and Evans 2016). In this instance it therefore appears that the social status of the deceased probably influenced the number and type of grave goods. For many other sites, however, the evidence is far more ambiguous, and it could have been that the

TABLE 6.4: SUMMARY OF RECORDED GRAVE GOOD TYPES BY REGION
(n=no. burials; complete records only)

Grave goods	Central Belt	Central West	East	North	North-East	South	South-West	Upland Wales & Marches	Total
Total no. burials with grave goods	**1138**	**46**	**828**	**161**	**131**	**1437**	**21**	**11**	**3773**
animal remains	192	34	94	9	39	222	1	1	592
bead/necklace	33	1	18	31	9	18	1		111
bracelet	81	1	21	2	13	43			161
brooch	94		43	6	5	130	17	1	296
coin	97	4	18	6	7	48	1	2	183
comb	12		1			7			20
finger ring	39		18	1	8	36	4	1	107
flint	7				1	8			16
glass vessel	34	4	37	41	10	57		1	184
hairpin	25		4		3	13			45
hobnails/shoe	307	19	71	54	11	275	3	1	741
knife	35		13	2	1	29			80
lighting	12	2	12		1	2		1	30
metal vessel	9		5	17		17			48
military	1			11	2	9	1		24
mirror	4		7			8	1		20
other personal object	19		7	10	2	17			55
plant remains	7	1	1		4	35			48
pottery vessel	503	25	656	76	45	941	3	2	2251
recreation	2		4			6			12
religious object	1		2	1	1	1			6
security	2		1	1	1	4			9
textile-processing object	11		2	1	1	13			28
toilet object	8		11	1		10			30
tool	12	2	6	1		19	1		41
wood vessel	1		1	3		13			18
writing	4		1		1	1			7

prevailing cultural values of local communities were of greater importance in the adoption of grave goods than the specific social status of the deceased, at least during the later Roman period.

If, in most cases, only a limited number of interments were selected for the provision of grave goods, then the types of objects accompanying the deceased were probably chosen with great care. On present evidence, there does not seem to have been any noticeable differentiation in grave good types between inhumation and cremation burials (cf. Weekes 2016, 438), though some previous studies have noted a degree of correlation between the types of grave good and the age and sex of the deceased individual (e.g. Philpott 1991, 232–3; Keegan 2002; A. Moore 2016). However, this is far from uniform, and osteological analysis of the human remains is always needed to confirm such details (cf. Cool 2011, 300–1). Any determination of ethnicity based upon grave goods has also proven to be very problematic, exemplified by the programme of isotopic analysis on the burials from Lankhills, Winchester, which showed a poor correlation between the origins of individuals and their funerary rituals, including the types of grave good (Booth et al. 2010, 509–16; Booth 2017, 196).

The types of grave good from all of the complete database burial records within the current project are quantified by region in TABLE 6.4, while the proportion of the most common types are shown in FIG. 6.47. There was clearly a wide range of objects that could be interred with the deceased, suggesting that there were no cultural barriers to the selection of different items. However, some types were clearly favoured over others, most notably ceramic vessels associated with eating and drinking. The range of funerary pottery from Romano-British graves has been studied extensively, notably by Biddulph (2002; 2005; 2015), whose analysis has indicated that, for the most part, pottery vessels were specifically selected out of the typical domestic range (e.g. jars, bowls, dishes, platters, beakers, cups and flagons), but

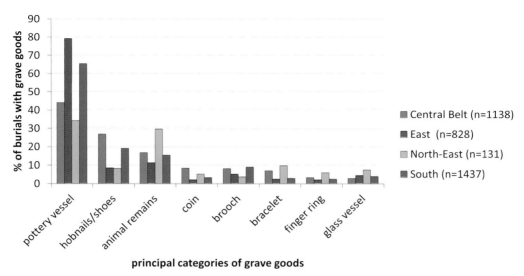

FIG. 6.47. Proportions of principal categories of grave goods by region (n=no. of burials with grave goods)

that different forms may have been chosen according to differing cultural traditions and status, at least in parts of south-east England. Furthermore it was argued that far from representing a universal concern with food and drink for the afterlife, the context of each burial with pottery must be assessed individually, as a range of different meanings and usages could be apparent (Biddulph 2002, 109).

Whatever the specific motivations, pottery was identified as a grave good in almost 80 per cent of furnished graves in the East region and 65 per cent of those in the South (FIG. 6.47). This falls to just 44 and 34 per cent of the Central Belt and North-East burials respectively, in part reflecting the general chronological decline in the provision of ceramics in graves during the later Roman period, discussed below, but also highlighting genuine regional variation in grave-good traditions. In the North-East, the relatively small numbers of burials with grave goods were almost as well furnished with animal remains as with pottery (see discussion of animal remains below, p. 271), while in the Central Belt hobnailed shoes are found in over a quarter of furnished graves. Details of whether these shoes were worn or placed within the grave, and thus whether they can be considered truly as grave goods or clothing, have not been systematically recorded, although clearly most of those in cremation graves – and not demonstrably burnt or mixed with cremated material – were placed. There are also many examples of inhumation burials with hobnailed shoes not found in the area of the feet, such as the grave of an adult male lying within a mausoleum at Binchester military *vicus*, where the shoes may have lain on top of the coffin (Wessex Archaeology 2008b). The conscious decision to place shoes

within the grave, worn or otherwise, has been argued by many (e.g. Philpott 1991, 172–3; van Driel-Murray 1999, 131) to relate to the journey of the deceased into the afterlife, and such provision was almost certainly more extensive than current evidence suggests, given the general lack of survival of most non-hobnailed footware (cf. Booth *et al.* 2010, 498).

Each of the other categories of grave good was represented in less than 10 per cent of furnished graves across the four regions with most burial evidence (FIG. 6.47), though brooches appear relatively common among the few furnished burials included from the South-West. The relative paucity of other grave goods from the East is particularly striking given that this region has particularly high levels of material culture (especially coins and brooches) from settlement contexts (Smith 2016c, 234–7), and suggests that there was not a simple correlation between the type and volume of objects from settlements and those from graves. There were, of course, individual cemeteries that had very different profiles from their regional 'average', with, for example, coins being found within six of the eleven furnished burials from Uffington in Oxfordshire (Miles *et al.* 2003), and in seven of the ten inhumation burials from the cemetery at Roden Downs in West Berkshire (Hood and Walton 1948; Booth 2001). The Uffington examples are recorded as having the coins originally placed within the mouth of the deceased, which is typically interpreted according to the Roman tradition as Charon's fee for the boat journey to the underworld (Cool 2011, 309), though even in cemeteries in Italy the provision of coins in graves is far from a universal burial rite (e.g. found in 15 per cent of graves in a cemetery at Emona; Miškec 2010).

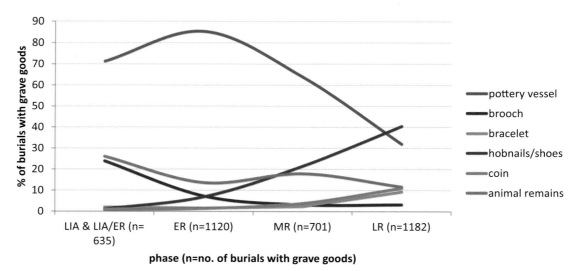

FIG. 6.48. Proportions of principal categories of grave goods by phase

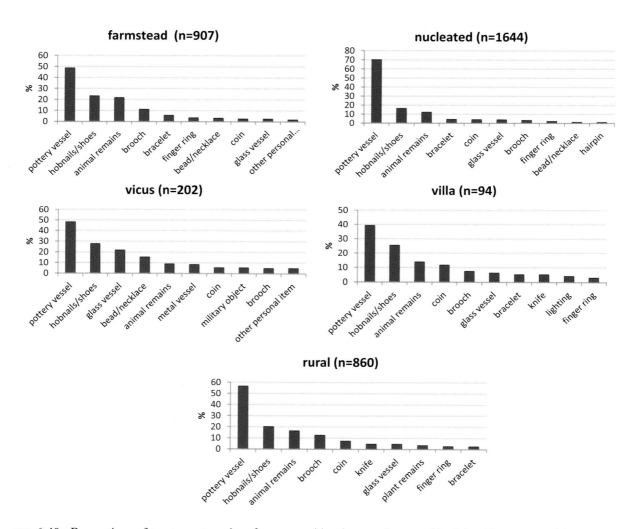

FIG. 6.49. Proportions of top ten categories of grave good by site type (n=no. of burials with grave goods)

Many of the other types of grave good fall within the overall category of 'personal objects', and if grouped together would be found in a significant proportion of furnished burials. These brooches, finger rings, bracelets, necklaces, hairpins, combs and the like each have varying patterns of distribution, though for the most part their numbers are so small as to probably represent the choices of individuals, or at least their grieving relatives, to have personal tokens taken with them to the grave. A study of urban cemeteries at Winchester and Colchester noted that jewellery was more readily associated with the graves of adult women and adolescents aged between 8 and 12 in particular (Gowland 2001, 159). In the case of the latter, the jewellery is suggested as possibly representing dowries for girls whose weddings would never come (Cool 2011, 311; A. Moore 2016, 328).

Brooches are among the more numerous types of personal object with funerary associations, particularly in the South region, where they have been recovered from 9 per cent of furnished graves. However, considering their ubiquity on many domestic sites – they have been recorded on *c.* 35 per cent, 44 per cent and 50 per cent of settlements in, respectively, the South, Central Belt and East regions (Smith *et al.* 2016, 122, 183, 235) – their use as grave goods still appears generally not to have been particularly favoured. As ever, there are plenty of individual exceptions, such as the brooches from eight of the twenty furnished early Roman cremation burials from the farmstead at Stansted Site DFS/SCS in Essex (Havis and Brooks 2004). Other jewellery items too were occasionally quite common grave goods, such as the bracelets found in ten of the thirteen furnished graves in the roadside settlement cemetery at Dunstable, many of these associated with children's burials (Matthews 1981). For the most part, however, jewellery items remain quite scarce as grave goods, although there are changes in use over time.

Although the overall number of furnished burials has been shown to have fallen over time, there are variations in the proportions of different grave good types (FIG. 6.48). While pottery vessels appear almost ubiquitous during the early Roman period, there was a marked decrease in their inclusion over time, being found in just over 30 per cent of furnished graves by the late Roman period; at this point they are overtaken by the presence of hobnailed shoes, although as just noted, not all of these can perhaps be considered as grave goods. The provision of animal remains, which mostly comprise the main meat-providing species (cattle, sheep, pig and domestic fowl), is a little more variable over time but seems to have been at its most prevalent during the late Iron Age and at its least important during the late Roman period (see below, p. 271). Such decline in grave goods associated with eating and drinking has been previously noted by Pearce (2013, 143–4), using data mostly from urban cemeteries, who suggested a shift towards dress items and ornaments, which were used to reinforce social hierarchy. In the rural dataset, there is an increase in the proportion of certain object types associated with display and status during the later Roman period, though the chronological patterns of most 'minor' grave good types appear to reflect more their varying patterns of consumption over time. Brooches, for example, were more prevalent in the late Iron Age, occurring in just under a quarter of furnished graves, this falling to *c.* 3 per cent of such graves by the later Roman period, when such artefacts were far less common. Bracelets and particularly coins were in greater circulation during the later Roman period, which presumably at least partly accounts for their increased use as grave goods, though even by this time both occur in only about 10 per cent of furnished graves. Although there are some differences in these patterns among the main regions with burial evidence, the same broad chronological trajectories are noted within all of them.

Analyses within Volume 1 (Smith *et al.* 2016) indicated that many of the differences observed concerning the volume and type of material culture within excavated rural sites could be attributed to the nature of the settlement. Villas and roadside settlements, for example, generally had quite different frequencies of artefact categories than at most farmsteads. In terms of grave good types, the differences between various classes of site are far less marked, with pottery vessels, hobnailed shoes and animal remains remaining the top three categories in all site types except military *vici*, where glass vessels appear somewhat more common (FIG. 6.49). There are differences in the relative proportions of the major grave-good types, with, for example, grave assemblages from nucleated settlements being more firmly dominated by pottery vessels and animal remains being more prevalent at farmsteads. Furthermore there is greater variation among the minor categories of grave goods, undoubtedly reflecting local traditions and the complexities of individual choice, with, for example, coins being more prolific at villas and brooches being more common at farmsteads and 'isolated' rural sites. Overall, however, the similarities between the different site types are remarkable, suggesting that there were certain widespread accepted notions of what sorts of item were deemed most appropriate to inter with the dead, albeit notions that seemed to have changed over time.

PLANTS IN BURIALS

By Lisa Lodwick

Plants can be preserved in cremation and inhumation burials from a range of sources – as pyre offerings, as pyre fuel, from surrounding vegetation, or as grave goods. Literary evidence indicates that plants were significant aspects of many Roman funerary rituals, including the use of fragrant plants to mask the smell of decay (Graham 2011). Most previous studies of Roman burial have barely mentioned the use of plants within funerary rituals (e.g. Philpott 1991), but following the widespread application of bulk sampling to funerary deposits in rural Roman Britain over recent decades, we can now evaluate the role of plants in funerary activities more systematically. That said, previous reviews of plant remains in Roman Britain have shown relatively limited evidence for the funerary use of plants (Van der Veen *et al.* 2008, 28), perhaps in part because of the lack of attention paid to non-burial deposits such as redeposited pyre debris (cf. McKinley 2000).

To clarify, in the case of cremation burials, plant remains can derive from two scenarios (Kreuz 2000; Rottoli and Castiglioni 2011). First, in *bustum* burials, the cremation process takes place above the grave pit, so that many of the plants burned on the pyre – as fuel or offerings – are deposited directly into this environment. Second, when cremation takes place in a separate area – an *ustrinum* – the deposition of plant remains relies upon the anthropogenic selection of ashes and pyre debris and deposition into the grave, as an urned or unurned burial. Beyond these instances, plants may also derive from subsequent activities taking place within the cemetery, such as funerary or grave-side feasting and festivals (Toynbee 1996, 50–1, 63–4; Williams 2004), with the example of ceramics demonstrating that it is possible for plant remains to be intrusive into the grave from such subsequent activities (Biddulph 2015). In inhumation burials, the absence of a burning event means plant remains are much less likely to be preserved, unless in rare instances of mineralisation. Charcoal derived from the funerary pyre can show key insights into fuel use (Kreuz 2000; Deforce and Haneca 2012), but was the not the focus of data collection in this project. This section reviews the evidence for plants in funerary rituals based on the selection of sites reviewed in the project database.

Cremation burials

Considering the substantial number of excavated late Iron Age and early Roman cremation cemeteries, there are surprisingly few cremation burials with definitive evidence for plants having played a role in funerary activities beyond that of pyre fuel. For instance, at Westhampnett, West Sussex, extensive sampling of pyre sites, pyre features and urns recovered only poorly preserved charred cereal grains, hazelnut shell and sloe-stone fragments, ranging in density from 5 items/L to 0.3 items/L. These plant remains were suggested as representing background noise, pyre offerings and/or cereal chaff used as fuel (Hinton 1997). Similarly, at Kingshill North, Cirencester, an adult cremation grave, radiocarbon dated to A.D. 86–247, produced a single barley grain and many wild taxa, at a density of 6.9 items/L. (W. Smith 2011). Occasionally, a high density of well-preserved plant items can be interpreted as everyday foods being used in offerings. For instance, at Nantwich, Kingsley Fields, Cheshire East, charred pea, pea/bean and barley were recovered from an older female cremation burial. Substantial quantities of large pieces of charcoal indicated the careful selection and deposition of pyre debris into the grave cut, which is most likely linked to the recovery of the plant food offerings (McKinley *et al.* 2012).

Where exotic plant foods occur in cremation burials and associated features, their derivation from background activity, local vegetation or use as fuel can be considered as much less likely, and an interpretation as pyre offerings is most probable. At early Roman Springhead Pepper Hill cemetery, Kent, charred remains of cereals, grapes, lentils, bean, pea and figs were recovered from an unurned cremation burial, and peas and beans were identified from another cremation burial alongside a chicken carcass and burnt pottery fragments. The presence of intact fruits was interpreted as evidence for the offering of unprocessed plant foods on the pyre (Biddulph 2006). Lentil was also recorded in two cremation graves at Ryknield Street, Wall, Staffordshire, alongside sloe and bramble seeds (Gray 2008). At Maryport military *vicus* in Cumbria, charred hazelnut shell and grapes were recovered from late Roman cremation burials, albeit at a very low density – being rare in a 10 L sample (Kirby 2011). Stone-pine nutshell has been recovered from a mid- to late Roman cremation burial at a farmstead at Horcott Quarry, Gloucestershire (Lodwick and Challinor 2017). The most substantial evidence for pyre offerings outside of urban contexts derives from a cremation cemetery associated with a fort at Doncaster in South Yorkshire, which spanned the later first and second centuries A.D. (Miller 2013). One group of cremation burials included charred pine nut, walnut, olive, date, fig, entire grapes and lentils, alongside ceramic lamps and flagons, while another group produced charred apple, date, lentil, hazelnut, pine nut and fig, alongside amphorae and unguentaria. The high quality preservation of such fragile plant foods was interpreted as showing that these were burnt separately, perhaps on an altar, and then added to the cremated bone in burial (*ibid.*).

Beyond pyre offerings, plant remains have also been interpreted as having derived from other aspects of funerary activity. An exceptional deposit of later second century A.D. date at Mucking, Essex, indicates the role of plants in a funerary feast. A charred deposit contained date stones, hazelnut shell and pine kernels, alongside a distinctive ceramic repertoire including platters, tazze, mica-dusted lamps, bag-shaped beakers, as well as nine *sestertii*. The small amount of burnt bone contributed to the preliminary interpretation of this assemblage as the remains of an *epulum* (ritual meal) deposit of ten place settings (Lucy and Evans 2016, 324). At Ryknield Street cemetery, Wall, in Staffordshire, the recovery of lentil, cereals, hazelnut, sloe and blackberry from ovens and enclosure ditches was also interpreted as the remains of funerary feasts (Stevens 2008).

Inhumation burials

The occasional presence of charred plant remains within inhumation burials has sometimes been interpreted as being ritual in origin. A late Iron Age site at Rushey Mead, Leicester, for example, had an inhumation burial that contained a high density (185–499 items/L) of well-preserved charred spelt wheat grains alongside loomweights and pieces of sawn antler, all believed to represent grave goods (Monckton 2001). An early twentieth-century excavation at Hailes, Gloucestershire, also recorded charred wheat grains overlying a late Iron Age inhumation (Clifford 1944), while charred wheat grains were reported from a number of Roman graves at Cranborne Chase (Pitt Rivers 1888). Elsewhere, the presence of charred cereal remains in burials is far more likely to derive from background noise or post-depositional processes, such as at High Wold, Bempton Lane, East Riding of Yorkshire, where just three charred barley grains from a neonate burial were suggested as a possible grave good (Roberts 2009).

Beyond plant foods, exceptional evidence comes from five sites for the inclusion of leaves of box (*Buxus sempervirens*) in inhumation burials, preserved through mineralisation in late Roman package burials (Lodwick 2017b). At Roden Downs, West Berkshire, a late Roman lead-lined coffin containing an elderly woman was lined with box leaves and young stems (Allison 1947), while box leaves appear to have been arranged as a wreath in an undated child burial at Cann, Dorset (Gray 1918), and in an early to mid-second century A.D. child inhumation at Scole, Norfolk,

alongside fruits of deadly nightshade (*Atropa belladonna*) (Fryer and Murphy 2014).

Conclusions

The accumulation of sampled cremation and inhumation burials demonstrate that plant foods and box leaves played a role in funerary rituals. The small number of sites restricts any clear observations of associations between social identity and plants, although it is noted that by far the most diverse range of plant foods recovered from cremation burials is from the military associated cemetery at Doncaster and from the individual at Watling Street, London (Giorgi 1997). Indeed, given the systematic sampling now undertaken of burials and the relatively abundant evidence for plant food offerings in Gaul, Germania Inferior and Italy (Bouby and Marinval 2004; Cooremans 2008; Preiss *et al.* 2005; Rottoli and Castiglioni 2011), it would appear that either the survival of plant foods is very rare in Britain or few people had access to imported plant foods, which would mirror the evidence from settlement contexts (Van der Veen *et al.* 2008). Beyond the evidence from plant macrofossils, chemical analysis has now produced evidence for resinous plant-derived substances from certain Roman burials, such as *Pistacia* resin from an infant inhumation near Arrington, Cambridgeshire (Brettell *et al.* 2014), *Boswellia* resin from burials at Alington Avenue, Dorchester, Dorset, *Pinaceae* resin at Poundbury, Dorchester, Dorset (Brettell *et al.* 2015) and frankincense from the cremation burial within a barrow at Mersea Island, Essex (Betrell *et al.* 2013).

ANIMALS IN BURIALS

By Martyn Allen

Animal bones are often found in association with human burials, although the meaning behind the deposition of animals in graves is rarely clear. Such interments may be made for a variety of reasons, such as the burial of companion animals alongside their 'masters', or animals selected as food offerings. Animals or animal parts may also have been chosen for their symbolic importance, such as deer antler or animal teeth, these possibly having amuletic, magical or even medicinal properties. Our understanding of animal remains in human burials relies on suitable preservation conditions and appropriate excavation and recording strategies. Animal bones may also become mixed with the backfill of a grave making them difficult to distinguish from deliberately interred specimens, although these could of course have important implications for matters such as funerary feasting around the graveside.

There are very few published surveys that have considered the role of animal remains in late Iron Age and Romano-British funerary contexts, one of the exceptions being Worley's (2008) PhD thesis, which showed that the study of animal remains in cremation burials can provide an important strand of evidence for our understanding of wider mortuary rites. Overall, however, zooarchaeological studies tend to ignore animal remains in burial contexts, focusing instead on the wider economic exploitation of animals (see Vol. 2 for in-depth analysis; Allen *et al.* 2017). Philpott's (1991) overview of Romano-British burials provides a catalogue of animal bones in graves where they have been mentioned in excavation reports, but for the most part, there has been far greater attention given to the role of animals placed in so-called 'special' or 'structured' deposits (see Ch. 5), although these can sometimes overlap with human burial contexts (Groot 2008; 2009; Maltby 2010a; 2012; Morris 2011; 2012; 2016; Serjeantson and Morris 2011; Wallace 2014, 126–8).

Despite the various taphonomic issues, animal bones are fairly well represented in late Iron Age to Romano-British funerary contexts, being recorded at almost a quarter of sites in the project database with inhumation burials, and at a third of sites with cremation burials. As noted above (p. 268), the overall pattern of animal remains in human burials appears quite variable over time, though they would seem to have been more prevalent within both cremation and inhumation burials during the late Iron Age/early period than in the late Roman period. For the most part, it is only the partial remains of animals that appear to have been interred with human burials, although complete carcasses are also known, with some examples noted below.

Animal species

Domestic animals are by far the most common category of animal found in human burials (FIG. 6.50). Sheep and chicken are the best represented in terms of their general presence within site burial records, followed by pigs and cattle. Sheep are approximately equally represented in inhumation and cremation burials, though chicken and pig are clearly a more common accompaniment of cremation burial (FIG. 6.51). In contrast, cattle, dog and horse are much better represented in inhumation burials. Cattle and horse bones are generally large and robust and this may bias their recovery from inhumation burials, while chicken bones tend to be more fragmentary. However, pig bones are also fairly robust and there is little reason why post-depositional bias should favour dogs over this species in inhumation burials.

The preference for pig and chicken to accompany cremation burials, and cattle, horse and dog in inhumation burials is likely to reflect differing cultural attitudes. The fact that cattle in general are relatively poorly represented in graves is at odds with their importance in the agricultural economy of Roman Britain. Cattle are generally the most common domestic animal, particularly during the mid- to late Roman period, when an increase in the frequency of cattle remains has been observed in most regions of southern and central England (Allen 2017). The greater importance of pig and chicken in many grave assemblages strongly suggests that certain animals were considered more appropriate for burial (or at least cremation with the deceased), probably in most cases intended as food offerings.

The likelihood that at least some of the differences in animal species representation in burial contexts were culturally motivated is borne out by some evidence for regional variation. In the South region, sheep are the most commonly-recovered animals from burial contexts, found at over 30 per cent of sites, followed closely by pig at 24 per cent. Cattle, chicken and dog are recovered at a similar percentage of burial sites, varying between 13 and 16 per cent. Sheep are also the most commonly encountered species at burial sites in the Central Belt (24 per cent) and in the North-East (22 per cent, though in these regions there is less variation in the relative occurrence of different species. In marked contrast, however, chicken, followed by pig, are the most common species used in burials in the East region, being found at over 30 per cent of sites. Sheep are found at less than 10 per cent of burial sites in this region, a similar proportion to cattle. The preference for chicken and pig in the East region may be accounted for by the relative prominence of cremation burial in this area, and perhaps by connections to the Continent, where these are the commonest species used in funerary ritual in northern Gaul (cf. Lepetz 1996), but the fact that sheep are so poorly represented cannot be readily explained.

Remains of wild animals are comparatively rare occurrences in burials. Deer bones have been recorded by the project in burials at five sites, four of which are late Roman in date, while several others have been previously noted (e.g. Philpott 1991, 198, 252). At two sites, Ridgeway Hill, Dorset (Brown *et al.* 2014), and Rushey Mead, Leicestershire (Pollard 2001), antlers were chosen for interment in inhumation burials. At the latter site, a late Iron Age pit burial comprised an adult male in his 40s or 50s buried with charred cereal grains, pottery and red deer antler that had been sawn and burnt. The authors argued that this

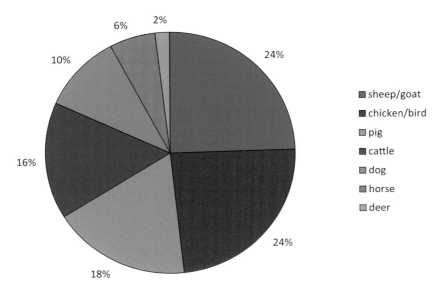

FIG. 6.50. Percentage of burial sites with different animal species present (no. sites = 152) (data include bones of unidentified birds; while wild birds may be represented in some burials, chickens dominate where bird bones have been identified to species)

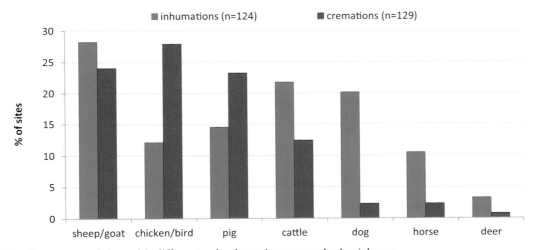

FIG. 6.51. Percentage of sites with different animal species present by burial type

burning was part of the burial rite (*ibid.*). The deliberate sawing and burning of deer antlers has been recorded elsewhere from Romano-British religious contexts (Luff 1999, 218), a practice which has been argued to have enhanced the sensory aspect of certain rituals (Allen 2014, 181).

Animals in cremation burials

While animal bones often form a component of the grave/pyre good assemblage from sites with cremation burials, the overall proportion of burials that include faunal remains is usually comparatively low (FIG. 6.52). Many animal bones may go unnoticed in cremation burials owing to an inability to discriminate between heavily burnt human skeletal remains and those from animals. In addition, much depends on animal remains

being collected from pyres and placed in the final deposits. Some cremation burials include unburnt animal remains indicating that food offerings were not always placed on pyres (pyre goods), but added to the burial afterwards (grave goods), such as at Stansted 99-04 Site MTCP, Essex (Cooke *et al.* 2008) and Westhampnett, West Sussex (Fitzpatrick 1997).

At the late Iron Age cremation cemetery at Westhampnett, West Sussex, animal remains were a relatively common feature, being present in 37 out of a total of 124 burials (Fitzpatrick 1997). Sheep/goat and pig remains were frequently encountered, while cattle was the only other species represented—the vast majority were found burnt. Of seventeen cremations excavated at the late Iron Age–early Roman cemetery at Bancroft,

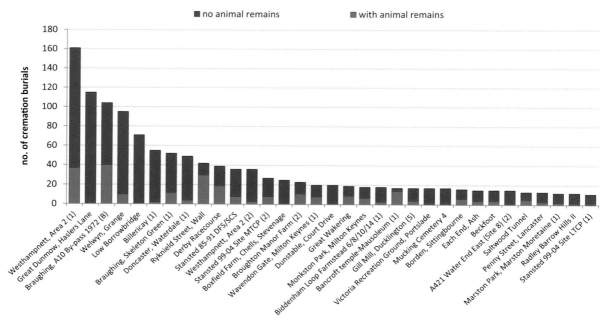

FIG. 6.52. Proportion of burials with animal remains at sites with ten or more cremation burials

Milton Keynes, fourteen included animal bones, comprising the remains of sheep/goat, bird, cattle and pig. Many of these burials were also accompanied by pottery vessels (including bowls, flasks, cups, jars, platters and beakers), brooches, jewellery and other personal items (Williams and Zeepvat 1994). Animal remains were a common accompaniment to cremation burials at two cemeteries excavated along the A10 Puckeridge By-pass at Braughing, Hertfordshire (Partridge 1977). A small early Roman (mid-first–second century A.D.), comparatively richly furnished cremation group included animal bones within each burial, while 40 per cent of a larger, mid-Roman (second–third century A.D.) burial group included remains of cattle, sheep/goat and chicken.

Cremation burials offer the opportunity to examine burial practices in areas of the country where bone survival is generally poor, particularly where acidic soils dominate. At Ryknield Street, Wall, Staffordshire, for instance, the majority of the 42 cremation burials were found to contain animal remains, included as pyre goods (McKinley 2008). The animals chosen for burial were restricted to pig, sheep/goat, cattle and domestic fowl; the remains indicate that complete animals were placed on some pyres, and more than one animal was placed with certain burials.

Military influences are apparent in burial practices at some sites, occasionally reflecting non-native tastes. Within the cemetery attached to the military *vicus* at Brougham, Cumbria, for example, the inclusion of animals in cremation burials represented both food offerings and companion animals (Cool 2004). Remains of cattle, birds, dogs, and pigs were all identified, though perhaps the most notable occurrence was the placement of complete horse carcasses on pyres. In several cases, women had been cremated accompanied by horses and military equipment.

Animals in inhumation burials

At sites with high numbers of inhumation burials, interments that include animal remains tend to be relatively few (FIG. 6.53). Nonetheless, as with cremation burial, there is some evidence that the inclusion of faunal remains in inhumation burials reflects particular cultural attitudes towards animals.

Animals feature prominently in the so-called 'Durotrigan' burials, which dominated in the Dorset region of southern England during the late Iron Age and early Roman period (Harding 2015, 83–7; see above p. 222). Chicken and pig were a particular feature in burials at Alington Avenue (Davies *et al.* 2002), while lambs appear to have been important at Whitcombe (Aitken and Aitken 1990) and Poundbury Farm (Dinwiddy and Bradley 2011). At some sites, articulated remains of horses, dogs and cattle have also been found in association with Durotrigan pit burials, such as at Gussage All Saints (Wainwright 1979), Flagstones (Smith *et al.* 1998) and Woodcuts (Pitt Rivers 1887).

Occasionally, animals were inhumed alongside people, either within the grave or on their own. At Mill Hill, Deal, Kent, a horse was buried in its own grave aligned with late Iron Age inhumation burials (Parfitt 1995), while a shallow pit containing horse skulls was a feature of the late

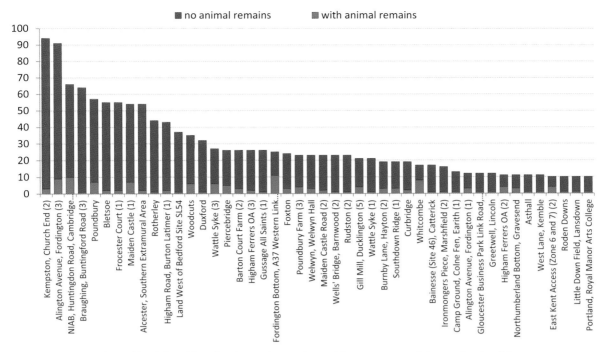

■ no animal remains ■ with animal remains

FIG. 6.53. Proportion of burials with animal remains at sites with ten or more inhumation burials

Roman inhumation cemetery at Vicar's Farm, Cambridge (Lucas 2001, 83; see FIG. 6.30). Within a ditch surrounding a late Roman cemetery by the roadside settlement at Dunstable, Central Bedfordshire, were the articulated remains of four horses and a dog, alongside a number of inhumations (Matthews 1981). Dog skeletons accompanying inhumations have also been identified at Reigate Road, Ewell, Surrey (Cotton 2001), A303 Stonehenge Area C1, Wiltshire (Wessex Archaeology 2002), and Figheldean, Hampshire (Graham and Newman 1993), while at Asthall in Oxfordshire a child inhumation burial was accompanied by two dog feet, thought to represent a dog skin in which the deceased was lain (Booth 1997, 73). The overall evidence certainly suggests that there were close social connections between dogs and people at some sites. At Wattle Syke, West Yorkshire, the late Iron Age burial of a young female was placed next to a 'pillow' of stones lain over a dog burial; this individual was the only burial of this date with accompanying grave goods, marking it out from others in the vicinity (Martin *et al.* 2013). Several female burials dating to the Roman period at Wattle Syke were found with chicken bones placed in their graves, perhaps indicating that gender may have occasionally played a role in the choice of animals selected for burial (*ibid.*).

'Amuletic' items

As well as food offerings and companion animals, some animal remains may have been interred because they were considered important as personal items. At Ridgeway Hill, Dorset, a fossilised shark tooth was found in one inhumation burial (Brown *et al.* 2014). The vertebrae of a small shark and a shark tooth were found to have been buried with two late Iron Age cremation burials at Marston Moretaine, Central Bedfordshire (Hounsell 2003). At Glen Garth, Hayton, East Riding of Yorkshire, an inhumed neonate was found to have been buried with a perforated animal tooth (Halkon *et al.* 2015).

THE UNBURIED DEAD

In his contextual analysis of Romano-British burial practice, Pearce (2013, 25) calculated that the ratio of excavated burials to the predicted original burial population was over forty times lower in rural contexts than in urban areas – in other words, there was a distinct lack of interred rural dead. Even with the mass of rural burial evidence collated for the current project, this conclusion remains the same for the vast majority of England and Wales. Weiss-Krejci (2013) discussed three of the possible scenarios for such 'unburied' dead, comprising 'people who are denied funerals', 'inaccessible corpses', and 'dead bodies on display'. There can surely be little doubt that the first two of these scenarios would have occurred in Roman Britain, perhaps including the exposure and dispersal of neonates, the disposal of criminals or other outcasts of society, and people lost as a result of warfare or other violence, or else drowned within rivers, lakes or the sea. Yet these are not routine events and would only account for a very small fraction of the rural population. The final scenario, that of displaying the dead, has often been seen as the most likely explanation for the relative absence of a buried population during the Iron Age, in the form of excarnation (Whimster 1981, 195). The resultant decaying body would then eventually be dispersed, either through anthropogenic or natural actions, leaving little or no trace in the archaeological record. Pearce (2008; 2013, 25, 145) has suggested that these 'invisible' Iron Age funerary traditions, which may also have included the dispersal of cremated remains or submersion within watery contexts, probably continued into the Roman period, particularly in rural areas, which would explain the relative paucity of burial remains.

Any attempt to try and assess the extent of such 'invisible' rites is, of course, fraught with difficulties, with the presence of disarticulated human bone being one of the very few possible indicators. Such data were systematically collected for the current project, being noted in 462 different excavated sites. The age, skeletal elements

and context vary significantly, though cranial fragments do seem slightly better represented, noted in 30 per cent of sites, with elements from infants/neonates also relatively common. Some remains have been suggested as having been deliberately placed in features, often alongside other objects as part of 'structured deposits', as discussed in Chapter 5 (p. 184), one example being a fragment of human cranium with evidence for trepanation found in a late Iron Age ditch terminus at Eysey Manor, Cricklade, Wiltshire (Pine 2011). Most of the human remains, however, appear on the face of it to be 'random' finds in ditches, pits and other features, inside and outside of settlements, though many of these could still represent more purposeful acts of deposition, perhaps guided by cosmological motivations (cf. Chadwick 2012).

The distribution of sites with evidence for disarticulated human bone is shown on FIG. 6.54. Many of these lie within the well-defined concentration of inhumation burials in the central part of the province and, indeed, some could represent the truncated and dispersed remains of

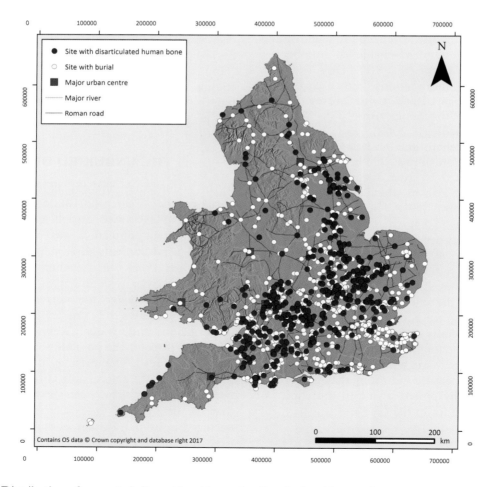

FIG. 6.54. Distribution of excavated sites with evidence for disarticulated human bone

formal burials. The lack of evidence from parts of the south-east is, however, notable, and given the reasonable quantity of animal bone from this area (cf. Smith and Fulford 2016, 399, fig. 12.12), is unlikely to be wholly explained by issues of poor preservation. Instead, it may reflect the particularly strong burial traditions from this region throughout the Roman period, and a resultant reduced tradition of alternative funerary rites like excarnation. By contrast, in the South-West, where the number of sites with formal burial appears quite limited, there are eight sites with evidence for disarticulated human remains, including two fragments of adult jawbone from a long-lived settlement at Lellizzick, Padstow (Wessex Archaeology 2008c), and fragments of burnt human bone suggestive of cremation or deliberate burning, thought likely to be of late Roman date, at Tintagel (Barrowman et al. 2007).

The records of disarticulated bone have been further sub-divided by phase where this has been possible, showing an approximately even distribution between the late Iron Age/early Roman and mid- to late Roman periods, which appears to be at odds with previous indications that such material was less abundant after the Roman conquest (Pearce 2013, 145). Indeed, assuming that this bone is representative of alternative funerary rites, it is suggestive of some degree of continuing practice from the Iron Age right through to at least the end of the Roman period.

Almost half of all sites with disarticulated bone comprised farmsteads (FIG. 6.55), and c. 30 per cent of these showed no evidence for any formal burial. Although the majority of 'isolated' rural sites with disarticulated human remains also had evidence for formal interment, including a number

with cemeteries, there were still many examples of human bones being found apparently isolated within field ditches as well as in other contexts such as caves (cf. Branigan 1992, 15–16). Excavations of a possible late Roman fishing weir close to the confluence of the Rivers Thames and Wey at Shepperton in Surrey encountered some disarticulated human bone from the silts (Bird 1999), providing some hint that rivers may have been used to carry the dead from the land of the living. Further examples of human remains from riverine contexts include those dating to the middle Iron Age found from the River Witham at Fiskerton in Lincolnshire, along with many other apparently deliberately placed deposits (Field and Parker Pearson 2003, 125–7), and Godwin Ridge in the Cambridgeshire Fens, which was suggested as an important site for mortuary rites involving riverine interment during the later Iron Age (Evans 2013b). The extent to which rivers were used to dispose of the dead in the Iron Age and Roman periods is far from certain, and the discovery of much human bone in Roman contexts within the Walbrook Stream in London is now believed to result from natural causes (i.e. erosion of burials lying close to the river bank) rather than a deliberate choice to use the river as a path to the afterlife (Harward et al. 2015).

Overall, the evidence suggests that funerary practices that did not result in the interment of the individual were a consistent feature of the countryside in most parts of Roman Britain, probably continuing on from Iron Age traditions. Just how far these can be viewed as 'mainstream' or 'alternative' practices remains uncertain and probably varied over time and between different communities, much the same as formal burial itself.

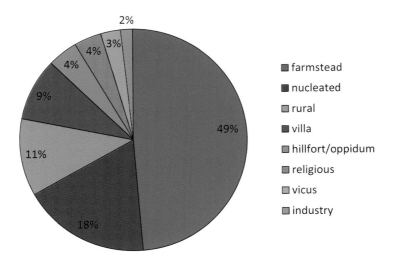

FIG. 6.55. Proportions of total number of sites with disarticulated human bone by site type (n=569)

CONCLUSIONS

If the response to death can be seen as a measure of societies' cultural values, then the sheer diversity and dynamism of funerary rites observed within late Iron Age and Roman Britain suggests a largely fragmented patchwork of communities across the province. The analysis presented in this chapter has focused upon the more archaeologically visible aspects of this funerary practice – notably the burials themselves, rather than the increasing evidence for wider mortuary rituals – and though there is now a substantial dataset of rural burials, there is also a growing awareness that such formal interment was probably not part of the 'normative' funerary process for large sections of the population. There was clearly a variable and complex attitude to the treatment of the dead, and a key question remains as to why certain communities, but not others, adopted formal burial practices. And what were the motivations that led communities who had lived within settlements for many generations to radically change funerary practices and start burying their dead, or at least a sizable number of them, in specialised cemetery zones, and in a variety of ways? Equally, why did some settlements and wider localities appear to have burial in certain phases, with little evidence for interments before and after, even when occupation clearly continued? Rarely before or since have societies undergone such momentous shifts in attitudes to the treatment of the dead as appears to have happened, on a piecemeal basis, across much of England and Wales over the course of the late Iron Age and Roman periods.

Many of the funerary practices seen within the Roman period stemmed from major changes that took place during the late Iron Age, though far from following an inherently conservative path of continuity into the post-conquest period, there continued to be dynamic developments right through to the fourth century and beyond. The number of burials overall certainly increased in the late Iron Age, and continued to do so in most areas into the later first and second centuries A.D., though, except for certain nucleated settlements such as Baldock and Braughing in Hertfordshire, rarely can these be considered as properly representative of the total populations of communities. It is only with the spike in burial numbers in large parts of central Britain, in particular, during the later Roman period that formal interment of the dead can start to be considered as a 'normative' funerary rite, and even then this was mostly restricted to some of the larger complex farmsteads, villas and nucleated settlements, paralleling the situation at larger Roman towns where substantial cemeteries also developed.

The increased use of defined burial zones, or cemeteries, appears to have been one of the key developments leading to the growth in the number of interments, though there was a definite hierarchy in terms of their use. They were present in almost all defended 'small towns', but were increasingly scarce at roadside settlements, villages and complex farmsteads, with very few at most other farmsteads. Here, if there was any burial evidence at all it was usually in the form of dispersed interments integrated within and around the settlement. The greater frequency of cemeteries at certain settlements appears not only linked to the scale of the site, and possibly to an increased population, but also to the levels of likely social and economic interactivity with other settlements, with cemeteries possibly used as part of wider mechanisms employed to enhance social standing. In certain areas the development of cemeteries can be linked to changes in surrounding settlements and landscapes, and perhaps even to shifts in the wider rural socio-economic system. Analysis in Volume 2, for example, highlighted the variable moves to more extensive farming practices in parts of southern and central Britain that were probably heavily dictated by the demands of the state (Allen and Lodwick 2017, 177). It is in these same areas that cemeteries associated with rural settlements were most common, particularly during the later Roman period, when a number of larger 'isolated' rural burial grounds also developed, some suggested here as possible communal cemeteries for surrounding farmsteads and villas. At this time there may have been tighter systems of control or management exerted over the rural population of these areas, especially the agricultural workforce, in order to meet the state's agrarian needs. The increased interment of the dead within larger, more organised cemeteries may represent one facet of this control, with funerary rituals being more carefully managed within certain agricultural estates, and individuals and families perhaps having less say in where their dead were buried.

Despite the shift towards larger cemeteries in certain areas, it is clear that there was still a great deal of variation within the burial rites employed, which was perhaps more a matter of local custom and individual choice. From the late Iron Age onwards there was a mix of cremation and inhumation burial, and though the latter came to dominate all areas by the later Roman period, there remained substantial chronological heterogeneity across different regions and landscapes, and there certainly was not always a linear progression between the two rites. The core area of cremation burial in the south-east had developed from the late Iron Age and is thought at this time to be representative of a distinctive cultural zone. However, by the late Roman period there were large parts of this zone that lack evidence for burial of any type, and there were no obvious traces of cultural cohesiveness remaining, at least not within the burial evidence. Instead the thin scatter of late Roman cremation burials lay mostly across the central part of the province, where they can be viewed as one of a number of funerary variants among the broad concentration of mostly inhumation burials. These variants also include the so called 'deviant' inhumation mortuary rites of decapitated and prone burial, which, despite having similar distribution patterns in central England, often display different characteristics. Decapitated burials are almost exclusively late Roman in date and are mostly found within defined cemeteries, especially those associated with nucleated settlements, whereas prone interments form a minor proportion of inhumation burial from the late Iron Age onwards, and are somewhat more likely to appear outside cemetery contexts. Despite many varied hypotheses, the possible motivations for the act of decapitation remain obscure, and were probably multifarious (but see Ch. 7, p. 283), though there are slightly greater indications to suggest that many of the individuals buried prone were likely to have been among the more marginalised members of society.

Further variation can be seen with the provision of grave containers and grave goods. The use of coffins, cinerary urns, caskets and cists display varied chronological and geographic patterns, probably governed by different social, cultural and economic factors. Both coffins and urns were more common in larger population centres where there may have been a slighter greater social impetus for the display of the dead. For the most part the same cannot be said for the provision of grave goods, which, despite displaying distinct regional and chronological patterning, shows remarkable consistency between most site types, both in the extent of provision and in the nature of the grave goods themselves. The use of grave goods may have been relatively restricted, particularly during the later Roman period, but their general consistency between different settlement types suggests that there may have been some more widely accepted conventions influencing the types of items thought most appropriate to inter with the dead, albeit conventions that changed over time.

Most of the variations in burial ritual just highlighted of course only represent differences relating to the act of interment, and not to the many other aspects of the funerary process, which were probably just as varied. Such heterogeneity undoubtedly reflects differences in individual choice, local customs and relative social status. Just how far the burial evidence informs upon social models within a rural context is difficult to determine. During the early to mid-Roman period, the act of burial itself may have been linked to enhanced social status, while there is also evidence for social differentiation through the type and quantity of grave goods (e.g. late second-century wooden casket cremation burial with a rich assemblage of grave goods found near to a possible villa at Creslow Manor Farm, Bucks; Booth and Champness 2014) and the use of funerary monuments (e.g. huge burial mounds at places like Bartlow Hills, Cambs.; Eckardt et al. 2009). Such features are less common, though not unheard of, during the later Roman period, and differences in status appear primarily to be marked by specific items of dress, such as crossbow brooches (though these remain particularly rare as grave goods in rural contexts), and by the use of lead-lined and stone coffins. Over half of all the 49 burial records with evidence for stone coffins were associated with villas or lay in rural contexts in areas where villas were most frequent, and these were often found either as single examples or in small groups, thereby heightening their 'separateness' from other sections of society. The various status indicators from burials do not by themselves, however, provide conclusive evidence for varying degrees of social inequality over time, and ultimately, the best indication for this is probably through detailed palaeopathological study of the human remains (see Ch. 7).

Variations in burial ritual may also have been at least partly dictated by religious beliefs, though this is very difficult to discern. The scant evidence for Christianity in rural Roman Britain was discussed in Chapter 5, and various studies (e.g. Watts 1991) have attempted to identify Christian communities on the basis of their burial traditions, notably the 'managed' late Roman cemeteries of well-ordered, east–west aligned inhumation burials with few or no grave goods and often with evidence for coffins. These tend to be found in the larger urban centres, with well-known examples at Poundbury outside Dorchester in Dorset (Farwell and Molleson 1993) and Butt Road, Colchester (Crummy et al. 1993), though such 'managed' late Roman east–west cemeteries have also been located at certain 'small towns' such as Queenford Farm, Dorchester-on-Thames in Oxfordshire (Chambers 1987) and Ashton in Northamptonshire (Petts 2003, 144). The problems in assigning a definite Christian label to such cemeteries have been highlighted by Petts (2003, 138–49; 2016, 672–3), who nevertheless suggested that they may be related to an increasing Christianisation of the imperial civil service, allowing the church to exert control over certain activities, including the organisation of burial grounds, although that was not to say that all who were buried in such cemeteries were necessarily Christian. Whether or not these 'managed' east–west cemeteries were associated with increasing church/state control, it is clear that the vast majority of the buried population in the late Roman countryside of Britain did not lie in such contexts, with grave orientation, location and the provision of burial containers and grave goods continuing to be markedly varied, both on an intra- and inter-site basis.

It was just noted how the relative 'cultural cohesiveness' of the south-east England cremation burial zone appears to have been eroded over time, and to a certain extent this can be seen in other areas such as Dorset, where the late Iron Age/early Roman Durotrigan types of burial had mostly disappeared by the later Roman period. Overall, it does seem that the decline of such distinct regional burial traditions corresponded with an increased integration of the various funerary rituals, primarily within the broad band of burial running through central England from the south-west to the north-east. But what this might mean in terms of cultural or ideological cohesiveness is another matter. Even within individual sites, deceased individuals could be cremated or inhumed, be laid out supine, flexed or prone, be decapitated, be buried with or without grave goods and with or without a container of varying form. This is, of course, assuming that they would have been afforded formal burial at all. Even during the late Roman period, when burials numbers in the central zone were at their height, it is very unlikely that all members of all communities would have been interred, though analysis of human skeletal remains can provide a vital insight into those who were.

CHAPTER 7

THE RURAL POPULATION

By Anna Rohnbogner

INTRODUCTION

The human skeleton offers a unique and multi-faceted resource that provides direct evidence for lived experiences in the past. Through use of the skeleton as physical evidence of morbidity (the disease rate within a population) and mortality (the frequency of death within a population) of the people who lived and died in Roman Britain, observations on social and biological relations can be made (see Larsen 1997; Gowland and Knüsel 2006; Gowland 2007). Palaeopathology, the study of trauma and disease in the past, allows us to explore a range of intrinsic and extrinsic factors that would have shaped life in the countryside of Roman Britain. Insights can be wide-ranging and include environmental factors, diet, migration and economy, climate, physical activity and access to medical treatment (Roberts and Manchester 2010).

Exposure to biocultural stress and infectious disease depends on the paucity of environmental factors, such as hygiene, sanitation or climate. The effects of both stress and disease further affect every individual differently depending on age, sex, genetic make-up, nutritional status and immune response. Risk of infection is greatly influenced by the synergistic relationship of poverty, poor diet and depressed immune function. In Roman Britain, exposure to new pathogens would have occurred through travel for migration and trade, or anthropogenic changes to the environment. Previous research on some of the urban settlements of Roman Britain has highlighted polluted, stressful and unsanitary living conditions. Osteologically, these can be observed via high levels of blood-borne diseases, enamel defects, respiratory and infectious diseases, and particularly the presence of tuberculosis in both adults and children (Roberts and Cox 2003, 118–19; Lewis 2011). We also see the first cases of leprosy reported in Britain at Roman Dorchester in Dorset, and Cirencester in Gloucestershire (Reader 1974; Manchester and Roberts 1986). The popular picture of Roman towns as centres of civilised public life, with running water, baths and toilets, has thus been challenged by the osteological data. Questions are being raised about our current perceptions of urban Romano-British life, but, as yet, we have little perspective on rural Roman

Britons, and whether they experienced the same, or altogether different, stresses.

Rural life should in theory boast a number of health benefits, with access to a balanced diet, generous living space and clean air, all while offering respite from noise, pollution and overcrowding. If Roman Britain was indeed marked by social inequality, the beneficial aspects of country living would have been reserved for a privileged, high-status minority. Current theories paint a picture of demanding physical labour, and perhaps oppressive living and working conditions for the majority of rural Roman Britons (Pitts and Griffin 2012; Redfern *et al.* 2015; Rohnbogner and Lewis 2016a). Indeed, a range of contemporary issues would have exerted pressure on the rural population. The men, women and children of the countryside may have been forced to shoulder the heavy burden of taxation and supply in an aggressive market economy (Miles 1982; Whittaker and Garnsey 1997; Scheidel and von Reden 2002). Events such as the fourth-century A.D. famine in the Rhineland must have impacted on Romano-British producers and suppliers (Fulford 2004, 316; Allen and Lodwick 2017). Wellbeing in rural contexts would have been shaped by short-term weather fluctuations, regionally specific land use, prosperity of individual settlements, and the psychological aspects of being ruled, conquered or oppressed (McCarthy 2013). Additionally, the socially stratified nature of rural Romano-British society, particularly during the fourth and early fifth centuries A.D., will have shaped resource distribution and consequently wellbeing (Miles 1982; Whittaker and Garnsey 1997; McCarthy 2013; Redfern *et al.* 2015). We also have to question how much autonomy the rural population truly enjoyed and it has been suggested that people were living in 'enslaved' conditions as *coloni* or bonded tenants under the auspices of a landlord or villa owner (Jones 1982; Whittaker and Garnsey 1997; Esmonde Cleary 2004).

Children offer a unique window into past population health. Growing bodies are more sensitive to adverse environmental conditions and therefore provide a more accurate and precise form of evidence (Mensforth *et al.* 1978; Lewis 2007). It may be argued that the palaeopathological signatures of the children of Roman Britain are a very good example of Mattingly's (2006; 2010) arguments on unequal power relations governing life in the province. Non-adult palaeopathology has produced interesting new findings, including biased access to resources and inequality between urban and rural societies, evidence for internal rural–urban migration, and the impact of working lives on the young (Rohnbogner and Lewis 2016a).

THE BIOARCHAEOLOGICAL LITERATURE

The comprehensive discussion of health in Britain through the ages by Roberts and Cox (2003) marks one of the greatest efforts to gain insight into ill-health and everyday life of the Romano-British population of both town and country. The Roman-period sample used in their study comprised an impressive 5716 individuals from 52 urban and rural sites. It is worth pointing out that the palaeopathological data were mainly derived from reports dating from the 1970s to 1990s. This in turn carries with it certain limitations, as fewer osteological methods were available to researchers and there was generally less of a focus on the recovery and recording of all human remains during excavations. With palaeopathological analysis being a relatively new and emerging field, a lack of detail in older skeletal reports often becomes apparent and would have had an impact on the quality of data available to Roberts and Cox. Nevertheless, their tracing of patterns of disease in the British past is a significant contribution to the palaeopathological literature and provides us with a much-needed starting point for exploring health in the rural Romano-British population. Higher levels of ill-health were apparent in the urban sample from their study; however, rural sites were not devoid of pathology. Zoonotic diseases, respiratory ailments, congenital and neoplastic disease were observed in the rural cohort (Roberts and Cox 2003). In Dorset, shortcomings in wellbeing from the Iron Age through to the end of the Roman period were observed. The later period yielded shorter female stature, increased male mortality, dietary change and a rise in infectious and metabolic diseases (Redfern 2008; Redfern et al. 2010; 2012; Redfern and DeWitte 2011a; 2011b). A 2015 study by Redfern and colleagues on ill-health in the same region demonstrated that rural populations were less stressed than their urban peers, with better dental health and fewer incidences of metabolic disease. However, pressure on the rural population was apparent as higher mortality risk and lower survivorship. Pitts and Griffin (2012) provided a national overview of health and inequality in late Roman Britain. Their inter-cemetery approach examined palaeopathology and burial practices across Roman England by incorporating both published and unpublished data from major urban, nucleated and smaller rural settlements. The overall verdict was compromised health in the countryside, which correlated with greater inequality in grave furnishings. Ultimately, the study demonstrated that settlement type and connectivity to road systems conditioned health in late Roman rural sites.

Diet and access to resources are sensitive indicators of social stratification (Twiss 2012). It has been suggested that status differences between urban and rural communities resulted in greater dietary variability in the towns, as demonstrated by archaeobotany (Van der Veen et al. 2008), and isotope analysis (Richards et al. 1998; Redfern et al. 2010; Cheung et al. 2012; Müldner 2013), with more animal products and refined carbohydrates being consumed in higher status and urbanised settlements (King 1984; 1999a; 2001; Maltby 1989b; Van der Veen 2007a; 2008; Van der Veen et al. 2007; 2008; Cummings 2009; Nehlich et al. 2011; Müldner 2013). Apart from informing on dietary variation, isotopic studies on cemetery populations of York (Leach et al. 2009; Müldner et al. 2011), London (Montgomery et al. 2010), and Gloucester (Chenery et al. 2009), have provided insights on migration to major urban centres. In contrast, many authors have lamented that our current knowledge on migration to and from rural Romano-British settlements is limited (Redfern and Roberts 2005; Eckardt 2010a; Gowland and Redfern 2010; Eckardt et al. 2014; Redfern et al. 2015; Rohnbogner and Lewis 2016a).

The peoples inhabiting the countryside of Roman Britain would have found employment in a variety of occupations. Although it is fair to claim that the vast majority was involved in agricultural labour, a considerable number of individuals would also have worked in extraction and construction industries, manufacture and as craftsmen or traders (McCarthy 2013; Smith 2017). Roberts and Cox (2003) found that trauma, along with spinal and joint degeneration, were relatively high in Roman Britain. This would of course be a general observation for inhabitants of both town and country. However, compared to earlier periods, the data demonstrate that the bones and joints of Roman Britons were under increasing stress and exposed to wear and tear through physical activity.

There is some evidence for access to medical care on rural settlements. Embryotomy, intended to save the mother's life during complications at birth, was identified at Yewden villa in Hambleden, Buckinghamshire (Mays et al. 2014). In addition, a case of amputation at the humerus was reported from Alington Avenue in Dorchester, Dorset (Waldron 1989), although this may have been accidental. Although examples are few, these cases highlight that surgery was practised on rural sites, allowing us to hypothesise that other means and methods of medicinal aid were also available.

A BRIEF NOTE ON PALAEOPATHOLOGY AND BURIAL PRACTICE

Attitudes towards the dead may be a reflection of their status, perception and treatment in life. The osteological record can be a helpful window into exploring whether physiological characteristics of the deceased influenced motivations behind any unusual burial rites. Prone burials, decapitated burials and furnished graves often spark debate about the social processes, for example marginalisation or hierarchies, which may have prompted this type of 'othering' in death (Milella et al. 2015). The reader is directed to Chapter 6 for a discussion of burial archaeology in rural Roman Britain, and an appraisal of the phasing and distribution of grave goods, prone and decapitated burials.

Prone burials carry the notion of a 'deviant' or somewhat less respectful rite, often found in close association with unusual features within or outside the formal cemetery area (Philpott 1991, 72; Aspöck 2008; see Ch. 6, p. 229). The practice tends to occur in adults from rural contexts (Boylston et al. 2000; Roberts and Cox 2003, 153), but was also identified in children with a disability, sometimes buried in elaborate graves (Farwell and Molleson 1993, 265; Southwell-Wright 2014). Taylor (2008, 110) suggested that prone burial in Roman Britain ensured security of the body, perhaps enabling a safer resting place or transition to the afterlife. The decision-making behind prone burial may involve complex processes, reflecting the unique characteristics of the deceased or even the grieving (Philpott 1991, 74; Strück 2000; Parker Pearson 2003, 54; also see Crerar 2016). Decapitated burials present additional challenges and may have occurred more frequently than the burial data currently suggest. Preservation often prevents us from differentiating peri- from post-mortem decapitation, or intentional removal and displacement of the head altogether (Milella et al. 2015). It is not possible to distinguish between decapitations that occurred during life and subsequently caused death, or immediately after death, as bone will react to trauma in the same way (see Boylston et al. 2000 for an appraisal of decapitation burials at Kempston, Bedford, and Anderson 2001 for two decapitated adult males from Towcester, Northamptonshire). Apart from some notable exceptions (see Wells 1982 for a discussion of six decapitated individuals from Roman Cirencester), it is generally accepted that decapitation in Romano-British inhumation burials rarely resulted from execution or warfare and was undertaken post-mortem (Boylston et al. 2000; for a contrary view see Tucker 2015). Rather than reserving it for capital punishment, or branding it as a rite for individuals on the fringes of society, a ritualistic aspect is assigned to these burials (Philpott 1991). Great media attention has been devoted to the unusual assemblage of the 46 'headless Romans' at Driffield Terrace, York, most notably due to isotopic and genome analyses that have revealed both local and non-local origins of the skeletons (Müldner et al. 2011; Martiniano et al. 2016). Some of these young and middle adult men suffered peri-mortem decapitation, meaning their injuries were sustained at the time of death, which allows us to speculate whether they were executed. Owing to their palaeopathology including ante- and peri-mortem trauma, and lesions indicative of early childhood stress, the group has been interpreted as possible gladiators or soldiers (Martiniano et al. 2016). Although we do not expect to find such sensational correlations between burial practice and skeletal lesions, it is of interest to evaluate the palaeopathology of the men, women and children afforded the same rite across rural Roman Britain.

INTERPRETATIVE FRAMEWORKS IN BIOARCHAEOLOGY

The study of skeletal remains as a means of measuring population health and demographics in Roman Britain has received considerable criticism (see Parkin 1992), and as Scheidel (2012) has advised, no standard Roman demographic pattern exists. Naturally, as with any data in archaeology, there is bias in the study of human remains. How representative a sample may be is influenced by a range of factors, such as preservation, burial practices and excavation strategies, all of which have a profound effect on the skeletal data available to osteoarchaeologists (Gowland 2001; Pinhasi and Bourbou 2008). The buried population from rural Roman Britain is in itself a biased sample, as much of the rural population would not have received a formal burial in the first instance (see Ch. 6). Other factors include the fluctuating rates of infant burials in both urban and rural Romano-British cemeteries, migration influencing the demographic and palaeopathological make-up within a cemetery, and burial grounds that may have served a number of satellite settlements (see a number of studies concerned with the topic, i.e. Philpott 1991, 101; Scott 1991, 120; Pearce 1999; 2013; Esmonde Cleary 2000; Redfern and Roberts 2005; Wileman 2005; Moore 2009; Gowland and Redfern 2010; Gowland et al. 2014; Millett and Gowland 2015; Redfern et al. 2015). Lastly, an osteological sample is never a true reflection of the people that lived and worked within any given temporal or spatial locale. People move, and chronic diseases yield skeletal changes, whereas acute illnesses may not act on the body for long enough to prompt skeletal responses prior to death. Essentially, a population with plenty of pathology reflects a cohort that was strong enough to live through chronic and acute health insults. However, this very same cohort is susceptible to ill-health in the first instance (Wood *et al.* 1992; Goodman 1993).

MATERIALS AND METHODS

THE SAMPLE

Only inhumation burials were included in the analysis, with age, sex and pathological data extracted from reports post-dating 1995. A cut-off date of the mid-1990s was initially sought as older reports often fail to present the human skeletal remains in appropriate detail. Sites with fewer than ten reported inhumation burials were excluded to enable faster recording of a bigger sample. Without late Iron Age burials, the selection process initially yielded a total of 135 sites with 5043 inhumations. Three regional case studies were selected, based on the biggest samples, notably the Central Belt, South and East (TABLE 7.1; FIG. 7.1). Regions were kept deliberately broad to provide meaningful sample sizes for an overview of bioarchaeological data. Patchy skeletal recording, preservation, and, unfortunately in some cases missing or reburied skeletal remains, meant that a total of 322 individuals were recorded for the East, 741 for the South, and 1654 for the Central Belt (TABLE 7.2). A breakdown of individual sites for each region, including a site bibliography, is provided electronically in the online data archive (Allen *et al.* 2016).

Farmsteads are discussed as one settlement type. However, as outlined in Volume 1 by Allen and Smith (2016), we see differences in material culture and aspects of environmental data between complex, enclosed and unenclosed farmsteads. Combining all farmsteads into one settlement type enables analysis of more meaningful sample sizes. Otherwise as many as ten different settlement categories are introduced per region, with some types of farmstead represented by a single site and as few as ten inhumation burials only. The supplementary online tables provide a breakdown of sites, detailing the different types of farmsteads included in each region.

AGE-AT-DEATH

Ages-at-death were summarised into age groups. Non-adults (0–17 years) were assigned to one of seven age groups, corresponding with developmental stages: perinate (<40 weeks gestation), 0.0–1.0 years, 1.1–2.5 years, 2.6–6.5 years, 6.6–10.5 years, 10.6–14.5 years and 14.6–17.0 years. For adults, the three broad age groups of 18–25 (young adult), 26–45 (middle adult) and >46 years (old adult) correspond with Pitts and Griffin's (2012) approach. Broad age groups were introduced to account for the difficulty associated with ageing fully developed skeletons. The age categories used are not an assumption of cultural ages or social transitions in the life course of Roman Britons, but reflect a biological construct that allows cross-comparison of the data and consolidates methodological discrepancies apparent in reports.

SEX

Sex was recorded in three categories, male (M) including probable and possible male, female (F) for probable and possible female, and unidentified/ambiguous (ua). Sex was not recorded in the children, as the accuracy of current sexing methods for immature skeletons remains debated (Sutter 2003; Lewis 2007).

THE PALAEOPATHOLOGY

Haematopoietic/blood-borne diseases

Pitting and porosity on the outer table of the skull (porotic hyperostosis, PH) and orbital roof (cribra orbitalia, CO), inform on blood-borne disorders. Non-adults display lesions more frequently due to a reduced capacity of sustaining higher red blood cell production. In adults, both CO and PH are therefore indicative of iron deficiency and megaloblastic anaemia in childhood. A largely plant-based diet, diarrhoeal disease and pathogen exposure, intestinal parasites and maladaptive breastfeeding and weaning practices may all contribute to blood-borne diseases, and in turn the formation of orbital and cranial lesions (Walker *et al.* 2009; Oxenham and Cavill 2010).

TABLE 7.1: POST-1995 SITES AND BURIALS BY REGION (EXCLUDING LATE IRON AGE SITES)

Region	Sites n	Inhumations n
Central Belt	67	2533
South	32	1420
East	15	687
North-East	14	333
Central West	2	29
North	1	20
South-West	1	21
Total	**132**	**5043**

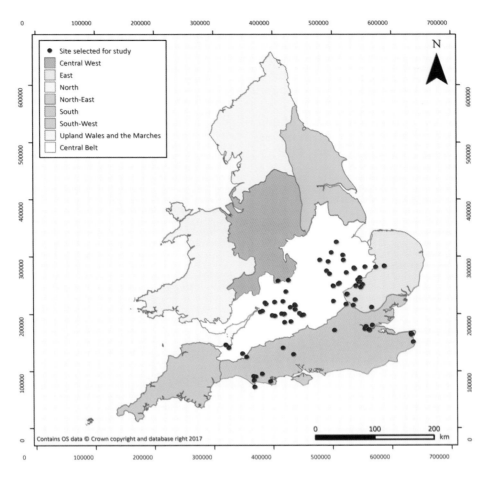

FIG. 7.1.   Distribution of study sites across the regions

TABLE 7.2: SETTLEMENT TYPES AND PHASING OF THE REGIONAL CASE STUDIES
% of total inhumations within each region; *cemetery site without associated information on settlement type

Site type	Central Belt Inh/sites n	%	South Inh/sites n	%	East Inh/sites n	%	Total Inh/sites n	%
Defended small town	16/1	0.9					16/1	
Farmstead	425/21	25.7	156/8	21.1	142/5	44.1	723/34	26.6
Funerary*	761/9	46.0	256/8	34.5	37/1	11.5	1054/18	38.8
Industry	11/1	0.7					11/1	0.4
Port	25/1	1.5					25/1	0.9
Religious			58/1	7.8			58/1	2.1
Roadside	221/11	13.4	90/4	12.1	112/5	34.8	423/20	15.6
Villa	161/3	9.7	67/1	9.0	24/1	7.5	252/5	9.3
Village	34/1	2.1	114/4	15.4	7/1	2.2	155/6	5.7
Total	**1654/48**		**741/26**		**322/13**		**2717/87**	
Phase								
LIA/ER			131/5	17.7	52/2	16.1	183/8	6.7
ER	55/5	3.3	92/7	12.4	22/1	6.8	169/13	6.2
E–MR			53/3	7.2			53/3	2.0
MR	73/5	4.4	53/3	7.2	52/1	16.1	178/9	6.6
M–LR	163/5	9.9	104/4	14.0	11/1	3.4	278/10	10.2
LR	1312/34	79.3	308/12	41.6	106/6	32.9	1726/52	63.5
Roman	51/4	3.1			79/3	24.5	130/7	4.8
Total	**1654/53**		**741/34**		**322/14**		**2717/102**	

Enamel hypoplasia

Enamel hypoplasia (EH) is a defect resulting in linear bands or pits in tooth crown enamel. Defects occur most commonly on the crowns of permanent incisors or canines, formed up until the age of around four years old. As such, EH provide a permanent retrospective record of non-specific early childhood stress through fever and malnutrition (Goodman and Rose 1991; Reid and Dean 2000; King *et al.* 2005).

Infections of non-specific origin

Endocranial lesions (EL) on the inner table of the skull and sub-periosteal new bone formation (SPNBF) anywhere on the skeleton are indicative of inflammatory responses. Lesions may arise secondary to infection, trauma, circulatory disorders, joint disease, haematological disease, skeletal dysplasia, and metabolic or neoplastic disease. Infection can affect the cortex of the bone (osteitis) and medullary cavity (osteomyelitis). Responses may be prompted by fungal infections, parasites, viruses and the staphylococcus, streptococcus and pneumococcus bacilli (Nelson 1990; Goodman and Martin 2002; Roberts and Manchester 2010, 168).

Leprosy, tuberculosis and respiratory disease

Infection with the human strains of *Mycobacterium leprae* results in the chronic disease of leprosy. Together with a depressed immune status, the infection may lead to lepromatous leprosy, its most debilitating form, affecting nerve endings, the skin, nose and bones. The infection may take 5–20 years to fully develop, and although only mildly infectious, the disease is spread via infected droplets of the mouth or nose (Ortner 2003). Because of the stigma associated with the disease, sufferers are often ostracised by their community. Finding lepromatous leprosy therefore informs on frequent and close contact with other carriers of the disease (Roberts 2002; 2011). Tuberculosis (TB) is a chronic infectious disease of the lungs, skin, lymph nodes, intestines, and in rare cases bones and joints (Turgut 2001). There are several strains within the TB complex and *Mycobacterium tuberculosis*, the bacterial genus specific to humans, is spread via exhaled airborne droplets, sputum or human waste, or can be transmitted from an infected mother to the foetus. Ingesting infected animal product will spread the animal equivalent bacillus, *Mycobacterium bovis*, from bovines to humans (Stead 2000). TB affects bones and joints following a secondary infection or depressed immune status after an initial primary infection earlier in life. TB is therefore a valuable indicator

for ongoing transmission and infection within a population (Santos and Roberts 2001; Roberts and Buikstra 2003).

Sinusitis of the maxillary sinuses, and new bone formation on the pleural surface of the ribs inform on respiratory ailments, such as bronchitis. Their presence informs on living environment and lifestyle, such as prolonged periods spent in low-quality air (Pfeiffer 1984; 1991; Boocock *et al.* 1995; Roberts *et al.* 1998a; 1998b).

Vitamin D deficiency (rickets and osteomalacia)

The prohormone vitamin D is vital to the formation and maintenance of healthy bone structure. It is absorbed via the intestine or formed by the skin's dermal cells in response to ultraviolet light (Brickley and Ives 2006). Rachitic children exhibit unmineralised bone that is porous in appearance and, when mechanical forces are applied, is prone to characteristic bending deformities (Thacher *et al.* 2006). Rickets can occur on a spectrum of vitamin D and calcium deficiency, therefore its presence not only points towards a lack of exposure to sunlight and associated cultural practices, but also calcium deficiency, maternal health, and child feeding practices (Kutluk *et al.* 2002; Pettifor 2004). Healed rickets can be observed in adults as the characteristic bowing of long bones; however, vitamin D deficiency at any age can be recognised as osteomalacia. Adult bone may soften as a result of calcium deficiency, either induced through dietary practices, malabsorption, loss from the body in kidney or intestinal disease, or indeed several pregnancies in close succession (Brickley and Ives 2008; Veselka *et al.* 2013).

Vitamin C deficiency (scurvy)

Vitamin C aids in the body's defence from infections, and is crucial for collagen formation and maintenance of body tissues. Collagen and osteoid synthesis is compromised in scorbutic individuals who also suffer from a reduced resistance to infections (Pimentel 2003). Skeletal growth is slowed down and sub-periosteal haematomas occur at weakened walls of small blood vessels, yielding characteristic porous patches of new bone, particularly in the skull (Brickley and Ives 2006). The skeletons of infants and young children are more likely to exhibit scorbutic lesions due to rapid growth (Brickley and Ives 2008; Stark 2014). Scurvy provides direct evidence for lack of fresh fruits and vegetables. In archaeological populations, widespread scurvy allows for exploration of dietary limitations shaped by resource stress, social hierarchies, ecology and behaviour (Crandall 2014; Halcrow *et al.* 2014).

Osteoporosis

Thinning of cortical bone and loss of trabecular structure is recognised as osteoporosis, resulting in lower bone density. Osteoporotic bone is more susceptible to fractures and characterised by a reduction of bone mass (Roberts and Manchester 2010). Osteoporosis is regarded as a chronic disease of advanced age, but the condition can also occur secondary to another underlying pathology, such as vitamin D deficiency in adults. The incidence of osteoporosis depends on age, lack of calcium in the diet, and various lifestyle factors, such as immobility, prolonged lactation and high number of pregnancies (Brickley 2002; Curate 2014).

Trauma

Dislocation, alteration to the shape of the bone, partial and complete breaks are distinct forms of skeletal injury observable in the osteological record (Ortner 2003). Most common are fractures in the upper limbs, hands and feet sustained by falls, rib fractures as a result of a direct blow to the thorax, and fractures of the lower limbs due to considerable force (Roberts and Manchester 2010). At times, the cause and severity of the injury can be discerned, allowing insight into activity patterns of past populations. For example, clay shovellers' fractures of the spinous process at the seventh cervical or first thoracic vertebra are caused by the repetitive strain of prolonged shovelling of heavy loads or similar motions that put a repeated strain on the back (Dellestable and Gaucher 1998; Jordana et al. 2006). Vertebrae may also separate into two parts at the lamina, the weakest point that connects the vertebral body and arch. The condition, termed spondylolysis, most commonly affects the fifth lumbar vertebra. Repetitive strain induced by lifting and bending at the site prompts stress fractures, which eventually lead to separation of the element (Waldron 1991a; Mays 2007). Osteochondritis dissecans (OCD), primarily a condition witnessed in young males, is a circular defect in the joint surface, commonly at the knee. Trauma causes disruption in the blood supply to the affected area, where affected bone tissue may die and separate from the joint area (Schenk and Goodnight 1996; Šlaus et al. 2010).

Joint degeneration

Degenerative joint disease is an expected occurrence of older age, where the strain of a physically active life will result in wear and tear or arthritic changes. However, if pronounced degeneration occurs in adolescents and young adults, it is an indicator of prolonged and demanding physical activity. Non-inflammatory joint disease can take on a variety of pathological processes owing to advancing age, strain or injury to a joint. Joint disease is primarily arthritic, occurring in the spine, upper or lower limbs, and extraspinal elements (Roberts and Manchester 2010). Osteoarthritis includes eburnation, osteophyte formation, pitting, deformation of the joint surface and new bone formation (Jurmain and Kilgore 1995; Weiss and Jurmain 2007). However, spinal joint disease does not always incur osteoarthritic changes but is also evident as degenerative disc disease (spondylosis), spinal osteophytosis and Schmorl's nodes among others (Burt et al. 2013, ch. 4). Degenerative disc disease is characterised by osteophytic lipping, and pitting and porosity of the vertebral body surface, sometimes accompanied by new bone formation (Rogers 2000). Osteophytosis at the margins of the vertebral bodies is a witness to the degeneration of the intervertebral joint capsule due to recurrent stress. Eventually, growth of bone is stimulated to compensate, and in extreme cases may lead to ankylosis of vertebral segments (Waldron 1991b). Schmorl's nodes indicate degeneration of the intervertebral discs. Disc herniation leads to the characteristic depressions on the superior or inferior aspect of vertebral bodies. Excessive loading of the spine in adolescence is thought to contribute to the formation of these lesions (Plomp et al. 2012).

Dental disease

Micro-organisms accumulate in the oral cavity. These may form plaque and mineralise on teeth as calculus (Hillson 1996). Diets high in protein and/or carbohydrates yield an alkaline environment that favours calculus deposition (Roberts and Manchester 2010, 71). Caries is an age-progressive infectious disease with localised demineralisation of dental hard tissues (Larsen 1997, 65). Streptococcus mutans and sobrinus in the oral cavity metabolise sugars and starches, creating an acidic environment leading to dental decay (Gussy et al. 2006). Ante-mortem tooth loss is caused by inflammation secondary to caries, periodontal disease, periapical lesions/abscesses and poor oral hygiene (Roberts and Manchester 2010, 74). Dental abscesses may form by bacterial infection of the pulp cavity secondary to caries. The inflammation produces pus and subsequent drainage, forming a cavity in the alveolar bone (Hillson 1996, 285–6). Abscesses are identified via radiographs or once they perforated the alveolar bone, meaning they may often go unnoticed in archaeological bone (Roberts and Manchester 2010, 70).

METHODS OF ANALYSIS

Morbidity and mortality were analysed as regional case studies. ArcGIS was used to visualise spatial distributions. Pathology was presented as crude prevalence rates by age and sex, as a percentage of the number of individuals affected in each region, site type and age category. The impact of periods of early childhood stress on survivorship was assessed by comparing non-adult and adult crude prevalence rates of enamel hypoplasia and cribra orbitalia.

The use of statistical testing will allow us to distinguish whether differences in lesion frequency between groups arose by chance, or, in the case of statistical significance, an underlying reason other than random chance. Differences between groups were tested using a non-parametric Chi-square test (X^2) at n-1 degrees of freedom (d.f.). The test was used sparingly, only when percentages suggested very different results. The number of degrees of freedom differs according to the number of independent values that are free to vary in a statistical calculation, such as, for example, the number of distinctive age groups or settlement classifications used. The confidence interval was set at 99.5 per cent (p<0.005) to avoid false positives. At 99.5 per cent confidence level, we only allow for a 0.05 per cent chance of uncertainty associated with the samples analysed.

RESULTS

General trends and statistical distributions in age-at-death, sex and palaeopathology are presented below, with brief descriptions of differences between groups. Crude prevalence rates are presented, as the nature of the skeletal data prevents more in-depth analysis. Some considerations on the biological data with respect to burial archaeology are described.

The East provided the smallest regional sample with 322 individuals and five different site types (TABLE 7.2). Funerary sites, villas and villages are represented by single examples, these being the village excavated at RAF Lakenheath, Caudle Head Mere, Suffolk, Chignal St James villa, Essex, and the cemetery site at Duxford, Cambridgeshire. The remaining sites comprise five farmsteads and five roadside settlements. A total of 741 individuals were reported for the South region. Only a single villa and religious site are represented, these comprising Bucknowle villa in Dorset, and Springhead Sanctuary complex in Kent. Since a large component of the infants and perinates from the Springhead Sanctuary complex were redeposited burials, their numbers were corrected for in the analysis and discussion. The Central Belt

region provided the largest sample with 1654 individuals. The associated sites types include a single defended small town at Alcester, Warwickshire, a nucleated 'village' at Gill Mill, Ducklington, Oxfordshire, an industry/villa site at Priors Hall, Weldon, Northamptonshire, and an inland port at Camp Ground, Colne Fen, Earith in Cambridgeshire. For the Central Belt, no individual data for cribra orbitalia, porotic hyperostosis, enamel hypoplasia and dental disease were available for the large Cannington cemetery in Somerset. The 359 adults from this funerary site were therefore excluded from analysis for the respective lesions. Raw data for tables and graphs are available in supplementary tables on the online resource. In non-adults, infants were excluded from analysis for dental disease due to eruption timings of the deciduous dentition. Perinates were excluded from analysis for crude prevalence rates of enamel hypoplasia.

The total number of adults for the provincial rural sample is 1759. The results are presented for the adult population of the three regions pooled together, before presenting regional patterns. This will allow comparison of crude lesion frequencies with the contemporary fourth-century A.D. urban cemetery at Lankhills, Winchester, and preceding populations, dating from the early Iron Age to the early Roman period. The contemporary urban sample comprises 220 adults from Lankhills, Winchester (Clough and Boyle 2010). Roberts and Cox (2003) provide regional data for 398 sexed Iron Age adults from Britain. The comparative samples carry with them a number of limitations. The Iron Age sample is collated from skeletal reports dating as far back as the 1940s which, as discussed above, had an impact on the quality of data available. In contrast, the cemetery at Lankhills was excavated between 2000 and 2005 and all palaeopathological analysis was undertaken following the latest and most comprehensive methods, generating very accurate and precise data.

PALAEOPATHOLOGY OVERVIEW – THE ADULTS

The contemporary comparative sample comprises 220 adults from the urban cemetery at Lankhills, Winchester (Clough and Boyle 2010). Roberts and Cox (2003) provide regional data for 398 sexed Iron Age adults from Britain. The total number of adults for the provincial rural sample is 1759.

No cases of metabolic disease, porotic hyperostosis, osteomyelitis or sinusitis were reported in the Iron Age adults. For the remainder of lesions, we see a general increase in frequencies between the Iron Age and rural Romano-British populations. In the Iron Age, the crude prevalence rates for cribra orbitalia (4.8 per cent, n=19), endocranial lesions (0.5 per cent, n=2) and rib periostitis (0.3 per cent, n=1) are only marginally lower than in the rural population of Roman date. Osteitis occurred at a slightly elevated rate in the earlier period (0.5 per cent, n=2), compared to 0.3 per cent (n=5) in the Roman period. Enamel hypoplasia was reported at 10.9 per cent (n=153), compared to only 1.8 per cent (n=7) in the Iron Age, which is statistically significant (X^2=32.67, p<0.001, d.f.=1). New bone formation affected significantly fewer Iron Age adults (1.0 per cent, n=4) compared with rural Roman Britons (7.1 per cent, n=125; X^2=22.17, p<0.001, d.f.=1). To date, one case of tuberculosis from Iron Age Tarrant Hinton has been reported, and marks the oldest find of the disease in the British Isles (0.3 per cent, n=1). Trauma also affected significantly more adults in the Roman period at 12.1 per cent (n=212) compared to the Iron Age (6.5 per cent, n=26; X^2=10.36, p<0.001, d.f.=1) (TABLE 7.3; FIG. 7.2).

Over time, the crude prevalence of Schmorl's nodes statistically increased from 1.5 per cent in the Iron Age to 8.1 per cent in rural Romano-British populations (X^2=22.70, p<0.001, d.f.=1). Spondylolysis affected a similar proportion of adults in both periods (rural 1.5 per cent, n=27/Iron Age 1.3 per cent, n=5). Overall, joint degeneration in the shoulder, hip and knee significantly increased from the Iron Age to affect 5.9 per cent (n=103), 7.0 per cent (n=124) and 4.9 per cent (n=87) of the rural adults respectively (shoulder: X^2=18.78, p<0.001, d.f.=1; hip: X^2=21.91, p<0.001, d.f.=1; knee: X^2=16.87,

p<0.001, d.f.=1). The pattern was reversed for spinal joint disease, although at a less striking rate. Vertebral degeneration affected 32.7 per cent (n=130) of adults during the Iron Age, compared to 25.6 per cent (n=450) in the Romano-British countryside (TABLE 7.3).

A distinct difference was also found in the distribution of dental disease. Calculus affected 4.1 per cent (n=17) of adults in the Iron Age, compared to 25.4 per cent (n=356) of rural Roman Britons (X^2=121.27, p<0.001, d.f.=1). Significantly lower rates of caries (rural 26.9 per cent, n=377/Iron Age 4.8 per cent, n=16; X^2=95.95, p<0.001, d.f.=1) and ante-mortem tooth loss (rural 20.4 per cent, n=286/Iron Age 3.5 per cent, n=14; X^2=64.21, p<0.001, d.f.=1) were also found in the earlier period. Abscesses and/or periapical lesions were reported at similar frequencies of 6.8 per cent (n=27) in the Iron Age and 10.4 per cent (n=145) in the rural population of Roman Britain (TABLE 7.3).

No cases of porotic hyperostosis, endocranial lesions, osteitis, tuberculosis or vitamin C deficiency were reported in the adult population buried at Lankhills, Winchester. These lesions occurred in the countryside, albeit at low frequencies of 1.6 per cent (n=23) for porotic hyperostosis, 0.9 per cent (n=16) for endocranial lesions, 0.3 per cent (n=5) for osteitis, 1.0 per cent (n=18) for tuberculosis and 0.3 per cent for possible and probable vitamin C deficiency. Cribra orbitalia affected proportionately more adults at Lankhills (11.8 per cent, n=26/rural 6.6 per cent, n=92). Enamel hypoplasia was statistically more frequent among the urban adults at 22.7 per cent (n=50/rural 10.9 per cent, n=153; X^2=23.57,

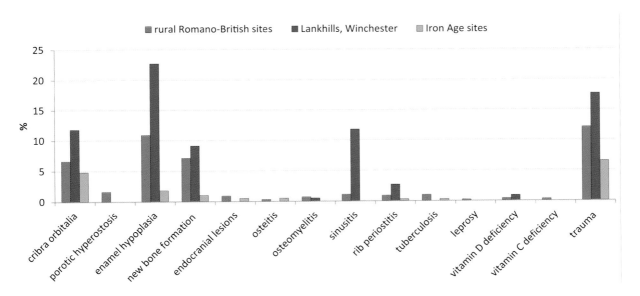

FIG. 7.2. Crude prevalence rates of pathology in the adult individuals from rural Roman Britain (all sites pooled), Lankhills, Winchester (Clough and Boyle 2010) and Iron Age Britain (Roberts and Cox 2003)

TABLE 7.3: THE ADULTS: POOLED PALAEOPATHOLOGY AND COMPARATIVE DATA
% of total number of adults observed; *n=6 secondary sinusitis due to dental abscess

	Rural Roman Britain			Lankhills, Winchester			Iron Age (British data pooled)		
	observed	affected	%	observed	affected	%	observed	affected	%
Cribra orbitalia	1400	92	6.6	220	26	11.8	398	19	4.8
Porotic hyperostosis	1400	23	1.6	220	0	0	398	0	0
Enamel hypoplasia	1400	153	10.9	220	50	22.7	398	7	1.8
Sub-periosteal new bone formation	1759	125	7.1	220	20	9.1	398	4	1.0
Endocranial lesions	1759	16	0.9	220	0	0	398	2	0.5
Osteitis	1759	5	0.3	220	0	0	398	2	0.5
Osteomyelitis	1759	13	0.7	220	1	0.5	398	0	0
Sinusitis	1759	19/25*	1.1	220	26	11.8	398	0	0
Rib periostitis	1759	16	0.9	220	6	2.7	398	1	0.3
Tuberculosis	1759	18	1.0	220	0	0	398	1	0.3
Vitamin D deficiency	1759	7	0.4	220	2	0.9	398	0	0
Vitamin C deficiency	1759	5	0.3	220	0	0	398	0	0
Trauma	1759	212	12.1	220	39	17.7	398	26	6.5
Joint stress									
Schmorl's nodes	1759	143	8.1	220	37	16.8	398	6	1.5
Spondylolysis	1759	27	1.5	220	5	2.3	398	5	1.3
Joint-specific rates of degeneration									
Shoulder	1759	103	5.9	220	8	3.6	398	2	0.5
Spine	1759	450	25.6	220	48	21.8	398	130	32.7
Hip	1759	124	7.0	220	3	1.4	398	4	1.0
Knee	1759	87	4.9	220	3	1.4	398	2	0.5
Dental disease									
Calculus	1400	356	25.4	220	63	28.6	398	17	4.1
Caries	1400	377	26.9	220	83	37.7	398	16	4.8
AMTL	1400	286	20.4	220	83	37.7	398	14	3.5
Abscess/PAL	1400	145	10.4	220	27	12.3	398	27	6.8

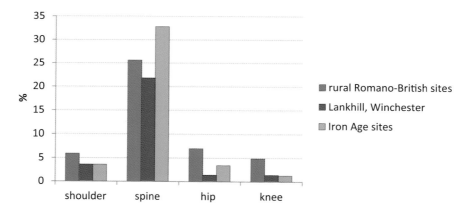

FIG. 7.3. Location-specific crude prevalence rates of joint degeneration in the adult individuals from rural Roman Britain (all sites pooled), Lankhills, Winchester (Clough and Boyle 2010) and Iron Age Britain (Roberts and Cox 2003)

p<0.001, d.f.=1). A marginally higher rate of subperiosteal new bone formation was apparent at Winchester (9.1 per cent, n=20), although osteomyelitis was proportionately more frequent in the rural sample (0.7 per cent, n=13). Sinusitis was reported significantly less often in the countryside at 1.1 per cent (n=19), compared to Winchester with 11.8 per cent (n=26) of adults affected (X^2=97.94, p<0.001, d.f.=1). Rates of periosteal new bone on the pleural aspect of ribs were also higher in the town (2.7 per cent, n=6). Vitamin D deficiency was equally low in the countryside (0.4 per cent, n=7) and at Lankhills (0.9 per cent, n=2) (TABLE 7.3; FIG. 7.2).

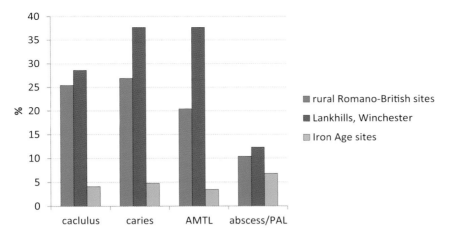

FIG. 7.4. Crude prevalence rates of dental disease in the adult individuals from rural Roman Britain (all sites pooled), Lankhills, Winchester (Clough and Boyle 2010) and Iron Age Britain (Roberts and Cox 2003)

Spondylolysis as a marker of joint stress affected the adults of the countryside and at Winchester at similar frequencies of 1.5 per cent (n=27) and 2.3 per cent (n=5) respectively. Although spinal joint stress apparent as Schmorl's nodes affected significantly more adults in the Lankhills cemetery (16.8 per cent, n=37/rural 8.1 per cent, n=143; X^2=17.20, p<0.001, d.f.=1), degeneration of the spine was reported in proportionately more adults from rural sites (25.6 per cent, n=450). Degeneration of the shoulder joint was less frequent at Roman Winchester 3.6 per cent, n=8) and statistically fewer adult individuals at the site were reported with degenerative joint disease at the hip and knee (1.4 per cent, n=3; hip: X^2=15.34, p<0.001, d.f.=1; knee: X^2=9.15, p<0.005, d.f.=1) (TABLE 7.3; FIG. 7.3).

Calculus and abscesses/periapical lesions were reported at similar frequencies between the urban and rural populations, at rates of 28.6 per cent (n=63)/25.4 per cent (n=356) and 12.3 per cent (n=27)/10.4 per cent (n=145) respectively. Caries and ante-mortem tooth loss were significantly more prevalent in the urban sample at 37.7 per cent (n=83), compared to 26.9 per cent (n=377) and 20.4 per cent (n=286) in the rural population (caries: X^2=10.74, p<0.005, d.f.=1; AMTL: X^2=31.96, p<0.001, d.f.=1) (TABLE 7.3; FIG. 7.4).

REGIONAL ANALYSIS

Age-at-death in the East

The East region includes 238 adults (73.9 per cent) and 70 non-adults (24.5 per cent). A total of 48.9 per cent (n=128) of adults died between 25 and 46 years old. Old adults were most frequently reported from complex and unclassified farmsteads (23.9 per cent, n=34), and the village at RAF Lakenheath, Caudle Head Mere, Suffolk (42.9 per cent, n=3), which is statistically significant (X^2=36.89, d.f.=4, p<0.001). Significantly more

middle adults stem from the funerary site at Duxford, Cambridgeshire, and Chignal St James villa in Essex (X^2=34.11, d.f.=4, p<0.001). Old adults are significantly more prevalent in the early Roman phase (n=9, 40.9 per cent; X^2=36.50, d.f.=5, p<0.001) (FIGS 7.5–7.6).

Perinates account for 27.8 per cent (n=22) of non-adult burials, with a further 31.6 per cent infants (n=25). Significantly more perinates were reported from roadside settlements (21.4 per cent, n=24; X^2=47.62, d.f.=4, p<0.001) (FIG. 7.5). Phasing of the perinate and infant cohort did not produce any useful results as the majority of individuals (96.0 per cent, n=24) fell within the 'Roman' phase (FIG. 7.6). Overall, fewer individuals died after infancy; however, we see slight increases in mortality rates at 2.6–6.5 years old to 2.5 per cent (n=8) and at 14.6–17.0 years old to 2.2 per cent (n=7).

Age-at-death in the South

The South region includes 388 adults (52.4 per cent) and 351 non-adults (47.4 per cent). The majority of adults died between 26 and 45 years old (53.6 per cent, n=173). Only a single young adult (1.7 per cent) was reported from the religious site at Springhead, Kent. High numbers of middle adults are apparent from complex, enclosed, unenclosed and unclassified farmsteads (26.9 per cent, n=42) and funerary sites (36.7 per cent, 94), although differences are not statistically significant (FIG. 7.7). The early Roman phase is characterised by low numbers of 18–25 year olds (3.3 per cent, n=3), particularly in comparison to young adult burials from the late Iron Age/early Roman phase (12.2 per cent, n=16) (FIG 7.8).

High numbers of infant burials were reported from Springhead Sanctuary complex (74.1 per cent, n=43), but the site was excluded from statistical analysis due to redeposition of burials.

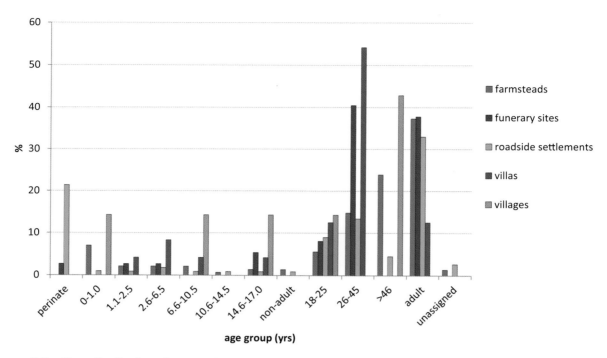

FIG. 7.5.   East: distribution of ages-at-death by site type

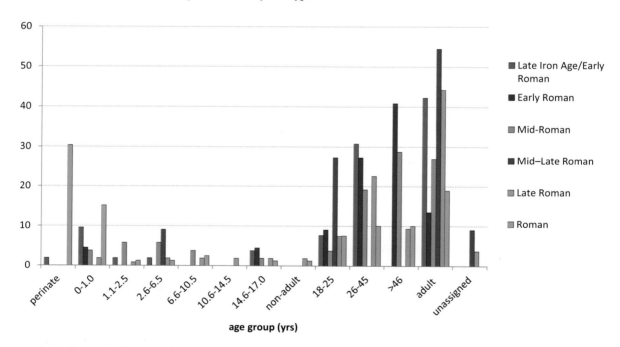

FIG. 7.6.   East: distribution of ages-at-death by phase

Perinate burials are proportionately low (10.2 per cent, n=30), compared to 57.0 per cent (n=167) infant burials, which were particularly high at Bucknowle Roman villa, Dorset (88.1 per cent, n=59). Funerary sites were devoid of perinate burials and held significantly fewer infant burials (5.9 per cent, n=15; X^2=226.99, p<0.001, d.f.=4) (FIG. 7.7). There are few perinate (1.6 per cent, n=5) and infant burials (9.4 per cent, n=5) of late Roman date, with significantly more infants reported from early to mid-Roman (66.0 per cent,

n=35) and mid- to late Roman contexts (58.7 per cent, n=61; X^2=161.48, p<0.001, d.f.=5) (FIG. 7.8). Mortality rates decline from infancy, with a slight increase in 2.6–6.5 years olds (3.6 per cent, n=27) and 10.6–14.5 year olds (3.0 per cent, n=22).

Age-at-death in the Central Belt

The Central Belt region includes 1133 adults (68.5 per cent) and 509 non-adults (30.8 per cent). The majority of adults died between 26 and 45 years

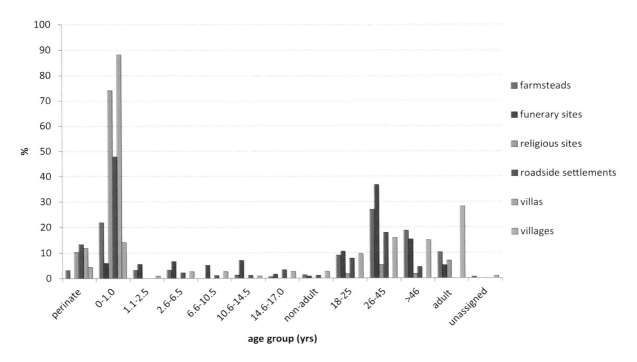

FIG. 7.7. South: distribution of ages-at-death by site type

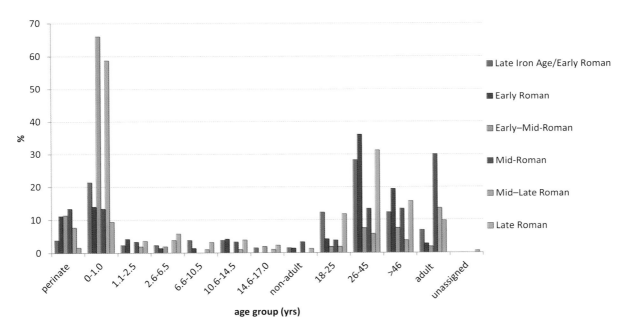

FIG. 7.8. South: distribution of ages-at-death by phase (corrected for redeposited burials from religious site)

old (23.8 per cent, n=394). A significantly lower number of middle adults was reported from villas (10.6 per cent, n=17; X^2=28.44, p<0.001, d.f.=6) (FIG. 7.9). The highest proportion of old adults stems from the industry/villa site at Priors Hall, Weldon, Northamptonshire (27.3 per cent, n=3). At the nucleated village at Gill Mill, Ducklington, Oxfordshire, young adult mortality was highest at 14.7 per cent (n=5). Since both these settlement types are represented by a single site each, we have to bear in mind small sample sizes.

Perinates (21.8 per cent, n=111) and infants (32.8 per cent, n=167) account for the majority of non-adult burials reported. Significantly lower rates of perinates were reported from complex and unclassified farmsteads (4.0 per cent, n=17), and funerary sites (2.9 per cent, n=22; X^2=120.15, p<0.001, d.f.=7). No perinates were reported at the industry/villa site at Priors Hall, whereas 40.0 per cent (n=10) of the individuals reported from the inland port at Camp Ground, Colne Fen in Cambridgeshire, were perinates. Statistically fewer

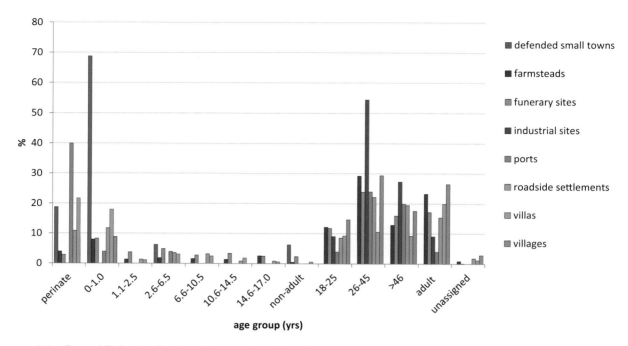

FIG. 7.9. Central Belt: distribution of ages-at-death by site type

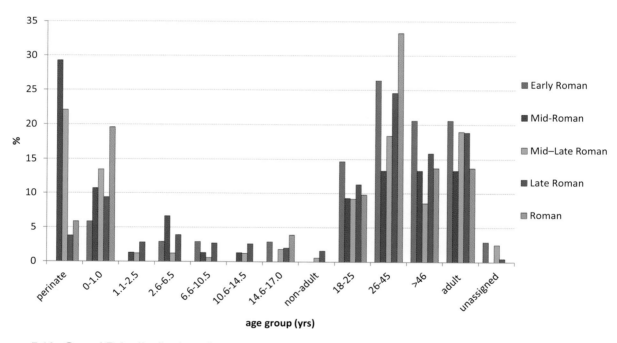

FIG. 7.10. Central Belt: distribution of ages-at-death by phase

perinate burials were of early (n=0) and late Roman date (3.8 per cent, n=50; X^2=139.64, p<0.001, d.f.=3). A significant proportion of burials at the only defended small town (Alcester) are infants (68.8 per cent, n=11; X^2=76.60, p<0.001, d.f.=7). Phasing of infant burials is uninformative owing to a large component in the dated 'Roman' group (19.6 per cent, n=10) (FIGS 7.9 and 7.10). In the non-adults, mortality rates decline after infancy, although there is a slight increase at 2.6–6.5 years old (3.6 per cent, n=60).

Sex distribution in the East

A total of 151 (63.4 per cent) of the 238 adults were sexed, with a slightly higher proportion of males (34.9 per cent, n=83) than females (28.6 per cent, n=68). Similar distributions are apparent at complex and unclassified farmsteads (male 32.7 per cent, n=38/female 30.2 per cent, n=35) and roadside settlements (male 25.4 per cent, n=17/female: 23.9 per cent, n=16) (FIG. 7.11). Twice as many males (50.0 per cent, n=16) were reported from the Duxford funerary

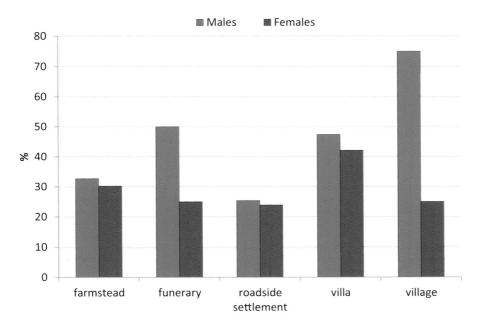

FIG. 7.11. East: adult sex distribution by site type

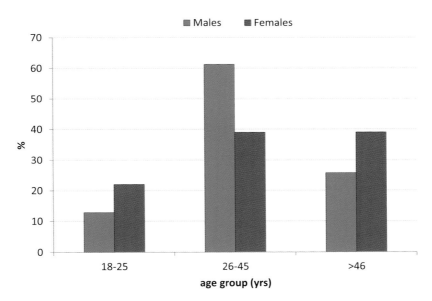

FIG. 7.12. East: sex distribution in the adults

site than females (25.0 per cent, n=8), which is a result of small sample sizes. The same issue applied to the only village site of the region, at RAF Lakenheath, Caudle Head Mere, in Suffolk, where 75.0 per cent (n=3) of the sample were reported as male, compared to only one female (FIG 7.11). More females were reported aged 18–25 years old (22.0 per cent, n=13) and over 46 years old (39.0 per cent, n=23) than males (FIG. 7.12). The majority of males died at 26–45 years old (61.3 per cent, n=38), whereas 39.0 per cent (n=23) of females fall into the 26–45 and >46 year age groups.

Sex distribution in the South

A total of 79.1 per cent (n=307) of adults were sexed, and more males (42.3 per cent, n=164) reported than females (36.9 per cent, n=143). This is also reflected by settlement type, although males (45.1 per cent, n=78) and females (43.9 per cent, n=76) were reported at similar frequencies at funerary sites (FIG. 7.13). Almost twice as many males (33.3 per cent, n=9) were from roadside settlements than females (18.5 per cent, n=5) but sample sizes are small. The same issue applies to the high rate of males (55.6 per cent, n=5) compared to females (11.1 per cent, n=1) at the

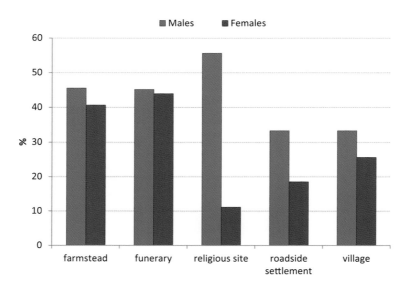

FIG. 7.13.   South: adult sex distribution by site type

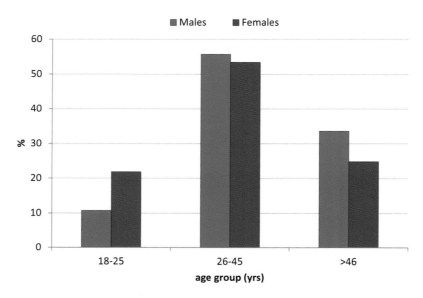

FIG. 7.14.   South: sex distribution in the adults

only religious site at Springhead Sanctuary complex in Kent. Proportionately more young adult females were present (21.8 per cent, n=29/young adult males: 10.7 per cent, n=16), and males were more frequently reported in the old adult age group (33.6 per cent, n=50/old adult females: 24.8 per cent, n=33) (FIG. 7.14).

Sex distribution in the Central Belt

A total of 886 (78.2 per cent) of the 1133 reported adults were sexed. Males and females were reported at similar frequencies (male: 39.3 per cent, n=445/female: 38.9 per cent, n=441). More young adult females were reported (25.5 per cent, n=92), compared to 17.2 per cent of young adult males (n=67). Proportionately more males were reported for the middle (55.7 per cent, n=83/female: 53.4 per cent, n=71) and old adult age

groups (33.6 per cent, n=50/female: 24.8 per cent, n=33) (FIG. 7.15). No adults were reported at the only defended small town of the region, Alcester, Warwickshire. Females outnumbered males in funerary sites (female: 45.3 per cent, n=238/male: 41.0 per cent, n=215), and villas (female: 39.2 per cent, n=31/male: 25.3 per cent, n=20). Twice as many males were reported from the industry/villa site at Priors Hall, Weldon, Northamptonshire; however, sample sizes are small (male: 60.0 per cent, n=6/female: 30.0 per cent n=3) (FIG. 7.16).

Non-adult palaeopathology in the East

Only a few non-adults were reported for the region, with low rates of palaeopathology. Cribra orbitalia was reported in a 1.1–2.5 year old from Chignal St James villa, Essex. Enamel hypoplasia was reported in three individuals, two aged 6.6–10.5 years old,

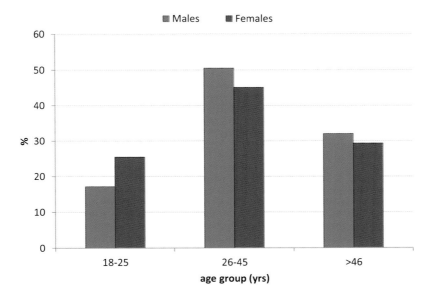

FIG. 7.15.   Central Belt: sex distribution in the adults

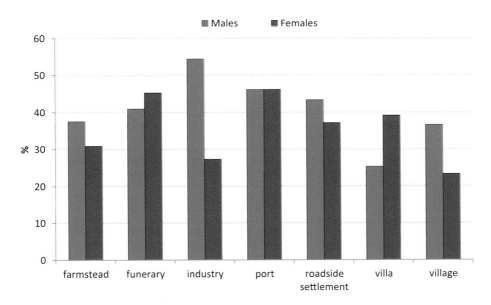

FIG. 7.16.   Central Belt: adult sex distribution by site type

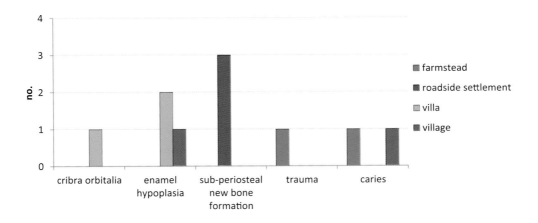

FIG. 7.17.   East: numbers of non-adults with pathology

and one 14.6–17.0 year old adolescent from Chignal St James (40.0 per cent) and the village site at RAF Lakenheath (33.3 per cent), with an overall rate of 5.6 per cent for the region. Sub-periosteal new bone formation exclusively affected three non-adults from roadside settlements (7.1 per cent), including an infant, a 10.6–14.5 and a 14.6–17.0 year old. An infant from the complex farmstead at Clay Farm, Trumpington in Cambridgeshire, was reported with abnormal bone turnover, possibly indicative of an unknown metabolic disorder. A healed but poorly aligned fracture to the left tibial mid-shaft was reported in an adolescent from the unclassified farmstead at Babraham, Cambridgeshire (4.2 per cent). This individual was decapitated and buried in a grave furnished with pottery (Timberlake *et al.* 2007). Dental disease was infrequent, with one adolescent from the same site reported with calculus. Caries was reported in two individuals, a 2.6–6.5 years old from the unclassified farmstead at Babraham (7.1 per cent), and a 14.6–17.0 year old from the village site at RAF Lakenheath (50.0 per cent), with an overall rate of 6.3 per cent for the region (FIG. 7.17).

Non-adult palaeopathology in the South

Similar to the East, non-adult pathology was low in the South region. Cribra orbitalia was reported in children from funerary, roadside and village sites at CPRs of 4.8 per cent (n=4), 1.6 per cent (n=1) and 8.6 per cent (n=3). The youngest individuals with cribrotic lesions were two 2.6–6.5 year olds from the funerary site at Zone 19, East Kent Access, and the village at Amesbury, Boscombe Down, Wiltshire. The highest rate of CO was found in 14.6–17.0 year olds. Enamel hypoplasia was reported for all age groups, most frequent in 2.6–6.5 year olds (18.5 per cent, n=5) and villages (10.0 per cent, n=3). Small sample sizes yielded high lesion frequencies by age groups (FIG 7.18).

Osteomyelitis was reported at 0.6 per cent (n=3), in infants and a perinate, which is questionable given the quality of infant bone (Wenaden *et al.* 2005). The highest frequency of endocranial lesions was reported for villages (5.7 per cent, n=2), and in 2.6–6.5 year olds (7.5 per cent, n=2). Sub-periosteal new bone formation was highest in 14.6–17.0 year olds (18.2 per cent, n=2) and reported in a range of settlement types. Infants and older children exhibited new bone formation and metabolic disease was reported in a scorbutic 2.6–6.5 year old from the funerary site at Zone 19, East Kent Access, and a rachitic infant from a village site at Zones 6 and 7 of the East Kent Access. Skeletal trauma was not reported.

Calculus affected those aged 6.6–10.5 years and older (11.8 per cent, n=2), peaking in 14.6–17.0 year olds (45.5 per cent, n=5). Calcified plaque was most prevalent in roadside settlements (37.5 per cent, n=3). Overall, caries prevalence was highest in the village sites (21.4 per cent, n=3) and mainly affected 14.6–17.0 year olds (27.3 per cent, n=3).

Non-adult palaeopathology in the Central Belt

A total of 39 (7.7 per cent) non-adults were reported with cribra orbitalia. Prevalence was highest in funerary sites (11.5 per cent, n=27) and 1.1–2.5 year olds (25.0 per cent, n=10), although we see a variation of rates across the ages and settlement types (FIG 7.19). Porotic hyperostosis affected 2.4 per cent (n=12) overall. Lesions were most frequent in 1.1–2.5 year olds (10.0 per cent, n=4), and at roadside settlements (4.2 per cent, n=3). Enamel hypoplasia was reported in 7.5 per cent (n=30) of non-adults, with the highest frequency in 6.6–10.5 year olds (23.1 per cent, n=9) and in funerary sites (9.5 per cent, n=19).

Osteomyelitis was reported in a perinate from the roadside settlement at Wanborough, Wiltshire

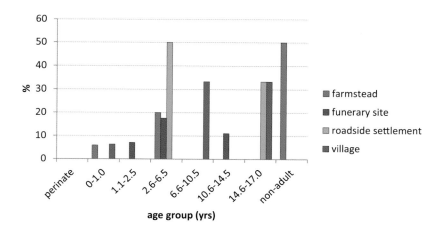

FIG. 7.18.   South: crude prevalence rates of enamel hypoplasia in non-adults

(1.4 per cent), and osteitis in a 10.6–14.5 year old from the unclassified farmstead at Bradley Hill, Somerset (1.1 per cent). Endocranial lesions were reported across a range of settlement types. Lesion frequency was highest in 10.6–14.5 year olds (8.1 per cent, n=3), all from funerary sites. Subperiosteal new bone formation was reported in 3.9 per cent (n=20) of non-adults, most prevalent at roadside settlements (5.6 per cent, n=4) and in 14.6–17.0 year olds (21.2 per cent, n=7). In total, four individuals (0.8 per cent) from funerary sites and an unclassified farmstead (Foxes Field, Stonehouse, Gloucestershire) were reported with visceral new bone formation on the ribs, including an infant, two adolescents and a 6.6–10.5 year old.

Vitamin D and vitamin C deficiencies were reported at 1.6 per cent (n=8) and 4.1 per cent (n=21). Rickets was present in infants and 1.1–2.5 year olds from the roadside settlement at Bourton-on-the-Water, Gloucestershire (3.8 per cent, n=1) and the funerary sites at Cannington, Somerset, and Radley Barrow Hills, Oxfordshire (6.3 per cent, n=4/10.3 per cent, n=3). Scurvy was most prevalent in 1.1–2.5 year olds (17.5 per cent, n=7), and the roadside settlement at Bourton-on-the-Water, Gloucestershire (6.9 per cent, n=5), and the funerary site at Cannington, Somerset (6.0 per cent, n=14). Infantile scurvy was present at the unclassified farmstead at Bradley Hill, Somerset (5.9 per cent, n=2), whereas Bourton-on-the-Water and Cannington had a greater dispersal of vitamin C deficiency across the age groups (FIG. 7.20).

Trauma was reported in five non-adults (1.0 per cent) from the funerary site at Cannington, Somerset (n=2), the villa at Watersmeet, Cambridgeshire (n=1), the roadside settlement at Kempston, Box End, Bedford (n=1) and the unclassified farmstead at Bradley Hill, Somerset (n=1). Fractures were most prevalent in 2.6–6.5 year olds (3.3 per cent, n=2). Infants presented with a dislocated femur and fractured clavicle. A clavicle fracture was also present in the 2.6–6.5 year olds, alongside a green-stick fracture to the

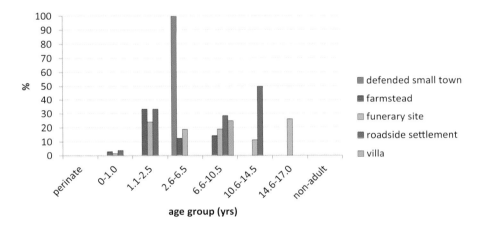

FIG. 7.19.   Central Belt: crude prevalence rates of cribra orbitalia in non-adults

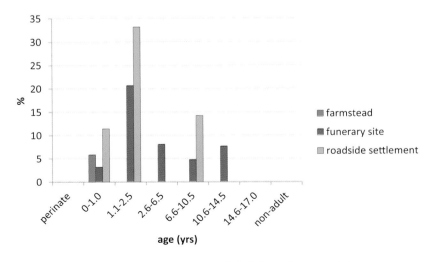

FIG. 7.20.   Central Belt: crude prevalence rates of vitamin C deficiency in non-adults

fibula. The oldest individual is a 10.6–14.5 year old with a Monteggia injury affecting the left ulna and radius.

Calculus (7.5 per cent, n=15), caries (6.0 per cent, n=12) and AMTL (1.0 per cent, n=2) were reported, with increasing frequencies in older children. Caries was highest at villa sites (12.5 per cent, n=2), and farmsteads yielded a significantly higher rate of calculus (17.5 per cent, n=7; X^2=19.35, p<0.005, d.f.=5) than elsewhere in the region. Nine of the 14 farmsteads with non-adults with calculus were complex farmsteads, and the remaining four unclassified.

Adult palaeopathology in the East

A total of 13 adults were reported with haematopoietic lesions, with similar frequencies in males (7.2 per cent, n=6) and females (7.4 per cent, n=5). Significantly more individuals from Chignal St James villa were reported with porotic hyperostosis (21.2 per cent, n=4; X^2=15.32, p<0.005, d.f.=4) and enamel hypoplasia (47.4 per cent, n=9; X^2=68.22, p<0.001, d.f.=4). Overall, enamel hypoplasia was reported in 13 individuals (5.5 per cent). The crude prevalence of enamel lesions was similar among the adults and non-adults (non-adult CPR 5.6 per cent/adult CPR5.5 per cent), and cribra orbitalia occurred at low frequencies in both groups (non-adult CPR 1.3 per cent/adult CPR 2.9 per cent). New bone formation was reported in 12 individuals (5.0 per cent) and affected 2.9 per cent (n=2) of females and 9.6 per cent (n=8) of males (TABLES 7.4 and 7.5). Periostitis was significantly more frequent at the village at RAF Lakenheath, Suffolk (50.0 per cent, n=2; X^2=15.11, p<0.005, d.f.=4) than elsewhere across the region. Both osteitis (n=2) and endocranial lesions (n=2) were reported at the complex farmstead at Clay Farm, Trumpington, Cambridgeshire (1.7 per cent) (TABLE 7.6). Tuberculosis was equally rare and identified in two young females (0.8 per cent) from the complex farmstead at Hutchison Site, Addenbrooke's in Cambridgeshire (n=1) and the funerary site at Duxford (n=1) (FIG. 7.21). Sinusitis and visceral new bone formation on the ribs affected one individual each (0.4 per cent) (TABLE 7.7). A middle adult female from The Tene, Baldock roadside settlement in Hertfordshire (1.5 per cent) was reported with vitamin C deficiency.

Trauma was most prevalent at Chignal St James villa (26.3 per cent, n=5), and more commonly

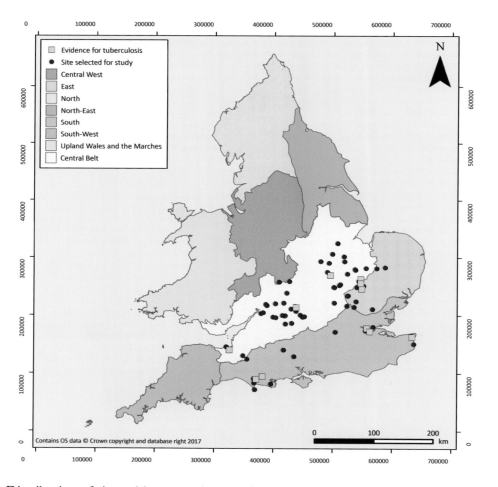

FIG.7.21. Distribution of sites with reported cases of tuberculosis

TABLE 7.4: ADULT CRUDE PREVALENCE RATES OF CRIBRA ORBITALIA AND POROTIC HYPEROSTOSIS
% of settlement type total

EAST	Observed n	Affected n	CPR %	M	F
Cribra orbitalia					
Farmstead	116	2	1.7	2	
Funerary	32	0	0		
Roadside	67	2	3.0		2
Villa	19	3	15.8	2	1
Village	4	0	0		
Total	**238**	**7**	**2.9**	**4**	**3**
Porotic hyperostosis					
Farmstead	116	1	0.9		
Funerary	32	0	0		
Roadside	67	0	0		
Villa	19	4	21.2	2	2
Village	4	0	0		
Total	**238**	**5**	**2.1**	**2**	**2**
SOUTH	Observed N	Affected n	CPR %	M	F
Cribra orbitalia					
Farmstead	101	8	7.9	5	3
Funerary	173	20	11.6	8	10
Religious	9	0	0		
Roadside	27	1	3.7	1	
Village	78	7	9.0	1	6
Total	**388**	**36**	**9.3**	**15**	**19**
Porotic hyperostosis					
Farmstead	101	0	0		
Funerary	173	2	1.2	1	1
Religious	9	0	0		
Roadside	27	0	0		
Village	78	2	2.6	2	
Total	**388**	**4**	**1.0**		
CENTRAL BELT	Observed n	Affected n	CPR %	M	F
Cribra orbitalia					
Farmstead	330	18	5.5	13	5
Funerary	166	10	6.0	4	6
Industry	11	0	0		
Port	13	0	0		
Roadside	145	17	11.7	9	8
Villa	79	3	3.8	1	2
Village	30	1	3.3		1
Total	**774**	**49**	**6.3**	**27**	**22**
Porotic hyperostosis					
Farmstead	330	6	1.8	5	
Funerary	166	0			
Industry	11	0			
Port	13	0			
Roadside	145	6	4.1	3	2
Villa	79	0			
Village	30	0			
Total	**774**	**12**	**1.6**	**9**	**2**

TABLE 7.5: ADULT CRUDE PREVALENCE RATES OF ENAMEL HYPOPLASIA
% of settlement type total

EAST	Observed n	Affected n	CPR %	M	F
Farmstead	116	1	0.9		1
Funerary	32	0	0		
Roadside	67	2	3.0		1
Villa	19	9	47.4	6	3
Village	4	1	25.0	1	
Total	**238**	**13**	**5.5**	**7**	**5**
SOUTH					
Farmstead	101	12	11.9	6	6
Funerary	173	21	12.1	8	11
Religious	9	1	11.1	1	
Roadside	27	2	7.4	2	
Village	78	8	10.3	4	4
Total	**388**	**44**	**11.3**	**21**	**21**
CENTRAL BELT					
Farmstead	330	32	9.7	20	10
Funerary	166	33	19.9	19	14
Industry	11	6	54.5	4	2
Port	13	0	0		
Roadside	145	22	15.2	13	7
Villa	79	1	1.3		1
Village	30	2	6.7		1
Total	**774**	**96**	**12.4**	**56**	**35**

TABLE 7.6: EAST: ADULT CRUDE PREVALENCE RATES OF NON-SPECIFIC INFECTION/INFLAMMATION
% of settlement type total

	Observed n	Affected n	CPR %	M	F
Sub-periosteal new bone formation					
Farmstead	116	7	6.0	5	
Funerary	32	0	0		
Roadside	67	3	4.5	1	2
Villa	19	0	0		
Village	4	2	50.0	2	
Total	**238**	**12**	**5.0**	**8**	**2**
Endocranial lesions					
Farmstead	116	2	1.7		
Funerary	32	0	0		
Roadside	67	0	0		
Villa	19	0	0		
Village	4	0	0		
Total	**238**	**2**	**0.8**		
Osteitis					
Farmstead	116	2	1.7	2	
Funerary	32	0	0		
Roadside	67	0	0		
Villa	19	0	0		
Village	4	0	0		
Total	**238**	**2**	**0.8**	**2**	

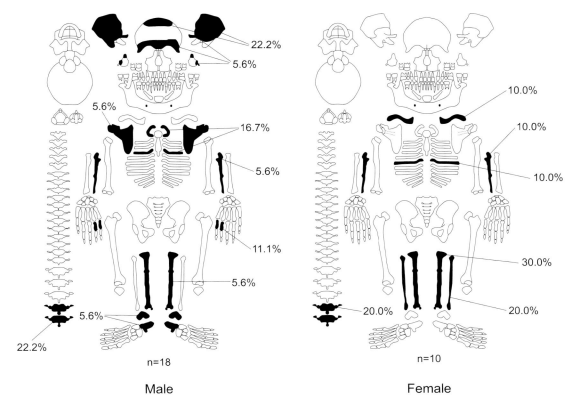

FIG. 7.22.   East: elements reported with fractures in adult males and females (per cent of total fractured elements reported)

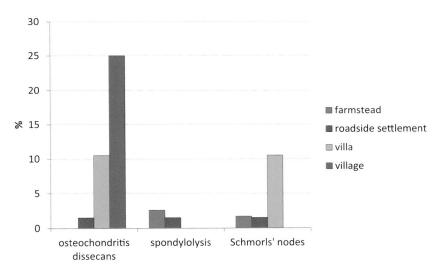

FIG. 7.23.   East: crude prevalence rates of joint stress in adults

reported in males (18.1 per cent, n=15) than females (10.3 per cent, n=7) (TABLE 7.8). In the region, 24 individuals (10.1 per cent) were affected, frequently at the spine (20.0 per cent, n=6). This fracture location was also most commonly reported in men (22.2 per cent, n=4) and at complex and unclassified farmsteads (37.5 per cent, n=6). Tibial fractures were most frequent at roadside settlements (28.6 per cent, n=2), Chignal St James villa (33.3 per cent, n=2) and in females (30.0 per cent, n=3) (TABLE 7.9). Sharp

force injuries to the cranium, facial region and scapulae were reported in the men (FIG. 7.22).

Joint stress was apparent in the men, the only affected woman being a middle adult female from the complex farmstead at Hutchison Site, Addenbrooke's in Cambridgeshire with spondylolysis. Schmorl's nodes were most prevalent in young adults (8.0 per cent, n=2) and most frequent at Chignal St James villa (10.5 per cent, n=2), whereas OCD in joints of the foot was reported from a range of settlement types.

TABLE 7.7: ADULT CRUDE PREVALENCE RATES OF RESPIRATORY DISEASE
% of settlement type total

EAST	Observed n	Affected n	CPR %	M	F
Tuberculosis					
Farmstead	116	1	0.9		1
Funerary	32	1	3.1		1
Roadside	67	0	0		
Villa	19	0	0		
Village	4	0	0		
Total	**238**	**2**	**0.8**		**2**
Sinusitis					
Farmstead	116	1	0.9		
Funerary	32	0	0		
Roadside	67	0	0		
Villa	19	0	0		
Village	4	0	0		
Total	**238**	**1**	**0.4**		
Rib periositis					
Farmstead	116	1	0.9	1	
Funerary	32	0	0		
Roadside	67	0	0		
Villa	19	0	0		
Village	4	0	0		
Total	**238**	**1**	**0.4**	**1**	
SOUTH	Observed n	Affected n	CPR %	M	F
Tuberculosis					
Farmstead	101	1	1.0	1	
Funerary	173	8	4.0	5	3
Religious	9	1	11.1	1	
Roadside	27	0			
Village	78	1	1.3		
Total	**388**	**11**	**2.8**	**7**	**3**
Sinusitis					
Farmstead	101	5	5.0	4	1
Funerary	173	2	1.2	1	1
Religious	9	0			
Roadside	27	0			
Village	78	1	1.3		1
Total	**388**	**8**	**2.0**	**5**	**3**
Rib periostitis					
Farmstead	101	0			
Funerary	173	2	1.2		2
Religious	9	0			
Roadside	27	0			
Village	78	2	2.6	2	
Total	**388**	**4**	**1.0**	**2**	**2**
CENTRAL BELT	Observed n	Affected n	CPR %	M	F
Tuberculosis					
Farmstead	330	1	0.3		1
Funerary	525	3	0.6	3	
Industry	11	0	0		
Port	13	0	0		
Roadside	145	1	0.7		1
Villa	79	0	0		
Village	30	0	0		
Total	**1133**	**5**	**0.4**	**3**	**2**

TABLE 7.7: (CONT'D)

CENTRAL BELT	Observed n	Affected n	CPR %	M	F
Sinusitis					
Farmstead	330	4	1.2	3	1
Funerary	525	2	0.4	1	1
Industry	11	0	0		
Port	13	0	0		
Roadside	145	7	4.8	5	2
Villa	79	3	3.8	1	2
Village	30	0	0		
Total	**1133**	**16**	**1.4**	**10**	**6**
Rib periostitis					
Farmstead	330	2	0.6	2	
Funerary	525	4	0.9	2	2
Industry	11	0	0		
Port	13	0	0		
Roadside	145	4	2.8	3	1
Villa	79	0	0		
Village	30	0	0		
Total	**1133**	**10**	**0.9**	**7**	**3**

TABLE 7.8: ADULT CRUDE PREVALENCE RATES OF SKELETAL TRAUMA
% of settlement type total

EAST	Observed n	Affected n	CPR %	M	F
Farmstead	116	13	11.2	9	2
Funerary	32	0	0		
Roadside	67	5	7.5	3	2
Villa	19	5	26.3	2	3
Village	4	1	25.0	1	
Total	**238**	**24**	**10.1**	**15**	**7**
SOUTH					
Farmstead	101	14	13.9	7	7
Funerary	173	24	13.8	17	7
Religious	9	1	11.1	1	
Roadside	27	1	3.7	1	
Village	78	9	11.5	5	3
Total	**388**	**49**	**12.6**	**31**	**17**
CENTRAL BELT					
Farmstead	330	38	11.5	27	8
Funerary	525	64	12.2	45	19
Industry	11	1	9.1	1	
Port	13	1	7.7	1	
Roadside	145	22	15.2	14	7
Villa	79	10	12.7	6	3
Village	30	3	10.0	3	
Total	**1133**	**139**	**12.3**	**97**	**37**

TABLE 7.9: EAST: TRAUMA LOCATIONS SPECIFIED IN ADULTS, BY SITE TYPE
% of total trauma locations by settlement type

Element	Farmstead n	Farmstead %	Roadside n	Roadside %	Villa n	Villa %	Village n	Village %	Total n	Total %
Cranium	4	25.0	1	14.3	0		0		5	16.7
Facial	1	6.3	0		0		0		1	3.3
Scapula	1	6.3	0		0		0		1	3.3
Clavicle	0		0		1	16.7	0		1	3.3
Rib	3	18.8	1	14.3	1	16.7	0		5	16.7
Spine	6	37.5	0		0		0		6	20.0
Ulna	1	6.3	1	14.3	0		0		2	6.7
Hand phalanx	0		1	14.3	1	16.7	0		2	6.7
Tibia	0		2	28.6	2	33.3	0		4	13.3
Fibula	0		1	14.3	1	16.7	0		2	6.7
Ankle (talus and calcaneus	0		0		0		1	100	1	3.3
Total	**16**		**7**		**6**		**1**		**30**	

TABLE 7.10: EAST: DEGENERATIVE JOINT DISEASE IN ADULTS
% of settlement type total

	Observed n	Affected n	CPR %	M	F
Extraspinal					
Sterno-costal					
Farmstead	116	1	0.9	1	
Total sterno-costal	**238**	**1**	**0.4**	**1**	
Spinal					
Vertebral					
Farmstead	116	25	21.6	12	12
Funerary	32	1	3.1	1	
Roadside	67	10	14.9	4	5
Villa	19	1	5.3	1	
Village	4	1	25.0	1	
Total spinal	**238**	**38**	**16.0**	**19**	**17**
Upper body					
Sterno-clavicular					
Village	4	3	75.0	1	1
Total sterno-clavicular	**238**	**3**	**1.3**	**1**	**1**
Acromio-clavicular					
Village	4	3	75.0	3	
Total acromio-clavicular	**238**	**3**	**1.3**	**3**	
Shoulder					
Farmstead	116	6	5.2	3	3
Funerary	32	3	9.4	3	
Village	4	3	75.0	1	1
Total shoulder	**238**	**12**	**5.0**	**7**	**4**
Elbow					
Farmstead	116	2	1.7		2
Roadside	67	1	1.5		1
Village	4	3	75.0	1	1
Total elbow	**238**	**6**	**2.5**	**1**	**4**
Wrist					
Farmstead	116	3	2.6	3	
Village	4	3	75.0	1	1
Total wrist	**238**	**6**	**2.5**	**4**	**1**
Hand					
Farmstead	116	4	3.4	1	3
Funerary	32	1	3.1	1	

TABLE 7.10: (CONT'D)

	Observed n	Affected n	CPR %	M	F
Hand					
Village	4	3	75.0	1	1
Total hand	**238**	**8**	**3.4**	**3**	**4**
Lower body					
Sacro-iliac					
Farmstead	116	1	0.9		1
Roadside	67	2	3.0		2
Village	4	3	75.0	1	1
Total sacro-iliac	**238**	**6**	**2.5**	**1**	**4**
Hip					
Farmstead	116	5	4.3	1	3
Funerary	32	3	9.4	3	
Roadside	67	3	4.5	1	2
Village	4	3	75.0	1	1
Total hip	**238**	**14**	**5.9**	**6**	**6**
Knee					
Farmstead	116	6	5.2	3	3
Village	4	3	75.0	1	1
Total knee	**238**	**9**	**3.8**	**4**	**4**
Ankle					
Farmstead	116	1	0.9	1	
Village	4	3	75.0	1	1
Total ankle	**238**	**4**	**1.7**	**2**	**1**
Foot					
Farmstead	116	5	4.3	3	2
Roadside	67	2	3.0	2	
Village	4	3	75.0	1	1
Total foot	**238**	**10**	**4.2**	**6**	**3**

TABLE 7.11: EAST: ADULT DENTAL DISEASE
% of settlement type total

	Observed n	Affected n	CPR %	M	F
Calculus					
Farmstead	80	22	27.5	13	9
Roadside	54	8	14.8	2	5
Village	4	2	50.0	2	
Total calculus	**157**	**32**	**20.4**	**17**	**14**
Caries					
Farmstead	80	13	16.3	7	6
Roadside	54	11	20.4	5	4
Village	4	2	50.0	2	
Total caries	**157**	**26**	**16.6**	**14**	**10**
AMTL					
Farmstead	80	24	30.0	10	14
Roadside	54	9	6.7	5	4
Village	4	2	50.0	2	
Total AMTL	**157**	**35**	**22.3**	**17**	**18**
PAL/abscess					
Farmstead	80	6	7.5	2	4
Roadside	54	6	11.1	5	1
Village	4	2	50.0	2	
Total PAL/abscess	**157**	**14**	**8.9**	**9**	**5**

Spondylolysis was identified in three adults from Cambridgeshire farmsteads (2.6 per cent), and an additional case was reported from the roadside settlement (1.5 per cent) at Braughing, Buntingford Road in Hertfordshire (FIG. 7.23).

Degenerative joint disease was reported in 16.0 per cent (n=4) of young adults, and increased to 64.3 per cent (n=27) in old age, affecting 33.8 per cent (n=23) of females, and 36.1 per cent (n=30) of males overall. By specified joint locations, degeneration occurred most frequently in the spine (16.0 per cent, n=38), followed by the hip (5.9 per cent, n=14) and shoulder (5.0 per cent, n=12). More women showed degeneration of the elbow and sacro-iliac joint (5.9 per cent, n=4/male: 1.2 per cent, n=1). Similar differences were also apparent in the hand, (female: 5.9 per cent, n=4/male: 3.6 per cent, n=3), hip and knee (female: 5.9 per cent, n=4/males: 4.8 per cent, n=4) (TABLE 7.10).

Dental disease was reported on in 157 individuals (male n=58, female n=54, not sexed n=45) (Table 7.11). Dental disease was consistently highest in the village at RAF Lakenheath, owing to small sample size, with two of four adults reported with dental disease. Calculus (27.5 per cent, n=22) and AMTL (30.0 per cent, n=24) were more prevalent at farmsteads, comprising Babraham (n=10) and Hutchison site, Addenbrooke's (n=12) in Cambridgeshire, and Melford Meadows, Brettenham, Thetford, in Norfolk (n=2). Proportionately more individuals with caries (20.4 per cent, n=11) and abscesses (11.1 per cent, n=6) were reported from roadside settlements. Prevalence rates for caries, AMTL and abscesses increase from young to old adults, with calculus most prevalent in middle adults (29.3 per cent, n=12). The rates for calculus (male: 29.3 per cent, n=17/female: 25.9 per cent, n=14), caries (male: 24.1 per cent, n=14/female: 18.5 per cent, n=10) and abscesses/PAL (male: 15.5 per cent, n=9/female: 9.3 per cent, n=5) are higher for males, whereas AMTL was reported more frequently in females (female: 33.3 per cent, n=18/male: 29.3 per cent, n=17).

Adult palaeopathology in the South

Haematopoietic lesions were reported in 40 individuals (CO: 9.3 per cent, n=36; PH: 1.0 per cent, n=4). Cribra orbitalia was most prevalent in funerary sites (11.6 per cent, n=20), and porotic hyperostosis in villages (2.6 per cent, n=2) (TABLE 7.4). Both CO and PH were more frequent in females (CO: 17.9 per cent, n=19; PH: 1.9 per cent, n=2). CO was highest in old adults (14.4 per cent, n=13), whereas PH was most prevalent in young adults (1.7 per cent, n=1). Enamel hypoplasia and new bone formation were reported in 44 adults (11.3 per cent). EH were most prevalent in young adults (23.3 per cent, n=14) and at funerary sites (12.2 per cent, n=21), and proportionately more women (14.7 per cent, n=21) exhibited hypoplastic lesions than men (12.8 per cent, n=21) (TABLE 7.5). In comparison to the non-adults, significantly more adults were reported with enamel hypoplasia (non-adult CPR 4.8 per cent, n=15/adult CPR 11.3 per cent, n=44; X^2=9.88, p<0.005, d.f.=1) and cribra orbitalia in the region (non-adult CPR 2.3 per cent, n=8/adult CPR 9.3 per cent, n=36; X^2=16.20, p<0.001, d.f.=1).

New bone formation was most frequently reported in old adults (21.1 per cent, n=19) and farmsteads (12.9 per cent, n=13). These include individuals from unenclosed (n=7), complex (n=4) and unclassified (n=2) farmsteads. Periostitis occurred at similar rates in males and females at 13.4 per cent (n=22) and 13.3 per cent (n=19) respectively. Six adults (1.5 per cent) were reported with endocranial lesions and four (1.1 per cent) with osteomyelitis (TABLE 7.12). Tuberculoid leprosy was described in an old adult male from the funerary site at West Thurrock, Essex, and possible tuberculosis was reported in 2.8 per cent (n=11) of individuals (FIGS 7.21, 7.24). The infectious disease was present in eight individuals (4.6 per cent) from funerary sites, and one adult each from the village site at Zones 6 and 7 of the East Kent Access (1.3 per cent), Springhead Sanctuary complex (11.1 per cent), and the enclosed farmstead at Alington Avenue, Fordington in Dorset (1.0 per cent). Sinusitis affected 2.0 per cent (n=8) of adults, and new bone formation on the pleural aspect of the ribs was reported in four individuals (1.0 per cent). Five of the eight individuals with sinusitis may have developed the condition secondary to a dental abscess (corrected for CPR 0.8 per cent, n=3). Both sinusitis and new bone formation on the ribs tended to be reported in young and middle adults, whereas tuberculosis was most prevalent in old adults (5.6 per cent, n=5). Tuberculosis and sinusitis were more frequent in males (4.3 per cent, n=7/1.2 per cent, n=2), whereas rib periostitis was more frequent in females (1.4 per cent, n=2) (TABLE 7.7).

Examples for metabolic disease were few (n=6, 1.5 per cent). Possible vitamin D and vitamin C deficiency was reported in an old adult male from the funerary context at Zone 19 of the East Kent Access. Healed childhood rickets was present in an old adult male from the funerary site at West Thurrock, Essex. Osteoporosis was reported in old (3.3 per cent, n=3) and middle adult males (0.6 per cent, n=1) from funerary sites.

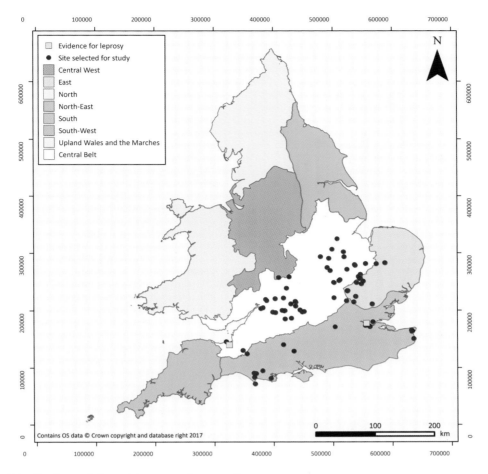

FIG. 7.24. Distributions of sites with reported cases of leprosy

TABLE 7.12: SOUTH: ADULT CRUDE PREVALENCE RATES OF NON-SPECIFIC INFECTION AND INFLAMMATION
% of settlement type total

	Observed n	Affected n	CPR %	M	F
Sub-periosteal new bone formation					
Farmstead	101	13	12.9	7	5
Funerary	173	19	11.0	11	8
Religious	9	1	11.1	1	
Roadside	27	3	11.1	2	
Village	78	8	10.3	1	6
Total	**388**	**44**	**11.3**	**22**	**19**
Endocranial lesions					
Farmstead	101	0	0		
Funerary	173	4	2.3	3	2
Religious	9	0	0		
Roadside	27	0	0		
Village	78	1	1.3		1
Total	**388**	**6**	**1.5**	**3**	**3**
Osteomyelitis					
Farmstead	101	4	4.0	2	1
Funerary	173	0	0		
Religious	9	0	0		
Roadside	27	0	0		
Village	78	0	0		
Total	**388**	**4**	**1.1**	**2**	**1**

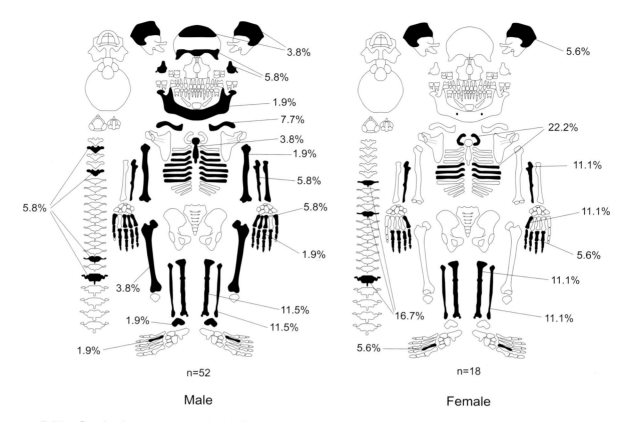

FIG. 7.25. South: elements reported with fractures in adult males and females (per cent of total fractures elements reported)

Trauma was reported in 49 (12.6 per cent) individuals, 18.9 per cent (n=31) of men, and 11.9 per cent (n=17) of women (TABLE 7.8). Overall, ribs were most commonly broken (24.3 per cent, n=17), a pattern also apparent between the sexes and at the settlement level, although fractured fibulae were most common at villages (40.0 per cent, n=4) (TABLE 7.13). Only one old adult female from the complex farmstead at East Kent Access Zones 9 and 10 was presented with multiple trauma of the spine and ribs, whereas multiple trauma affected 11 males. Women had higher rates of spinal fractures (16.7 per cent, n=3) and trauma affecting the forearm, hands and feet. Facial trauma was reported in males only (7.7 per cent, n=4) (FIG. 7.25). Notable cases include the published case of amputation at the humeral mid-shaft in an old adult male from Alington Avenue, Dorset (Waldron 1989), and weapon trauma in a middle adult and four old adult males.

Osteochondritis dissecans in the feet and ankles was reported in 1.8 per cent (n=7), at funerary sites and Springhead Sanctuary complex only, mostly in young adults (6.7 per cent, n=4). OCD was reported in five males (3.0 per cent), as opposed to one female (0.7 per cent). Spondylolysis affected 2.8 per cent (n=11) of adults in the region, mostly at funerary sites (4.0 per cent, n=7). The condition affected more males (4.9 per

cent, n=8) than females (2.1 per cent, n=3) and was most common in middle adults (4.6 per cent, n=8). Schmorl's nodes were recorded in 11.9 per cent (n=46) of individuals, 15.9 per cent (n=26) of males and 14.0 per cent (n=20) of females. The distribution of lesions varies slightly according to age and settlement type, where crude prevalence was highest at funerary sites (16.2 per cent, n=28) and in middle adults (14.5 per cent, n=25) (FIG. 7.26).

Degenerative joint disease was reported in 141 individuals (36.3 per cent), in young adults at 10.0 per cent (n=6), and 64.4 per cent (n=58) in old adults. Joint degeneration affected 42.7 per cent (n=61) of females, and 45.7 per cent (n=75) of males. Degenerative changes were most frequently recorded in the spine (27.6 per cent, n=107), followed by the hip (9.3 per cent, n=36) and shoulder (8.8 per cent, n=34). In villages, 50.0 per cent (n=10) of females had evidence for joint disease, as opposed to 30.8 per cent (n=8) of males. More females exhibited joint disease of the shoulder (11.2 per cent, n=16/male: 10.4 per cent, n=17), acromio-clavicular (7.0 per cent, n=10/male: 3.7 per cent, n=6), and sterno-clavicular joints (4.9 per cent, n=7/male: n=0). Between the sexes, the distribution for the sterno-clavicular joint is statistically significant (X^2=8.22, p<0.005, d.f.=1) (TABLE 7.14).

TABLE 7.13: SOUTH: TRAUMA LOCATIONS SPECIFIED IN ADULTS, BY SITE TYPE
% of total trauma locations by settlement type

Element	Farmstead n	Farmstead %	Funerary n	Funerary %	Religious n	Religious %	Roadside n	Roadside %	Village n	Village %	Total n	Total %
Cranium	0		2	5.6	1	33.3	0		0		3	4.3
Mandible	0		1	2.8								
Facial	2	10.0	1	2.8	0		0		0		4	5.7
Clavicle	0		3	8.3	0		0		1	10.0	4	5.7
Sternum	1	5.0	1	2.8	0		0		0		2	2.9
Rib	7	35.0	7	19.4	1	33.3	0		2	20.0	17	24.3
Spine	2	10.0	4	11.1	0		0		0		6	8.6
Humerus	0		1	2.8	0		0		0		1	1.4
Ulna	0		4	11.1	0		1	100	0		5	7.1
Metacarpal	2	10.0	3	8.3	0		0		0		5	7.1
Hand phalanx	1	5.0	1	2.8	0		0		0		2	2.9
Femur	1	5.0	1	2.8	0		0		0		2	2.9
Tibia	2	10.0	3	8.3	1	33.3	0		2	20.0	8	11.4
Fibula	2	10.0	2	5.6	0		0		4	40.0	8	11.4
Ankle (Talus)	0		1	2.8	0		0		0		1	1.4
Metatarsal	0		1	2.8	0		0		1	10.0	2	2.9
Total	**20**		**36**		**3**		**1**		**10**		**70**	

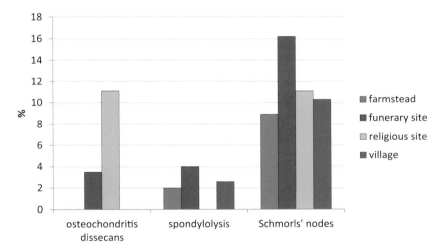

FIG. 7.26.   South: crude prevalence rates of joint stress in adults

Dental disease was reported on in 289 individuals (male n=133, female n=106, not sexed n=50) and calculus and caries affected over 30 per cent of adults. AMTL was seen in 29.8 per cent (n=86) of individuals, and 17.6 per cent (n=51) suffered from an abscess or periapical lesion. Calculus was most frequent in young adults (48.9 per cent, n=22), whereas caries, AMTL, abscesses/PAL increase with age. The lowest rate for calculus was observed in farmsteads (23.1 per cent, n=18; complex n=10, unenclosed n=6, unclassified n=2), compared to 41.8 per cent (n=51) at funerary sites. Caries most frequently affected individuals from Springhead Sanctuary complex (55.6 per cent, n=5), and was lowest in roadside settlements (7.4 per cent, n=2). AMTL was least prevalent in adults from roadside settlements (7.4 per cent, n=2), compared to 37.7 per cent (n=46) at funerary sites. At Springhead Sanctuary complex, 22.2 per cent (n=2) of adults had dental abscesses/PAL. Both calculus and caries were more frequent in females at rates of 41.5 per cent (n=44) and 47.2 per cent (n=50), compared to 36.1 per cent (n=48) and 36.8 per cent (n=49) in males (TABLE 7.15).

DISH (diffuse idiopathic skeletal hyperostosis) was reported in two old adult males from contexts along the East Kent Access. One relates to the early to mid-Roman complex farmstead at Zones 9 and 10, and the other to the early Roman

TABLE 7.14: SOUTH: DEGENERATIVE JOINT DISEASE IN ADULTS
% of settlement type total

	Observed n	Affected n	%	M	F
Extraspinal					
TMJ					
Farmstead	101	5	5	1	4
Funerary	173	7	4	5	2
Roadside	27	1	3.7	1	0
Village	78	1	1.3	0	1
Total TMJ	**388**	**14**	**3.6**	**7**	**7**
Sterno-costal					
Farmstead	101	7	6.7	6	1
Funerary	173	14	8.1	5	9
Religious	9	1	11.1	1	0
Village	78	5	6.4	3	1
Total sterno-costal	**388**	**27**	**7.0**	**15**	**11**
Spinal					
Vertebral					
Farmstead	101	32	31.7	20	12
Funerary	173	58	33.5	29	28
Religious	9	1	11.1	1	0
Roadside	27	2	7.4	2	0
Village	78	14	17.9	7	6
Total spinal	**388**	**107**	**27.6**	**59**	**46**
Upper body					
Sterno-clavicular					
Farmstead	101	6	5.9	0	6
Funerary	**173**	**1**	**0.6**	**0**	**1**
Total sterno-clavicular	**388**	**7**	**1.8**	**0**	**7**
Acromio-clavicular					
Farmstead	101	7	6.9	1	6
Funerary	**173**	**9**	**5.2**	**5**	**4**
Total acromio-clavicular	**388**	**16**	**4.1**	**6**	**10**
Shoulder					
Farmstead	101	18	17.8	9	8
Funerary	173	13	7.5	6	7
Religious	9	1	11.1	1	0
Roadside	27	1	3.7	1	0
Village	78	1	1.3	0	1
Total shoulder	**388**	**34**	**8.8**	**17**	**16**
Elbow					
Farmstead	101	8	7.9	5	3
Funerary	173	4	2.3	3	1
Village	78	3	3.8	1	2
Total Elbow	**388**	**15**	**3.9**	**9**	**6**
Wrist					
Farmstead	101	6	5.9	3	3
Funerary	173	6	3.5	6	0
Religious	9	1	11.1	1	0
Total wrist	**388**	**13**	**3.4**	**10**	**3**
Hand					
Farmstead	101	13	12.9	9	4
Funerary	173	7	4.0	4	3
Religious	9	1	11.1	1	0
Roadside	27	1	3.7	1	0
Village	78	4	5.1	1	1
Total hand	**388**	**26**	**6.7**	**16**	**8**

TABLE 7.14: (CONT'D)

	Observed n	Affected n	%	M	F
Sacro-iliac					
Farmstead	101	11	10.9	6	5
Funerary	173	1	0.6	0	1
Total sacro-iliac	**388**	**12**	**3.1**	**6**	**6**
Hip					
Farmstead	101	20	19.8	11	8
Funerary	173	10	5.8	8	2
Religious	9	1	11.1	1	0
Roadside	27	2	7.4	2	0
Village	78	3	3.8	2	0
Total hip	**388**	**36**	**9.3**	**24**	**10**
Knee					
Farmstead	101	9	8.9	5	4
Funerary	173	7	4.0	6	1
Religious	9	1	11.1	1	0
Roadside	27	1	3.7	1	0
Village	78	9	11.5	4	4
Total knee	**388**	**27**	**7.0**	**17**	**9**
Ankle					
Farmstead	101	5	5.0	4	1
Roadside	27	1	3.7	1	0
Village	78				
Total ankle	**388**	**6**	**1.5**	**5**	**1**
Foot					
Farmstead	101	9	8.9	6	3
Funerary	173	8	4.6	4	4
Religious	9	1	11.1	1	0
Roadside	27	1	3.7	1	0
Village	78	2	2.6	1	1
Total foot	**388**	**21**	**5.4**	**13**	**8**

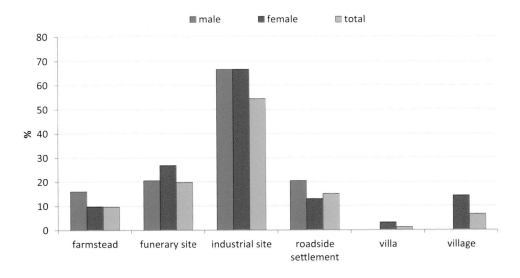

FIG. 7.27. Central Belt: crude prevalence rates of enamel hypoplasia in adults

TABLE 7.15: SOUTH: DENTAL DISEASE IN ADULTS
% of settlement type total

	Observed n	Affected n	CPR %	M	F
Calculus					
Farmstead	78	18	23.1	9	9
Funerary	122	51	41.8	21	26
Religious	9	3	33.3	3	0
Roadside	27	11	40.7	6	4
Village	53	14	26.4	9	5
Total calculus	**289**	**97**	**33.6**	**48**	**44**
Caries					
Farmstead	78	26	33.3	14	13
Funerary	122	54	44.3	24	26
Religious	9	5	55.6	4	1
Roadside	27	2	7.4	1	0
Village	53	17	32.1	6	11
Total caries	**289**	**104**	**36.0**	**49**	**50**
AMTL					
Farmstead	78	26	33.3	14	12
Funerary	122	46	37.7	27	19
Religious	9	1	11.1	1	0
Roadside	27	2	7.4	2	0
Village	53	11	20.8	5	5
Total N AMTL	**289**	**86**	**29.8**	**49**	**36**
Abscess/PAL					
Farmstead	78	17	21.8	9	8
Funerary	122	25	20.5	15	10
Religious	9	2	22.2	2	0
Roadside	27	0	0	0	0
Village	53	7	13.2	3	4
Total abscess/PAL	**289**	**51**	**17.6**	**29**	**22**

funerary site at Zone 19. The condition is characterised by ligament ossification of the spine leading to ankylosis (Ortner 2003).

Adult palaeopathology in the Central Belt

Porotic hyperostosis was only reported in the adults from roadside settlements (4.1 per cent, n=6) and complex, enclosed and unclassified farmsteads (1.8 per cent, n=6). Cribra orbitalia was most frequent in young adults (8.7 per cent, n=10), and was reported at similar rates for males (8.4 per cent, n=27) and females (8.6 per cent, n=22). The highest relative frequency of 11.7 per cent (n=17) was reported for roadside settlements, whereas no lesions were reported from either the industry/villa site at Priors Hall, Weldon, Northamptonshire, or the inland port at Camp Ground, Colne Fen in Cambridgeshire (TABLE 7.4). Enamel hypoplasia affected 12.4 per cent (n=96) of adults, with the statistically highest prevalence reported from the industry/villa site at Priors Hall, Weldon (54.5 per cent, n=6; X^2=43.19,

p<0.001, d.f.=6) (FIG. 7.27). Enamel lesions were slightly more prevalent in males (17.4 per cent, n=56) than females (13.7 per cent, n=35) and in old adults (18.8 per cent, n=36), compared to younger individuals (TABLE 7.5). In comparison to the non-adults, proportionately more adults were reported with enamel hypoplasia (non-adult CPR 7.5 per cent/adult CPR 12.4 per cent). Cribra orbitalia was slightly more frequent among the non-adults (non-adult CPR 7.7 per cent/adult CPR 6.3 per cent).

Relative frequencies of osteitis (0.3 per cent, n=3), osteomyelitis (0.8 per cent, n=9) and endocranial lesions (0.7 per cent, n=8) were low. New bone formation was reported in 69 (6.1 per cent) individuals, and most prevalent at the inland port at Camp Ground, Colne Fen (23.1 per cent, n=3) and roadside settlements (13.1 per cent, n=19), which is statistically significant (X^2=24.71, p<0.001, d.f.=6) (TABLE 7.16). New bone formation was most frequent in old adults at 8.4 per cent (n=21) and statistically more prevalent in males (9.9 per cent, n=44) than females (4.5 per cent,

TABLE 7.16: CENTRAL BELT: ADULT CRUDE PREVALENCE RATES OF NON-SPECIFIC INFECTION/INFLAMMATION
% of settlement type total

	Observed n	Affected n	CPR %	M	F
Sub-periosteal new bone formation					
Farmstead	330	20	6.1	11	5
Funerary	525	25	4.8	17	8
Industry	11	1	9.1	1	
Port	13	3	23.1	2	1
Roadside	145	19	13.1	12	6
Villa	79	1	1.3	1	
Village	30	0	0		
Total	**1133**	**69**	**6.1**	**44**	**20**
Endocranial lesions					
Farmstead	330	4	1.2	4	
Funerary	525	2	0.4	1	1
Industry	11	0	0		
Port	13	0	0		
Roadside	145	2	1.4	1	1
Villa	79	0	0		
Village	30	0	0		
Total	**1133**	**8**	**0.7**	**6**	**2**
Osteitis					
Farmstead	330	1	0.3		1
Funerary	525	0	0		
Industry	11	0	0		
Port	13	0	0		
Roadside	145	1	0.7		1
Villa	79	1	1.3		1
Village	30	0	0		
Total	**1133**	**3**	**0.3**		**3**
Osteomyelitis					
Farmstead	330	4	1.2	1	3
Funerary	525	2	0.4	2	
Industry	11	0	0		
Port	13	0	0		
Roadside	145	1	0.7	1	
Villa	79	2	2.5	1	1
Village	30	0	0		
Total	**1133**	**9**	**0.8**	**5**	**4**

n=20; X^2=9.49, p<0.005, d.f.=1). Leprosy affected two middle adult males and a young adult female from the funerary site at Cannington, Somerset (FIG. 7.24). Tuberculosis was reported in 0.4 per cent (n=5) of the sample, reported in two males from the funerary site at Cannington, a young adult male from the funerary site at Shakenoak Farm, Oxfordshire, and two old adult females from the unclassified farmstead at Milton, East Waste, Cambridgeshire, and the roadside settlement at Higham Ferrers in Northamptonshire (FIG. 7.21). A total of 10 (0.9 per cent) adults presented with rib periostitis, and 16 (n=1.4 per cent) with sinusitis. Roadside settlements (4.8 per cent, n=7) and villas (3.8 per cent, n=3), showed significantly higher prevalence of sinusitis compared to other settlement types (X^2=24.08, p<0.001, d.f.=6) (TABLE 7.7).

Only a few individuals were reported with metabolic disease, i.e. vitamin D (0.4 per cent, n=5) and vitamin C deficiency (0.3 per cent, n=3). Three cases of healed rickets were reported from the funerary sites at Cannington (n=2) and Horcott Quarry, Gloucestershire (n=1), whereas possible osteomalacia was reported in two individuals described as elderly from Cannington and the villa at Frocester Court, Gloucestershire. Probable and possible vitamin C deficiency affected an elderly individual from the same site, and both a young and old adult male from the roadside settlement at Bourton-on-the-Water, Gloucestershire. Osteoporosis was more frequent

TABLE 7.17: CENTRAL BELT: ADULT CRUDE PREVALENCE RATES OF METABOLIC DISEASE
% of settlement type total

	Observed n	Affected n	CPR %	M	F
Vitamin D deficiency					
Farmstead	330	0	0		
Funerary	525	4	0.8	2	1
Industry	11	0	0		
Port	13	0	0		
Roadside	145	0	0		
Villa	79	1	1.3		1
Village	30	0	0		
Total	**1133**	**5**	**0.4**	**2**	**2**
Vitamin C deficiency					
Farmstead	330	0	0		
Funerary	525	1	0.2		
Industry	11	0	0		
Port	13	0	0		
Roadside	145	2	1.4	2	
Villa	79	0	0		
Village	30	0	0		
Total	**1133**	**3**	**0.3**	**2**	
Osteoporosis					
Farmstead	330	2	1.5		1
Funerary	525	2	0.4	1	1
Industry	11	0	0		
Port	13	0	0		
Roadside	145	2	1.4		2
Villa	79	0	0		
Village	30	0	0		
Total	**1133**	**6**	**0.5**	**1**	**4**

in females (0.9 per cent, n=4), than males (0.2 per cent, n=1), and affected 1.6 per cent (n=4) of old adults (TABLE 7.17).

Trauma was reported in 139 individuals (12.3 per cent). Rates were highest in roadside settlements (15.2 per cent, n=22) and lowest at the single port site (5.0 per cent, n=1) (TABLE 7.7). Trauma was most frequent in old adults (23.7 per cent, n=59), and statistically more prevalent in men (21.8 per cent, n=97; X^2=31.03, p<0.001, d.f.=1). Ribs were the most common fracture from sites overall (17.6 per cent, n=35), and also in men (19.0 per cent, n=28). However, spinal trauma was most common in women (17.0 per cent, n=8) and on roadside settlements (18.9 per cent, n=7). Sharp and blunt force trauma indicative of weapon injury to the ulna was reported in a middle adult female from the villa at Frocester Court, Gloucestershire. A middle adult male was reported with a cut at the knee from the same site. At Asthall roadside settlement in Oxfordshire, a possible blade injury to the sixth and seventh cervical vertebra was reported in a middle adult male. Facial trauma affected males and females at similar frequencies of

4.8 per cent (n=7) and 4.3 per cent (n=2) respectively (FIG 7.28). Weapon injury to facial and cranial bones was reported in four males from the village at Gill Mill, Ducklington, Oxfordshire, the funerary sites at Cannington, Somerset, and Horcott Quarry, Gloucestershire, and the roadside settlement at Bourton-on-the-Water, Gloucestershire. Amputation of two hand phalanges was reported in old adult males from a funerary site at Horcott Quarry, Gloucestershire (TABLE 7.18).

Osteochondritis dissecans in the knee, elbow, wrist or ankle joints was reported in fifteen (1.3 per cent) individuals. The condition was more prevalent in middle adults (1.8 per cent, n=7), males (1.8 per cent, n=8) and at roadside settlements (4.1 per cent n=6). Spondylolysis was reported in 1.1 per cent (n=13) of adults, and was more frequent in females (1.6 per cent, n=7) and at funerary sites (1.7 per cent, n=9). Only a single case of a clay shoveller's fracture was identified, in an old adult male from the funerary site at Horcott Quarry. Schmorl's nodes were recorded in 8.1 per cent (n=92) of adults, and most common in

TABLE 7.18: CENTRAL BELT: TRAUMA LOCATIONS SPECIFIED IN ADULTS, BY SITE TYPE
% of total trauma locations by settlement type

Element	Farmstead		Funerary		Industry		Port		Roadside		Villa		Village		Total	
	n	%	n	%	n	%	n	%	n	%	n	%	n	%	n	%
Cranium	0		3	3.2	0		0		4	10.8	0		1	33.3	8	4
Mandible	0		2	2.1	0		0		0		0		0		2	1
Facial	2	3.9	5	5.3	0		0		1	2.7	1	9.1	0		9	4.5
Scapula	1	2.0	4	4.2	0		0		0		0		0		5	2.5
Clavicle	2	3.9	8	8.4	0		1	100	2	5.4	0		0		13	6.5
Sternum	0		1	1.1	0		0		0		0		0		1	0.5
Rib	10	19.6	20	21.1	0		0		2	5.4	2	18.2	1	33.3	35	17.6
Spine	10	19.6	0		0		0		7	18.9	1	9.1	0		18	9
Humerus	1	2.0	6	6.3	0		0		0		0		0		7	3.5
Radius	1	2.0	6	6.3	0		0		1	2.7	1	9.1	0		9	4.5
Ulna	2	3.9	7	7.4	0		0		1	2.7	4	36.4	0		14	7
Metacarpal	4	7.8	2	2.1	0		0		1	2.7	0		0		7	3.5
Hand phalanx	7	13.7	4	4.2	0		0		2	5.4	0		0		13	6.5
Hip	0		1	1.1	0		0		1	2.7	2	18.2	0		4	2
Femur	2	3.9	4	4.2	0		0		1	2.7	0		0		7	3.5
Patella	0		2	2.1	0		0		0		0		0		2	1
Tibia	4	7.8	7	7.4	0		0		5	13.5	0		0		16	8
Fibula	3	5.9	6	6.3	0		0		4	10.8	0		1	33.3	14	7
Ankle (talus, calcaneus)	1	2.0	1	1.1	0		0		2	5.4	0		0		4	2
Metatarsal	1	2.0	3	3.2	0		0		2	5.4	0		0		6	3
Foot phalanx	0		3	3.2	1	100	0		1	2.7	0		0		5	2.5
Total	**51**		**95**		**1**		**1**		**37**		**11**		**3**		**199**	

TABLE 7.19: CENTRAL BELT: DEGENERATIVE JOINT DISEASE IN ADULTS
% of settlement type total

	Observed n	Affected n	CPR %	M	F
Extraspinal					
TMJ					
Farmstead	330	5	1.5	5	
Funerary	525	10	1.9	6	4
Port	13	0	0		
Roadside	145	6	4.1	3	3
Total TMJ	**1133**	**21**	**1.9**	**14**	**7**
Sterno-costal					
Farmstead	330	4	1.2	2	2
Funerary	525	4	0.8	4	
Port	13	1	7.7		1
Roadside	145	4	2.8		3
Village	30	1	3.3	1	
Total sterno-costal	**1133**	**14**	**1.2**	**7**	**6**
Spinal					
Vertebral					
Farmstead	330	80	24.2	33	40
Funerary	525	148	28.2	82	62
Industry	11	4	36.4	4	
Port	13	7	53.8	4	3
Roadside	145	51	35.2	24	25
Villa	79	16	20.3	6	9
Village	30	1	3.3	1	
Total spinal	**1133**	**305**	**26.9**	**153**	**138**
Upper body					
Sterno-clavicular					
Farmstead	330	6	1.8	2	4
Funerary	525	4	0.8	4	
Roadside	145	7	4.8	4	3
Total sterno-clavicular	**1133**	**17**	**1.5**	**10**	**7**
Acromio-clavicular					
Farmstead	330	2	0.6	2	
Funerary	525	4	0.8	4	
Roadside	145	15	10.3	6	9
Village	30	1	3.3	1	
Total acromio-clavicular	**1133**	**22**	**1.9**	**13**	**9**
Shoulder					
Farmstead	330	18	5.5	12	4
Funerary	525	22	4.2	10	12
Roadside	145	14	9.7	6	8
Villa	79	3	3.8		3
Total shoulder	**1133**	**57**	**5.0**	**28**	**27**
Elbow					
Farmstead	330	8	2.4	4	4
Funerary	525	21	4.0	14	5
Roadside	145	9	6.2	5	4
Villa	79	5	6.3		5
Village	30	1	3.3	1	
Total elbow	**1133**	**44**	**3.9**	**24**	**18**

TABLE 7.19: (CONT'D)

	Observed n	*Affected n*	*CPR %*	*M*	*F*
Wrist					
Farmstead	330	13	3.9	10	3
Funerary	525	26	5.0	16	10
Port	13	1	7.7		1
Industry	11	1	9.1	1	
Roadside	145	15	10.3	7	8
Villa	79	1	1.3		1
Total wrist	**1133**	**57**	**5.0**	**34**	**23**
Hand					
Farmstead	330	18	5.5	8	8
Funerary	525	23	4.4	10	13
Roadside	145	15	10.3	5	10
Villa	79	5	6.3	1	3
Village	30	1	3.3	1	
Total hand	**1133**	**62**	**5.5**	**25**	**34**
Sacro-iliac					
Farmstead	330	3	0.9	3	
Funerary	525	4	0.8	2	2
Roadside	145	3	2.1		3
Villa	79	1	1.3		
Total sacro-iliac	**1133**	**11**	**1.0**	**5**	**5**
Hip					
Farmstead	330	21	6.4	13	5
Funerary	525	27	5.1	23	4
Port	13	1	7.7	1	
Roadside	145	18	12.4	8	10
Villa	79	7	8.9	2	3
Total hip	**1133**	**74**	**6.5**	**47**	**22**
Knee					
Farmstead	330	8	2.4	7	1
Funerary	525	23	4.4	13	10
Industry	11	2	18.2	2	
Roadside	145	12	8.3	5	7
Villa	79	4	5.1		3
Village	30	2	6.7	2	
Total knee	**1113**	**51**	**4.5**	**29**	**21**
Ankle					
Farmstead	330	4	1.2	3	1
Funerary	525	9	1.7	5	4
Roadside	145	8	5.5	3	4
Villa	79	1	1.3		
Village	30	1	3.3	1	
Total ankle	**1133**	**23**	**2.0**	**12**	**9**
Foot					
Farmstead	330	7	2.1	5	1
Funerary	525	23	4.4	13	10
Port	13	2	15.4	2	
Roadside	145	9	6.2	3	5
Villa	79	1	1.3		
Total foot	**1133**	**42**	**3.7**	**23**	**16**

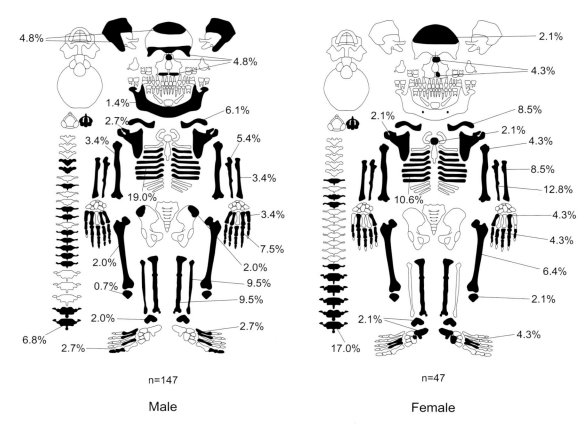

FIG. 7.28. Central Belt: elements reported with fractures in adult males and females (per cent of total fractures elements reported)

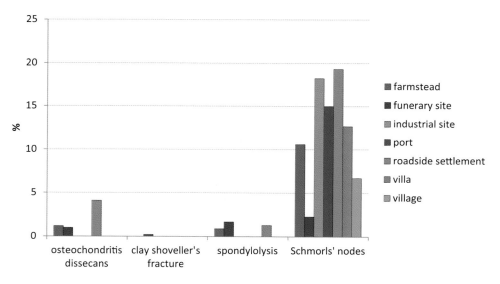

FIG. 7.29. Central Belt: crude prevalence rates of joint stress in adults

middle adults (12.2 per cent, n=48) and males (10.8 per cent, n=48). The inland port at Camp Ground, Colne Fen in Cambridgeshire, has the highest rate of spinal lesions at 23.1 per cent, although only three individuals were affected. Schmorl's nodes were also frequent on roadside settlements (19.3 per cent, n=28) (FIG. 7.29).

Degenerative changes were noted in 400 individuals, 35.5 per cent overall. As expected, joint

disease advanced with age, and was most frequent in old adults (67.1 per cent, n=167), although 33.3 per cent (n=5) of young adults at villas are already affected. Significantly fewer women (37.6 per cent, n=166) had joint disease than men (47.2 per cent, n=210; X^2=8.27, p<0.005, d.f.=1). However, 66.7 per cent (n=4) of men and women at the inland port at Camp Ground, Colne Fen, had joint degeneration, and more women (55.6,

TABLE 7.20: CENTRAL BELT: DENTAL DISEASE IN ADULTS
% of settlement type total

	Observed n	Affected n	CPR %	M	F
Calculus					
Farmstead	315	104	33.0	52	43
Funerary	166	53	31.9	35	17
Industry	11	4	36.4	4	0
Port	13	4	30.8	3	1
Roadside	145	40	27.6	20	19
Villa	79	17	21.5	3	13
Village	30	4	13.3	2	1
Total calculus	**759**	**226**	**29.8**	**119**	**94**
Caries					
Farmstead	315	106	33.7	57	37
Funerary	166	69	41.6	43	26
Industry	11	6	54.5	4	2
Port	13	2	15.4	2	
Roadside	145	40	27.6	19	19
Villa	79	49	62.0	3	11
Village	30	23	76.7	3	4
Total caries	**759**	**247**	**32.5**	**131**	**99**
AMTL					
Farmstead	315	54	17.1	30	20
Funerary	166	62	37.3	35	27
Industry	11	3	27.3	3	0
Port	13	8	61.5	5	3
Roadside	145	23	15.9	12	11
Villa	79	10	12.7	1	9
Village	30	5	16.7	4	1
Total AMTL	**759**	**165**	**27.8**	**78**	**84**
Abscess/PAL					
Farmstead	315	12	3.8	8	4
Funerary	166	46	27.7	26	20
Industry	11	0	0		
Port	13	1	7.7		1
Roadside	145	15	10.3	6	9
Villa	79	6	7.6	2	6
Village	30	0	0		
Total abscess/PAL	**759**	**80**	**10.5**	**42**	**38**

n=30) from roadside settlements presented with degeneration than men (42.9 per cent, n=27). The spine was the most frequently cited location of joint degeneration (26.9 per cent, n=305), followed by the hip (6.5 per cent, n=74) and hand (5.5 per cent, n=62). This pattern is mimicked at the site level, although the knee joint is most frequently affected at the only village site at Gill Mill, Ducklington, in Oxfordshire (25.0 per cent, n=2). Degeneration in the hand is more frequent in females (7.7 per cent, n=34) than males (5.6 per cent, n=25) (TABLE 7.19).

Dental disease was reported on in 759 adults (male n=314, female n=249, unsexed n=196). Caries was most frequent, affecting 32.5 per cent (n=247) of adults, compared to 10.5 per cent

(n=80) for abscesses/PAL. Dental disease became more frequent with advancing age, apart from calculus which was most prevalent in middle adults (43.5 per cent, n=110). Both calculus and caries were slightly more prevalent in men, at 37.9 per cent (n=119) and 41.7 per cent (n=131), compared to rates of 37.8 per cent (n=94) and 39.8 per cent (n=99) in females. Tooth loss and abscesses were, however, more frequently identified in the female cohort at rates of 33.7 per cent (n=84) and 15.3 per cent (n=38). Caries affected significantly more individuals at the industry/villa site at Priors Hall, Weldon, Northamptonshire (54.5 per cent, n=6; X^2=54.03, p<0.001, d.f.=6). Camp Ground, Colne Fen (61.5 per cent, n=8), and funerary sites (37.7 per cent, n=62) showed significantly higher rates of AMTL (X^2=42.83, p<0.001, d.f.=6). Abscesses and periapical lesions were statistically more prevalent at funerary sites, particularly at Horcott Quarry in Gloucestershire and Radley Barrow Hills in Oxfordshire (27.7 per cent, n=46; X^2=80.43, p<0.001, d.f.=6) (TABLE 7.20).

PALAEOPATHOLOGY AND BURIAL ARCHAEOLOGY

Burial practice in rural Roman Britain is discussed in detail in Chapter 6 of this volume. Patterns in the distribution of ages-at-death, sex, and palaeopathology in relation to burial practice are presented below. These are based on the subsample of rural Romano-British inhumation burials outlined above.

Palaeopathology and burial archaeology in the East

The subsample discussed here includes six prone (positioned face down) adult burials from the complex farmsteads (5.2 per cent) at Clay Farm, Trumpington (n=1) and Hutchison site, Addenbrooke's (n=4) in Cambridgeshire, and Melford Meadows, Norfolk (n=1). The practice was apparent in every adult age group (TABLES 7.21 and 7.22). Women were buried prone in 5.9 per cent (n=4) of cases, whereas only one adult

TABLE 7.21: EAST: PALAEOPATHOLOGY SUBSAMPLE OF PRONE AND DECAPITATED BURIALS, AND BURIALS WITH GRAVE GOODS
% of observed total

Prone	Observed n	Affected n	%
Sex			
Adult	238	6	2.5
M	83	1	1.2
F	68	4	5.9
Decapitation	*Observed n*	*Affected n*	*%*
Sex			
Total	322	24	7.5
Non-adult	79	2	2.5
Adult	238	21	8.8
M	83	7	8.4
F	68	9	13.2
Grave goods	*Observed n*	*Affected n*	*%*
Sex			
Total	322	65	20.2
Non-adult	79	11	13.9
Adult	238	53	22.3
M	83	13	15.7
F	68	18	26.5

TABLE 7.22: EAST: PRONE BURIALS BY AGE AND SETTLEMENT TYPE
% of observed total

	Farmstead observed	affected	%	Total observed	affected	%
18–25	8	1	12.5	25	1	4.0
26–45	21	1	4.8	64	1	1.6
>46	34	2	5.9	42	2	4.8
Adult	53	2	3.8	107	2	1.9
Total n	**116**	**6**	**5.2**	**238**	**6**	**2.5**

TABLE 7.23: EAST: PRONE BURIALS BY AGE AND SETTLEMENT TYPE
% of observed total

	Farmstead observed	affected	%	Villa observed	affected	%	Total observed	affected	%Non-adult
Non-adult									
10.6–14.5	1	1	100	0			2	1	50.0
14.6–17.0	2	1	50.0	1	0	0	7	1	14.3
Total	**24**	**2**	**8.3**	**5**	**0**	**0**	**79**	**2**	**2.5**
Adult									
18–25	8	1	12.5	3	2	66.7	25	3	12.0
26–45	21	4	19.0	13	3	23.1	64	7	10.9
>46	34	6	17.6	0			42	6	14.3
Adult	53	5	9.4	3	0	0	107	5	4.7
Total	**116**	**16**	**13.8**	**19**	**5**	**26.3**	**238**	**21**	**8.8**

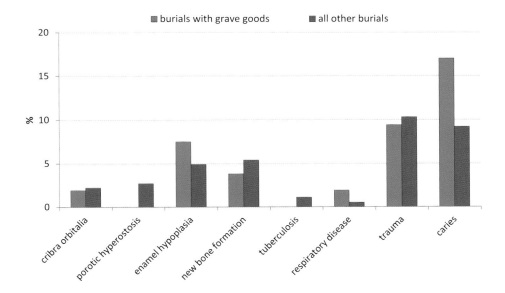

■ burials with grave goods   ■ all other burials

FIG. 7.30. East: crude prevalence rates of palaeopathology in adult inhumations with grave goods

male (1.2 per cent) was interred face down. Palaeopathology in this cohort was low overall, with enamel hypoplasia, caries and joint disease affecting one individual each. Notably, one young adult female was reported with tuberculosis.

A total of 7.5 per cent (n=24) of burials in the sample were of decapitated individuals, 19 from unclassified and complex farmsteads (13.8 per cent) and five from Chignal St James villa (26.3 per cent). These include two older children (2.5 per cent), one unaged individual, and 21 (8.8 per cent) adults. Decapitation was more frequent in adult females (13.2 per cent, n=9) (TABLE 7.22). The rite was most prevalent in children aged 10.6–14.5 years old (50.0 per cent, n=1), although sample sizes are small for this cohort (TABLES 7.21, 7.23). Decapitated adults showed proportionally higher rates of porotic hyperostosis (9.5 per cent, n=2), enamel hypoplasia (19.0 per cent, n=4), respiratory disease (4.8 per cent, n=1) and caries (14.3 per cent n=3), although sample sizes are small.

Grave goods were present in 65 (20.2 per cent) burials. Fewer child burials were furnished (13.9 per cent, n=11), than those of adults (22.3 per cent, n=53). Women (26.5 per cent, n=18) were more often accompanied by grave goods than men (15.7 per cent, n=13) (TABLE 7.21). In non-adults, those buried in furnished graves exhibited higher frequencies of EH, trauma and caries, although each of these cases is represented by only one individual each. In the adults, frequencies of EH (7.5 per cent, n=4), respiratory disease (1.9 per cent, n=1) and caries (17.0 per cent, n=9) were higher in the cohort buried with grave goods (FIG. 7.30). Again, sample sizes are small and may not be representative.

TABLE 7.24: SOUTH: PALAEOPATHOLOGY SUBSAMPLE OF PRONE AND DECAPITATED BURIALS, AND BURIALS WITH GRAVE GOODS
% of observed total

Prone	Observed n	Affected n	%
Sex			
Total	741	8	1.1
Non-adult	351	2	0.6
Adult	388	6	1.5
M	164	1	0.6
F	143	5	3.5
Decapitation	Observed n	Affected n	%
Sex			
Total	741	3	0.4
Adult	388	3	0.8
M	164	1	0.6
F	143	2	1.4
Grave goods	Observed n	Affected n	%
Sex			
Total	741	101	13.6
Non-adult	351	16	4.6
Adult	388	85	21.9
M	164	27	16.5
F	143	43	30.1

Palaeopathology and burial archaeology in the South

A total of eight (1.1 per cent) prone burials were reported, including two 14.6–17.0 year olds and six (1.5 per cent) adults. Prone burial was most frequent in adolescents (18.2 per cent, n=2), and at complex and unenclosed farmsteads (2.6 per cent, n=4). In this subsample, more adult females (3.5 per cent, n=5) were buried face down than males (0.6 per cent, n=1) (TABLES 7.24 and 7.25).

TABLE 7.25: SOUTH: PRONE AND DECAPITATED BURIALS BY AGE AND SETTLEMENT TYPE
% of observed total

Prone	Farmstead observed	affected	%	Funerary observed	affected	%	Village observed	affected	%	Total n	affected	%
14.6–17.0	1	0	0	4	0	0	3	2	66.7	11	2	18.2
18–25	14	1	7.1	27	0	0	11	0	0	60	1	1.7
26–45	42	1	2.4	94	1	1.1	18	0	0	173	2	1.2
>46	29	2	6.9	39	1	2.6	17	0	0	90	3	3.3
Total n	**156**	**4**	**2.6**	**256**	**2**	**0.8**	**114**	**2**	**1.8**	**741**	**8**	**1.1**
Decapitation												
26–45	42	1	2.4	94	0	0	18	0	0	173	1	0.6
>46	29	0	0	39	1	2.6	17	1	5.9	90	2	2.2
Total n	**156**	**1**	**0.6**	**256**	**1**	**0.4**	**114**	**1**	**0.9**	**741**	**3**	**0.4**

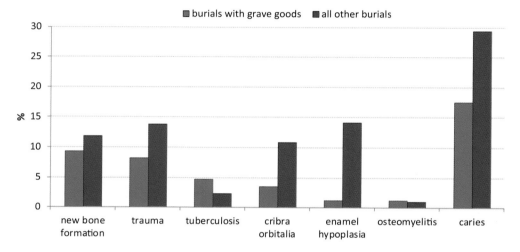

FIG. 7.31. South: crude prevalence rates of palaeopathology in adult inhumations with grave goods

In the adults, frequencies for haematopoietic lesions, enamel defects, new bone formation, bone infections, respiratory disease, TB, metabolic disease, trauma and caries were consistently higher in the prone cohort. However, sample sizes are small.

Three (0.4 per cent) decapitated burials were reported, one each from the complex farmstead at Zones 9 and 10 of the East Kent Access (0.6 per cent), the funerary site at Alington Avenue, Fordington in Dorset (0.4 per cent), and the village at Mucking, Essex (0.9 per cent). Decapitation occurred in adults only (0.8 per cent), and was identified in one male (0.6 per cent) and two females (1.4 per cent) (TABLE 7.24). The highest frequency of this burial rite was observed in old adults (2.2 per cent, n=2) (TABLE 7.25). Palaeopathology is negligible in this sample, with one individual affected by dental disease.

Grave goods were reported in 101 (13.6 per cent) burials. Significantly more adult burials (21.9 per cent, n=85; X^2=47.07, p<0.001, d.f.=1) and female burials (30.1 per cent, n=43; X^2=8.02,

p<0.005, d.f.=1) were furnished (TABLE 7.24). Furnishings were most frequent in 18–25 year olds (23.3 per cent, n=14). Both osteomyelitis (1.2 per cent, n=1) and tuberculosis (4.7 per cent, n=4) were more frequent in the adults that were accompanied by goods. Enamel hypoplasia was significantly more frequent in unfurnished burials (14.2 per cent, n=43) than in those with grave goods (1.2 per cent, n=1; X^2=11.78, p<0.001, d.f.=1) (FIG. 7.31).

Palaeopathology and burial archaeology in the Central Belt

A total of 63 individuals (3.8 per cent) were reported prone in the subsample for the Central Belt. Six children were buried prone, compared to 57 adults (5.0 per cent), which is statistically significant (X^2=14.51, p<0.001, d.f.=1). In the children, prevalence was highest in 2.6–6.5 year olds from villas (20.0 per cent, n=1) (TABLES 7.26 and 7.27). Palaeopathology includes one case of dental disease, and Schmorl's nodes in the adolescent from the complex farmstead at Higham

TABLE 7.26: CENTRAL BELT: DISTRIBUTION OF PRONE BURIALS IN NON-ADULT GRAVES
% of observed total

	Farmstead observed	affected	%	Funerary observed	affected	%	Villa observed	affected	%t
Perinate	17	1	5.6	22	0	0	35	1	2.9
0–1.0	34	0	0	63	1	1.6	29	0	0
1.1–2.5	6	0	0	29	0	0	2	0	0
2.6–6.5	8	0	0	37	0	0	5	1	20.0
6.6–10.5	7	0	0	21	1	4.8	4	0	0
10.6–14.5	6	0	0	26	0	0	3	0	0
14.6–17.0	11	1	9.1	19	0	0	1	0	0
Non-adult	2	0	0	18	0	0	1	0	0
Total n	**91**	**2**	**2.2**	**235**	**2**	**0.9**	**80**	**2**	**2.5**

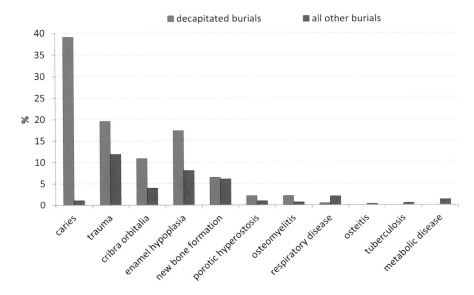

FIG. 7.32.   Central Belt: crude prevalence rates of palaeopathology in adult decapitated burials

Road, Burton Latimer in Northamptonshire. In the adults, slightly higher numbers of males were reported prone (6.7 per cent, n=30), and the rite was most frequent in old adults (8.0 per cent, n=20). Sample sizes are small, but it is apparent that lesions are more frequent in adults that were interred face down, particularly for cribra orbitalia (10.5 per cent, n=6/4.0 per cent, n=43), trauma (28.1 per cent, n=16/11.4 per cent, n=123) and caries (36.8 per cent, n=21/21.0 per cent, n=226).

Decapitation was reported in 48 individuals (2.9 per cent). Two children were decapitated (0.4 per cent), including a 6.6–10.5 year old with enamel hypoplasia. Overall, significantly more adults (4.1 per cent, n=46) than children were decapitated (X^2=17.13, p<0.001, d.f.=1). The rite was slightly more frequent among males (4.7 per cent, n=21), and old adults (6.4 per cent, n=16) (TABLE 7.26). Significantly higher rates of enamel hypoplasia (17.4 per cent, n=8; X^2=48.13, p<0.001, d.f.=1), trauma (19.6 per cent, n=9, X^2=96.43, p<0.001,

d.f.=1) and caries (39.1 per cent, n=18, X^2=266.40, p<0.001, d.f.=1) were reported in the decapitated adult cohort (FIG. 7.32).

Overall, 11.0 per cent (n=182) of burials were furnished. Grave goods were significantly more frequent in the adult cohort (14.2 per cent, n=161), compared to the children (4.1 per cent, n=21; X^2=36.55, p<0.001, d.f.=1) (TABLE 7.26). No perinates were buried with grave goods. Old adults have the highest frequency of furnished graves at 16.5 per cent (n=41), whereas 6.6–10.5 year olds mark the non-adult group with most furnished graves (12.8 per cent, n=5).

In the non-adults, higher rates for cribra orbitalia (14.3 per cent, n=3/7.4 per cent, n=36), enamel hypoplasia (9.5 per cent, n=2/5.7 per cent, n=28), endocranial lesions (9.5 per cent, n=2/5.7 per cent, n=28), respiratory disease (4.8 per cent, n=1/0.4 per cent, n=2) and caries (4.8 per cent, n=1/2.3 per cent, n=11) were reported in those buried with grave goods. In the adult cohort,

TABLE 7.27: CENTRAL BELT: PALAEOPATHOLOGY
SUBSAMPLE OF PRONE AND DECAPITATED BURIALS, AND
BURIALS WITH GRAVE GOODS
% of observed total

Prone	Observed n	Affected n	%
Sex			
Total	1654	63	3.8
Non-adult	509	6	1.2
Adult	1133	57	5.0
M	445	30	6.7
F	441	19	4.3
Decapitation	Observed n	Affected n	%
Sex			
Total	1654	48	2.9
Non-adult	509	2	0.4
Adult	1133	46	4.1
M	445	21	4.7
F	441	16	3.6
Grave goods	Observed n	Affected n	%
Sex			
Total	1654	182	11.0
Non-adult	509	21	4.1
Adult	1133	161	14.2
M	445	56	12.6
F	441	74	16.8

pathology rates are similar between furnished and unfurnished inhumation burials. All the adults diagnosed with tuberculosis (0.5 per cent, n=5) were buried without grave goods, although a higher rate of respiratory disease is apparent in furnished graves (3.8 per cent, n=6).

DISCUSSION

The current study marks the first effort in providing a focused analysis of adult and child health in rural Roman Britain. It gives much needed reference points for ages-at-death, sex distributions, and palaeopathology in three regional case studies, the East, South and Central Belt of England. As discussed in Chapter 6, the pre-Roman Iron Age is characterised by a paucity of archaeologically detectable burial rites across much of Britain, and it is likely that a large proportion of rural Roman Britons may have been afforded similar forms of treatment in death. The skeletal data available for the study are, therefore, biased. We observe the biological signatures of only a selected dead population, which may not accurately reflect population size, structure and health in rural Roman Britain (Chamberlain 2001).

Additional limitations arise due to variations in sample sizes, with some settlement types being represented by just one site, and by differences in

the recording and reporting of bioarchaeological data. Discrepancies exist between the methods used, particularly with regard to non-adult skeletal remains. However, by consolidating the data into standardised age groups, and discussing crude as opposed to true prevalence rates, we are able to grasp health and wellbeing in the largest sample of men, women and children of the Romano-British countryside to date.

BURIAL RITES AND PALAEOPATHOLOGY

Perinatal and infant burial: distinct rites or evidence for absence?

Extremes in the representation of newborn and infant burials in Romano-British cemeteries are the subject of ongoing debate (see Gilmore and Halcrow 2014). Rates may vary from complete absence of infants and perinates in designated cemetery sites, to burial grounds entirely composed of those who have not survived the first year of life. These trends have previously been noted by Rohnbogner and Lewis (2016a) in an analysis of ages-at-death in urban and rural Romano-British children. In fact, major urban burial grounds held significantly fewer infant burials than those from rural sites. Observations in the current study expand on this, and demonstrate that even within the rural cohort itself, significant variation in the rate of burial and recovery of both infants and perinates exists. Major differences were found in the spatial and temporal distribution of perinate and infant burials across the regions, suggesting fluctuations in biological (i.e. endogenous) and environmental (i.e. exogenous) factors that determine survival at birth and during the first year of life (Bourgeois-Pichat 1951; Vögele 1994; Murray and Frenk 2002). Ill-health of the mother, birth trauma and congenital disease will raise mortality at birth (Frenzen and Hogan 1982), whereas death in infancy is profoundly affected by infection, poisoning, accidents and shortcomings in nutrition (Scott and Duncan 1999). Mortality at birth must have been low in settlements and phases with only very few perinate burials. Accordingly, this would suggest that the risks of congenital diseases, birth trauma and maternal ill-health did not pose a hazard to newborns in early and late Roman periods, at all settlement types in the East except roadside settlements, and at the farmsteads and funerary sites of the South and Central Belt (FIG. 7.33).

Extremes are also reported for the representation of infant burials (FIG. 7.34). In the South, early to mid-Roman and mid- to late Roman phases and villa sites were reported with high numbers of infant burials. This could on the face of it suggest that a high infant mortality risk only occurred

FIG. 7.33. Distribution of sites with at least one perinate burial reported

FIG. 7.34. Distribution of sites with at least one infant burial reported

during specific phases and at one particular settlement type. The defended small town at Alcester, Warwickshire, was also characterised by high infant mortality, which could suggest that infections, accidents or nutritional problems were having a significant impact on infant wellbeing at this site. In contrast, low numbers of infant burials at funerary sites and during early and late Roman phases are apparent across all three regions. This could mean that environmental risk factors for infant survival were low, but only in sites of early or late Roman date, and in those unknown satellite settlements served by a dedicated cemetery site.

Such extreme fluctuations in the proportions of perinate and infant burials, and therefore biological and environmental factors, seem unlikely in a pre-industrial rural society (Vögele 1994; Lewis and Gowland 2007; Humphrey et al. 2012). Perhaps it is not differential mortality risk at birth and during infancy that we observe, but rather differences in the burial and recovery of those dying very young. Several earlier studies discuss the inherent problems faced when interpreting demographic profiles of Romano-British sites, with high proportions of perinates and infants on one side, and their complete absence on the other (see Philpott 1991, 101; Scott 1991, 120; Esmonde Cleary 2000; Pearce 2001; 2013; Wileman 2005, 80–1, 99; Moore 2009; Gowland et al. 2014; Millett and Gowland 2015; see also Ch. 6, p. 231).

In his *Naturalis Historia* VII [15], Pliny describes children as lacking a soul until teething at around six months old. Perhaps this crucial point in the lifecourse of children marked those who did not attain it as separate, i.e. without a soul. Those who died prior to teething may, therefore, have been treated differently in death and excluded from formal cemeteries (Philpott 1991, 101). Regarding the low numbers of infants reported from funerary sites, it has been suggested that a set of distinct infant burial rites may have been practised in rural Roman Britain. If the objective was to protect the child in the afterlife, particularly if he or she was without a soul, a burial location that allows the infant to remain with the living may have been favoured (Millett and Gowland 2015). Additionally, beliefs about fruitfulness and fecundity of the women and the land may have come into play, perhaps placing infants in the domestic or agricultural sphere rather than formal burial grounds (Finlay 2000; Tibbetts 2008; Chadwick 2012). Regardless of motivation, this may lead to areas of a site or cemetery with a high density of perinate or infant burials. Examples of these are apparent across the regions. The villa at Frocester Court in Gloucestershire is characterised by high numbers of perinates (n=35) who make up 85.4 per cent of the non-adult population (n=41).

This is even more intriguing since no infants were reported at the site. Perinates were often interred in oval graves, scattered throughout the site at Frocester Court, in association with ditches and building structures of Roman date (Reece 2000, 204–5). At Baldock roadside settlement in Hertfordshire, 24 (70.6 per cent) of the 34 reported non-adult burials were those of perinates. As discussed in Chapter 6, this roadside settlement is characterised by a large number of cemeteries around its periphery, as well as burials reported from within the settlement itself (Stead and Rigby 1986, 81; Burleigh and Fitzpatrick-Matthews 2010, 31). At Camp Ground, Colne Fen, the inland port in Cambridgeshire, perinates accounted for 83.3 per cent (n=10) of the non-adult sample (n=12). It is likely that the site had a formal burial ground, lying either to the south or west, which remains to be discovered, and this would indicate that the perinates were those newborns excluded from the formal cemetery. Interestingly, these perinates were also distributed throughout the site, associated with postholes, enclosures and ditches (Evans 2013a, 230). The villas at Bucknowle in Dorset and at Itter Crescent, Peterborough, in Cambridgeshire, have high numbers of post-neonatal and infant burials, accounting for 88.1 per cent (n=59, n=67) and 95.5 per cent (n=21, n=22) of the total non-adult burials. Burial was observed within buildings at Bucknowle villa (Robb and Rogers 2009), while infants were recovered from pits and ditches, as foundation deposits, and in association with the tile kiln and stone villa building at Itter Crescent (Webb forthcoming). The roadside settlement at Staines, Surrey, saw sixteen burials of infants aged seven months and younger, who formed the majority of human burials reported from the site (Chapman 2010).

With the spread of Christianity during the later Roman period, we may expect inclusion of infants in formal cemeteries, alongside adults and older children (Petts 2004; see Ch. 6, p. 279). However, at the third to fifth century A.D. urban cemetery at Poundbury Camp, Dorchester, Dorset, Molleson (1989) suggested baptism as a rite of passage that dictated inclusion of infants in the formal cemetery. Burying unbaptised children away from baptised members of the community is a long-standing Christian tradition (Finlay 2000), though distinguishing such unbaptised children of Christian communities from other 'pagan' infant burials found integrated within settlement contexts is of course impossible. As discussed in Chapter 5, there is also great uncertainty as to the actual impact of Christianity on the rural population, as we cannot measure how widespread this new belief system actually was across rural communities of the province.

The highly variable proportions of infants and perinates in the burial grounds of rural Roman Britain may be a confirmation of one of the major limitations of the study. Perhaps the youngest members of society were awarded archaeologically invisible funerary rites, which varied through both time and space. This may have caused their under-representation or absence at times, particularly within cemeteries. Dedicated 'infant corners' may have been created within some of the larger, formal burial grounds, although so far evidence for this is lacking (Philpott 1991; Esmonde Cleary 2000; Moore 2009; Pearce 2013). High numbers of perinates and infants at certain sites would seem to be a reflection of dedicated burial space within the settlement itself, or in association with boundary features, such as at Barton Court Farm in Oxfordshire (see Ch. 6, p. 248). If these kinds of burial locations were favoured, then we are going to observe high numbers of infants or perinates for a site where no formal cemetery has been excavated. These burials are not hasty and haphazard disposals of unwanted babies, but mark a community's effort to maintain a close bond between the living and those who have died very young (Carroll 2011).

Ultimately, the underlying reasons behind differential burial rites for babies have still to be fully explored. The withholding of perinates and infants from the rest of the dead community may have had many underlying motivations and were probably not the result of a single belief or cultural identity.

Palaeopathology of the buried population: prone burial, decapitation and grave goods

As discussed in Chapter 6 (p. 226), decapitated and prone burials are of great interest to archaeologists and the public alike. Equally, elaborate inhumation burials with an array of grave goods seem to warrant greater attention, as we often perceive these individuals to have been outstanding in both life and death. A way of investigating if the men, women and children buried in these unusual graves were 'different' is by evaluating their biological data in comparison to those buried in 'standardised' inhumation graves (Parker Pearson 2003; Pearce 2008).

At Kempston, Bedford, Boylston et al. (2000) observed that neither sex was favoured for prone burial or decapitation, a trend also apparent across the regions. The lack of patterning we have observed in prone and decapitation burials regarding sex distributions acts as a reminder that these particular rites may not have had a gendered origin in rural societies. Decapitated and prone burial were primarily reserved for adults, and frequently associated with old age. A higher likelihood of prone burial in older individuals was also noted at Kempston, although decapitation affected individuals of all ages (ibid.). It is likely that both prone and decapitated burials were a minor part of the normative funerary practice of particular communities, possibly negotiated by cultural, regional, social and biological factors (Strück 2000; Milella et al. 2015; Crerar 2016; see Ch. 6, p. 279).

Overall, those of older age were more frequently accompanied by grave goods. This is interesting as the opposite has been noted at the fourth to fifth century A.D. cemetery at Butt Road, Colchester, and in the 1967–1972 excavations of the fourth-century A.D. cemetery at Lankhills, Winchester (Clarke 1979; Crummy et al. 1993; Gowland 2007). Perhaps a range of attributes, like marriage or parenthood, had to be acquired through the lifecourse, and older age therefore correlated with a more secure or higher social status that warranted the offering of grave goods in older individuals in rural communities (Harlow and Laurence 2007). Although grave goods were statistically more frequent in the adults of the Central Belt and South regions, burials of children as young as infants were furnished across all areas. In the children of the South and East regions, the highest frequency of grave goods was apparent in those that would have been weaned, i.e. 2.6–6.5 years old (Fuller et al. 2006; Nehlich et al. 2011; Redfern et al. 2012; Powell et al. 2014). The distribution of grave goods among the children of the Central Belt differed, and 6.6–10.5 year olds stand out. It was suggested by Rohnbogner and Lewis (2016a) that children may have commenced their working lives within this age group. If this was indeed the case, death in association with this important milestone in the Romano-British lifecourse may have incurred the need for grave goods (Redfern and Gowland 2012).

When discussing palaeopathology in furnished, prone or decapitated burials, we have to consider small sample sizes. Unusual burials may also generate greater interest from excavators and specialists, which may result in a more detailed skeletal analysis and subsequent bias with palaeopathological data. A prone body position has been reported in child burials where the palaeopathology suggests a disability (Southwell-Wright 2014). Examples include a congenitally deaf 6-year-old from Poundbury Camp, Dorchester, buried prone in a cist constructed of limestone roof tiles (Farwell and Molleson 1993, 29, 188). At Lankhills, Winchester, a 4–7 year old with scaphocephaly, a form of premature cranial suture fusion, was placed in the grave prone. The child, believed to be a girl based on the grave goods, was wearing bracelets and finger-rings

(Clough and Boyle 2010, 372). A range of congenital conditions do not translate into the skeletal record, although they would have had an impact on social and cultural relationships while alive, perhaps marking certain individuals as different or 'other' (Foucault 1988).

In the Central Belt, significantly higher rates of enamel hypoplasia, trauma and caries were observed in the decapitated adults, attesting to early childhood stress through fever or infection, hazardous activity and poor oral health exacerbated by weakened enamel and the caries-promoting function of stress (Hong *et al.* 2009). Perhaps this may indicate an overall lower status and somewhat more physical lifestyle for these individuals. In the South, instances of enamel hypoplasia were significantly lower in adults buried with grave goods, suggesting differences in the early childhood experience between those afforded grave goods, and those without. Grave goods are often used as an indicator of higher status, and less exposure to early childhood stress in those given grave goods supports this hypothesis.

Burial rites and palaeopathology: summary

We are still speculating about the social, cultural or religious reasons that initiated changes in the burial rites or location of resting places of infants and newborns. The study has demonstrated that the issue is no longer one of urban–rural difference as previously suggested by Rohnbogner and Lewis (2016a). It is apparent that differences in burial practice existed within rural communities themselves, and future work must explore these further to try and understand the underlying motivations. The issue is complex, however, as recording and reporting of infant burials is fraught with inconsistencies regarding the ageing of perinate and infant skeletons. Often, these little bones will end up on the spoil heap, are only recognised during sieving, or are wrongly identified as those of animals during excavation. Context for these important burials is therefore lost, and contributes little to our efforts in reconstructing the beliefs and behaviours associated with the decision to bury an infant or perinate differently from older children or adults.

Regarding prone and decapitated burial, and the gifting of grave goods, observed trends in sex distributions and age-at-death confirm that 'deviant' or high-status rites were probably not reserved for a particular group. However, we do see a limited relationship between ill-health in life and the funerary rite awarded, albeit one that is regionally confined. Exposure to early childhood stressors was lower in those afforded grave goods in the South, and we would associate higher status with better health. However, we would expect to

see similar results across the regions, and not only southern sites. In contrast, the palaeopathology of the decapitated adults of the Central Belt suggests a physically active group with poor dental health and episodes of ill-health in childhood. Overall, these factors may be indicative of a lower status group, although we have to question why these patterns are only apparent in Central Belt sites. The regional variation in relationships between burial rites and health highlight the fluidity of these practices.

THE CHILDREN – GROWING UP IN THE EAST, SOUTH AND CENTRAL BELT

The skeletal remains of children (i.e. non-adults ages 0–17 years) provide a unique window into observing environmental pressures on past populations. However, the nature of the data available, with a large amount of missing information, and crude prevalence rates as our sole means of discussing palaeopathology in the non-adults, makes this a difficult pursuit. The methods used for recording non-adult palaeopathology differed widely, resulting in unintentional under-representation and omission of lesions in the children. A greater range and higher frequency of non-adult palaeopathology is apparent in the Central Belt. This has to be treated cautiously, as the large non-adult cohort of the Cannington cemetery, Somerset, was re-analysed by the author and therefore yielded a detailed record of palaeopathology. However, this is an important new dataset and the biggest of its kind, allowing general observations on childhood health and lifeways beyond the urban centres of Roman Britain for the first time.

Infancy and the weaning period

Transitional feeding becomes necessary at six months old, as breast milk alone no longer meets the nutritional requirements of the growing child (Sellen 2007; Katzenberg 2012). The weaning period itself is a perilous stage in childhood development, characterised by malnutrition–infection interactions that impact on wellbeing and ultimately survival of the child (McDade and Worthman 1998; Fewtrell *et al.* 2007). A number of regional isotopic studies for Roman London (Powell *et al.* 2014), Queenford Farm, Oxfordshire (Fuller *et al.* 2006; Nehlich *et al.* 2011), and several sites across Dorset (Redfern *et al.* 2012) suggest that weaning was completed between 2 and 4 years old. At this point, it is also worth considering the results from fourth to second century B.C. Wetwang Slack in the East Riding of Yorkshire, where isotope analysis suggested that weaning would have been complete by 2.5 years old.

The introduction of supplementary foods would have also occurred very early in infancy at the site (Jay *et al.* 2008). A very specific onset for supplementation is given for Roman London, where solid foods were first introduced at six months old (Powell *et al.* 2014). This is in accordance with the second-century A.D. Greek physician Soranus' recommended weaning timeframe (Temkin 1991, 117). Some of the expected shortcomings of the weaning process are reflected in the palaeopathology and the representation of ages-at-death in the rural non-adult cohort. We see a slight increase in mortality rates after infancy at 2.6–6.5 years old, indicating raised mortality towards the end of the weaning period. Additionally, by 1.1–2.5 years old, supplementary feeding would have been well underway, and an increase in haematopoietic lesions, inflammation, infection and metabolic disease was observed. In combination, these suggest elevated morbidity during the weaning process, requiring a consideration of the different factors that may have contributed to this.

Lesions not only indicate maladaptive infant feeding practices, but also compromise health in breastfeeding women. Mothers may not have been well enough to produce breast milk, forcing the administration of other, less holistic and ultimately more harmful foods. The milk of cow, sheep or goat cannot be tolerated well by the developing infant gut flora, leading to diarrhoeal disease, malnutrition and infection (Fewtrell *et al.* 2007; Stevens *et al.* 2009). However, if the cultural norm was to introduce supplementary foods earlier than six months, we would expect to see similar consequences for the child. In fact, the isotopic study of non-adults younger than six years old from Iron Age Wetwang Slack attests to very early supplementation with animal milk and plant foods (Jay *et al.* 2008). Especially in young infants, early reliance on cereal-based foods would have interfered with the intestinal absorption of iron through high intake of phytates (Facchini *et al.* 2004; Nielsen *et al.* 2013). The result would have been chronic iron-deficiency anaemia, apparent as cribra orbitalia and porotic hyperostosis in those of weaning age. Retention of Iron Age practices in the rural population may therefore also have had a negative impact on health and wellbeing of weanlings. A greater body of work on the palaeopathology of Iron Age non-adults, particularly those of weaning age would help us to better integrate these observations. Earlier weaning in a rural context would make sense as it would have allowed mothers to return to work.

On the other hand, some of the mothers may have followed Soranus' advice of starving the newborn, feeding the infant with goats' milk and honey, or avoiding colostrum, a form of milk produced in late pregnancy and the few days after giving birth (Temkin 1991, 88–90). Withholding colostrum may have an effect on passive immunity of the newborn, as this early type of breast milk is particularly nutrient-dense and rich in antibodies. It helps to protect the newborn against bacteria and viruses, and lowers the risk for jaundice (Swishers and Lauwers 2011, 188–9). Honey, whether raw or boiled, may cause infant botulism, resulting in muscle paralysis and, in extreme cases, respiratory arrest (Aureli *et al.* 2002; Nevas *et al.* 2002). Perhaps maternal wellbeing was under greater threat in areas of the South and Central Belt. During pregnancy, severe malnourishment and extreme depletion of vitamin D status can cause the transfer of scurvy and vitamin D deficiency from mother to child (Wagner and Greer 2008; Robbins Schug and Blevins 2016). Equally, micronutrient content in breast milk, particularly of iron and vitamins B6/B12, is subject to maternal diet (Kumar *et al.* 2008; Allen 2012). Both iron and vitamin B6/12 deficiency in the mothers may have contributed to the haematopoietic lesions observed in young children of farmstead and roadside settlements of the Central Belt and perhaps at Chignal St James villa in the East.

Soranus' recommended weaning diet based on cereal foods was isotopically validated at Roman London (Powell *et al.* 2014), and may be traced via dental disease in young children. Infection with *S. mutans*, the main caries-causing bacteria is highest at around two years old, and lesions will develop from 13–16 months after colonisation (Kawashita *et al.* 2011). The presence of caries in 2.6–6.5 year olds therefore suggests that cariogenic foods may have been given as part of the transitional diet. These would have been in the form of soft carbohydrate-rich foods, most likely porridge or bread soaked in milk, wine or honey (Temkin 1991, 117–19; Garnsey 1999; Freeman and Stevens 2008).

No cases of metabolic disease were reported in the children from villas. Sampling bias may be partly responsible for the absence of reported cases, as 86.2 per cent (n=131) of the 152 non-adults from villa sites were perinates and infants. Diagnosing vitamin C or D deficiency in these young individuals is notoriously difficult. Porous new bone is deposited rapidly due to natural growth in this age group, and may mimic or mask pathological lesions (Ortner *et al.* 1999; 2001; Kwon *et al.* 2002; Rana *et al.* 2009). Rickets and scurvy were reported in the villages, farmsteads and roadside settlements of the South and Central Belt. Apart from diet, these conditions also inform on early childhood rearing practices and socio-cultural factors. Rickets has been linked to low socioeconomic status that prompts inadequate nutrition, i.e. calcium deficiency and too little time spent outdoors (Urnaa *et al.* 2006; van Sleuwen *et al.* 2007). Scurvy should be absent in a rural environment, which may suggest more general mal- or under-nutrition in these young children, perhaps due to preferential feeding and resource allocation within the household or community (Crandall and Klaus 2014; Stark 2014). Appropriate foods may not have been available at times, and young children, perhaps being generally poorly, may have been kept indoors or carried in a sling for prolonged periods, leading to both rickets and scurvy on these rural sites.

Later childhood and adolescence

Few older children and adolescents were reported across all regions. This result was expected as mortality should tail off after the perilous periods of birth, infancy and the weaning period (Lewis 2010). Haematopoietic and non-specific stress, observed as cribra orbitalia, porotic hyperostosis and enamel hypoplasia were seen across all regions, and most ages and settlement types. An overview of enamel hypoplasia in children from contemporary major urban sites yielded a CPR of 17.8 per cent (Rohnbogner 2015), which is significantly higher than the rates of 5.6 per cent reported in the East, 4.8 per cent in the South, and 7.5 per cent in the Central Belt (X^2=33.99, p<0.001, d.f.=3). Early childhood stress may have been less severe on rural sites. Equally, this may be a weaker cohort, where children succumbed to stress before lesions were able to form (Goodman *et al.* 1988; Wood *et al.* 1992).

Cribra orbitalia and porotic hyperostosis affected 1.3 per cent (n=1) of children in the East, 2.3 per cent (n=8) in the South, and 10.0 per cent (n=51) in the Central Belt, which is significant (X^2=25.63, p<0.001, d.f.=2). We have to acknowledge the possibility of sampling bias for this result as the large Cannington funerary site was re-examined by the author during PhD research. Yet the distribution may be an indicator for regional variation in childhood health in rural Roman Britain. Collectively the children of the Central Belt may have been under greater haematopoietic stress as demonstrated by cribra orbitalia and porotic hyperostosis at complex and unclassified farmsteads, funerary sites, roadside settlements, villas and the defended small town at Alcester. This could have been brought about by a variety of factors, including parasitic infection, diarrhoeal disease, and mal- or under-nutrition (Walker *et al.* 2009; Oxenham and Cavill 2010). We see further evidence for dietary shortcomings in older ages at 6.6–10.5, and 10.6–14.5 years,

where scurvy was reported in the roadside settlement at Bourton-on-the-Water, Gloucestershire, and the funerary site at Cannington, Somerset. The withholding of foods and resources and more widespread mal- or under-nutrition have to be considered here (Crandall and Klaus 2014; Halcrow *et al.* 2014), as access to foods rich in vitamin C should be plentiful in a rural setting. In a market economy, this relationship may be reversed, and result in shortages or lower quality produce available to the farming population, and hitting those reliant on the care of others the hardest (Stark 2014).

In the East and South, mortality rates are raised slightly in adolescents and 10.6–14.5 year olds. From the age of 6.6–10.5 years onwards, we see a general decline in health. This may have been due to a change in lifestyle, as for example the start of working life, resulting in greater exposure to pathogens, environmental, dietary and occupational stress. Cases of respiratory disease were reported in 6.6–10.5 and 14.6–17.0 year olds, highlighting that a prolonged amount of time was spent in smoke- and particle-polluted air (Roberts and Manchester 2010, 18). Children may have done so to either rest from illness, or to fulfil chores. Fractures attest to falls and accidents that may have been sustained either during play or work. Further evidence for strenuous activity comes from a 16-year-old female at Cannington, Somerset, who was reported with Schmorl's nodes (Brothwell *et al.* 2000, 203), pointing to prolonged strain on the back (Plomp *et al.* 2012).

A build-up of dental plaque (calculus) and caries serve as indicators of oral health and diet (Halcrow *et al.* 2013), with both conditions reported across all regions, and more frequent in older age groups. We would expect to see this pattern due to the age-progressive nature of dental disease and calcified plaque (Larsen 1997; White 1997). Overall, in comparison with children from major urban sites with a reported CPR of 14.8 per cent (Rohnbogner and Lewis 2016b), caries frequencies are lower in the East (6.3 per cent), South (6.7 per cent) and Central Belt (6.0 per cent), although the result is not significant (X^2=11.16, d.f.=3). It is likely that rural children ate a different diet than children in urban settlements. Fibrous and tough foods, and low and infrequent intake of sweetened, soft and refined foods, would have resulted in lower caries frequencies (Powell 1985; Duray 1992; Moynihan 2000). Access to foods was linked with social status (King 1984; 1999a; 2001; Cummings 2009), and the dental health of the rural children, coupled with evidence for vitamin C deficiency, may be a reminder of lower social standing of the rural population (Klaus 2012). In the Central

Belt, calculus was reported at significantly higher rates in children from complex and unclassified farmsteads. This may suggest dietary variation within the settlement types of the region, as calculus deposits are more likely to form when a high-protein or high-carbohydrate diet is consumed (Roberts and Manchester 2010, 71). Only in the Central Belt do we see dental disease in children of the villa sites, affecting two individuals (12.5 per cent) in this settlement type. These are very small sample sizes, and we have to be careful not to over-interpret this result as evidence for the consumption of higher status foods by these children. Similar to the limitations with metabolic disease, the result is influenced by the availability of only 21 non-adults from villas with a reported age over one year old for dental eruption.

The children: summary

Overall, children of the countryside exhibited low rates of pathology, and experienced similar stresses across the regions. Dietary deficiencies may be indicative of shortcomings in access to resources, maternal health and infant feeding and weaning practices. A point to remember is that infant feeding and the weaning process are highly variable, depending on the individual and unique characteristics of both mother and child. However, we do see an increase in morbidity in the weaning age group of 1.1–2.5 years old, and an increase in mortality at 2.6–6.5 years old, which would correspond with the suggested timeframe for the complete cessation of breastfeeding. Rural Romano-British weanlings may have been fed on inappropriate supplementary foods, the mothers themselves may have been poorly resulting in breast milk low in nutrients, or inadequate weaning strategies were in place such as supplementing too early, or prolonged feeding with breast milk past the age of six months old. Without the insight of isotopic analysis on a large sample of weanlings and their mothers, it is difficult, perhaps even impossible, to tease apart the specific underlying causes of lesions in those of weaning age. What is interesting is that we cannot rule out either Roman or native Iron Age practices for weaning in a rural environment. Perhaps an amalgamation of recommended Roman and local long-established behaviours were adopted towards weaning and early child rearing.

Older children were equally sensitive to dietary and environmental pressures. Compared to urban children, those growing up in a rural environment may have experienced fewer episodes of early childhood stress in the form of fever or infection. Some of the skeletal evidence suggests that children may have experienced a shift in lifestyle from 6.6–10.5 years old, possibly an indication of commencing work or being tasked with carrying out chores. Particularly in the Central Belt, resource stress in the form of food shortages or lower quality foods may have affected the children. Additionally, dental disease rates attest to a simpler diet eaten by the children in the countryside compared to their urban peers. These observations may be taken as a reminder of lower social standing of the rural population under Roman administration.

THE ADULT POPULATION OF THE EAST, SOUTH AND CENTRAL BELT

Demography: age-at-death and sex

The information we can glean from mortality rates and sex distributions of the rural population is limited by our ability to provide accurate and precise age estimates in adult skeletons (Chamberlain 2000). Villa sites stand out in the East and Central Belt for providing us with conflicting mortality patterns. In the East, the only records from a villa site saw high mortality in the middle adult age group, although significantly fewer middle adults were observed on villas in the Central Belt. Several formal burial locations were identified at Chignal St James Roman villa in Essex, which may have had an impact on the demographic data available to us (Clarke 1998). Equally, we only have a limited sample available for villas in the Central Belt. At Watersmeet in Cambridgeshire, burials were found in the cemetery area and outlying ditches (Nicholson 2006b), whereas no formal cemetery area was identified at Frocester Court, Gloucestershire, with infant remains scattered throughout the site (Price 2000). At Itter Crescent, Peterborough, in Cambridgeshire, intra-mural burial of non-adults was observed, alongside adult inhumation burials spread across the site, some of which were disturbed or disarticulated (Pickstone 2011). Mortality patterns on villa sites should therefore be approached with caution, as bias in burial and excavation would have influenced the results. Despite these limitations, the significantly higher mortality rate of middle adults at Chignal St James villa compared to other settlement types of the East, and to villas in the Central Belt, is interesting. Perhaps the buried population at Chignal St James experienced a particularly strenuous lifestyle. To an extent, this is also reflected in the adult palaeopathology at the site, and has led Clarke (1998, 140–1) to suggest that the skeletal population may have been bonded tenants (*coloni*) of the villa estate. This is certainly an interesting interpretation, and ideally should be contextualised using data from villas throughout the province. However, in the absence of meaningful sample sizes for this settlement type, we currently cannot comment any further.

In young adults, the number of women within the buried population outnumbered men in all regions. This may be a result of female depletion over time due to multiple cycles of pregnancy and lactation, and the risks associated with childbirth (Chamberlain 2006). Pre- and post-partum hazards such as toxaemia or haemorrhage do not affect the skeleton, therefore preventing us from testing this hypothesis on the skeletons of these young women (Slaus 2000). We also have to consider migration here, as young men may have migrated from rural settlements for economic reasons (see Eckardt 2010a; McCarthy 2013). However, it is worth stating here that the skeletons of young adult males may in fact look rather gracile and lean towards feminine traits for sex determination, which may have influenced the sex ratios in this age group (Walker 1995; 2005).

Old age was more frequently attained by men in the South and Central Belt, as opposed to women in the East. Before we discuss underlying factors of the demographic differences, we have to consider some site-specific caveats. Only a few women were reported from the village site at RAF Lakenheath, Caudle Head Mere in the East, the Springhead Sanctuary complex in the South, and the industry/villa site at Priors Hall, Weldon, in the Central Belt. Perhaps unsurprisingly, more men would have lived and died at the late Iron Age/ early Roman ironworking site of Priors Hall, Weldon (Hall 2006). However, the inhumation graves at the site are badly preserved. The latter may have caused discrepant sex ratios, rather than being a true representation of demography of the living population at the site. The sex distribution at Springhead Sanctuary complex also has to be approached with caution owing to the nature of the site and frequent redeposition of burials (Barnett et al. 2011; McKinley 2011). Reports on the excavations at the village site at RAF Lakenheath in the East remark on disturbance of the areas under investigation, and dispersed locations of the burials recovered (Tester 1993). Together, these factors would have affected the demographic profile of the reported burials at the site. Similar to the issues of sexing young adult males, more robust and masculine features may be apparent in old adult females, perhaps raising the proportionate representation of old adult males across the sites and therefore regions (Effros 2000; Walker 2005). With these caveats in mind, more women in old adulthood in the East may be a result of the physically more demanding lives men may have led. In turn, the sex distribution in the South and Central Belt may signify that women

were leading equally strenuous lives, causing fewer of them to live into old age. We can only say that these men and women were older than 46 years on average, rather than commenting on all of them being elderly. Frailty, illness and disability may have affected all these individuals differently, as would have the level and quality of care they received.

Childhood stress and survivorship

Cribra orbitalia affected both sexes at similar rates in the East and Central Belt, although the highest percentage of affected individuals was in the South (9.3 per cent). Within this region, the greatest discrepancy between men (11.3 per cent) and women (17.9 per cent) was observed. Similar trends are apparent in the distribution of enamel hypoplasia, which was significantly more frequent at Chignal St James villa (47.4 per cent) than elsewhere in the East. Notably, an old adult male from the only village site in the region was reported with hypoplasia of the third molar, which is formed between 10–12 years old (Moorrees et al. 1963). Chronic biocultural stress in childhood affected the inhabitants at Chignal St James villa to a greater extent than elsewhere in the East (Salvadei et al. 2001; Steckel 2005). Indeed, Clarke (1998, 140–1) described exploitative conditions at the site, based on the palaeopathology of the inhabitants (see above, p. 333). The ironworking site at Priors Hall, Weldon, was characterised by significantly higher rates of individuals with enamel defects. Elevated stress in childhood is not unexpected, considering the metallurgy and industrial exploitation at the site, which was followed or even coincided with a villa estate at nearby Weldon (Hall 2006).

In comparison to the children, significantly more adults were reported with enamel hypoplasia and cribra orbitalia in the South, and we see proportionately more adults with enamel lesions in the Central Belt. This does conform with the 'Barker hypothesis' that ascribes an early childhood origin to illnesses in later life, which may have had an impact on mortality risk (Armelagos et al. 2009; Gowland 2015). Watts (2015) stated that enamel hypoplasia reflects early childhood short-term periods of stress that may not be disruptive enough to cause long-term damage to health, which may have been the case for these adult individuals. The men and women of the South and Central Belt may reflect the overall stronger cohort, as despite experiencing chronic biocultural stress during childhood, these individuals were able to flourish and attain adulthood (Paine and Boldsen 2002). The higher rate of cribrotic lesions in the adult cohort of the South compared to the children may have arisen due to similar reasons, or alternatively migration to the area. Another theory that may be considered is the presence of malaria in southern England, particularly the marshlands around Kent and Essex where it became known as 'marsh fever' (Dobson 1980; Mendis *et al.* 2001; Sallares 2002). High prevalence of malaria within a population is selective towards individuals with acquired or genetic anaemias that enable resistance (Ayi *et al.* 2004; Harinarayan *et al.* 2007), resulting in high rates of cribra orbitalia and porotic hyperostosis (Soren 2003; Gowland and Garnsey 2010). Periosteal new bone formation is also prevalent in populations where malaria is endemic (Smith-Guzmán 2015), and was reported at 11.3 per cent of burials in the South, compared to 5.0 per cent in the East and 6.1 per cent in the Central Belt. Although cribra orbitalia was more frequent in southern adults than in any other region, porotic hyperostosis only affected 1.0 per cent. In contrast, over twice the rate was reported in the East (2.1 per cent). Demographic data, and palaeopathological studies of Roman, Anglo-Saxon and late medieval cemeteries around the fens and marshlands of Cambridgeshire and Lincolnshire, demonstrated acquired immunity to endemic malaria in local populations (Kuhn *et al.* 2003; Kendall 2014). Therefore, we should also be seeing significant rates of cribra orbitalia in the children, and particularly adults of the East. This was only observed at Chignal St James Roman villa, where porotic hyperostosis was reported in 21.2 per cent of adults, and cribra orbitalia affected 20.0 per cent of children and 15.8 per cent of adults. It would be unlikely for malaria to affect the inhabitants of a single site only, especially as Chignal St James villa is situated away from the coastal marshes. The generally low rates of cribrotic lesions in the East may therefore indicate the absence of endemic malaria in the selected study sites of the region. We also have to bear in mind the limitations that would have influenced these observations. Crude prevalence rates are heavily influenced by preservation on each study site, which is a major limitation. Inherent discrepancy in recording and reporting of non-adult versus adult skeletal remains would have also resulted in the under-representation of palaeopathology in the children.

Living environment: infection and respiratory disease

Bone infections (i.e. osteitis, osteomyelitis and endocranial lesions) were rare across the regions, perhaps pointing to a low risk for contracting infections, parasites and other diseases (Nelson 1990; Goodman and Martin 2002; Roberts and Manchester 2010, 168). New bone formation is a skeletal response to trauma, joint disease,

circulatory disorders, skeletal dysplasia, haematological, neoplastic, metabolic or infectious disease. In the Central Belt, higher rates of new bone formation in the men may be a result of the various stressors and disease causing periosteal reactions, perhaps alongside a greater risk of soft-tissue injuries sustained at work (Weston 2008). The larger populations of nucleated roadside settlements may have prompted increased stress for their inhabitants and harboured a potentially more unsanitary living environment (Roberts 2000).

Leprosy was a disease well known during Roman times and described by Greco-Roman medical writers such as Celsus in the second century A.D. (Dirckx 1983). Lepromatous and tuberculoid leprosy were reported in four adults out of a total of 2717 individuals. The dating of the burials is of interest here. The old adult male with tuberculoid leprosy is from West Thurrock, Essex, a funerary site in the South of early Roman date, whereas the remainder are from the late and post-Roman cemetery at Cannington, Somerset, in the Central Belt. So far, only two additional cases of leprosy were reported, from Cirencester and Poundbury, dating to the fourth century A.D. (Reader 1974; Manchester and Roberts 1986; Roberts 2002). This would make the West Thurrock male the earliest find of leprosy in Roman Britain and he must have had close and frequent contact with others infected with *M. leprae* (Robbins Schug 2016). The individual was buried flexed on his left side in an unfurnished grave, cut into the top of a late Bronze Age/early Iron Age ditch. The dating of the burial stems from pottery and brooches in the cemetery, which revealed a first century B.C. to second half of the first century A.D. date for the burial ground (McKinley 2009, 28–30; Andrews 2009b). This could mean that the disease had an earlier origin in Roman Britain than previously thought, and was more widespread across rural settlements than we have so far anticipated. Since only a few cases are reported for Roman Britain generally, we have to consider that these individuals may have migrated with the disease and contracted it in crowded and unsanitary living quarters elsewhere (Roberts 2002). In fact, West Thurrock is situated relatively close to the River Thames and the entry into Roman London, which may make migration a likely route for the illness into the site.

Cases of tuberculosis in every region add further evidence for crowding and poor hygiene, particularly since tuberculosis requires re-infection of the latent primary infection to yield soft tissue, and in rare cases, bony lesions (Resnick 2002; Roberts and Buikstra 2003). Adult tuberculosis was reported in all sexes, ages and a range of settlement types, i.e. funerary sites, roadside settlements, farmsteads and villages, suggesting that close contact with livestock and ingestion of infected animal products contributed to the spread of the disease (Grange 2001; de la Rua-Domenech 2006). Significantly more adults from the South (2.8 per cent, n=11; X^2=15.62, p<0.001, d.f.=2) were reported with the disease compared to the Central Belt (0.4 per cent, n=5) and the East (0.8 per cent, n=2). Zooarchaeological evidence suggests that dairying of cattle took place around Winchester and Dorchester (Maltby 1994; 2010b), and it is possible that if cattle dairying was a more widespread part of the subsistence economy in the region, i.e. in rural settlements surrounding the towns, then perhaps bovine tuberculosis was more endemic in the South (Shitaye *et al.* 2007; cf. Allen 2017, 113–14). Subsequently, more frequent transmission from animal to human would have occurred. Human infection with the bovine strain is also more likely to produce skeletal lesions (Stead 2000), which allows us to identify the disease more readily. Again, early Roman West Thurrock in Essex is of interest here as two cases of possible tuberculosis were reported that could not be differentiated from brucellosis. The latter is a zoonotic infectious disease, spread by *Brucella* bacteria, contracted through the same mechanisms as bovine tuberculosis (Wilkinson 1993). In the south of England, *brucella* may have been present in animals since the Iron Age (Bendrey *et al.* 2008), possibly accounting for infection with brucellosis in the two cases. The dating of tuberculosis is also of interest, with all cases from the East dating to the late Iron Age and early Roman periods. A further five individuals of early Roman date come from the Central Belt (Milton, East Waste, Cambridgeshire) and South (West Thurrock, Essex, and Alington Avenue, Dorset). Although the earliest published skeletal find of tuberculosis is from Iron Age Tarrant Hinton in Dorset (Mays and Taylor 2003), these early Roman cases are important in confirming the antiquity of the disease in Britain.

Sinusitis and rib periostitis were present in every region, albeit at low rates. Maxillary sinusitis affected 0.4 per cent of adults in the East, 0.8 per cent in the South and 1.4 per cent in the Central Belt. Within the Central Belt, the roadside settlement at Higham Ferrers, Northamptonshire, and the villa at Itter Crescent, Peterborough in Cambridgeshire, saw significantly higher rates of sinusitis. Inhabitants at these sites may have been more frequently exposed to low-quality particle-polluted air and subsequent inflammation and infections. However, maxillary sinusitis may also arise secondary to a fistula or other periapical lesions affecting the maxillary dentition, which

may have been the case for some of these individuals (Liebe-Harkort 2012). Other respiratory infections such as pneumonia or bronchitis would have led to new bone formation on the ribs (Roberts *et al.* 1994; Santos and Roberts 2001; Matos and Santos 2006). Lesions are, however, non-specific and were found in less than 1.0 per cent of individuals. Nevertheless, open hearths in crowded living quarters, or long hours spent working with industrial ovens or kilns, could have prompted respiratory infections on rural sites.

Diet: metabolic and dental disease

Nutritional deficiency diseases were almost absent in the adults. Yet, high rates of porotic hyperostosis were reported at Chignal St James villa in the East, tying in with additional skeletal evidence for dietary and environmental stress at the site, i.e. cribra orbitalia and enamel hypoplasia. Porotic hyperostosis in the adults at Chignal St James villa may have been a result of dietary deficiencies, an underlying genetic anaemia, or infection and inflammation (Ortner 2003, 89). Indeed, if we look to classical literary accounts describing life on villas in Italy and the Continent, descriptions of hard physical labour and unfavourable conditions prevail (Whittaker and Garnsey 1997, 284). However, if Chignal St James villa was representative of health on all villa sites, we would expect to see similarly high lesion frequencies in the villa sites of the South and Central Belt.

Although only a few cases of adult scurvy were reported, there is a trend for old adults and men to be affected, particularly around Somerset, Gloucestershire and the Isle of Thanet in Kent (East Kent Access). This mimics the distribution of vitamin C deficiency in the children, with non-adult scurvy prevalent at a funerary and village site along the East Kent Access Road, the roadside settlement at Bourton-on-the-Water in Gloucestershire and the Somerset sites of Bradley Hill (unclassified farmstead) and Cannington cemetery. Scurvy may develop in the elderly owing to the need for assisted feeding, poverty, poor access to adequate foods, reclusiveness and absent or poor dentition (Hirschmann and Raugi 1999). It is often termed 'bachelor' or 'widower' scurvy because of its frequent occurrence in elderly men (Richardson *et al.* 2002). Healed blunt force trauma to the left parietal was apparent in the old adult male with possible scurvy from the funerary site at Zone 19, East Kent Access (Dinwiddy 2015). He also suffered from a dental abscess, ante-mortem tooth loss and caries. Perhaps this individual struggled to recover from the consequences of the injury and was unable to chew foods properly, resulting in dietary deficiency.

Scurvy in adult skeletons is notoriously difficult to identify, so we have to be reminded that the disease may go unrecognised owing to poor preservation and the non-specific nature of new bone formation (Brickley et al. 2016). Vitamin D deficiency was reported in the South along the East Kent Access and at West Thurrock in Essex, and Bourton-on-the-Water roadside settlement and Cannington cemetery in the Central Belt, somewhat mirroring the distribution observed for the children. The metabolic disease was either reported as healed childhood rickets, or suspected osteomalacia with an onset in adulthood. The latter group were described as elderly, and perhaps were housebound and therefore experienced inadequate exposure to sunlight, whereas the former recovered from rickets in childhood (Gloth et al. 1995; Ortner 2003). A case of DISH was identified in one of the two elderly individuals from a funerary site along the East Kent Access (Zone 19). The only other example of this type of spinal ossification and ankylosis stems from an old adult male recovered from a farmstead at Zones 9 and 10 of the same project. These mark the only two affected individuals in the study sample (CPR 0.1 per cent for rural Roman Britain). In comparison, the crude prevalence of DISH at fourth-century A.D. Lankhills, Winchester, is 1.4 per cent (n=3 of 220). The aetiology of this type of spinal fusion and extra bone formation is interesting as it is linked with Type 2 diabetes and obesity (Rogers and Waldron 2001). Perhaps both of these old adult males were incomers to the area, or had access to a richer diet than the rest of the community.

Loss in bone density, described as osteoporosis, was reported in both males and females of old age, although only ten individuals from the South and Central Belt were affected overall. Osteoporosis often affects post-menopausal women, but is also seen in men as senile osteoporosis due to advancing age (Riggs et al. 1982). One of the elderly women presented with a femoral neck fracture, and another with wedging of lumbar vertebrae, both common fracture locations in patients with osteoporosis today (Center et al. 1999). The loss in bone density observed in the men and women may have been a result of hormonal changes, old age, immobilisation and subsequent vitamin D shortage through time spent indoors, and a diet insufficient in calcium or too high in protein (Roberts and Manchester 2010, 243).

There is clear evidence for regional dietary variation across Roman Britain, ranging from archaeobotanical and isotopic studies, to differences in butchery practices and material culture (King 1984; 1999a; 2001; Cool 2006; Van der Veen et al. 2007; 2008; Van der Veen 2008; Alcock 2010; Müldner 2013; also see Allen 2017

and Lodwick 2017c). Across the regions, caries and its associated lesions (i.e. tooth loss and periapical lesions/abscesses) were on the rise with increasing age, reflecting the age-progressive nature of dental disease (Larsen 1997, 65). Generally, the rate of dental disease was similar in men and women. Calculus was reported at comparable frequencies across the regions (South 33.6 per cent, Central Belt 29.8 per cent) although there is a trend for lower rates in the East (20.4 per cent). We actually see significantly lower numbers of adults with caries in the region at 16.6 per cent, compared to 36.0 per cent in the South and 32.5 per cent in the Central Belt (X^2=19.53, p<0.001, d.f.=2). A variety of factors contribute to the formation of caries, including fluoride content of food and drink, the prevalence of cariogenic bacteria, dental variants in shape and structure of teeth, diet, oral hygiene and genetic factors (Sreebny 1983; Powell 1985). Perhaps fewer food sugars were available in the diet of rural Roman Britons of the East, and soft and carbohydrate-rich foods were less frequently consumed. Natural fluoride content of ground water varies across England, and parts of East Anglia are characterised by raised fluoride concentrations, according to the Drinking Water Inspectorate (2013). Apart from diet, it may be equally likely that availability of calcium fluoride to individuals in the East lowered caries progression in childhood and therefore later in life.

Abscesses or pericapical lesions affected 8.9 per cent of adults in the East, 17.6 per cent in the South, and 10.5 per cent in the Central Belt. In fact, periapical lesions were statistically more frequent in the South than in the other regions (X^2=11.60, p<0.005, d.f.=2). This complements the findings on calculus and caries distributions for the South, as these dental pathologies will predispose a population to higher rates of dental abscesses and cysts. Perhaps, attrition, trauma and periodontal disease plagued people in the South more frequently than elsewhere and contributed to abscess formation (Roberts and Manchester 2010, 70). Some periapical lesions would have been benign, whereas some abscesses may have caused severe pain and secondary sinusitis (Melén et al. 1986). An important limitation of the data is the fact that periapical lesions and abscesses are only visible to the naked eye when they perforate the alveolar bone. If no systematic radiography was undertaken to assess dental disease (which it rarely is), a large proportion of lesions are missed.

Periodontal disease, caries and abscesses ultimately cause a tooth to die and be lost, evident as healing and remodelling of tooth sockets in archaeological bone (Roberts and Manchester 2010, 74). The discussion of ante-mortem tooth loss is problematic in this context. Tooth loss is recorded by total number of sockets observable, rather than by individuals as had to be done in this study. Ante-mortem tooth loss was highest in the South, which is in keeping with trends for dental disease in this region. However, more individuals in the East were reported with teeth lost ante-mortem than in the Central Belt. The relatively high rate of tooth loss in the East may have contributed to low rates of caries and calculus observed in this region owing to the absence of observable teeth.

In the Central Belt, statistically significant patterns between settlement types were apparent. It would seem that dietary variation existed within the region. High rates of caries in the industry/villa site at Priors Hall, Weldon, in Northamptonshire may be site-specific, and a result of discussing crude rather than true prevalence rates. High numbers of periapical lesions/abscesses in funerary sites, including Horcott Quarry, Gloucestershire, and Radley Barrow Hills, Oxfordshire, are complemented by high prevalence of caries and ante-mortem tooth loss. Within this cohort, dental health may have been generally poor. However, the larger funerary sites may have served a range of unknown satellite settlements (see Ch. 6, p. 249), and we cannot make inferences on the socio-cultural environment of these people. Nevertheless, it seems that those buried in such 'isolated' rural funerary sites had higher rates of dental disease than those who were not. Perhaps a richer diet, with greater sugar content and refined foods was eaten by certain parts of the population. The high rate of abscesses in the single port site of Camp Ground, Colne Fen, Cambridgeshire, is interesting as both caries and ante-mortem tooth loss were comparatively infrequent here. It may be likely that attrition and trauma influenced dental health at this site.

Working lives

Traumatic injuries and joint degeneration during life enable us to comment on activity levels in past populations. The crude prevalence for skeletal trauma is similar across the regions, and men exhibited trauma more frequently than women, significantly so in the Central Belt region. Activity patterns associated with the division of labour and risk-taking in men may have caused these distributions (Harris *et al.* 2006). Men may have been more often involved in high-risk activities as part of their working lives, for example in extraction industries, construction, ploughing or the clearing of woodland (McCarthy 2013). Women may have been in charge of the day-to-day running of the farm, tending to crops, animals and domestic chores (Allason-Jones 2005). Although these

activities also carry risks of injury, perhaps, on the whole, women were less often exposed to accidents and injury, whether work-related or not. Spinal trauma is commonly sustained in falls and was most frequent in the East (Dryden *et al.* 2003), whereas rib fractures requiring significant blunt force to the thorax were most prevalent in the South and Central Belt (Sirmali *et al.* 2003). Both types of injuries can be sustained in accidents related to agricultural labour and working with traction animals. Tibial fractures, which were most frequently observed in the women of the East, require a considerable amount of force, often occurring in road traffic accidents and sports injuries today (Court-Brown and McBirnie 1995). Tibial fractures at Chignal St James were reported in two adult females, which may attest to the working environment to which these women were exposed. Rib fractures commonly affected women in the South and spinal compression fractures in the Central Belt. We see that women engaged in physical activity and associated hazards and were perhaps exposed to occupational risks. A higher rate of inter-personal violence was encountered by men in the East, resulting in high rates of cranial trauma alongside spinal injuries. Ante-mortem, and one case of sharp force peri-mortem, trauma to the temporal, parietal and frontal bones were reported in four adult males, which indicate a degree of inter-personal violence not witnessed in the women of the region (Alvrus 1999). A similar trend for gendered division of weapon trauma and inter-personal violence was observed in the South. The amputation of a right humerus at the mid-shaft in an old adult male at Alington Avenue in Dorset is a reminder that medical care was indeed available on rural sites. We also have to consider accidental amputation in this context, which attests to perhaps occupational hazards rather than treatment and care. However, well-aligned, healed long-bone fractures indicate that those with injuries were cared for, by immobilising joints and allowing broken bones to heal. Two additional cases of amputations of fingers were reported at Horcott Quarry, Gloucestershire. Amputations like these most commonly occur accidentally at work, frequently seen in circular saw injuries today and somewhat of an occupational hazard (Boyle *et al.* 2000). Weapon trauma not only affected men in the Central Belt, but also a woman with evidence for sharp force trauma to the ulna that resulted in infection. Trauma to the face was equally frequent among both sexes in the region. Yet, we do not know whether women experience facial and cranial trauma as a result of accidents, combat or abuse (Ochs *et al.* 1996).

In the East, joint stress primarily affected men, a pattern that was not apparent across the South or Central Belt, where females were equally likely to display lesions. Osteochondritis dissecans as a result of continued weightbearing and stress was limited to the feet in the East, whereas joints of the lower and upper limbs were affected elsewhere, particularly in the Central Belt (Hangody *et al.* 2001). The spondylolysis observed at farmsteads, villas, roadside settlements and villages across the regions attests to prolonged and repeated stress on the spine through lifting and bending (Waldron 1991a; Mays 2007). More women exhibited spondylolysis in the South than men, a pattern that was reversed in the Central Belt. Both sexes were therefore under similar strain regarding activity that required loading of the spine. Only a single case of clay shoveller's fracture was apparent in an old adult male from a funerary site of the Central Belt. Although the injury is informative in terms of injury mechanism, as the name suggests, it is not representative and remains an exception. Schmorl's nodes were reported in only 2.1 per cent of individuals in the East, compared to 8.1 per cent in the Central Belt, and 11.9 per cent in the South, which is statistically significant (X^2=19.08, p<0.001, d.f.=2). Schmorl's nodes would form as early as adolescence in response to spinal strain (Dar *et al.* 2010). The result is probably influenced by preservation and recording of lesions, as spinal strain was certainly present in select groups of the East, particularly young men from Chignal St James villa, a witness to perhaps strenuous physical labour at the site that required participation from an early age. Schmorl's nodes affected both sexes and were reported at most settlement types. Overall, the distribution of joint stress suggests that physical activity and associated strain on the bones and joints were a common occurrence in Romano-British rural life.

As expected, the frequency of degenerative joint disease increased with advancing age. However, 10.0 per cent of young adults in the South were already affected by degenerative changes, compared to 16.0 per cent of young adults in the East, and 20.0 per cent in the Central Belt. An early onset of joint disease may indicate strenuous activity undertaken from an early age. In line with a physically active population undertaking a range of occupations, we see spinal degeneration most prominently, followed by joint disease in the hip (9.3 per cent) and shoulder (8.8 per cent) in the East and South, and the hip (6.5 per cent) and hand (5.5 per cent) in the Central Belt. These very broad patterns are generally mimicked at the site level, although joint disease in the knee was high in the village site at Gill Mill, Ducklington, Oxfordshire, in the Central Belt. Comparison with urban populations may be fruitful in this context. At Butt Road, Colchester, spinal degeneration

affected 13.0 per cent of the adult population (Pinter-Bellows 1993), similar to the 16.0 per cent of adults reported with spinal joint disease in the East, though less than the 27.6 per cent in the South and 26.9 per cent in the Central Belt. Some settlement types of the East follow the pattern from the South and Central Belt regions, i.e. farmsteads (21.6 per cent) and the only village site at RAF Lakenheath, Caudle Head Mere, Suffolk (25.0 per cent). For Roman Britain overall, Roberts and Cox (2003, 148–9) reported on 56 individuals (N=2664, CPR 2.1 per cent) with joint disease in the shoulder, 96 in the hip (N=3289, CPR 2.9 per cent), and 78 in the hand (N=2911, CPR 2.7 per cent). The data by Roberts and Cox (2003) yields lower prevalence rates than those reported for the rural regions. Their data are primarily based on urban populations, and the discrepant rates are perhaps a result of greater wear and tear on the joints of the spine, hips, shoulders and hands of the rural population.

General variation in the location of joint disease exists between the sexes, where women showed higher rates for degeneration of the upper limbs than men across the regions. In the Central Belt, we see significantly fewer women with joint disease than men, and degeneration at the sterno-clavicular joint was significantly higher in women of the South. Repetitive work and subsequent stress on the shoulders, arms and hands more frequently applied to the women (Stock 1991). This may be indicative of certain divisions in activity, and perhaps labour, between the sexes.

The adult population: summary

An important observation of this study is the poor availability of adult skeletons from villa sites, with the health of the inhabitants at this particular site type remaining largely unstudied. Chignal St James in Essex provides the only sample from a villa with a meaningful adult, as opposed to perinate and infant, population. We must therefore remain cautious and cannot assume that the high rates of lesions, trauma and joint disease at this site are representative of villas across the province.

As expected, there was a higher number of young adult females across all the regions, likely to be the result of the risks associated with childbirth and multiple pregnancies. Old age was attained by both men and women, and across all regions and settlement types. Contrary to what we often assume about past societies, rural Roman Britons were able to live into older age (46 years +). Not only does this inform about life expectancy in rural Roman Britain, but also reminds us of social and familial structures. Some of these older individuals may have been elderly and were cared for by their community or family.

Interestingly, we may be seeing evidence for malaria in the South, particularly around the Kent and Essex marshlands, although this should not come as a surprise, as it has been suggested previously that malaria was endemic in Roman Britain. This would have primarily applied to the marshes of the South, the Fenlands in the East and the Severn estuary wetlands. However, skeletal populations from the latter two areas are minimal. Those included in this study from the Fens were not displaying haematopoietic lesions and new bone formation to the extent we would anticipate in a region with endemic malaria. Rather than evidence of absence, we should be approaching this as absence of evidence as the adult sample from the region was particularly small.

Low-quality, particle-polluted air may have been a problem at times, as demonstrated by the presence of new bone formation on the pleural aspect of the ribs and sinusitis. Respiratory disease affected fewer individuals than it did in urban environments, but it nevertheless attests to perhaps industrial activity in smoke-filled environments, and time spent in domestic dwellings with smoke from the hearth. Non-specific bone infection was low in rural Roman Britain, but we see examples of tuberculosis infection across the regions, and leprosy was apparent in late Roman Somerset and late Iron Age/early Roman Essex. These diseases attest to crowded and unsanitary living conditions, where frequent contact with infected persons was common. Tuberculosis would have also been contracted through ingestion of infected animal products, and seems to have occurred more frequently in the South where cattle dairying may have been undertaken more intensively. The case of tuberculoid leprosy at West Thurrock, Essex, is of particular interest, as this old adult male would mark the earliest case of the disease in Roman Britain, and confirms the antiquity of leprosy in the British Isles.

The incidence of metabolic disease in rural Roman Britons was low overall, although, as expected, loss in bone density, reported as osteoporosis, was observed in a small number of older individuals. The aetiology of this condition includes calcium and vitamin deficiency, the latter also being observed in older adults in the Central Belt. Immobilisation, reliance on care, complications when eating and prolonged periods spent indoors may have contributed to both osteoporosis and osteomalacia in this context. We see further evidence for shortcomings in diet and inadequate exposure to sunlight, concentrated in settlements in Gloucestershire and Somerset, more specifically the roadside settlement at Bourton-on-the-Water and Cannington cemetery. At times, healed rickets was observed, attesting to

a childhood episode of vitamin D or calcium deficiency. Scurvy in older individuals may be a result of complications when eating, where dietary intake of foods containing vitamin C is restricted. At the other end of the spectrum, two old adult males from the East Kent Access excavations were reported with DISH, which is related to obesity and diabetes. This suggests that rich diets were also consumed in rural Roman Britain, reminding us of status differences within the rural population. Dental disease rates are a further facet in the discussion of diet in rural Roman Britain. Although variation in dental disease rates was observed between the settlement types of the Central Belt and East, a relatively similar diet may have been eaten across rural sites. However, dental disease was elevated in settlements of the South, perhaps a direct result of more intensive milling in the region. Inhabitants of southern sites may therefore have eaten a more refined diet, which increases carious lesion frequency and associated dental pathologies such as abscesses and tooth loss.

As a general observation, rural Roman Britons led active lives, as demonstrated by frequent fractures, stress and degeneration of joints. Fractures, some of which would have required considerable force, indicate accidents and perhaps work-related risks. Although skeletal injury and fractures were apparent in both sexes, men may have experienced an elevated risk of skeletal trauma. Traumatic evidence for inter-personal violence and the use of weapons was reported in both men and women, which raises questions on abuse or participation in combat. An identification of the specific activities undertaken by the men and women in the countryside is beyond the remit of the study, but we see degeneration and stress affecting the joints of rural Roman Britons from a young age. Lesions were apparent in every region and a broad range of settlement types, which confirms that this would have been a physically active population involved in agricultural and domestic labour.

RURAL PEOPLE IN PERSPECTIVE: IRON AGE PARALLELS AND CONTEMPORARY URBAN–RURAL DIFFERENCES

Before moving on to any concluding thoughts on health and disease in the countryside of Roman Britain, we ought to contextualise the dataset used for study. The adult sample was therefore tested against the published results for contemporary adults from the 2000–2005 Oxford Archaeology excavations at Lankhills, Winchester in Hampshire (Booth et al. 2010), and Roberts and Cox' (2003) observations on pathology in adults from Iron Age Britain. The latter is a sample entirely composed of sexed adults only, which impacted on the sample size available for comparison. Nevertheless, this is the only and most comprehensive set of adult palaeopathology data for the period. Naturally, by comparing the rural Romano-British sample to the bioarchaeological data obtained from the Lankhills cemetery, we must be aware that the urban sample is composed of a single site only. This may lead to site-specific patterns being compared to a broad regional sample.

Some very broad but interesting patterns are observed in the distribution of disease within adults from rural Roman contexts, contemporary urban contexts, and those from Iron Age sites. Perhaps the most striking observation is that the variety and frequency of pathological lesions increased considerably between the Iron Age and later rural Romano-British populations. Similarly, the buried dead from rural contexts have a greater range of pathological lesions than those from late Roman Winchester. We have to bear in mind that these differences may be a result of smaller sample sizes for the Iron Age (n=398) and Roman urban (n=220) samples.

Early childhood bio-cultural stress resulting in the disruption of enamel deposition for tooth crown formation increased over time, with the highest rate reported from the urban cohort (22.7 per cent). To an extent, stress in early childhood may have correlated with socio-cultural and environmental changes brought about by Roman administration generally, and urbanisation more specifically (Addyman 1989). This confirms previous research on the urban living environment as unsanitary and unfavourable (Lewis 2010; 2012). Rates of cribra orbitalia as a result of childhood haematopoietic stress remain relatively constant across the Iron Age (4.8 per cent) and rural Roman Britain (6.6 per cent), but increase in an urban living environment (11.8 per cent). Blood-borne diseases resulting from mal- or under-nutrition, along with parasites or infections, may have affected rural Roman and preceding Iron Age populations to a similar extent, while iron-deficiency anaemia, or vitamin B6/B12 deficiency, affected the residents of towns at a more pressing scale (Holland and O'Brien 1997; Facchini et al. 2004; Mahmud et al. 2013). Again, this may be a result of more health hazards in the urban environment. However, we also have to take into account the possibility that fewer rural children lived through these stresses to acquire lesions and display them as adults (Wood et al. 1992; Wright and Yoder 2003).

Similar rates in rib periostitis may be a result of respiratory infections occurring at a somewhat constant rate over time, including conditions such as pneumonia or bronchitis (Roberts et al. 1994; Santos and Roberts 2001; Matos and Santos

2006). However, upper respiratory tract infections leading to sinusitis were only identified in the Roman period, which suggests a change in the exposure to air pollution with the Roman conquest (Lanza and Kennedy 1997; Bhattacharyya 2009). This may have been linked to occupational risks that required time to be spent in particle-polluted air, or smoke-filled domestic dwellings (see Ch. 3, p. 55). As demonstrated by the significantly lower rates of sinusitis on rural sites, upper respiratory tract infections may have been more frequent at Roman Winchester than in the countryside (Roberts 2007). Air pollution may have affected Winchester residents to a greater degree, perhaps owing to more intensive industrial activity. In contrast, however, 2.4 per cent of the adults at Butt Road, Colchester, were reported with sinusitis (Pinter-Bellows 1993), which is only marginally higher than the 1.1 per cent of affected individuals from rural sites. Discrepant results may have arisen owing to varying preservation conditions, and differing methods for recording sinusitis (Liebe-Harkort 2012). However, we have to take into account that air pollution, and therefore respiratory infections, may have varied depending on site-specific industrial and living environments.

Contrary to what we would expect, evidence for infection in the form of endocranial lesions, osteomyelitis, leprosy and tuberculosis, was absent among the Winchester adults. Bone infection, and conditions that lead to the inflammation of the dura mater surrounding the brain, such as meningitis, may have been more frequent in a rural environment (Schultz 2003). Similar, albeit low, rates of endocranial lesions and osteitis were reported from rural Roman and Iron Age sites, suggesting that non-specific infection may have been a low but steady risk. Since tuberculosis can be transmitted from animal to human, we would expect to encounter the disease in a rural environment (Grange 2001; Shitaye et al. 2007). However, human to human transmission in the crowded and unsanitary living quarters of Roman Winchester could also be anticipated (Roberts and Buikstra 2003). Although no skeletal evidence for the disease was brought forward in the adults, a diagnosis for tuberculosis is suggested in a 6–7 year old child from Lankhills (Clough and Boyle 2010, 388). Childhood tuberculosis informs on the ongoing rate of transmission of the infection within a population and suggests an adult pool with the disease (Nelson and Wells 2004). However, in the absence of any skeletal evidence for tuberculosis in the Winchester adults, the results suggest a greater threat of tuberculosis infection on rural sites.

Leprosy may have been a new and emerging disease that was introduced with increasing contact with populations on the Continent. The disease remains rare in the Romano-British skeletal record, with only two cases from the urban sites of Cirencester, Gloucestershire, and Poundbury Camp, Dorchester, Dorset, reported to date (Reader 1974; Manchester and Roberts 1986). Finding leprosy on rural sites may indicate that the disease was more widespread than previously anticipated. However, those with leprosy may have travelled with the disease and contracted it elsewhere.

Both porotic hyperostosis and vitamin C deficiency were absent at Lankhills, and vitamin D deficiency occurred at similar rates in the town and the countryside. If we use porotic hyperostosis as an indicator for blood-borne disease arising from iron-deficiency anaemia or vitamin B9/B12 deficiency, these differences may indicate a degree of dietary variation between town and country. Rural populations may have relied on a more plant-based diet, with greater pathogen load, parasitic infections and diarrhoeal disease (Walker et al. 2009; Oxenham and Cavill 2010). The fact that vitamin C deficiency was not reported from the urban context suggests that adequate resources in the form of fresh produce, i.e. fruits and vegetables, were available to the population at Winchester. In contrast, a small number of rural residents had skeletal signs that may be indicative of the deficiency. These could have arisen from a variety of possible causes, including difficulty eating, religious practices, fussy eaters or illness that required higher intake of the vitamin (Halcrow et al. 2014). Additionally, access to resources may have been restricted at times, impacting on the foods available to the men and women of rural settlements (Crandall and Klaus 2014; Stark 2014). The absence of metabolic disease in the Iron Age further attests to unequal resource distribution between the later urban and rural populations.

Dietary variation could have also caused the apparent differences in the distribution of dental disease. Sugar would have been accessible in the forms of *sapa*/*defrutum*, fruit and fruit juices, honey as the main sweetener in contemporary cuisine, and in the form of refined carbohydrates as finely milled grains (Moore and Corbett 1973; Roberts and Cox 2003, 129; Cool 2006, 67–8; Carreck 2008; Alcock 2010, 29–30; Crane 2013, 251). We assume that these foods were less frequently eaten by the population in the countryside, which should be reflected in dental disease rates (Rohnbogner and Lewis 2016b). Yet, intensive milling may have taken place in the South (Shaffrey 2015), potentially impacting on dental disease rates in the countryside. The rural population must have undergone considerable dietary change between the Iron Age and Roman

period to yield significantly higher rates of tooth decay, calculus deposits and tooth loss (Hillson 1996). More refined carbohydrates, softer foods, and foodstuffs with higher sugar content, may have been eaten during the Roman occupation. Honey would not only have been the main sweetener but also used for its medicinal properties (Baker 2016; Lodwick 2017c, 81). This is further amplified in the urban settlement, as caries and subsequent tooth loss were significantly elevated at Lankhills. The adults at Winchester presented a caries rate of 37.7 per cent, compared to 26.9 per cent in the rural sample, possibly a reflection of the link between caries prevalence and urbanisation (Miura et al. 1997). Perhaps fruit, refined carbohydrates and honey were economically important foods reserved for trade, therefore more accessible in towns and less often eaten in the countryside. Altogether, along with the relatively high incidence of metabolic disease, it seems likely that the occupants of the countryside of Roman Britain had a less adequate diet than during the Iron Age, and also when compared with the inhabitants of urban centres, or Winchester at least. This signals a decline in diet over time, while also highlighting the stratified nature of access to resources in Romano-British society.

Activity patterns may have changed since the Iron Age, as the men and women of rural Roman Britain presented with more Schmorl's nodes. Lesions stem from continuous stress on the spine during adolescence and early adulthood (Plomp et al. 2012). This pattern was amplified for Roman Winchester. Similar observations were made for the prevalence of spondylolysis, with stress fractures in the spine being most frequent in the Lankhills sample. Overall, the results may indicate an even greater spinal strain on young people on this site, and perhaps an early start to continuous loading of the spine, which may have been an occupational risk.

Spinal joint disease actually decreased from the Iron Age (32.7 per cent), but rural Roman Britons (25.6 per cent) were more likely to suffer from spinal degeneration than their urban peers (21.8 per cent). At Butt Road, Colchester, spinal degeneration was in fact even lower at 13.0 per cent (Pinter-Bellows 1993). Rural inhabitants of all regions were more predisposed to spinal degeneration, which may be a result of strenuous activity and general joint stress. Joint disease in the shoulder, hip and knee affected rural Roman Britons to the greatest extent. Although we see that Iron Age populations endured considerable wear and tear to their spines, later rural residents were experiencing greater strain on their upper and lower limbs. This may well be related to increases in agricultural production during the Roman period, as outlined in Volume 2 (Allen *et al.* 2017), which would have created a greater burden on manpower. Ultimately this may have led to greater strain on the joints of the rural population. When comparing these patterns to urban Winchester, it is apparent that activity and labour may have differed between town and country, perhaps a reflection of the different occupations held by town dwellers and rural residents.

The rural people in perspective: summary

The comparison of trends in the palaeopathology of Iron Age, rural Romano-British and urban Romano-British adults has yielded some fruitful insights. Generally, elevated levels of pathology are reported from rural Roman Britain compared to Iron Age populations, indicative of a decline in health. Bio-cultural stress may have increased during Roman rule, which also came with greater stress on the joints of the rural population, a more refined but less wholesome diet, and higher rates of infection. In some respects, these decreases in health were further amplified in the urban environment at Roman Winchester. Here, respiratory infections were on the rise, although non-specific infections and tuberculosis were more frequent on rural settlements. Access to resources in the form of certain foods may have differed between town and country, reflected in the differences in dental pathology and metabolic disease. Previously, the urban Romano-British living environment was believed to be responsible for adverse effects on health. Ill-health did in fact extend beyond the city walls, as demonstrated by this brief comparison, and rural Romano-British populations may have experienced greater stress and unfavourable conditions overall. Contrary to popular belief, the countryside may not have provided a significantly better living environment, perhaps reflecting the social status of the peasant population.

Future work is strongly recommended to contextualise the findings of this chapter. Comparison with bioarchaeological data from rural, particularly early medieval sites collated in a similar fashion would be very welcome. Similar to the Roman period, the general population of the medieval countryside has received considerably less attention than their urban and high-born counterparts.

CONCLUSIONS

Osteological data for 2717 individuals from 102 settlements of early to late Roman date were observed from the South, East and Central Belt regions. The majority of these were late Roman.

Sample sizes varied between the regions, with 1654 individuals reported from Central Belt sites, 741 from the South and 322 from the East. Only sites with a report date of 1995 and later, and with a minimum number of 10 individuals, were included. This covered the more in-depth anthropological data reported since the mid-1990s and enabled faster recording of a bigger sample. Nevertheless, the detail of the bioarchaeological and particularly palaeopathological data varied greatly between reports, especially for non-adults. The analysis presented here is, therefore, restricted to a discussion of crude prevalence rates only. No doubt a more detailed and in-depth analysis would allow for the observation of much more nuanced patterns in ill-health, and therefore lifeways, between men and women, adults and children, and the populations of different types of settlement.

Despite the limitations, this study utilises the largest and most comprehensive osteological dataset for rural Roman Britain to date. The data allow us to put a more personal note on the people who lived and worked in the countryside of Roman Britain. A number of important new observations are further helping us to understand the rural living environment, diet and the range of daily stressors that impacted on wellbeing in the countryside.

An effort was made to evaluate the relationship between different burial rites and the age, sex and palaeopathology of rural Roman Britons. Differential burial rites for infants are apparent, characterised by exclusion from formal cemetery areas, inhumation in dedicated infant burial clusters, and intra-mural burial. The relative frequency of infant burials varied by region, settlement type and phase, from a complete absence of perinates and older infants, to accounting for almost the entire buried population of a site. These vastly different rates suggest changing attitudes towards death in infancy, and particularly around the time of birth. The motivations behind the decision to exclude the youngest children from formal cemeteries, bury them within the settlement, or reserve a dedicated infant burial site, may have been complex. It is likely that these practices reflect a mix of local, regional and imported social, cultural and religious beliefs.

It is only in the Central Belt where a relationship between burial practice, in this case decapitation, and palaeopathology is apparent. Decapitated individuals in the Central Belt tended to show higher rates of skeletal trauma, enamel hypoplasia and caries. This would attest to higher rates of bio-cultural stress in childhood, exposure to accidents and hazardous activity, and poor oral health, linked with the consumption of soft and refined carbohydrate-rich foods. These indications may suggest a generally lower social status for the decapitated cohort. In the South region, those buried with grave goods were less likely to exhibit enamel hypoplasia. This may attest to fewer episodes of stress in early childhood of those awarded grave goods, perhaps a reflection of higher status having a positive effect on childhood health. In children, grave goods may have been given in association with milestones in the lifecourse, such as weaning and perhaps the transition into working life.

A common link between prone body position, decapitation and the presence of grave goods was that they were all more frequent in individuals of older age. Although this may suggest some correlation between people's age and the types of burial treatment to be expected in Romano-British rural society, it has to be emphasised that a range of physical attributes of the deceased may have influenced a community's decision to bury an individual in a certain way, which is not always manifested osteologically. Burial rites would have been chosen carefully by the community, and 'unusual' rites are associated with individuals demonstrating a range of ages, sexes and palaeopathological lesions.

The palaeopathology of the children (0–17 years) allows us to explore important developmental milestones in the childhood experience, while providing a multi-faceted resource for the study of health and disease in the countryside of Roman Britain. Lesion frequencies in the children were low overall, probably a result of recording and reporting of non-adult skeletons and pathological changes. Elevated levels in mortality and morbidity are apparent in 1.1–2.5 year olds, and 2.6–6.5 year olds. These remind us of the dangers that come with the introduction of supplementary feeding and the cessation of breast milk in the childhood diet. Weanlings endured infection, haematopoietic disorders and metabolic disease, which prompted elevated mortality. Inadequate weaning strategies and foods may have been in place, and the mothers themselves may have been nutritionally deprived. The weaning process would have been culturally mediated, and may have been an amalgamation of Roman and native practices. We have to bear in mind that the children we are basing our observations on were those who did not survive the weaning period and are therefore likely to show maladaptive practices. Practices may have been Roman or native in origin, and would have been influenced by individual characteristics of mother and child, their environment and access to resources. Although we should refrain from generalising too much, we do see that many rural Romano-British weanlings were exposed to pathogens and inadequate nutrition once breast milk was supplemented.

Older children of the South, East and Central Belt regions experienced a range of health problems, albeit at relatively low frequencies. Unexpectedly, metabolic disease affected children in the Central Belt, particularly from Somerset and Gloucestershire sites. We have to consider that these may have been children affected by a range of conditions that yield secondary vitamin C deficiency. Equally, resource stress may have affected these children more severely than their peers, resulting in scurvy as a result of a lack of fresh fruits and vegetables in the diet. In comparison to a sample of children from urban sites, the simpler diet of the rural cohort translates into discrepant rates of dental disease. Ultimately this may attest to a lower social status of rural children. From the age of 6.6–10.5 years, slightly elevated rates in morbidity and mortality suggest a shift in the childhood experience. It is likely that adverse health effects in these age groups are due to the early start of working lives in the countryside.

Within the corpus of adult burials, older ages were attained across a range of settlement types in every region. Mortality rates are slightly elevated for young adult females, which may be a product of the dangers of pregnancy and childbirth. Similar to the children, some regional variations in the prevalence of certain diseases are apparent. Interestingly, we see osteological evidence for malaria in the South. Within the region, the adult population sustained significantly more lesions indicative of haematopoietic disease than the children. Although the Kent and Essex marshlands provide favourable conditions for malaria, higher levels of cribra orbitalia may also stem from migration of adult individuals to the area.

The living environment in rural Roman Britain permitted infections to spread. Although non-specific bone infections, leprosy and tuberculosis were rare, they highlight an existing threat for contamination, lack of hygiene and potentially crowded living quarters. Tuberculosis was certainly more widespread than anticipated, particularly in the South. It is likely that a relationship between tuberculosis infection in humans and animal husbandry existed in the region. The earliest diagnosis to date for leprosy in the Romano-British skeletal record also stems from a rural site, late Iron Age/early Roman West Thurrock in Essex. Although this is only an isolated find, it may pinpoint the antiquity of the disease in Roman Britain, which affected rural and urban residents alike. Other respiratory ailments yielding inflammation of the maxillary and frontal sinuses or pleural aspects of the ribs were equally rare.

However, the inhabitants at the roadside settlement at Higham Ferrers, Northamptonshire, and the villa at Itter Crescent, Peterborough, in Cambridgeshire, were more predisposed to sinusitis than elsewhere. Particle-polluted air leading to upper respiratory tract infections may have been a product of hearths in living quarters or occupational hazards at these sites.

The presence of metabolic disease in the adults from certain parts of the Central Belt region is approximately coterminous with the areas where children were affected by rickets and scurvy. Some of these adult individuals were affected by shortages of sunlight or calcium in childhood, whereas others may have acquired vitamin D or vitamin C deficiencies as a result of old age. Similarly, osteoporosis was predominantly identified in old adults. In contrast to deficiency diseases, DISH was noted in two old adult males from a funerary site and farmstead along the East Kent Access. This type of spinal hyperostosis is linked with obesity and diabetes, attesting to a rich diet. Perhaps these men were distinguished members of Romano-British rural society, although we cannot rule out immigration.

Dental disease rates reveal a fairly uniform diet across the regions and settlement types of the East and Central Belt. The South is characterised by proportionately more individuals with caries and abscesses/periapical lesions. Tooth decay and associated pathologies arise more frequently with the consumption of refined carbohydrates and softer foods. Caries may have progressed more rapidly in the region due to the greater availability of finely milled flour as an everyday staple.

Skeletal injury, joint stress and joint degeneration attest to a physically active population. We cannot pinpoint the specific activity patterns of the men and women living and working in rural Roman Britain, but stress, injury and degeneration affected both sexes from a young age, and were seen across all regions and all site types. Spines, hips, shoulders, hands and knees were mostly affected by joint degeneration, perhaps influenced by the heavy demands of agricultural labour. Generally, joint disease affected the men more severely, yet the upper limbs of women seemed to be more prone to degeneration than those of the men. It is likely that different activities were undertaken according to sex, which placed distinct stresses on the skeletons of men and women.

In comparison with Iron Age and Romano-British urban adults, significant shortcomings in the health of the adult residents of the countryside become apparent. A considerable decline in health, measured as a significant increase in the frequency and variety of pathological lesions between the Iron Age and rural Roman Britain, was reported. The literature often focuses on the urban environment as the harbour for ill-health in Roman Britain, being the antithesis of Iron Age lifeways. Although it is often assumed that Roman rural lifeways were not too far removed from those of earlier Iron Age populations, the Roman occupation marked a significant change for the wellbeing of the men and women of the countryside. Furthermore, in comparison with urban populations, as represented by burials from Lankhills, Winchester, rural living appears to have had even more deleterious effects on health. Surprisingly, the rural settlements of the East, South and Central Belt regions were characterised by a higher rate of infections, metabolic disease, and joint degeneration. Some environmental pressures may have been amplified on rural sites, perhaps exacerbated by the demands of physical labour and at times inadequate diet and resource allocation.

Rural life was certainly not without a number of problems regarding health, but equally, it is clear that at least some of the population was managing reasonably well. In other cases this is not so apparent, as, for example, with the vitamin C deficiency in the children of the Central Belt. We see a population with tuberculosis and other infections, early childhood stress, nutritional deficiencies, work-related injuries, degeneration and stress on joints. Living quarters and working environments may have been polluted and crowded, and access to food and resources perhaps restricted.

CHAPTER 8

CONCLUSIONS

By Alexander Smith and Michael Fulford

INTRODUCTION

One of the overarching themes running through this and other volumes in the *New Visions* series is that the countryside of Roman Britain – its settlements, farming regimes, industries, social structures and ritual practices – is a great deal more varied and complex than previous syntheses have concluded. In many ways the increased awareness of its complexity is a natural consequence of the collection and synthesis of thousands of excavation reports of late Iron Age and Roman sites from across England and Wales. We now have many more pieces of the jigsaw, though it remains a very incomplete picture, and one with significant changes over the four hundred year timeframe under review. As with Volume 2 (Allen *et al.* 2017), this volume has utilised the framework set out in Volume 1 (Smith *et al.* 2016), with its eight regions and range of different settlement types, in order to facilitate more readily comparison and understanding of geographic and social variation across the Roman province. But whereas the previous volumes have focused on characterising the settlements and economic life of the countryside, here we have put the people firmly at the heart of the analysis – how they looked, lived, interacted with the material and spiritual worlds surrounding them, and also how they died, and what their physical remains can tell us.

A book concerned with life and death in the countryside of Roman Britain has a very wide potential remit, but analysis has largely focused upon certain aspects of identity, lifestyle and ritual practices that best correlate with the types and quantities of data collected for this project. As previously noted (Fulford and Allen 2016, 2–3), much of these data derive from development-led archaeological investigations of the past 30 years, which have been particularly successful in revealing large numbers of Roman-period farmsteads of differing forms across England and Wales. When it comes to understanding life and death in Roman Britain, this has had a fundamental impact, as most previous accounts relate to urban, military or high-status (i.e. villa) rural settlements. Life and death within lower status farmsteads – where the vast majority of the population would have resided – has been largely ignored (with notable exceptions such as Mattingly 2006, 353–490; Gerrard 2013,

236–43; McCarthy 2013), mostly for lack of evidence. This is a world that has rarely been explored before, and never in as much depth as has been possible here, resulting in a picture of the countryside of Roman Britain that is – for the most part – quite removed from the bucolic scenes of villa life, such as that depicted in the reconstruction of Great Witcombe villa in Gloucestershire, shown in FIG. 8.1.

IDENTITY AND DIVERSITY: THEMES FROM THE CURRENT VOLUME

Brindle's analysis in Chapter 2 used various categories of object associated with dress and personal display – particularly brooches – to highlight the great diversity of peoples in the Roman province. In general terms, it was pointed out that people living in much of southern and eastern Britain would seem to have had very different ways of dressing than most of those further north and west. In the South and Central Belt it is possible to go further. During the late Iron Age and early Roman period there was a difference in the clothing worn by the inhabitants of different types of settlement. The clothes of those living in farmsteads would typically have required brooches as fasteners, while those living in other settlements, notably villas, complex farmsteads and nucleated settlements, were more likely to have also worn other items of dress accessory, such as metal bracelets and finger rings. In addition, the presence of hairpins, particularly at villas, points to more elaborate hairstyles for elite woman. On this basis, it was suggested that the occupants of these settlements in the Central Belt or South regions, for instance, would have been able to distinguish themselves from the occupants of an enclosed farmstead, based upon their appearance.

In the north and west of the Roman province, there is very little evidence for anybody's personal appearance, except at forts and associated *vici*, suggesting that traditional styles of dress continued, with little influence from the substantial military population, although this may have been a product of tight military control and a lack of access to certain dress accessories. However, the Roman occupation did result in some changes to people's appearance, in the form of the relatively widespread

FIG. 8.1. Artist's reconstruction of Great Witcombe villa, Gloucestershire © Historic England (illustration by Ivan Lapper)

use of glass bangles (if they were indeed a form of dress accessory), which, together with the distribution of metal torcs, may reflect the conscious construction of new group identities to counter the more 'Roman'-inspired dress of the military communities.

Such cultural identities and social strategies could be defined and manipulated through many different media, including domestic environments and lifestyle choices. This has been explored in Chapter 3, which focused upon variations in domestic homes, including aspects such as security, lighting and the existence of gardens, alongside evidence for eating and drinking, recreation and literacy. The multiplicity of lifestyles in rural Roman Britain was made clear, though it is true to say that most country dwellers continued to live in fairly simple, and probably multi-functional, houses with minimal architectural elaboration or decoration, albeit with a progressively greater tendency for rectilinear building forms in most areas. Many aspects of lifestyle are likely to have remained largely unaltered from the pre-conquest period, though settlements with greater socio-economic connectivity – notably those that developed into villas, complex farmsteads and particularly nucleated settlements on the road network – were

clearly associated with a greater range of opportunities and pace of lifestyle change. Increased use of locks and keys, for example, suggests both greater affluence and a greater need for security, while more evidence for lighting equipment may have impacted upon aspects such as the length of the working day and social activities like reading and dining.

Evidence for recreational activities is relatively sparse, presumably since the majority of the rural population would not have had much in the way of leisure time, certainly as suggested by skeletal pathologies, which, as highlighted below, indicated a harsh working life for most rural inhabitants. This is not to say that there would not have been any 'down-time', but rather that any entertainment was perhaps more based upon traditional activities, such as music and story-telling around the hearth fire, rather than 'Roman' games. Social bathing is often seen as a typically 'Roman' past-time, yet bathhouses were largely restricted to urban populations and the few wealthy rural elite; it is possible that some villa estate workers in the south may have had occasional access to bathing establishments, but it seems certain that the vast majority of country folk did not.

Analysis of the evidence for Latin and literacy has shown a strong correlation with the road system and its associated settlements, including roadside settlements, larger urban centres and military sites, undoubtedly reflecting their key role in the bureaucracy and management of the province. The ability to read and write Latin at rural settlements away from the main communications routes was largely restricted to a few rural elite.

The cultural diversity and dynamism of rural Roman Britain can also be expressed through people's relations with the world around them, and Allen's analysis in Chapter 4 has ably demonstrated this through a study of the social connections of people with animals and the natural environment. As discussed at length in Volume 2 (Allen *et al.* 2017), farming was by far the most important economic activity in Roman Britain, and the major developments in farming practices would have had far-reaching social implications. Cattle, for example, are likely to have been utilised as a form of wealth and prestige during the Iron Age, only to be slaughtered for feasting during social exchanges. They became steadily more common, at least from the second century A.D. onwards, in response to a widespread expansion of arable agriculture across southern and central England, where they switched to being 'beasts of burden', used as traction for ploughing and haulage, thereby marking a complete social change in human–animal relationships. They may have become a shared resource between rural households in these areas in order to shoulder the increasing agricultural burden, which was in part dictated by demands of the state. In such circumstances it is thought likely that farmers would have built up strong social bonds with their cattle, which would have differentiated them from urban dwellers, where cattle were likely to have been viewed purely as a commodity for meat, leather etc.

It is thus the case that attitudes toward animals and nature in towns and forts may have been quite different to much of the countryside. The occupants of villas, however, also demonstrate a distinctive relationship with the natural world, as seen through evidence for keeping 'exotic' wildlife and hunting wild animals. The increased exploitation of wild resources is thought to be consistent with changes associated with an increased emphasis on the accumulation of landed wealth, and deer hunting may have thus become a means of expressing land rights. It all seems a very clear ideological shift from the Iron Age worldview, where wild animals are thought to have been regarded with reverence.

This is not to say that religious ideologies were any less significant in the countryside of Roman Britain than they were in the Iron Age, with all aspects of rural life being intimately connected with a belief in the supernatural. The assessment of religion in rural Roman Britain in Chapter 5 thus lies at the heart of this volume. It focuses upon analyses of sacred space, along with the material culture, plant and animal remains that either formed part of ritual practices, or else had some other religious associations.

The first point to highlight is that certain elements of religious expression changed significantly into and throughout the Roman period, and exhibited a great deal of variation, some on a regional scale, others reflecting local traditions and individual choices. People appear, for the most part, to have been able to exert considerable control over many aspects of their religious lives, from the use of religious objects, including figurines and amulets, to the performance of rituals involving sacrifice and the deposition of artefacts and ecofacts. Such 'structured deposition' was widespread and could clearly be performed in a variety of contexts, though there were regional and chronological patterns noted in the types of features generally used for the deposits.

Structured deposits were certainly not confined to religious sites, although these are, nevertheless, numerous in certain parts of the Roman province, their geographic variability reflecting the traditions and choices of individual families and communities. Those places defined here as shrines are relatively widely distributed, in the Roman period at least, and take on a variety of different forms, from buildings and enclosures to sites merely defined by concentrations of finds. Some small rural shrines appear relatively isolated in the landscape, and may have been visited fairly infrequently, but they presumably marked places of special significance. Most of the shrines directly associated with farmsteads lay within the Central Belt region, the majority of these farms being of complex type. Such shrines likely served just the families and other workers on these agricultural settlements, but there were also other sacred places in the landscape reserved for much larger scale ritual activities, probably designed to ensure the welfare of the wider community. In the East region these were largely confined to the towns and other nucleated settlements, while in parts of the South and Central Belt regions, religious complexes developed in the wider countryside, some of these developing to a scale where they can barely be differentiated from 'small towns'. The majority of these complexes have temples of Romano-Celtic form, and might have attracted worshippers from some distance; they were, perhaps, under some level of *civitas* control, or may even have been largely independent communities. Such Romano-Celtic temples have typically been regarded as the 'standard' form of religious architecture in Roman

Britain, though it is now clear that they only represent a relatively small fraction of sacred sites, usually associated with public sanctuaries and other forms of 'elite' architectural display.

The depth of pagan religious beliefs and practices in the countryside undoubtedly remained strong into the late and post-Roman periods. While most of the major sanctuaries went into physical decline before the end of the Roman period, this was often contemporaneous with surrounding settlements, and there is no discernible evidence for any friction with Christianity. Indeed there is only fairly limited evidence for Christian communities beyond villas and nucleated settlements, and it would be some time after the Roman period before this religion took a deep and lasting hold in the countryside.

While the majority of this volume is concerned with the lives of the peoples of rural Roman Britain, Chapters 6 and 7 assess evidence for the dead. In Chapter 6, the various rituals associated with death are considered, and burial rites examined. The late Iron Age and Roman periods were particularly dynamic in terms of changing attitudes to the disposal of dead, developing from many different local and regional funerary traditions, to a somewhat more widespread but heterogeneous burial tradition, which was particularly marked across the Central Belt and western part of the South region. Perhaps one of the biggest changes in many areas was that the dead were being increasingly interred within graves, whether as cremated remains or as a body, whereas previously they had left little trace, the remains presumably being disposed of in ways that are archaeologically invisible. Yet, even though – in some places at least – there was clearly an increase in burial during the late Iron Age and early Roman periods, it is unlikely in most cases that these burials represent the total deceased populations of their communities, with traditional 'invisible' funerary rites, such as excarnation and dispersal, continuing as before. Why certain communities chose to start to bury at least a proportion of their dead, and how these individuals were selected, remain difficult questions for future research.

The spike in burial numbers in large parts of central Britain, in particular, during the later Roman period is notable. At this time, formal interment of the dead may have been considered as a 'normative' (though far from exclusive) funerary rite within many communities, particularly those living within some of the larger complex farmsteads, villas and nucleated settlements, paralleling the substantial numbers of late Roman burials at larger towns. Much of this general increase in interments is due to the greater use of defined burial zones, or cemeteries, as opposed to more dispersed burial within and around the settlements and fields. The use of cemeteries is certainly linked to the scale of the site, and possibly to an increased population, but is also associated with higher levels of likely social and economic interactivity with other settlements, with burial grounds perhaps used as part of wider mechanisms employed to enhance social standing. Rural cemeteries may also, however, have been used to exert an element of control over sections of the agricultural workforce.

Osteological data for 2717 individuals, from 102 settlements of primarily mid- to late Roman date in the South, East and Central Belt regions, were analysed by Rohnbogner in Chapter 7, making it the most comprehensive osteological dataset for rural Roman Britain to date. Although analysis was obviously limited to those selected members of communities who had been formally interred as complete, un-cremated individuals, it has provided important new observations on the rural living environment of Roman Britain, including aspects of diet and the range of daily stressors that impacted on wellbeing in the countryside.

Elevated levels in mortality and morbidity were generally apparent in infants (1.1–2.5 year olds) and younger children (2.6–6.5 year olds), indicating the dangers of exposure to pathogens and inadequate nutrition that follows the cessation of breast milk and introduction of supplementary feeding in the childhood diet. Older children (6.6–10.5 years) were also seen to have experienced a range of health problems, though these may be more regionally specific, with, for example, greater occurrence of metabolic disease in western parts of the Central Belt, some perhaps linked with a lack of fresh fruit and vegetables in the diet. Crucially, in comparison with children from urban sites, the more simple diets of rural children may hint at a lower social status. In addition, it would seem that the adverse health effects evident in older children probably attest to the early start of their working lives.

It is clear from adult buried remains that older ages (46 years +) could be achieved across all of the areas studied, though, as with the children, there was regional variation in the prevalence of certain diseases, such as malaria and tuberculosis in parts of the South, and metabolic disease in western parts of the Central Belt. Of course there was also much individual variation, with, for example, the deceased from the roadside settlement at Higham Ferrers, Northants, seemingly being more disposed to upper respiratory tract infections, probably caused by increased pollutants (e.g. smoke). Overall, the palaeopathology of the rural adult population indicates a physically hard, strenuous lifestyle, probably dictated by the heavy demands of agricultural labour. Furthermore, although both men and women suffered stress, differences suggest that divisions of activities were undertaken according to sex. Compared with both the preceding Iron Age and the contemporary adult urban populations, the rural peoples of later Roman Britain, although 'coping', were clearly more stressed, with significant short-comings in their health.

CULTURAL LANDSCAPES AND SOCIAL CONNECTIVITY

The analyses presented in this volume have demonstrated major heterogeneity in the social construct of rural Roman Britain, on a regional, local and individual basis. People in various parts of the countryside would have had differences in appearance, diet, forms of dwelling, methods of interaction with the spiritual world, and concepts of dealing with their dead, among many other aspects of their existence. Any corresponding shared cultural characteristics may have created levels of social cohesiveness among peoples in certain areas, although defining broader, cultural landscapes across the province is difficult. The distinctive, late Iron Age, so called 'Aylesford-Swarling Culture' of south-east England (notably Kent, Essex and Hertfordshire), defined primarily by the presence of cremation burial and distinctive wheel-turned pottery, certainly indicates a level of cultural cohesion, one that appears to have been partly stimulated by the transformation of existing links with northern Gaul, where there seems to have been a broadly similar social organisation (Champion 2016, 161). However, there was still considerable diversity within the burial and settlement evidence of the south-east at this time, and the distinctive developments in this region form part of wider cultural changes found across different parts of Britain – there is certainly little to suggest that they were initiated by any mass movement of population from Gaul to Britain (Caesar's 'Belgic migration', *BGall* 5.12; Hill 2007, 24; T. Moore 2016, 264).

As previously demonstrated (Smith and Fulford 2016, 402–3), it has not been possible to conclusively identify the extent of any named 'tribes' or *civitates* (Roman administrative districts) within the distribution of archaeological data, perhaps because these were not based upon any underlying, consistent, shared cultural values. Indeed, Moore (2011, following Roymans 2004 for the Batavians) has argued that such larger socio-political entities may have had fairly limited periods of relevance, developing towards the very end of the Iron Age, in response to expanding Roman power, and becoming less important by the third century A.D. (see below, p. 351). Although certain people, particularly those of higher social status, may have had some sense of identity associated with a particular *civitas*, especially during the earlier Roman period, it is likely that most rural peoples' 'worldview' remained on a fairly local scale.

Nevertheless, although the identification of particular *civitates* remains elusive within the archaeological record, there are some forms of evidence that suggest there were areas where people shared certain cultural values, as seen, for example, with burial practice. Analysis in Chapter 6 highlighted various late Iron Age and early Roman mortuary rites that had strong and well-known regional associations, including, as just noted, a concentration of cremation burial in the south-east, of 'Durotrigan' burial in parts of Dorset, and of cist burial further to the south-west. Yet, even within these areas, there is still considerable variety in funerary rites, and it is highly unlikely that all such burial traditions belonged to separate, culturally homogeneous zones. The reality was undoubtedly far more complex. Other evidence often used to suggest regional cultural coherency during the late Iron Age includes distinctive pottery types and different coin series, the distributions of which would broadly correlate with some of the burial traditions in, for example, parts of the south-east and in Dorset (Cunliffe 2005, 144–77; Creighton 2000; Papworth 2008). However, Lein's analysis of late Iron Age coins has indicated a far more complex and shifting network of social groupings (Leins 2008), and the ceramic evidence is seen more to represent networks of social exchange rather than defining specific cultural groups (Hill 2006; Moore 2007). Attempts to map these fluid social groupings through such material culture are certainly problematic (Moore 2011, 350), which can be further demonstrated through the lack of geographic correlation between late Iron Age/early Roman burial traditions and evidence relating to personal appearance and religious expression. All of this is hardly surprising, as we should not expect neat and discrete 'cultural packages' (Roberts and Vander Linden 2011, 3).

As expressed via a number of different, and sometime conflicting, forms of evidence, there was clearly a strong element of diversity across England and Wales, particularly during the late Iron Age and early Roman period. At its broadest level, this is demonstrated by the major differentiation in the types and quantities of material culture and settlement architecture between parts of the north and west, and regions to the south and east. There is also more specific variation broadly corresponding with the regions utilised in this project (see Ch. 1), such as the concentration of Dragonesque brooch types in the North-East (see Ch. 2, p. 30) and the high proportion of religious enclosures in the East. Ultimately, however, a great many differences are revealed on a more localised, landscape scale, as seen, for example, with the many variances in burial ritual, such as the relative paucity of late Iron Age to early Roman cemeteries in landscapes like the Thames and Avon Vales, compared with others such as the North Kent Plain, where such burial groups are far more common. Overall, this would suggest that while there may have been broad and, perhaps, deep-rooted cultural divisions between the north and west on one hand, and the south and east on the other, there were also many divergent sub-regions and landscapes, each with certain culturally distinctive traits, albeit traits that in some areas were gradually eroded over time.

None of the regions remained culturally static over the course of the Roman period, though some areas would appear more dynamic than others. Incorporation into the empire brought great social change, and the diverse nature of this change in part reflects the variable character of the regions and landscapes during the Iron Age (cf. Mattingly 2004, 22; Sharples 2010, 310–17). Parts of the Central Belt and South and East regions would appear especially dynamic in terms of social development, particularly from the second century A.D., when rural settlement numbers, and, by proxy, population size, reached their height, as discussed in Volume 1 (Smith and Fulford 2016, 404–5). This also coincided with a period of significant development in agricultural practices, as indicated in Volume 2 (Allen and Lodwick 2017, 170). These are undoubtedly inter-related, and together herald the start of a gradual but significant cultural shift from the late Iron Age/early Roman period. The regional diversity that was such a strong feature of this earlier period, although certainly still evident, appears to begin to break down across much of south, central and eastern Britain, so that by the later Roman period, the main concentrations of settlement in these areas exhibited increased levels of broad cultural conformity, as expressed by the built environment, material culture, religious behaviour and burial practice, albeit still with considerable individuality. Aspects such as people's appearance, religious practices, and funerary rites appear to be less dictated by previous cultural traditions but more by social hierarchies and individual choice. Such changes were probably down to a multitude of factors, but were largely driven by the degree of social connectivity between settlements.

Throughout many of the analyses in this volume, settlement types could often be differentiated through variations in material culture, environmental remains, and articulations of religious expression and burial practices, even within the same regions and landscapes. Those settlements exhibiting greater dynamism were generally those that developed into complex farmsteads, villas and nucleated settlements, especially those along the main, arterial roads of the provincial network. The inhabitants of these sites would appear to have been far more connected, not only physically, through the existence of trackways and roads, but also economically and socially, as seen through the types and quantities of objects and ecofacts recovered. This all suggests that peoples living in these sites interacted with others on a far more regular basis than those at other settlements, with this interactivity acting as a catalyst for social change. Roadside settlements in particular are probably the key to more widespread social developments in the countryside of south, east and central Britain, just as they were key to certain economic developments, as discussed in Volume 2 (Allen *et al.* 2017). They would have had regular flows of people and provided opportunities for social interaction at markets, religious sites and perhaps hostelries. Some certainly had bathing establishments, though, as noted in Chapter 3, it is uncertain how accessible these would have been to much of the population. The unfortunate fact is that there are still relatively few of these sites to have been comprehensively excavated, and this must form a priority for future research. More multi-isotope analysis in particular is needed on the buried populations of such settlements, which may shed light on just how transient the occupants were (see below, p. 352).

The conditions for the 'success' of these roadside settlements, in terms of their acting as social catalysts, seem to have been largely limited to much of the South, Central Belt and East regions. In the North-East region, roadside settlements along the major north–south routes also had important social and economic functions, although their reach into the countryside appears somewhat limited, reflecting a general lack of integration (Allen 2016b, 280). The paucity of such settlements further north and west probably reflects differences in pre-existing social and cultural conditions. Military *vici*, as the major type of nucleated settlement in these areas, are a very different type of site, being largely inward looking towards the military community and certainly not acting as conduits for social change within the surrounding rural communities. This is not to say that the rural populations in these areas underwent no social change as a result of the significant military presence, as indicated by the slight evidence for shifts in personal appearance, noted above and in Chapter 2. However, these changes would appear more concerned with countering the *Romanitas* of the military communities rather than emulating them. Furthermore, the potentially devastating social disruption that the Roman military could have had on rural communities in these areas is seen, for example, in the abandonment of certain settlements just to the north of Hadrian's Wall during the second century A.D. (Hodgson *et al.* 2013; Brindle 2016a, 315). Added to this social disruption may have been the movements of peoples from elsewhere in the province (or from outside) to these military-dominated zones, as suggested by the inscriptions relating to southern *civitates* on Hadrian's Wall and large numbers of roundhouses from Vindolanda (Bidwell 1985, 28–31; Fulford 2006; Smith and Fulford 2016, 417).

POPULATION MOBILITY IN THE COUNTRYSIDE

It has been suggested above that social connectivity between settlements may have been key to wider cultural change within certain parts of the Roman province. Such connectivity would of course rely upon the movements of people, a topic that has received considerable attention in recent years, in particular the Diaspora Project at the University of Reading, which explored the diversity of the Romano-British population using a combination of techniques (cf. papers in Eckardt 2010b; Eckardt and Müldner 2016). The principal methods of assessing population mobility and the extent of migration comprise the analysis of epigraphic data – for example, inscriptions on tombstones or altars identifying the origins of individuals – alongside aspects of material culture (e.g. objects associated with certain ways of dressing and eating), and, perhaps most importantly, the scientific application of stable isotope analysis (particularly strontium and oxygen) in order to distinguish between locals and foreigners (Eckardt 2010a). Although each set of data has its own problems and limitations (cf. Eckardt and Müldner 2016, 204–11), taken together it is clear that there was substantial mobility within the Roman Empire. Approximately half of the 155 skeletons analysed from five Romano-British sites for the Diaspora project, for example, were of non-local (more than 30 km) origin, mostly thought to have been from other parts of Britain, but also with some individuals from cooler and warmer climates (Eckardt 2010a, table 7.2). However, as the authors of this project

readily admit, much of our evidence for population mobility derives from military and urban sites, and is thus not representative of the Romano-British population as a whole. It may be expected that persons associated with military sites and those living in major cities are more likely to have had non-local origins, including soldiers, traders, craftsmen, officials and their dependents, that may have come from all parts of the Roman world. But what of those living in rural areas? Unfortunately, here we are left with relatively little evidence, and although isotopic analysis is far from a perfect indicator of origin, its more widespread application on skeletons from rural contexts would be hugely beneficial in understanding mobility in the countryside.

Most of the few isotopic studies of rural Roman burials have concentrated on analysis of carbon and nitrogen values, used to evaluate differences in diet, though this can also be useful for assessing origins. At Horcott Quarry in Gloucestershire, for example, the variable levels of $\delta^{13}C$ isotopes were used to suggest that an unusual triple burial comprised individuals who had diets early in life possibly consistent with an external origin (Cheung *et al.* 2012; Hayden *et al.* 2017, 420). In addition, analysis of a small mid- to late Roman rural cemetery at Gravesend in Kent revealed one skeleton with a diet that included a substantial C_4 component, completely different from the remaining eleven individuals, suggesting a non-local origin (Pollard *et al.* 2011). Interestingly, subsequent $\delta^{18}O_c$ and $^{87}Sr/^{86}Sr$ measurements of the particular individual were consistent with a local origin, or from a region sharing similar isotopic values, highlighting the value of obtaining a suite of isotopic signatures.

These few studies, along with certain other indications, such as the occasional inscription and graffito (Noy 2010), and evidence for continental craftsmen (Birley 1979, 129–36; Fulford 2010), does suggest that there was some movement of people from outside the province into the countryside of Roman Britain. There was undoubtedly a huge influx of incomers into Britain from the earliest post-conquest period, with at least 40,000 military and over 100,000 camp followers, traders, craft-workers, slaves and the like (Fulford 2010, 68). Although the great majority of these would have settled in military sites and the rapidly developing urban centres, many may have ended up residing in the countryside. Retirements from the army, arguably amounting to several hundreds every year, presented opportunities for veterans to invest their *praemia militiae* in land and build appropriate accommodation (Black 1994; Fulford 1999). In addition, slaves from other parts of the empire would have been brought in for various duties, although there was almost certainly not a lack of British slaves at this time (see below). All of this could have had a significant effect on rural society (cf. Mattingly 2006, 355).

It is, of course, not only incomers from other parts of the empire that could cause social disruption, but also movement of peoples from within the province. The Diaspora project demonstrated that there was certainly some movement of peoples from different parts of the province into the cities (Eckardt 2010a, 112–24), though there is nothing to suggest mass rural–urban migration. Discussion in Volume 1 (Smith and Fulford 2016, 417) highlighted some slight evidence for larger scale population movements within the province, much of which may have been involuntary and for specific purposes. As noted above, the epigraphic evidence from Hadrian's Wall referring to the Catuvellauni, Dumnonii and Dutrotriges from the south of the province suggests that people were moved up to help with the monumental building work, while over 200 roundhouses from Vindolanda on the Stanegate are thought to relate to levies brought in from elsewhere to help with rebuilding work during the Severan period. Of course, whether these were temporary relocations for specific purposes, or permanent forced migrations, remains uncertain; the social impact of the latter scenario on surrounding communities would surely have been much greater, though there is little archaeological evidence for this. One area where there may be signs of larger scale, permanent population movement is that to the south and east of the Fens. Here, the prevalence and persistence of circular buildings was noted in Volume 1 (Smith 2016d, 168), and, taken together with the incidences of flexed burials and cist graves, is indicative of certain cultural characteristics more typically found further north and west. Whether this is due to, presumably forced, population movement from these areas is unknown, but further programmes of stable isotope analysis on these 'unusual' burials would certainly be beneficial.

Population movement within the province is rarely likely to have been on any large scale. The extent of small-scale migrations – families and individuals – is impossible to ascertain, but it was certainly occurring, as attested by the Diaspora project. Some communities in rural upland areas may have followed a semi-nomadic existence, moving with their livestock between summer and winter pastures. Further south, there is limited evidence from strontium isotope analyses (notably from Owslebury, Hampshire) to suggest that livestock were transported some distances in the Roman period (Minniti *et al.* 2014; see Allen 2017, 86), perhaps, therefore, suggesting the existence of professional drovers, driving cattle across parts of the province. Many traders would certainly have moved around the province to different markets at various times, while there is also evidence for itinerant craftsmen, such as the specialist mortaria makers who migrated from Colchester to the Verulamium region or from the Verulamium region to Mancetter, Warwickshire (Tyers 1996, 61–2), or the tile maker Cabriabanus, whose stamped voussoir tiles have been found at various sites in Kent and London (Davies 2004). The occasional occurrence of an unusual finds assemblage from a settlement may attest to other examples of small-scale population movement, such as the atypically large group of 'non-local' brooches and pottery from the farmstead at St Mawgan-in-Pydar, Cornwall, noted in Chapter 2 (p. 47). Of course, in these cases, it remains uncertain if this represents movement of people or just objects, but in either case it points to a higher degree of connectivity with other parts of the province. It is still, nevertheless, likely that most of the rural population remained fairly static, especially those of lower social status, who may have found themselves increasingly tied to the land. Greater mobility may have been generally reserved for certain groups higher up the social and economic spectrum – particularly elements of the populations from villas, nucleated roadside centres and complex farmsteads.

THE SOCIAL CLASS SYSTEM

The position of certain individuals within society in Roman Britain can be gleaned from evidence such as inscriptions on tombstones or altars (e.g. the altar recording a *beneficiarius consularis* from Dorchester-on-Thames, Oxon.; *RIB* 235; Henig and Booth 2000, 40), or more generally from, for example, the context and material culture associated with burials (e.g. high-status barrow burials near to a villa at Bartlow Hills, Cambs.; Eckardt *et al.* 2009). Establishing a broader understanding of social and tenurial structures across the Roman province is, however, far harder to achieve, partly due to the paucity of written evidence. When viewed on an empire-wide scale, it is typically thought that 'Roman society evolved into one of the most hierarchic and status conscious social orders in human history', albeit one that allowed significant degrees of social mobility, both formally and illicitly (Reinhold 2002, 25). By the later Roman period, this social order appears at its most hierarchical, from the 'super-rich' at the uppermost end of the empire's elite (cf. Scott 2004), to the bonded-tenant farmers, or *coloni*, and slaves at the lowest end of the social spectrum. It has recently been estimated that the imperial 'super-rich' of this period represented 1.5 per cent of the empire's population, and owned about half of all the slaves (Harper 2012, 59).

Despite the highly stratified nature of 'Roman' society, we cannot simply transpose social orders that are known primarily from literary evidence pertaining to the Mediterranean world directly onto far-flung provinces. As has been made clear, the Britain that Claudius invaded in A.D. 43 was a cultural patchwork, whose social systems would have reacted in many different ways to inclusion within the Roman Empire. If we can use settlement form and architecture as one set of indicators for social change, then the marked development of complex farmsteads and multi-room buildings in parts of the Central Belt during the second century A.D., for instance, suggests a particular growth of the 'middle classes', perhaps entrepreneurs (both native and incomers, including veterans) exploiting new social and economic opportunities within the Roman province. In parts of south-east Britain, there appears to have been a slightly greater socio-economic gap between those living in settlements that developed more sophisticated villa architecture and those in mostly simple, enclosed farmsteads. Meanwhile, to the north and west of the Central Belt this gap, between those living on farmsteads and those in towns, roadside settlements, military sites, and the occasional villa, was even more marked, reflecting the general lack of connectivity and integration in these areas, noted above.

Over time, in parts of central, southern and eastern Britain at least, the archaeological evidence does appear to conform to wider patterns across the Roman world, with much deeper inequalities between the social classes by the later third and fourth centuries A.D. (cf. Gerrard 2013, 243). There is a rise in the number of rural settlements that had significant capital investment in villa architecture, including – by British standards at least – a number of 'palatial' multi-courtyard villas (Smith 2016b, 71–4), with luxurious mosaics, painted walls and statuary, ably demonstrating the appropriate cultural and social knowledge (*paideia*) needed to compete within the upper echelons of Roman society (Scott 2004, 52). Although the economic basis of these villas is usually unclear, it is likely that many were centres of agricultural estates. These estates may have expanded at the expense of smaller farmsteads, whose numbers had declined from a second century A.D. high, in order to fulfil the growing state demand for agricultural produce (Allen and Lodwick 2017, 173). It may have been the case that, within the context of a steadily dwindling population,

agricultural labour became more concentrated within such villa estates rather than on dispersed 'independent' farmsteads, a process that may, for example, account for the development of the villages on Salisbury Plain (McOmish *et al.* 2002, 87–108). The later Roman period was certainly a time of agricultural innovation in crop cultivation, enabling greater production per unit (Lodwick 2017c, 48). The growth of arable production may have occurred through improved processing and storage infrastructure, more technological innovation, and greater economic integration (*ibid.*, 83), but it was also undoubtedly only made possible through the increased exploitation of the rural workforce; analysis of human palaeopathology in Chapter 7 certainly suggests a harsh working life for the average rural resident; the evidence of spinal strain and high mortality rate among the middle adult age group at the Chignall St James villa, Essex, is a case in point (p. 353).

The Roman state's increasing demands for agricultural produce may have necessitated greater control over the rural workforce, possibly involving occasional deployment of military personnel. The *beneficiarius* inscription from Dorchester-on-Thames noted above attests to the presence of officials in local small towns, while the recovery of Roman military equipment from excavated rural sites has long attracted attention (Bishop 1991; Black 1994; Cool 2007, 348). Within the current dataset, possible Roman military equipment (fittings, armour, *armillae*, weapons, etc.) was recovered at *c.* 60 per cent of defended small towns, *c.* 40 per cent of roadside settlements, *c.* 23 per cent of villas and *c.* 10 per cent of farmsteads. Such equipment has been argued to indicate the presence of retired military personnel (Black 1994), though it could also represent army detachments sent to police important local activities such as agricultural supply networks (Bishop 1991, 26; Haynes 2003, 342). In this respect, the relative prevalence of military equipment at farmsteads in the Central Belt (*c.* 50 per cent of the 200 farmsteads with military objects), which was the agricultural heartland of the Roman province, may be of significance, although this may also be due to the high numbers of farmsteads that have been excavated in this region.

The actual status of the 'typical' agricultural worker in late Roman Britain remains uncertain. Tenant farmers, termed *coloni*, who leased their lands from larger landowners (mostly villa owners), are known to have existed in Britain (*Theo. Cod.* XI.7.2; Gerrard 2013, 237), though these do not represent a single homogeneous group, only being unified in an official sense for the sake of tax collection purposes (Sirks 1993; Rio 2017, 5).

Nevertheless, it is generally thought that, from the reign of Diocletian (A.D. 284–305), many *coloni* were increasingly tied to the land, with a gradual erosion of status and rights (Salway 1981, 606). Some have viewed such people as being in a position of de facto slavery in the fourth century (McCarthy 2013, 130–2), though of course there would also have been plenty of actual slaves engaged in a multitude of tasks within Romano-British society.

Roman society is generally thought of as a 'slave society', though in actuality this probably only applied to Italy and possibly some of the Mediterranean provinces, where slaves have been estimated to have made up over 20 per cent of the population (Joshel 2010, 7–8). The proportion of slaves within the population of Roman Britain is generally considered to have been less, with the province instead being described as a 'slave-using society' (Mattingly 2006, 294). Regardless of overall numbers, it is likely that the use of slaves was relatively widespread in parts of Roman Britain, with the occasional finding of slave chains suggesting that it was also far from unknown prior to the Claudian conquest.

Roman literary sources clearly indicate the wide-ranging use of slaves in Italy, with those working on agricultural estates and in mines being of fundamental importance in the creation of wealth for private individuals and the state. They would have formed an integral part of the agricultural labour force, particularly in the late Republic and early imperial period, working alongside tenant farmers (*coloni*) and seasonal labourers (Joshel 2010, 8). There are a number of literary references by the likes of Varro, Pliny and Columella in the first century A.D. to large agricultural estates (*latifundia*) in parts of Italy and the Mediterranean provinces that used extensive slave workforces, these mostly being deplored by these writers as symbols of moral degeneracy (Garnsey and Saller 1987, 67). Although relatively large agricultural estates undoubtedly existed in parts of Roman Gaul and Britain, there is no specific evidence for any slave-based *latifundia*, and in any case, it would seem that the overall use of slaves as a rural workforce declined over the course of the empire, with much greater reliance on *coloni* (Alfoldy 1985, 175). Other uses of slaves, however, would appear to have remained prevalent within the upper reaches of society right through to the late antique period, including those serving as domestic servants, administrators, financial agents, tutors and many additional roles. Such slaves may not have added to the intrinsic wealth of elite families – indeed they could have been a considerable drain on resources – but they served a very important role as expressions of wealth, status and power – 'slaves figure importantly as animate possessions that signal wealth and power, as symbols of excessive spending, as evidence of good or finicky taste, or as a means to best one's social peers or inferiors' (Joshel and Petersen 2014, 163).

The paucity of social commentary within the few classical literary references to Britain means that the only direct evidence for slavery (slaves and freedmen) in this province comes from a small amount of epigraphic and iconographic material, alongside the occasional finding of objects such as slave chains and shackles. In addition, Webster (2005) has suggested that the numerous examples of roundhouses on otherwise 'Roman-style' settlements such as villas (and the 200 roundhouses from Vindolanda *vicus* noted above, p. 352) may have been built and used by slaves, while certain other structures, including some aisled buildings, may have been dedicated slave-quarters (*ergastula*).

Much of the epigraphic and iconographic evidence for slavery has been found in military or urban contexts, and is earlier Roman in date, such as the tombstone of Martialis, a 14-year-old slave, depicted at the foot of a couch containing his master, Gaius Cilonius, found in a cemetery outside Gloucester (Henig and Tomlin 2008). A particularly well-preserved wooden writing tablet from No. 1 Poultry in London records the contract for the sale of a Gallic slave-girl called Fortunata to a man named Vegetus, who was a Roman official, though also himself the slave of a slave of the Emperor (most likely Domitian or Trajan; Tomlin 2003). The existence of slavery in the countryside of Roman Britain is, however, suggested by the occasional religious curse tablet, notably from the temple at Uley in Gloucestershire, where the phrase 'whether slave or free' is used a number of times (e.g. Hassall and Tomlin 1979, 343).

Iron objects described as shackles (a metal link used to secure a chain or rope to something) have been recovered from seventeen sites recorded in the project's database, though their original use is not always certain. Some, such as that from the nucleated 'village' at Butterfield Down, Amesbury, Wiltshire, were suggested as being used for animals (Rawlings and Fitzpatrick 1996), while others, like the two finds from a roadside settlement at Higham Ferrers, Northamptonshire, were interpreted as for slaves or prisoners (Lawrence and Smith 2009). Very occasionally, some still have chains attached, such as that at Park Street, Hertfordshire, found in a mid-first century A.D. pit, pre-dating the villa (O'Neil 1947). Such objects are more commonly found in nucleated settlements (7), though have also been recovered from farmsteads (4), villas (3), temples (2) and a single industrial site, occurring in a range of phases, from first to fourth century A.D. Even supposing that most of these artefacts were associated with slavery, the evidence is still slight, and other indications occasionally put forward are even more tentative. An aisled building on a villa complex at Houghton Down, Longstock, Hants, for example, was suggested as possibly being used for slaves/servants during the fourth century A.D. (Cunliffe and Poole 2008c), while a mid-Roman cemetery of 24 individuals in a roadside settlement at Stainfield, Lincolnshire, was thought to possibly include slaves due to an excess number of young adult males (APS 1995). Given the vagaries of all this evidence, how common slaves would actually have been in the countryside of Roman Britain remains uncertain.

Even if we cannot attach particular labels to individuals, such as those in the Stainfield cemetery, the burial evidence, particularly when burial practice and palaeopathology correlate, does suggest the presence of distinctive social groups among the non-elite in late Roman Britain. Rohnbogner has observed that decapitated individuals in the Central Belt show higher rates of skeletal trauma, enamel hypoplasia and caries, characteristics that indicate biocultural stress in childhood (Ch. 7, p. 343). She interprets these traits as indicative of a lower social status for these individuals. By contrast, in the South region she sees evidence of higher social status among those buried with grave goods. Such individuals also lacked evidence of enamel hypoplasia, an indication of fewer episodes of stress in early childhood.

Ultimately, whatever their status, it seems clear that life for the majority of workers in rural Roman Britain was generally harsh and unrelenting, and a world away from the lifestyles of those higher up the social scale. This increased hierarchy within late Roman society may have been instrumental in the breakdown of certain elements of regional cultural expression, as noted above (p. 351). This is certainly not to say that regional differences disappeared, but just that in parts of central, southern and eastern Britain it probably became more important for many people to be identified by their position in society rather than by any shared, geographic-based, cultural bond, which may in any case have been gradually eroded by over 200 years of Roman rule.

With events on the Continent in the early fifth century leading to Britain ceding from the Roman Empire, there would have been a seismic shock to the social system, or at least to its upper echelons. The collapse of Roman authority would have quickly led to a breakdown of social and economic connectivity within the diocese, and with that a rapid fragmentation of power. There would have been significantly less demand for agricultural output, which was no longer dictated by the state, and this in turn would have had major effects on the rural workforce, especially in the primary agricultural lands of central Britain. There is little doubt that they continued with agricultural production, but on a far less intensive scale (cf. Rippon *et al.* 2015, 312) and probably with greater emphasis on self-sufficient, mixed farming regimes. The social bonds between land-owners and tenant farmers may have continued in some areas for some time, though many were undoubtedly renegotiated as power structures, economies and social networks adjusted to fit the new world order.

CONCLUDING REMARKS

Since the outset of this project we have been very conscious of the disparities in the quantities of available data, particularly between the Central Belt and South regions and elsewhere, and the extent to which we can draw generalisations or address what might be considered as 'big' questions, one of which might be quality of life. In developing her conclusion that the countryside of Roman Britain saw a decline in health compared with the Iron Age, Rohnbogner was drawing on a population sample from three regions in the south of the province: the Central Belt, the South and the East. We question whether it is legitimate to extrapolate from this sample and conclude that similar conditions prevailed in the north, west and south-west, where we have already seen in Volumes 1 and 2 how little rural settlement patterns and evidence of agricultural activity had changed from the Iron Age. It might be reasonable to speculate that the health of the population in these regions had not changed for the worse since the Roman conquest; that there was an expectation of better health in the regions apparently least affected by the Roman occupation. Yet such an optimistic view is immediately tempered by the knowledge that the Romans did draw on the manpower from these regions and not all the people, who are the source of the data regarding elevated levels of pathology analysed in Chapter 7, will have lived all their lives in the farmsteads and settlements where they died in central and south-eastern Britain (above, p. 352; Smith and Fulford 2016, 417).

Our information regarding the health of the population is not only confined to three southern regions, but it is also largely limited to the later Roman period when the rite of inhumation was prevalent. As skeletal data cannot yet address change over time within the Roman period, we have to consider the usefulness of other sources in providing possible insights into the wellbeing of the rural population before the late third and fourth centuries. Was the quality of life worse in the fourth century than it was in, say, the second century? One significant dataset that we have analysed in this project is brooches (Ch. 2), which are common finds both from excavations and as reported to the Portable Antiquities Scheme between the first and early third centuries, but become rare thereafter. A number of explanations, such as rejection of the fashion or a change to forms of clothing that did not require fastening in the same way, can be invoked to explain the change, but the period of transition also coincides with other changes such as the reduction in long distance trade, evidenced, for example, by the marked decline in the importation of pottery, whether as containers of wine, olive oil or other foodstuffs, or as tableware. Were brooches no longer as affordable as they were? Support for a relative impoverishment of material culture in the late Roman period comes from the finds assemblages of late Roman farmsteads, which are dominated by just two categories of finds not related to structures (such as iron nails): bronze coins and pottery. The burial record shows a similar pattern with a reduction in the use of grave goods, and with simple pottery vessels the most frequent find in those graves that were furnished. While a decrease in the availability of certain material goods, such as dress and toilet items, may not have had a major impact on day-to-day life, it would have had if clothing, the means of keeping warm in winter, was similarly affected. In this regard we may note the decline in the evidence for spinning and weaving in the countryside in the Roman period, suggested as coinciding with increased centralised production. The incidence of spindlewhorls in the Roman period declines generally, and their relative scarcity at farmsteads, in particular, across the province, except in Upland Wales and the Marches and the South-West, is striking (Brindle and Lodwick 2017, 226–8, figs 5.30–2). Whereas previously the rural population could look to the household to provide clothing, now it was vulnerable to the price fluctuations of the market place. That the loss of textiles and articles of clothing was a source of grief, in the second century as well as later, is evidenced by the incidence of the theft of these, the largest and most distinctive category of stolen items, on the curse tablets from Bath (Tomlin 1988, 79–81). Stricter control over woodland and the commodification of timber may also be part of the explanation for the adoption of inhumation burial from the second century onwards; securing wood for the purposes of cooking and heating may have taken priority over meeting the needs of funerary rituals. While life for the peasantry was undoubtedly hard even in the second century, the above examples of changing conditions suggest it was even more difficult in the fourth century.

This focus on the condition of the rural population of Roman Britain, which is a major theme of this volume, also necessarily points up similarities and differences with life in the towns of the provinces. We have seen, for example, that the varieties of burial practice – decapitated, prone, cremation burials – observed in the countryside are paralleled in the towns, where the informal practices collectively termed as 'structured deposition', one of the few behaviours, incidentally, that can be mapped in all the regions of Roman Britain, are also widely recorded (Fulford 2001). Although there are some differences reported between the health of the rural and urban populations, these do not appear very significant: while a higher rate of early childhood stress and upper respiratory infection is reported from the urban cohort, vitamin C deficiency is absent and there is no difference in vitamin D deficiency between town and country. However, the more varied urban diet, including of sweeteners, is reflected in a higher incidence of caries and tooth loss than in the countryside. Spinal joint disease affected a slightly higher proportion of the rural population who were more predisposed to spinal degeneration than their urban counterparts.

Although the benefits of Roman civilisation are widely and repeatedly trumpeted, it is clear that these did not impact favourably on the mass of the population of Roman Britain. Paradoxically, those who lived outside the areas of intensive agricultural production in the south and east of Britain and were apparently least affected by the Roman occupation may have enjoyed slightly better health and quality of life, comparable to that of their Iron Age ancestors.

BIBLIOGRAPHY

ABBREVIATIONS

CBA	Council for British Archaeology
BAR	British Archaeological Reports
RCHME	Royal Commission on the Historical Monuments of England
WYAS	West Yorkshire Archaeological Service

Primary sources

RIB	Collingwood, R.G. and Wright, R.P. 1965: *The Roman Inscriptions of Britain. I Inscriptions on Stone* (Oxford)
RIB II.7	Frere, S.S. and Tomlin, R. 1995: *The Roman Inscriptions of Britain. Vol. 2 Fascicule 7: Graffiti on coarse pottery cut before and after firing; stamp on coarse pottery* (Stroud)
RIB II.8	Frere, S.S. and Tomlin, R. 1995: *The Roman Inscriptions of Britain. Vol. 2 Fascicule 8: Graffiti on samian ware* (Stroud)
Caes. *BGall.*	Caesar: *The Gallic War*, trans. H.J. Edwards 1917, Loeb Classical Library (Cambridge, Mass.)
Celsus, *Med.*	Celsus: *De Medicina* On Medicine, trans. W.G. Spenser 1935, Loeb Classical Library (Cambridge, Mass.)
Columella, *Rust.*	Columella – *De Re Rustica: On Agriculture*, trans. H.B. Ash 1941, Loeb Classical Library (Cambridge, Mass.)
Ov., *Ars am.*	Ovid: *Ars Amatoria Art of Love*, trans. J.H. Mozley 1929, Loeb Classical Library (Cambridge, Mass.)
Mart., *Spect.*	Martial: *Epigrams, Volume II. Spectacles 6–10*, trans. D.R. Shackleton Bailey 1993, Loeb Classical Library (Cambridge, Mass.)
Pliny, *Nat. Hist.*	Pliny: *Naturalis Historia* Natural History, Volume II: Books 3–7, trans. H. Rackham 1942, Loeb Classical Library (Cambridge, Mass.)
Pliny, *Ep.*	Pliny: *Letters, Books VIII–X and Panegyricus*, trans. B. Radice 1976, Loeb Classical Library (Cambridge, Mass.)
Sor., *Gyn.*	Soranus: *Gynaecology* trans. O. Temkin 1991, Johns Hopkins University Press (Baltimore)
Strabo, *Geog.*	Strabo: *Geography*, trans. H. Leonard Jones 1989, 2nd edn, Loeb Classical Library (Cambridge, Mass.)
Suetonius, *Dom.*	Suetonius: *Lives of the Caesars, Volume II*, trans. J.C. Rolfe, Loeb Classical Library (Cambridge, Mass.)
Tac., *Agr. Germ.*	Tacitus: *Agricola. Germania. Dialogue on Oratory*, trans. M. Hutton and W.
	Peterson 1914 (revised by R.M. Ogilvie, E.H. Warmington and M. Winterbottom), Loeb Classical Library (Cambridge, Mass.)
Theo. Cod. XI.7.2	*The Theodosian Code and Novels and the Sirmondian Constitutions*. A translation with commentary, glossary, and bibliography by C. Pharr 1952 (Princeton)
Varro, *Rust.*	Cato and Varro: *Res Rustica: On Agriculture*, trans. W.D. Hooper 1934, Loeb Classical Library (Cambridge, Mass.)

Printed works

Abbink, J. 2003: 'Love and death of cattle: the paradox in Suri attitudes toward livestock', *Ethnos* 68.3, 341–64

Adams, G.W. 2009: *Power and Religious Acculturation in Romano-Celtic Society. An Examination of Archaeological Sites in Gloucestershire*, BAR British Series 477 (Oxford)

Adams, J.N. 2007: *The Regional Diversification of Latin 200 BC–AD 600* (Cambridge)

— 2013: *Social Variation and the Latin Language* (Cambridge)

Adams, S.A. 2013: *The First Brooches in Britain: From Manufacture to Deposition in the Early and Middle Iron Age*, unpublished PhD thesis, University of Leicester

Addyman, P.V. 1989: 'The archaeology of public health at York, England', *World Archaeology* 21(2), 244–63

Aitchison, N.B. 1988: 'Roman wealth, native ritual: coin hoards within and beyond Britain', *World Archaeology* 20(2), 270–83

Aitken, G.M. and Aitkin, G.N. 1990: 'Excavations at Whitcombe, 1965–1967', *Proceedings of the Dorset Natural History and Archaeological Society* 112, 57–94

Albarella, U. 1997: 'Size, power, wool and veal: zooarchaeological evidence for late medieval innovations', in G. De Boe and F. Verhaeghe (eds), *Environment and Subsistence in Medieval Europe*, Institute for the Archaeological Heritage of Flanders (Brugge), 19–30

— 2005: 'Alternate fortunes? The role of domestic ducks and geese from Roman to medieval times in Britain', in G. Grupe and J. Peters (eds), *Documenta Archaeobiologiae III: Feathers, Grit and Symbolism* (Munchen), 249–58

— 2007: 'The end of the sheep age: people and animals in the late Iron Age', in Haselgrove and Moore (eds) 2007, 389–403

—, Johnstone, C. and Vickers, K. 2008: 'The development of animal husbandry from the Late Iron Age to the end of the Roman period: a case study from South-East Britain', *Journal of Archaeological Science* 35, 1828–48

—, Dobney, K. and Rowley-Conwy, P. 2009: 'Size and shape of the Eurasian wild boar (*Sus scrofa*), with a view to the reconstruction of its Holocene history', *Environmental Archaeology* 14(2), 103–36

Alcock, J.P. 2006: *Life in Roman Britain* (Stroud)

— 2010: *Food in Roman Britain* (Stroud)

Aldhouse-Green, M. 1999: *Pilgrims in Stone*, BAR International Series 754 (Oxford)

— 2001a: *Dying for the Gods. Human Sacrifice in Iron Age and Roman Europe* (Stroud)

— 2001b: 'Cosmovision and metaphor: monsters and shamans in Gallo-British cult-expression', *European Journal of Archaeology* 4(2), 203–31

— 2004a: 'Gallo-British deities and their shrines', in Todd (ed.) 2004, 194–219

— 2004b: *An Archaeology of Images: Iconology and Cosmology in Iron Age and Roman Europe* (London)

— 2010: *Caesar's Druids* (Yale)

— 2012: '"Singing stones": contexting body-language in Romano-British iconography', *Britannia* 43, 115–34

Aldridge, N. 2005: 'A Belgic cremation cemetery and iron bloomery furnace at Jubilee Corner, Ulcombe', *Archaeologia Cantiana* 125, 173–82

Alexander, J. and Pullinger, J. 2000: 'Roman Cambridge. Excavations on Castle Hill 1956–1988', *Proceedings of the Cambridge Antiquarian Society* 88

Alfoldy, G. 1985: *The Social History of Rome* (London)

Allason-Jones, L. 1991: 'Roman and native interaction in Northumberland', in V.A. Maxfield and M.J. Dobson (eds), *Roman Frontier Studies: Proceedings of the XVth International Congress of Roman Frontier Studies*, (Exeter), 1–5

— 2005: *Women in Roman Britain* (York)

— (ed.) 2011a: *Artefacts in Roman Britain: Their Purpose and Use* (Cambridge)

— 2011b: 'Recreation', in Allason-Jones (ed.) 2011a, 219–42

— 2014: 'Zoomorphic brooches in Roman Britain: decoration or religious ideology?', in S. Marzel and G. Stiebel (eds) *Fashion and Ideology* (London), 69–86

— and McKay, B. 1985: *Coventina's Well: A Shrine on Hadrian's Wall Chesters* (Hexham)

Allen, H.A. 2012: 'B vitamins in breast milk: relative importance of maternal status and intake, and effects on infant status and function', *Advances in Nutrition* 3, 362–69

Allen, M.G. 2011: *Animalscapes and Empire: New Perspectives on the Iron Age/Romano-British Transition*, unpublished PhD thesis, University of Nottingham

— 2014: 'Chasing Sylvia's stag: placing deer in the countryside of Roman Britain', in K. Baker, R. Carden and R. Madgwick (eds), *Deer and People* (Oxford), 174–86

— 2016a: 'The South', in Smith *et al.* 2016, 75–140

— 2016b: 'The North-East', in Smith *et al.* 2016, 242–81

— 2017: 'Pastoral farming', in Allen *et al.* 2017, 85–141

— forthcoming: 'Animal bones', in G. Anelay (ed.), *The Selhurst Park Project: Middle Barn, Selhurst Park Farm, Eartham, West Sussex 2005–2008*

— and Lodwick, L. 2017: 'Agricultural strategies in Roman Britain', in Allen *et al.* 2017, 142–77

— and Smith, A. 2016: 'Rural settlement in Roman Britain: morphological classification and overview', in Smith *et al.* 2016, 17–43

— and Sykes, N. 2011: 'New animals, new landscapes and new worldviews: the Iron Age to Roman transition at Fishbourne', *Sussex Archaeological Collections* 149, 7–24

—, Blick, N., Brindle, T., Evans, T., Fulford, M., Holbrook, N., Richards, J.D. and Smith, A. 2016: *The Rural Settlement of Roman Britain: an online resource*, Archaeology Data Service (http://archaeology dataservice.ac.uk/archives/view/romangl/)

—, Lodwick, L., Brindle, T., Fulford, M. and Smith, A. 2017: *The Rural Economy of Roman Britain. Vol. 2*, Britannia Monograph Series 30 (London)

Allen, M. and Palmer-Brown, C. 2001: *Archaeological Evaluation Report: Land West of Ermine Street, Chapel Heath, Navenby, Lincolnshire*, Pre-Construct Archaeology

Allen, M. and Rylatt, J. 2002: *Archaeological Excavation Report: Phase 5, The Bridles, St Barnabas Road, Barnetby le Wold, North Lincolnshire*, Pre-Construct Archaeology

Allen, T.G., Darvill, T.C., Green, L.S. and Jones, M.U. 1993: *Excavations at Roughground Farm, Lechlade, Gloucestershire: a Prehistoric and Roman landscape*, Oxford Archaeology Thames Valley Landscapes 1 (Oxford)

Allen, T., Donnelly, M., Hardy, A., Hayden, C. and Powell, K. 2012: *A Road through the Past: Archaeological Discoveries on the A2 Pepperhill to Cobham Road-Scheme in Kent*, Oxford Archaeology Monograph 16 (Oxford)

Allison, J. 1947: '*Buxus sempervirens* in a late Roman burial in Berkshire: data for the study of post-glacial history of British vegetation. XI', *New Phytologist* 46(1), 122

Alvrus, A. 1999: 'Fracture patterns among the Nubians of Semna South, Sudanese Nubia', *International Journal of Osteoarchaeology* 9(6), 417–29

Ambrey, C., Fell, D., Ross, S., Speed, G. and Wood, P.N. 2011: *A1 Dishforth to Barton Improvement Post-excavation Assessment Report, Volume 1: Results Draft*, Northern Archaeological Associates Rep. NAA 11/90

Ancel, M-J. 2012: *Pratiques et Espaces Funéraires; La Cremation dans les Campagnes Romaines de la Gaule Belgique* (Montagnac)

Anderson, A.S., Wacher, J.S. and Fitzpatrick A.P. 2001: *The Romano-British 'Small Town' at Wanborough, Wiltshire*, Britannia Monograph Series 19 (London)

Anderson, K. 1985: *Hunting in the Ancient World* (Berkeley)

Anderson, K., Hinman, M. and Pankhurst, N. 2013: *Further Excavations at Skeleton Green – Assessment of an Archaeological Excavation at Buntingford Road, Puckeridge, Hertfordshire*, PCA Report no. R11228

Anderson, K., Woolhouse, T., Marter-Brown, K. and Quinn, P. 2016: 'Continental potters? First-century Roman flagon production at Duxford, Cambridgeshire', *Britannia* 47, 43–69

Anderson, T. 2001: 'Two decapitations from Roman Towcester', *International Journal of Osteoarchaeology* 11(6), 400–5

Ando, C. 2007: 'Exporting Roman religion', in J. Rüpke (ed.), *A Companion to Roman Religion* (Oxford), 429–45

Andrews, C. 2012: *Roman Seal Boxes in Britain*, BAR British Series 567 (Oxford)

Andrews, P. 2009a: 'The discovery, excavation and preservation of a detached Roman bath-house at Truckle Hill, North Wraxall', *Wiltshire Archaeological and Natural History Magazine* 102, 129–49

— 2009b: 'West Thurrock: late prehistoric settlement, Roman burials and medieval manor houses, Channel Tunnel Rail Link Excavations 2002', *Transactions of the Essex Society for Archaeology and History* 40, 1–77

— and Smith, A. 2011: 'The development of Springhead', in Andrews *et al.* 2011, 189–211

—, Dinwiddy, K.E., Ellis, C., Hutcheson, A., Philpotts, C., Powell, A.B. and Schuster, J. 2009: *Kentish Sites and Sites of Kent: A Miscellany of Four Archaeological Excavations*, Wessex Archaeology Report 24 (Salisbury)

—, Biddulph, E., Hardy, A. and Brown, R. 2011: *Settling the Ebbsfleet Valley: High Speed I Excavations at Springhead and Northfleet, Kent. The Late Iron Age, Roman, Saxon, and Medieval Landscape. Vol. 1: The Sites* (Oxford/Salisbury)

—, Booth, P., Fitzpatrick, A.P. and Welsh, K. 2015: *Digging at the Gateway. Archaeological Landscapes of South Thanet. The Archaeology of East Kent Access (Phase II)*, Oxford Wessex Archaeology Monograph 8 (Oxford/Salisbury)

Andrews, P. and Bello, S. 2006: 'Pattern in human burial practice', in Gowland and Knüsel (eds) 2006, 16–29

Anelay, G. 2010: *Middle Barn, Selhurst Park Farm, Eartham, West Sussex, 2005–2008*, West Sussex Archaeology

Annable, F.K. 1966: 'A Romano-British interment at Bradford-on-Avon', *Wiltshire Archaeological and Natural History Magazine* 61, 95–6

APS 1995: *Archaeological Excavation at Hangman's Lane, Stainfield, Lincolnshire*, Archaeological Project Services

Apsimon, A.M. 1965: 'The Roman temple on Brean Down, Somerset', *Proceedings of the University of Bristol Speleaological Society* 10(3), 195–258

Armelagos, G.J., Goodman, A.H., Harper, K.H. and Blakey, M.L. 2009: 'Enamel hypoplasia and early mortality: bioarchaeological support for the Barker Hypothesis', *Evolutionary Anthropology* 18, 261–71

Armstrong Oma, K. 2010: 'Between trust and domination: social contracts between humans and animals', *World Archaeology* 42(2), 175–87

Ashbee, P. 1954: 'The excavation of a cist-grave cemetery and associated structures near Hughtown, St Mary's, Isles of Scilly, 1949–50', *The Archaeological Journal* 111, 1–25

— 1979: 'The Porth Cressa cist-graves, St Mary's, Isles of Scilly: a postscript', *Cornish Archaeology* 18, 61–80

— 1996: 'Halangy Down, St Mary's, Isles of Scilly, excavations 1964–1977', *Cornish Archaeology* 35, 9–201

Ashby, T., Hudd, A and King, F. 1910: 'Excavations at Caerwent, Monmouthshire, on the site of the Romano-British city of *Venta Silurum*, in the year 1908', *Archaeologia* 86, 1–20

Ashdown, R. 1981: 'Avian bones', in C. Partridge, *Skeleton Green. A Late Iron Age and Romano-British Site*, Britannia Monograph Series 2 (London), 235–42

Ashwin, T. and Tester, A. 2014: *A Romano-British Settlement in the Waveney Valley: Excavations at Scole, 1993–4*, East Anglian Archaeology 152 (Dereham)

Ashworth, H.W. and Crampton, D.M. 1964: 'Excavations at Hole Ground, Wookey Hole', *Wells Archaeological and Natural History Society Annual Report* 75/6, 4–25

Askew, P., Morris, J. and Thorp, A. 2014: 'Excavations at South Marston Industrial Park, (Plots D, E and F), Swindon, Wiltshire', *Wiltshire Archaeological and Natural History Magazine* 107, 50–65

Aspöck, E. 2008: 'What actually is a "deviant burial"? Comparing German-language and Anglophone research on "deviant burials"', in E.M. Murphy (ed.), *Deviant Burial in the Archaeological Record* (Oxford), 17–34

Atkins, R. 2014: *Roman Settlements at WIX021, WTL010 and BYG030* (draft report), Oxford Archaeology East

— and Mudd, A. 2003: 'An Iron Age and Romano-British settlement at Prickwillow Road, Ely, Cambridgeshire: excavations 1999–2000', *Proceedings of the Cambridge Antiquarian Society* 92, 5–55

—, Popescu, E., Rees, G. and Stansbie, D. 2014: *Broughton, Milton Keynes, Buckinghamshire: The Evolution of a South Midlands Landscape*, Oxford Archaeology Monograph 22 (Oxford)

Atkinson, D. 1916: *The Romano-British Site on Lowbury Hill in Berkshire* (Reading)

Atkinson, M. and Preston, S. 2015: *Heybridge, a Late Iron Age and Roman Settlement: Excavations at Elms Farm 1993–5, Vol. 1*, East Anglian Archaeology 154 (Colchester)

Atkinson, R.J.C. 1952/3: 'Excavations in Barrow Hills Field, Radley, Berks, 1944–5', *Oxoniensia* 17/18, 14–35

Aureli, P., Fanciosa, G. and Fenicia, L. 2002: 'Infant botulism and honey in Europe: a commentary', *Pediatric Infectious Disease Journal* 21(9), 866–68

Ayi, K., Turrini, F., Piga, A. and Arese, P. 2004: 'Enhanced phagocytosis of ring-parasitized mutant erythrocytes: a common mechanism that may explain protection against falciparum malaria in sickle trait and beta-thalassemia trait', *Blood* 104(10), 3364–71

Baddeley, C. 1930: 'The Romano-British temple, Chedworth', *Transactions of the Bristol and Gloucester Archaeology Society* 52, 255–64

Bagnall-Smith, J. 1995: 'Interim report on the votive material from Romano-Celtic temple sites in Oxfordshire', *Oxoniensia* 60, 172–204

— 1999: 'More votive finds from Woodeaton, Oxfordshire', *Oxoniensia* 63, 147–85

— 2008: 'Aspects of votive offering in South-East Britain', in Rudling (ed.) 2008a, 153–70

Bailliot, M. 2015: 'Roman magic figurines from the western provinces of the Roman Empire', *Britannia* 46, 93–110

Baker, C.A. 2006: *Investigation of an Iron Age Pit and Roman Cave at Spratling Court Farm, Manston, Kent,* unpublished report for Kent Archaeological Society

Baker, P. 2016: 'Medicine', in Millett *et al.* (eds) 2016, 555–72

Banerjea, R.Y. 2011: 'The changing use of internal urban space: a microscopic perspective from early Roman timber building 4', in Fulford and Clarke 2011, 63–95

Banks, T. 2001: 'Property rights and the environment in pastoral China: evidence from the field', *Development and Change* 32, 717–40

Barber, A. and Hart, J. 2014: *South Wales Gas Pipeline Project Site 503. Land East of Vaynor Farm Llanddowror Carmarthenshire. Archaeological Excavation,* Cotswold Archaeology Report 13328

Barber, L. 1998: 'An early Romano-British salt-working site at Scotney Court', *Archaeologia Cantiana* 118, 327–53

Barfield, F. 2006: 'Bays Meadow villa, Droitwich: excavations 1967–77', in D. Hurst (ed.), *Roman Droitwich: Dodderhill Fort, Bays Meadow Villa, and Roadside Settlement,* CBA Research Report 146 (York), 78–242

Barfield, T.J. 2011: 'Nomadic pastoralism in Mongolia and beyond', in P.L.W. Sabloff (ed.) *Mapping Mongolia: Situating Mongolia in the World Geologic Time to the Present* (Philadelphia), 104–24

Barford, P.M. 2002: *Excavations at Little Oakley, Essex, 1951–78. Roman Villa and Saxon Settlement,* East Anglian Archaeology 98 (Chelmsford)

Barker, J. and Meckseper, C. 2015: *Huntingdon Road/ NIAB (Darwin Green), Cambridge, Cambridgeshire. Assessment of Potential and Updated Project Design,* Albion Archaeology Report 2015/48

Barnett, C., McKinley, J.I., Stafford, E., Grimm, J.M. and Stevens, C.J. 2011: *Settling the Ebbsfleet Valley. High Speed 1 Excavations at Springhead and Northfleet, Kent. The Late Iron Age, Roman, Saxon, and Medieval Landscape. Volume 3: Late Iron Age to Roman Human Remains and Environmental Reports* (Oxford/ Salisbury)

Barratt, J., Freeman, P.W.M. and Woodward, A. 2000: *Cadbury Castle, Somerset. The Late Prehistoric and Early Historic Archaeology,* English Heritage Archaeological Report 20 (Swindon)

Barrett, J.H. and Boon, G.C. 1972: 'A Roman counterfeiters' den. Part 1. White Woman's Hole, near Leighton, Mendip Hills, Somerset', *Proceedings of the University of Bristol Spelaeological Society* 13(i), 61–9

Barrowman, R.C., Batey, C.E. and Morris, C.D. 2007: *Excavations at Tintagel Castle, Cornwall, 1990–1999* (London)

Bartosiewicz, L. 2000: 'Metric variability in Roman period dogs in Pannonia Province and the Barbaricum (Hungary)', in Crockford (ed.) 2000, 181–9

Bateman, N.C.W. 1997: 'The London amphitheatre: excavations 1987–1996', *Britannia* 28, 51–85

Baxter, I.L. 2002: 'A dwarf hound skeleton from a Romano-British grave at York Road, Leicester, England, U.K., with a discussion of other Roman small dog types and speculation regarding their respective aetiologies', in L.M. Snyder and E.A. Moore (eds), *Dogs and People in Social, Working, Economic or Symbolic Interaction* (Oxford), 12–23

— 2003: 'Animal bone', in Hinman 2003 (ed.), 99–103

Bayley, J. and Butcher, S. 2004: *Roman Brooches in Britain: A Technological and Typological Study Based on the Richborough Collection,* Reports of the Research Committee of the Society of Antiquaries of London 68 (London)

Bedwin, O. and Holgate, R. 1985: 'Excavations at Copse Farm, Oving, West Sussex', *Proceedings of the Prehistoric Society* 51, 215–45

Belcastro, M.G. and Ortalli, J. (eds) 2010: *Sepolture Anomale: Indagini archeologiche e antropologiche dall'epoca classica al Medioevo in Emilia Romagna* (Borgo San Lorenzo)

Bell, M. 1977: 'Excavations at Bishopstone', *Sussex Archaeological Collections* 115, 83–117

Bendrey, R. 2003: 'The identification of fallow deer (*Dama dama*) remains from Roman Monkton, the Isle of Thanet, Kent', in I.D. Riddler (ed.), *Materials of Manufacture. The Choice of Materials in the Working of Bone and Antler in Northern and Central Europe during the First Millennium AD,* BAR International Series 1193 (Oxford), 15–18

—, Hayes, T.E. and Palmer, M. 2009: 'Patterns of Iron Age horse supply: an analysis of strontium isotope ratios in teeth', *Archaeometry* 51(1), 140–50

—, Taylor, G.M., Bouwman, A.S. and Cassidy, J.P. 2008: 'Suspected bacterial disease in two archaeological horse skeletons from southern England: palaeopathological and biomolecular studies', *Journal of Archaeological Science* 35(6), 1581–90

Bennett, D. and Timm, R.M. 2016: 'The dogs of Roman Vindolanda, Part II: time-stratigraphic occurrence, ethnographic comparisons, and biotype reconstruction', *Archaeofauna* 25, 107–26

Bennett, J. 1983: 'The end of Roman settlement in north England', in J.C. Chapman and H.C. Mytum (eds), *Settlement in North Britain, 1000 BC–AD 1000,* BAR British Series 118 (Oxford), 205–22

Bennett, P., Clark, P., Hicks, A., Rady, J. and Riddler, I. 2008: *At the Great Crossroads: Prehistoric, Roman and Medieval Discoveries on the Isle of Thanet 1994–95,* Canterbury Archaeological Trust Occasional Paper 4 (Canterbury)

Bennett, P., Riddler, I. and Sparey-Green, C. 2010: *The Roman Watermills and Settlement at Ickham, Kent,* Canterbury Archaeological Trust Monograph 5 (Canterbury)

Berg, D. and Major, P. 2006: *River Idle Washlands, Bawtry, South Yorkshire: Archaeological Watching Brief,* Archaeological Services WYAS

Bergmann, B. 1994: 'Painted perspectives of a villa visit: landscape as status and metaphor', in E.K. Gadza (ed.), *Roman Art in the Private Sphere: New Perspectives on the Architecture and Décor of the Domus, Villa and Insula* (Michigan), 49–69

Bhattacharyya, N. 2009: 'Air quality influences the prevalence of hay fever and sinusitis', *Laryngoscope* 119(3), 429–33

Biddulph, E. 2002: 'One for the road? Providing food and drink for the final journey', *Archaeologia Cantiana* 122, 101–11

— 2005: 'Last orders: choosing pottery for funerals in Roman Essex', *Oxford Journal of Archaeology* 24(1), 23–45

— 2006: *The Roman Cemetery at Pepper Hill, Southfleet, Kent*, CTRL Integrated Site Report Series, doi. org/10.5284/1008714

— 2012: 'On cultural selection: examining the process of cultural evolution through funerary evidence', in M. Duggan, F. McIntosh and D.J. Rohl (eds), *TRAC 2011: Proceedings of the Twenty-First Annual Theoretical Roman Archaeology Conference* (Oxford), 76–90

— 2015: 'Residual or ritual? Pottery from the backfills of graves and other features in Roman cemeteries', in T. Brindle, M. Allen, E. Durham and A. Smith (eds), *Proceedings of the Twenty-Fourth Annual Theoretical Roman Archaeology Conference* (Oxford), 41–53

—, Brady, K., Ford, B.M. and Murray, P. 2010: 'Roman settlement, pottery production, and a cemetery in the Beam valley, Dagenham' *Essex Archaeology and History* (4th series) 1, 109–65

—, Foreman, S., Stafford, E., Stansbie, D. and Nicholson, R. 2012: *London Gateway: Iron Age and Roman Salt Making in the Thames Estuary. Excavation at Stanford Wharf Nature Reserve, Essex*, Oxford Archaeology Monograph 18 (Oxford)

—, Seager Smith, R. and Schuster, J. 2011: *Settling the Ebbsfleet Valley. High Speed 1 Excavations at Springhead and Northfleet, Kent: The Late Iron Age, Roman, Saxon, and Medieval Landscape. Vol. 2: Late Iron Age to Roman Finds Reports* (Oxford/Salisbury)

Bidwell, P. 1985: *The Roman Fort of Vindolanda at Chesterholm, Northumberland*, English Heritage Archaeological Report 1 (London)

— 2017: 'Rural settlement and the Roman army in the North: external supply and regional self-sufficiency', in Allen *et al.* 2017, 290–305

Bille, M. and Sørensen, T.F. 2016: 'Into the fog of architecture', in M. Bille, M. and T.F. Sørensen (eds), *Elements of Architecture: Assembling Archaeology, Atmosphere and the Performance of Building Spaces* (Abingdon), 1–29

Birbeck, V. 2009: *Friars Wash, Redbourn, Hertfordshire. Archaeological Evaluation and Assessment of Results*, Wessex Archaeology Report 68735.01 (Salisbury)

Bird, D.G. 1999: 'Possible late Roman or early Saxon fish weirs at Ferry Lane, Shepperton', *Surrey Archaeological Collections* 86, 105–23

— 2004a: 'Roman religious sites in the landscape', in J. Cotton, G. Crocker and A. Graham (eds), *Aspects of Archaeology and History in Surrey: Towards a Research Framework for the County* (Guildford), 77–90

— 2004b: *Roman Surrey* (Stroud)

— 2008: 'Roman-period temples and religion in Surrey', in Rudling (ed.) 2008a, 63–86

Bird, J. 1996: 'Roman objects from Wanborough: a supplementary note', *Surrey Archaeological Collections* 83, 240–3

— 2011: 'Religious objects', in Allason-Jones (ed.) 2011a, 269–94

Birley, A.R. 1979: *The People of Roman Britain* (London)

Birley, E.B. and Keeney, G.S. 1935: 'Fourth report on excavations at Housesteads', *Archaeologia Aeliana* (4th series) 12, 204–59

Birley, R. 2009: *Vindolanda: A Roman Frontier Fort on Hadrian's Wall* (Stroud)

Bishop, M.C. 1991: 'Soldiers and military equipment in the towns of Roman Britain', in V.A. Maxfield and M.J. Dobson (eds), *Roman Frontier Studies, Proceedings of the XVth International Congress Frontier Studies 1989* (Exeter), 21–8

Black, E.W. 1986: 'Romano-British burial customs and religious beliefs in South-East England', *The Archaeological Journal* 143, 201–39

— 1994: 'Villa-owners: Romano-British gentlemen and officers', *Britannia* 25, 99–110

— 2008: 'Pagan religion in rural south-east Britain: contexts, deities and belief', in Rudling (ed.) 2008a, 1–26

Blagg, T.F.C. 1986: 'Roman religious sites in the British landscape', *Landscape History* 8, 15–25

— 1990: 'Architectural munifence in Roman Britain', *Britannia* 21, 13–31

Blake, B. 1960: 'Excavations of native (Iron Age) sites in Cumberland, 1956–58', *Transactions of the Cumberland and Westmorland Antiquarian and Archaeological Society* 59, 1–14

Bland, R. 2013: 'Presidential address 2013: hoarding in Britain: an overview', *British Numismatic Journal* 83, 214–38

Blockley, K. 1985: *Marshfield Ironmongers Piece Excavations 1982–3. An Iron Age and Romano-British settlement in the South Cotswolds*, BAR British Series 141 (Oxford)

Boocock, P., Roberts, C.A. and Manchester, K. 1995: 'Maxillary sinusitis in medieval Chichester, England', *American Journal of Physical Anthropology* 98(4), 483–95

Boon, G.C. 1975: 'Segontium fifty years on: I. A Roman stave of larchwood and other unpublished finds mainly of organic materials, together with a note of late barracks', *Archaeologia Cambrensis* 124, 52–67

— 1983: 'Some Romano-British domestic shrines and their inhabitants', in B. Hartley and J. Wacher (eds), *Rome and her Northern Provinces, Papers presented to Sheppard Frere in honour of his Retirement from the Chair of Archaeology of the Roman Empire, University of Oxford, 1983* (Gloucester), 33–55

— 1989: 'A Roman sculpture rehabilitated: the Pagans Hill dog', *Britannia* 20, 201–17

Booth, A.L. 2014: *Reassessing the Long Chronology of the Penannular Brooch in Britain: Exploring Changing Styles, Use and Meaning across a Millennium*, unpublished PhD thesis, University of Leicester

Booth, P. 1993–4: 'A Roman burial near Welford-on-Avon, Warwickshire', *Transactions of the Birmingham and Warwickshire Archaeological Society* 98, 37–50

— 1997: *Asthall, Oxfordshire: Excavations in a Roman 'Small Town'*, Oxford Archaeology Thames Valley Landscapes Monograph 9 (Oxford)

— 2001: 'Late Roman cemeteries in Oxfordshire: a review', *Oxoniensia* 66, 13–42

— 2011a: 'Romano-British trackways in the Upper Thames Valley', *Oxoniensia* 74, 1–14

— 2011b: 'The late Iron Age and Roman periods', in P. Booth, T. Champion, S. Foreman, P. Garwood, H. Glass, J. Munby and A. Reynolds, *On Track. The Archaeology of High Speed 1 Section 1 in Kent*, Oxford Wessex Archaeology Monograph 4 (Oxford/ Salisbury), 243–340

— 2016: 'A probable cattle-handling settlement in the Windrush Valley, Oxfordshire: a brief summary of 25 years work at Gill Mill Quarry, Ducklington and South Leigh', *Britannia* 47, 253–61

— 2017: 'Some recent work on Romano-British cemeteries', in Pearce and Weekes (eds) 2017, 174–207

— and Champness, C. 2014: *Creslow Manor Farm Buckinghamshire. Archaeological Excavation Report*, Oxford Archaeology

— and Lawrence, S. 2006: *The Iron Age Settlement and Roman Villa at Thurnham, Kent*, CTRL Integrated Site Report Series, Oxford/Wessex Archaeology, http://dx.doi.org/10.5284/1008824

— and Simmonds, A. 2018: *Later Prehistoric Landscape and a Roman Nucleated Settlement in the Lower Windrush Valley at Gill Mill, near Witney, Oxfordshire*, Oxford Archaeology Thames Valley Landscapes Monograph (Oxford)

—, Dodd, A., Robinson, M. and Smith, A. 2007: *Thames through Time: The Archaeology of the Gravel Terraces of the Upper and Middle Thames. The Early Historical Period AD 1–1000*, Oxford Archaeology Thames Valley Landscapes Monograph (Oxford)

—, Bingham, A-M. and Lawrence, S. 2008: *The Roman Roadside Settlement at Westhawk Farm, Ashford, Kent, Excavations 1998–9*, Oxford Archaeology Monograph 2 (Oxford)

—, Simmonds, A., Boyle, A., Clough, S., Cool, H.E.M. and Poore, D. 2010: *The Late Roman Cemetery at Lankhills, Winchester, Excavations 2000–2005*, Oxford Archaeology Monograph 10 (Oxford)

Bouby, L. and Marinval, P. 2004: 'Fruits and seeds from Roman cremations in Limagne (Massif Central) and the spatial variability of plant offerings in France', *Journal of Archaeological Science* 31, 77–86

Boudet, R. 1988: 'Iberian-type brooches', in Cunliffe 1988a, 62

Bourgeois-Pichat, J. 1951: 'La measure de la mortalité infantile: I. Principes et méthodes', *Population* 6, 233–48

Bowden, W. 2011: 'Architectural innovation in the land of the Iceni: a new complex near Venta Icenorum (Norfolk)', *Journal of Roman Archaeology* 24, 382–8

Bowman, A.K. 1994: *Life and Letters on the Roman Frontier: Vindolanda and Its People* (London)

—, Thomas, J.D. and Pearce, J. 2003: *The Vindolanda Writing Tablets (Tabulae Vindolandenses)* Vol. 3 (London)

Boyle, D., Parker, D., Larson, C. and Pessao-Brandão, L. 2000: 'Nature, incidence, and cause of work-related amputations in Minnesota', *American Journal of Industrial Medicine* 37(5), 542–50

Boylston, A., Knüsel C.J., Roberts, C.A. and Dawson, M. 2000: 'Investigation of a Romano-British rural ritual in Bedford, England', *Journal of Archaeological Science* 27(3), 241–54

Bradford, J.P.S. and Goodchild, R.G. 1939: 'Excavations at Frilford, Berks, 1937–8', *Oxoniensia* 4, 1–70

Bradley, R. 1998: *The Passage of Arms: Archaeological Analysis of Prehistoric Hoards and Votive Deposits* (Oxford)

— 2000: *An Archaeology of Natural Places* (London)

— 2002: *The Past in Prehistoric Societies* (Abingdon)

— 2007: *The Prehistory of Britain and Ireland* (Cambridge)

Branigan, K. 1972: 'The Romano-British villa at Brislington', *Proceedings of Somerset Archaeology and Natural History Society* 116, 78–85

— 1992: *Romano-British Cavemen* (Oxford)

Branigan, K. and Dearne, M.J. 1991a: 'The Romano-British finds from Wookey Hole: a re-appraisal', *Somerset Archaeology and Natural History* 134, 57–80

— 1991b: 'The small finds from Thirst House Cave, Deepdale: a reappraisal', in K. Smith and R. Hodges (eds), *Recent Developments in the Archaeology of the Peak District* (Sheffield), 85–100

Breese, C.E. and Anwyl, E. 1909: 'Roman building at Glasfryn, Tremadoc, Caernarvonshire', *Archaeologia Cambrensis* 6(9), 473–94

Brettell, R.C., Stern, B. and Heron, C.P. 2013: 'Mersea Island barrow: molecular evidence for frankincense', *Essex Society for Archaeology and History Transactions* (4th Series) 4, 81–7

Brettell, R.C., Stern, B., Reifarth, N. and Heron, C. 2014: 'The "Semblance of Immortality"? resinous materials and mortuary rites in Roman Britain', *Archaeometry* 56(3), 444–9, http://doi.org/10.1111/arcm.12027

Brettell, R.C., Schotsmans, E.M.J., Walton Rogers, P., Reifarth, N., Redfern, R.C., Stern, B. and Heron, C.P. 2015: '"Choicest unguents": molecular evidence for the use of resinous plant exudates in late Roman mortuary rites in Britain', *Journal of Archaeological Science* 53, 639–48

Brickley, M. 2002: 'An investigation of historical and archaeological evidence for age-related bone loss and osteoporosis', *International Journal of Osteoarchaeology* 12(5), 364–71

— and Ives, R. 2006: 'Skeletal manifestations of infantile scurvy', *American Journal of Physical Anthropology* 129, 163–72

— and Ives, R. 2008: *The Bioarchaeology of Metabolic Bone Disease* (London)

—, Schattmann, A. and Ingram, J. 2016: 'Possible scurvy in the prisoners of Old Quebec: a re-evaluation of evidence in adult skeletal remains', *International Journal of Paleopathology* 15 doi: 10.1016/j.ipp.2016.10.001

Brickstock, R., Brown, K., Campbell, G., Dungworth, D., Fell, V., Graham, K., Hamilton, D., Hammon, A., Harding, P., Hembrey, N., Hill, B., Jennings, S., Linford, N., Linford, P., Martin, L., Morley, G., Robinson, D.E., Schuster, J., Timby, J. and Wilson, P. 2006: *Groundwell Ridge Roman Villa, Swindon. Excavations 2003–2005*, English Heritage Research Department Report 77/2006

Brindle, T. 2014: *The Portable Antiquities Scheme and Roman Britain* (London)

— 2016a: 'The North', in Smith *et al.* 2016, 308–30

— 2016b: 'The Central West', in Smith *et al.* 2016, 282–307

— 2016c: 'Upland Wales and the Marches', in Smith *et al.* 2016, 359–84

— 2016d: 'The South-West', in Smith *et al.* 2016, 331–58

— 2017a: 'Coins and markets in the countryside', in Allen *et al.* 2017, 237–80

— 2017b: 'Imported pottery in the Romano-British countryside: a consideration of samian and amphorae', in Allen *et al.* 2017, 282–90

— and Lodwick, L. 2017: 'Textile production', in Allen *et al.* 2017, 221–30

—, Payne, N. and Hinds, K. 2013: 'A new Romano-British ritual site at Great Bedwyn/Shalbourne, Wiltshire', *Wiltshire Archaeology and History Magazine* 106, 81–8

Britnell, J. 1989: *Caersws Vicus, Powys: Excavations at the Old Primary School, 1985–86*, BAR British Series 205 (Oxford)

Brodribb, G. and Cleere, H. 1988: 'The '*Classis Britannica*' bath-house at Beauport Park, East Sussex', *Britannia* 19, 217–74

Brothwell, D.R., Powers, R. and Hirst, S.M. 2000: 'The pathology', in Rahtz *et al.* 2000, 195–239

Brown, F., Howard-Davis, C., Brennand, M., Boyle, A., Evans, T., O'Connor, S., Spence, A., Heawood, R. and Lupton, A. 2007: *The Archaeology of the A1(M): Darrington to Dishforth DBFO Road Scheme*, Lancaster Imprints 12 (Lancaster)

Brown, J. 2008: *Late Iron Age Occupation and the Emergence of a Roman Farming Settlement at Broadway Fields, Yaxley, Huntingdonshire. Final Report*, Northamptonshire Archaeology Report 08/135

Brown, L., Hayden, C. and Score, D. 2014: '*Down to Weymouth Town by Ridgeway': Prehistoric, Roman and Later Sites along the Weymouth Relief Road*, Dorset Natural History and Archaeological Society Monograph Series 23 (Dorchester)

Brown, N.R. 1999: *The Archaeology of Ardleigh, Essex. Excavations 1955–1980*, East Anglian Archaeology 90 (Colchester)

Bruce-Mitford, R. and Bruce-Mitford, M. 1970: 'The Sutton Hoo lyre, Beowulf, and the origins of the frame harp', *Antiquity* 44, 7–13

Brunaux, J.L. 1989: 'Les Enceintes Carrées sont elles des lieux de culte?', in O. Buchenshutz (ed.), *Les viereckshanzen et les Enceintes quadrilaterales en Europe Celtique* (Paris), 11–14

Buckland-Wright, J.C. 1987: 'The animal bones', in C. Sparey-Green, *Excavations at Poundbury, Dorchester, Dorset 1966–82, Vol. I: The Settlements* (Dorchester), microfiche 4–6

— 1990: 'The animal bones', in G.M. Aitken and G.N. Aitken (eds), 'Excavations at Whitcombe, 1965–7', *Proceedings of the Dorset Natural History and Archaeology Society* 112, 57–94

Buglass, J. and West, J. 2014: 'Pet cats in Roman villas: a North Yorkshire candidate', *Forum: The Journal of Council for British Archaeology Yorkshire* 4, 85–8

Bull, R. and Davis, S. 2006: *Becoming Roman. Excavation of a Late Iron Age to Romano-British Landscape at Monkston Park, Milton Keynes*, Museum of London Archaeology Study Series 16 (London)

Burleigh, G. 2015: 'Burials, ditches and deities: defining the boundaries of Iron Age and Roman Baldock', in K. Lockyear (ed.), *Archaeology in Hertfordshire Recent Research* (Welwyn), 89–117

— and Fitzpatrick-Mattthews, K.J. 2010: *Excavations at Baldock, Hertfordshire, 1978–1994. Vol. 1. An Iron Age and Romano-British Cemetery at Wallington Road* (Letchworth)

Burnham, B.C. and Davies, J.L. (eds) 2010: *Roman Frontiers in Wales and the Marches* (Aberystwyth)

Burnham, B. and Wacher, J. 1990: *The 'Small Towns' of Roman Britain* (London)

Burstow, G.P. and Hollyman, G.A. 1957: 'Muntham Court', *Sussex Notes and Queries* 14(12), 232–3

Burt, N.M., Semple, D., Waterhouse, K. and Lovell, N.C. 2013: *Identification and Interpretation of Joint Disease in Paleopathology and Forensic Anthropology* (Springfield)

Burton, J.W. 1981: 'Ethnicity on the hoof: on the economics of Nuer identity', *Ethnology* 20(2), 157–62

Busby, P., de Moulins, D., Lyne, M., McPhillips, S. and Scaife, R. 2001: 'Excavations at Clatterford Roman villa, Isle of Wight', *Proceedings of the Hampshire Field Club and Archaeology Society* 56, 95–128

Butcher, S. 2004a: 'Nornour, Isles of Scilly: a reconsideration', *Cornish Archaeology* 39–40, 5–44

— 2004b: 'Brooches', in Quinnell 2004, 70–2

Buteux, V., and Hemmingway, J. 1992: *A Roman Site at Dunley Road, Arley Kings, Worcester*, Hereford and Worcester County Council Archaeological Service Report 91 https://doi.org/10.5284/1026839

Campbell, R. 2008: 'Manufacturing evidence of Romano-British glass bangles from Thearne, near Beverley, East Yorkshire', *Yorkshire Archaeological Society Roman Antiquities Section Bulletin* 24, 12–17

Carlyle, S. 2011: *Rutland Water Habitat Creation, Lagoon B: An Iron Age Enclosure and Romano-British Shrine near Egleton, Rutland, May To July 2008*, Northamptonshire Archaeology

Carlyon, P. 1987: 'Finds from the earthwork at Carvossa, Probus', *Cornish Archaeology* 26, 103–41

Carmichael, D., Hubert, J., Reeves, B. and Schanche, A. (eds) 1994: *Sacred Sites, Sacred Places* (Abingdon)

Carr, G.C. 2003: 'Creolisation, pidginisation and the interpretation of unique artefacts in early Roman Britain', in G. Carr, E. Swift and J. Weekes (eds), *TRAC 2002: the Twelfth Proceedings of the Theoretical Roman Archaeology Conference, Canterbury 2002* (Oxford), 113–25

— 2006: *Creolised Bodies and Hybrid Identities: Examining the Early Roman Period in Essex and Hertfordshire*, BAR British Series 418 (Oxford)

— 2007: 'Creolising the body in early Roman Britain', in R. Hingley and S. Willis (eds), *Roman Finds: Context and Theory* (Oxford), 106–15

Carreck, N.L. 2008: 'Are honey bees (*Apis mellifera* L.) native to the British Isles?', *Journal of Apicultural Research* 47(4), 318–22

Carrington, P. 2012: 'Fortress, canabae and hinterland', in S.W. Ward, D.J.P. Mason, J. McPeake and P.

Carrington, *Excavations at Chester: The Western and Southern Roman Extramural Settlements: a Roman Community on the Edge of the World: Excavations 1964–1989 and Other Investigations*, BAR British Series 553 (Oxford), 338–415

Carroll, M., 2011: 'Infant death and burial in Roman Italy', *Journal of Roman Archaeology* 24, 99–120

— and Graham, E.J. (eds) 2014: *Infant Health and Death in Roman Italy and Beyond*, Journal of Roman Archaeology Supplementary Series 98 (Portsmouth, RI)

Cartmill, M. 1993: *A View to a Death in the Morning: Hunting and Nature through History* (Cambridge)

Cartwright, C. 2013: 'Folded bark objects', in Pickstone and Drummond-Murray 2013, 56

Carver, M., Hills, C. and Scheschkewitz, J. 2009: *Wasperton: A Roman, British and Anglo-Saxon Community in Central England* (Woodbridge)

Casswell, C. and Daniel, P. 2010: *'Stone was the One Crop that Never Failed': the Archaeology of a Trans-Pennine Pipeline* (Oxford)

Center, J., Nguyen, T.V., Scheider, D., Sambrook, P.N. and Eisman, J.A. 1999: 'Mortality after all major types of osteoporotic fracture in men and women: an observational study', *The Lancet* 353(9156), 878–82

Chadwick, A.M. 2010: *Fields for Discourse. Landscape and Materialities of Being in South and West Yorkshire and Nottinghamshire during the Iron Age and Romano-British Periods. A Study of People and Place*, unpublished PhD thesis, University of Wales, Newport, http://archaeologydataservice.ac.uk/archives/view/chadwick_phd_2010/metadata.cfm

— 2012: 'Routine magic, mundane ritual: towards a unified notion of depositional practice', *Oxford Journal of Archaeology* 31(3) 283–315

— 2015: 'Doorways, ditches and dead dogs – material manifestations of practical magic in Iron Age and Roman Britain', in Houlbrook and Armitage (eds) 2015, 37–64

Chamberlain, A. 2000: 'Problems and prospects in paleodemography', in Cox and Mays (eds) 2000, 101–15

— 2001: 'Palaeodemography', in D. Brothwell and A.M. Pollard (eds), *Handbook of Archaeological Sciences* (Chichester), 259–68

— 2006: *Demography in Archaeology* (Cambridge)

Chambers, R.A. 1987: 'The late- and sub-Roman cemetery at Queenford Farm, Dorchester-on-Thames, Oxon', *Oxoniensia* 52, 35–69

— and McAdam, E. 2007: *Excavations at Barrow Hills, Radley, Oxfordshire, 1983–5. Vol. 2: The Romano-British Cemetery and Anglo-Saxon Settlement*, Oxford Archaeology Thames Valley Landscapes Monograph 25 (Oxford)

Champion, T. 2016: 'Britain before the Romans', in Millett *et al.* 2016 (eds), 150–78

Chandler, B. 2008: 'A late Romano-British inhumation burial from Hookhills, Paignton', *Proceedings of the Devon Archaeological Society* 66, 59–68

Chaplin, R.E. and Barnetson, L.P. 1980: 'Animal bones', in I.M. Stead, *Rudston Roman Villa* (York), 149–61

Chapman, J. 2010: 'The human bones', in Jones 2010, 171, 232

Chapman, J. and Smith, S. 1988: 'Finds from a Roman well in Staines', *London Archaeologist* 6(1), 3–6

Charlton, D.B. and Mitcheson, M.M. 1983: 'Yardhope. A shrine to Cocidius?', *Britannia* 14, 143–53

— 1984: 'The Roman cemetery at Petty Knowes, Rochester, Northumberland', *Archaeologia Aeliana* (5th series) 12, 1–30

Chenery, C., Müldner, G., Evans, J., Eckardt, H. and Lewis, M. 2009: 'Strontium and stable isotope evidence for diet and mobility in Roman Gloucester, UK', *Journal of Archaeological Science* 37, 150–63

Cheung, C., Schroeder, H. and Hedges, R.E.M. 2012: 'Diet, social differentiation and social change in Roman Britain: new isotopic evidence from Gloucestershire', *Archaeological and Anthropological Sciences* 4, 61–73

Chryssides, G.D. and Geaves, R. 2014: *The Study of Religion: An Introduction to Key Ideas and Methods* (2nd edn) (London)

Clapham, A. and Gleason, K.L. 1997: 'Archaeobotanical evidence', in E. Hostetter and T.N. Howe, *The Romano-British Villa at Castle Copse, Great Bedwyn* (Bloomington and Indianapolis), 345–58

Clark, K.M. 1995: 'The later prehistoric and protohistoric dog: the emergence of canine diversity', *Archaeozoologia* 7(2), 9–32

— 2000: 'Dogged persistence: the phenomenon of canine skeletal uniformity in British prehistory', in Crockford (ed.) 2000, 163–9

— 2011: 'The dog assemblage', in Fulford and Clarke 2011, 474–84

— 2012: 'A review of the Romano-British dog', in Fulford (ed.) 2012, 165–83

Clarke, C.P. 1998: *Excavations to the South of Chignall Roman Villa, Essex, 1977–1981*, East Anglian Archaeology 83 (Chelmsford)

Clarke, G. 1979: *Winchester Studies 3 – Pre-Roman and Roman Winchester – Part II – The Roman Cemetery at Lankhills* (Oxford)

Clifford, E.M. 1944: 'Graves found at Hailes, Gloucestershire', *Transactions of the Bristol and Gloucestershire Archaeological Society* 65, 187–98

Close, R.S. 1972: 'Excavation of Iron Age hut circles at Percy Rigg, Kildale', *Yorkshire Archaeological Journal* 44, 23–31

Clough, S. and Boyle, A. 2010: 'Inhumations and disarticulated human bone', in Booth *et al.* 2010, 339–99

Clutton-Brock, J. 1999: *A Natural History of Domesticated Mammals* (2nd edn) (Cambridge)

Cocks, A.H. 1921: 'A Romano-British homestead, in the Hambleden Valley, Bucks', *Archaeologia* 71, 141–98

Coleman, K.M. 2011: 'Public entertainments', in Peachin (ed.) 2011, 335–57

Collingwood, R.G. and Richmond, I. 1969: *The Archaeology of Roman Britain* (2nd edn) (London)

Colonese, A.C., Lucquin, A. and Craig, O.E. in press. 'Organic residue of ceramic vessels', in M. Fulford, A. Clarke, E. Durham and N. Pankhurst, *Late Iron Age Calleva. 1. The Pre-Conquest Occupation at Silchester Insula IX*, Britannia Monograph Series 31 (London)

Cooke, N., Brown, F. and Phillpotts, C. 2008: *From Hunter Gatherers to Huntsmen: A History of the Stansted Landscape*, Framework Archaeology Monograph 2 (Oxford/Salisbury)

Cool, H.E.M. 1990: 'Roman metal hair pins from southern Britain', *The Archaeological Journal* 147, 148–82

— 2004: *The Roman Cemetery at Brougham, Cumbria: Excavations 1966–67*, Britannia Monograph Series 21 (London)

— 2006: *Eating and Drinking in Roman Britain* (Cambridge)

— 2007: 'Metal and glass small finds', in Miles *et al.* 2007, 134–44, 190–3, 342–50

— 2010: 'Objects of glass, shale, bone and metal (except nails)', in Booth *et al.* 2010, 267–309

— 2011: 'Funerary contexts', in Allason-Jones (ed.) 2011a, 293–312

— 2016: 'Clothing and identity', in Millett *et al.* (eds) 2016, 406–24

— and Baxter, M.J. 2016: 'Brooches and Britannia', *Britannia* 47, 71–98

— and Mason, D.J.P. 2008: *Roman Piercebridge. Excavations by D.W. Harding and P. Scott 1969–1981*, Architectural and Archaeological Society of Durham and Northumberland Research Report 7 (Durham)

— and Philo, C. 1998: *Roman Castleford, Vol. I: excavations 1974–85. The Small Finds* (Leeds)

— and Richardson, J.E. 2013: 'Exploring ritual deposits in a well at Rothwell Haigh, Leeds', *Britannia* 44, 191–217

Cooremans, B. 2008: 'The Roman cemeteries of Tienen and Tongeren: results from the archaeobotanical analysis of the cremation graves', *Vegetation History and Archaeobotany* 17(1), 3–13

Corney, M. 2009: *Archaeological Investigations off Church Road, Caldicot, Monmouthshire*, AC Archaeology

Cosivi, O., Grange, J.M., Daborn, C.J., Raviglione, M.C., Fujikura, T., Cousins, D., Robinson, R.A., Huchzermeyer, H.F.A.K., de Kantor, I. and Meslin, F.X. 1998: 'Zoonotic tuberculosis due to mycobacterium bovis in developing countries', *Emerging Infectious Diseases* 4, 59–70

Cotton, J. 2001: 'Prehistoric and Roman settlement in Reigate Road, Ewell', *Surrey Archaeological Collections* 88, 1–42

— n.d.: *Prehistoric and Roman Settlement at Tothill Street, Minster in Thanet, Kent*, Museum of London Archaeology Report. http://www.kentarchaeology.org.uk/10/042.pdf, accessed 13/12/2016

— and Sheldon, H. 2006, *Archaeology at Hatch Furlong, Ewell, 2006: Interim Report*, Birbeck College, University of London/Epsom and Ewell History and Archaeology Society/Surrey Archaeology Society

Cotton, M.A. and Gathercole, P.W. 1958: *Excavations at Clausentum, Southampton, 1951–54* (London)

Cottrell, T., Broomhead, R.A. and Hawkes, J.W. 1996: *Archaeological Observations during the Laying of an Outfall Drain at Wint Hill, near Banwell, Avon*, AC Archaeology

Court-Brown, M.C. and McBirnie, J. 1995: 'The epidemiology of tibial fractures', *Bone and Joint Journal* 77(3), 417–21

Cowell, R. 2009: *M62 Junction 6 Improvements Scheme: Archaeological Post-Excavation Assessment Report on Excavations in 2007*, National Museums Liverpool Field Archaeology Unit

Cox, A. 1998: *Keynsham Cemetery, Durley Hill, Keynsham, Bath and North East Somerset. Archaeological Evaluation Project*, Avon Archaeological Unit Limited, doi: 10.5284/1029136

Cox, M. and Mays, S. (eds) 2000: *Human Osteology in Archaeology and Forensic Science* (London)

Coy, J. 1984: 'The small mammals and amphibians', in Cunliffe 1984, 526–31

Cram, L. 2000: 'Varieties of dogs in Roman Britain', in Crockford (ed.) 2000, 171–80

Cram, C.L. 2005: 'Animal bones', in A.C.C. Brodribb, A.R. Hands and D.R. Walker (eds), *The Roman Villa at Shakenoak Farm, Oxfordshire: Excavations 1960–76*, BAR British Series 395 (Oxford), 384–401, 498–528

Cram, L. and Fulford, M. 1979: 'Silchester tile making – the faunal environment', in A. McWhirr (ed.), *Roman Brick and Tile. Studies in Manufacture, Distribution and Use in the Western Empire*, BAR International Series 68 (Oxford), 201–10

Cramp, L.J.E., Evershed, R.P. and Eckardt, H. 2011: 'What was a mortarium used for? Organic residues and cultural change in Iron Age and Roman Britain', *Antiquity* 85(330), 1339–52

Crandall, J.J. 2014: 'Scurvy in the Greater American Southwest: modelling micronutrition and biosocial processes in contexts of resource stress', *International Journal of Palaeopathology* 5, 46–54

Crandall, J.J. and Klaus, H.D. 2014: 'Advancements, challenges and prospects in the paleopathology of scurvy: current perspectives on vitamin C deficiency in human skeletal remains', *International Journal of Palaeopathology* 5, 1–8

Crane, E.E. 2013: *The World History of Beekeeping and Honey Hunting* (London)

Creighton, J. 1995: 'Visions of power: imagery and symbols in late Iron Age Britain', *Britannia* 26, 285–301

— 2000: *Coins and Power in Late Iron Age Britain* (Cambridge)

— with Fry, R. 2016: *Silchester: Changing Visions of a Roman Town. Integrating Geophysics and Archaeology – the Results of the Silchester Mapping Project 2005–10*, Britannia Monograph Series 28 (London)

Crerar, B. 2016: 'Deviancy in late Romano-British burial', in Millett *et al.* (eds) 2016, 381–405, doi: 10.1093/oxfordhb/9780199697713.013.023

Crockford, S.J. (ed.) 2000: *Dogs Through Time: An Archaeological Perspective*, BAR International Series 889 (Oxford)

Crosby, V. and Muldowney, L. 2011: *Stanwick Quarry, Northampton. Raunds Area Project: Phasing the Iron Age and Romano-British Settlement at Stanwick, Northamptonshire (Excavations 1984–1992): Vol. 1*, English Heritage Research Department Report Series 54–2011

Cross, P.J. 2011: 'Horse burial in first millennium AD Britain: issues of interpretation', *European Journal of Archaeology* 14(1–2), 190–209

Crummy, N. 1983: *The Roman Small Finds from Excavations in Colchester 1971–79*, Colchester Archaeological Report 2 (Colchester)

— 2007: 'Brooches and the cult of Mercury', *Britannia* 38, 225–30

— 2010: 'Bears and coins: the iconography of protection in late Roman infant burials', *Britannia* 41, 37–93

— 2011: 'Travel and transport', in Allason-Jones (ed.) 2011, 46–67

— 2013: 'Attitudes to the hare in town and country', in H. Eckardt and S. Rippon (eds), *Living and Working in the Roman World: Essays in Honour of Michael Fulford on his 65th Birthday*. Journal of Roman Archaeology Supplementary Series 95 (Portsmouth, RI), 111–28

— and Eckardt, H. 2003: 'Regional identities and technologies of the self: nail cleaners in Roman Britain', *The Archaeological Journal* 160, 44–69

—, Crummy, P. and Crossan, C. 1993: *Excavations of Roman and Later Cemeteries, Churches and Monastic Sites in Colchester, 1971–88*, Colchester Archaeological Report 9 (Colchester)

Crummy, P. 2008: 'The Roman circus at Colchester', *Britannia* 39, 15–31

—, Benfield, S., Crummy, N., Rigby, V. and Shimmin, D. 2007: *Stanway: An Elite Burial Site at Camulodunum*, Britannia Monograph Series 24 (London)

Cummings, C. 2009: 'Meat consumption in Roman Britain: the evidence from stable isotopes', in M. Driessen, S. Heeren, J. Hendriks, F. Kemmers and R. Visser (eds), *TRAC 2008: Proceedings of the Eighteenth Annual Theoretical Roman Archaeology Conference, Amsterdam 2008* (Oxford), 73–83

Cunliffe, B. 1969: *Roman Bath* (Oxford)

— 1971: *Excavations at Fishbourne. Vols I and II*, Reports of the Research Committee of the Society of the Antiquaries of London 26–27 (London)

— 1975: *Excavations at Portchester Castle 1: Roman*, Report of the Research Committee of the Society of Antiquaries of London 32 (London)

— 1981: 'Roman gardens in Britain: a review of the evidence', in E.B. Macdougall and W.M.F. Jashemski (eds), *Ancient Roman Gardens* (Washington), 97–108

— 1984: *Danebury: An Iron Age Hillfort in Hampshire. Vol. 2: The Excavations 1968–1978: The Finds*, CBA Research Report 52 (London)

— 1988a: *Mount Batten, Plymouth: A Prehistoric and Roman Port*, Oxford University Committee for Archaeology Monograph 26 (Oxford)

— 1988b: *The Temple of Sulis Minerva at Bath. Vol. 2. The Finds from the Sacred Spring*, Oxford University Committee for Archaeology Monograph 16 (Oxford)

— 1992: 'Pits, preconceptions and propitiation in the British Iron Age', *Oxford Journal of Archaeology* 11, 69–83

— 1993: *Wessex to AD 1000 – A Regional History of England* (London)

— 1995: *Danebury an Iron Age Hillfort in Hampshire, Volume 6: A Hillfort Community in Perspective*, CBA Research Report 102 (York)

— 2005: *Iron Age Communities in Britain: An Account of England, Scotland and Wales* (4th edn) (London)

— and Davenport, P. 1985: *The Temple of Sulis Minerva at Bath. Vol. 1 The Site*, Oxford University Committee for Archaeology Monograph 7 (Oxford)

Cunliffe, B. and Poole, C. 1991: *Danebury: an Iron Age hillfort in Hampshire, Volume 5: The Excavations 1979–1988: The Finds*, CBA Research Report 73b (York)

— 2000: *The Danebury Environs Programme: The Prehistory of a Wessex Landscape. Vol. 2, Part 2: Bury Hill, Upper Clatford, Hampshire, 1990*, Oxford University Committee for Archaeology Monograph 49 (Oxford)

— 2008a: *The Danebury Environs Roman Programme, A Wessex Landscape during the Roman Era, Vol. 2, Part 4: Thruxton, Hants, 2002*, Oxford University School of Archaeology Monograph 71 (Oxford)

— 2008b: *The Danebury Environs Roman Programme, A Wessex Landscape during the Roman Era, Vol. 2, Part 7: Dunkirt Barn, Abbotts Ann, Hants, 2005 and 2006*, Oxford University School of Archaeology Monograph 71 (Oxford)

— 2008c: *The Danebury Environs Roman Programme, A Wessex Landscape during the Roman Era, Vol. 2, Part 1: Houghton Down, Longstock, Hants, 1997*, Oxford University School of Archaeology Monograph 71 (Oxford)

Cunliffe, B., Down, A. and Rudkin, D. 1996: *Excavations at Fishbourne 1969–1988*, Chichester Excavations IX (Chichester)

Curate, F. 2014: 'Osteoporosis and paleopathology: a review', *Journal of Anthropological Sciences* 92, 119–46

Current Arch. 2014: 'Maryport's mystery monuments', *Current Archaeology* 289, April 2014, https://www.archaeology.co.uk/articles/features/maryports-mystery-monuments.htm

— 2017: 'Roman ritual at Red Lodge, Suffolk', *Current Archaeology* 331, October 2017, 16–17

Cuttler, R., Davidson, A. and Hughes, G. 2012: *A Corridor through Time: The Archaeology of the A55 Anglesey Road Scheme* (Oxford)

Dagless, N., Brown, L. and Fitzpatrick, A.P. 2003: *New School Site, Boscombe Down, Wiltshire: Archaeological Excavation*, Wessex Archaeology

Dalby, A. 2000: *Empire of Pleasures* (London)

Dar, G., Masharawi, Y., Peleg, S., Steinberg, N., May, H., Medlej, B., Peled, N. and Hershkovitz, I. 2010: 'Schmorl's nodes distribution in the human spine and its possible etiology', *European Spine Journal* 19(4), 670–5

Darvill, T. 2010: *Prehistoric Britain* (London)

Daubney, A. 2010: 'The cult of Totatis: evidence for tribal identity in mid Roman Britain', in S. Worrell, G. Egan, J. Naylor, K. Leahy and M. Lewis (eds), *A Decade of Discovery: Proceedings of the Portable Antiquities Scheme Conference 2007*, BAR British Series 520 (Oxford), 109–20

Davenport, P. 2000: '*Aquae Sulis*: the origins and development of a Roman town', *Bath History* 8, 6–26

Davies, G. 2013: *Excavations at Waterdale, Doncaster: Excavation Report*, ArcHeritage Report 2013/13.3

Davies, M. 2004: 'Cabriabanus – a Romano-British tile craftsman in Kent', *Archæologia Cantiana* 124, 163–84

Davies, S. 2005: 'Late and post-Roman burial to 19th century brickmaking: excavations at the site of 40

Queen Street, Hitchin, SG4', *Hertfordshire Archaeology and History* 14, 57–74

Davies, S.M., Bellamy, P.S., Heaton, M.J. and Woodward, P.J. 2002: *Excavations at Alington Avenue, Fordington, Dorchester, Dorset, 1984–87*, Dorset Natural History and Archaeology Society Monograph 15 (Dorchester)

Davis, S.J.M. 1997: *Animal Bones from the Roman Site at Redlands Farm, Stanwick, Northamptonshire, 1990 Excavations*, English Heritage, Ancient Monument Laboratory Report Series 106/97

— 2005: *Animal Bones from Roman São Pedro, Fronteira, Alentejo*, Trabalhos do CIPA 88 (Lisbon)

Dawson, M. 1994: *A Late Roman Cemetery at Bletsoe*, Bedfordshire Archaeology Monograph 1 (Bedford)

— 2004: *Archaeology in the Bedford Region*, BAR British Series 373 (Oxford)

De Grozzi Mazorin, J. and Tagliacozzo, A. 2000: 'Morphological and osteological changes in the dog from the Neolithic to the Roman period in Italy', in Crockford (ed.) 2000, 141–61

de la Bédoyère, G. 2015: *The Real Lives of Roman Britain* (Yale)

de la Rua-Domenech, R. 2006: 'Human *mycobacterium bovis* infection in the United Kingdom: incidence, risks, control measures and review of the zoonotic aspects of bovine tuberculosis', *Tuberculosis* 86(2), 77–109

Dean, M. and Gorin, M.S. 2000: 'Site 1: Empingham Romano-British farmstead', in N. Cooper, *The Archaeology of Rutland Water*, Leicestershire Archaeology Monograph 6, 4–16

Dearne, M.J. and Lord, T.C. 1998: *The Romano-British Archaeology of Victoria Cave, Settle*, BAR British Series 273 (Oxford)

Deforce, K. and Haneca, K. 2012: 'Ashes to ashes. Fuelwood selection in Roman cremation rituals in northern Gaul', *Journal of Archaeological Science* 39(5), 1338–48

Dellestable, F. and Gaucher, A. 1998: 'Clay-shoveler's fracture. Stress fracture of the lower cervical and upper thoracic spinous processes', *Revue du Rhumatisme (English edn)* 65(10), 575–82

Deniger, V. 1997: *Amphitheatres of Roman Britain. A Study of their Classes, Architecture and Uses*, unpublished MA thesis, Queen's University, Kingston, Ontario

Derks, T. 1995: 'The ritual of the vow in Gallo-Roman religion', in J. Metzler, M. Millett, N.G.A.M. Roymans and J. Slofstra (eds), *Integration in the Early Roman West. The Role of Culture and Ideology*, Dossier d'archéologie du Musée National d'Histoire et d'Art 4 (Luxembourg), 111–27

— 1998: *Gods, Temples and Ritual Practices: The Transformation of Religious Ideas and Values in Roman Gaul* (Amsterdam)

— and Roymans, N. (eds) 2009: *Ethnic Constructs in Antiquity: The Role of Power and Tradition* (Amsterdam)

Detienne, M. 1989: 'Culinary practices and the spirit of sacrifice', in M. Detienne and J.-P. Vernant (eds), *The Cuisine of Sacrifice among the Greeks* (Chicago/London)

Diamond, H.W. 1847: 'Account of wells or pits, containing Roman remains, discovered at Ewell in Surrey', *Archaeologia* 32, 451–5

Dickson, C. 1994: 'Macroscopic fossils of garden plants from British Roman and medieval deposits', in D. Moe, J. Dickson and P.M. Jorgensen (eds), *Garden History: Garden Plants, Species, Forms and Varieties from Pompeii to 1800* (Rixensart), 47–62

Dimbleby, G. 1978: *Plants and Archaeology* (London)

Dinwiddy, K.E. 2009: *A Late Roman Cemetery at Little Keep, Dorchester, Dorset*, Wessex Archaeology, http://www.wessexarch.co.uk/reports/64913/little-keep-dorchester

— 2015: 'Roman', in J.I. McKinley and K.E. Dinwiddy, 'Human bone', in Andrews *et al.* 2015, 374–406

— and Bradley, P. 2011: *Prehistoric Activity and a Romano-British Settlement at Poundbury Farm, Dorchester, Dorset*, Wessex Archaeology Report 28 (Salisbury)

Dirckx, J.H. 1983: 'Dermatologic terms in the De Medicina of Celsus', *Dermatology in Historical Perspective* 5(4), 363–70

Dobney, K. 2001: 'A place at the table: the role of vertebrate zooarchaeology within a Roman research agenda for Britain', in James and Millett (eds) 2001, 36–45

— and Ervynck, A. 2007: 'To fish or not to fish? Evidence for the possible avoidance of fish consumption during the Iron Age around the North Sea', in Haselgrove and Moore (eds) 2007, 403–18

— and Jaques, D. 1996: 'The mammal bones', in R.J. Williams, P.J. Hart and A.T.L. Williams, *Wavendon Gate: a Late Iron Age and Roman Settlement in Milton Keynes*, Buckinghamshire Archaeology Society Monograph 10 (Aylesbury), 203–30

—, Jaques, D. and Irving, B. 1996: *Of Butchers and Breeds. Report on Vertebrate Remains from Various Sites in the City of Lincoln*, Lincoln Archaeological Studies 5 (Lincoln)

—, Hall, A. and Kenward, H. 1999: 'It's all garbage... a review of bioarchaeology in the four English Colonia towns', in H. Hurst (ed.), *The Coloniae of Roman Britain: New Studies and a Review*, Journal of Roman Archaeology Supplementary Series 36 (Portsmouth, RI), 15–35

Dobson, M. 1980: '"Marsh Fever" – the geography of malaria in England', *Journal of Historical Geography* 6(4), 357–89

Doherty, G. 1987: 'The pine-scales', in Meates 1987, 318

Dool, J. 1978: 'Roman material from Rainster Rocks, Brassington', *Derbyshire Archaeological Journal* 96, 17–22

Douglas, A., Gerrard, J. and Sudds, B. 2011: *A Roman Settlement and Bath House at Shadwell: Excavations at Tobacco Dock and Babe Ruth Restaurant, The Highway, London*, Pre-Construct Archaeology Monograph 12 (London)

Down, A. 1979: *Chichester Excavations IV* (Chichester)

Draper, J. 1985: *Excavations at Hill Farm, Gestingthorpe, Essex*, East Anglian Archaeology 25 (Chelmsford)

Drew, C.D. 1932: 'The excavations at Jordan Hill and Preston, 1932', *Proceedings of the Dorset Natural History and Archaeological Society* 54, 15–34

Drinking Water Inspectorate 2013: *Fluoridation of Drinking Water* (London)

Dryden, D.M., Saunders, L.D., Rowe, B.H., May, L.A., Yiannakoulias, N., Svenson, L.W., Schopflocher, D.P. and Voaklander, D.C. 2003: 'The epidemiology of traumatic spinal cord injury in Alberta, Canada', *Canadian Journal of Neurological Sciences* 30(2), 113–21

Ducos, P. 1978: '"Domestication" defined and methodological approaches to its recognition in faunal assemblages', in R.H. Meadow and M.A. Zeder (eds), *Approaches to Faunal Analysis in the Middle East*. Peabody Museum Bulletin 2 (Cambridge, MA), 53–6

Duday, H. 2009: *The Archaeology of the Dead: Lectures in Archaeothanatology* (Oxford)

Dundes, A. 1994: *The Cockfight: a Casebook* (Madison, WI)

Duray, S.M. 1992: 'Enamel defects and caries etiology: an historical perspective', in A.H. Goodman and L.L. Capasso (eds), *Recent Contributions to the Study of Enamel Developmental Defects*, Journal of Palaeopathology Monographic Publications 2, 307–20

Durham, E. 2012: 'Depicting the gods: metal figurines in Roman Britain', *Internet Archaeology* 31, http://dx.doi.org/10.11141/ia.31.2

— 2013: 'Symbols of power: the Silchester bronze eagle and eagles in Roman Britain', *The Archaeological Journal* 170(1), 78–105

Dütting, M.K. and Hoss, S. 2014: 'Lead net-sinkers as an indicator of fishing activities', *Journal of Roman Archaeology* 27, 429–42

Dyer, M.J. 1999: *Archaeological Observation and Recording of a Residential Development Between Peel Close and Orchard Way, Topsham, Exeter*, Exeter Archaeology Report 99.83 (Exeter)

ECC 2003: *Former Council Depot, Haslers Lane, Great Dunmow. Archaeological Excavation*, Essex County Council Field Archaeology Unit

Eckardt, H. 2002: *Illuminating Roman Britain*, Monographies instrumentum 23 (Montagnac)

— 2005: 'The social distribution of Roman artefacts: the case of nail-cleaners and brooches in Britain', *Journal of Roman Archaeology* 18, 139–60

— 2006: 'The character, chronology, and use of the late Roman pits: the Silchester finds assemblage', in M. Fulford, A. Clarke and H. Eckardt, *Life and Labour in Late Roman Silchester. Excavations in Insula IX since 1997*, Britannia Monograph 22 (London), 221–45, 380–3

— 2008: 'Technologies of the body: Iron Age and Roman grooming and display', in Garrow *et al.* (eds) 2008, 113–28

— 2010a: 'A long way from home: diaspora communities in Roman Britain', in Eckardt (ed.) 2010b, 99–130

— (ed.) 2010b: *Roman Diasporas. Archaeological Approaches to Mobility and Diversity in the Roman Empire*, Journal of Roman Archaeology Supplementary Series 78 (Portsmouth, RI)

— 2011: 'Heating and lighting', in Allason-Jones (ed.) 2011a, 180–93

— 2014: *Objects and Identities: Roman Britain and the North-Western Provinces* (Cambridge)

— 2017: *Writing and Power in the Roman World: Literacies and Material Culture* (Cambridge)

— and Crummy, N. 2008: *Styling the Body in Late Iron Age and Roman Britain: A Contextual Approach to Toilet Instruments*, Monographies instrumentum 36 (Montagnac)

— and Müldner, G. 2016: 'Mobility, migration and diasporas in Roman Britain', in Millett *et al.* (eds) 2016, 203–23, doi 10.1093/oxfordhb/9780199697731.001.0001

—, Brewer, P., Hay, S. and Poppy, S. 2009: 'Roman barrows and their landscape context: a GIS case study at Bartlow, Cambridgeshire', *Britannia* 40, 65–98

—, Müldner, G. and Lewis, M. 2014: 'People on the move in Roman Britain', *World Archaeology* 46(4), 534–50

—, Müldner, G. and Speed, G. 2015: 'The late Roman Field Army in northern Britain? Material culture and multi-isotope analysis at Scorton (N Yorks.)', *Britannia* 46, 191–223

Effros, B. 2000: 'Skeletal sex and gender in Merovingian mortuary archaeology', *Antiquity* 74(285), 632–9

Ekengren, F. 2013: 'Contextualizing grave goods: theoretical perspectives and methodological implications', in Nilsson Stutz and Tarlow (eds), 2013, 173–94, doi: 10.1093/oxfordhb/9780199569069.013.0010

El-Harami, J. 2015: 'Entertainment and recreation in the classical world – tourism products', *Journal of Management and Sustainability* 5(1), 168–78

Elliot, L. 2004: *Archaeological Evaluation at Sturton Le Steeple, Nottinghamshire*, Trent and Peak Archaeological Unit

— and Malone, S. 2005: 'Iron Age/Romano-British features and a fourth century AD Christian lead tank from Flawborough, Nottinghamshire', *Transactions of the Thoroton Society* 109, 25–43

Ellis, C.J. and Rawlings, M. 2001: 'Excavations at Balksbury Camp, Andover 1995-97', *Proceedings of the Hampshire Field Club and Archaeological Society* 56, 21–94

Ellis, P. and King, R. 2016: 'A Romano-British rural cemetery at Well's Bridge, Barnwood: excavations 1998-9', *Transactions of the Bristol and Gloucestershire Archaeological Society* 134, 113–26

Ellis, P., Henig, M. and Hayward, K. forthcoming (2017): 'The Well's Bridge ash-chest and cremation cylinder', *Transactions of the Bristol and Gloucestershire Archaeological Society* 135

Elsner, J. (ed.) 2008: *Pilgrimage in Graeco-Roman and Early Christian Antiquity: Seeing the Gods* (Oxford)

— 2012: 'Sacrifice in late Roman art', in C.A. Faraone and F.S. Naiden (eds), *Greek and Roman Animal Sacrifice: Ancient Victims, Modern Observers*, (Cambridge), 120–63

Epplett, C. 2001: 'The capture of animals by the Roman military', *Greece and Rome* 48, 210–22

Esmonde Cleary, S. 2000: Putting the dead in their place: burial location in Roman Britain, in Pearce *et al.* (eds) 2000, 127–42

— 2004: 'Britain in the fourth century', in Todd (ed.) 2004, 409–47

— 2005: 'Beating the bounds: ritual and the articulation of urban space in Roman Britain', in A. MacMahon and J. Price (eds), *Roman Working Lives and Urban Living* (Oxford), 1–17

— 2013: *Chedworth. Life in a Roman Villa* (Stroud)

Esposito, A. 2016: 'A context for Roman priestly regalia: depositional practices and spatial distribution of assemblages from Roman Britain', in Mandich *et al.* (eds) 2016, 92–110

Evans, C. 2013a: *Process and History. Romano-British Communities at Colne Fen, Earith: An Inland Port and Supply Farm*, The Archaeology of the Lower Ouse Valley Vol. 2 (Cambridge)

— 2013b: 'Delivering bodies unto waters: a late Bronze Age mid-stream midden settlement and Iron Age ritual complex in the fens', *The Antiquaries Journal* 93, 55–79

— and Hodder, I. 2006: *Marshland Communities and Cultural Landscapes* (Cambridge)

— and Newman, R. 2010: *North-west Cambridge, University of Cambridge. Archaeological Evaluation Fieldwork*, Cambridge Archaeological Unit Report 921

—, Mackay, D. and Appleby, G. 2006: *Longstanton, Cambridgeshire. A Village Hinterland (I, II and III). 2004, 2005 and 2006 Investigations*, Cambridge Archaeological Unit

Evans, J. 1987: 'Graffiti and the evidence of literacy and pottery use in Roman Britain', *The Archaeological Journal* 144, 191–204

Eyers, J.E. 2011: *Romans in the Hambleden Valley. Yewden Roman Villa*, Chiltern Archaeology Monograph 1 (High Wycombe)

Facchini, F., Rastelli, E. and Brsili, P. 2004: 'Cribra orbitalia and cribra cranii in Roman skeletal remains from the Ravenna area and Rimini (I–IV century AD)', *International Journal of Osteoarchaeology* 14, 126–36

Fagan, G.G. 1999: *Bathing in Public in the Roman World* (Michigan)

— 2011: 'Socialising at the baths', in Peachin (ed.) 2011, 358–76

Farley, J. 2011: 'The deposition of miniature weaponry in Iron Age Lincolnshire', in A.C. Smith and M.E. Bergeron (eds), *The Gods of Small Things*, Pallas 86 (Paris), http://pallas.revues.org/2108

Farrar, L. 2011: *Ancient Roman Gardens* (Stroud)

Farwell, D.E. and Molleson, T.I. 1993: *Poundbury Vol. 2: The cemeteries*, Dorset Natural History and Archaeology Society Monograph Series 11 (Dorchester)

Fasham, P.J., Kelly, R.S., Mason, M.A. and White, R.B. 1998: *The Graeanog Ridge: the Evolution of a Farming Landscape and its Settlements in North-West Wales*, Cambrian Archaeological Monographs 6 (Bangor)

Fauduet, I. 2014: 'Gaul at the time of the Berthouville Sanctuary', in K. Lapatin (ed.), *The Berthouville Silver Treasure and Roman Luxury* (Los Angeles), 69–88

Feachem, R.W. de F. 1951: 'Dragonesque fibulae', *Antiquaries Journal* 31, 32–44

— 1968: 'Dragonesque fibulae', *Antiquaries Journal* 48, 100–2

Fenton-Thomas, C. 2011: *Where Sky and Yorkshire and Water Meet: The Story of the Melton Landscape from Prehistory to the Present*, On-Site Archaeology Monograph 2 (York)

Ferris, I.M. 1986: 'Horse-and-Rider brooches in Britain: a new example from Rocester, Staffordshire', *Transactions Staffordshire Archaeological and Historical Society* 28, 1–10

— 2012: *Roman Britain Through Its Objects* (Stroud)

—, Bevan, L. and Cuttler, R. 2000: *The Excavation of a Romano-British Shrine at Orton's Pasture, Rocester, Staffordshire*, BAR British Series 314 (Oxford)

Fewtrell, M.S., Morgan, J.B., Duggan, C., Gunnlaugsson, G., Hibberd, P.L., Lucas, A. and Kleinman, R.E. 2007: 'Optimal duration of exclusive breastfeeding: what is the evidence to support current recommendations?', *American Journal of Clinical Nutrition* 85(2), 635–8

Field, N. and Parker Pearson, M. 2003: *An Iron Age Timber Causeway with Iron Age and Roman Votive Offerings: the 1981 Excavations* (Oxford)

Fillery-Travis, R. 2012: 'Multidisciplinary analysis of Roman Horse-and-Rider brooches from Bosworth', in I. Schrüfer-Kolb (ed.) *More than just Numbers? The role of Science in Roman Archaeology*, Journal of Roman Archaeology Supplementary Series 91 (Portsmouth, RI), 135–62

Finlay, N. 2000: 'Outside of life: traditions of infant burial in Ireland from cillin to cist', *World Archaeology* 31(3), 407–22

Fishwick, D. 1961: 'The imperial cult in Roman Britain', *Phoenix* 15 (3 and 4), 159–73, 213–29

— 1995: 'The temple of Divus Claudius at Camulodunum', *Britannia* 26, 11–27

Fittock, M.G. 2015: 'Broken deities: the pipe-clay figurines from Roman London', *Britannia* 46, 111–34

Fitzpatrick, A.P. 1991: "Celtic (Iron Age) religion' – traditional and timeless?', *Scottish Archaeological Review* 8, 123–25

— 1997: *Archaeological Excavations on the Route of the A27 Westhampnett Bypass, West Sussex, 1992, Vol. 2: The Cemeteries*, Wessex Archaeology Report 12 (Salisbury)

— 2004: 'The tombstones and inscribed stones', in Cool 2004, 405–35

— 2007: 'Druids: towards an archaeology', in C. Gosden, H. Hamerow, P. de Jersey, and G. Lock (eds), *Communities and Connections: Essays in Honour of Barry Cunliffe* (Oxford), 287–315

—, Powell, A.B., and Allen, M.J. 2008: *Archaeological Excavations on the Route of the A27 Westhampnett Bypass, West Sussex, 1992, Vol. 1: The Late Upper Palaeolithic–Saxon*, Wessex Archaeology Report 21 (Salisbury)

Ford, S., Cass, S., Lewis, J., Mumford, J., Preston, S. and Taylor, A. 2016: *Roman Occupation at Chapel Farm, Blunsden, Swindon, Wiltshire (Lower Widhill Farm), Excavations 2004–2012*, Thames Valley Archaeological Services Monograph 22 (Reading)

Foster, J. 1977: *Bronze Boar Figurines in Iron Age and Roman Britain*, BAR British Series 39 (Oxford)

Foster, M. 1989: 'Alchester, Oxon: a brief review and new aerial evidence', *Britannia* 20, 141–7

Foster, S. 1989: 'Analysis of spatial patterns in buildings (access analysis) as an insight into social structure:

examples from the Scottish Atlantic Iron Age', *Antiquity* 63, 40–50

Foucault, M. 1988: *Madness and Civilisation: A History of Insanity in the Age of Reason* (New York)

Fowler, C. 2013: 'Identities in transformation: identities, funerary rites, and the mortuary process', in Nilsson Stutz and Tarlow (eds) 2013, 511–26, doi: 10.1093/oxfordhb/9780199569069.013.0028

Fox, A. 1952: 'Roman objects from Cadbury Castle', *Report and Transactions of the Devonshire Association for the Advancement of Science, Literature and Art* 84, 105–14

Fox, N.P. 1967: 'The ritual shaft at Warbank, Keston', *Archaeologia Cantiana* 82, 184–91

Fradley, M. 2009: 'The field archaeology of the Romano-British settlement at Charterhouse-on-Mendip', *Britannia* 40, 99–122

France, N.E. and Gobel, B. 1985: *The Romano-British Temple at Harlow* (Stroud)

Frankfurter, D. 2006: 'Traditional cult', in D.S. Potter (ed.), *A Companion to the Roman Empire* (Oxford), 543–64

Fraser, J. and George, R. 2013: *Archaeological Investigations at the Caythorpe Gas Storage Project, Low Caythorpe, East Riding of Yorkshire, 2009–2010: Post-Excavation Assessment*, Humber Field Archaeology

Fraser, R. and Speed, G. 1997: *A69 Haltwhistle Bypass. Archaeological Watching Brief (1996 and 1997)*, Northern Archaeological Associates

Freeman, R. and Stevens, A. 2008: 'Nursing caries and buying time: an emerging theory of prolonged bottle feeding', *Community Dentistry and Oral Epidemiology* 36, 425–33

Frenzen, P.D. and Hogan, D.P. 1982: 'The impact of class, education, and health care on infant mortality in a developing society: the case of rural Thailand', *Demography* 19(3), 391–408

Frere, S. 1967: *Britannia. A History of Roman Britain* (first edn) (London)

Frere, S.S. and Tomlin, R. 1995a: *The Roman Inscriptions of Britain Vol. 2 Fascicule 7: Graffiti on coarse pottery cut before and after firing; stamp on coarse pottery* (Stroud)

— 1995b: *The Roman Inscriptions of Britain Vol. 2 Fascicule 8: Graffiti on samian ware* (Stroud)

Friendship-Taylor, R.M. 1999: *Iron Age and Roman Quinton: The Evidence for the Ritual Use of the Site (Site 'E' 1978–1981)*, Upper Nene Archaeological Society (Northampton)

Fryer, V. and Murphy, P. 2014: 'Plant macrofossils', in Ashwin and Tester 2014, 400–2

Fudge, E. 2013: 'The animal face of early modern England', *Theory, Culture and Society* 30(7–8), 177–98

Fulford, M. 1989a: 'A Roman shipwreck off Nornour, Isles of Scilly?', *Britannia* 20, 245–9

— 1989b: *Silchester Amphitheatre: Excavations 1979–85*, Britannia Monograph Series 10 (London)

— 1999: 'Veteran settlement in 1st-c. Britain and the foundations of Gloucester and Lincoln', in H. Hurst (ed.), *The* Coloniae *of Roman Britain: New Studies and a Review*, Journal of Roman Archaeology Supplementary Series 36 (Portsmouth, RI), 177–80

— 2001: 'Pervasive "ritual" behaviour in Roman Britain', *Britannia* 32, 199–218

— 2004: 'Economic structures', in Todd (ed.) 2004, 309–26

— 2006: 'Corvées and *civitates*', in R.J.A. Wilson (ed.), *Romanitas. Essays on Roman Archaeology in Honour of Sheppard Frere on the Occasion of his Ninetieth Birthday* (Oxford), 65–71

— 2010: 'Roman Britain: immigration and material culture', in Eckardt (ed.) 2010b, 67–80

— (ed.) 2012: *Silchester and the Study of Romano-British Urbanism*, Journal of Roman Archaeology Supplementary Series 50 (Portsmouth, RI)

— 2017: 'Conclusions', in Allen *et al.* 2017, 358–63

— and Allen, J. 1992: 'Iron-making at the Chesters villa, Woolaston, Gloucestershire: survey and excavation 1987–91', *Britannia* 23, 159–215

— and Clarke, A.S. 2011: *City in Transition: The Mid-Roman Occupation of Insula IX, c. A.D. 125–250/300: A Report on Excavations Undertaken Since 1997*, Britannia Monograph Series 25 (London)

— and Rippon, S.J. 1994: 'Lowbury Hill, Oxon: a re-assessment of the probable Romano-Celtic temple and the Anglo-Saxon barrow', *The Archaeological Journal* 151, 158–211

—, Powell, A.B., Entwistle, R. and Raymond, F. 2006: *Iron Age and Romano-British Settlements and Landscapes of Salisbury Plain*, Wessex Archaeology Report 20 (Salisbury)

Fuller, B.T., Molleson, T.I., Harris, D.A., Gilmour, L.T. and Hedges, R.E.M. 2006: 'Isotopic evidence for breastfeeding and possible adult dietary differences from late/sub-Roman Britain', *American Journal of Physical Anthropology* 129, 45–54

Gage Rokewode, J. 1842: 'Account of the final excavations made at the Bartlow Hills', *Archaeologia* 29, 1–4

Gaffney, V., White, R.H. and Goodchild, H. 2007: *Wroxeter, The Cornovii, and the Urban Process: Final Report on the Wroxeter Hinterland Project 1994–1997. Vol. 1 Researching the Hinterland*, Journal of Roman Archaeology Supplementary Series 68 (Portsmouth, RI)

García Sanjuán, L., Garrido González, P. and Lozano Gómez, F. 2008: 'The use of prehistoric ritual and funerary sites in Roman Spain: discussing tradition, memory and identity in Roman society', in C. Fenwick, M. Wiggins, and D. Wythe (eds), *TRAC 2007 Proceedings of the Seventeenth Theoretical Roman Archaeology Conference* (Oxford), 1–14

Gardner, A. 2007: *An Archaeology of Identity: Soldiers and Society in Late Roman Britain* (Walnut Creek, CA)

Garland, N. 2013: 'Ritual landscapes of pre-Roman Britain: the margins of practice on the margins of the empire', in A. Bokern, M. Bolder-Boos, S. Krmnicek, D. Maschek and S. Page (eds), *TRAC 2012 Proceedings of the Twenty-Second Theoretical Roman Archaeology Conference* (Oxford), 183–98

Garner, D. and Reid, M. 2012: 'Roman Middlewich: reassessing its form, function and chronology', *Journal of the Chester Archaeological Society* 83, 37–93

Garnsey, P. 1999: *Food and Society in Classical Antiquity* (Cambridge)

— and Saller, R. 1987: *The Roman Empire: Economy, Society, and Culture* (Berkeley)

Garrow, D. 2012: 'Odd deposits and average practice. A critical history of the concept of structured deposition', *Archaeological Dialogues* 19(2), 85–115

—, Gosden, C. and Hill, J.D. (eds) 2008: *Rethinking Celtic Art* (Oxford)

Gerrard, J. 2005: 'Bradley, Hill Somerset, and the end of Roman Britain: a study in continuity?', *Proceedings of the Somerset Archaeological and Natural History Society* 148, 1–10

— 2013: *The Ruin of Roman Britain* (Oxford)

Ghey, E. 2005: 'Beyond the temple: blurring the boundaries of "sacred space"', in J. Bruhn, B. Croxford and D. Grigoropoulos (eds), *TRAC 2004. Proceedings of the Fourteenth Annual Theoretical Roman Archaeology Conference, Durham 2004* (Oxford), 109–18

— 2007: 'Empty spaces or meaningful places? A broader perspective on continuity', in Haeussler and King (eds) 2007, 19–30

Gibson, C. and Manning, A. 2005: *Boscombe Down Phase V excavations, Amesbury, Wiltshire, Post-excavation Assessment Report*, Wessex Archaeology Report 56240

Gibson, D. and Knight, M. 2002: *Prehistoric and Roman Archaeology at Stonald Field King's Dyke West, Whittlesey*, Cambridge Archaeological Unit Report 498

Gidney, L. 2000: 'Economic trends, craft specialisation and social status: bone assemblages from Leicester', in P. Rowley-Conwy (ed.), *Animal Bones, Human Societies* (London), 170–8

— 2008: 'The animal bone', in D.W. Harding, 'The Holme House villa', in Cool and Mason 2008, 127–58

Giecco, F. 2000: *Report on an Archaeological Watching Brief at Skye Road, Wigton, Cumbria*, Carlisle Archaeology Report 46/00

—, Zant, J., Craddock, G. and Wigfield, N. 2001: *Interim Report on Archaeological Excavation between Mary Street and Tait Street, Botchergate, Carlisle*, Carlisle Archaeology Ltd

Giles M. 2007: 'Good fences make good neighbours? Exploring the ladder enclosures of late Iron Age East Yorkshire', in Haselgrove and Moore (eds) 2007, 235–49

Gilhus, I.S. 2006: *Animals, Gods and Humans: Changing Attitudes to Animals in Greek, Roman and Early Christian Ideas* (London)

Gilmore, H. and Halcrow, S.E. 2014: 'Interpretations of infanticide in the past', in J.L. Thompson, M.P. Alfonso-Durruty and J.J. Crandall (eds), *Tracing Childhood: Bioarchaeological Investigations of Early Lives in Antiquity* (Gainesville), 123–38

Giorgi, J. 1997: 'The plant remains', in A. Mackinder, *A Romano-British Cemetery on Watling Street: Excavations at 166 Great Dover Street, Southwark, London*, MoLAS Archaeology Studies Series 4 (London), 65–6

Girling, M. and Straker, V. 1993: 'Plant macrofossils, arthropods and charcoal', in Woodward and Leach 1993, 250–3

Gloth, F.M., Gundberg, C.M., Hollis, B.W., Haddad, J.G. and Tobin, J.D. 1995: 'Vitamin D deficiency in homebound elderly persons', *Journal of the American Medical Association* 274(21), 1683–6

Going, C.J. and Hunn, J.R. 1999: *Excavations at Boxfield Farm, Chells, Stevenage, Hertfordshire*, Hertfordshire Archaeological Trust Report 2 (Hertford)

Goodman, A.H. 1993: 'On the interpretation of health from skeletal remains', *Current Anthropology* 34(3), 281–8

— and Martin, D.L. 2002: 'Reconstructing health profiles from skeletal remains', in R. Steckel and J. Rose (eds), *The Backbone of History: Health and Nutrition in the Western Hemisphere* (Cambridge), 11–60

— and Rose, J.C. 1991: 'Dental enamel hypoplasias as indicators of nutritional status', in M.A. Kelley and C.S. Larsen (eds), *Advances in Dental Anthropology* (New York), 279–93

—, Brooke Thomas, R., Swedlund, A.C. and Armelagos, G.J. 1988: 'Biocultural perspectives on stress in prehistorical, historical and contemporary population research, *Yearbook of Physical Anthropology* 31, 169–202

Gosden, C. and Lock, G. 2013: *Histories in the Making: Excavations at Alfred's Castle 1998–2000*, Oxford University School of Archaeology Monograph 79 (Oxford)

Gosden, C. and Marshall, Y. 1999: 'The cultural biography of objects', *World Archaeology* 31(2), 169–78

Gowland, R. 2001:'Playing dead: implications of mortuary evidence for the social construction of childhood in Roman Britain', in D. Davies, A. Gardner and K. Lockyear (eds), *TRAC 2000: Proceedings of the Tenth Annual Theoretical Roman Archaeology Conference, London 2000* (Oxford), 152–68

— 2007:'Age, ageism and osteological bias: the evidence from late Roman Britain', in M. Harlow and R. Laurence (eds), *Age and Ageing in the Roman Empire*, Journal of Roman Archaeology Supplementary Series 65 (Portsmouth, RI), 153–69

— 2015: 'Entangled lives: implications of the developmental origins of health and disease hypothesis for bioarchaeology and the life course', *American Journal of Physical Anthropology* 158(4), 530–40

— and Garnsey, P. 2010: 'Skeletal evidence for health, nutritional status and malaria in Rome and the Empire', in Eckardt (ed.) 2010b, 131–56

— and Knüsel, C. (eds) 2006: *The Social Archaeology of Funerary Remains* (Oxford)

— and Redfern, R. 2010: 'Childhood health in the Roman world: perspectives from the centre and margin of the Empire', *Childhood in the Past* 3, 15–42

—, Chamberlain, A.T. and Redfern, R.C. 2014: 'On the brink of being: re-evaluating infant death and infanticide in Roman Britain', in Carroll and Graham (eds) 2014, 69–88

Graham, A. 2006: *The Excavation of Five Beaker Burials, the Iron Age and Romano-British Settlements, and the 4th century Courtyard Villa at Barton Field, Tarrant Hinton, Dorset, 1968–1984*, Dorset Natural History and Archaeological Society Monograph 17 (Dorchester)

— and Newman, C. 1993: 'Recent excavations of Iron Age and Romano-British enclosures in the Avon

Valley', *Wiltshire Archaeological and Natural History Magazine* 86, 8–57

Graham, D. 2001: 'Frensham Manor', *Bulletin of the Surrey Archaeological Society* 352, 12–13

Graham, E.-J. 2011: 'Memory and materiality: re-embodying the Roman funeral', in V.M. Hope and J. Huskinson (eds), *Memory and Mourning: Studies on Roman Death* (Oxford), 21–39

Grahame, M. 2000: *Reading Space: Social Interaction and Identity in the Houses of Roman Pompeii: A Syntactical Approach to the Analysis and Interpretation of Built Space*, BAR International Series 886 (Oxford)

Grange, J.M. 2001: '*Mycobacterium bovis* infection in human beings', *Tuberculosis* 81(1/2), 71–77

Grant, A. 1975: 'The faunal remains', in B. Cunliffe, *Excavations at Portchester Castle Vol. 1: Roman*, Reports of the Research Committee of the Society of Antiquaries of London 32 (London), 378–406

— 1981: 'The significance of deer remains at occupation sites of the Iron Age to the Anglo-Saxon period', in M. Jones and G.W. Dimbleby (eds), *The Environment of Man: The Iron Age to the Anglo-Saxon Period*, BAR British Series 87 (Oxford), 205–13

— 1984: 'Animal husbandry', in Cunliffe 1984, 102–19

— 1991: 'Animal husbandry', in Cunliffe and Poole 1991, 447–87

— 2000: 'Diet, economy and ritual evidence from the faunal remains', in M. Fulford and J. Timby, *Late Iron Age and Roman Silchester: Excavations on the Site of the Forum-Basilica 1977, 1980–86*, Britannia Monograph Series 15 (London), 425–82

Gray, H.S.G. 1918: 'Leaden coffin found at Cann, near Shaftesbury', *Proceedings of the Dorset Natural History and Antiquarian Field Club* 38, 68–73

Gray, L. 2008: 'Charred plant remains', in Powell *et al.* 2008, 173–6

Gray, M. 1999: 'Pilgimage: a comparative perspective', in Aldhouse-Green 1999, 101–10

Green, C.W. 1966: 'A Romano-Celtic temple at Bourton Grounds, Buckingham', *Records of Buckinghamshire* 17(5), 356–66

Green, F.J., Hanna, H. and Brown, D. 2009: 'Environmental samples', in Light and Ellis 2009, 165–72

Green, F.M.L. and Boreham, S. forthcoming: 'Pollen', in Hinman and Zant, forthcoming

Green, H.J.M. 1975: 'Roman Godmanchester', in W. Rodwell and T. Rowley (eds), *The 'Small Towns' of Roman Britain. Papers presented to a Conference, Oxford 1975*, BAR British Series 15 (Oxford), 183–210

Green, M.J. 1986: *The Gods of the Celts* (Gloucester)

— 1992: *Animals in Celtic Life and Myth* (London)

— 1993: *Celtic Myths* (London)

— 1994: 'The religious symbolism of Llyn Cerrig Bach and other early sacred water sites', *Holy Wells Journal* 1, http://people.bath.ac.uk/liskmj/living-spring/sourcearchive/ns1/ns1mg1.htm

— 1999: 'Religion and deities', in Turner 1999, 255–7

Gregory, R.A. 2007: *Roman Manchester: The University of Manchester's Excavations within the Vicus 2001–5* (Oxford)

Gregory, T. 1991: *Excavations in Thetford, 1980–1982, Fison Way*, East Anglian Archaeology 53 (Dereham)

Griffith, F.M. 1988: 'A Romano-British villa near Crediton', *Proceedings of Devon Archaeological Society* 46, 137–42

Griffiths, D., Philpott, R.A. and Egan, G. 2007: *Meols: The Archaeology of the North Wirral Coast – Discoveries and Observations in the 19th and 20th Centuries; with a Catalogue of Collections*, Oxford University School of Archaeology Monograph 68 (Oxford)

Grimes, W. 1968: *The Excavation of Roman and Mediaeval London* (Abingdon)

— and Close-Brooks, J. 1993: 'The excavations of Caesar's camp, Heathrow, Harmondsworth, Middlesex, 1944', *Proceedings of the Prehistoric Society* 59, 303–60

Grimm, J. and Worley, F. 2011: 'Animal bone', in Barnett *et al.* 2011, 15–52

Groot, M. 2008: *Animals in Ritual and Economy in a Roman Frontier Community: Excavations in Tiel-Passewaaij*, Amsterdam Archaeological Studies 12 (Amsterdam)

— 2009: Searching for patterns among special animal deposits in the Dutch River area during the Roman period, *Journal of Archaeology in the Low Countries* 1(2), 49–81

Gurney, D. 1986a: 'A Romano-Celtic temple site at Caistor St Edmund', in T. Gregory and D. Gurney (eds), *Excavations at Thornham, Warham, Wighton and Caistor St Edmund, Norfolk*, East Anglian Archaeology Report 30 (Dereham), 37–55

— 1986b: *Settlement, Religion and Industry on the Roman Fen Edge, Norfolk*, East Anglian Archaeology 31 (Dereham)

Gussy, M.G., Waters, E.G., Walsh, O. and Kilpatrick, N.M. 2006: 'Early childhood caries: current evidence for aetiology and prevention', *Journal of Paediatrics and Child Health* 42, 37–43

Gwilt, A. and Haselgrove, C. (eds), *Reconstructing Iron Age Societies*, Oxbow Monograph 71 (Oxford)

Haeussler, R. 2013: *Becoming Roman? Diverging Identities and Experiences in Ancient Northwest Italy* (London)

— and King, A.C. (eds) 2007: *Continuity and Innovation in Religion in the Roman West: Vols 1–2*, Archaeological and Regional Studies, Journal of Roman Archaeology Supplementary Series 67 (Portsmouth, RI)

Hair, N. and Howard-Davis, C. 1996: 'The Roman cemetery at Low Borrowbridge near Tebay: excavation of the Roman cemetery in 1991 and 1992', in J. Lambert (ed.), *Transect through Time: The Archaeological Landscape of the Shell North Western Ethylene Pipeline*, Lancaster Imprints 1 (Lancaster), 122–5

Halcrow, S.E., Harris, N.J., Tayles, N., Ikehara-Quebral, R. and Pietrusewsky, M. 2013: From the mouths of babes: dental caries in infants and children and the intensification of agriculture in mainland Southeast Asia', *American Journal of Physical Anthropology* 150, 409–20

Halcrow, S.E., Harris, N.J., Beavan, N. and Buckley, H.R. 2014: 'First bioarchaeological evidence of probable scurvy in Southeast Asia: multifactorial etiologies of vitamin C deficiency in a tropical environment', *International Journal of Palaeopathology* 5, 63–71

Halkon, P. 2013: *The Parisi: Britons and Romans in Eastern Yorkshire* (Stroud)

—, Millett, M. and Woodhouse, H. 2015: *Hayton: The Archaeology of an Iron Age and Roman Landscape in East Yorkshire*, Yorkshire Archaeological Report 6–7 (Leeds)

Hall, A. and Huntley, J. 2007: *A Review of the Evidence for Macrofossil Plant Remains from Archaeological Deposits in Northern England*, English Heritage Research Department Report Series 87/–2007

Hall, A. and Kenward, H. 1990: *Environmental Evidence from the Colonia: Tanner Row and Rougier Street* (London)

Hall, M. 1994: *South West Oxfordshire Reservoir Proposal: An Archaeological Evaluation of Site 110 for Thames Water Utilities Limited*, Thames Valley Archaeological Services, doi: 10.5284/1028267

Hall, N. 2007: *Stratton Farm, Godstone, Surrey: Archaeological Evaluation and Assessment of Results*, Wessex Archaeology

Hall, R. 2006: *Excavations at Priors Hall, Northamptonshire, 2006: An Iron Age and Romano-British Ironworking Complex*, Archaeological Project Services Report, doi: 10.5284/1023760

Halstead, P. 1996: 'Pastoralism or household herding? Problems of scale and specialization in early Greek animal husbandry', *World Archaeology* 28(1), 20–42

— 2014: *Two Oxen Ahead: Pre-Mechanized Farming in the Mediterranean* (Chichester)

Hambleton, E. 2008: *Review of Middle Bronze Age–Late Iron Age Faunal Assemblages from Southern Britain*, English Heritage Research Department Report 71/2008

Hamilakis, Y. 2003: 'The sacred geography of hunting: wild animals, social power and gender in early farming societies', in E. Kotjabopoulou, Y. Hamilakis, P. Halstead, C. Gamble and V. Elefanti (eds) *Zooarchaeology in Greece: Recent Advances* (London), 239–47

Hamilton J. 2000a: 'Animal bones', in Cunliffe and Poole 2000, 67–73

— 2000b: 'The animal bones', in B. Cunliffe and C. Poole, *Nettlebank Copse, Wherwell, Hants, 1993: The Danebury Environs Programme: A Wessex landscape during the Roman era, Vol. 2, part 5*, Oxford University School of Archaeology Monograph 49 (Oxford), 101–16

Hamilton, R. 1971: 'Animal remains', in K. Branigan (ed.), *Latimer: Belgic, Roman, Dark Age, and Early Modern Farm* (Chess Valley), 163–6

Hamilton, S. 1998: 'Using elderly databases: Iron Age pit deposits at the Caburn, East Sussex and related sites', *Sussex Archaeological Collections* 136, 23–39

Hamilton-Dyer, S. 1993: 'The animal bone', in J.D. Zienkiewicz, J. Hillam, E. Besly, B.M. Dickinson, P.V. Webster, S.A. Fox, S. Hamilton-Dyer, A.E. Caseldine and P.A. Busby (eds), 'Excavations in the *Scamnum Tribunorum* at Caerleon: the Legionary Museum Site 1983–5', *Britannia* 24, 132–6

Hammon, A. 2008a: 'The animal bones', in Cunliffe and Poole 2008c, 97–111

— 2008b: 'The animal bones', in B. Cunliffe and C. Poole, *Fullerton, Hants, 2000 and 2001: The Danebury Environs Roman Programme: A Wessex Landscape during*

the Roman era, Vol. 2, part 3, Oxford University School of Archaeology Monograph 71 (Oxford), 150–61

— 2010: 'The brown bear', in O'Connor and Sykes (eds) 2010, 95–103

Hammond, S. and Preston, S. 2010: 'Excavation of Roman landscape and prehistoric features at Elsenham Quarry, Elsenham, Essex', *Essex Archaeology and History* 1, 16–50

Hands, A.R. 2004: *The Romano-British Roadside Settlement at Wilcote, Oxfordshire Vol. 3*, BAR British Series 370 (Oxford)

Hangody, L. Kish, G., Módis, L., Szerb, I., Gáspár, L., Diószegi, Z. and Kendik, Z. 2001: 'Mosaicplasty for the treatment of osteochondritis dissecans of the talus: two to seven year results in 36 patients', *Foot and Ankle International* 22(7), 552–8

Hanson, W. S. and Conolly, R. 2002: 'Language and literacy in Roman Britain: some archaeological considerations', in A.E. Cooley (ed.), *Becoming Roman, Writing Latin? Literacy and Epigraphy in the Roman West*, Journal of Roman Archaeology Supplementary Series 48 (Portsmouth, RI), 151–64

Harcourt R. 1974: 'The dog in prehistoric and early historic Britain', *Journal of Archaeological Science* 1, 151–75

— 1979: 'The animal bones', in Wainwright 1979, 150–60

Harding, D.W. 1987: *Excavations in Oxfordshire, 1964-66*, University of Edinburgh occasional paper 15 (Edinburgh)

— 2008: 'The Holme House villa', in Cool and Mason 2008, 127–58

— 2015: *Death and Burial in Iron Age Britain* (Oxford)

Harinayaran, C.V., Ramalakshmi, T., Prasad, U.V., Sudhakar, D., Srinivasarao, P.V., Sarma, K.V.S. and Kumar, E.G.T. 2007: 'High prevalence of low dietary calcium, high phytate consumption, and vitamin D deficiency in healthy south Indians', *American Journal of Clinical Nutrition* 85, 1062–7

Harlow M. and Laurence R. 2007: 'Age and ageing in the Roman Empire', in M. Harlow and R. Laurence (eds), *Age and Ageing in the Roman Empire*, Journal of Roman Archaeology Supplementary Series 65 (Portsmouth, RI), 9–24

Harman, M. 1996: 'Mammal bones', in May 1996, 141–65

—, Molleson, T. and Price, J.L. 1981: 'Burials, bodies and beheadings in Romano-British and Anglo-Saxon cemeteries', *Bulletin of the British Museum Natural History (Geology)* 35(3), 145–88

Harper, K. 2012: *Slavery in the Late Roman World, AD 275–425* (Cambridge)

Harris, C.R., Jenkins M. and Glaser, D. 2006: 'Gender differences in risk assessment: why do women take fewer risks than men?', *Judgement and Decision Making* 1, 48–63

Hart, G.D. 1970: 'A hermatological artefact from 4th century Britain', *Bulletin of the History of Medicine* 63, 76–9

Hart, J., Geber, J. and Holbrook, N. 2017: 'Iron Age settlement and a Romano-British cemetery at The Cotswold School, Bourton-on-the-Water: excavation in 2011', *Transactions of the Bristol and Gloucestershire Archaeology Society* 134, 77–111

Hartridge, R. 1978: 'Excavations at the prehistoric and Romano-British site at Slonk Hill, Shoreham, Sussex', *Sussex Archaeological Collections* 116, 69–141

Harward, C., Powers, N. and Watson, S. 2015: *The Upper Walbrook Valley Cemetery of Roman London. Excavations at Finsbury Circus, City of London, 1987– 2007*, Museum of London Archaeology Monograph 69 (London)

Haselgrove, C. 1993: 'The development of British Iron Age coinage', *The Numismatic Chronicle* 153, 31–63

— 2005: 'A trio of temples: a reassessment of Iron Age coin deposition at Hayling Island, Harlow and Wanborough', in C. Haselgrove and D. Wigg-Wolf (eds), *Iron Age Coinage and Ritual Practices* (Mainz am Rhein), 381–418

— 2016: *Cartimandua's Capital? The Late Iron Age Royal Site at Stanwick, North Yorkshire, Fieldwork and Analysis 1981–2011* (Oxford)

— and Allon, V.L. 1982: 'An Iron Age settlement at West House, Coxhoe, County Durham', *Archaeologia Aeliana* (5th series) 10, 25–51

— and Moore, T. (eds) 2007: *The Later Iron Age in Britain and Beyond* (Oxford)

Haslam, A. 2009: *Land at Residential Phase II (Southern Parcel), Waterstone Park, Stone Castle, Kent: Archaeological Excavation*, Pre-Construct Archaeology

Hassall, M.W.C. 1980: 'Altars, curses and other epigraphic evidence', in Rodwell (ed.) 1980, 79–90

— 1981: 'The inscribed pot', in Matthews 1981, 46–8

— and Tomlin, R. 1979: 'Inscriptions', *Britannia* 10, 339–56

Hattatt, R. 1982: *Ancient and Romano-British Brooches* (Sherbourne)

— 1985: *Iron Age and Roman Brooches* (Oxford)

— 1987: *Brooches of Antiquity* (Oxford)

— 1989: *Ancient Brooches and Other Artefacts* (Oxford)

Haverfield, F. 1905: *Victoria County History of Derbyshire I* (London)

— 1912: *The Romanization of Roman Britain* (Oxford)

Havis, R. and Brooks, H. 2004: *Excavations at Stansted Airport 1986–91*, East Anglian Archaeology 107 (Colchester)

Hayden, C., Early, R., Biddulph, E., Booth, P., Dodd, A., Smith, A., Laws, G. and Welsh, K. 2017: *Horcott Quarry, Fairford and Arkell's Land, Kempsford: Prehistoric, Roman and Anglo-Saxon Settlement and Burial in the Upper Thames Valley in Gloucestershire*, Oxford Archaeology Thames Valley Landscapes Monograph 40 (Oxford)

Haynes, I. 1999: 'Military service and cultural identity in the auxilia', in A.K. Goldsworthy and I. Haynes (eds), *The Roman Army as a Community*, Journal of Roman Archaeolology Supplementary Series 341 (Portsmouth, RI), 65–74

— 2003: 'War and peace', in G. Woolf (ed.), *Roman World* (Cambridge), 320–51

— 2014: 'Characterising cult communities in the Roman provinces: some observations on small finds evidence from the sanctuary of Liber Pater, Apulum', in R. Collins and F. McIntosh (eds), *Life in the Limes: Studies of the People and Objects of the Roman Frontiers* (Oxford), 87–95

— and Wilmott, T. 2012: 'The Maryport altars: an archaeological myth dispelled', *Studia Universitatis Babes-Bolyai, Historia* 51(1), 25–37

Hayward, L.C. 1982: *Ilchester Mead Roman Villa* (Beaminster)

Hearne, C.M. and Birbeck, V. 1999: *A35 Tolpuddle to Puddletown Bypass DBFO, Dorset, 1996–8, incorporating Excavations at Tolpuddle Ball 1993*, Wessex Archaeology Report 15 (Salisbury)

Heighway, C. 2003: 'Not Angels but Anglicans – the origins of the Christian church in Gloucestershire', in M. Ecclestone (ed.), *The Land of the Dobunni* (Gloucester), 49–55

Helm, R. 2014: *Outside the Town. Roman Industry, Burial and Religion at Augustine House, Rodaus Town, Canterbury*, Canterbury Archaeological Trust Occasional Paper 10 (Canterbury)

Helms, M.W. 1993: *Craft and the Kingly Ideal: Art, Trade and Power* (Austin)

Henderson, K. 2010: 'Importance of leisure to individuals and society', in Human Kinetics, *Dimensions of Leisure for Life. Individuals and Society* (Champaign), 3–26

Henig, M. 1993: 'Votive objects: images and inscriptions', in Woodward and Leach 1993, 88–112

— 1999: 'A new star shining over Bath', *Oxford Journal of Archaeology* 18(4), 419–25

— 2008: '"And did those feet in ancient times": Christian churches and pagan shrines in south-east Britain', in Rudling (ed.) 2008a, 191–206

— and Booth, P. 2000: *Roman Oxfordshire* (Stroud)

— and King, A. (eds) 1986: *Pagan Gods and Shrines of the Roman Empire*, Oxford University Committee for Archaeology Monograph 8 (Oxford)

— and Tomlin, R. 2008: 'The sculptural stone', in A. Simmonds, N. Marquez-Grant and L. Loe, *Life and Death in a Roman City. Excavation of a Roman Cemetery with a Mass Grave at 120–122 London Road, Gloucester*, Oxford Archaeology Monograph 6 (Oxford), 116–18

Herbert, A.N. 2011: 'Excavations and discoveries at the Romano-British cemetery, East Hill, Dartford', *Archaeologia Cantiana* 131, 85–110

Hersch, K.K. 2010: 'The woolworker bride', in L. Larsson Lovén and A. Strömberg (eds), *Ancient Marriage in Myth and Reality* (Newcastle upon Tyne), 122–35

Hesse, R. 2011: 'Reconsidering animal husbandry and diet in the northwest provinces', *Journal of Roman Archaeology* 24, 215–48

Hetherington, H. 2010: 'The lynx', in O'Connor and Sykes (eds) 2010, 75–82

Hey, G., Dennis, C. and Mayes, A. 2007: 'Archaeological investigations on Whiteleaf Hill, Princes Risborough, Buckinghamshire, 2002–6', *Records of Buckinghamshire* 47(2), 1–80

Higbee, L. 2013: 'Animal bones', in Evans 2013a, 116–33

Higgins, P. 2005: 'Other environmental evidence', in S. Teague, 'Manor Farm, Monk Sherborne, Hampshire: archaeological investigations in 1996', *Proceedings of the Hampshire Field Club and Archaeological Society* 60, 115–19

Higham, N.J. 1989: 'Roman and native in England north of the Tees: acculturation and its limitations', in J. Barrett, A.P. Fitzpatrick and L. MacInnes (eds), *Barbarians and Romans in North-West Europe from the Late Republic to Late Antiquity'*, BAR International Series 471 (Oxford), 153–74

Hill, J.D. 1995a: *Ritual and Rubbish in the Iron Age of Wessex: A Study on the Formation of a Specific Archaeological Record*, BAR British Series 242 (Oxford)

— 1995b: 'The pre-Roman Iron Age in Britain and Ireland (ca. 800 BC to AD 100): an overview', *Journal of World Prehistory* 9(1), 47–98

— 1997: 'The end of one kind of body and the beginning of another kind of body? Toilet instruments and "Romanization"', in Gwilt and Haselgrove (eds), 96–107

— 2001: 'Romanisation, gender and class: recent approaches to identity in Britain and their possible consequences', in James and Millett (eds) 2001, 12–18

— 2006: 'Are we any closer to understanding how later Iron Age societies worked (or did not work)?', in C. Haselgrove (ed.) *Celtes et Gaulois, L'Archéologie Face à l'Histoire. Les Mutations de la Fin de L'âge du Fer. Actes de la Table Ronde de Cambridge, 7–8 Juillet 2005*, Collection Bibracte 12/4 (Glux-en-Glenne), 169–80

— 2007: 'The dynamics of social change in later Iron Age eastern and south-eastern England, c 300 BC–AD 43', in Haselgrove and Moore (eds) 2007, 16–39

Hillson, S. 1996: *Dental Anthropology* (Cambridge)

Hingley R. 1989: *Rural Settlement in Roman Britain* (London)

— 1990: 'Public and private space: domestic organisation and gender relations among Iron Age and Romano-British households', in R. Samson (ed.), *The Social Archaeology of Houses* (Edinburgh), 125–48

— 2006: 'The deposition of iron objects in Britain during the later prehistoric and Roman periods: contextual analysis and the significance of iron', *Britannia* 37, 213–57

— 2011: 'Rome: Imperial and local religions', in T. Insoll (ed.), *The Oxford Handbook of the Archaeology of Ritual and Religion* (Oxford), 745–57, doi: 10.1093/oxfordhb/9780199232444.013.0047

Hinman, M. 2003: *A Late Iron Age Farmstead and Romano-British site at Haddon, Peterborough*, BAR British Series 358 (Oxford)

— and Zant, J. forthcoming: *Conquering the Claylands: Excavations at Love's Farm, St Neots, Cambridgeshire*, East Anglian Archaeology

Hinton, P. 1997: 'Charred plant remains', in Fitzpatrick 1997, 83–9

Hirschmann, J. and Raugi, G.J. 1999: 'Adult scurvy', *Journal of the American Academy of Dermatology* 41(6), 895–910

Hoaen, A. and Loney, H. 2010: 'Excavations of Iron Age and Roman Iron Age levels at a settlement in Glencoyne Park, Ullswater, Cumbria', *Transactions of the Cumberland and Westmorland Antiquarian and Archaeological Society* (3rd series) 10, 93–102

Hobbs, R. 2006: *Late Roman Precious Metal Deposits, AD 200–700: Changes over Time and Space*, BAR International Series 1504 (Oxford)

— and Jackson, R. 2010: *Roman Britain* (London)

Hobley, B. 1975: 'Lunt Roman Fort: interim report', *Transactions of Bristol and Gloucestershire Archaeological Society* 87, 1–46

Hodder, I. 1977: 'The distribution of material culture items in the Baringo District, Western Kenya', *Man* (new series) 12(2), 239–69

Hodgson, N. 2009: *Hadrian's Wall 1999–2009: A Summary of Excavation and Research Prepared for the Thirteenth Pilgrimage of Hadrian's Wall, 8–14 August 2009* (Kendal)

— 2012: 'Assessing the contribution of commercial archaeology to the study of Roman South and West Yorkshire, 1990–2004', *Yorkshire Archaeological Journal* 84, 38–58

—, McKelvey, J. and Muncaster, W. 2013: *The Iron Age on the Northumberland Coastal Plain*, Tyne and Wear Archives and Museums Archaeological Monographs 3 (Newcastle)

Hogg, A.H.A. 1942: 'The native settlement at Gunnar Peak', *Archaeologia Aeliana* (4th series) 20, 155–73

Holbrook, N. 2006: 'The Roman period', in N. Holbrook and J. Jurica (eds), *Twenty-five Years of Archaeology in Gloucestershire. A Review of New Discoveries and New Thinking in Gloucestershire, South Gloucestershire and Bristol* (Stroud), 97–131

—, McSloy, E. and Geber, J. 2013: 'Corinium's dead: excavating the Tetbury Road Roman cemetery', *Current Archaeology* 281, 28–34

Holland, T.D. and O'Brien, M.J. 1997: 'Parasites, porotic hyperostosis, and the implications of changing perspectives', *American Antiquity* 62(2), 183–93

Hood, S. and Walton, H. 1948: 'A Romano-British cremating place on Roden Downs, Berkshire', *Transactions of the Newbury District Field Club* 9(1), 10–62

Hong, L., Levy, S.M., Warren, J.J. and Broffitt, B. 2009: 'Association between enamel hypoplasia and dental caries in primary second molars: a cohort study', *Caries Research* 43, 345–53

Hope, V.M. 2016: 'Inscriptions and identity', in Millett et al. (eds) 2016, 285–302, doi: 10.1093/oxfordhb/9780199697731.013.018

Horster, M. 2010: 'Religious landscape and sacred ground: relationships between space and cult in the Greek world', *Revue de l'histoire des religions* 4, 435–58

— 2016: 'Cult economy in the Eastern Provinces', conference paper presented at *The Economics of Roman Religion*, University of Oxford, 22–23 September 2016 (unpublished)

Houlbrook, C. and Armitage, N. (eds) 2015: *The Materiality of Magic: an Artefactual Investigation into Ritual Practices and Popular Beliefs* (Oxford)

Hounsell, D. 2003: *Land East of Bedford Road Marston Moretaine Archaeological Field Evaluation*, Albion Archaeology Report 2003/64 (Bedford)

Howell, I. 2005, *Prehistoric Landscape to Roman Villa: Excavations at Beddington, Surrey, 1981–7*, MoLAS Monograph 26 (London)

Hughes, G. 1996: *The Excavation of a Late Prehistoric and Romano-British Settlement at Thornwell Farm, Chepstow, Gwent*, BAR British Series 224 (Oxford)

Hughes, H. 1923: 'Prehistoric remains on Penmaenmawr (known as Braich y Dinas): fifth report on the survey and excavations', *Archaeologia Cambrensis* 78, 243–68

Hughes, S. 2015: 'A prehistoric and Romano-British settlement at Aller Cross, Kingskerswell', *Proceedings of the Devon Archaeological Society* 73, 91–184

Humphrey, L., Bello, S. and Rousham, E. 2012: 'Sex differences in infant mortality in Spitalfields, London, 1750–1839', *Journal of Biosocial Science* 44(1), 95–119

Hunt, A. 2016: *Reviving Roman Religion. Sacred Trees in the Roman World* (Cambridge)

Hunter, F. 2008: 'Celtic art in Roman Britain', in Garrow *et al.* (eds) 2008, 129–45

— 2009: 'Traprain Law and the Roman world', in W.S. Hanson (ed.), *The Army and Frontiers of Rome*, Journal of Roman Archaeology Supplementary Series 74 (Portsmouth, RI), 225–40

— 2010: 'Changing objects in changing worlds: Dragonesque brooches and beaded torcs', in S. Worrell, G. Egan, J. Naylor, K. Leahy and M. Lewis (eds), *A Decade of Discovery: Proceedings of the Portable Antiquities Scheme Conference 2007*, BAR British Series 520 (Oxford), 91–107

— 2016: 'Beyond Hadrian's Wall', in Millett *et al.* (eds) 2016, 179–202, doi: 10.1093/oxfordhb/9780199697731.013.011

Hunter-Mann, K. 2015: *Driffield Terrace Web Report*, York Archaeological Trust, http://www.yorkarchaeology.co.uk/wp-content/uploads/2016/01/Kurt-Web-Doc.pdf

Hurst, D. 2016: 'A Roman pond at Wyre Piddle, Worcestershire, with a brief survey of ponds in Roman Britain', *Britannia* 47, 169–91

Hutcheson, N.C.G., 2004, *Later Iron Age Norfolk: Metalwork, Landscape and Society*, BAR British Series 361 (Oxford)

Hutton, R. 2011: 'Romano-British reuse of prehistoric ritual sites', *Britannia* 42, 1–22

Ingham, D., Oetgen, J. and Slowikowski, A. 2016: *Newnham: a Roman Bath House and Estate Centre East of Bedford*, East Anglian Archaeology 158 (Bedford)

Ingold T. 2000: *The Perception of the Environment: Essays in Livelihood, Dwelling and Skill* (Abingdon)

Ingrem, C. 2011: 'The animal bone', in Fulford and Clarke 2011, 244–70

— 2012: 'Animals in the economy and culture of Roman Britain: a case study from southern England', in Fulford 2012, 184–212

— 2013: 'Fish bone', in Evans 2013a, 132–3

Ireland, S. 2008: *Roman Britain. A Sourcebook* (3rd edn) (Abingdon)

Ivarsdotter, A. 2004: 'And the cattle follow her, for they know her voice…on communication between women and cattle in Scandinavian pastures', in B.S. Frizell (ed.), *Man and Animal in Antiquity*, *Proceedings of the Conference at the Swedish Institute in Rome, September 9–12, 2002* (Rome), 146–9

Jackson, D.A. and Tylecote, R.F. 1988: 'Two new Romano-British iron-working sites in Northamptonshire – a new type of furnace?', *Britannia* 19, 275–98

Jackson, K.H. 1953: *Language and History in Early Britain* (Edinburgh)

Jackson, R. 2012: *Ariconium, Herefordshire: an Iron Age Settlement and Romano-British 'Small Town'* (Oxford)

— and Burleigh, G. 2017: *Dea Senuna: Treasure, Cult and Ritual at Ashwell, Hertfordshire* (London)

Jackson, R.P.J. and Potter, T.W. 1996: *Excavations at Stonea, Cambridgeshire 1980–85* (London)

James, S. 2001: 'Soldiers and civilians: identity and interaction in Roman Britain', in James and Millett (eds) 2001, 77–89

— and Millett, M. (eds) 2001: *Britons and Romans: Advancing the Archaeological Agenda*, CBA Research Report 125 (York)

Jarvis, M. 1995: *Excavation of a Late Iron Age/Romano-British Settlement at Mill Drove, Bourne*, Lindsey Archaeological Services

Jashemski, W.F. 1981: 'The Campanian peristyle garden', in E.B. Macdougall and W.M.F. Jashemski (eds), *Ancient Roman Gardens* (Washington), 31–48

Jay, M., Fuller, B.T., Richards, M.P., Knüsel, C.J. and King, S.S. 2008: 'Iron Age breast feeding practices in Britain: isotopic evidence from Wetwang Slack, East Yorkshire', *American Journal of Physical Anthropology* 136(3), 327–37

Jay, M., Haselgrove, C., Hamilton, D., Hill, J.D. and Dent, J. 2012: 'Chariots and context: new radiocarbon dates from Wetwang and the chronology of Iron Age burials and brooches in East Yorkshire', *Oxford Journal of Archaeology* 31(2), 161–89

Jenkins, C. 2013: *Great Chilton, County Durham: Archaeological Excavation and Geophysical Survey*, Archaeological Services Durham University Report 3078

Jobey, G. 1973: 'A native settlement at Hartburn and the Devil's Causeway, Northumberland 1971', *Archaeologia Aeliana* (5th series) 1, 11–53

— 1982: 'The settlement at Doubstead and Romano-British settlement on the coastal plain between Tyne and Forth', *Archaeologia Aeliana* (5th series) 10, 1–24

Jobey, I. and Jobey, G. 1988: 'Gowenburn River Camp: an Iron Age, Romano-British and more recent settlement in North Tynedale, Northumberland', *Archaeologia Aeliana* 16, 11–28

Johns, C. 1994: 'Treasure: Romano-British precious-metal hoards: some comments on Martin Millett's paper', in S. Cottam, D. Dungworth, S. Scott, and J. Taylor (eds), *TRAC 94: Proceedings of the Fourth Annual Theoretical Roman Archaeology Conference* (Oxford), 107–17

— 1995: 'Mounted men and sitting ducks: the iconography of Romano-British plate-brooches', in B. Raftery, V. Megaw, and V. Rigby (eds), *Sites and Sights of the Iron Age: Essays on Fieldwork and Museum Research presented to Ian Mathieson Stead* (Oxford), 103–9

— 1996a: *The Jewellery of Roman Britain: Celtic and Classical Traditions* (Abingdon)

— 1996b: 'The classification and interpretation of Romano-British treasures', *Britannia* 27, 1–16

— 2006: 'An Iron Age sword and mirror cist burial from Bryher, Isles of Scilly', *Cornish Archaeology* 41–42, 1–79

— and Potter, T. 1983: *The Thetford Treasure: Roman Jewellery and Silver* (London)

Johnson, A. 1983: *Roman Forts of the 1st and 2nd Centuries AD in Britain and the Roman Provinces* (London)

Jones, A. 1999: 'Greensforge: investigations in the Romano-British civilian settlement, 1994', *Transactions of the Staffordshire Archaeological and Historical Society* 38, 12–31

— 2001: 'A Romano-Celtic shrine and settlements at Little Paxton Quarry, Diddington, Cambridgeshire', *Proceedings of the Cambridge Antiquarian Society* 90, 5–27

Jones, M. 1982: 'Crop production in Roman Britain', in D. Miles (ed.), *The Romano-British Countryside – Studies in Rural Settlement and Economy*, BAR British Series 103 (Oxford), 97–108

— 1996: 'Plant exploitation', in T.C. Champion and J.R. Collis (eds), *The Iron Age in Britain and Ireland: Recent Trends* (Sheffield) 29–40

Jones, N.W. 1996: 'Excavations within the Roman vicus at Caersws, 1989–93', *Montgomeryshire Collections* 84, 1–36

— 2011: 'Romano-British settlement at Plas Coch, Wrexham: excavations 1994–96', *Archaeologia Cambrensis* 160, 51–113

Jones, P. 2010: *Roman and Medieval Staines: The Development of the Town* (Woking)

Jordana, X., Galtés, I., Busquets, F., Isidro, A. and Malgosa, A. 2006: 'Clay-shoveler's fracture: an uncommon diagnosis in palaeopathology', *International Journal of Osteoarchaeology* 16(4), 366–72

Joshel, S.R. 2010: *Slavery in the Roman World* (Cambridge)

— and Petersen, L.H. 2014: *The Material Life of Roman Slaves* (Cambridge)

Joy, J. 2011: 'The Iron Age', in T. Insoll (ed.), *The Oxford Handbook of the Archaeology of Ritual and Religion* (Oxford), 405–21, doi: 10.1093/oxfordhb/9780199232444.013.0027

Joyce, S., Sheldon, S., and Reynish, S. 2012: *Hinckley Point C Somerset. Archaeological Works: Excavations SPE1–SPE5 Interim Statement*, Cotswold Archaeology

Jundi, S. and Hill, J.D. 1998: 'Brooches and identities in first century AD Britain: more than meets the eye?', in C. Forcey, J. Hawthorne and R. Witcher (eds), *TRAC 97: Proceedings of the Seventh Annual Theoretical Roman Archaeology Conference* (Oxford), 125–37

Jurmain, R.D. and Kilgore, L. 1995: 'Skeletal evidence of osteoarthritis: a palaeopathological perspective', *Annals of the Rheumatic Diseases* 54(6), 443–50

Kamash, Z. 2008: 'What lies beneath? Perceptions of the ontological paradox of water', *World Archaeology* 40(2), 224–35

— 2016: 'Memories of the past in Roman Britain', in Millett *et al.* (eds) 2016, 681–98, doi: 10.1093/oxfordhb/9780199697731.013.037

—, Gosden, C. and Lock, G. 2010: 'Continuity and religious practices in Roman Britain: the case of the rural religious complex at Marcham/Frilford, Oxfordshire', *Britannia* 41, 95–125

Katzenberg, M.A. 2012: 'The ecological approach: understanding past diet and the relationship between diet and disease', in A.L. Grauer (ed.), *A Companion to Paleopathology* (Chichester), 97–113

Kawashita, Y., Kitamura, M. and Saito, T. 2011: 'Early childhood caries', *International Journal of Dentistry* 2011, 1–7

Keegan, S.L. 2002: *Inhumation Rites in Late Roman Britain: The Treatment of the Engendered Body*, BAR British Series 335 (Oxford)

Kelly, E. and Dudley, C. 1981: 'Two Romano-British burials', *Sussex Archaeological Collections* 119, 65–88

Kendall, R. 2014: *Past Endemic Malaria and Adaptive Responses in the Fens and Marshlands of Eastern England*, unpublished PhD thesis, Durham University

Kiernan, P. 2009: *Miniature Votive Offerings in the Roman North-West* (Mainz)

Kilbride-Jones, H.E. 1938a: 'Glass armlets in Britain', *Proceedings of the Society of Antiquaries of Scotland* 72, 366–95

— 1938b: 'Excavation of a native settlement at Milking Gap, Northumberland', *Archaeologia Aeliana* (4th series) 15, 303–50

Killock, D., Shepherd, J., Gerrard, J., Hayward, K., Rielly, K. and Ridgeway, V. 2015: *Temples and Suburbs. Excavations at Tabard Square, Southwark* (London)

King, A.C. 1984: 'Animal bones and the dietary identity of military and civilian groups in Roman Britain, Germany and Gaul', in T.F.C. Blagg and A.C. King (eds), *Military and Civilian in Roman Britain: Cultural Relationships in a Frontier Province*, BAR British Series 136 (Oxford), 187–217

— 1991: 'Food production and consumption – meat', in R.F.J. Jones (ed.), *Britain in the Roman Period: Recent Trends* (Sheffield), 14–19

— 1999a: 'Diet in the Roman world: a regional inter-site comparison of the mammal bones', *Journal of Roman Archaeology* 12, 168–202

— 1999b, 'Animals and the Roman army: the evidence of animal bones', in A. Goldsworthy and I. Haynes (eds), *The Roman Army as a Community*, Journal of Roman Archaeology Supplementary Series 34 (Portsmouth, RI), 139–49

— 2001: 'The Romanization of diet in the Western Empire: comparative archaeological studies', in S. Keay and N. Terrenato (eds), *Italy and the West – Comparative Issues in Romanization* (Oxford), 210–26

— 2005: 'Animal remains from temples in Roman Britain', *Britannia* 36, 329–69

— 2007a: 'Romano-Celtic temples in Britain: Gallo-Roman influence or indigenous development?', in Haeussler and King (eds) 2007, 13–18

— 2007b: 'Coins and coin hoards from Romano-Celtic temples in Britain', in Haeussler and King (eds) 2007, 25–42

— 2016: 'Sacred flocks and herds? The implications of animal sacrifice at remote rural Romano-Celtic shrines', conference paper presented at *The Economics of Roman Religion*, University of Oxford, 22–23 September 2016 (unpublished)

— and Soffe, G. 2013: *A Sacred Island. Iron Age, Roman and Saxon Temples and Ritual on Hayling Island* (Winchester)

King, J. 1996: 'The animal bones', in Mackreth 1996, 216–19

King, T., Humphrey, L.T. and Hillson, S. 2005: 'Linear enamel hypoplasias as indicators of systemic physiological stress: evidence from two known age-at-death and sex populations from postmedieval London', *American Journal of Physical Anthropology* 128(3), 547–59

Kirby, M. 2011: *Land off Netherhall Road, Maryport, Cumbria. Archaeological Evaluation*, CFA Archaeology Ltd, Report 1772, doi: 10.5284/1030349

Kislev, M. 1988: '*Pinus pinea* in agriculture, culture and cult', in H. Kuster (ed.), *Der Prähistorische Mensch und seine Umwelt. Fetschrift für Udelgard Körber Grohne zum 65. Geburtstag* (Stuttgart), 73–9

Kitchener, A. and O'Connor, T. 2010: 'Wildcats, domestic and feral cats', in O'Connor and Sykes (eds) 2010, 83–94

—, Yamaguchi, N., Ward, J.M. and Macdonald, D.W. 2005: 'A diagnosis for the Scottish wildcat (*Felis silvestris*): a tool for conservation action for a critically-endangered felid', *Animal Conservation* 8, 223–37

Klaus, H.D. 2012: 'The bioarchaeology of structural violence – a theoretical model and a case study', in D.I. Martin, R.P. Harrod and V.R. Pérez (eds), *The Bioarchaeology of Violence* (Gainesville), 29–62

Knowles, A.K. 1977: 'The Roman settlement at Brampton, Norfolk: interim report', *Britannia* 8, 209–221

Kowalski, N. 2010: 'Picking up the trail: an introduction to hunting – philosophy for everyone', in N. Kowalski (ed.), *Hunting: Philosophy for Everyone* (Chichester), 1–8

Kreuz, A. 2000: 'Functional and conceptual archaeobotanical data from Roman cremations', in Pearce *et al.* 2000, 45–51

Kuhn, K.G., Campbell-Lendrum, D.H., Armstrong, B. and Davies, C.R. 2003: 'Malaria in Britain: past, present, and future', *Proceedings of the National Academy of Sciences (U.S.)* 100, 9997–10001

Kumar, A.R., Basu A.K., Dash, S., Singh, D. and Saran, J. 2008: 'Cord blood and breast milk iron status in maternal anemia', *Pediatrics* 121(3), e673–e677

Kutluk, G., Feyzullah, C. and Muzaffer, B. 2002: 'Comparisons of oral calcium, high dose vitamin D and a combination of these in the treatment of nutritional rickets in children', *Journal of Tropical Pediatrics* 48(6), 351–3

Kvium, C. 2008: 'The ownership of sacred things. Observations on sacred, public and private property in the late Roman Republic and Early Empire', in A.H. Rasmussen and S.W. Rasmussen (eds), *Religion and Society. Rituals, Resources and Identity in the Ancient Greco-Roman world. The BOMOS-Conferences 2002–2005* (Rome), 159–66

Kwon, D.S., Spevak, M.R., Fletcher, K. and Kleinman, P.K. 2002: 'Physiologic subperiosteal new bone formation: prevalence, distribution, and thickness in neonates and infants', *American Journal of Roentgenology* 179, 985–8

La Trobe-Bateman, E. and Niblett, R. 2016: *Bath: An Archaeological Assessment: a study of settlement around the sacred hot springs from the Mesolithic to the 17th century AD* (Oxford)

Lambert, R. 2009: *An Archaeological Excavation in 2009 at Farnham Quarry, Runfold, Surrey*, Surrey County Archaeological Unit

Lambrick, G. and Robinson, M. 1979: *Iron Age and Roman Riverside Settlements at Farmoor, Oxford*, CBA Research Report 32 (London)

Lane-Fox, R. 1996: 'Ancient hunting: from Homer to Polybios', in G. Shipley and J. Salmon (eds), *Human Landscapes in Classical Antiquity: Environment and Culture* (London) 119–53

Langton, B. and Holbrook, N. 1997: 'A prehistoric and Roman occupation and burial site at Heybridge: excavations at Langford Road, 1994', *Essex Archaeology and History* 28, 12–46

Lanza, D.C. and Kennedy, D. 1997: 'Adult rhinosinusitis defined', *Journal of Otolaryngology Head and Neck Surgery* 117, S1–S7

Large, F., Kenward, H., Carrott, J., Nicholson, C. and Kent, P. 2009: *Insect and Other Invertebrate Remains from the Roman Fort at Ribchester, Lancashire (Site Code RB89): Technical Report*, Reports from the Environmental Archaeology Unit, York 94/11

Larsen, C.S. 1997: *Bioarchaeology: Interpreting Behaviour from the Human Skeleton* (Cambridge)

Lawrence, S. and Smith, A. 2009: *Between Villa and Town: Excavations of a Roman Roadside Settlement and Shrine at Higham Ferrers, Northamptonshire*, Oxford Archaeology Monograph 7 (Oxford)

Leach, P. 2003: 'Excavations at Hillyfields, Upper Holway, Taunton', *Somerset Archaeology and Natural History* 145, 57–82

— and Evans, C.J. 2001: *Fosse Lane, Shepton Mallet 1990*, Britannia Monograph Series 18 (London)

Leach, S., Lewis, M., Chenery, C., Müldner, G. and Eckardt, H. 2009: 'Migration and diversity in Roman Britain: a multidisciplinary approach to the identification of immigrants in Roman York, England', *American Journal of Physical Anthropology* 140, 546–61

Lee, R. 2009: *Production, Use and Disposal of Romano-British Pewter Tableware*, BAR British Series 478 (Oxford)

Leech, R. 1981: 'The excavation of a Romano-British farmstead and cemetery on Bradley Hill, Somerton, Somerset', *Britannia* 12, 177–252

— 1986: 'The excavation of a Romano-Celtic temple and a later cemetery on Lamyatt Beacon, Somerset', *Britannia* 17, 259–328

Leins, I. 2008: 'What can be inferred from the regional stylistic diversity of Iron Age coinage?', in Garrow *et al.* (eds) 2008, 100–12

Lepetz, S. 1996: *L'animal dans la société gallo-romaine de la France du nord*, Revue archéologique de Picardie Spécial 12 (Amiens)

Levitan, B. 1989: 'The vertebrate remains from Chichester Cattlemarket', in A. Down, *Chichester Excavations VI* (Chichester), 242–76

— 1993: 'The vertebrate remains' in Woodward and Leach 1993, 257–301

Lewis, J., Leivers, M., Brown, L., Smith, A., Cramp, K., Mepham, L. and Phillpotts, C. 2010: *Landscape Evolution in the Middle Thames Valley: Heathrow Terminal 5 Excavations. Vol. 2*, Framework Archaeology Monograph 3 (Oxford/Salisbury)

Lewis, M.E. 2007: *The Bioarchaeology of Children – Perspectives from Biological and Forensic Anthropology* (Cambridge)

— 2010: 'Life and death in a civitas capital: metabolic disease and trauma in the children from late Roman Dorchester, Dorset', *American Journal of Physical Anthropology* 142, 405–16

— 2011: 'Tuberculosis in the non-adults from Romano-British Poundbury Camp, Dorset, England', *International Journal of Palaeopathology* 1, 12–23

— 2012: 'Thalassaemia: its diagnosis and interpretation in past skeletal populations', *International Journal of Osteoarchaeology* 22, 685–93

— and Gowland, R. 2007: 'Brief and precarious lives: infant mortality in contrasting sites from medieval and post-medieval England (AD 850–1859)', *American Journal of Physical Anthropology* 134, 117–29

Lewis, M.J.T. 1966: *Temples in Roman Britain* (Cambridge)

Liddle, J., Ainsley, C. and Reilly, K. 2009: 'Animal bone', in C. Cowan, F. Seeley, A. Wardle, A. Westman and L. Wheeler, *Roman Southwark Settlement and Economy: Excavations in Southwark 1973–91*, MoLA Monograph 42 (London), 244–8

Liebe-Harkort, C. 2012: 'Cribra orbitalia, sinusitis and linear enamel hypoplasia in Swedish Roman Iron Age adults and subadults', *International Journal of Osteoarchaeology* 22(4), 387–97

Light, T. and Ellis, P. 2009: *Bucknowle: A Romano-British Villa and its Antecedents, Excavations 1976–1991*, Dorset Natural History and Archaeological Society Monograph 18 (Dorchester)

Lindstrøm, T.C. 2010: 'The animals of the arena: how and why could their destruction and death be endured and enjoyed?', *World Archaeology* 42, 310–23

Livarda, A. 2013: 'Date, rituals and socio-cultural identity in the north-western Roman provinces', *Oxford Journal of Archaeology* 32(1), 101–17, http://doi.org/10.1111/ojoa.12004

Liversidge, J. 1968: *Britain in the Roman Empire* (London)

Loader, E. 1999: 'Copper alloy objects', in Hearne and Birbeck 1999, 102–5

Locker, A. 1990: 'Gorhambury villa: the fish bones', unpublished report, Historic England

— 1991: 'The animal bone', in Philp *et al.* 1991, 285–92

— 1999: 'Fish bones', in R. Broomhead, 'Ilchester, Great Yard archaeological excavations 1995', *Proceedings of the Somerset Archaeological and Natural History Society* 142, 165–6

— 2007, '*In Piscibus Diversis*: the bone evidence for fish consumption in Roman Britain', *Britannia* 38, 141–80

Lodwick, L. 2015: 'Identifying ritual deposition of plant remains: a case study of stone pine cones in Roman Britain', in T. Brindle, M. Allen, E. Durham and A. Smith (eds), *TRAC 2014: Proceedings of the Twenty-Fourth Annual Theoretical Roman Archaeology Conference* (Oxford), 54–69

— 2017a: '"The debatable territory where geology and archaeology meet": reassessing the early archaeobotanical work of Clement Reid and Arthur Lyell at Roman Silchester', *Environmental Archaeology* 22(1), 56–78, doi: 10.1080/14614103.2015.1116218

— 2017b:'Evergreen plants in Roman Britain: movement, meaning and materiality', *Britannia online,* doi: https://doi.org/10.1017/S0068113X17000101

— 2017c: 'Arable farming, plant foods and resources', in Allen *et al.* 2017, 11–84

— and Challinor, D. 2017: '*Pinus pinea* (stone pine) and other charred plant remains from cremation burials 3343 and 4593', in Hayden *et al.* 2017, 357–8

Lokuruka, M.N.I. 2006: 'Meat is the meal and status is by meat: recognition of rank, wealth and respect through meat in Turkana culture', *Food and Foodways* 14, 201–29

Lucas, G. 2001: *Excavations at Vicar's Farm, West Cambridge,* draft publication, Cambridge Archaeological Unit

Lucas, R.N. 1993: *The Romano-British Villa at Halstock, Dorset: Excavations 1967–1985*, Dorset Natural History and Archaeological Society Monograph 13 (Dorchester)

Lucy, S. and Evans, C. 2016: *Romano-British Settlement and Cemeteries at Mucking. Excavations by Margaret and Tom Jones, 1965–1978* (Oxford)

Luff, R.M. 1985: 'The fauna', in R. Niblett, *Sheepen: an early Roman industrial site at Camulodunum*, CBA Research Report 57 (London), 143–9

— 1999, 'Animal and human bones', in Turner 1999, 204–23

Luke, M. 2009: *Life in the Loop: Investigation of a Prehistoric and Roman-British Landscape at Biddenham Loop, Bedfordshire*, East Anglian Archaeology 125 (Bedford)

— 2016: *Close to the Loop: 6000 years of Landscape and Settlement Evolution beside the Biddenham Loop, west of Bedford*, East Anglian Archaeology 156 (Bedford)

— and Preece, T. 2010: 'Iron Age, Roman and Saxo-Norman settlement on the Oxford Clay at Luton Road, Bedford', *Bedfordshire Archaeology* 26, 99–165

— and Preece, T. 2011: *Farm and Forge: Late Iron Age/ Romano-British farmsteads at Marsh Leys, Kempston, Bedfordshire*, East Anglian Archaeology 138 (Bedford)

—, Cockings, S. and Sayer, E. 2015: *A Roman Site at Manton Lane, Bedford: Preliminary Report on the Archaeological Investigations*, draft report, Bedford Archaeological Council

Lundock, J. 2015: *A Study of the Deposition and Distribution of Copper Alloy Vessels in Roman Britain*, Roman Archaeology 9 (Oxford)

Lyons, A. 2011: *Life and Afterlife at Duxford, Cambridgeshire: Archaeology and History in a Chalkland Community*, East Anglian Archaeology 141 (Cambridge)

— 2014: *Godmanchester, Cambridgeshire: Excavations at Rectory Farm 1988–1995. Summary report*, Oxford Archaeology East

Macaulay-Lewis, E. 2008: 'The fruits of victory: generals, plants and power in the Roman World', in E. Bragg, L. Hay and E. Macaulay-Lewis (eds), *Beyond the Battlefields: New Perspectives on Warfare and Society in the Graeco-Roman World* (Newcastle upon Tyne), 205–25

MacDonald, P. 2007: *Llyn Cerrig Bach: A Study of the Copper Alloy Artefacts from the Insular La Tène Assemblage* (Cardiff)

Mackey, R. 1999: 'The Welton villa – a view of social and economic change during the Roman period in East Yorkshire', in P. Halkon (ed.), *Further Light on the Parisi: Recent Research in Iron Age and Roman East Yorkshire* (Hull), 21–32

MacKinnon, M. 2004: *Production and Consumption of Animals in Roman Italy: Integrating the Zooarchaeological and Textual Evidence*, Journal of Roman Archaeology Supplementary Series 54 (Portsmouth, RI)

— 2010:'"Sick as a dog": zooarchaeological evidence for pet dog health and welfare in the Roman world', *World Archaeology* 42(2), 290–309

Mackreth, D.F. 1986: 'Brooches', in D. Gurney, *Settlement, Religion and Industry on the Fen-Edge; Three Romano-British Sites in Norfolk*, East Anglian Archaeology 31 (Dereham), 61–7

— 1996: *Orton Hall Farm: A Roman and Early Anglo-Saxon Farmstead*, East Anglian Archaeology 76 (Peterborough)

— 2011: *Brooches in Late Iron Age and Roman Britain* (Oxford)

— 2012: 'Dragonesque brooches', *Lucerna* 43, 11–12

MacRae, D. 2016: *Legible Religion* (Harvard)

Madgwick R. 2008: 'Patterns in the modification of animal and human bones in Iron Age Wessex: revisiting the excarnation debate', in O.P. Davis, N.M. Sharples and K.E. Waddington (eds), *Changing Perspectives on the First Millennium BC* (Oxford), 99–118

—, Sykes, N., Miller, H., Symmons, R., Morris, J. and Lamb, A. 2013: 'Fallow deer (*Dama dama dama*) management in Roman south-east Britain', *Archaeological and Anthropological Sciences* 5(2), 111–22

Magilton, J. 2006: 'A Romano-Celtic temple and settlement at Grimstock Hill, Coleshill, Warwickshire', *Birmingham and Warwickshire Archaeological Society Transactions* 110, 1–236

Mahmud, M.A., Spigt, M., Bezabih, A.M., Pavon, I.L., Dinant, G. and Velasco, R.B. 2013: 'Risk factors for intestinal parasitosis, anaemia, and malnutrition among school children in Ethiopia', *Pathogens and Global Health* 107(2), 58–65

Mainland, I., and Halstead, P. 2004: 'The diet and management of domestic sheep and goats in Neolithic Makriyalos', in J. Davies (ed.), *Diet and Health in Past Animal Populations: Current Research and Future Directions* (Oxford), 104–12

Makepeace, G.A.M. 1998: 'Romano-British rural settlements in the Peak District and North East Staffordshire', *Derbyshire Archaeological Journal* 108, 127–9

Malim, T. 2006: 'A Romano-British temple complex and Anglo-Saxon burials at Gallows Hill, Swaffham Prior', *Proceedings of the Cambridge Antiquarian Society* 95, 91–114

Maltby, M. 1979: *The Animal Bones from Exeter 1971–1975*, Exeter Archaeological Reports 2 (Sheffield)

— 1984: 'Animal bones and the Romano-British economy', in C. Grigson and J. Clutton-Brock (eds), *Animals and Archaeology: 4. Husbandry in Europe*, BAR International Series 227 (Oxford), 125–38

— 1987: *The Animal Bones from the Excavations at Owslebury, Hants. An Iron Age and Early Romano-British Settlement*, English Heritage Ancient Monuments Laboratory Report 6/87

— 1989a: 'The animal bones', in P.J., Fasham, D.E. Farwell and R.J.B. Whinney (eds), *The Archaeological Site at Easton Lane, Winchester*, Hampshire Field Club and Archaeological Society Monograph 6 (Gloucester), 122–31

— 1989b: 'Urban–rural variations in the butchering of cattle in Romano-British Hampshire', in D. Serjeantson and T. Waldron (eds), *Diet and Crafts in Towns – The Evidence of Animal Remains from the Roman to the Post-medieval Period*, BAR British Series 199 (Oxford), 75–107

— 1993a: 'The animal bones', in P.J. Woodward, S.M. Davies and A.H. Graham, *Excavations at the Old Methodist Chapel and Greyhound Yard, Dorchester 1981–4* (Dorchester), 315–40 and microfiche A2–D14

— 1993b: 'The animal bones from a Romano-British well at Oakridge II, Basingstoke', *Proceedings of the Hampshire Field Club Archaeological Society* 49, 47–76

— 1994: 'The meat supply in Roman Dorchester and Winchester', in A.R. Hall and H.K. Kenward (eds), *Urban-Rural Connexions: Perspectives from Environmental Archaeology* (Oxford), 85–102

— 1997: 'Domestic fowl on Romano-British sites: inter-site comparisons of abundance', *International Journal of Osteoarchaeology* 7, 402–14

— 2007: 'Chop and change: specialist cattle carcass processing in Roman Britain', in B. Croxford, N. Ray, R. Roth and N. White (eds), *TRAC 2006: Proceedings of the Sixteenth Annual Theoretical Roman Archaeology Conference* (Oxford), 59–76

— 2009: 'Mammals, birds and fish', in S. Palmer, *Excavation of an Enigmatic Multi-Period Site on the Isle of Portland, Dorset*, BAR British Series 499 (Oxford), 27–43

— 2010a: 'Zooarchaeology and the interpretation of depositions in shafts', in J. Morris and M. Maltby (eds), *Integrating Social and Environmental Archaeologies: Reconsidering Deposition*, BAR International Series S2077 (Oxford), 24–32

— 2010b: *Feeding a Roman Town: Environmental Evidence from Excavations in Winchester, 1972–1985* (Winchester)

— 2012: 'Sheep foundation burials in Roman Winchester', in A. Pluskowski (ed.), *The Ritual Killing and Burial of Animals: European Perspectives* (Oxford), 152–63

— 2015: 'Commercial archaeology, zooarchaeology and the study of Romano-British towns', in M. Fulford and N. Holbrook (eds), *The Towns of Roman Britain: the Contribution of Commercial Archaeology since 1990*, Britannia Monograph Series 27 (London), 175–93

— 2016: 'The exploitation of animals in Roman Britain', in Millett *et al.* 2016, 791–806, doi: 10.1093/oxfordhb/9780199697731.013.045

— and Hamilton-Dyer, S. 2012: 'Big fish and great auks: exploitation of birds and fish on the Isle of Portland, Dorset, during the Romano-British period', *Environmental Archaeology* 17, 168–76

Manchester, K.A. and Roberts, C. 1986: *Palaeopathological Evidence of Leprosy and Tuberculosis in Britain*, SERC Report for Grant Number 337.367

Mandich, M.J., Gonzalez Sanchez, S., Zampieri, E., Savani, G. and Derrick, T.J. (eds) 2016: *TRAC 2015: Proceedings of the Twenty-fifth Annual Theoretical Roman Archaeology Conference* (Oxford)

Manning, W.H. 1985: *Catalogue of Romano-British Iron Tools, Fittings and Weapons in the British Museum* (London)

MAP Arch. Con. 1997: *Garden Lane, Sherburn in Elmet, North Yorkshire: Archaeological Excavations*, MAP Archaeological Consultancy Report 8/058

Martin, L., Richardson, J. and Roberts, I. 2013: *Iron Age and Roman Settlements at Wattle Syke. Archaeological Excavations during the A1 Bramham to Wetherby Upgrading Scheme*, Yorkshire Archaeology 11 (Leeds)

Martiniano, R., Caffell, A., Holst, M., Hunter-Mann, K., Montgomery, J., Müldner, G., McLaughlin, R.L., Teasdale, M.D., van Rheenen, W. and Veldink, J.H. 2016: 'Genomic signals of migration and continuity in Britain before the Anglo-Saxons', *Nature Communications* 7, doi: 10.1038/ncomms10326

Marvin, G. 2000: 'The problem of foxes: legitimate and illegitimate killing in the English countryside', in J. Knight (ed.), *Natural Enemies: People-Wildlife Conflict in Anthropological Perspective* (London), 189–211

Marzano, A. 2014: 'Roman gardens, military conquests, and elite self-representation', in K. Coleman (ed.), *Le Jardin dans l'Antiquité*, Entretiens sur l'Antiquité Classique 60 (Geneva), 195–244

Masson Phillips, E.N. 1966: 'Excavation of a Romano-British site at Lower Well Farm, Stoke Gabriel, Devon', *Proceedings of the Devon Archaeological Society* 23, 3–34

Matos, V. and Santos, V.L. 2006: 'On the trail of pulmonary tuberculosis based on rib lesions: results from the Human Identified Skeletal Collection from the Museu Bocage (Lisbon, Portugal)', *American Journal of Physical Anthropology* 130, 190–200

Matthews, C.L. 1981: 'A Romano-British inhumation cemetery at Dunstable', *Bedfordshire Archaeological Journal* 15, 1–74

Mattingly, D. 2004: 'Being Roman: expressing identity in a provincial setting', *Journal of Roman Archaeology* 17, 5–25

— 2006: *An Imperial Possession: Britain in the Roman Empire, 54 BC–AD 409* (London)

— 2010: *Imperialism, Power, and Identity: Experiencing the Roman Empire* (Princeton)

May, J. 1996: *Dragonby: Report on Excavations at an Iron Age and Romano-British Settlement in North Lincolnshire*, Oxbow Monograph 61 (Oxford)

Mays, S. 2007: 'Lysis at the anterior vertebral body margin: evidence for brucellar spondylitis?', *International Journal of Osteoarchaeology* 17(2), 107–18

— and Eyers, J. 2011: 'Perinatal infant death at the Roman villa site at Hambleden, Buckinghamshire, England', *Journal of Archaeological Science* 38, 1931–8

— and Taylor, G.M. 2003: 'A first prehistoric case of tuberculosis from Britain', *International Journal of Osteoarchaeology* 13(4), 189–96

—, Robson-Brown, K., Vincent, S., Eyers, J., King, H. and Roberts, A. 2014: 'An infant femur bearing cut marks from Roman Hambleden, England', *International Journal of Osteoarchaeology* 24, 111–15

McCarthy, M. 2013. *The Romano-British Peasant: Towards a Study of People, Landscapes and Work during the Roman Occupation of Britain* (Oxford)

McDade, T.W. and Worthman, C.M. 1998: 'The weanling's dilemma reconsidered: a biocultural analysis of breastfeeding ecology', *Journal of Developmental and Behavioural Pediatrics* 19(4), 286–99

McIntosh, F. and Ponting, M. 2014: 'The Wirral Brooch: the form, distribution and role of a regional Romano-British brooch type', *The Archaeological Journal* 171(1), 111–50

McKinley, J.I. 2000: 'Phoenix rising. Aspects of cremation burial in Roman Britain', in Pearce *et al.* 2000, 38–44

— 2006: 'Cremation … the cheap option?', in Gowland and Knüsel 2006, 81–8

— 2008: 'Ryknield Street, Wall (Site 12)', in Powell *et al.* 2008, 87–190

— 2009: 'Human bone', in Andrews 2009, 1–77

— 2011: 'Human bone', in Barnett *et al.* 2011, 1–14

— 2013: 'Cremation: excavation, analysis, and interpretation of material from cremation-related contexts', in Nilsson Stutz and Tarlow 2013, 147–72, doi: 10.1093/oxfordhb/9780199569069.013.0009

— and Heaton, M. 1996: 'A Romano-British farmstead and associated burials at Maddington Farm, Shrewton', *Wiltshire Archaeological and Natural History Magazine* 89, 44–72

—, with Barnett, C. and Pelling, R. 2012 'Cremated remains', in P. Arrowsmith and D. Power, *Roman Nantwich: A Salt-Making Settlement. Excavations at Kingsley Fields 2002*, BAR British Series 557 (Oxford), 100–7

McLeod, G. 1989: 'Wild and tame animals and birds in Roman law', in P. Birks (ed.), *New Perspectives in the Roman Law of Property: Essays for Barry Nicholas* (Oxford), 169–76

McOmish, D., Field, D. and Brown, G. 2002: *The Field Archaeology of the Salisbury Plain Training Area* (Swindon),

Meates, G.W. 1979: *The Lullingstone Roman Villa. Vol. 1: The Site*, Monograph Series of the Kent Archaeological Society 1 (Maidstone)

— 1987: *The Lullingstone Roman Villa. Vol. 2: The Wall Paintings and Finds*, Monograph Series of the Kent Archaeological Society 3 (Maidstone)

Meddens, B. 2002: 'Animal bones from Bainesse (Site 46)', in P.R. Wilson (ed.), *Cataractonium: Roman Catterick and its Hinterland. Excavations and Research 1958–1997, Part II*, CBA Research Report 129 (York), 419–25

Medlycott, M. 2011: *The Roman Town of Great Chesterford*, East Anglian Archaeology 137 (Chelmsford)

Melén, I., Lindahl, L. Andréasson, L. and Rundcrantz, H. 1986: 'Chronic maxillary sinusitis: definition, diagnosis and relation to dental infections and nasal polyposis', *Acta Oto-Laryngologica* 101(3–4), 320–7

Mendis, K., Sina, B.J., Marchesini, P. and Carter, R. 2001: 'The neglected burden of *Plasmodium vivax* malaria', *The American Journal of Tropical Medicine and Hygiene* 64(1), 97–106

Meniel, P. 2002: 'La chasse en Gaule, une activité aristocratique?', in V. Guichard, F. Perrin and J.-C. Decourt (eds), *L'Aristocratie Celte à la Fin de l'Âge du Fer*, Collection Bibracte 5 (Glux-en-Glenne), 223–30

Mensforth, R.P., Lovejoy, C.O., Lallo, J.W. and Armelagos, G.J. 1978: 'The role of constitutional factors, diet, and infectious disease in the etiology of porotic hyperostosis and periosteal reactions in prehistoric infants and children', *Medical Anthropology* 2(1), 1–59

Mighall, T. and Chambers, F. 1989: 'The environmental impact of iron-working at Bryn y Castell hillfort, Merioneth', *Archaeology in Wales* 29, 17–21

Milella, M., Mariotti, V., Belcastro, M.G. and Knüsel, C.J. 2015: 'Patterns of irregular burials in Western Europe (1st–5th century A.D.)', *PloS One* 10(6), doi: e0130616

Miles, D. (ed) 1982: *The Romano-British Countryside – Studies in Rural Settlement and Economy*, BAR British Series 103 (Oxford)

— (ed.) 1986: *Archaeology at Barton Court Farm, Abingdon, Oxon*, Oxford Archaeological Unit Report 3/CBA Research Report 50 (London/Oxford)

—, Palmer, S., Lock, G., Gosden. C. and Cromarty, A.M. 2003: *Uffington White Horse Hill and its Landscape: investigations at White Horse Hill, Uffington, 1989–95 and Tower Hill, Ashbury, 1993–4, Oxfordshire*, Oxford Archaeology Thames Valley Landscapes Monograph 18 (Oxford)

—, Palmer, S., Smith, A. and Perpetua Jones, G. 2007: *Iron Age and Roman Settlement in the Upper Thames Valley, Excavations at Claydon Pike and other Sites within the Cotswold Water Park*, Oxford Archaeology Thames Valley Landscapes Monograph 26 (Oxford)

Miller, D., Griffin, L. and Pearson, E. 2004: 'Excavation at Stonebridge Cross, Westwood, Worcestershire: an Iron Age and Romano-British settlement', *Transactions of the Worcestershire Archaeological Society* 19, 1–44

Miller, J. 2013: 'Appendix 18 – Botanical analysis of cremation deposits', in Davies 2013, doi: 10.5284/1029314, 117–24

Millett, M. 1990: *The Romanization of Britain: An Essay in Archaeological Interpretation* (Cambridge)

— 1994: 'Interpreting Roman hoards', in S. Cottam, D. Dungworth, S. Scott, and J. Taylor (eds), *TRAC 94: Proceedings of the Fourth Annual Theoretical Roman Archaeology Conference* (Oxford), 99–106

— 2016: '"By small things revealed": rural settlement and society', in Millett *et al.* 2016, 699–719, doi: 10.1093/oxfordhb/9780199697713.013.038

— and Gowland, R. 2015: 'Infant and child burial rites in Roman Britain: a study from East Yorkshire', *Britannia* 46, 171–89

—, Revell, L. and Moore, A. (eds) 2016: *The Oxford Handbook of Roman Britain* (Oxford) (on line, doi: 10.1093/oxfordhb/9780199697731.001.0001)

Minniti, C., Valenzuela-Lamas, S., Evans, J. and Albarella, U. 2014: 'Widening the market. Strontium isotope analysis on cattle teeth from Owslebury (Hampshire, UK) highlights changes in livestock supply between the Iron Age and the Roman period', *Journal of Archaeological Science* 42, 305–14

Miškec, A. 2010: 'Analysis of the coin finds from the graves in the northern cemetery of Emona', in I. Lazar and B. Županek (eds), *Emona – between Aquileia and Pannonia*, 133–42

Miura, H., Araki, Y., Haraguchi, K., Arai, Y. and Umenai, T. 1997: 'Socioeconomic factors and dental caries in developing countries: a cross-national study', *Social Science and Medicine* 44(2), 269–72

Moffatt, B. and Heaton, M. 2003: *Sand Hill Farm, Longbridge Deverill, Wiltshire. Evaluation of Lead Coffin Burial*, Pathfinders Archaeological Reconnaisance

Molleson, T. 1989: 'Social implications of mortality patterns of juveniles from Poundbury Camp, Romano-British cemetery', *Anthropologischer Anzeiger* 47(1), 27–38

Monckton, A. 1999: 'Oysters from Causeway Lane', in A. Connor and R. Buckley (eds), *Roman and Medieval Occupation at Causeway Lane, Leicester*, University of Leicester Archaeology Monographs 5 (Leicester), 337–41

— 2001: 'The charred plant remains', in Pollard 2001, 29–31

Montgomery, J., Evans, J.A., Chenery, S.R., Pashley, V. and Killgrove, K. 2010: '"Gleaming, white and deadly": using lead to track human exposure and geographic origins in the Roman period in Britain', in Eckardt (ed.) 2010b, 199–226

Mooketsi, C. 2001: 'Butchery styles and the processing of cattle carcasses in Botswana', *Pula Journal* 15(1), 108–24

Moore, A. 2009: 'Hearth and home: the burial of infants within Romano-British domestic contexts', *Childhood in the Past* 2(1), 33–54

— 2016: 'The life course', in Millett *et al.* (eds) 2016, 321–40, doi: 10.1093/oxfordhb/9780199697731. 013.015

Moore, T. 2001: 'An archaeological assessment of Hailey Wood Camp, Sapperton, Gloucestershire: a Roman temple complex in the Cotswolds?', *Transactions of the Bristol and Gloucestershire Archaeological Society* 119, 83–93

— 2003: 'Rectangular houses in the British Iron Age – "squaring the circle"', in J. Humphrey (ed.), *Re-searching the Iron Age*, Leicester Archaeology Monographs 11 (Leicester), 47–58

— 2007: 'Life on the edge? Exchange, settlement and identity in the later Iron Age of the Severn Cotswolds', in Haselgrove and Moore 2007, 41–61

— 2011: 'Detribalizing the later prehistoric past: concepts of tribes in Iron Age and Roman studies', *Journal of Social Archaeology* 11(3), 334–60

— 2016: 'Britain, Gaul, and Germany: cultural interactions', in Millett *et al.* 2016, 262–82

Moore, W.J. and Corbett, E. 1973: 'The distribution of dental caries in ancient British populations – II. Iron Age, Romano-British and mediaeval periods', *Caries Research* 7, 139–53

Moorrees, C.F.A., Fanning, E.A. and Hunt, E.E. 1963: 'Age variation of formation stages for ten permanent teeth', *Journal of Dental Research* 42, 1490–1502

Morey, D.D.F. 2010: *Dogs: Domestication and the Development of a Social Bond* (Cambridge)

Morris, E.L. and Gelling, P.S. 1991: 'A note on The Berth', *Shropshire Archaeology and History* 67, 58–62

Morris J. 2008: *Re-examining Associated Bone Groups from Southern England and Yorkshire, c. 4000 BC to AD 1550*, unpublished PhD thesis, University of Bournemouth

— 2011: *Investigating Animal Burials: Ritual, Mundane and Beyond*, BAR British Series 535 (Oxford)

— 2012: 'Animal "ritual" killing: from remains to meanings', in A. Plukowski (ed.), *The Ritual Killing and Burial of Animals: European Perspectives* (Oxford), 8–21

— 2016: 'Mourning the sacrifice. Behaviour and meaning behind animal burials', in M. DeMello (ed.), *Mourning Animals: Rituals and Practices Surrounding Animal Death. The Animal Turn* (East Lansing), 11–20

Morris, M., Buckley, R. and Codd, M. 2011: *Visions of Ancient Leicester. Reconstructing Life in the Roman and Medieval Town from the Archaeology of the Highcross Leicester Excavations* (Leicester)

Morris, S. and Meadows, I. 2012: *Iron Age and Roman Landscapes at Victoria Park, Irchester, Northamptonshire; Excavations September 2004 to May 2005*, Northamptonshire Archaeology report

Morrison, W. A. 2013: 'A fresh eye on familiar objects: rethinking toiletry sets in Roman Britain', *Oxford Journal of Archaeology* 32, 221–30

Mould, Q. 2011: 'Domestic life', in Allason-Jones 2011a, 153–79

Moyes, H. (ed.) 2012a: *Sacred Darkness: A Global Perspective on the Ritual use of Caves* (Colorado)

— 2012b: 'Introduction', in Moyes 2012a, 1–11

Moynihan, P. 2000: 'Foods and factors that protect against dental caries', *British Nutrition Foundation Nutrition Bulletin* 25, 281–6

Mudd, A. 2002: *Excavations at Melford Meadows, Brettenham, 1994: Romano-British and Early Saxon Occupations*, East Anglian Archaeology 99 (Oxford)

Müldner, G. 2013: 'Stable isotopes and diet: their contribution to Romano-British research', *Antiquity* 87, 137–49

—, Chenery, C. and Eckardt, H. 2011: 'The "Headless Romans": multi-isotope investigations of an unusual burial ground from Roman Britain', *Journal of Archaeological Science* 38(2), 280–90

Mulkeen, S. and O'Connor, T.P. 1997: 'Raptors in towns: towards an ecological model', *International Journal of Osteoarchaeology* 7(4), 440–9

Mullen, A. 2016: 'Sociolinguistics', in Millett *et al.* 2016, 573–98, doi: 10.1093/oxfordhb/9780199697731.013.032

Mullin, M.H. 1999: 'Mirrors and windows: sociocultural studies of human-animal relationships', *Annual Review of Anthropology* 28, 201–24

Mulville, J. and Levitan, B. 2004: 'The animal bone', in G. Lambrick and T. Allen (eds), *Gravelly Guy, Stanton Harcourt: the Development of a Prehistoric and Romano-British Community*, Oxford Archaeology, Thames Valley Landscape Monograph 21. Oxford Archaeological Unit, 263–479

Munyeme, M., Muma, J.B., Skjerve, E., Nambota, A.M., Phiri, I.G., Samui, K.L., Dorny, P. and Tryland, M.

2008: 'Risk factors associated with bovine tuberculosis in traditional cattle of the livestock/wildlife interface areas in the Kafue basin of Zambia', *Preventive Veterinary Medicine* 85(3–4), 317–28

Murphy, K. 1993: 'Plas Gogerddan, Dyfed: a multi-period burial and ritual site', *The Archaeological Journal* 149, 1–38

Murphy, P. 1998: *A Review of Plant Macrofossils from Archaeological Sites in the Eastern Counties*, Centre of East Anglian Studies, University of East Anglia (Norwich)

— 2001: *Review of Wood and Macroscopic Wood Charcoal from Archaeological Sites in the West and East Midlands Regions and the East of England* (Portsmouth)

— and Scaife, R. 1991: 'The environmental archaeology of gardens', in A.E. Brown (ed.), *Garden Archaeology: Papers Presented to a Conference at Knutston Hall, Northamptonshire, April 1988*, CBA Research Report 78 (London), 83–99

—, Albarella, U. and Germany, M. 2000: 'Production, imports and status: biological remains from a late Roman farm at Great Holts Farm, Essex, UK', *Environmental Archaeology* 5, 35–48

Murray, C. and Frenk, J. 2002: 'Summary measures of population health in the context of the WHO framework for health system performance assessment', in C.J. Murray, J.A. Salomon, C.D. Mathers and A.D. Lopex (eds), *Summary Measures of Population Health. Concepts, Ethics, Measurement and Application* (Geneva), 1–12

Musty, J. 1977: 'The Roman pond and dipping well at Armsley, Godshill, Hampshire', *Proceedings of the Hampshire Field Club and Archaeological Society* 30, 35–8

Nan Kivell, R. deC. 1927: 'Objects found during excavations on the Romano-British site at Cold Kitchen Hill, Brixton, Deverill, 1924', *Wiltshire Archaeology and Natural History Magazine* 43, 180–91 and 327–32

— 1929: 'Objects found during excavations on the Romano-British site at Cold Kitchen Hill, Brixton, Deverill, 1926', *Wiltshire Archaeology and Natural History Magazine* 44, 138–42

Neal, D.S. 1976: 'Northchurch, Bowmoor, and Hemel Hempstead Station: the excavation of three Roman buildings in the Bulbourne Valley', *Hertfordshire Archaeology* 4, 1–135

— 1984: 'A sanctuary at Wood Lane End, Hemel Hempstead', *Britannia* 15, 193–215

— 1989: 'The Stanwick Villa, Northants: an interim report on the excavations of 1984–88', *Britannia* 20, 149–68

— and Cosh, S.R. 2009: *Roman Mosaics of Britain Vol. III: South-East Britain* (London)

Nehlich, O., Fuller, B.T., Jay, M., Mora, A., Nicholson, R.A., Smith, C.I. and Richards, M.P. 2011: 'Application of sulphur isotope ratios to examine weaning patterns and freshwater fish consumption in Roman Oxfordshire, UK', *Geochimica et Cosmochimica Acta* 75, 4963–77

Nelson, J.D. 1990: 'Acute osteomyelitis in children', *Infectious Disease Clinics of North America* 4(3), 513–22

Nelson, L.J. and Wells, C.D. 2004: 'Global epidemiology of childhood tuberculosis', *International Journal of Tuberculosis and Lung Disease* 8(5), 636–47

Nevas, M., Hielm, S., Linström, M., Horn, H., Koivulehto, K. and Korkeala, H. 2002: 'High prevalence of *Clostridium botulinum* types A and B in honey samples detected by polymerase chain reaction', *International Journal of Food Microbiology* 72(1–2), 45–52

Niblett, R. 1999: *The Excavation of a Ceremonial Site at Folly Lane, Verulamium*, Britannia Monograph Series 14 (London)

Nicholson, K. 2006a: 'An Iron Age site at South Witham Quarry, Lincolnshire', *Lincolnshire Archaeology and History* 41, 22–40

— 2006b: 'A late Roman cemetery at Watersmeet, Mill Common, Huntingdon', *Proceedings of the Cambridge Antiquarian Society* 95, 57–90

— and Woolhouse, T. 2016: *A Late Iron Age and Romano-British Farmstead at Cedars Park, Stowmarket, Suffolk*, East Anglian Archaeology 160 (Bury St Edmunds)

Nielsen, A.V.F., Tetens, I. and Meyer, A.S. 2013: 'Potential of phytase-mediated iron release from cereal-based foods: a quantitative view', *Nutrients* 5(8), 3074–98

Nilsson Stutz, L. and Tarlow, S. (eds) 2013: *The Oxford Handbook of the Archaeology of Death and Burial* (Oxford)

Noddle, B. 2006: 'Animal bone', in D. Hurst (ed.), *Roman Droitwich: Dodderhill Fort, Bays Meadow Villa, and Roadside Settlement*, CBA Research Report 146 (York), 216–20

Noel Hume, I. 1956: 'Ritual burials on the Upchurch Marshes', *Archaeologia Cantiana* 70, 160–7

North, J.A. 2000: *Roman Religion* (Oxford)

— 2005: 'Religion and rusticity', in T.J. Cornell and K. Lomas (eds), *Urban Society in Roman Italy* (London), 141–56

Nowakowski, J.A. 1991: 'Trethellan Farm, Newquay: excavation of a lowland Bronze Age settlement and Iron Age cemetery', *Cornish Archaeology* 30, 5–242

Noy, D. 2010: 'Epigraphic evidence for immigrants at Rome and in Roman Britain', in Eckardt 2010b, 13–26

Ochs, H.A., Neuenschwander, M.C. and Dodson, T.B. 1996: 'Are head, neck and facial injuries markers of domestic violence?', *The Journal of the American Dental Association* 127(6), 757–61

O'Connell, M.G. and Bird, J. 1994: 'The Roman temple at Wanborough, excavation 1985–1986', *Surrey Archaeological Collections* 82, 1–168

O'Connor, T.P. 1988: *Bones from the General Accident Site, Tanner Row*, The Archaeology of York 15/2 (London)

— 1992: 'Provisioning urban communities: a topic in search of a model', *Anthropozoologica (L'Homme et L'Animal)* 16, 101–6

— 2010: 'The house mouse', in O'Connor and Sykes (eds) 2010, 127–33

— and Sykes, N.J. 2010: *Extinctions and Invasions: The Social History of British Fauna* (Oxford)

Oliver, M. 1992: 'The Iron Age and Romano-British settlement at Oakridge', *Proceedings of the Hampshire Field Club and Archaeological Society* 48, 55–94

Oloya, J., Kazwala, R., Lund, A., Opuda-Asibo, J., Demelash, B., Skjerve, E., Johansen, T.B. and Djønne, B. 2007: 'Characterisation of mycobacteria isolated from slaughter cattle in pastoral regions of Uganda', *BMC Microbiology* 7(1), 95

O'Neill, B.H. St J. 1933: 'The Roman villa at Magor Farm, near Camborne, Cornwall', *Journal of the British Archaeological Association* 39, 117–75

O'Neil. H. 1947: 'The Roman villa at Park Street near St Albans', *The Archaeological Journal* 102, 21–110

Orlin, E.M. 2002: *Temples, Religion, and Politics in the Roman Republic* (Boston/Leiden)

— (ed.) 2015: *Routledge Encyclopedia of Ancient Mediterranean Religions* (Abingdon)

Ortner, D.J. 2003: *Identification of Pathological Conditions in Human Skeletal Remains* (2nd edn) (San Diego)

—, Kimmerle, E. and Diez, M. 1999: 'Probable evidence of scurvy in subadults from archaeological sites in Peru', *American Journal of Physical Anthropology* 108, 321–31

—, Butler, W., Cafarella, J. and Milligan, L. 2001: 'Evidence of probable scurvy in subadults from archaeological sites in North America', *American Journal of Physical Anthropology* 114, 343–51

Orton, C. 1997: 'Ewell, King William IV site', *Surrey Archaeological Collections* 84, 89–122

Orton, D. 2006: 'A local barrow for local people? The Ferry Fryston cattle in context', in B. Croxford, N. Ray, R. Roth and N. White (eds), *TRAC 2006: Proceedings of the Sixteenth Annual Theoretical Roman Archaeology Conference, Cambridge* (Oxford), 77–91

O'Shea, J. 1989: 'The role of wild resources in small-scale agricultural systems: tales from the lakes and the plains', in J. O'Shea and P. Halstead (eds), *Bad Year Economics* (Cambridge), 57–67

Oswald, A. 1949: 'A re-excavation of the Roman villa at Mansfield Woodhouse, Nottinghamshire, 1936–39', *Transactions of the Thoroton Society* 53, 1–14

Ottaway, P.J., Qualmann, K.E., Rees, H. and Scobie, G.D. 2012: *The Roman Cemeteries and Suburbs of Winchester. Excavations 1971–86*, Winchester Museums (Winchester)

Owen, W.J., Schwab, I., and Sheldon, H. 1973: 'Roman burials from Old Ford, E3. February and May 1972', *Transactions London and Middlesex Archaeological Society* 24, 135–45

Oxenham, M.F. and Cavill, I. 2010: 'Porotic hyperostosis and cribra orbitalia: the erythropoietic response to iron-deficiency anaemia', *Anthropological Science* 118(3), 199–200

Paine, R.R. and Boldsen, J.L. 2002: 'Linking age-at-death distributions and ancient population dynamics: a case study', in R.D. Hoppa and J.W. Vaupel (eds), *Paleodemography – Age Distributions from Skeletal Samples* (Cambridge), 169–80

Palmer, S.C. 2000: 'Archaeological excavations in the Arrow Valley, Warwickshire', *Birmingham and Warwickshire Archaeological Society Transactions* 103, 1–231

Papaioannou, S. 2016: 'Introduction', in P.A. Johnston, A. Mastrocinque and S. Papaioannou (eds), *Animals in Greek and Roman Religion and Myth: Proceedings of the Symposium Grumentinum Grumento Nova*

(Potenza) 5–7 June 2013 (Newcastle-upon-Tyne), 1–18

Papworth, M. 2008: *Deconstructing the Durotriges: a Definition of Iron Age Communities within the Dorset Environs*, BAR British Series 462 (Oxford)

Parfitt, K. 1995: *Iron Age Burials from Mill Hill, Deal* (London)

— and Green, M. 1987: 'A chalk figurine from Upper Deal, Kent', *Britannia* 18, 295–8

Parker, A. J. 1988: 'The birds of Roman Britain', *Oxford Journal of Archaeology* 7, 197–226

Parker Pearson, M. 2003: *The Archaeology of Death and Burial* (2nd edn) (Stroud)

— and Richards, C. (eds) 1994: *Architecture and Order: Approaches to Social Space* (London)

Parkhouse, J. and Evans, E. (eds) 1996: *Excavations in Cowbridge, South Glamorgan, 1977–88*, BAR British Series 245 (Oxford)

Parkin, T.G. 1992: *Demography and Roman Society* (London)

Parsons, D.N. 2011: 'Sabrina in the Thorns: place-names as evidence for British and Latin in Roman Britain', *Transactions of the Philological Society* 109, 113–37

Partridge, C. 1977: 'Excavations and fieldwork at Braughing, 1968–73', *Hertfordshire Archaeology* 5, 22–108

Pascal, C.B., 1981: 'October horse', *Harvard Studies in Classical Philology* 85, 261–91

Peachin, M. (ed.) 2011: *The Oxford Handbook of Social Relations in the Roman World* (Oxford)

Peacock, D. 2013: *The Stone of Life: the Archaeology of Querns, Mills and Flour Production in Europe up to c. 500 A.D.*, Southampton Monographs in Archaeology 1 (Southampton)

Pearce, J. 1997: 'Death and time: the structure of late Iron Age mortuary ritual', in Gwilt and Haselgrove (eds), 174–80

— 1999: 'The dispersed dead: preliminary observations on burial and settlement space in rural Roman Britain', in P. Baker, C. Forcey, S. Jundi and R. Witcher (eds), *TRAC 98: Proceedings of the Eighth Annual Theoretical Roman Archaeology Conference, Leicester 1998* (Oxford), 151–62

— 2001: 'Infants, cemeteries and communities in the Roman provinces', in D. Davies, A. Gardner and K. Lockyear (eds), *TRAC 2000: Proceedings of the Tenth Annual Theoretical Roman Archaeology Conference, London 2000* (Oxford), 125–42

— 2004: 'Archaeology, writing tablets and literacy in Roman Britain', *Gallia* 61, 43–51

— 2008: 'Burial evidence from Roman Britain: the un-numbered dead', in J. Scheid (ed.), *Pour une archéologie du rite. Nouvelles perspectives de l'archéologie funéraire*, Collection de l'Ecole Francaise de Rome 407 (Rome), 29–42

— 2011: 'Marking the dead: tombs and topography in the Roman provinces', in M. Carroll and J. Rempel (eds), *Living Through the Dead: Burial and Commemoration in the Classical World* (Oxford), 134–58

— 2013: *Contextual Archaeology of Burial Practice. Case Studies from Roman Britain*, BAR British Series 588 (Oxford)

— 2014a: 'A "civilised" death? The interpretation of provincial Roman grave goods assemblages', in J. Rasmus Brandt, H. Roland and M. Prusac (eds), *Death and Changing Rituals: Function and Meaning in Ancient Funerary Practices* (Oxford), 223–47

— 2014b: 'Commemorating the dead in Britain: monuments and their setting', in J. Álvarez, T. Nogales and I. Rodà (eds), *Centro y periferia en el mundo clásico/Centre and periphery in the ancient world*, *Proceedings of the 18th International Congress of Classical Archaeology* (Merida), 1209–12

— 2015: 'Urban exits: commercial archaeology and the study of death rituals and the dead in the towns of Roman Britain', in M. Fulford and N. Holbrook (eds), *The Towns of Roman Britain. The Contribution of Commercial Archaeology since 1990*, Britannia Monograph Series 27 (London), 138–66

— 2016: 'Status and burial', in Millett *et al.* 2016, 341–62, doi: 10.1093/oxfordhb/9780199697713.013.021

— 2017: 'Introduction: death as a process in Roman funerary archaeology', in Pearce and Weekes 2017, 1–26

— and Weekes, J. (eds): 2017: *Death as a Process. The Archaeology of the Roman Funeral* (Oxford)

—, Millett, M. and Strück, M. (eds) 2000: *Burial, Society and Context in the Roman world* (Oxford)

Pearson, E. and Robinson, M. 1994: 'Environmental evidence from the villa', in Williams and Zeepvat 1994, 565–84

Pelling, R. 2008: 'Charred and waterlogged plant remains', in Booth *et al.* 2008, 349–57

— 2013: 'The charred plant remains', in Gosden and Lock 2013, 157–63

Penn, W.S. 1957: 'The Romano-British settlement at Springhead, excavation of the Bakery Site A', *Archaeologia Cantiana* 7, 53–105

— 1962: 'Springhead: Temples II and V', *Archaeolgia Cantiana* 77, 110–32

— 1964: 'Springhead: the temple ditch site', *Archaeologia Cantiana* 79, 170–89

Perring, D. 1989: 'Cellars and cults in Roman Britain', *The Archaeological Journal* 146, 279–301

— 2002: *The Roman House in Britain* (London)

— 2011: 'Two studies on Roman London. A: London's military origins. B: Population decline and ritual landscapes in Antonine London', *Journal of Roman Archaeology* 24, 249–82

Pettifor, J.M. 2004: 'Nutritional rickets: deficiency of vitamin D, calcium, or both?', *American Journal of Clinical Nutrition* 80, S1725–S1729

Petts, D. 2002: 'Cemeteries and boundaries in western Britain', in S. Lucy and A. Reynolds (eds), *Burial in Early Medieval England and Wales*, Society for Medieval Archaeology Monograph Series 17 (Leeds), 24–46

— 2003: *Christianity in Roman Britain* (Stroud)

— 2004: 'Burial in western Britain, AD 400–800. Late Antique or early medieval', in R. Collins and J. Gerrard (eds), *Debating Late Antiquity in Britain AD 300–700*, BAR British Series 365 (Oxford), 77–88

— 2016: 'Christianity in Roman Britain', in Millett *et al.* (eds) 2016, 660–81, doi: 10.1093/oxfordhb/9780199697731.013.033

Pfeiffer, S. 1984: 'Paleopathology in an Iroquoian ossuary, with special reference to tuberculosis', *American Journal of Physical Anthropology* 65, 181–9

— 1991: 'Rib lesions and New World tuberculosis', *International Journal of Osteoarchaeology* 1, 191–8

Phillips, T. 2014: *Late Iron Age and Roman Settlement at Land off Broadway, Yaxley, Peterborough. Excavation Report*, Oxford Archaeology East Report 1312

Philo, C. and Wilbert, C. 2000: 'Animal spaces and beastly places: an introduction', in C. Philo and C. Wilbert (eds), *Animal Spaces and Beastly Places* (London), 1–34

Philp, B. 1973: *Excavations in West Kent, 1960–1970: The Discovery and Excavation of Prehistoric, Roman, Saxon and Medieval Sites, mainly in the Bromley area and the Darent Valley*, Kent Archaeological Rescue Unit 4 (Dover)

— 2010: *Isle of Grain: The Discovery of a Major Roman Cemetery in 1981*, Kent Archaeological Rescue Unit, Special Subject Series 18 (Dover)

—, Parfitt, K., Willson, J., Dutto, M. and Williams, W. 1991: *The Roman Villa site at Keston, Kent. First report (Excavations 1968–1978)*, Kent Monograph Series 6 (Dover)

— , Parfitt, K., Willson, J. and Williams, W. 1999: *The Roman Villa site at Keston, Kent. Second report (Excavations 1967 and 1978–1990)*, Kent Monograph Series 8 (Dover)

Philpott, R.A. 1991: *Burial Practices in Roman Britain: A Survey of Grave Treatment and Furnishing A.D. 43–410*, BAR British Series 219 (Oxford)

— 1999: 'A Romano-British brooch type from North Western and Northern England', *Britannia* 30, 274–86

— 2000: 'Ochre Brook, Tarbock', in R. Cowell and R.A. Philpott, *Prehistoric, Romano-British and Medieval Settlement in Lowland North West England: Archaeological Excavations along the A5300 road corridor in Merseyside, Liverpool* (Liverpool), 67–116

Pickstone, A. 2011: *Land Adjacent to Itter Crescent, Peterborough. Archaeological Evaluation Interim Statement*, Oxford Archaeology East Report 1290

— and Drummond-Murray, J. 2013: 'A late Roman well or cistern and ritual deposition at Bretton Way, Peterborough', *Proceedings of the Cambridge Antiquarian Society* 102, 37–66

Pieper, J. 2009: *Leisure: The Basis of Culture* (revised edn) (San Francisco)

Piggott, S. 1968: *The Druids* (London)

Pimentel, L. 2003: 'Scurvy: historical review and current diagnostic approach', *American Journal of Emergency Medicine* 21, 328–32

Pine, J. 2011: *Eysey Manor, Cricklade, Wiltshire. A Post-Excavation Assessment* (phases 1–4: 2008–2011), Thames Valley Archaeological Services

— and Preston, P. 2015: *An Iron Age Round House and Roman Villa at Chilton Fields, Oxfordshire*, Thames Valley Archaeological Services Monograph 21 (Reading)

Pinhasi, R. and Bourbou, C. 2008: 'How representative are human skeletal assemblages for population analysis?', in R. Pinhasi and S. Mays (eds), *Advances in Human Palaeopathology* (Chichester), 31–44

Pinter-Bellows, S. 1993: 'The human skeletons', in Crummy *et al.* 1993, 62–91

Pitt-Rivers, A.H.L.-F. 1887: *Excavations in Cranborne Chase near Rushmore on the Borders of Dorset and Wiltshire 1880–1888. Vol 1: Excavations in the Romano-British Village on Woodcuts Common, and Romano-British Antiquities in Rushmore Park* (London)

— 1888: *Excavations in Cranborne Chase near Rushmore on the Borders of Dorset and Wiltshire 1880–1888. Vol. 2: Excavations in Barrows near Rushmore; in Romano-British village, Rotherley; in Winkelbury camp; in British Barrows and Anglo-Saxon cemetery, Winkelbury Hill* (London)

Pitts, M. 2005: 'Pots and pits: drinking and deposition in late Iron Age south-east Britain', *Oxford Journal of Archaeology* 24(2), 143–61

— and Griffin, R. 2012: 'Exploring health and social well-being in late Roman Britain: an intercemetery approach', *American Journal of Archaeology* 116, 253–76

Platell, A. 2014: 'Archaeological investigations along the Roman road through Chester-le-Street, County Durham', *Durham Archaeological Journal* 19, 43–104

Plomp, K.A., Roberts, C.A. and Vidarsdóttir, U.S. 2012: 'Vertebral morphology influences the development of Schmorl's nodes in the lower thoracic vertebrae', *American Journal of Physical Anthropology* 149(4), 572–82

Plouviez, J. 2004: 'Brooches', in T. Blagg, J. Plouviez and A. Tester, *Excavations at a Large Romano-British Settlement at Hacheston, Suffolk, 1973–74*, East Anglian Archaeology 106 (Dereham), 87–108

Pluskowski, A.G. 2006: 'Where are the wolves? Investigating the scarcity of European Grey Wolf (*Canis lupus lupus*) remains in medieval archaeological contexts and its implications', *International Journal of Osteoarchaeology* 16, 279–95

— 2010: 'The wolf', in O'Connor and Sykes (eds) 2010, 68–74

—, Boas, A. and Gerrard, C. 2011: 'The ecology of crusading: investigating the environmental impact of holy war and colonisation at the frontiers of medieval Europe', *Medieval Archaeology* 55, 192–225

Pollard, A.M., Ditchfield, P., Allen, T., Gibson, M., Boston, C., Clough, S., Marquez-Grant, N. and Nicholson, R.A. 2011: '"These boots were made for walking": the isotopic analysis of a C4 Roman inhumation from Gravesend, Kent, UK', *American Journal of Physical Anthropology* 146, 446–56

Pollard, R. 2001: 'An Iron Age inhumation from Rushey Mead, Leicester', *Transactions of the Leicestershire Archaeological and Historical Society* 75, 20–35

Pollock, K.J. 2006: *The Evolution and Role of Burial Practice in Roman Wales*, BAR British Series 426 (Oxford)

Poole, K. 2010: 'Bird introductions', in O'Connor and Sykes (eds) 2010, 156–65

Poulton, R. and Bird, J. 2007: 'Farley Heath Roman temple', *Surrey Archaeological Collections* 92, 1–147

Poulton, R. and Scott, E. 1993: 'The hoarding, deposition and use of pewter in Roman Britain', in E. Scott (ed.), *Theoretical Roman Archaeology: First Conference Proceedings*, Worldwide Archaeology Series 4 (Aldershot), 115–32

Powell, A. and Clark, K.M. 1996: *Exploitation of Domestic Animals in the Iron Age at Rooksdown*, unpublished Centre for Human Ecology report, Southampton

Powell, A.B., Booth, P., Fitzpatrick, A.P. and Crockett, A.D. (eds) 2008: *The Archaeology of the M6 Toll, 2000–2003*, Oxford-Wessex Archaeology Monograph 2 (Oxford/Salisbury)

Powell, K., Smith, A. and Laws, G. 2010: *Evolution of a Farming Community in the Upper Thames Valley. Excavation of a Prehistoric, Roman and post-Roman Landscape at Cotswold Community, Gloucestershire and Wiltshire*, Thames Valley Landscapes Monograph 31 (Oxford)

Powell, L.A., Redfern, R.C., Millard, A.R. and Gröcke, D.R. 2014: 'Infant feeding practices in Roman London: evidence from isotopic analyses', in Carroll and Graham (eds) 2014, 89–110

Powell, M.L. 1985: 'The analysis of dental wear and caries for dietary reconstruction', in R.I. Gilbert and J.H. Mielke (eds), *The Analysis of Prehistoric Diets* (Orlando), 307–88

Powlesland, D. 1998: 'The West Heslerton assessment', *Internet Archaeology* 5, http://dx.doi.org/10.11141/ia.5.4

— 2003: *25 Years of Archaeological Research on the Sands and Gravels of Heslerton* (Colchester)

—, Lyall, J., Hopkinson, G., Donoghue, D., Beck, M., Harte, A. and Stott, D. 2006: *Beneath the Sand: Remote Sensing, Archaeology, Aggregates and Sustainability: A Case Study from Heslerton, the Vale of Pickering, North Yorkshire, England*, Landscape Research Centre Report (London)

Preiss, S., Matterne, V. and Latron, F. 2005: 'An approach to funerary rituals in the Roman provinces: plant remains from a Gallo-Roman cemetery at Faulquemont (Moselle, France)', *Vegetation History and Archaeobotany* 144, 362–72

Price, E. 2000: *Frocester. A Romano-British Settlement, its Antecedents and Successors* (Stonehouse)

Price, J. 1988: 'Romano-British glass bangles from East Yorkshire', in J. Price and P. Wilson (eds), *Recent Research in Roman Yorkshire*, BAR British Series 193 (Oxford), 339–66

— 2003: 'Broken bottles and quartz sand: glass production in Yorkshire and the North in the Roman period', in P. Wilson and J. Price (eds), *Aspects of Industry in Roman Yorkshire and the North* (Oxford), 81–93

Proctor, K. 2012: *Faverdale, Darlington. Excavations at a Major Settlement in the Northern Frontier Zone of Roman Britain*, Pre-Construct Archaeology Limited Monograph 15 (London)

Prummel, W. 1997: 'Evidence of hawking (falconry) from bird and mammal bones', *International Journal of Osteoarchaeology* 7, 333–8

Pugsley, P. 2003: *Roman Domestic Wood: Analysis of the Morphology, Manufacture and Use of Selected Categories of Domestic Wooden Artefacts with Particular Reference to the Material from Roman Britain*, BAR International Series 1118 (Oxford)

Purcell, N. 1994: 'The Roman villa and the landscape of production', in E.K. Gadza (ed.), *Roman Art in the Private Sphere: New Perspectives on the Architecture and Décor of the Domus, Villa and Insula* (Michigan), 151–79

Puttock, S. 2002: *Ritual Significance of Personal Ornament in Roman Britain*, BAR British Series 327 (Oxford)

Quinnell, H. 1991: 'The villa and temple at Cosgrove, Northamptonshire', *Northamptonshire Archaeology* 23, 4–66

— 2004: *Trethurgy: Excavations at Trethurgy Round, St Austell: Community and Status in Roman and Post-Roman Cornwall* (Truro)

Rackham, J. 1998: 'Appendix 7. Environmental archaeology assessment', in J. Hunn, *Hartsfield JMI School, Baldock, Herts. Post-Excavation Assessment and Research Design*, Heritage Network, Report 50, 68–88, https://doi.org/10.5284/1021898

Rahtz, P., Hirst, S. and Wright, S.M. 2000: *Cannington Cemetery: Excavations 1962–3 of Prehistoric, Roman, Post-Roman and Later Features at Cannington Park Quarry, Near Bridgwater, Somerset*, Britannia Monograph Series 17 (London)

Raja, R. and Rüpke, J. 2015: *A Companion to the Archaeology of Religion in the Ancient World* (Oxford)

Rana, R.S., Wu, J.S. and Eisenberg, R.L. 2009: 'Periosteal reaction', *American Journal of Roentgenology* 193, 259–72

Ranson, C. 2008: *The Waste Management Park, Ely Road, Waterbeach, Cambridge: An Archaeological Excavation*, Cambridge Archaeological Unit

Rapoport, A. 1969: *House Form and Culture* (New Jersey)

Rawes, B. 1991: 'A prehistoric and Romano-British settlement at Vineyards Farm, Charlton Kings, Gloucestershire', *Transactions of the Bristol and Gloucestershire Archaeological Society* 109, 25–89

Rawlings, M. and Fitzpatrick, A.P. 1996: 'Prehistoric sites and Romano-British settlement at Butterfield Down, Amesbury', *Wiltshire Archaeology and Natural History Magazine* 89, 1–43

Ray, N. and Farley, J. 2012: *Exploratory Excavations at Bosworth Roman Temple, Leics*, School of History and Archaeology, University of Leicester

Raybould, M. 1999: *A Study of Inscribed Material from Roman Britain: An Inquiry into Some Aspects of Literacy in Romano-British Society*, BAR British Series 281 (Oxford)

RCHME 1983: 'West Park Roman Villa, Rockbourne, Hampshire', *The Archaeological Journal* 140, 129–50

Reader, R. 1974: 'New evidence for the antiquity of leprosy in early Britain', *Journal of Archaeological Science* 1, 205–7

Redfern, R. 2008: 'A bioarchaeological investigation of cultural change in Dorset, England (mid-to-late fourth century B.C. to the end of the fourth century A.D.)', *Britannia* 39, 161–91

— 2011: 'A re-appraisal of the evidence for violence in the late Iron Age human remains from Maiden Castle Hillfort, Dorset, England', *Proceedings of the Prehistoric Society* 77, 111–38

— and DeWitte, S.N. 2011a: 'A new approach to the study of Romanization in Britain: a regional perspective of cultural change in late Iron Age and Roman Dorset using the Siler and Gompertz-Makeham models of mortality', *American Journal of Physical Anthropology* 144, 269–85

— and DeWitte, S.N. 2011b: 'Status and health in Roman Dorset: the effect of status on risk of mortality in post-conquest populations', *American Journal of Physical Anthropology* 146, 197–208

— and Gowland, R.L. 2012: 'A bioarchaeological perspective on the pre-adult stages of the life course: implications for the care and health of children in the Roman Empire', in M. Harlow and L. Larsson Loven (eds), *Families in the Roman and Late Antique World* (London), 111–40

— and Roberts, C.A. 2005: 'Health in Romano-British urban communities: reflections from the cemeteries', in D.N. Smith, M.B. Brickley and W. Smith (eds), *Fertile Ground: Papers in Honour of Susan Limbey* (Oxford), 115–29

—, Hamlin, C. and Beavan-Athfield, N. 2010: 'Temporal changes in diet: a stable isotope analysis of late Iron Age and Roman Dorset, Britain', *Journal of Archaeological Science* 37, 1149–60

—, Millard, A.R. and Hamlin, C. 2012: 'A regional investigation of subadult dietary patterns and health in late Iron Age and Roman Dorset', *Journal of Archaeological Science* 39, 1249–59

—, DeWitte, S.N., Pearce, J., Hamlin, C. and Dinwiddy, K.E. 2015: 'Urban-rural differences in Roman Dorset, England: a bioarchaeological perspective on Roman settlements', *American Journal of Physical Anthropology* 157, 107–20

Reece, R. 1988: 'Interpreting coin hoards', *World Archaeology* 20(2), 261–9

— 2000: 'The Frocester cemetery and rural burial in Roman Britain', in Price 2000, 205–16

— 2002: *The Coinage of Roman Britain* (Stroud)

Rees, G. 2008: 'Enclosure boundaries and settlement individuality in the Iron Age', in O. Davis, N. Sharples and K. Waddington (eds), *Changing Perspectives on the First Millennium BC* (Oxford), 61–82

Reid, D.J. and Dean, M.C. 2000: 'Brief communication: the timing of linear enamel hypoplasias on human anterior teeth', *American Journal of Physical Anthropology* 113, 135–9

Reid, M.L. 1989: 'A room with a view: an examination of round-houses, with particular reference to northern Britain', *Oxford Journal of Archaeology* 8(1), 1–40

Reinhold, M. 2002: *Studies in Classical History and Society*, American Philological Association American Classical Studies 45 (Oxford)

Renfrew, C. 1994: 'The archaeology of religion', in C. Renfrew and E. Zubrow (eds), *The Ancient Mind. Elements of Cognitive Archaeology* (Cambridge), 47–54

Resnick, D. 2002: *Diagnosis of Bone and Joint Disorders – Vol. 3* (4th edn) (Philadelphia)

Revell, L. 2007: 'Religion and ritual in the western provinces', *Greece and Rome* 54(2), 210–28

Reynolds, A. 2001: *Newquay Sewage Treatment Scheme, Cornwall: Archaeological Mitigation*, Cornwall Archaeological Unit, Report 2001R062

Reynolds, P. 1996: 'Plant remains', in Cunliffe *et al.* 1996, 236

Richards, M.P., Hedges, R.E.M., Molleson, T.I. and Vogel, J.C. 1998: 'Stable isotope analysis reveals variations in human diet at the Poundbury Camp Cemetery Site', *Journal of Archaeological Science* 25, 1247–52

Richardson, J. 2011: 'Bronze Age cremations, Iron Age and Roman settlement and early medieval inhumations at the Langeled Receiving Facilities, Easington, East Riding of Yorkshire', *Yorkshire Archaeological Journal* 83, 59–100

— 2012: *Iron Age and Roman Settlement Activity at Newbridge Quarry, Pickering, North Yorkshire*, Archaeological Services WYAS Publication 12 (Leeds)

Richardson, T.I.L., Ball, L. and Rosenfeld, T. 2002: 'Will an orange a day keep the doctor away?', *Postgraduate Medical Journal* 78(919), 292–4

Richmond, I. and Gillam, J. 1951: 'The temple of Mithras at Carrawburgh', *Archaeologia Aeliana* 29, 1–92

Richmond, I.A. and Wright, W.P. 1948: 'Two Roman shrines to Vinotonus on Scargill Moor, near Bowes', *Yorkshire Archaeological Journal* 37, 107–16

Rielly, K. 2008: 'The Drapers Garden Bear', *London Archaeologist* 11(12), 318

— 2010: 'The black rat', in O'Connor and Sykes (eds) 2010, 134–45

Riggs, B.L., Wahner, H.W., Seeman, E., Offord, K.P., Dunn, W.L., Mazess, R.B., Johnson, K.A. and Melton, L.J. 1982: 'Changes in bone mineral density of the proximal femur and spine with aging: differences between the postmenopausal and senile osteoporosis syndromes', *Journal of Clinical Investigation* 70(4), 716–23

Rio, A. 2017: *Slavery After Rome, 500–1100* (Oxford)

Rippon, S., Smart, C. and Pears, B. 2015: *The Fields of Britannia* (Oxford)

Ritvo H. 1987: *The Animal Estate: The English and Other Creatures in the Victorian Age* (Cambridge)

Rives, J. 2000: 'Religion in the Roman world', in J. Huskinson (ed.), *Experiencing Rome: Culture, Identity and Power in the Roman Empire* (London), 245–76

— 2007: *Religion in the Roman Empire* (Oxford)

Rivet, A.L.F. 1958: *Town and Country in Roman Britain* (London)

— and Smith, C. 1979: *The Place-Names of Roman Britain* (London)

Robb, J. and Rogers, J.M. 2009: 'Human bones', in Light and Ellis 2009, 155–8

Robbins Schug, G. 2016: 'Begotten of corruption? Bioarchaeology and "othering" of leprosy in South Asia', *International Journal of Paleopathology* 15, 1–9

— and Blevins, K. 2016: 'The center cannot hold: a bioarchaeological perspective on environmental crisis in the second millennium BCE, South Asia', in G. Robbins Schug and S.R. Walimbe (eds), *A Companion to South Asia in the Past* (Chichester), 255–73

Roberts, B.W. and Vander Linden, M. 2011: 'Investigating archaeological cultures: material culture, variability and transmission', in B.W. Roberts and M. Vander Linden (eds), *Investigating Archaeological Cultures: Material Culture, Variability and Transmission* (London), 1–22

Roberts, C.A. 2000: 'Infectious disease in biocultural perspective: past, present and future work in Britain', in Cox and Mays 2000, 145–62

— 2002: 'The antiquity of leprosy in Britain: the skeletal evidence', in C.A. Roberts, M.E. Lewis and K. Manchester, *The Past and Present of Leprosy: Archaeological, Historical, Palaeopathological and Clinical Approaches*, BAR International Series 1054 (Oxford), 213–22

— 2007: 'A bioarchaeological study of maxillary sinusitis', *American Journal of Physical Anthropology* 133, 792–807

— 2011: 'The bioarchaeology of leprosy and tuberculosis – a comparative study of perceptions, stigma, diagnosis, and treatment', in S.C. Agarwal and B.A. Glencross (eds), *Social Bioarchaeology* (Chichester), 252–82

— and Buikstra, J.E. 2003: *The Bioarchaeology of Tuberculosis – A Global View on a Re-emerging Disease* (Gainesville)

— and Cox, M. 2003: *Health and Disease in Britain – From Prehistory to the Present Day* (Stroud)

— and Manchester, K. 2010: *The Archaeology of Disease* (3rd edn) (Stroud)

—, Lucy, D. and Manchester, K. 1994: 'Inflammatory lesions of ribs: an analysis of the Terry Collection', *American Journal of Physical Anthropology* 95, 169–82

—, Boylston, A., Buckley, L., Chamberlain, A.C. and Murphy, E.M. 1998a: 'Rib lesions and tuberculosis: the palaeopathological evidence', *Tuberculosis and Lung Disease* 79.1, 55–60

—, Lewis, M.E. and Boocock, P. 1998b: 'Infectious disease, sex and gender: the complexity of it all', in A. Grauer and P. Stuart-Macadam, *Sex and Gender in Paleopathological Perspective* (Cambridge), 93–113

Roberts, I. 2003: *Excavations at Topham Farm, Sykehouse, South Yorkshire. A Late Iron Age and Romano-British Settlement in the Humberhead Levels*, Archaeological Services WYAS Publications 3 (Morley)

— 2009: 'A late Iron Age and Romano-British settlement at High Wold, Bempton Lane, Bridlington, East Yorkshire', *Yorkshire Archaeological Journal* 81, 47–137

Roberts, T. 2013: *Excavation Report Nesley Farm, 2009–2011*, Archeoscan

Robertson, I. 2008: *The Roman Villa at Blacksmith's Corner, Walberton, West Sussex: An Interim Report on the 2008/2009 Excavations*, Worthing Archaeological Society

Robinson, M. 2004: 'The plant and invertebrate remains', in D. Jennings, J. Muir, S. Palmer and A. Smith, *Thornhill Farm, Fairford, Gloucestershire: An Iron Age and Roman Pastoral site in the Upper Thames Valley*, Thames Valley Landscapes Monograph 23 (Oxford), 133–46

— 2006: 'The macroscopic plant remains', in Fulford *et al.* 2006, 206–18

— 2007: 'The environmental archaeology of the Cotswold Water Park', in Miles *et al.* 2007, 204–5, 355–64

— 2011a: 'Charred and waterlogged remains', in Luke and Preece 2011, 128–34

— 2011b: 'The macroscopic plant and invertebrate remains', in Fulford and Clarke 2011, 281–93

Rodwell, W. (ed.) 1980: *Temples, Churches and Religion in Roman Britain*, BAR British Series 77 (Oxford)

Rogers, A. 2007: 'Beyond the economic in the Roman fenland: reconsidering land, water, hoards and religion', in A. Fleming and R. Hingley (eds), *The Making of the British Landscape: Fifty Years After Hoskins: Prehistoric and Roman periods* (Macclesfield), 113–30

— 2013: *Water and Roman Urbanism: Towns, Waterscapes, Land Transformation and Experience in Roman Britain* (Leiden)

Rogers, J. 2000: 'The palaeopathology of joint disease', in Cox and Mays 2000, 163–82

— and Waldron, T. 2001: 'DISH and the monastic way of life', *International Journal of Osteoarchaeology* 11, 357–65

Rohnbogner, A. 2015: *Dying Young – A Palaeopathological Analysis of Child Health in Roman Britain*, unpublished PhD thesis, University of Reading

Rohnbogner, A. and Lewis, M.E. 2016a: 'Poundbury Camp in context – a new perspective on the lives of children from urban and rural Roman England, *American Journal of Physical Anthropology* 162, doi: 10.1002/ajpa.23106

— 2016b: 'Dental caries as a measure of diet, health, and difference in non-adults from urban and rural Roman Britain', *Dental Anthropology* 29(1), 16–31

Rook, T. 1986: 'The Roman villa at Dicket Mead, Lockleys, Welwyn', *Hertfordshire Archaeology* 9, 79–175

Rose, D.S. 2016: 'Lieux de mémoire, central places, and the sanctuary of Ribemont-sur-Ancre', in Mandich *et al.* 2016, 57–75

Roskams, S., Neal, C., Richardson, J. and Leary, R. 2013: 'A late Roman well at Heslington East, York: ritual or routine practices?', *Internet Archaeology* 34, http://dx.doi.org/10.11141/ia.34.5

Ross, A. 1967: *Pagan Celtic Britain* (London)

— 1968: 'Shafts, pits, wells – sanctuaries of the Belgic Britons?', in J.M. Coles and D.D.A. Simpson (eds), *Studies in Ancient Europe* (Leicester), 255–85

Rothe, U. 2009: *Dress and Cultural Identity in the Rhine-Moselle Region of the Roman Empire*, BAR International Series 2038 (Oxford)

— 2012: 'Dress and cultural identity in the Roman Empire', in M. Harlow (ed.), *Dress and Identity*, BAR International Series 2356/IAA Interdisciplinary Series: Studies in Archaeology, History, Literature and Art 2 (Oxford), 59–68

Rottoli, M. and Castiglioni, E. 2011: 'Plant offerings from Roman cremations in northern Italy: a review', *Vegetation History and Archaeobotany* 20(5), 495–506

Roymans, N. 2004: *Ethnic Identity and Imperial Power. The Batavians in the Early Roman Empire* (Amsterdam)

Rudling, D. 1998: 'Roman villas in Sussex', *Sussex Archaeological Collections* 136, 41–65

— 2001: 'Chanctonbury Ring revisited: the excavations of 1988–91', *Sussex Archaeological Collections* 139, 75–121

— (ed.) 2008a: *Ritual Landscapes of Roman South-East Britain* (Oxford)

— 2008b: 'Roman-period temples, shrines and religion in Sussex', in Rudling 2008a, 95–137

Russell, B. 2010: 'Sarcophagi in Roman Britain', *Bollettino di Archeologia* on line Volume speciale E/

E10/2, www.archeologia.beniculturali.it/pages/pubblicazioni.html

Russell, N. 2012: *Social Zooarchaeology: Humans and Animals in Prehistory* (Cambridge)

Sage, A. and Allan, J. 2004: 'The early Roman military defences, late Roman cemetery and later features at the Topsham School, Topsham', *Proceedings of the Devon Archaeological Society* 62, 1–39

Sallares, R. 2002: *Malaria and Rome: a History of Malaria in Ancient Italy* (Oxford)

Salvadei, L., Ricci, F. and Manzi, G. 2001: 'Porotic hyperostosis as a marker of health and nutritional conditions during childhood: studies at the transition between Imperial Rome and the early Middle Ages', *American Journal of Human Biology* 13(6), 709–17

Salway, P. 1967: 'Excavations at Hockwold-cum-Wilton, Norfolk, 1961–62', *Proceedings of the Cambridge Antiquarian Society* 60, 39–80

— 1981: *Roman Britain* (Oxford)

Sanders, D. 1990: 'Behaviorable conventions and archaeology: methods for the analysis of ancient architecture', in S. Kent (ed.), *Domestic Architecture and the Use of Space* (Cambridge), 43–72

Santos, A.L. and Roberts, C.A. 2001: 'A picture of tuberculosis in young Portuguese people in the early 20th century: a multidisciplinary study of the skeletal and historical evidence', *American Journal of Physical Anthropology* 115, 38–49

Schädler, U. 2007: 'The doctor's game: new light on the history of ancient board games', in Crummy *et al.* 2007, 359–75

Scheidel, W. 2012: 'Epigraphy and demography: birth, marriage, family, and death,' in J. Davies and J. Wilkes (eds), *Epigraphy and the Historical Sciences*, Proceedings of the British Academy 177, 101–29

— and von Reden, S. (eds) 2002: *The Ancient Economy* (New York)

Schenck, R.C. and Goodnight, M.C. 1996: 'Current concept review – osteochondritis dissecans', *Journal of Bone and Joint Surgery* 78(3), 439–56

Schultz, C.E. 2016: 'Roman sacrifice, inside and out', *Journal of Roman Studies* 106, 58–76

Schultz, M. 2003: 'Light microscopic analysis in skeletal palaeopathology', in D.J. Ortner, *Identification of Pathological Conditions in Human Skeletal Remains* (2nd edn) (London), 73–107

Score, V. 2011: *Hoards, Hounds and Helmets: A Conquest-Period Ritual Site at Hallaton, Leicestershire*, Leicester Archaeology Monograph 21 (Leicester)

Scott, E. 1991: 'Animal and infant burials in Romano-British villas: a revitalization movement', in P. Garwood (ed.), *Sacred and Profane: Proceedings of a Conference on Archaeology, Ritual and Religion, Oxford*, Oxford University Committee for Archaeology Monograph 32 (Oxford), 115–21

— 1999: *The Archaeology of Infancy and Infant Death* (Oxford)

Scott, S. 2000: *Art and Society in Fourth-Century Britain: Villa Mosaics in Context*, Oxford University School of Archaeology Monograph 53 (Oxford)

— 2004: 'Elites, exhibitionism and the society of the late Roman villa', in N. Christie (ed.), *Landscapes of Change: Rural Evolution in Late Antiquity and the Early Middle Ages* (London), 39–65

Scott, S. and Duncan, C.J. 1999: 'Malnutrition, pregnancy and infant mortality: a biometric model', *Journal of Interdisciplinary History* 30, 37–60

Sealey, P.R. 2007: 'The amphoras', in Crummy *et al.* 2007, 297–305

Seetah, K. 2004: 'Meat in history – the butchery trade in the Romano-British period', *Food and History* 2(2), 19–34

— 2005: 'Butchery as a tool for understanding the changing views of animals: cattle in Roman Britain', in A. Pluskowski (ed.), *Just Skin and Bones? New Perspectives on Human-Animal Relations in the Historical Past*, BAR International Series 1410 (Oxford), 1–8

Sellen, D.W. 2007: 'Evolution of infant and young child feeding: implications for contemporary public health', *Annual Review of Nutrition* 27, 123–48

Serjeantson D. 1991: 'The bird bones', in Cunliffe and Poole 1991, 479–81

— 1998: 'Birds: a seasonal resource', *Environmental Archaeology* 3, 23–33

— 2000: 'The bird bones', in M. Fulford and J. Timby, *Late Iron Age and Roman Silchester: Excavations on the site of the Forum-Basilica 1977, 1980–86*, Britannia Monograph Series 15 (London), 484–500

— 2006: 'Animal remains', in Evans and Hodder 2006, 213–48, 288–91

— 2009: *Birds* (Cambridge)

— and Morris, J. 2011: 'Ravens and crows in Iron Age and Roman Britain', *Oxford Journal of Archaeology* 30(1), 85–107

Serpell, J. 1986: *In the Company of Animals. A Study of Human-Animal Relationships* (Oxford)

Shaffrey, R. 2015: 'Intensive milling practices in the Romano-British landscape of southern England: using newly established criteria for distinguishing millstones from rotary querns', *Britannia* 46, 55–92

Sharples, N. 1991: *Maiden Castle* (London)

— 2010: *Social Relations in Later Prehistory* (Oxford)

Shitaye, J.E., Tsegaye, W. and Pavlik, I. 2007: 'Bovine tuberculosis infection in animal and human populations in Ethiopia: a review', *Veterinari Medicina* 52, 317–32

Shotter, D. 2005: 'Salt proprietors in Cheshire. Realities and possibilities', in M. Nevell and A.P. Fielding (eds), *Brine in Britannia: Recent Archaeological Work on the Roman Salt Industry in Cheshire* (Manchester), 41–6

Silvester, R.J. 1986: 'The later prehistoric and Roman material from Kent's Cavern, Torquay', *Proceedings of Devon Archaeological Society* 44, 9–38

Simmonds, A., Anderson-Whymark, H. and Norton, A. 2011: 'Excavations at Tubney Wood Quarry, Oxfordshire, 2001–2009', *Oxoniensia* 76, 105–72

Simpson, G. and Blance, B. 1998: 'Do brooches have ritual associations?', in J. Bird (ed.), *Form and Fabric: Studies in Rome's Material Past in Honour of B.R. Hartley* (Oxford), 267–79

Sirks, B. 1993: 'Reconsidering the Roman Colonate', *Zeitschrift der Savigny-Stiftung für Rechtsgeschichte. Romanistische Abteilung* 110(1), 331–69, accessed 5 June 2017, from doi: 10.7767/zrgra.1993.110.1.331

Sirmali, M., Türüt, H., Topçu, S., Gülhan, E., Yazici, Ü., Kaya, S. and Taştepe, I. 2003: 'A comprehensive analysis of traumatic rib fractures: morbidity, mortality and management', *European Journal of Cardio-Thoracic Surgery* 24(1), 133–8

Šlaus, M. 2000: 'Biocultural analysis of sex differences in mortality profiles and stress levels in the late medieval population from Nova Raca, Croatia', *American Journal of Physical Anthropology* 111(2), 193–210

—, Cicvara-Pećina, T., Lucijanić I. and Strinović D. 2010: 'Osteochondritis dissecans of the knee in a subadult from a medieval (ninth century AD) site in Croatia', *Acta Clinica Croatica* 49(2), 189–96

Smith, A.T. 2001: *The Differential Use of Constructed Sacred Space in Southern Britain from the Late Iron Age to the Fourth Century A.D.*, BAR British Series 318 (Oxford)

— 2008: 'The fate of pagan temples in South-East Britain during the late and post-Roman period', in Rudling (ed.) 2008a, 171–90

— 2016a: 'Ritual deposition', in Millett *et al.* (eds) 2016, 641–59, doi: 10.1093/oxfordhb/9780199697731.013.035

— 2016b: 'Buildings in the countryside', in Smith *et al.* 2016, 44–74

— 2016c: 'The East', in Smith *et al.* 2016, 208–41

— 2016d: 'The Central Belt', in Smith *et al.* 2016, 141–207

— 2017: 'Rural crafts and industry', in Allen *et al.* 2017, 178–236

— and Fulford, M. 2016: 'Conclusions: the rural settlement of Roman Britain', in Smith *et al.* 2016, 385–420

—, Allen, M., Brindle, T. and Fulford, M. 2016: *The Rural Settlement of Roman Britain, New Visions of the Countryside of Roman Britain. Vol. 1*, Britannia Monograph Series 29 (London)

Smith, R.J.C., Healy, F., Allen, M.J., Morris, E.L., Barnes, I. and Woodward, P.J. 1998: *Excavations along the Route of the Dorchester By-Pass, Dorset, 1986–8*, Wessex Archaeology Report 11 (Salisbury)

Smith, W. 2011: 'Charred plant remains', in E. Biddulph and K. Welsh (eds), *Cirencester Before Corinium: Excavations at Kingshill North, Cirencester, Gloucestershire*, Oxford Archaeology Thames Valley Landscapes Monograph 34 (Oxford), 89–94

Smith-Guzmán, N.E. 2015: 'The skeletal manifestation of malaria: an epidemiological approach using documented skeletal collections', *American Journal of Physical Anthropology* 158, 624–35

Smithson, P. and Branigan, K. 1991: 'Poole's Cavern, Buxton – investigation of a Romano-British working environment', *Derbyshire Archaeological Journal* 111, 40–5

Somerville, E.M. 1997: 'The oysters', in M.G. Fulford, S. Rippon, S. Ford, J. Timby and B. Williams, 'Silchester: excavations at the North Gate, on the north walls, and in the northern suburbs 1988 and 1991–3', *Britannia* 28, 135–9

— 2005: 'Marine shell from the late Iron Age ditch', in J. Manley and D. Rudkin, 'A pre-AD 43 ditch at Fishbourne Roman Palace, Chichester', *Britannia* 36, 91

Somerville, E.M. and Bonell, J. 2005: 'Marine shell', in J. Manley and D. Rudkin, 'Facing the Palace: excavations in front of Fishbourne Roman palace (Sussex, UK) 1995–99', *Sussex Archaeological Collections* 141, 123–4

— 2006: 'The marine shell', in J. Manley and D. Rudkin, 'More buildings facing the Palace', *Sussex Archaeological Collections* 144, 94–7

Soren, D. 2003: 'Can archaeologists excavate evidence of malaria?', *World Archaeology* 35(2), 193–209

Southwell-Wright, W. 2014: 'Perceptions of infant disability in Roman Britain', in Carroll and Graham (eds) 2014, 111–30

Sparey-Green, C. 1989: 'The early Christian cemetery at Poundbury', in *Actes du XIe congrès international d'archéologie chrétienne, Lyon, Vienne, Grenoble, Genève, Aoste, 21–28 septembre 1986*, Publications de l'École française de Rome, 123 (Rome), 2073–5

— 2003: 'Where are the Christians? Late Roman cemeteries in Britain', in M. Carver (ed.), *The Cross Goes North: Processes of Conversion in Northern Europe, AD 300–1300* (Woodbridge), 93–107

Sprague, R. 2005: *Burial Terminology: A Guide for Researchers* (Lanham, MD)

Sreebny, L.M. 1983: 'Sugar and human dental caries', *World Review of Nutrition and Diet* 40, 19–65

Stallibrass, S. 2002: 'An overview of the animal bones: what would we like to know, what do we know so far, and where do we go from here?', in P.R. Wilson, *Cataractonium: Roman Catterick and its Hinterland. Excavations and Research 1958–1997, Part 2*, CBA Research Report 129 (York), 392–438

— 2009: 'The way to a Roman soldier's heart: a post-medieval model for cattle droving to the Hadrian's Wall area', in M. Driessen, S. Heeren, J. Hendriks, F. Kemmers and R. Visser (eds), *TRAC 2008: Proceedings of the Eighteenth Annual Theoretical Roman Archaeology Conference, Amsterdam 2008* (Oxford), 101–12

Stamatis, C., Suchentrunk, F., Moutou, K.A., Giacometti, M., Haerer, G., Djan, M., Vapa, L., Vukovic, M., Tvrtković, N., Sert, H., Alves, P.C. and Mamuris, Z. 2009: 'Phylogeography of the brown hare (*Lepus europaeus*) in Europe: a legacy of south-eastern Mediterranean refugia?', *Journal of Biogeography* 36(3), 515–28

Stamper, J.W. 2005: *The Architecture of Roman Temples: The Republic to the Middle Empire* (Cambridge)

Stanford, S.C. 1974: *Croft Ambrey* (Hereford)

— 1981: *Midsummer Hill: An Iron Age hillfort in the Malverns* (Malvern)

Stansbie, D., Smith, A., Laws, G. and Haines, T. 2008: 'Excavation of Iron-Age and Roman occupation at Coln Gravel, Thornhill Farm, Fairford, Gloucestershire, 2003 and 2004', *Transactions of the Bristol and Gloucestershire Archaeological Society* 126, 31–81

Stant, M.Y. and Metcalfe, C.R. 1977: 'Seeds and other plant debris', in P.A. Rahtz and E. Greenfield (eds), *Excavations at Chew Valley Lake Somerset*, Department of the Environmental Archaeological Reports 8 (London), 372–3

Stark, R.J. 2014: 'A proposed framework for the study of paleopathological cases of subadult scurvy', *International Journal of Palaeopathology* 5, 18–26

Starr, R.J. 1992: 'Sylvia's Deer (Vergil, Aeneid 7.479–502): game parks and Roman law', *The American Journal of Philology* 113, 435–9

Statton, M. 2012: 'Mackreth, D. 2011. Brooches in Late Iron Age and Roman Britain', *Papers from the Institute of Archaeology* 21, 106–9, doi: http://doi.org/10.5334/pia.384

Stead, I.M. 1988: 'Chalk figurines of the Parisi', *The Antiquaries Journal* 68(1), 9–29

— 1991: *Iron Age Cemeteries in East Yorkshire* (London)

— 1998: *The Salisbury Hoard* (London)

Stead, I.M. and Rigby, V. 1986: *Baldock: the Excavation of a Roman and Pre-Roman Settlement, 1968–72*, Britannia Monograph Series 7 (London)

— 1989: *Verulamium: the King Harry Lane Site*, English Heritage Archaeology Report 12 (London)

Stead, W.W. 2000: 'What's in a name: confusion of *Mycobacterium tuberculosis* and *Mycobacterium bovis* in ancient DNA analysis', *Palaeopathology Association Newsletter* 110, 13–16

Steckel, R.H. 2005: 'Young adult mortality following severe physiological stress in childhood: the evidence', *Economics and Human Biology* 3(2), 314–28

Steele, P. 2012: *Llyn Cerrig Bach: Treasure from the Iron Age* (Anglesey)

Stephens, J. 2008: 'Ancient Roman hairdressing: on (hair)pins and needles', *Journal of Roman Archaeology* 21, 110–32

Stevens, C. 2008: 'Environment and agricultural economy', in Powell *et al.* 2008, 457–60

— 2011: 'Charred plant remains from Springhead', in Barnett *et al.* 2011, 95–105

Stevens, E.E., Patrick, T.E. and Pickler, R. 2009: 'A history of infant feeding', *Journal of Perinatal Education* 18(2), 32–9

Stevenson, R.B.K. 1956: 'Native bangles and Roman glass', *Proceedings of the Society of Antiquaries of Scotland* 88, 208–21

— 1976: 'Romano-British glass bangles', *Glasgow Archaeological Journal* 4, 45–54

Stock, S.R. 1991: 'Workplace ergonomic factors and the development of musculoskeletal disorders of the neck and upper limbs: a meta-analysis', *American Journal of Industrial Medicine* 19(1), 87–107

Stoertz, C. 1997: *Ancient Landscapes of the Yorkshire Wolds: Aerial Photographic Transcription and Analysis* (London)

Strid, L. 2011: 'Section 11: mammal and bird bones', in B. Ford and S. Teague, *Winchester, A City in the Making: Archaeological Excavations Between 2002–2007 on the Sites of Northgate House, Staple Gardens and the Former Winchester Library, Jewry St*, Oxford Archaeology Monograph 12 (Oxford), https://library.thehumanjourney.net/663/1/Animal_Bone_Report.pdfA.pdf

— 2015: 'Animal bone', in Andrews *et al.* 2015, 433–80

Strück, M. 2000: 'High status burials in Roman Britain (first–third century AD) – potential interpretation', in Pearce *et al.* (eds) 2000, 85–96

Summer, G. and D'Amato, R. 2009: *Arms and Armour of the Imperial Roman Soldier: From Marius to Commodus* (Barnsley)

Sutter, R.C. 2003: 'Nonmetric subadult skeletal sexing traits: I. A blind test of the accuracy of eight previously proposed methods using prehistoric known-sex mummies from northern Chile', *Journal of Forensic Science* 48(5), 1–9

Swift, E. 2017: *Roman Artefacts and Society* (Oxford)

Swishers, A. and Lauwers, J. 2011: *Counselling the Nursing Mother: A Lactation Consultant's Guide* (Sudbury)

Sykes, N.J. 2004: 'The introduction of fallow deer (*Dama dama*): a zooarchaeological perspective', *Environmental Archaeology* 9, 75–83

— 2005: 'The animal remains', in J. Manley and D. Rudkin, 'A pre-AD 43 ditch at Fishbourne Roman Palace, Chichester', *Britannia* 36, 84

— 2007: 'Animal bone' in Miles *et al.* 2007, 53–4, 84–5, 151–3, 203–4

— 2009: 'Worldviews in transition: the impact of exotic plants and animals on Iron Age/Romano-British landscapes', *Landscapes* 10(2), 19–36

— 2010: 'Fallow deer', in O'Connor and Sykes (eds) 2010, 51–8

— 2012: 'A social perspective on the introduction of exotic animals: the case of the chicken', *World Archaeology* 44(1), 158–69

— 2014: *Beastly Questions: Animal Answers to Archaeological Questions* (London)

— and Curl J. 2010: 'The rabbit', in O'Connor and Sykes (eds) 2010, 116–26

—, White, J. Hayes, T. and Palmer, M. 2006: 'Tracking animals using strontium isotopes in teeth: the role of fallow deer (*Dama dama*) in Roman Britain', *Antiquity* 80, 948–59

—, Baker, K.H., Carden, R.F., Higham, T.F.G., Hoelzel, A.R. and Stevens, R.E. 2011: 'New evidence for the establishment and management of the European fallow deer (*Dama dama dama*) in Roman Britain', *Journal of Archaeological Science* 38(1), 156–65

Symons, M. 2002: 'Cutting up cultures', *Journal of Historical Sociology* 15(4), 431–50

Tabor, R. 2002: 'Sigwells, Charlton Horethorne: the identification, interpretation and testing of Bronze Age to Early Medieval landscapes by geophysical survey and excavation', *Proceedings of Somerset Archaeology and Natural History* 144, 1–24

Tabor, J.L. 2009: 'Romano-British remains at Burton Fleming', *East Riding Archaeologist* 12, 87–96

Taylor, A. 2008: 'Aspects of deviant burial in Roman Britain', in E.M. Murphy (ed.), *Deviant Burial in the Archaeological Record* (Oxford), 91–114

Taylor, J. 2001: 'Rural society in Roman Britain', in James and Millett (eds) 2001, 46–59

— 2013: 'Encountering Romanitas: characterising the role of agricultural communities in Roman Britain', *Britannia* 44, 171–90

Taylor, S.R. 2012: 'Excavations of a Roman and post-Roman site at Penlee House, Tregony: a cremation burial and other burning issues', *Cornish Archaeology* 51, 125–63

Temkin, O. 1991: *Soranus' Gynecology* (Baltimore)

Tester, A. 1993: *R.A.F. Lakenheath Industrial Maintenance Workshop. Archaeological Excavation Report*, Suffolk County Council Archaeological Services Report 93/46

Thacher, T.D., Fischer, P.R., Strand, M.A. and Pettifor, J.M. 2006: 'Nutritional rickets around the world:

causes and future directions', *Paediatrics and International Child Health* 26(1), 1–16

Thatcher, C., Popescu, E. and Hounsell, D. 2014: 'Excavations along the Hardwick to Marsh Gibbon Pipeline: an Iron Age to Roman landscape', *Records of Buckinghamshire* 54, 1–60

Thomas, A., Holbrook, N. and Bateman, C. 2003: *Late Prehistoric and Romano-British Burial and Settlement at Hucclecote, Gloucestershire. Excavations in advance of the Gloucester Business Park Link Road, 1998*, Bristol and Gloucestershire Archaeological Report 2 (Kemble)

Thomas, R. 2005: 'Zooarchaeology, improvement and the British Agricultural Revolution', *International Journal of Historical Archaeology* 9(2), 71–88

— and Wilson, A. 1994: 'Water supply for Roman farms in Latium and South Etruria', *Papers of the British School at Rome* 62, 139–96

Thomas, S. 2016: 'From treasured items to trash? The use of brooches in Roman Cornwall in the creation of identity and social memory', in Mandich *et al.* 2016, 111–24

Thorne, A. 2009: 'A Roman cremation cemetery at 11–15 Offington Lane, Worthing, West Sussex', *Sussex Archaeological Collections* 147, 37–49

Threipland, L.M. 1956: 'An excavation at St Mawgan-in-Pyder, North Cornwall', *The Archaeological Journal* 113, 33–80

Thurston, T. 2009: 'Unity and diversity in the European Iron Age: out of the mists, some clarity?', *Journal of Archaeological Research* 17(4), 347–423

Tibbetts, B. 2008: 'Infant burials in Iron Age Britain', in K. Bacvarov (ed.), *Babies Reborn: Infant/Child Burials in Pre- and Protohistory*, BAR International Series 1832 (Oxford), 189–94

Timberlake, S., Dodwell, N. and Armour, N. 2007: *The Roman Cemetery, The Babraham Institute, Cambridgeshire. An Archaeological Excavation*, Cambridge Archaeological Unit Rep. 754

Timby, J. 1998: *Excavations at Kingscote and Wycomb, Gloucestershire* (Kemble)

— 2017: 'What's on the table? A review of Roman pottery in the Western Central Belt', in Allen *et al.* 2017, 305–36

—, Brown, R., Biddulph, E., Hardy, A. and Powell, A. 2007a: *A Slice of Rural Essex: Archaeological Discoveries from the A120 Between Stansted Airport and Braintree*, Oxford-Wessex Monograph 1 (Oxford/Salisbury)

—, Brown, R., Hardy, A., Leech, S., Poole, C. and Webley, L. 2007b: *A421: Archaeology along the Great Barford Bypass, Oxford Archaeology*, Bedfordshire Archaeology Monograph 8 (Oxford)

Todd, M. 1981: *Roman Britain (55 BC–AD 400)* (1st edn) (London)

— (ed.) 2004: *A Companion to Roman Britain* (Oxford)

Todd, N.B. 1978: 'An ecological, behavioural genetic model for the domestication of the cat', *Carnivore* 1, 52–60

Toller, H. 1977: *Roman Lead Coffins and Ossuaria in Britain*, BAR British Series 38 (Oxford)

Tomlin, R.S.O. 1988: 'The curse tablets', in Cunliffe 1988b, 59–280

— 1993: 'The inscribed lead tablets: an interim report', in Woodward and Leach 1993, 113–30

— 2002: 'Writing to the gods in Britain', in A.E. Cooley (ed.), *Becoming Roman, Writing Latin? Literacy and Epigraphy in the Roman West*, Journal of Roman Archaeology Supplementary Series 48 (Portsmouth, RI), 151–79

— 2003: '"The girl in question": a new text from Roman London', *Britannia* 34, 41–51

— 2008: 'Dea Senuna: a new goddess from Britain', in M. Hainzmann and R. Wedenig (eds), *Instrumenta Inscripta Latina II: Akten des 2. Internationalen Kolloquiums, Klagenfurt, 5.–8. Mai 2005* (Klagenfurt), Band 36, 305–15

— 2009: 'The lead sheets', in Lawrence and Smith 2009, 213

— 2011: 'Writing and communication', in Allason-Jones 2011a, 133–52

— 2016: *Roman London's First Voices: Writing Tablets from the Bloomberg Excavations, 2010–14* (London)

Tomlinson, R.A. 1976: *Greek Sanctuaries* (London)

Toner, J.P. 1995: *Leisure and Ancient Rome* (Cambridge)

— 2009: *Popular Culture in Ancient Rome* (Cambridge)

Toynbee, J.M.C. 1971: *Death and Burial in the Roman World* (London)

— 1973: *Animals in Roman Life and Art* (London)

— 1996: *Death and Burial in the Roman World* (new edn) (Baltimore)

Tracey, J. 2012: 'New evidence for Iron Age burial and propitiation practices in southern Britain', *Oxford Journal of Archaeology* 31(4), 367–79

Trevarthen, M. 2008: *Suburban Life in Roman Durnovaria: Excavations at the Former County Hospital Site, Dorchester, Dorset, 2000–2001* (Salisbury)

— 2015: *Excavation of Later Prehistoric Remains and a Roman Cemetery at East Hill, Dartford, 2006*, Wessex Archaeology, http://www.kentarchaeology.org. uk/10/011.pdf#sthash.wLLe0pON.dpuf

Tuck, S. 2005: 'The origins of imperial hunting imagery: Domitian and the redefinition of *Virtus* under the Principate', *Greece and Rome* 52.2, 221–45

Tucker, K. 2015: *An Archaeological Study of Human Decapitation Burials* (Barnsley)

Turgut, M. 2001: 'Spinal tuberculosis (Pott's disease): its clinical presentation, surgical management, and outcome: a survey study on 694 patients', *Neurosurgical Review* 24, 8–13

Turner, R. 1990: 'A Romano-British cemetery at Lanchester', *Archaeologia Aeliana* 18, 63–77

— 1999: *Excavations of an Iron Age Settlement and Roman Religious Complex at Ivy Chimneys, Witham, Essex 1978–83*, East Anglian Archaeology 88 (Chelmsford)

Turner, S.C. 2003: *Christianity and the Landscape of Early Medieval South-West Britain*, unpublished PhD thesis, University of York, http://etheses.whiterose. ac.uk/9848/78/411475_vol1.pdf

Twiss, K. 2007: 'We are what we eat', in K. Twiss (ed.), *The Archaeology of Food and Identity*, Center for Archaeological Investigations Occasional Paper 34 (Illinois), 1–15

— 2012: 'The archaeology of food and social diversity', *Journal of Archaeological Research* 20(4), 357–95

Tyacke, A., Bayley, J. and Butcher, S. 2011: 'Romano-British brooches – of Cornish origin?', in S. Pearce (ed.), *Recent Archaeological Work in South-Western Britain: Papers in Honour of Henrietta Quinnell*, BAR British Series 548 (Oxford), 139–49

Tyers, P. 1996: *Roman Pottery in Britain* (London)

Upex, S. 1994: *Excavations at a Roman and Saxon site at Haddon, Cambridgeshire, 1992–1993*, Nene Valley Research Committee (Northampton)

— 2011: 'The Praetorium of Edmund Artis: a summary of excavations and surveys of the palatial Roman structure at Castor, Cambridgeshire 1828–2008', *Britannia* 42, 23–112

Urnaa, V., Kizuki, M., Nakamuro, K., Kaneko, A., Inose, T., Seino, K. and Takano, T. 2006: 'Association of swaddling, rickets onset and bone properties in children in Ulaanbaatar, Mongolia', *Public Health* 120(9), 834–40

Valentin, J. and Robinson, S. 2002: 'Excavations in 1999 on land adjacent to Wayside Farm, Nurseed Road, Devizes', *Wiltshire Archaeology and Natural History Magazine* 95, 147–213

Van der Veen, M. 2007a: 'Formation processes of desiccated and carbonized plant remains – the identification of routine practice', *Journal of Archaeological Science* 34(6), 968–90

— 2007b: 'Food as an instrument of social change', in K. Twiss (ed.), *The Archaeology of Food and Identity*, Center for Archaeological Investigations Occasional Paper 34 (Illinois), 112–29

— 2008: 'Food as embodied material culture: diversity and change in plant food consumption in Roman Britain', *Journal of Roman Archaeology* 21, 83–109

—, Livarda, A. and Hill, A. 2007: 'The archaeobotany of Roman Britain: current state and identification of research priorities', *Britannia* 38, 181–210

—, Livarda, A. and Hill, A. 2008: 'New plant foods in Roman Britain — dispersal and social access', *Environmental Archaeology* 13(1), 11–36

van Driel-Murray, C. 1999: 'And did those feet in ancient time… Feet and shoes as a material projection of the self', in P. Baker, C. Forcey, S. Jundi and R. Witcher (eds), *TRAC 98. Proceedings of the Eighth Annual Theoretical Roman Archaeology Conference Leicester 1998* (Oxford), 131–40

Van Sleuwen, B.E., Engelberts, A.C., Boere-Boonekamp, M.M., Kuis, W., Schulpen, T.W.J. and L'Hoir, M.P. 2007: 'Swaddling: a systematic review', *Pediatrics* 120(4), 1097–106

Varner, G.R. 2009: *Sacred Wells: A Study in the History, Meaning, and Mythology of Holy Wells* (New York)

Vatcher, F. de M. 1963: 'The excavation of the Roman earthwork at Winterslow, Wilts.', *Antiquaries Journal* 43, 197–213

Venclova, N. 1993: 'Celtic shrines in Europe: a sceptical approach', *Oxford Journal of Archaeology* 12, 55–65

Veselka, B., Hoogland, M.L.P. and Waters-Rist, A.L. 2013: 'Rural rickets: Vitamin D deficiency in a post-medieval farming community from the Netherlands', *International Journal of Osteoarchaeology* 25, doi: 10.1002/oa.2329

Vögele, J.P. 1994: 'Urban infant mortality in Imperial Germany', *Social History of Medicine* 7, 401–26

Waddelove, A.C. and Waddelove, E. 1985: 'Roman roads in Delamere Forest and neighbourhood: a century after Edward Kirk', *Transactions of the Lancashire and Cheshire Antiquarian Society* 83, 161–85

Wagner, C.L. and Greer F.R. 2008: 'Prevention of rickets and vitamin D deficiency in infants, children, and adolescents', *Pediatrics* 122(5), 1142–52

Wainwright, G.J. 1967: *Coygan Camp. A Prehistoric, Romano-British and Dark Age Settlement in Carmarthenshire* (Cardiff)

— 1979: *Gussage All Saints: an Iron Age Settlement in Dorset*, Department of the Environment Archaeological Reports 10 (London)

— and Davies, S.M. 1995: *Balksbury Camp, Hampshire: Excavations 1973 and 1981*, English Heritage Archaeological Report 4 (London)

Wainwright, J. 2010: *Archaeological Investigations at West Mercia Police HQ, Hindlip, Worcestershire*, Worcestershire Archaeology Service Report 1755, https://doi.org/10.5284/1017994

Wait, G.A. 1985: *Ritual and Religion in Iron Age Britain*, BAR British Series 149 (Oxford)

Waldron, H.A. 1989: *The Human Remains from Alington Avenue*, unpublished report

— 1991a: 'Variations in the prevalence of spondylolysis in early British populations', *Journal of the Royal Society of Medicine* 84.9, 547–9

— 1991b: 'The prevalence of, and the relationship between some spinal diseases in a human skeletal population from London', *International Journal of Osteoarchaeology* 1(2), 103–10

Walker, P.L. 1995: 'Problems of preservation and sexism in sexing: some lessons from historical collections for palaeodemographics', in S. Saunders and A. Herring (eds), *Grave Reflections: Portraying the Past through Cemetery Studies* (Toronto), 31–47

— 2005: 'Greater sciatic notch morphology: sex, age and population differences', *American Journal of Physical anthropology* 127, 385–91

—, Bathurst, R.R., Richman, R., Gjerdrum, T. and Andrushko, V.A. 2009: 'The causes of porotic hyperostosis and cribra orbitalia: a reappraisal of the iron-deficiency-anemia hypothesis', *American Journal of Physical Anthropology* 139, 109–25

Wallace, L. 2014: *The Origins of Roman London* (Cambridge)

Wallis, H. 2011: *Romano-British and Saxon Occupation at Billingford, Central Norfolk. Excavation (1991–2 and 1997) and Watching Brief (1995–2002)*, East Anglian Archaeology 135 (Dereham)

Walton, P. 2016: 'Is the Piercebridge assemblage a military votive deposit?', in X.P. Jensen and T. Grane (eds), *Imitation and Inspiration. Proceedings of the 18th International Roman Military Equipment Conference held in Copenhagen, Denmark, 9th–14th June 2013*, Journal of Roman Military Equipment Studies 17, 191–4

Ward, M. 1998: 'Some finds from the Roman works-depot at Holt', *Studia Celtica* 32, 43–84

Watts, D. 1991: *Christians and Pagans in Roman Britain* (London)

— 1998: *Religion in Late Roman Britain: Forces of Change* (London)

— 2005: *Boudicca's Heirs: Women in Early Britain* (London)

Watts, R. 2015: 'The long-term impact of developmental stress. Evidence from later medieval and post-medieval London (AD 1117–1853)', *American Journal of Physical Anthropology* 158, 569–80

Webb, H. forthcoming: *Itter Crescent, Peterborough, Cambridgeshire (PETITC11), Specialist Report on the Human Remains*, Oxford Archaeology

Webster, G. 1981: 'Further light on the Roman site at Greensforge', *Transactions of the Birmingham and Warwickshire Archaeological Society* 91, 126–32

— 1986: *The British Celts and their Gods under Rome* (London)

Webster, J. 1992: *The Identification of Ritual in the Later Iron Age, with specific reference to selected themes in proto-historic Gaul and Britain*, unpublished PhD thesis, University of Edinburgh

— 1995a: 'Translation and subjection: interpretation and the Celtic gods', in J.D. Hill and C.G. Cumberpatch (eds), *Different Iron Ages: Studies on the Iron Age in Temperate Europe*, BAR International Series 602 (Oxford), 175–84

— 1995b: 'Sanctuaries and sacred places', in M. Green (ed.), *The Celtic World* (London), 445–64

— 1997: 'Text expectations: the archaeology of "Celtic" ritual wells and shafts', in Gwilt and Haselgrove (eds), 134–44

— 2001: 'Creolizing the Roman Provinces', *American Journal of Archaeology*, 105(2), 209–25

— 2005: 'Archaeologies of slavery and servitude: bringing "New World" perspectives to Roman Britain', *Journal of Roman Archaeology* 18, 161–79

Wedlake, W.J. 1982: *The Excavation of the Shrine at Nettleton, Wiltshire, 1956–1971*, Reports of the Research Committee of the Society of Antiquaries of London 40 (London)

Weekes, J. 2008: 'Classification and analysis of archaeological contexts for the reconstruction of early Romano-British cremation funerals', *Britannia* 39, 145–60

— 2011: 'A review of Canterbury's Romano-British cemeteries', *Archaeologia Cantiana* 131, 23–42

— 2016: 'Cemeteries and funerary practice', in Millett *et al.* (eds) 2016, 425–47, doi: 10.1093/oxfordhb/9780199697713.013.025

Weiss, E. and Jurmain, R. 2007: 'Osteoarthritis revisited: a contemporary review of aetiology', *International Journal of Osteoarchaeology* 17(5), 437–50

Weiss-Krejci, E. 2013: 'The unburied dead', in Nilsson Stutz and Tarlow (eds) 2013, 281–302, doi: 10.1093/oxfordhb/9780199569069.013.0016

Wells, C. 1982: 'The human burials', in D. McWhirr, L. Viner and C. Wells, *Romano-British Cemeteries at Cirencester*, Cirencester Excavations 2 (Cirencester), 135–202

Wenaden, A.E.T., Szyszko, T.A. and Saifuddin, A. 2005: 'Imaging of periosteal reactions associated with focal lesions of bone', *Clinical Radiology* 60(4), 439–56

Wessex Archaeology, 2002: *A303 Stonehenge Archaeological Surveys. Archaeological Evaluation Report: Area C1. Salisbury*, Wessex Archaeology Report 50157.01

— 2008a: *Boscombe Down Phase VI Excavation, Amesbury, Wiltshire, 2006–7. Interim Assessment on the Results of the Byway 20 Romano-British Cemetery Excavations*, Wessex Archaeology Report 56246.04

— 2008b: *Binchester Roman Fort, County Durham. Archaeological Evaluation and Assessment of Results*, Wessex Archaeology Report 65302.01

— 2008c: *Lellizzick, near Padstow, Cornwall: Archaeological Evaluation and Assessment of Results*, Wessex Archaeology Report 65312.01

— 2010: *Litlington, Cambridgeshire. Archaeological Evaluation and Assessment of Results*, Wessex Archaeology Report 71511

Westell, W.P. 1931: 'A Romano-British cemetery at Baldock, Herts', *The Archaeological Journal* 88, 24–301

Weston, D.A. 2008: 'Investigating the specificity of periosteal reactions in pathology museum specimens', *American Journal of Physical Anthropology* 137, 48–59

Wheeler, M. 1943: *Maiden Castle, Dorset*, Reports of the Research Committee of the Society of Antiquaries of London (London)

Wheeler, R.E.M and Wheeler, T.V. 1932: *Report on the Excavation of the Prehistoric, Roman and Post-Roman Site at Lydney Park, Gloucestershire*, Reports of the Research Committee of the Society of Antiquaries of London 9 (London)

— 1936: *Verulamium. A Belgic and Two Roman Cities*, Reports of the Research Committee of the Society of Antiquaries of London 11 (London)

Whimster, R. 1977: 'Harlyn Bay reconsidered: the excavations of 1900–1905 in the light of recent work', *Cornish Archaeology* 16, 61–88

— 1981: *Burial Practices in Iron Age Britain*, BAR British Series 90 (Oxford)

White, J.D. 1997: 'Dental calculus: recent insights into occurrence, formation, prevention, removal and oral health effects of supragingival and subgingival deposits', *European Journal of Oral Sciences* 105(5), 508–22

White, R. and Barker, P. 2000: *Wroxeter: Life and Death of a Roman City* (Stroud)

—, Gaffney, C. and Gaffney, V.L. 2013: *Wroxeter, the Cornovii and the Urban Process* (Oxford)

White, S.I. and Smith, G. 1999: 'A funerary and ceremonial centre at Capel Eithin, Gaerwen, Anglesey: excavations of Neolithic, Bronze Age, Roman and early medieval features in 1980 and 1981', *Transactions of the Anglesey Antiquarian Society*, 9–166

Whitehouse, R.D. 1996: 'Ritual objects. Archaeological joke or neglected evidence?', in J. Wilkins (ed.), *Approaches to the Study of Ritual: Italy and the Ancient Mediterranean* (London), 9–30

Whiting, W., Hawley, W. and May, T. 1931: *Report on the Excavation of the Roman Cemetery at Ospringe, Kent*, Reports of the Research Committee of the Society of Antiquaries of London 8 (London)

Whittaker, C.R. 1997: 'Imperialism and culture: the Roman initiative', in D.J. Mattingly and S.E. Alcock (eds), *Dialogues in Roman Imperialism: Power, Discourse, and Discrepant Experience in the Roman Empire*, Journal of Roman Archaeology Supplementary Series 23 (Portsmouth, RI), 143–63

— and Garnsey, P. 1997: 'Rural life in the later Roman Empire', in A. Cameron and P. Garnsey (eds), *The*

Cambridge Ancient History 13. The Late Empire, AD 337–425 (Cambridge), 277–311

Wickenden, N.P. 1992: *The Temple and other Sites in the North-Eastern Sector of Caesaromagus*, CBA Research Report 75 (York)

Wickham C. 1994: *Land and Power; Studies in Italian and European Social History, 400–1200* (London)

Wild, J.P. 1968: 'Clothing in the north-west provinces of the Roman Empire', *Bonner Jahrbucher* 168, 166–240

— 2002: 'The textile industries of Roman Britain', *Britannia* 33, 1–42

Wileman, J. 2005: *Hide and Seek – The Archaeology of Childhood* (Stroud)

Wilkes, J. 2005: 'The Roman Danube: an archaeological survey', *Journal of Roman Studies* 95, 124–225

Wilkinson, L. 1993: 'Brucellosis', in K. Kiple (ed.), *The Cambridge World History of Human Disease* (Cambridge), 625–8

Wilkinson, P. 2009: *An Archaeological Investigation of the Roman Octagonal Bath-House at Bax Farm, Teynham, Kent 2006 and 2009*, Kent Archaeological Field School (Faversham)

— 2013: *The Roman Religious Sanctuary at 'Blacklands', School Farm, Graveney Road, Faversham, Kent*, Kent Archaeological Field School (Faversham)

Willerslev, R. 2004: 'Not animal, not not-animal: hunting, imitation and empathetic knowledge among Siberian Yukaghirs', *Journal of the Royal Anthropological Institute* 10(3), 629–52

Williams, H.M.R. 1998: 'The ancient monument in Romano-British ritual practices' in C. Forcey, J. Hawthorne, and R. Witcher (eds), *TRAC 97 Proceedings of the Seventh Annual Theoretical Roman Archaeology Conference* (Oxford), 71–86

— 2004: 'Potted histories: cremation, ceramics and social memory in early Roman Britain', *Oxford Journal of Archaeology* 23(4), 417–27

— 2007: 'Introduction: themes in the archaeology of early medieval death and burial', in S. Semple and H. Williams (eds), *Early Medieval Mortuary Practices: Anglo-Saxon Studies in Archaeology and History 14* (Oxford), 1–11

— 2013: 'Death, memory, and material culture: catalytic commemoration and the cremated Dead', in Nilsson Stutz and Tarlow (eds) 2013, 195–208, doi: 10.1093/oxfordhb/9780199569069. 013.0011

Williams, M. 2003: 'Growing metaphors: the agricultural cycle as metaphor in the later prehistoric period of Britain and north-western Europe', *Journal of Social Archaeology* 3(2), 223–55

Williams, M. and Reid, M. 2008: *Salt: Life and Industry: Excavations at King Street, Middlewich, Cheshire, 2001–2002*, BAR British Series 456 (Oxford)

Williams, R.J. and Zeepvat, R.J. 1994: *Bancroft. A Late Bronze Age/Iron Age Settlement, Roman Villa and Temple-Mausoleum*, Buckinghamshire Archaeological Society Monograph 7 (Milton Keynes)

Willis, S. 1998: 'Samian pottery in Britain: exploring its distribution and archaeological potential', *The Archaeological Journal* 155, 82–133

— 2005: 'The context of writing and written records in ink: the archaeology of samian inkwells in Roman Britain', *The Archaeological Journal* 162, 96–145

— 2007: 'Sea, coast, estuary, land and culture in Iron Age Britain', in Haselgrove and Moore (eds) 2007, 107–29

— 2011: 'Samian ware and society in Roman Britain and beyond', *Britannia* 42, 167–242

— 2013a: 'Red from the green field: samian ware at villas and other rural sites in Roman Britain. An examination of site evidence and general trends', in M. Fulford and E. Durham (eds), *Seeing Red: New Economic and Social Perspectives on Terra Sigillata*, Bulletin of the Institute of Classical Studies Supplement 102 (London), 224–41

— 2013b: *The Roman Roadside Settlement and Multi-Period Ritual Complex at Nettleton and Rothwell, Lincolnshire: The Central Lincolnshire Wolds Research Project. Vol. 1* (London)

Wilmott, T. 2008: *The Roman Amphitheatre in Britain* (Stroud)

— 2010: 'Birdoswald Roman cemetery', *English Heritage Research News* 14, 16–19, https://content.historicengland.org.uk/images-books/publications/research-news-14/researchnews14.pdf/

Wilson, B. 1986: 'Faunal remains: animals and marine shells', in Miles 1986, microfiche ch. VI

— 1999: 'Displayed or concealed? Cross cultural evidence for symbolic and ritual activity depositing Iron Age animal bones', *Oxford Journal of Archaeology* 18(3), 297–305

Wilson, D.R. 1975: 'Romano-Celtic temple architecture', *Journal of the Roman Archaeological Association* 38 (3rd series), 3–27

— 2004: 'The North Leigh Roman villa: its plan reviewed', *Britannia* 35, 77–113

—, Bagnall, A. and Taylor, B. 2014: *Report on the Excavation of a Romano-British Site at Wortley, South Gloucestershire*, BAR British Series 591 (Oxford)

Wilson, R. 1990: *Sicily under the Roman Empire: The Archaeology of a Roman Province, 36 BC–AD 535* (Warminster)

Winder, J.M. 1992: *A Study in the Variation of Oyster Shells from Archaeological Sites and a Discussion of Oyster Exploitation*, unpublished PhD thesis, University of Southampton

Wintle, W.A. 2013: *Becoming Romano-British: The Landscape of the Late Prehistoric and Romano-British Periods in the Vale of the White Horse*, unpublished DPhil thesis, University of Oxford

Winton, H. 2001: 'A possible Roman small town at Sansom's Platt, Tackley, Oxon', *Britannia* 32, 304–9

Witcher, R. 2013: 'On Rome's ecological contribution to British flora and fauna: landscape, legacy and identity', *Landscape History* 34(2), 5–26

Wolch, J. and Emel, J. (eds) 1998: *Animal Geographies: Place, Politics and Identity in the Nature-Culture Borderlands* (London)

Wood, J.W., Milner, G.R., Harpending, H.C. and Weiss, K.M. 1992: 'The osteological paradox-problems of inferring prehistoric health from skeletal samples', *Current Anthropology* 33(4), 343–70

Woodfield, C. and Johnson, C. 1989: 'A Roman site at Stanton Low, on the Great Ouse, Buckinghamshire', *The Archaeological Journal* 146, 135–278

Woodward, A. 1992: *Shrines and Sacrifice* (London)

— 1993: 'Part 3: Discussion', in Farwell and Molleson 1993, 215–39

— and Leach, P. 1993: *The Uley Shrines: Excavation of a Ritual Complex on West Hill, Uley, Gloucestershire: 1977–9*, English Heritage Archaeological Report 17 (London)

Woodward, P. and Woodward, A. 2004: 'Dedicating the town: urban foundation deposits in Roman Britain', *World Archaeology* 36, 68–86

Worley, F. 2008: *Taken to the Grave: An Archaeozoological Approach Assessing the Role of Animals as Crematory Offerings in First Millennium AD Britain*, unpublished PhD thesis, University of Bradford

Wright, J., Leivers, M., Seager Smith, R. and Stevens, C.J. 2009: *Cambourne New Settlement. Iron Age and Romano-British Settlement on the Clay Uplands of West Cambridgeshire*, Wessex Archaeology Report 23 (Salisbury)

Wright, L.E. and Yoder, C.J. 2003: 'Recent progress in bioarchaeology: approaches to the osteological paradox', *Journal of Archaeological Research* 11(1), 43–70

Wright, N. 2008: 'A lead lined stone coffin cremation burial from Harnhill, Gloucestershire', *Transactions of Bristol and Gloucestershire Archaeology Society* 126, 83–90

Wright, R.P. and Gillam, J.P. 1953: 'Third report on the Roman site at Old Durham', *Archaeologia Aeliana* 31, 116–26

WYAS, 2001: *Leadenham Quarry vols 1–2, Leadenham Welbourn, Lincolnshire. Archaeological Excavation*, West Yorkshire Archaeological Services

Wythe, D. 2007: 'An analysis of coin finds from 75 Roman temple sites in Britain', in Haeussler and King 2007, 43–66

Yalden, D. 1999: *The History of British Mammals* (London)

— and Albarella, U. 2009: *The History of British Birds* (Oxford)

Yates, A. 2000: 'Little Bulmore Farm, Bulmore', *Archaeology in Wales* 40, 98–9

Zeepvat, R.J. 1991: 'Roman gardens in Britain', in A.E. Brown (ed.), *Garden Archaeology*, CBA Research Report 78 (London), 53–9

Zienkiewicz, J.D. 1986: *The Legionary Fortress Baths at Caerleon. Vol I: The Buildings and Vol 2: The Finds* (Cardiff)

Zohary, D., Tchernov, E. and Kolska Horwitz, I. 1998: 'The role of unconscious selection in the domestication of sheep and goats', *Journal of Zoology* 245, 129–35

Zoll, A. 1995: 'A view through inscriptions: the epigraphic evidence for religion at Hadrian's Wall', in J. Metzler, M. Millett, N.G.A.M. Roymans and J. Slofstra (eds), *Integration in the Early Roman West. The Role of Culture and Ideology* (Luxembourg), 129–50

— 2016: 'Names of gods', in Millett *et al.* (eds) 2016, 619–40, doi: 10.1093/oxfordhb/9780199697731.013.034

INDEX

Page numbers in *italics* denote illustrations.